For Reference

Not to be taken from this room

DEMCO

Dictionary Of Literary Biography Yearbook: 1982

Dictionary of Literary Biography

DICTIONARY OF LITERARY BIOGRAPHY YEARBOOK: 1982

Edited by
Richard Ziegfeld

Associate Editors:
Jean W. Ross
Lynne C. Zeigler

A Bruccoli Clark Book
Gale Research Company • Book Tower • Detroit, Michigan 48226
1983

Matthew J. Bruccoli and Richard Layman, *Editorial Directors*
C. E. Frazer Clark, Jr., *Managing Editor*

Manufactured by Edwards Brothers, Inc.
Ann Arbor, Michigan
Printed in the United States of America

Library of Congress Catalog Card Number 82-645185
ISBN 0-8103-1626-9
ISSN 0731-7867

Contents

Foreword

The *DLB Yearbook* is guided by the same three principles that have provided the basic rationale for the entire *DLB* series: 1) the literature of a nation represents an inexhaustible resource of permanent worth; 2) the surest way to trace the outlines of literary history is by a comprehensive scholarly treatment of the lives and works of those who contributed to it; and 3) the greatest service the series can provide is to make literary achievement better understood and more accessible to students and the literate public, while serving the needs of scholars. In keeping with those principles, the *Yearbook* has been designed to augment *DLB* by reflecting the vitality of contemporary literature and summarizing current literary activity. In 1982 nearly four thousand books among the twenty-nine thousand new hardbacks published in America have some claim to literary importance, whether as belles lettres or as literary studies. The librarian, scholar, or student attempting to stay abreast of literary developments is faced with an enormous, never-ending task. The purpose of *DLB Yearbook* is to help.

DLB Yearbook is divided into three sections: articles about the past year's literary topics: updates of entries previously published in *DLB*; and new author entries. Beginning in the 1982 *Yearbook*, the articles section will feature essays which discuss the year's work in literary biography, fiction, poetry, and drama. The *Yearbook* will also endeavor to cover important prizes and conferences; in this volume there are articles about the 1982 Nobel Prize in Literature (including the Swedish Academy's citation, Gabriel García Márquez's acceptance speech, and appreciations of his work) and the Drue Heinz Literature Prize established to promote fiction (including a statement about the prize, an interview with the first winner, and an excerpt from his novel). In addition, there is coverage of the F. Scott Fitzgerald conference in St. Paul, Minnesota, the James Joyce Centenary conference in Dublin, and the Jack Kerouac conference at the Naropa Institute. Each year a literary archive will be described; the 1982 *Yearbook* includes a description of the Humanities Research Center at the University of Texas, which holds over 9 million literary manuscripts. Literary topics of current interest will also be explored: in this *Yearbook* there are interviews with five spokesmen for organizations concerned with censorship in school libraries, offering their opinions about the Supreme Court decision in the Island Trees case; charges of plagiarism against D. M. Thomas, author of *The White Hotel*, are reported. In addition, there is a poll of authors, asking their

views on "the most powerful book review in America" and a review of Emerson scholarship on the 100th anniversary of his death.

Updated Entries in the second section are designed to complement the *DLB* series with current information about the literary activities of authors who have entries in previously published DLB volumes. Each Updated Entry takes as its point of departure an already published *DLB* entry, updating primary and secondary bibliographical information, providing descriptions and assessments of new works, and, when necessary, reevaluating an author's works. In the Updated Entries section, exclusive interviews are frequently included; Peter DeVries, James Dickey, and Anne Tyler are interviewed for the 1982 *Yearbook*. The death of a major literary figure prompts a summation of his achievement, and one of the functions of Updated Entries is to provide fresh, authoritative appraisals of the careers of recently deceased authors. Comments from the authors' contemporaries are solicited, as in the cases of John Cheever, John Gardner, Archibald MacLeish, and Kenneth Rexroth in this volume. The form of entry in Updated Entries is similar to that in the standard *DLB* series. Each Updated Entry is preceded by a reference to the *DLB* volume in which the basic entry on the subject appears. Readers seeking information about an author's entire career should consult the basic entry along with the Updated Entry for complete biographical and bibliographical information.

The third section is devoted to New Entries on figures not previously included in *DLB*. These entries follow the well-established format for the series: emphasis is placed on biography and syntheses of the critical reception of the authors' works; primary bibliographies precede each entry, a list of references follows the entry. As with Updated Entries, New Entries are frequently followed by exclusive interviews conducted by the *DLB* staff. The 1982 *Yearbook* includes interviews with Doris Betts, Jim Harrison, Shirley Hazzard, Lee Pennington, and John Rechy.

Each Yearbook includes a necrology and a checklist of books about literary history and biography published during the year.

From the outset, the *DLB* series has undertaken the responsibility to compile our literary history as it is revealed in the lives and works of authors. The *Yearbook* supports that commitment by extending *DLB* coverage up to the present, recording literary history as it happens.

Permissions

The following people and institutions generously permitted the reproduction of illustrations and other materials: The Nobel Foundation, p. 4, © 1982, The Nobel Foundation; University of Pittsburgh Press, pp. 11, 13, © 1982, University of Pittsburgh Press; Donald Stetzer, p. 14; Michael Metzer, p. 19; Indiana News Bureau, p. 23; Joseph Thomas, p. 25; Naropa Institute, pp. 52, 53, 54, 55, 56, 57, 58, 59, © 1982 Naropa Institute and © 1982 John Schoenwalter; *Irish Times*, p. 65; Humanities Research Center, University of Texas at Austin, pp. 73, 76; Frank Armstrong, Information Service, University of Texas, pp. 74, 77; Joyce Ravid, pp. 79, 278; Susan Cook, p. 94; Gerry Goodstein, p. 95; Layle Silbert, p. 121; Black Star, p. 123; Harold Strauss, p. 127; Evelyn Floret / People Weekly, Time, Inc., p. 133; Steve Hunt, Columbia Newspapers, p. 138; James Dickey, p. 142, © 1983, James Dickey; Tom Victor, pp. 147, 165, 206; Morgan and Keiko Gibson, p. 179; Helen Marcus, p. 188; Michael Chikiris, p. 195; Jade Albert, p. 203; James Benford, p. 213; Mark Morrow, p. 219; Camera North, p. 227; Nancy Crampton, p. 233; Richard Sutor, p. 240; Ian Berry, p. 244; Lloyd Arnold, p. 246; Jo Ellen Gent, p. 251; Sally Stone Halverson, p. 255; *Miami Herald*, p. 261; Bob Wargo, p. 266; James Heidish, p. 288; Mary Vann Hunter, p. 291; Loew's, Inc., p. 293; Michael J. Elderman, p. 300; Michelle Ryder, p. 306; John Nichols, p. 316; Don Anderson, p. 334; Peter Southwick, p. 343; Tony Korody, p. 349; Tappy Phillips, p. 358; Peter Simons, p. 362; Town and Country Studios, Chapel Hill, North Carolina, p. 367; Karsh, Ottawa, p. 383; Holly Wright, p. 389.

Acknowledgments

This book was produced by BC Research. Karen L. Rood is senior editor for the *Dictionary of Literary Biography* series.

The production staff included Mary Betts, Joseph Caldwell, Patricia Coate, Angela Dixon, Lynn Felder, Joyce Fowler, Nancy L. Houghton, Sharon K. Kirkland, Cynthia D. Lybrand, Alice A. Parsons, Joycelyn R. Smith, Debra D. Straw, Robin A. Sumner, and Meredith Walker. Charles L. Wentworth is photography editor.

Walter W. Ross did the library research with the assistance of the staff at the Thomas Cooper Library of the University of South Carolina: Michael Freeman, Gary Geer, Alexander M. Gilchrist, W. Michael Havener, David Lincove, Donna Nance, Harriet B. Oglesbee, Jean Rhyne, Paula Swope, Jane Thesing, Ellen Tillett, Beth S. Woodard, and especially Joseph Pukl.

Special thanks are due to the Swedish Academy, to Frederick A. Hetzel of the University of Pittsburgh Press, to Winnifred King at the University of South Carolina Bookstore, and to William McKeever at the Naropa Institute.

DICTIONARY OF LITERARY BIOGRAPHY
YEARBOOK: 1982

Dictionary of Literary Biography

The 1982 Nobel Prize in Literature

ANNOUNCEMENT BY
THE SWEDISH ACADEMY

With this year's Nobel prize in literature to the Colombian writer *Gabriel García Márquez* (b. 1928) the Swedish Academy cannot be said to bring forward an unknown writer.

García Márquez achieved unusual international success as a writer with his novel *Cien años de soledad* in 1967 (*One Hundred Years of Solitude*). The novel has been translated into a large number of languages and has sold millions of copies. It is still being reprinted and read with undiminished interest by new readers. Such a success with a single book could be fatal for a writer with less resources than those possessed by García Márquez. He has, however, gradually confirmed his position as a rare storyteller richly endowed with a material, from imagination and experience, which seems inexhaustible. In breadth and epic richness, for instance, the novel *El ontoño del patriarca*, 1975 (*The Autumn of the Patriarch*), compares favorably with the first-mentioned work. Short novels such as *El coronel no tiene quien le escriba*, 1961 (*No One Writes to the Colonel*), *La mala hora*, 1962 (*In an Evil Hour*), or *Crónica de una muerte anunciada* (*Chronicle of a Death Foretold*), complement the picture of a writer who combines the copious, almost overwhelming narrative talent with the mastery of the conscious, disciplined and widely read artist of language. A large number of short stories, published in several collections or in magazines, give further proof of the great versatility of García Márquez' narrative gift. His international successes have continued. Each new work of his is received by expectant critics and readers as an event of world importance, is trans-lated into many languages and published as quickly as possible in large editions.

Nor can it be said that any unknown literary continent or province is brought to light with the prize to Gabriel García Márquez. For a long time

Gabriel García Márquez

Latin American literature has shown a vigour as in few other literary spheres, having won acclaim in the cultural life of today. Many impulses and traditions cross each other. Folk culture, including oral storytelling, reminiscences from old Indian culture, currents from Spanish baroque in different epochs, influences from European surrealism and other modernism are blended into a spiced and life-giving brew from which García Márquez and other Spanish-American writers derive material and inspiration. The violent conflicts of a political nature—social and economic—raise the temperature of the intellectual climate. Like most of the other important writers in the Latin American world, García Márquez is strongly committed politically on the side of the poor and the weak against domestic oppression and foreign economic exploitation. Apart from his fictional production he has been very active as a journalist, his writings being many-sided, inventive, often provocative and by no means limited to political subjects.

The great novels remind one of William Faulkner. García Márquez has created a world of his own round the imaginary town of Macondo. Since the end of the 1940s his novels and short stories have led us into this peculiar place where the miraculous and the real converge: the extravagant flight of his own fantasy, traditional folk tales and facts, literary allusions, tangible—at times obtrusively graphic—descriptions approaching the matter-of-factness of reportage. As with Faulkner, or why not Balzac, the same chief characters and minor persons crop up in different stories, brought forward into the light in various ways—sometimes in dramatically revealing situations, sometimes in comic and grotesque complications of a kind that only the wildest imagination or shameless reality itself can achieve. Manias and passions harass them. Absurdities of war let courage change shape with craziness, infamy with chivalry, cunning with madness. Death is perhaps the most important director behind the scenes in García Márquez' invented and discovered world. Often his stories revolve around a dead person—someone who has died, is dying or will die. A tragic sense of life characterizes Garcia Marquez' books—a sense of the incorruptible superiority of fate and the inhuman, inexorable ravages of history. But this awareness of death and tragic sense of life is broken by the narrative's apparently unlimited, ingenious vitality, which in its turn is a representative of the at once frightening and edifying vital force of reality and life itself. The comedy and grotesqueness in García Márquez can

be cruel, but can also glide over into a conciliating humour.

With his stories Gabriel García Márquez has created a world of his own which is a microcosmos. In its tumultuous, bewildering yet graphically convincing authenticity it reflects a continent and its human riches and poverty.

Perhaps more than that: a cosmos in which the human heart and the combined forces of history time and again burst the bounds of chaos—killing and procreation.

ENGLISH TRANSLATIONS OF BOOKS: *No One Writes to the Colonel and Other Stories* (New York: Harper & Row, 1968; London: Cape, 1971); *One Hundred Years of Solitude* (New York: Harper & Row, 1970; London: Cape, 1970); *Leaf Storm and Other Stories* (New York: Harper & Row, 1976; London: Cape, 1977); *The Autumn of the Patriarch* (New York: Harper & Row, 1976); *Innocent Eréndira and Other Stories* (New York: Harper & Row, 1978; London: Cape, 1979); *In an Evil Hour* (New York: Harper & Row, 1979); *Chronicle of a Death Foretold* (London: Cape, 1982; New York: Knopf, forthcoming 1983).

NOBEL LECTURE 1982:
THE SOLITUDE OF LATIN AMERICA
by
Gabriel García Márquez

Antonio Pigafetta, a Florentine navigator who went with Magellan on the first voyage around the world, wrote, upon his passage through our southern lands of America, a strictly accurate account that nonetheless resembles a venture into fantasy. In it he recorded that he had seen hogs with navels on their haunches, clawless birds whose hens laid eggs on the backs of their mates, and others still, resembling tongueless pelicans, with beaks like spoons. He wrote of having seen a misbegotten creature with the head and ears of a mule, a camel's body, the legs of a deer and the whinny of a horse. He described how the first native encountered in Patagonia was confronted with a mirror, whereupon that impassioned giant lost his senses to the terror of his own image.

This short and fascinating book, which even

then contained the seeds of our present-day novels, is by no means the most staggering account of our reality in that age. The Chroniclers of the Indies left us countless others. Eldorado, our so avidly sought and illusory land, appeared on numerous maps for many a long year, shifting its place and form to suit the fantasy of cartographers. In his search for the fountain of eternal youth, the mythical Alvar Núñez Cabeza de Vaca explored the north of Mexico for eight years, in a deluded expedition whose members devoured each other and only five of whom returned, of the six hundred who had undertaken it. One of the many unfathomed mysteries is that of the eleven thousand mules, each loaded with one hundred pounds of gold, that left Cuzco one day to pay the ransom of Atahualpa and never reached their destination. Subsequently, in colonial times, hens were sold in Cartagena de Indias, that had been raised on alluvial land and whose gizzards contained tiny lumps of gold. Our founders' lust for gold beset us until recently. As late as the last century, a German mission appointed to study the construction of an interoceanic railroad across the Isthmus of Panama concluded that the project was feasible on one condition: that the rails not be made of iron, which was scarce in the region, but of gold.

Our independence from Spanish domination did not put us beyond the reach of madness. General Antonio López de Santana, three times dictator of Mexico, held a magnificent funeral for the right leg he had lost in the so-called Pastry War. General Gabriel García Moreno ruled Ecuador for sixteen years as an absolute monarch; at his wake, the corpse was seated on the presidential chair, decked out in full-dress uniform and a protective layer of medals. General Maximiliano Hernández Martínez, the theosophical despot of El Salvador who had thirty thousand peasants slaughtered in a savage massacre, invented a pendulum to detect poison in his food, and had streetlamps draped in red paper to defeat an epidemic of scarlet fever. The statue to General Francisco Morazán erected in the main square of Tegucigalpa is actually one of Marshal Ney, purchased at a Paris warehouse of second-hand sculptures.

Eleven years ago, the Chilean Pablo Neruda, one of the outstanding poets of our time, enlightened this audience with his word. Since then, the Europeans of good will—and sometimes those of bad, as well—have been struck, with ever greater force, by the unearthly tidings of Latin America, that boundless realm of haunted men and historic women, whose unending obstinacy blurs into legend. We have not had a moment's rest. A prometheical president, entrenched in his burning palace, died fighting an entire army, alone; and two suspicious airplane accidents, yet to be explained, cut short the life of another great-hearted president and that of a democratic soldier who had revived the dignity of his people. There have been five wars and seventeen military coups; there emerged a diabolic dictator who is carrying out, in God's name, the first Latin American ethnocide of our time. In the meantime, twenty million Latin American children died before the age of one—more than have been born in Europe since 1970. Those missing because of repression number nearly one hundred and twenty thousand, which is as if no one could account for all the inhabitants of Upsala. Numerous women arrested while pregnant have given birth in Argentinian prisons, yet nobody knows the whereabouts and identity of their children, who were furtively adopted or sent to an orphanage by order of the military authorities. Because they tried to change this state of things, nearly two hundred thousand men and women have died throughout the continent, and over one hundred thousand have lost their lives in three small and illfated countries of Central America: Nicaragua, El Salvador and Guatemala. If this had happened in the United States, the corresponding figure would be that of one million six hundred thousand violent deaths in four years.

One million people have fled Chile, a country with a tradition of hospitality—that is, ten per cent of its population. Uruguay, a tiny nation of two and a half million inhabitants which considered itself the continent's most civilized country, has lost to exile one out of every five citizens. Since 1979, the civil war in El Salvador has produced almost one refugee every twenty minutes. The country that could be formed of all the exiles and forced emigrants of Latin America would have a population larger than that of Norway.

I dare to think that it is this outsized reality, and not just its literary expression, that has deserved the attention of the Swedish Academy of Letters. A reality not of paper, but one that lives within us and determines each instant of our countless daily deaths, and that nourishes a source of insatiable creativity, full of sorrow and beauty, of which this roving and nostalgic Colombian is but one cipher more, singled out by fortune. Poets and beggars, musicians and prophets, warriors and scoundrels, all creatures of that unbridled reality, we have had to ask but little of imagination, for our crucial problem has been a lack of conventional means to render our lives believable. This, my friends, is the crux of our solitude.

And if these difficulties, whose essence we share, hinder us, it is understandable that the rational talents on this side of the world, exalted in the contemplation of their own cultures, should have found themselves without a valid means to interpret us. It is only natural that they insist on measuring us with the yardstick that they use for themselves, forgetting that the ravages of life are not the same for all, and that the quest of our own identity is just as arduous and bloody for us as it was for them. The interpretation of our reality through patterns not our own serves only to make us ever more unknown, ever less free, ever more solitary. Venerable Europe would perhaps be more perceptive if it tried to see us in its own past. If only it recalled that London took three hundred years to build its first city wall, and three hundred years more to acquire a bishop; that Rome labored in a gloom of uncertainty for twenty centuries, until an Etruscan King anchored it in history; and that the peaceful Swiss of today, who feast us with their mild cheeses and apathetic watches, bloodied Europe as soldiers of fortune, as late as the nineteenth century. Even at the height of the Renaissance, twelve thousand lansquenets in the pay of the imperial armies sacked and devastated Rome and put eight thousand of its inhabitants to the sword.

I do not mean to embody the illusions of Tonio Kröger, whose dreams of uniting a chaste north to a passionate south were exalted here, fifty-three years ago, by Thomas Mann. But I do believe that those clearsighted Europeans who struggle, here as well, for a more just and humane homeland, could help us far better if they reconsidered their way of seeing us. Solidarity with our dreams will not make us feel less alone, as long as it is not translated into concrete acts of legitimate support for all the peoples that assume the illusions of having a life of their own in the distribution of the world.

Latin America neither wants, nor has any reason, to be a pawn without a will of its own; nor is it merely wishful thinking that its quest for independence and originality should become a Western aspiration. However, the navigational advances that have narrowed such distances between our Americas and Europe seem, conversely, to have accentuated our cultural remoteness. Why is the originality so readily granted us in literature so mistrustfully denied us in our difficult attempts at social change? Why think that the social justice sought by progressive Europeans for their own countries cannot also be a goal for Latin America, with different methods for dissimilar conditions? No: the immeasurable violence and pain of our history are the result of age-old inequities and untold bitterness, and not a conspiracy plotted three thousand leagues from our home. But many European leaders and thinkers have thought so, with the childishness of oldtimers who have forgotten the fruitful excesses of their youth as if it were impossible to find another destiny than to live at the mercy of the two great masters of the world. This, my friends, is the very scale of our solitude.

In spite of this, to oppression, plundering and abandonment, we respond with life. Neither floods nor plagues, famines nor cataclysms, nor even the eternal wars of century upon century, have been able to subdue the persistent advantage of life over death. An advantage that grows and quickens: every year, there are seventy-four million more births than deaths, a sufficient number of new lives to multiply each year, the population of New York sevenfold. Most of these births occur in the countries of least resources—including, of course, those of Latin America. Conversely, the most prosperous countries have succeeded in accumulating powers of destruction such as to annihilate, a hundred times over, not only all the human beings that have existed to this day, but also the totality of all living beings that have ever drawn breath on this planet of misfortune.

On a day like today, my master William Faulkner said, "I decline to accept the end of man." I would feel unworthy of standing in this place that was his, if I were not fully aware that the colossal tragedy he refused to recognize thirty-two years ago is now, for the first time since the beginning of humanity, nothing more than a simple scientific possibility. Faced with this awesome reality that must have seemed a mere utopia through all of human time, we, the inventors of tales, who will believe anything, feel entitled to believe that it is not yet too late to engage in the creation of the opposite utopia. A new and sweeping utopia of life, where no one will be able to decide for others how they die, where love will prove true and happiness be possible, and where the races condemned to one hundred years of solitude will have, at last and forever, a second opportunity on earth.

(Translated from the Spanish by Marina Castañeda; ©The Nobel Foundation, 1982.)

Many years later, as he faced the firing squad, Colonel Aureliano Buendía was to remember that distant afternoon when his father took him to discover ice. At that time Macondo was a village of twenty adobe houses, built on the bank of a river of clear water that ran along a bed of polished stones, which were white and enormous, like prehistoric eggs. The world was so recent that many things lacked names, and in order to indicate them it was necessary to point. Every year during the month of March a family of ragged gypsies would set up their tents near the village, and with a great uproar of pipes and kettledrums they would display new inventions. First they brought the magnet. A heavy gypsy with an untamed beard and sparrow hands, who introduced himself as Melquíades, put on a bold public demonstration of what he himself called the eighth wonder of the learned alchemists of Macedonia. He went from house to house dragging two metal ingots and everybody was amazed to see pots, pans, tongs, and braziers tumble down from their places and beams creak from the desperation of nails and screws trying to emerge, and even objects that had been lost for a long time appeared from where they had been searched for most and went dragging along in turbulent confusion behind Melquíades' magical irons. "Things have a life of their own," the gypsy proclaimed with a harsh accent. "It's simply a matter of waking up their souls."

—*from* One Hundred Years of Solitude

THE MAGICAL WORLD OF MACONDO

Juan Loveluck
University of South Carolina

Since its earliest manifestations, at the beginning of the sixteenth century, the literature of Latin America has shown two distinct and well-defined directions: one is the cultivated, elitist and scriptural; the other is the colloquial, almost "oral" and lighthearted, that has a strong conversational aspect, full of fantasy and joy. Contemporary Latin American fiction, without doubt, reflects these two possible directions and we can mention a pair of very famous writers, already translated into more than thirty languages, as its most eminent representatives: Jorge Luis Borges and Gabriel García Márquez. The latter has just received—at the age of fifty-four—the maximum literary recognition, the Nobel Prize. In granting this prize, the Swedish Academy expressed that García Márquez was being honored "for his novels and short stories, in which the fantastic and the realistic are combined in a richly composed world of imagination, reflecting a continent's life and conflicts."

There is no doubt that the Swedish academics, in explaining the reasons for this award, had in mind the fact that Gabriel García Márquez has powerfully universalized a small area of Colombia (in the Magdalena province) where he was born in 1928: Aracataca. This forgotten place that barely appears in regional maps is, in the imaginary universe created by the author, the mythical and magic town of Macondo, poetical cipher of the cosmos and supreme elevation of a regional element to an intense representation of universal and meaningful values.

In the manner of William Faulkner—one of García Márquez's idols—and his obsession to create a geographical and universal metaphor of the world (the county of Yoknapatawpha and the lineage of the Sartoris family), the Colombian writer has maintained a rare and obsessive fidelity to "Macondo" and its magical atmosphere, its endless rain, the torturing passage of time, its violences and crimes, its "biblical pestilences," and its marvelous occurrences.

In an early short story popularized by the Chilean critic Ricardo A. Latcham in his *Anthology of the Latin American Short Story* (1958), and whose title is "Monolog of Isabel Seeing the Rain Fall in Macondo" (1955), we already find, with mature and definite traits, the conception of a world in which geography and climate are its salient features: the intolerable heat, the rains that fall for years and centuries (in our imagination), time that elapses with cruel lentitude.

I would like to translate a short and meaningful paragraph of this narrative, in which the characters, under the mythical rain, eternalized in tedium, lose all objective notions or perceive (as we will read many years later in *One Hundred Years of Solitude*) that "time is revolving in perfect circles." Isabel, after many days suffering the rain, meditates in the following way:

7

At Thursday's dawning the aromas ceased, and the sense of distances was lost. The notion of time twisted since the day before, completely disappeared. Then there was no Thursday. What should have been Thursday was a physical and gelatinous thing that could have been opened with the hands in order to peer upon Friday.

Here we have, in a 1955 text, a conception of the Colombian and Latin American world which the author will preserve as an imaginary system until the creation of *One Hundred Years of Solitude* (1967) and later works. The manifest temporal obsession that we find in the fictitious world of the Colombian writer is not so much a dialogue with other texts (those of Defoe, Joyce, Woolf, and Faulkner) if we think of "intertextuality." It is the conception of time that extends itself in the solitude of a cruel history, social injustices, and endless hope. A time that meanders in search of that hope: when will dictatorships and wars end?; when will abuses and deprivations end? The extraordinary book that García Márquez made known in 1967 directs itself to the expression of that peculiar aspect of solitude. (Another form of solitude has always attracted García Márquez: the tremendous solitude of power;

this is the center of the book that the author considers his best "poetic novel," *The Autumn of the Patriarch*.) For such a reason, in *One Hundred Years of Solitude*, time and times—history, but the particular history of the New World—are basic elements. If Macondo is indeed an *axis mundi* and if the Buendías' lineage metaphorizes the entire human race and avatars of history, the time that regulates that world assumes distinct imaginary projections that make it the center and the reason of the novel.

One is the mythical time of foundations: pure genesis and origin, without possible inscription in history and chronology. Another one is the time of the Buendías' lineage, with Ursula Iguarán as the cohesive figure. Yet another is the time that controls solitude and an endless wait. Finally, the time of the destruction and punishment: the apocalypse and fall of Macondo, that lost paradise.

The structural canon that rules this timeless world of myth is the one of exaggeration, gigantism, and hyperbole. For that reason some critics (obsessed with the old-fashioned idea of "influences") have recalled Rabelais's *Gargantua* that the writer offers in *One Hundred Years of Solitude* as the text taken by a fictionalized "Gabriel" to Paris. García Márquez—who enjoys teasing his critics—has corrected the opinions of these and has put them on the

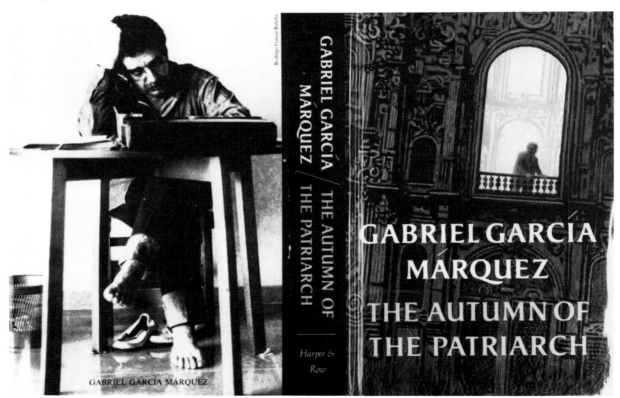

Dust jacket for García Márquez's second novel: "my only book which I have not lived myself"

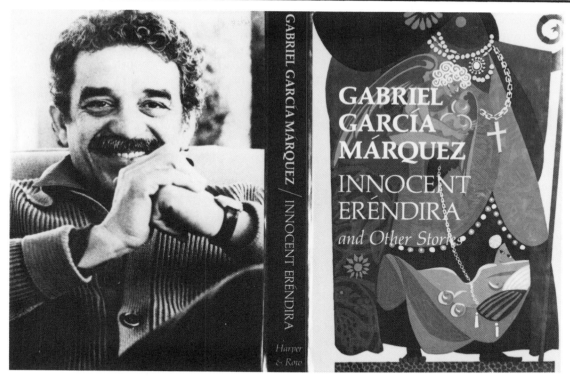

Dust jacket for García Márquez's third volume of short stories translated into English (1978)

right critical path, that of the early Spanish chivalric novel, and the most primitive and beautiful of these: *Amadís de Gaule*. In this book, in an ordinary level of life, the most incredible and exaggerated things occur: wars, love, adventures, deeds. A "total" fiction (no human aspect is left aside, sex included) in which every detail of common existence is connected with fantasy, exaggeration, and miracles. I should also mention the early chronicles of the New World, starting with Antonio Pigafetta, the navigator who accompanied Magellan on the first voyage around the world. In his Stockholm address García Márquez has indicated his literary debt toward that "short and fascinating book in which one can see already the germs of our novels of today." Pigafetta and the chroniclers—Cortés, Díaz del Castillo, Sahagún, etc.—began the catalogue of wonders that the magical realist novel of Latin America is still trying to decipher within its imaginary space.

This is the poetic world that originates García Márquez's fiction. But we must add the fantastic universe of the writer's infancy, the stories that the grandparents told him, the maids' gossip, and the phantasmagoric space of "the house"—that was the title of the novel in its early versions—in which

Dust jacket for the 1979 English translation of García Márquez's 1962 short novel, La mala hora

García Márquez stayed until the death of his maternal grandparents. For years that magic cosmos stayed in the imagination of the boy. When he was twenty or twenty-one he returned to Aracataca with his mother, to sell "the house." That visit and the contrast between the Aracataca kept in his memory and the somnolent town he saw one humid afternoon resulted in the creation of a perfect short story: "Tuesday's Afternoon."

An incredible amount of reading would explain that a book like *One Hundred Years of Solitude* is the place of recurrence and fusion of all the novels that have been written, of all the things that have been imagined, and of all that has been told. In summation, a book-universe in which one finds all that has been invented by men and all that is left to imagine: an infinite opening to our power of fantasy.

A TRIBUTE
to GABRIEL GARCÍA MÁRQUEZ

The selection of Gabriel García Márquez for the 1982 Nobel Prize in Literature indirectly brings honor to the Swedish Academy of Letters while directly conferring literature's highest recognition on one of the most renowned novelists since World War II. Too often the Nobel Prize goes to authors—for example Vicente Aleixandre and Harry Edmund Martinson—who for a variety of reasons will never be read beyond their severely limited spheres of influence. Conversely, too often the Swedish Academy overlooks writers—for example James Joyce and Vladimir Nabokov—whose work is applauded by serious readers everywhere. Such is not the case with García Márquez. Author of seven books, he has permanently affected the genre of fiction with his masterwork, *One Hundred Years of Solitude* (1967).

His is a towering achievement. The Swedish Academy said that it honored García Márquez because in his fiction the fantastic and the real are "combined in a richly composed world of imagination, reflecting a continent's life and conflicts," but his accomplishment goes beyond such generalizations. His great contemporary Vargas Llosa has spoken more to the point: "*One Hundred Years of Solitude* is a *total* novel, in the direct line of those dimensionally ambitious creations which compete with reality on an equal footing, confronting it with the image of a qualitatively equivalent vastness, vitality, and complexity."

García Márquez's exuberant sighting of the marvelous in the real—*lo real maravilloso*—of the inevitable union of the surreal and the street, of the freedom of fantasy in the confines of the mundane, has its origin in his youth. Born in Aracataca, Colombia, in 1928 to a family with sixteen children, he lived his first eight years with maternal grandparents Colonel Nicolas Márquez Iguaran and Doña Tranquilina Iguaran Cotes. These eight years were crucial. For in addition to hearing of his grandfather's heroic exploits in the disastrous civil war of 1899-1903, called the War of a Thousand Days, García Márquez also absorbed the old man's readings from *The Thousand and One Nights*. Myth and reality merged in such proportions that facing the hard facts of the moment in later years only embellished rather than blunted his grasp of the magical in the everyday.

From *la Violencia* in Colombia in the 1950s through the fall of Perez Jimenez in Venezuela and the overthrow of Batista in Cuba, to the fascism of Franco's Spain and the receipt of death threats in Mexico where he now lives, García Márquez has rushed through a life that is as adventuresome and bizarre as the fiction of two of his literary heroes, Ernest Hemingway and William Faulkner: "Faulkner is a writer who has had much to do with my soul, but Hemingway is the one who had the most to do with my craft." Add his love of such comic-book heroes as Dick Tracy and Tarzan to this mixture of violent history and innovative art, and one understands the primary source of the galloping pace in his vigorous tales.

For while García Márquez is today a political journalist with left-wing leanings, his enormous stature rests on the energy of his limitless imagination. Like Laurence Sterne in the 1760s, Herman Melville in the 1850s, and James Joyce in the 1920s, he has once again opened up authors and readers to the possibilities of the novel. In his hands, fiction is not merely a vehicle for social observation but also an opportunity for showing that art may be as colossal, as mysterious, and as unpredictable as life itself. The perimeters of time and the logic of sentence structure are not limitations to crouch within but invitations to leap beyond. And leap he does, until, in especially *One Hundred Years of Solitude* and *The Autumn of the Patriarch* (1975), García Márquez's imagination soars above the minuteness of the quotidian and carries it to a realm where real and surreal merge, where time is freed from clocks, where man transcends his boundaries, and where, finally, flying carpets in the jungle are as common as dictators and fools.

—Donald J. Greiner

The Drue Heinz Literature Prize

Beginning its fourth year, the Drue Heinz Literature Prize is the answer of Pittsburgh to the neglect of short fiction by the national publishing community. The Prize was established in 1980 by the Howard Heinz Endowment of Pittsburgh and the University of Pittsburgh Press as an award to the writers of short stories or novellas. It consists of $5,000 and publication by the Press.

Frederick A. Hetzel, Director of the University of Pittsburgh Press, calls the short story and the novella "stepchildren" in the world of literature. William Lafe, Associate Director of the Endowment, agrees. But the impetus for the Prize originated with Mrs. Drue Heinz. At a board meeting of the Endowment in 1979, she asked what support was being given to the field of literature. The question led Lafe to enlist Hetzel's help in coming up with an appropriate idea.

"We chose fiction because the need was there,"

explains Hetzel. "About ten to fifteen years ago, the need for new publications in poetry existed. The University of Pittsburgh Press developed the Pitt Poetry Series in response. Now the need is with short fiction."

On the part of the Howard Heinz Endowment, the venture was an unusual one. "This is the only prize that we offer, and the only grant that has a national impact," says Lafe. "All our other grants are regional ones. Yet it is very much in keeping with the things we do, because it is part of our broad, on-going support of the arts."

The first competition was judged by Robert Penn Warren and three screeners, all published novelists, from some 300 manuscripts. The winning entry was David Bosworth's *The Death of Descartes*, a collection of four short stories and one novella, which gives the book its title. The author is thirty-three years old, a graduate of Brown Univer-

Frederick A. Hetzel, Director of the University of Pittsburgh Press, and Robley Wilson, Jr.

sity who lives in Cambridge, Massachusetts. He is superintendent of an apartment house and devotes all his spare time to writing.

The publication of *The Death of Descartes* spectacularly launched both David Bosworth's career as a writer and the Drue Heinz Literature Prize. Peter S. Prescott reviewed the book in *Newsweek*, in itself an unusual recognition for a university press book, and commented: "Bosworth shows . . . a fierce talent. His stories are fresh, well shaped and extremely well written. The book that contains them is handsomely made, but because it comes from a university press I fear it may be hard to find in the stores. Do not be deterred: make a fuss. Demand that the book be produced. Bosworth will prove worth the trouble."

Choice wrote of Bosworth's "undeniable authority," adding that the publication of *The Death of Descartes* "bodes well for the years to come" with the Drue Heinz Literature Prize. The *Nation* found that the judges' choice "was a wise and . . . strategic decision, for not only will the book honor the Prize but it will set a precedent for publishing work marked by independence and imagination." The *Christian Science Monitor* acclaimed the book as "one of this season's finest fiction debuts," while the *Boston Globe* found Bosworth to be "one of the two or three best American writers of his generation." The *New York Times* noted Bosworth's "tragic power." The *Detroit Free Press* adjured its readers to "remember the name David Bosworth"; and *Publishers Weekly* called Bosworth "a precise and lyrical writer."

Hetzel believes that *The Death of Descartes* offered its reviewers an unusual chance of discovery and excitement, but he is equally pleased with the second winner, Robley Wilson, Jr.'s *Dancing For Men*, a collection of short stories, which will be published early in 1983. Wilson says of his book: "These are stories about the circumstances that join and divide men and women—stories of politics, sexual and otherwise; of age differences; of the weight of custom; of contempts whether vicious or polite." The second competition was judged by Raymond Carver.

Editor of the *North American Review* and a teacher at the University of Northern Iowa, Wilson has published two collections of short stories and three books of poems. Hetzel finds the contrast between the first two winners of the Heinz Prize exciting: "In its first two years," he says, "the Prize has served both the unpublished writer—Bosworth—and the experienced writer—Wilson. I look forward to our third winner."

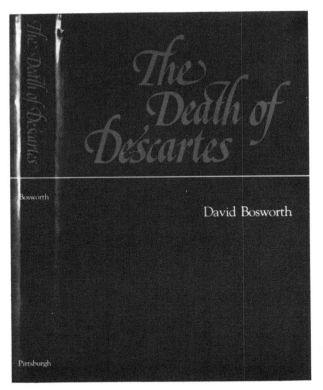

Dust jacket for the story collection that won the first Drue Heinz Literature Prize

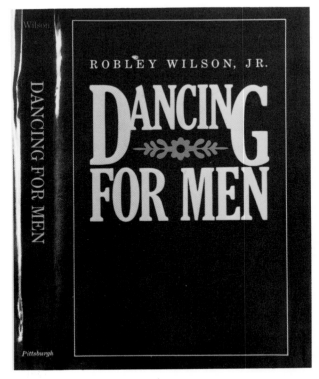

Dust jacket for the novel that won the 1981 Drue Heinz Literature Prize

Exhibit 2b-324: a child's worn catcher's mitt. Its thumb is split, its leather dried and cracked, the inside rotted from sweat, its Del Crandall signature barely legible as though the abraded inscription on an ancient statue. To the best of my recollection, I receive Exhibit 2b-324 when I'm eleven years old, on a Saturday afternoon in the spring of '59, spring of Little League and presidential primaries, Joe Kennedy out following the hustings, buying his son the nomination. *My* father buys me a catcher's mitt and, while taking a break from raking our lawn, presents it to me. He is his eyes that afternoon, no flickering sneers, no resigned cynicism, animated and intense, a keeper of mysteries. He cradles the glove in his hands as if it were some family totem or a royal diadem on a satin pillow whose transfer requires this special ritual, fatherly advice for the heir apparent. He smiles—a small, knowing, wonderful smile—unaware that his gift is a sexist one, unaware that he is oppressing me with this age-old macho knowledge he brings: how to break a glove in by rubbing it again and again, pausing to take in the commingled, exquisite scent of calfskin and linseed oil; how to admire a thing well-made, not just with your eyes but with your hands, your fingertips, the feel and flex, the sensual caress of softened leather.

He is his eyes that afternoon; the years of silence have been broken through. We sit together on the back steps, immense cumulus clouds passing overhead; our raked piles of splintered twigs, of dead grass and cracked leaves, lay abandoned, spring's ritual of readying the lawn delayed for a moment. For not yet aware of the fascist character of American sport, we, my father and I, are discussing the intricacies of the foul tip, of picking runners off second base, how to dig a curve out of the dirt, all the lore and craftsmanship of catching a baseball game. And when we're finished and the time has come to transfer the glove from father to son, he holds Exhibit 2b-324 above my hands, and pausing, gives me his final words, both a benediction and a warning, a standard of truth and an invocation of responsibility:

"You have to take care of a glove like this."

—from "Excerpts from a Report of the Commission," in Bosworth's *The Death of Descartes*

AN INTERVIEW
with DAVID BOSWORTH

DLB: Where did your initial impulse to write come from?

BOSWORTH: That's a complicated question. I think most writers start out as people who love to read, and I certainly loved to read as a kid. And, like many, I eventually felt a need to express somehow my strong response to this strange reality we've all been born to. Beyond that, I've always been fascinated by small worlds. Model boats and cars, paperweight globes; later, biology with its intricate working environments—ant colonies, beehives, the life-soup of a pond. My childhood was a sea of failed and frustrated projects in this regard: dead turtles and tadpoles in cages and jars; model kits messed up and finally disregarded. (I was a singularly inept model builder.) It wasn't until college and after that all these desires began to come together, that my need for a means of expression, my love of reading, and my fascination with model worlds were united and satisfied by my fiction writing.

DLB: Had you done any writing before college?

BOSWORTH: Not really, just school assignments. And not that much in college either. When I was fifteen or sixteen, I discovered my love of serious fiction and later nurtured a vague ambition to write "someday"; but I lacked the necessary discipline,

David Bosworth

was too involved with identity and sex and social display, too paralyzed by all the profound philosophical questions which affect "sensitive" young men coming of age. And I felt no social pressure to write—the contrary, in fact—since I didn't hang out with a literary set of friends, a situation which has had both its advantages and its liabilities.

DLB: How so?

BOSWORTH: The distinct advantage is that I came to writing from my own perspective, less mired in the fads and fashions of the day. Just as important, I think, my writing was not infected by a quest for social prestige. Since my friends weren't literary, my standing with them never depended on my writing ability. As a consequence, my fiction didn't become, as it does for some young writers, a social defense, a gesture to gain acceptance or exact revenge. Instead, it was something special and very private which I practiced because it mattered to me, be-

cause I liked it. In the long run, this background of isolation has helped me retain the right values in relation to my work; made it easier to distinguish what's good for the soul from what's merely good for the ego or for the bank account.

On the other hand, I began writing seriously later (twenty-five or so) than I might have otherwise. And, more importantly, I've been deprived of meeting some very interesting writers who, undoubtedly, would have enriched my life.

DLB: You had a National Endowment for the Arts fellowship in 1979-1980, and then the honor of winning the first Drue Heinz Literature Prize, in 1980, for *The Death of Descartes*. There were 268 manuscripts submitted for that prize. How did it feel to win?

BOSWORTH: Winning the fellowship and the prize were tremendous thrills—a child's delight at Christmastime recaptured as an adult. Having pursued my writing in a private way, the public recognition, award dinners and the like, were a pleasant change of pace, and there was the much deeper satisfaction of seeing my stories in print. I must admit, though, that I feel a general uneasiness about the book's success. Good reviews, requests for interviews, etc., are like candy—you want more and more; they never quite satisfy. I'm instinctively wary, afraid of bad habits.

DLB: Many young writers support their habit by teaching, but you manage an apartment house. Does that give you plenty of time to write?

BOSWORTH: Yes and no. I'm energetic and disciplined and, after ten years of managing the building, rather well organized. The physical work gets done early in the morning or late in the afternoon, theoretically leaving me five or six hours behind the desk. But this time is frequently interrupted by workmen, tenants, meter readers and the like. I can never indulge my secret desire to unplug the phone, never seal myself off from the outside world, which is what every writer has to do. All in all, this situation has been very good for me; but you always pay a price when you work two jobs. My life isn't as tranquil as I'd like.

DLB: Your fiction is rich in settings observed as if they were paintings or were being analyzed and assessed by a painter. Are you also an artist?

BOSWORTH: No. But like a painter, I'm intrigued by the physical world, by landscapes, cityscapes, the whole feast of sense brought to us by our eyes and ears. Like the Puritans, who thought nature was God's book, something to be studied, to be read, I keep seeing lessons, moral metaphors, in the smallest details of the environment. And beyond those glints of meaning is the overwhelming force of reality's beauty; I find it hard *not* to respond to the sheer sensual splendor of it all. Having a new baby now, a daily witness to *his* intense witnessing of the world, I'm all the more aware of how remarkable it is to be alive at all. But a child's curiosity is a gift, is instinctive; the older we grow, the more we have to choose and will an attitude toward the world. Writing fiction is, for me, a way to retain and sophisticate our oldest and finest instincts—our drives to explore, to know, to feel. The act of writing, at its best, is an act of prolonged, intense perception. It celebrates the world by being true to it.

DLB: You use movie and photography terms in your fiction: stills, frozen frames, transparencies. Your settings are sometimes built piece by piece—like the bar-restaurant in "Dice"—just as movie sets are. Have movies been a great influence on your work?

BOSWORTH: Not in any self-conscious sense. I grew up in America and, like most Americans, have seen hundreds of movies and watched thousands of hours of TV. It's probably impossible not to have one's visual sense altered in some way by all this exposure. In *The Death of Descartes*, for example, the image of the frozen frame obviously comes from photography and perhaps even from sports on TV; it seemed useful to me because it's an accurate metaphor for the way the rational mind, the detective's mind, operates—always wanting to stop reality in order to analyze it. I don't see the influence of movies, though, in "Dice." The construction of the setting in that story is distinctly verbal, not cinematic.

DLB: Are there literary influences you can pinpoint?

BOSWORTH: That's a difficult question. All good fiction is inspiring in some way and, I suspect, has a subtle effect. Conrad comes to mind because he was an early favorite and because I admire the high seriousness of his work and the intensity with which

he observes his environment. His introduction to *The Nigger of the Narcissus* inspired my one real literary essay. I was reading John Barth, who is a genuine virtuoso, when I first started writing and learned a lot about fictional form from his *Lost in the Funhouse*. Further back, as a sophomore in college, I was assigned Marguerite Duras's *Moderato Contabile*. It has occurred to me only recently, upon rereading, that that short and musical masterpiece may have had a profound if subliminal effect on my perception of what a story should be.

DLB: The Drue Heinz Literature Prize was established to promote the recognition of good short stories and novellas, which University of Pittsburgh Press director Frederick A. Hetzel has called the "stepchildren" of literature. Why have you concentrated on short fiction rather than the novel?

BOSWORTH: Actually I haven't. As a fiction writer, I don't self-consciously limit myself to a certain length before I start, but rather try to discover the scope each story requires. Fred's comment, though, is a perceptive one. This freedom of discovery I cherish so much is definitely circumscribed by the marketplace. For whatever reason, publishers these days want novels, not story collections. I'm particularly fond of novellas, and they're the bane of booksellers. The Heinz Prize, and a few others, have come to the aid of short fiction when it was most needed. Their importance, though, isn't just to subsidize the short-story writer as opposed to the novelist, but to promote the freedom of choice necessary for high-quality literature.

DLB: Is there work in progress that you'd like to talk about?

BOSWORTH: I've just finished a 125-page—what should I call it to make it more marketable?—"short novel." It's a lyrical meditation on fathers and sons, written in honor of (and frequently interrupted by) our first baby. It was a particularly difficult and ambitious project—although perhaps they all seem that way to me when I'm finishing. I'm also in the middle of two other novels and have a number of ideas for other stories. A lack of projects has never been one of my problems as a writer. The difficulty lies in doing the job right—the job must be done right. And that takes endless rewrites, so much time.

–Jean W. Ross

SUMMARY OF YOUR BOOK (350-500 words)

It is from this description of the book that the promotion staff will get much of the information used in writing advertising copy.

In addition to summarizing the book, please include a brief comment about its purpose, method, special source material. What distinguishes it from other books in its field? What is its "first" quality? What contribution does it make to knowledge in its field?

If it is a nonscholarly book such as poetry, is there anything you wish to say about the intent or content of your work, your working habits, your background, and your reason for writing the book that might be used in the jacket copy?

I'm not sure how this applies to fiction, and would prefer to have someone else "summarize" the collection — although I would be happy to comment on advertising copy sent me. (Perhaps the prize's judges would be best qualified to describe it.)

Excerpt from David Bosworth's application for the Drue Heinz Literature Prize

SUMMARY OF YOUR BOOK (350-500 words)

It is from this description of the book that the promotion staff will get much of the information used in writing advertising copy.

In addition to summarizing the book, please include a brief comment about its purpose, method, special source material. What distinguishes it from other books in its field? What is its "first" quality. What contribution does it make to knowledge in its field?

If it is a nonscholarly book such as poetry, is there anything you wish to say about the intent or content of your work, your working habits, your background, and your reason for writing the book that might be used in the jacket copy?

These are stories about the circumstances that join and divide men and women--stories of politics, sexual and otherwise; of age differences; of the weight of custom; of contempts whether vicious or polite.

Excerpt from Robley Wilson's application for the Drue Heinz Literature Prize

The Island Trees Case: A Symposium on School Library Censorship

Jean W. Ross

In September 1975, three members of the Island Trees, Long Island, school board attended a conference sponsored by Parents of New York-United, where they received a list of books which that organization considered objectionable reading for high school students. Shortly after the conference, two members of the board checked the high school library and found that it contained some of the books listed. At a meeting in February 1976 the board requested that the junior and senior high school principals remove eleven books from the library's shelves: *The Fixer* by Bernard Malamud (winner of the 1976 Pulitzer Prize for fiction and assigned reading in one senior English course at the time); *Slaughterhouse-Five* by Kurt Vonnegut; *Soul on Ice* by Eldridge Cleaver; *The Naked Ape* by Desmond Morris; *Down These Mean Streets* by Piri Thomas; *Best Short Stories by Negro Writers*, edited by Langston Hughes; the anonymous *Go Ask Alice*; *A Hero Ain't Nothin' But a Sandwich* by Alice Childress; *Black Boy* by Richard Wright; *Laughing Boy* by Oliver La Farge; and *A Reader for Writers*, edited by Jerome Archer.

The objections of school superintendent Richard Morrow resulted in the formation of a committee of eight—four school staff members and four parents—appointed jointly by the superintendent and the board. This committee was asked to read the books, consider their suitability for educational purposes, and make recommendations to the board. When the committee presented its recommendations, the board overruled them on several points and finally removed all but two of the books—*Laughing Boy* and *Black Boy*—from the library.

The board's action triggered a series of legal moves that ultimately reached the United States Supreme Court. Represented by the New York Civil Liberties Union, five students brought suit against the Island Trees school board, charging that the students' First Amendment rights had been violated by the board's removal of the books. This suit was dismissed without a trial by the district court, which held the board's action to be within its rights and obligations.

The next move was an appeal, heard by a three-judge panel. The decision was split, with one of the judges upholding the school board's right to determine matters of student curriculum under its authority. Judge Charles B. Sifton, who wrote the panel's opinion, strongly questioned the school board's motives and methods in removing the books. The panel remanded the case to the lower court for trial. In response to the school board's petition, a second court of appeals hearing was held, this time before a full panel of ten. This panel's evenly divided opinion allowed the earlier panel's decision to stand. At this point the school board appealed to the United States Supreme Court, which agreed to hear the case.

The Island Trees case has attracted nationwide attention for several reasons. With very few exceptions, the authority of local school boards in matters of curriculum and the selection of texts and other books has gone unchallenged. Any dissatisfaction with the actions of board members has traditionally been expressed at the next election. The suit against the Island Trees school board not only threatened the board's authority but also raised the charge that it was attempting to suppress ideas. Judge Sifton, in his appeals court opinion, asserted that books cannot be removed from school libraries because of the ideas contained in them. This point is central to the basic controversy, with the school board acting as custodian of community morals and standards, and the students protesting what they perceived as the violation of their First Amendment right to receive information and ideas.

The Supreme Court has generally avoided intervening in cases involving the jurisdiction of local school boards. Since previous school-library cases had failed to produce a consensus guideline in the lower courts, a clear Supreme Court decision on the Island Trees issues could stand as a signal and precedent for the future. It is extremely significant, further, in coming at a time when the heightened activity of conservative political and religious groups has reawakened concern about censorship and book banning. The *New Yorker* (26 April 1982) has described it as a time when "a contagion of prudery, anxiety, and silliness . . . has forced librarians—mostly school librarians—to remove books from their shelves." Some groups, conversely, claim to be the victims of censorship by omission when books expressing their views are excluded from school libraries in the selection process. The Reverend Lamarr Mooneyham, chairman of the North Carolina chapter of the Moral Majority, says, "Let's be fair, let's be balanced. You are what you read. It's not healthy to have just a single viewpoint."

In July 1981 the Association of American Publishers, the American Library Association, and the Association for Supervision and Curriculum Development released a report entitled "Limiting What Students Shall Read: Books and Other Learning Materials in Our Public Schools: How They Are Selected and How They Are Removed." To gather data, the sponsoring groups conducted nationwide surveys of elementary and secondary public school librarians, library supervisors, principals, district superintendents, and state-level administrators. Survey results indicated that during 1978-1980, the period covered, nearly one administrator in five and nearly one librarian in three had experienced some challenge to classroom or library materials. Further, more than half the challenges resulted in censorship or restriction to some extent.

The United States Supreme Court handed down its decision on Island Trees in June 1982. In a 5-4 vote, it ordered a lower court trial of the case. Justice William Brennan wrote in the majority opinion: "In brief, we hold that local school boards may not remove books from school library shelves simply because they dislike the ideas contained in those books and seek by their removal to 'prescribe what shall be orthodox in politics, nationalism, religion, or other matters of opinion.' *West Virginia* v. *Barnette*, 319 U.S., at 642." The court failed to produce a ruling on the merits of the case, however, because Justice Byron White, though joining in the majority opinion for remanding the case to the lower court for trial, saw no necessity for issuing "a dissertation on the extent to which the First Amendment limits the discretion of the school board to remove books from the school library." The dissenting justices upheld the school board's right to remove books from the school library at its discretion.

As an assessment of the ruling in the September-October 1982 *Authors Guild Bulletin* points out, the Supreme Court's decision failed to resolve the basic issues in the case, and its affirmation of the appeals court ruling in ordering a trial is weak because of the decision's close split. "The

opinions in the Island Trees appeal," it concludes, "are not likely to discourage intolerant school boards from removing library books they disapprove of."

In August 1982 the Island Trees school board voted 6-1 to return the previously banned books to the library, with the provision that librarians notify the parents of students who checked them out. According to a *New York Times* account, the board's attorney had strongly advised against further court exposure for the case. In January 1983, after New York Attorney General Robert Abrams had stated that the personal notification requirement violated a law on confidentiality of library records, the school board voted 4-3 that the books could remain on the library shelves with no restrictions on their use. At that time lawyers for the school board and the New York Civil Liberties Union were still trying to negotiate a formal settlement of the case.

The larger issues that kept this case alive for seven years are still unresolved, as are a host of related problems: for example, proper procedure in determining what books are suitable for students' use in schools, censorship in the selection process, and the right of parents and other citizens to intervene in matters of required reading for students. For their thoughts on these questions, *DLB* talked with people who have been actively involved in the issues.

AN INTERVIEW
with JUDITH KRUG

Judith Krug is director of the American Library Association's Office for Intellectual Freedom and editor of the Newsletter on Intellectual Freedom.

DLB: In the spring of 1980 the American Library Association, the Association of American Publishers, and the Association for Supervision and Curriculum Development undertook a nationwide survey to "investigate the relationship between censorship pressures and book selection in the schools" (*Newsletter on Intellectual Freedom*, September 1981). The findings were reported in summer 1981 in "Limiting What Students Shall Read: Books and Other Learning Materials in Our Public Schools: How They Are Selected and How They Are Removed." How does the current number of challenges to books compare with the number reported in that study?

KRUG: I can only report what's happening in the

Judith Krug

Office for Intellectual Freedom; I have no additional evidence to change the figures we came up with in "Limiting What Students Shall Read." Interestingly, in the years 1978-1980, approximately 300 incidents per year were being reported to this office. I would stress that this figure came from simply going through our files and counting the number of incidents of which we were aware. In the period from late 1980 through the present, the number of incidents reported to this office has increased approximately threefold, to between 900 and 1,000 incidents in 1981 and 1982. However, I don't feel that you can really equate the figures in "Limiting" with what we do in the office; they are two different kinds of figures.

Secondly, Lee Burress, a professor of English at the University of Wisconsin, has just completed and released his fourth survey of high school librarians. His last survey was in 1977. The number of high school librarians reporting censorship pressures has increased four percent, from thirty percent in the 1977 survey to thirty-four percent in the 1982 survey. Unfortunately, the only figures available from Lee's most recent study are the most obvious ones: *x* number of librarians reported pressures, and the names of books usually attacked.

What he's planning to do is a very careful analysis which will include some socioeconomic analyses—tie the figures into community size, economic status of the community per se and the complainants individually, etc. I think this is going to be extremely valuable, but it will not be available until late summer 1983.

DLB: Conservative groups challenge liberal groups' definition of censorship, claiming that the real censorship has already taken place in the selection process. How would the ALA define censorship?

KRUG: We go back to Lester Asheim's original article "Not Censorship But Selection," published back in 1953. I honestly have not found anything better than Les's basic description of the differences between censorship and selection: a censor looks for something which will allow him or her to remove or exclude the material; a selector looks for that thing within the overall collection-building guidelines that will make or keep the material a part of the collection. It's one's attitude. I know it's very easy to say, "You're a censor"; it's much more difficult to identify the difference between a censor and a selector. I feel that anyone is a censor who says someone else may not read or view or listen to material because that material is offensive or deemed inaccurate for whatever minor reason.

DLB: Teachers and administrators are said sometimes to invoke First Amendment rights as a means of evading the question of appropriateness in the case of some book selections. Does the ALA consider parents to have a right to question the appropriateness of books selected for the instruction of their children?

KRUG: We are concerned with library materials, and your question is taken to apply to textual materials. But our basic position in regard to what students shall read is that it is the right and responsibility of parents or guardians, and only parents or guardians, to guide their children, and only *their* children, in appropriate reading material. To extrapolate that to the classroom: we recommend that if a parent is sorely exercised over particular novels, for instance, that a child will read in the classroom, then the teacher should make alternate selections available.

Many of our current complaints are about textual materials in their aggregate. One of the problems is that public education is responsible for educating all the children, not only those whose parents have the loudest voices or are the most powerful in a given community or, indeed, comprise the majority. Public education and public libraries must serve the needs of the entire community, whether that community is the school community per se, the students in a given classroom, or the broader based community. We live in a constitutional republic, which strives within broad parameters to provide to each individual citizen the greatest possible individual freedom. It is a balancing act. We must make sure that despite the loudness, the ferocity of complaints, and the power behind the complaints, we continue to try to educate all the children and fulfill the needs of all the community. We are not a homogeneous society. And students are even less so than the adult population.

DLB: Are clearer selection guidelines and involving parents in the selection process at least a partial means of reasonably preventing book challenges?

KRUG: I think it is important for parents to have at least some degree of input. I do not believe that parents, by virtue of the fact that they are parents, are capable of identifying appropriate educational materials for all children. I feel very strongly about that. This is not to say, however, that parents shouldn't have some degree of input. At the same time, this is a democracy, to use the phrase of some of our protesters. Well, in some ways it is: we elect people by majority, and school board members are in most instances elected, to represent the public's—including parents'—interest in the schools. The great push to involve parents today is, in some ways, rather amusing to me; parents have *always* been involved in the process by means of electing school board members to represent them. What is really being said by the protesters is not we want to be represented in the process, but we want to control the process. If you do not do what we want, without question, your actions are verboten. I will not accept that.

DLB: How does the ALA feel about the Supreme Court decision in the Island Trees case?

KRUG: If the institution that is ALA had a position, it would be that it is a victory. It is a victory by virtue of the issue that was before the Court: whether school boards have absolute authority—that is, could the Island Trees school board remove materials because they personally did not like them? What the Supreme Court said is, we have to go back for trial. But in the process of saying that, they said,

in effect, no, school boards do not have absolute authority to remove whatever they wish.

At the outset, it's a victory. Think what would happen if the Supreme Court had said that a school board could do whatever it wanted. Of course there were previous decisions which indicated that no school board could systematically eliminate areas of study with which they disagreed from the curriculum or from the library. But in some ways the Court has not only strengthened this principle but broadened it, in that it extends beyond areas of study to materials representative of their class that may not be what school board members would personally like to see being made available to students.

But starting from the proposition that we have a victory, I think the next point is that it is indeed a very tenuous victory. The plurality opinion secured the votes of merely three justices, with Blackman concurring in part but writing his own brief in part, which became part of the plurality; and White saying, in effect, these are all interesting issues, but I don't have enough information on which to base any decision, and in order to get such information, we have to go back to court. So in effect you have a four-four split. The Court did limit the decision to library materials. Even Brennan, in his plurality decision, made it very clear that he was not dealing with curriculum materials but with library materials. There were some aspects of the decision which I thought were unnecessary, since there were not facts concerning these areas to begin with: for example, that books could be removed if they were educationally unsound or "pervasively" vulgar. I don't believe that these phrases have any meaning. I cannot imagine materials being in the schools that are "educationally unsound." Vulgarity, in terms of school materials, is in the mind of the beholder, just as are truth and beauty and justice. This means we're right back to subjective judgments.

The Supreme Court—Justice Brennan, at least—had an interesting point regarding the process by which materials are not only selected but also reviewed. It's very clear that materials selection policy and procedures are going to be more important, at least in the foreseeable future, because they do guarantee some degree of fairness. I don't think we can hope for much more. But it's also going to mean (again I'm extrapolating from Brennan) that if you develop policy and procedures, you must carry them through to their logical end. You cannot go through the review process and receive the opinions of reviewers and then, because you don't like those opinions, just go ahead and act on the basis of what you feel is more important.

I think Justice Burger's opinion was one of the most vitriolic I have ever read. I was particularly concerned with his view that students may *not* have the right to receive information, but if they do, there are other sources through which to receive the information. I was terribly concerned with the tone of Burger's decision. I think it showed more clearly than almost any other case I've read recently the deep philosophical split on the Supreme Court. And I do not think this bodes well.

AN INTERVIEW
with PHYLLIS SCHLAFLY

Phyllis Schlafly is the founder and president of Eagle Forum, a national organization that promotes profamily values and standards through education and legislation. She is the author of The Power of the Positive Woman *and eight other books.*

DLB: How actively is the Eagle Forum involved in monitoring high school libraries and attempting to have books added or removed?

SCHLAFLY: We are a national profamily organization of volunteers, so there is immense local autonomy; members may do different things that are not directed by national officers. I would say a great many of our members are very interested in education, in curriculum, in textbooks, and in libraries because the majority of our members have children. There is no instance that I know of where any of our members tried to get rid of any book at any time, with the sole exception of the book *Show Me!*, which the local chapter wanted to have removed from the children's section of a library. *Show Me!* has since been withdrawn from sale by the publisher because it is child pornography forbidden by the statute unanimously upheld by the U.S. Supreme Court in *New York* v. *Ferber.*

Our main effort is to try to stop the tremendous censorship that has been going on for years of the books, the ideas, the concepts, and the values that we think are properly part of any educational system or library. We have discovered large areas in which the things we think are important and valid in schools and libraries have been effectively censored out by the prevailing establishment.

DLB: Are you saying, then, that you are actively involved in an effort to see that all points of view are represented in school and library materials?

SCHLAFLY: Yes, we are. There are several fundamental principles here. We feel that anybody who is spending tax dollars is accountable to the public. We believe that libraries should have an obligation very much akin to the Fairness Doctrine that applies to television and radio.

DLB: In the *Phyllis Schlafly Report* you have listed books that you feel should be in libraries. Do you offer specific guidelines for the selection of books for high school libraries?

SCHLAFLY: We have not done that. But I would say that we feel very strongly about the selection of books for the first grade, because one of the most effective areas of censorship in the last several years has been the censorship of first-grade phonics readers and the phonics system. We have a large program of encouraging parents to teach their own children to read by the phonics method when they discover that this method has been censored out of their local schools.

DLB: Part of your concern is for what is called basic education?

SCHLAFLY: Yes; I'm a long-time supporter of basic

Phyllis Schlafly

education, if by that you mean that the first responsibility of schools is to teach children to read and write the English language, to add and subtract—to have the basic verbal and mathematical skills. The illiteracy rate in America today is shocking.

DLB: Would you like to comment on the United States Supreme Court's decision in the Island Trees case?

SCHLAFLY: It is a very confused decision. I think the real issue in the case is whether the final responsibility for book selection should be in the hands of school boards, who are elected by the constituency they serve, or in the hands of the judiciary and special-interest liberal groups like the American Civil Liberties Union. I operate from the principle that all those spending tax money are responsible to the public. They have no right to complain when the public looks over their shoulder and questions the way they spent it. They should carry out the duties their constituents elected them for; if they default on that responsibility, they can be turned out of office at the next election. I find intolerable the whole notion that the responsibility of selecting school curriculum and books can be moved into the hands of federal judges to be decided by litigation.

DLB: How much of a direct voice do you think parents should have in cases where they feel reading or teaching material is questionable?

SCHLAFLY: I think they should have plenty of input. That's their right and responsibility, because they are the ultimate guardians of their children. I don't feel any teacher has the right to teach a child something that is obnoxious to the values of the parent. I think the school board, which is the elected body, should have the responsibility of resolving those conflicts of opinion. I also believe that the world is full of books. There are millions of books. The notion that some particular liberal book, which may become a cause célèbre, is a sine qua non for graduation is absolutely ridiculous. There's no reason schools cannot select books acceptable to parents. I see no reason of any kind why any child should be forced to read a book which is obnoxious to the values of the child's parents. There are too many fine books available from which to select.

DLB: Sometimes, however, parents complain about a book without having read it. Books are attacked on the basis of information from some source outside

the immediate community, as in the Island Trees case. Do you think that's fair?

SCHLAFLY: I think that's irrelevant. I don't think anybody has a right to look into the motives of the parent. Parents have a right to oppose a book on second-hand information just as much as on first-hand information. I don't see any reason why the parent, who is hard-working, trying to earn a living, trying to keep a house, is obligated to read controversial books in order to have an opinion. If it's understood that a book is offensive to their religion, to their values, to their morals, why should parents waste time reading it?

DLB: In an editorial in *Christian Century*, 20 May 1981, James M. Wall affirmed the need for schools "to be sensitive to material made available to young people," but went on to say that "what groups like the Moral Majority and Eagle Forum propose to do is turn back the cultural clock, raiding schools and libraries and demanding adherence to a narrow, limited view of sexuality." How would you answer?

SCHLAFLY: It is, of course, simply false. If he wants to talk about sex education, Eagle Forum has published a flyer on herpes which gives students the facts which the so-called sex educators have declined to give them. They have censored out of the sex-ed materials the fact that herpes is currently incurable. I have examined hundreds of sex-ed materials, and the overwhelming majority do not tell children that. What James Wall said is simply a smokescreen to cover up the censorship that *they* have carried on in order to present promiscuous life-styles, values and attitudes which are offensive to many parents. It is offensive to many parents to present children—and they are children; they're not adults—with the notion that premarital sex is OK as long as they use contraceptives, and if you make a mistake, antibiotics or abortion clinics will take care of it. That is a lie, but that is a fair inference of the overwhelming majority of sex-education material. It is *they* who have censored out the facts about VD, the incurability of herpes, the incidence of cervical cancer among young girls who are promiscuous, and the tremendous psychological and physical consequences of promiscuity.

DLB: Are there any other comments you'd like to make?

SCHLAFLY: Most of what you have read in the press

about me and about Eagle Forum in relation to censorship is completely false. Irresponsible journalists have used my name to make their articles appear newsworthy. They have said things that were completely false and have implied in article after article that we were trying to remove books such as *Huckleberry Finn* and *Mary Poppins*, which is a total fabrication. We call our committee the Stop Textbook Censorship Committee. Our effort is to *stop* the censorship, which is very real, at different levels, such as censorship of the phonics reading method, the censorship out of libraries of anything opposed to the Equal Rights Amendment, the censorship of materials presenting traditional values, and the censorship of the facts about VD.

The whole subject of censorship, in the way that word is used in current articles, is a smokescreen. A teacher or librarian who likes certain material and buys certain books is engaging right at that moment in "preemptive censorship," that is, selecting the books he or she wants the children to read and the public to have access to, and censoring all other books. Most of the censorship goes on at that point. The whole notion that a librarian or a teacher—both of whom get their salaries from tax funds and who are spending tax funds—is not accountable to the public is intolerable in a free society.

Edward B. Jenkinson

AN INTERVIEW

with EDWARD B. JENKINSON

Edward B. Jenkinson is Professor of English Education and director of the English Curriculum Study Center at Indiana University. From 1976 to 1978 he served as chairperson of the National Council of Teachers of English Committee Against Censorship, and he is the author of Censor in the Classroom.

DLB: You've expressed concern that censorship of books in schools is on the rise over the past several years. Do you think most of it is coming from individuals or from groups?

JENKINSON: According to surveys taken by Professor Lee Burress at the University of Wisconsin-Stevens Point and by others, approximately eighty percent of the attempts to remove books from school libraries and classrooms seems to come from individuals. However, that's very hard to ascertain since many individuals do object to books on the basis of reviews prepared and distributed by one or more organizations. The objections made during statewide adoptions of textbooks are more easily detected. They come primarily from organized groups. There is considerable evidence that organized groups throughout the country have increased their attempts to remove materials. As I speak throughout the country, teachers come up to me quietly and tell me about the problems that they are currently experiencing. In one state, for example, which I won't identify, I was told by the state chairperson of the coalition against censorship that he did not know of any activities in his state at that time, but he said that the coalition hadn't had a meeting yet to find out what was going on. Within twenty-four hours I was informed by individual teachers about sixteen incidents. By the time I left, the number was rapidly approaching thirty. That's not unusual. Attacks on the so-called religion of secular humanism are on the rise, and books that allegedly reflect that religion are primary targets of organizations. Thus, it is not surprising that Phyllis Schlafly's Stop Textbook Censorship Committee is attacking sex education as a part of the secular humanism charge.

DLB: One faction charges censorship and the other says no, just the right of parents as guardians and taxpayers to a voice in the educational process. Drawing the line, it seems, is at the heart of the problem. What really constitutes censorship, and where does the parent's right end?

JENKINSON: I came to the study of censorship primarily as a parent and not as an educator. I have three children, one grown and two small ones in school, and I'd been very much concerned about what was happening throughout the country. I feel that, as a parent, I have the right to be concerned about what my children are studying in school and, yes, I have the right to complain—perhaps I even have the *duty* to be concerned and to complain—if I think something is wrong. However, I think that my rights as a parent extend only to my children and not to all the children in my daughter's class, for example, or in the county, or in the state, or—as is the case with Mel and Norma Gabler—in the entire nation. I think I have the right to request alternate assignments where appropriate. But if I call for the removal of something, I am indeed setting myself up as an authority who knows what's right for all.

DLB: You consider alternate assignments, then, a viable solution in some cases in which parents are unhappy with what their children are being asked to read?

JENKINSON: In some cases, yes, particularly with novels. I've talked with English teachers all over the country, and they're willing to make alternate assignments if a parent finds a book objectionable. But when it comes to a prescribed textbook, that's a different matter, and the courts have not dealt with that fully. I think I know how the courts would deal with a parent who objected to a prescribed, state-adopted textbook in a course required for graduation: I don't think the school or the teacher would have to supply an alternate textbook in such a situation.

DLB: How do you feel about the United States Supreme Court's decision in the Island Trees case? What does it imply for the future?

JENKINSON: I was disturbed by the lack of direction in that decision. If I read the majority opinion correctly, it indicates a couple of things: one, that students apparently do have the right to sue for their rights to know and for access to information; two, that there is an indication that school boards

had better develop policies and procedures and follow them. That's one interpretation I read from a First Amendment lawyer; others had not picked up on that. I think school boards throughout this nation need specific procedures for dealing with complaints against school materials, and they must also have materials-selection policies. Professional organizations have been calling for such policies and procedures for nearly two decades. I estimate that at least fifty percent of the schools do not have them. The ALA-ASCD-AAP report "Limiting What Students Shall Read" indicates that seventy-five percent of the school systems have them. I was really surprised by that figure; I think it's quite high.

DLB: You've spoken out on the need for schools and parents to work together. How can it best be done?

JENKINSON: I've had comments from administrators and teachers who have appointed parents to curriculum-planning and textbook-selection committees. The educators indicate that in most instances when parents are faced with the responsibility of reading the materials and deciding what students should be reading and learning, they are for the most part in agreement with the educators about what should be done. Of course we run the risk of having people on these committees who have axes to grind, who have specific points of view to express. But that's a risk we have to take in a democratic society. One of the things that concerns me most is that many people object to books and ideas without having read the books or explored the ideas. When we involve such people in the curriculum process, we expose them for what they are.

DLB: The charge is made that teachers sometimes hide behind the concept of First Amendment rights rather than confront the question of appropriateness of books they assign their students for supplemental reading. Is it justified?

JENKINSON: I'm certain that with as many teachers as we have in this country, there must be some who have hidden behind First Amendment rights. But I think for the most part those teachers who have attempted to match their educational objectives to their teaching materials do not hide behind First Amendment rights. They do not hide behind jargon or anything else. They stand up for their rights and those of their students. Some people don't understand the First Amendment to begin with, and they think it's a ruse teachers and administrators are using.

DLB: Are there any other comments you'd like to make?

JENKINSON: Yes. One of my major concerns in this is that many individuals read textbooks, novels, and everything else solely from their own religious and political points of view and object to anything that does not coincide perfectly with those points of view. I indicate in my speeches that I am very grateful to have been trained by my teachers to read for information, for knowledge, for ideas, for the possibility of broadening my horizons. I was taught *not* to go seeking those things that would only reaffirm my own small view of the world. It seems to me after ten years of studying this issue that one of our particular problems is the great number of people looking at the world and at ideas through blinders. I am also concerned with the distortions of fact that some schoolbook protesters include in their objections. I frequently wonder if they and I are reading the same books.

AN INTERVIEW ————————
with LAMARR MOONEYHAM

Lamarr Mooneyham is state chairman of the Moral Majority of North Carolina and pastor of the Tri-City Baptist Church in Durham.

DLB: It was reported in the Newsletter on Intellectual Freedom, published by the American Library Association's Office for Intellectual Freedom, that early in 1981 the North Carolina chapter of the Moral Majority began a campaign to remove books from the state's schools. According to the report, the Moral Majority's plan was to issue a list of proscribed books, which it did, and then enlist parents to confront local school boards with this list. This raises, among other points, the question of whether it is fair to attack books through agents who in many cases will not have read the books.

MOONEYHAM: No, it isn't, and we have not attempted to do that. We have never engaged in any program to remove books or resource material, and we don't intend to. We fear the removal of books probably as much as some of the conscientious people on the Left do. Unethical people on the Left use statements like these to scare their supporters, I guess, into making contributions. Norman Lear is an expert at that. But we have never in any speech or in any printed material, including the material on

Lamarr Mooneyham

textbooks that was mailed to parents, advocated the removal of a book.

It is correct that we got involved in the issue early in 1981. It was our plan to issue a list of books most complained about by parents in North Carolina. We did not decide on the titles; they were titles actually complained about by parents. We lifted statements out of the books. We encouraged parents to read their children's books, as we do today, and then take whatever action they felt was warranted. If a compliment was warranted, pay a compliment. And there were more books that deserved compliments than books that deserved criticism.

DLB: You're saying that the reports were inaccurate as to the intent and method of the North Carolina Moral Majority in this instance?

MOONEYHAM: They have been from the beginning. I was involved with the agency you've just spoken of, in a gathering in Atlanta in 1981, along with the Columbia Graduate School of Journalism. We repeatedly stated our purpose, but they have preconceived ideas and don't listen to what we say.

They have their minds made up that we want to burn books. I have been invited to places to speak on censorship only to burst my opponents' balloon in the first five minutes by saying, "I don't promote censorship." But these reports have been circulated, and much to my sorrow, it's a very difficult impression to correct. I don't think it *can* be corrected among those who want to believe it.

DLB: What are you trying to achieve where school books are concerned?

MOONEYHAM: It's impossible to "unbuy" a book that has been purchased, but we can get involved in the future selection process. As an agency, we have no claims on the school children. We have said this from the beginning: we resent any organization, whether it be a feminist group, a religious group, or whatever, coming into the schools and trying to press for a particular book's removal. We see parents as the only people who have a right to get involved in that. They have a vested interest in the school—their children. Consequently, we encourage parents to get involved at the local school level. The PTA has been promoting this for years.

We did put out the twenty-eight-page book review to raise the awareness level, to say, "Folks, you might be concerned that this sort of thing exists." But we've found that when you do a book review, if you're on the right of center, it's a hit list; if you're left of center, it's a publication that will aid in positive selection. It depends on which side of the issue you're on.

DLB: Surely some of the parents who receive such a publication, however, go to the schools and press for the removal of books listed in it without any real firsthand knowledge of what they're attacking.

MOONEYHAM: I'm sure that happens. But again, we fall back on our original intent. In every piece of literature that we've ever mailed out—and we can document this—we've encouraged parents to read the books. Personally, as a parent of three, I don't think I have a right to speak until I am familiar with my children's reading material. That's part of the problem in public education today: the parents have removed themselves from the picture altogether, and that is tragic.

DLB: The Moral Majority and other organizations are accused of wanting to manipulate book selection in favor of books that express the viewpoints and ideas they espouse, which could, carried to its possi-

ble extreme, eliminate any presentation of dissenting views. How do you respond to this charge?

MOONEYHAM: We are dedicated to pluralism. We have never objected and do not object now to the opposing point of view being placed beside our point of view, which is the conservative, Judeo-Christian point of view. What we're asking is to be part of the plural. Censorship *has* taken place, but it has been hidden censorship. It's been a slow process over a period of years. Mr. Craig Phillips [the head of the Department of Public Instruction] knows this, but he refuses to come out of his office to talk with us. He likes to tell reporters that "kids need to have access to the world around them." Well, I'll say amen to that. But *I'm* part of the world around them, and I have a large number of people who espouse the same principles I do. We'd like kids to have access to that conservative point of view. Our opponents say most of our points of view are religious, and "surely we couldn't bring religion into the classroom." That would violate the illusory principle of the separation of church and state. Scientific creationism is a good point of view, but it doesn't matter to these people how scientific it is; they're not going to allow it no matter what is proven. We don't blush at evolution. "Make your speech," we say to the evolutionists. "But let us make ours." We're going to get involved, we're going to get people to run for the school board, and we're going to have our voice.

DLB: What is the Moral Majority of North Carolina's current involvement in the selection and control of books for high school libraries?

MOONEYHAM: We're primarily concerned with the elementary school library. We're concerned about all students, but we recognize a point at which a student is grown, for all practical purposes. If students haven't made up their minds at that point, there's very little you can legislate to them. We're particularly concerned with children in the formative years. What we're doing is two-fold. We're encouraging parents to take an interest. In everything we do, every speech we make, we ask the simple question, "Your child's textbooks—have you read them?" And we leave it at that.

The second phase of what we're doing has to do with the selection of books. We are trying to press for legislation that would abolish the textbook commission appointed by the governor. It consists of fourteen people across the state, all of them the governor's friends, hard workers in his campaign—trinket appointments. These fourteen solicit help from fifty-six people on the grass-roots level. They're supposed to approve all of the books that go on the reading list. What we're saying is this: appoint a dogcatcher, but *elect* the people who are responsible for the academic future of all North Carolina schoolchildren. We're suggesting the election of one textbook committee member from each of the eleven congressional districts. Let candidates run for office; allow them to explain their philosophy of education, because that will determine what kind of books they approve and reject. Elect this committee, and then let the committee incorporate a larger number of people on the county level—there are one hundred counties, so perhaps two hundred lay people, volunteers who can help in the process of selection of books.

We also advocate that parents have an opportunity to see the materials that will be used through the school year. The teachers know now what they're going to be using next year. Have a PTA meeting and lay the materials out for parents to see. That's the parents' right, and this may take care of the problems before they happen. We are frightened at the attitude of some of the educators here. For years they've had it their way. When parents begin to question why their children aren't functioning as they should academically, educators don't want them snooping around. Many educators have exhibited an attitude of infallibility, as if they knew it all and parents couldn't possibly add anything to the school program. In New Hanover County, one set of parents received a letter from the school principal saying that they could *not* see the reading materials, that he had talked with the attorney general's office and determined that they had no such right. That's what it has come to in our state, and that's why a lot of parents we talk with don't have it in them to complain or fight. They just wait until next September and put their children in a nonpublic school. Every year in Durham and Orange County the enrollment in the public schools goes down.

DLB: Would you like to comment on the outcome of the Island Trees case and any implications it might have for the future?

MOONEYHAM: I think probably the best nine friends the nonpublic school movement has are the Supreme Court justices. I do not follow their logic in declaring the case a violation of the First Amendment. The school boards I know about are elected, and they should have the power to act. If their

action isn't acceptable to the community, they can be replaced. But when you strip the school board of its power, what you've really done is declare the Supreme Court the national school board. That's totalitarian. Where does that leave representative government? It leaves it in the same ditch as the Arkansas Creationism Bill that passed the legislature, passed the senate, and was signed into law by the governor; then the ACLU circumvented the legislature and the senate, and a judge—who was neither elected nor reelected—overturned it. Where does that leave representative government? You don't have any. You have judges making laws as they go.

The Island Trees case is horrible. I cannot see how the students' rights were violated; they don't occupy seats on the school board, and they don't buy the books. I'm familiar with many of the books in that case, and they're just vulgarity. There's no academic value in those novels. If a high school student wants to buy that sort of thing, then I guess he's free to do that, but I don't think taxpayers ought to be forced to.

DLB: Would you like to make any additional comments?

MOONEYHAM: Yes. We really wonder about the motives of the other side when they put up such a resistance to our getting involved. Every time we dare to open our mouth, we're accused of censorship, and nothing could be farther from the truth. There have been some radicals who have claimed our name, but there's no documentation that they were ever part of our group. This is not our style. We don't see censorship as the solution; it's the problem. And in the years to come we want to see the books that reflect the well-rounded presentation educators talk so much about. We're not sure what they mean when they say well-rounded, but what *we* mean is both sides. And then let the students make up their minds. We know that when they're confronted with both sides, invariably they'll choose that set of principles and absolutes that makes sense.

AN INTERVIEW ———————————
                    with HARRIET BERNSTEIN

Harriet Bernstein is Senior Associate at the Council for Basic Education. From 1972-1976 she served as an elected school board member in Montgomery County, Maryland.

DLB: Would you describe the Council for Basic Education's general aims and its philosophy on the question of censorship in high school libraries?

BERNSTEIN: Our position is to preserve the free marketplace of ideas for books in school libraries and their availability to students, subject only to their appropriateness to students' level of maturity.

DLB: You've expressed what you call a "plague on both their houses" attitude toward the factions concerned with the issue of censorship. Why so?

BERNSTEIN: If you assume that we don't want to prevent children from reading books that contain ideas departing from majoritarian sentiments in the United States, that it's OK for kids to read about political and economic ideas at variance with the norms, that it's OK for kids to read about viewpoints of subgroups within the country that vary from the majority culture, then you're left with the question of appropriateness to the age level of students. And that's a debate that doesn't take place. Part of my frustration is that the people who would be my

Harriet Bernstein

natural philosophical allies, such as the American Library Association and other groups opposed to censorship, get so wrapped up in the First Amendment question and in "professional prerogative" that their attitude becomes, how dare an ignorant parent come in and question my judgment? Educators theoretically ought to be, even more so than parents, the experts on the psychological, social, sexual maturity levels of children, because they study child development and psychology, and they see kids en masse at given age and grade levels. They also have a feeling about community standards. So they should be able to offer opinions on appropriateness, but they don't.

Let me give you an example. You could probably get one hundred percent of elementary school librarians to say that *Playboy* would not be appropriate for elementary school libraries. But when it comes to Judy Blume, when the question isn't so grotesque, how do you determine appropriateness? Teachers and librarians clearly accept the principle that certain things are not appropriate for children at certain ages and stages of their growing up. But you can't engage them in an objective discussion—at least I have never been able to.

Another example: When I was on the school board, there were some right-wingers who challenged the assignment of *Deliverance* to a tenth-grade English literature class. *Deliverance* has an anal rape. Well, the objectors were too embarrassed to say what their objection was, but the staff never engaged in any discussion other than saying, "First Amendment rights" and "professional authority." There is a real question to be answered there, and nobody discussed it.

On one hand you have people who are prudish and easy to make fun of saying, "I don't want children exposed to that. That's dirty; that's disgusting." On the other you have people saying, "I am a professional. This is an award-winning book. Besides, there's the First Amendment and you're limiting what students shall read." You have a complicated issue here that concerns appropriateness—not alien political philosophy or alien economic theory or anything like that, but a question of whether tenth-graders will be harmed in their growth and development if they are exposed to that material. But nobody discussed it! That's why I get annoyed. People talk past each other, one group speaking legalisms and claims to professional authority, the other speaking of their personal beliefs of appropriateness, but there's no real joining together to discuss the issue.

DLB: How do you feel about the Supreme Court ruling on the Island Trees case?

BERNSTEIN: I was disappointed that the Supreme Court didn't resolve the issue.

DLB: As a school board member, you were called upon to deal with challenges to library books from various citizen lobbies representing right-wing groups, minority groups, women's groups, and religious groups. Were there many challenges from individual parents or small groups of parents that didn't seem motivated by some larger organization?

BERNSTEIN: Yes, there were. To give you the flavor of the kind of challenges we had, there was a newly formed Hispanic task force, because we were beginning to get a Cuban influx in our county. They found some Spanish textbooks that had photographs of students at the University of Puerto Rico who all looked terribly Castilian—there was not a single dark-skinned student. They violently objected to that and wanted us to remove those books from use and replace them with books that reflected the variety of skin colors at the University of Puerto Rico. While we agreed with them in principle, we didn't believe that the issue rose to the level of requiring us to spend money to replace a fairly new set of books.

DLB: Did parents generally seem to be well informed about the books they expressed concern about?

BERNSTEIN: Yes, in our case. Of course it is a very highly educated, very articulate, very affluent community. I would say that we didn't have many people coming forward on the basis of some newsletter from the Gablers or something similar telling them to demand that the school board ban this or that book. I would say that all the people who came forth as challengers appeared to have read the book and to know what they were talking about. It was just a question of philosophical disagreement.

DLB: Does the Council for Basic Education offer guidelines for the selection of books to be used in school curricula and for dealing with threats to those books from outside?

BERNSTEIN: No. We keep up with what's recommended, and we certainly support the general notion that a school district ought to have a clear policy and ought to provide a mechanism agreed upon by the people of that community for determining appropriateness and community standards, and for processing complaints. A school district ought to be receptive to complaints, to see them as positive, and not assume that all wisdom inheres in the profession. And the profession ought to be willing to engage in serious debate rather than draw in the wagons and wrap themselves in the flag.

The Most Powerful Book Review in America

Christopher Surr

To state that the *New York Times Book Review* is the most powerful book-review publication in America is not to make a great claim. The competition is meager. The *New York Review of Books* is not interested in literature and has lost its sense of mission since the cessation of the Vietnam and Watergate hostilities.

If "power" is defined as selling power, the *NYTBR* exercises it. A front-page review sells a lot of books; any *NYTBR* review—even a bad one—sells books. A generally accepted rule in publishing is that a Sunday *Times* review cannot break a book, but can make it. The worst thing the *Times* can do to a book is ignore it. Many buyers—including librarians and bookshop owners—use the *NYTBR* as an order catalog. Books-By-Phone has run an ad in the *NYTBR* inviting readers to "Think of This Week's Review As Our Catalog."

The charges that have been brought against the *NYTBR* are familiar: that it is insular (the borough of Manhattan is the biggest hick town in America); that it operates on the buddy system—or the enemy system; that its coverage is too limited; that its reputation is greater than its actual influence.

DLB invited comments on these charges, and the replies reveal a general feeling that the *NYTBR* does the best it can given the difficulties of its job: too many books to be considered for review, the complexities of the literary life, and tender authorial egos. Herbert Gold made the point that the *NYTBR* is by default the victim of its prominence. "The *New York Times Book Review* is not written by the ideal critic, Posterity. Human beings do it, even though readers say, 'The New York Times says. . . .' The problem, for readers, writers, and I daresay for the editors of the *New York Times Book Review*, is its awful power. If there were a countervailing force, its human failings could be forgiven more easily. Alas, every other review medium is just as subject to caprice, favoritism, and insularity; and none has any power to compare with the *NYTBR*."

One writer, Mary McCarthy, addressed herself to the interest value of the supplement: "My main objection to the *Times Book Review* has nothing to do with unfairness or lack of 'responsibility'; it's merely that it's so boring."

Malcolm Cowley, a participant in the publishing scene for some fifty years, observed that under the editorship of Harvey Shapiro the *NYTBR* has become more responsive to literature. "His predecessors mostly chose 'big' books, those with big subjects from the standpoint of politics and current events, especially when they were deciding what to feature on the front page. The general Sunday editor rode herd on them, always demanding book reviews that were 'in the news.' Shapiro seems to have more latitude, and perhaps he goes too far in featuring experimental novels that nobody much enjoys reading. He seems to have little political bias, and that is a great virtue in these days of embittered ideologists."

Howard Kaminsky, president of Warner Books, recently commented, "I see no hope for the *New York Times Book Review* until Harvey Ginzburg [*sic*] retires permanently to Yaddo" (*Publishers Weekly*, 17 December 1982). Only one publisher responded to the *DLB* survey, Roger W. Straus, president of Farrar, Straus & Giroux. He observed, "I believe the *New York Times Book Review* does live up to its responsibility. One can always quibble from time to time, but in the main I think that they do a good job both in the selection of the reviewers and in the selections of books that they review, and therefore the *Times* does serve the national audience. My only major difference of opinion with

their policy would be that they should use their extraordinarily valuable space more for reviews than for the essays and interviews which could well go as fill-in material in the daily *Times*. And they should pay more attention to the 'new wave' of publishing which is and will remain in the near foreseeable future trade paperback publishing."

JOHN GARDNER:

Does the New York Times Book Review *live up to its responsibility as the country's most influential book review publication?*

First let me say that only in a narrow sense, it seems to me, is the *NYT Book Review* the country's most influential book review publication. It is indeed read by a great many people in all parts of the country, but on sensitive issues it very often stands alone, or so it seems to me, with book reviews ranging from the *Philadelphia Enquirer* to the *Chicago Trib Book World* to the *LA Times BR* on the other side. I lived for years in the Far West and Midwest, and I think there the *NYTBR* is perceived as a fairly trustworthy spokesman for an, excuse the expression, Eastern Establishment position. I myself certainly perceived it that way, and still do, now that I'm an Easterner again. I think it's definitely a good thing that the *NYTBR* represent, with fair predictability, not the whole country but a section of it— after all, it's a very big country. It's true that *NYTBR* uses, with some regularity, reviewers not strictly Eastern. Even so, the tone seems to me distinctly Eastern. If the *Times Book Review* gives Westerners or Midwesterners a fair shake it does so, I think, in an honest effort not to be *too* provincial. In answer to your question, then, I would say the *NYTBR* does not have the responsibility your question claims for it. A dog is not responsible for seeing colors in the same way as a man from Oklahoma. The two are not looking at the same reality; to see the same thing, then, one or the other would have to lie.

Do you find the reviews to be fair?

Often not, but fairness is a relative matter. Anyone who regularly follows the *NYTBR* can tell horror stories. Though I myself have sometimes criticized the writer Maxine Kumin, I once read a piece in the *NYTBR* so savage that, as I read, I lost feeling in my hands. Another time Helen Vendler, a critic for whom I have the greatest respect, felt, apparently, an inexplicable urge to go after the poetry of Joyce Carol Oates. Granted Miss Oates is far better at fiction than at poetry, but the Vendler-Oates contest was, to say the least, unequal, and I think it was bad taste to publish Miss Vendler's review. On yet another occasion, a bad writer who had been flunked in creative writing by Nicholas Delbanco was assigned review of a Nicholas Delbanco novel. I know all the people involved, the writer, the reviewer, and the assigner of the review, and I am as certain as one can be about these things that the resulting hatchet job was no surprise to the *NYTBR*. No regular follower of the *NYTBR* is surprised to see a novel reviewed by one of the novelist's closest friends or most outspoken enemies, depending, of course, on the review assigner's opinion of the writer. On the other hand, I know at first hand of many cases where the *NYTBR* editors rejected a review for its patent unfairness. I think the bottom line—in general at least—is this: the *NYTBR* is essentially in the business of selling good books and discouraging bad ones, and the editors do, by their lights, the best job possible. To their credit it can be said that they're subjective. Art *is* subjective. When my dear and close friend Richard Locke, a former editor of the *NYTBR*, listed the hundred or so best novelists in America, he did not include me. He cannot help having known that my feelings would be hurt, and I think it's impossible that the omission was anything but intentional, but he stands where he stands, for which reason I forgive him. Stupidity is bad, but dishonesty is worse. I'm absolutely convinced that the *NYTBR* is as fair as it knows how to be. Even when it wiggles to achieve the results it wants, it does it from idealism. If someone were to argue that the *NYTBR* is profoundly stupid, I might not be able to think of an effective counterargument except that, from time to time, it has had intelligent editors. But I do not think the *NYTBR* is intentionally unfair. To the contrary, it bends over backward to be fair, by its lights.

What do you think of the selection process—the books to be reviewed and the people selected to review them?

I have frequently visited the *NYTBR* floor, mostly to ask friends there to come play with me—have a drink, go to supper. No one who has not seen that place can understand or imagine, I swear to you, what problems they face with regard to selection. The whole huge room—the size of a football field—is divided into cubicles, each of which is piled high with books. A hundred people in each cubicle could not read all the books there, from major publishers and small presses. Around every desk—perhaps fifty desks—books are piled in six-foot stacks, maybe ten or fifteen stacks. Every one of the sub-subeditors at the *NYTBR* reads as much as he/she can in the available time, but inevitably, since they can't get through everything, they mainly read two kinds of books—the book sent by a major publisher whose reputation can be respected, or the book some friend has suggested they pay close attention to. Reading and judging every book published is a physical impossibility. In fact, reading only the most highly recommended books of the most responsible publishers is almost beyond human means. So on the whole I would say they select books for review as well and honorably as they can. As for whom they select for reviewing, well, that is, as we say these days, iffy. If it's a major novel, the people at the *NYTBR* are likely to choose, as I've already indicated, people who will be interesting—that is, close friends or deep enemies. Not that that always happens. The *NYTBR* has a policy favoring objectivity—they mean to avoid friends or enemies. More often than not, I think, that policy is subverted; but for idealistic reasons. Their way of working is too complex—too human and intuitive—for hard description, but some of the factors involved are these: If the editor in question loves or hates a given book, it is hard for him/her to assign it to someone who might not feel likewise. In all honesty, who wouldn't do much the same? Long ago, Melville's *Moby-Dick* was assigned to a writer who liked a book called *Helen's Babies* much better. What editor wants to make a mistake like that? Slightly less long ago, the whole work of Dostoevski was unfavorably compared to *Mein Kampf*. If I, a person of strong opinions, were an editor of the *NYTBR*, I would do my best to get a proper review, by my lights. However famous he may be, I would not ask Stanley Fish to review anything. . . . Or Harold Bloom. And so on. The people who assign reviews at the *NYTBR* care deeply about books. Perhaps they think they're objective, but the truth is they're desperately serious people, and they'll do anything—for the most part unconsciously—to get the right thing said about a given book. I say, Terrific!

With one reservation. The *NYTBR* is not so good at poetry. The best thing they can do for poetry—which they regularly do, to their credit—is say nothing at all. (I've said many times in print that Helen Vendler is a superb critic of poetry; but her pieces were rare, and she's now retired.) I have often voiced in private conversation the speculation that perhaps Harvey Shapiro, one of the worst poets who ever lived, and editor of the *NYTBR*, may secretly think that by savaging every poet in America he may make room for his own verses. Second only to opera, in my crank opinion, poetry is the greatest art known to humanity. The greatest civilizations that ever thrived thrived on poetry. To this day even the stupid Russians do. So do we at society's bottom level. Think of the best songs of Stevie Wonder, or Arkansas unknowns who write splendid lines like "My gal took my heart and she stomped that sucker flat." We are—all academia to the contrary—a deeply poetic people, and we have among us some of the greatest poets who ever lived. For some queer reason (up-mobility, I think) we scorn poetry if we're "smart." Imagine a poetry section of the *NYTBR* edited by Galway Kinnell! Or Carl Dennis, or James Dickey—and so on. Businessmen understand. A major paper manufacturer recently hired Dickey to do a piece on how to understand poetry. (Beware of writing off businessmen.) The *New York Times Book Review* is scared to death of real poetry. It's there—and only there, I think—that you see their vulgarity. I'm a Welshman, and I used to think the secret of my people's greatness was poetry (and it is). But then I chanced to notice the secret of the Irish (we used to eat them), and the Germans and French, Vietnamese and Koreans, even, God help us, Englishmen. I don't say everyone should appreciate Robert Frost or Wallace Stevens; but surely

no one doubts that the greatness of the Beatles has partly to do with the words. Or listen to Grace Slick. And so on. If I despise the *New York Times*, which I don't really, it's because it's pale and intellectual, it has no roots in what is really American. High-class poetry is nothing but a wonderful refinement of normal human poetry, and the *NYTBR* has no room for either. It's better, in this regard, than most papers. (*Rolling Stone* tries, but it's not interesting.) The *New York Times Book Review*, in short, is very very good, very fair, very honest, but—in my opinion—out of touch. I think the editors of the *New York Times Book Review* would be embarrassed to hear that most Americans love poetry—bad and good (almost equally). And even if they believed me, what could they do? Galway Kinnell is not likely to give up his art for regular reviewing. Dickey might—but it's not likely. Anthony Hecht reviewed for them once, but he found it too unpleasant to face poets he'd honestly criticized—and why not? He likes them and would never criticize them except to make them better, but he found that his criticism hurt their feelings.

So I think the *NYTBR* is as good as it can be on poetry, however lousy.

Does the New York Times Book Review *serve a national audience? Should it do so?*

No.

GEORGE V. HIGGINS:

I think the *NYT Book Review* fulfills its obligation of impartiality about as well as can be expected, which is to say: not very well. The editors, when all is said and done, must commonly rely upon the scruples of the reviewers they select; while they are certainly aware of the notables in the New York literary mafia, who praise each others' books with a shamelessness that would gag a goat and torpedo the works of those who labor outside the pale, they cannot possibly keep track of new affections and grudges and seductions daily arising among those legions who have never been to tea at Diana Trilling's or dinner at Elaine's. They must depend upon the writers to make full disclosure (*e.g.*, "This son of a bitch gored me the last time and now I'm gonna clean his clock for him in this review"; or "I've had Harold in my pocket since my first book, and by God I'm gonna give him a nice smooth ride on his new book.")

Sad to state, writers are about as honorable as

Congressmen. There is just as large a proportionate number of logrollers and snipers in the groves where the muses wander as in the U.S. Capitol membership. When the reviewer discloses his potential bias, the *Review* often withdraws the offer, no matter whether the bias be for good or for ill. I know because Yolanda Andrews offered me a book by a gentleman for whom I have been lying in ambush for some time, and later on a book by a fellow whose work I admire extravagantly and who is a friend of mine as well. In each instance, I told her what she was doing, and what the probable result would be, and I fully accorded with her decision to withdraw each of the offers notwithstanding my stated intention to include a declaration of my bias in the reviews. Significantly, the first time the issue cropped up, she appeared startled by my response; this makes me think that conflict of interest is not a condition which greatly vexes the consciences of some other reviewers, who lie low and get their innings in when the chances present themselves. But there is nothing the *Book Review* can do about such intellectual venality, and it should not be criticized for failure to perform a task beyond human capacity.

Where I do fault the *Review* is in its policy of giving the reviewer the last word. My Watergate book was assigned to a pal of Sam Dash, whom I treated with scorn; the reviewer, without disclosing what he was doing (in which case I would have had no complaint) shotgunned the book. I demanded equal time to describe the coziness of the two and learned that the reviewer would be afforded the chance to reply to my reply. This does not seem fair—he'd had his shot, and I think I was entitled to take mine.

I think the *Review* serves a national audience about as well as any publication so specialized— there aren't many book buyers among 220 million citizens. Most, I think, are sufficiently sophisticated to use it more as a catalog of current new books which contains some opinions quite possibly at variance with those of any sane human being, than as Received Wisdom. Those who are not deserve what they get; they're in over their intellectual depths the minute they open it.

THOMAS BERGER:

Insofar as I am competent to answer your questions about the *New York Times Book Review*, which, frankly, I rarely see (as I rarely see the book-review sections or columns of any other publica-

tion), I should answer them as follows, portmanteau-fashion: the *Book Review* probably does as good a job as could be done, in responsibility, fairness, selection of reviewers, and serving a national audience. In any case, I am sure that the editors make a strenuous and sincere effort to do a good job. But it is inevitable that unfortunate things will happen. And I think I can make that statement with unassailable authority, for I had to publish *five* novels before getting my first favorable review in that literary supplement. Yet at no time during those deplorable years (1958-1970) did I take this as the effect of intentional malice on the part of anyone: I recognized it as simply the cretin fecklessness with which my work was so often greeted in those days (though I must say that no other publication was so consistently negative towards me).

But in justice I should add that the *NYTBR* has in the years since made handsome atonement for its early miscreance.

ISHMAEL REED:

Yesterday, I went into the Old Harbor bookstore here in Sitka, Alaska, and asked for the *New York Times Book Review*. The store owner gave me a free copy; he said, "I can't give it away." I get the *Book Review* in Berkeley free because the storeowners tell me it doesn't sell independently of the rest of the sections.

I think that this shows how much the Book Review is out of contact with the national culture, at a time when American writing is undergoing a renaissance due to the strong representation of Native-American, Chicano, Asian-American, student, feminist, and other groups who have, up to now, been excluded from the American writing scene.

The response to the *New York Times Book Review* to this movement has been hostile when not ignoring it altogether. Paul Zweig, a critic, used Richard Rodriguez's book as an opportunity to lambast Spanish, black English, and Affirmative Action. When Mark Harris wrote an unsympathetic article about student writing, I wrote a letter taking him to task. The letter wasn't printed, and when I sent an anthology of student writing to Harvey Shapiro, to prove that Mark Harris was wrong in writing that students weren't interested in writing, the anthology was ignored.

Most recently, Benjamin DeMott, in a review of Diane Johnson's *Terrorists and Novelists*, said that anyone who saw racism in the proposal that black leadership had failed to impart educational values to the black masses was "simpleminded." Benjamin DeMott may not be simpleminded, but he is wrong. "Black political leadership" as a group, from Ph.D. W. E. B. Du Bois to Ph.D. Huey Newton, possesses more advanced degrees than "white political leadership" as a group, and has promoted educational values from Frederick Douglass, a brilliant, self-taught slave who risked his life on behalf of literacy, to Dr. Martin Luther King, Jr., who received a Nobel Prize.

I think it is a shame that critics and periodicals in England, France, Italy, Belgium, Spain, and the Netherlands have a broader notion of what constitutes the American writing scene than Eastern critics who know little about American culture outside of the contributions made by members of their own class, and yet are always calling people "minority," "ethnic," and "simpleminded."

The *Book Review* is also very very white. Critic Michiko Kakutani wrote an article on "Faction" without mentioning black writer Alex Haley, who coined the term.

I could go on and on.

* * *

No generalization can be drawn from this limited sampling. *The New York Times Book Review* is regarded by the authors who replied—with the exception of Reed—as a well-intentioned compromise. Is there a model for what it should be? The London *Times Literary Supplement*—scholarly in scope and content—is the best book-review supplement in the English-speaking world; but the people who want the *TLS* read the *TLS*. It is far from certain that an Americanized *TLS* would thrive. The *New York Times Book Review* is what it is—and perhaps what it is supposed to be: the Sunday book-review section of the *Times*, a New York paper with a national readership. Undoubtedly the *NYTBR* is complacent and a bit dull; but that's what happens to institutions.

The Practice of Biography

AN INTERVIEW
with STANLEY WEINTRAUB

Stanley Weintraub is a biographer and a teacher of biography. An authority on George Bernard Shaw and other figures of the late 1800s and early 1900s, he is currently Research Professor and Director of the Institute for the Arts and Humanistic Studies at Pennsylvania State University. His biographies include *Private Shaw and Public Shaw: A Dual Portrait of Lawrence of Arabia and George Bernard Shaw*; *Reggie: A Portrait of Reginald Turner*; *Aubrey Beardsley: Imp of the Perverse*; *Whistler*; *Four Rossettis*; and *The Unexpected Shaw*. He is editor of *Shaw: The Annual of Bernard Shaw Studies* and has contributed articles to the *Times Literary Supplement*, the *New Republic*, and other journals. In December 1982, Weintraub talked with *DLB* about the art and practice of biography.

DLB: How did you become a biographer? Did you begin with an ambition to write fiction and get sidetracked, or was biography what you aspired to all along?

Stanley Weintraub

WEINTRAUB: I don't think I aspired to biography or to fiction. I am not sure how one normally gets involved with writing biography. I've seen examples of people beginning with fiction and turning to biography or beginning with criticism and turning to biography. In my case, I think the origin really lay in curiosity. One of the major qualities a biographer needs in the first place is curiosity—about behavior, about motivation, and so on.

I began very early in my writing to write biography. When I was working on my doctorate, I wandered down the open stacks in our library looking for something I might work on in the nineteenth-century novel and discovered that Bernard Shaw, the playwright, had been of all things a novelist in his early career. I was curious enough to do a paper on the subject, and the paper led to a doctoral dissertation which was actually a biographical study of Shaw's novelistic career. At that point I was hooked on biography.

DLB: And the dissertation led to the next project?

WEINTRAUB: I had used so much unpublished material in the dissertation that I couldn't get permission to publish it. So I had to find a way to use my material and continue in the same line I had been working in. I did manage to publish Shaw's fragmentary, unfinished novel which he had abandoned and which ended his career as a novelist, and I was able to pull out other material.

I'd had one of those fortunate breaks that sometimes occurs: T. E. Hanley, a collector of rare books and manuscripts, found out that I was working on Shaw the novelist and wrote to me to say that he had hundreds of unpublished Shaw letters; would I like to come look at them? Of course I was delighted to come look at them. (These are now, by the way, at the University of Texas.) I was able to utilize some of his material in my doctoral work.

I mentally filed away the fact that he had more material, finished my dissertation, and began doing what every new full-time teacher must do—prepare classes. That took a great deal of time away from following up the biographical leads that I had gotten. But one thing fascinated me. I had discovered that there was another Shaw: T. E. Shaw. In the 1920s, T. E. Lawrence had legally changed his name to Shaw. I wondered whether this had anything to do with Bernard Shaw—curiosity again. And I thought, maybe an article could be written on the subject if there turns out to be a connection. Well, it turned out there was a great deal of

connection—that Lawrence of Arabia had been in effect a surrogate son to Mr. and Mrs. Shaw and this relationship was a very close and very profound one that had implications for both men. That resulted in *Private Shaw and Public Shaw*, my first real biography.

DLB: You've said before that you sometimes find the subject for your next biography in the index to your last one. Did this happen with that first biography?

WEINTRAUB: That wasn't actually true in the case of *Private Shaw and Public Shaw*, but in working on Shaw I was naturally led to his earlier years and earlier relationships, such as his relationship with Oscar Wilde. And working on Shaw and Wilde I saw again the importance of cultivating the private collectors of material in one's areas of work. The biographer can always find the public collections; it's the private ones that are so difficult to know about and get access to. One private collector of Arnold Bennett material showed me a postcard that I was puzzled by. It was from Arnold Bennett to a person then unknown to me, Reggie Turner, a friend of Oscar Wilde's. It said something to the effect that "Dorothy has had a little girl. Her name is going to be Virginia, and we wanted you to be the first to know." Arnold Bennett wasn't married to the actress Dorothy Cheston, because he couldn't get a divorce from his wife. But Bennett and Dorothy lived together as man and wife. She changed her name legally to Bennett so that she could be called Dorothy Cheston Bennett. Their child was illegitimate, of course, but Bennett adopted Dorothy Cheston as his daughter, and in effect his *daughter* became his *granddaughter*, a very strange situation.

In any case, I had no idea who Reggie Turner was or why he would be told this very scandalous information, but I thought I'd try to find out. The result of my curiosity about a postcard was the biography *Reggie*, which is a study of two literary circles. Reggie Turner was a part of Oscar Wilde's circle—he was at Wilde's bedside when he died—and was later a part of the D. H. Lawrence literary circle in Italy, when Lawrence was in exile from England.

Reggie was involved in the circle of 1890s Aesthetes and contributed to the *Yellow Book*, for which Aubrey Beardsley was art editor. That led me to write a biography of Beardsley. *Beardsley* led me then to *Whistler*. Beardsley doted on Whistler; Whistler was a kind of god to him. As I went on, again the index to one led me to the subject of another biography. At the same time I was continuing to work on Shaw, which has led now to my latest book, *The Unexpected Shaw*. I've really had two parallel biographical directions.

DLB: What do you consider the biographer's responsibilities to the reader?

WEINTRAUB: First he has to tell a good story. He has to tell a truthful story, and to find significance in the way a life is lived. There ought to be something beyond fact in the life of a biographical subject that we can learn, and that doesn't have to be shown in any moralistic way. I don't believe, as the earliest English biographers did, that one has to preach a sermon in a biography. But every life has some kind of significance. The biographer should infer it and not deal with it in any more direct way.

He also owes something to the genre of biography. To write *authentic* biography, for one thing. By that I mean that there should not be invented dialogue. There should not be invented incidents, details, background, and other novelistic embellishments that are not factual. Interesting examples of this occur regularly in Lytton Strachey's work. Strachey is often paid tribute for what is called the detachment and the concision and the exquisite poise and the sustained irony of his biographies. But I think they're intellectually dishonest. He dramatized scenes that life had already made dramatic enough. He rearranged his facts in a novelistic way. In other words, if things didn't work quite in the way he thought they should have worked, he turned them around. He gave characters thoughts that they probably never had. In a lot of ways he was a caricaturist, a cartoonist.

I think Strachey caused a great deal of difficulty for later biographical practice because he was so successful that people followed him. I noticed in a book just published—I don't think we need to mention the name, but it's called a biography—this line from a love scene: "They made love tenderly and fiercely and both of them laughed and cried and whispered enduring promises." A line from a *love scene*. Now how can the biographer know that? And some of the best biographers have done that sort of thing. One, a well-known biographer of English kings, has done something on this order about one of the Richards. This is not an exact quotation but close enough to indicate the kind of invention I'm referring to: "Out of the mist loomed the great banner of the house of York." How did he know it loomed out of the *mist*? "A giant figure strode for-

ward. Pushing his visor up, Richard saw that the king was smiling at him in brotherly pride." That was invented by the author. He assumed that brotherly pride was likely, so it's there. These are novelistic devices; I don't believe they belong in a biography.

I know of another example where someone tried to edit letters that Shaw had written to a woman friend. The Shaw estate refused to provide permission. The author then wrote a novel based on the letters, using quotations from the letters as conversations. This has happened more than once in a biography, and I probably would get myself involved in a libel suit if I pointed to similar cases chapter and verse. But people don't speak the way they write letters. When one reads a biography and sees that kind of language, it's quite likely that it was stolen from letters.

This has been done in American biography. It's been done in English biography. It's dishonest. One owes one's sources the proper use of these sources, and that means to be honest in indicating what the source is; to use good taste without being dishonest, especially in dealing with living people; to credit your sources; to ask permission of your sources in advance or after the fact; and to quote accurately. Quoting accurately is often something of a problem when one must cut a quotation in length. It's important to retain the original intent of a quotation when it's cut. These are all important things to do, and I try to stress them when I teach biographical writing.

DLB: To what extent is it possible to teach students to write biography?

WEINTRAUB: It may be that biographical writing can't be taught too easily, but there are certain things one can teach: to be truthful, to credit your sources, to use your sources honestly, to avoid the temptation to invent. One can give students the injunction to keep events in proportion and in balance, which can be difficult. For example, if someone in a biography is paid a certain amount of money for a book or a picture, or gets a certain amount as income, that has to be related to the value of money at the time it occurred. What did a loaf of bread cost at that time, or something else common to the reader today? The novelist L. P. Hartley said, "The past is a foreign country. They do things differently there." This is the problem, you see. The ethics of another time may have been quite different from ours. Something that would have been considered proper then might be considered blatant prejudice today. The attitude of a man toward a woman may have been that of an owner toward chattel. Today man and wife have a different relationship. The biographer must put these things into perspective, and we can at least alert students to this. We can also caution students to collect documents without prejudgment or bias. That's a problem any biographer has to face.

DLB: In his 1928 lectures at Trinity College, Cambridge (published as *Aspects of Biography*, 1929), André Maurois discussed the biographer's need to have some empathy with his subject. Can this present a problem of bias?

WEINTRAUB: Empathy suggests almost a prejudgment, a bias. I don't think that empathy is as important as curiosity about the subject. But it is interesting how biography often affects the writer in such a way that he develops empathy with a subject with whom that didn't seem possible at first. I do worry about the prejudice of beginning with empathy. This is much less likely when you're writing a historical biography. Then you're dealing with somebody who is a bit distant—the dust has already settled. That can be done quite differently from a biography about a person who is alive now or who was recently alive.

I knew the novelist C. P. Snow very well, for about twenty years. Toward the end of his life, when I was visiting him once in London, he said to me, "I don't want you to be annoyed with me, but I want you to know that I have permitted somebody else to begin writing a biography of me." I said, "Why would you think that I'd be upset?" And he said, "Well, you have known me longer than anybody else who's been writing biography." Then he added, "I thought you knew me too well." He wanted someone with distance, and he was quite right. The biography written by a friend or a relative has a built-in bias. It might be useful in that such a writer can contribute a lot of firsthand information that nobody else can, but it can't be the definitive biography. It can only contribute toward a fuller, more objective one.

DLB: One question in writing about living people or people recently alive is dealing with information that might be embarrassing to living relatives and might even subject the biographer to libel suits. Does this problem come up a lot?

WEINTRAUB: It does, and there are a number of ways to deal with it. I just finished reading a biog-

raphy in which somebody is referred to only by the letter P, because "P" is still alive. Here's a major figure who is only vaguely identified. As a result, you know there are holes in this work that will need to be filled in later. But the relationship between the subject and "P" was clearly a dubious one and privacy had to be insisted upon. There are problems of the law. One can invade the privacy of a public figure, because a public figure has deliberately made himself or herself unprivate. But a person who is private remains private.

I once tried to get information for *Reggie* about Reggie Turner from a writer who knew him. This person would not respond to me, but instead wrote to somebody who was a mutual friend, "A young professor in America is trying to get information out of me on Reggie Turner, but I'm not going to tell him, because Reggie was an essentially private person whose private life shouldn't be invaded." My feeling is that anybody who writes a dozen novels, even if they were unsuccessful, and who is otherwise involved in public life is not essentially private, but that was the writer's insistence. Nevertheless, the writer went on to tell our mutual friend everything I wanted to know. The mutual friend then told me. I was able to use the information in *Reggie*, but I had to credit it to a private source; I had no other way to keep from invading that privacy.

It's very difficult to write about people who are close to our own time. I think that in some cases the best commercial possibilities are to write about contemporaries or near contemporaries, if one wants to write commercial biography, but the limitations are there. One knows one has to write a partial work because of living people who are involved who may sue or may prevent your material from being used. I think it was W. H. Auden who said he didn't think a biographer should read private letters. He thought they had nothing to do with the life of a creative person, that the person's life was in his or her work—in the same way, let's say, that the general or the admiral has no other life than his military activities.

Auden was trying, of course, to prevent his own biography from being written, but he was unsuccessful. All this does is cause a little bit of delay. He hasn't been dead very long, and there are already at least two biographies of him. Somerset Maugham declared in his will that none of his letters could be published and no biography could be written, but within a few years of his death his nephew and a number of friends had already published memoirs and biographies of him. Finally his literary executor gave a biographer permission to write a biography. So much had already been written that the executor wanted to get all the facts straight.

George Orwell did the same thing, declaring that no biography of him could be written. We now have an authorized biography. It was authorized by his widow, who is now dead also, because there had been other books about Orwell which confused the issues. There is no way to prevent a life from being written. It's just going to be done more or less fully, and the unavailability of private letters is not going to stop anybody. T. S. Eliot's widow has tried to prevent a biography of Eliot. She is looking for an authorized biographer, but that hasn't stopped several biographies from coming out. She says she wants somebody who is in sympathy with Eliot's political and religious views to write the authorized biography. She will find her biographer, but clearly that will be a biography that will have to be superseded by another biography.

That's the fun of being a biographer. No subject is out of range for an interested biographer just because he or she has already been written about. One interprets the past and people in the past anew, with new information and new perspectives. That makes it fun. The problem of picking a subject is not whether it's been done before, but whether it's commercial—whether it can be sold.

DLB: How would you feel about doing an authorized biography?

WEINTRAUB: I've never written a biography that I was asked to write. Still, one's visibility as a biographer very often will result in his being asked to write a biography, as has happened in my case. Some people find this a good thing to do. I'm not so sure. I went so far in one case as to talk to the widow after some people wanted to commission me to write a biography. I decided I didn't want to get that close to a situation in which I would have to deal with legal aspects of privacy and be under the censorship thumb of the family morally if not actually. I stayed out of it.

DLB: Would you name some biographies you consider the best?

WEINTRAUB: I'm not sure I'd like to hold up one or two and say they're the best biographies ever done. I think our perspectives change. Probably nobody is going to write a biography as good as Boswell's *Johnson* from the standpoint of a person

who lived at the elbow of the subject. But that's now a work of art that's looked at at a distance. Very few people ever read Boswell's *Johnson* unless they read it in a class, and then, probably, only an abridgment is read. Many of the old classic biographies which are still considered great works were written by people close to the subject, and they are just too long to be read. Lockhart's *Scott*, written by Scott's son-in-law, is an example.

Strachey did one thing that was healthy. He destroyed the old-fashioned life-and-letters biography that was volume after volume of recital of dull facts combined with the publication of complete letters strung together one after another with some commentary. There was very little in the way of motivation, of psychology, of color. There was no flesh and blood to those books. Strachey did them in. But I think he did them in only very briefly, because when we look around us we see that the copious life-and-letters biography is back. In different form, maybe, but we see a lot of them again, and some of the first in this country were not as good as they should have been. I think that Mark Schorer's *Sinclair Lewis* was one of the earliest big, fat, compendious biographies to come back into fashion. It wasn't as readable as some of the ones that followed; yet some of the later biographers in this country learned from Schorer. Richard Ellmann's remarkable *James Joyce* is probably one of the best biographies by an American. For the *best* biography by an American, I'd have to go with Leon Edel's *Henry James*. It has grace and style and is the product of an immense amount of detective work. Someone will way, "That's in multiple volumes. How can you say it's not a life-and-letters on the old Victorian order?" Actually, Edel insists to me—and I haven't counted the words to prove him—that there are about the same number of words in his multivolume *James* as there are in the one volume of Ellmann's *Joyce*. But they're packaged differently. One of them has larger print, smaller format, more space between the lines; the other one has smaller print, larger format, thinner pages, and so on.

So the big, full-detailed work that Strachey thought he had done away with when he published *Eminent Victorians* in 1918 is really back, but the oversized biography of today is more readable. It fleshes out the person. It has more psychological realism to it. It's not a scissors-and-paste job of stringing letters together with bland commentary. There's more analysis, more homework. I think the American tendency to longer biographies has been a result, of all things, of the *New Yorker* magazine profiles, some of them running six or seven issues in length. There's been a racy sophistication, irreverence, a passion for detail, a spacious unconcern about pagination limitations that make these different from the English biographies today, and much more readable than many of the English biographies. One of my favorites of those *New Yorker* profiles is A. J. Liebling's *The Earl of Louisiana*. It's about Earl Long, the brother of Huey Long, who was governor of Louisiana. Another is S. N. Behrman's *Duveen*, about the great and flamboyant art dealer Sam Duveen, later Lord Duveen. It's a marvel of wit and learning, and it conveys an irreverent charm that suggests its *New Yorker* origin.

DLB: Is the biographer sometimes tempted to stay immersed in his research longer than he should, past the time when he should have started writing?

WEINTRAUB: I think so. I remember reading not long ago, in the *Chronicle of Higher Education*, an interview with a biographer and teacher of biography who said that he analyzes everything before he sets about writing. I don't think that's possible. Setting about writing at a point where you think you have a sufficient critical mass of material to make it possible enables you to find out what you're missing, to know where the holes are. I continue to do research as I write. In fact, I continue to do research right through to the end. And when I reread my first draft, I know where I still need to do research. When I was working on *The London Yankees* and was dealing, toward the end of the book, with T. S. Eliot's arrival in England, where he was going to stay the rest of his life, I wrote to Eliot's widow and said that I'd like permission to look at the Eliot letters that are sealed in the Harvard Library—just the letters dealing with the period of August to December 1914—because I wanted to use them in completing *The London Yankees*. Her answer was, "I won't let you use them because I'm going to use some of those letters myself in my edition of Eliot's letters. Just wait until the edition of Eliot's letters is out. Then you can use whatever you like." Well, *The London Yankees* was published in 1979. The edition of Eliot's letters that she said she was working on hasn't appeared. I would still be waiting.

Similarly, when I was working on *Reggie*, quite a long time ago now, I wrote to the novelist Sir Compton Mackenzie asking whether he had any knowledge of Reggie Turner that would be useful for my biography. I knew he had. I was particularly interested in stories about Reggie as a conversationalist; I knew he had told good stories, but conversation is hard to fill in. Mackenzie wrote me

back saying that he was planning to do an eight-to-ten-volume autobiography, that he was in volume one at that time, and that he planned to put Reggie in volume four. If I would only wait, I would get the anecdotes I wanted in volume four. Well, I could not wait for his volume four. He was also in his eighties and I didn't know whether the mortality tables were such that I could reasonably *expect* a volume four. It turned out that he lived to be nearly ninety and published volume four as well as the rest. Did the whole job. And the anecdotes are there to be seen. But I couldn't wait.

There are cases like these when you can't do all the research. It's just not possible. Then you have to work around it. In some cases you can fill in the material as you go; in others you may never get it. When *Private Shaw and Public Shaw* was published, I heard from people who had refused to answer my inquiries while I was doing the research. They said, in effect, "It's a very good book. I'm sorry now that I didn't contribute to it." This is the fate of a great many biographers writing about people who have lived in the near present. Because survivors do remain. They are suspicious of your motives. They don't know whether you're going to treat their friend or their relative the way they would like to see the person treated, so they will not help you. But then they'll be indulgent later.

In some cases it's possible to write a biography again and use the material that turned up too late for the first version. I've done three versions of *Beardsley* for that reason. The amusing thing about it, to me, is that when *Beardsley* was first published, in 1967, there was a front-page review of it in the *New York Times Book Review* in which the reviewer said, "As a biography this needs no successor." That's very pleasant for the writer to hear, but I knew it needed a successor. I knew that there was information I could not get my hands on. In the third version, which is in print now, I quoted that line in the new introduction, because I wanted to make the point that every biography needs a successor if new data can be found that alter one's perspective and fill in the picture. That was true of the third version, which I even gave a new title: *Aubrey Beardsley: Imp of the Perverse*. I wanted to use that title with the first version, but the publisher wouldn't let me. That's an interesting thing one runs into now and then. The publisher said that the subtitle was too provocative, that it would suggest something about Beardsley that might not have been the case. I said I was only suggesting the "imp" portion of it, not the "perverse." In any case, I wasn't permitted. Similarly, the publisher originally

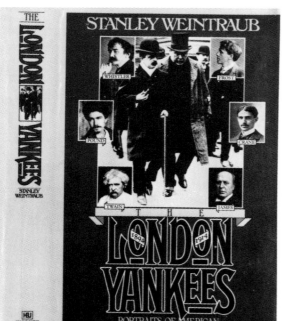

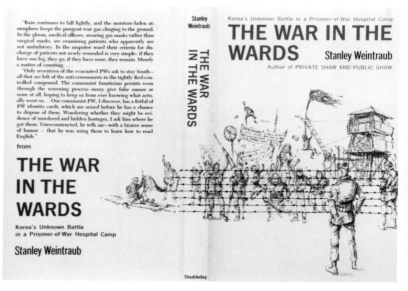

Dust jackets for biographies by Stanley Weintraub

wouldn't let me use some of the illustrations that Beardsley had done for Aristophanes' *Lysistrata*, because he felt that "lady librarians" wouldn't buy the book. Times change, you see, and as times change a new biography becomes possible. That's why picking a subject is not as much of a problem as it might seem to be. One can always return to a fascinating figure if the figure remains fascinating and look at him again from a new perspective and possibly with new data.

DLB: Let's talk about autobiography. Is it true, as Johnson said, that "every man's life should be best written by himself?"

WEINTRAUB: I can't imagine anybody being more prejudiced in his or her own favor than the autobiographer. But the autobiographer is likely to provide information that nobody else is going to have. Even if we don't believe him, we're going to get a lot more from him than we'll get from biographies. He is going to tell us something about motive, something about his thoughts at the time—whether or not they're true. He is going to dredge down into memories that he would not have revealed to biographers. In some ways the autobiography is the most honest, the most genuine of biographies, because this is the subject talking. But he can be dishonest. Vladimir Nabokov wrote two autobiographies, many years apart, dealing with the same events. And they're different. He changed his mind about what he wanted to say. So one of them is dishonest. The question is, which one? And this is a matter for biographers to take up.

The autobiography is in some ways like the interview, if the interview is well done. That is, if you have confidence in the interviewer and you have enough ego just to go on talking, eventually your defenses will crumble and you will reveal more of yourself than you intended to reveal, even though you started with your guard up.

One problem with autobiography is similar to that of the biography of a person who is near our time or alive now. You're dealing with living people—your relations with living people—and you may either have to be reticent or use some disguises. I wrote a little autobiography myself, a memoir of a period I spent in Korea during the Korean War, called *The War in the Wards*. I had to deal with many people who were alive at the time that I wrote my chronicle. In fact, what I did was reproduce portions of a diary I had kept at the time, which I then had to edit. I had to edit out real names. There were a few names I could use, such as names of generals,

because they were public figures. But I could not use the names of other people; I would have needed their permission and they might or might not have granted it. I finally decided I would change all the names except the names of people who were in the news and therefore not eligible for that consideration of privacy. Here is a case of an autobiography very close to me because I perpetrated it, in which I know there are people described by names not their own. Nobody else knows them. In a sense, then, this is not factual. Further, I've made cuts in it because I didn't want to draw attention to particular people who would have been easily identified. That makes it even more a partial picture. Autobiography, I think, has to be a partial picture, but it's nevertheless a very valuable one. And the art of autobiography is one of the great literary arts. There ought to be more college courses in biography and autobiography—just in reading some of the great works of both genres.

DLB: What do you think of the so-called nonfiction novels, such as Mailer's *Executioner's Song*?

WEINTRAUB: I dislike them intensely. I think a book has to be either fiction or nonfiction, and one should not try to blur the line between the two. One owes a duty to authenticity in biography, as I commented earlier. I remember talking with the late Catherine Drinker Bowen, who was a great lady and a fine biographer in her later years, though not so much in her earlier years. She confided to me (I think she later put it in writing, so it wasn't all that much of a confession) that she was very sorry indeed for the early biographies that she wrote. Particularly she mentioned one on Tchaikovsky, which was called *Beloved Friend*. She said she invented all the conversations in it and she passed this off as biography. She said she was ashamed of herself for doing that and was making amends in her later work. She did a biography on Sir Edward Coke, the English jurist, called *The Lion and the Throne*, which is one of the finest American biographies. It is chock-full of documentation. There is no question but that she was making amends in her later work for the earlier stuff where she was inventing things.

If one is going to write a biographical novel, let's call it a biographical novel but not blur the terms by calling it a nonfiction novel. Those two terms are contradictory. I don't like the genre: Truman Capote's *In Cold Blood*, Mailer's *Executioner's Song*, and so on. I think invented dialogue has to be identified as such, and that invented motivation and invented incidents have to be exactly that, and one should call it a biography or call it a novel. A biography must have not only the ring of authenticity but the documentation of authenticity, or it's unreliable. It's untrustworthy. It's not biography; it's fiction. And *Beloved Friend* by Catherine Drinker Bowen, as she confessed later, was really fiction.

DLB: Biography seems vulnerable to criticism on more points than fiction. How well do you think reviews and serious criticism of biography are done?

WEINTRAUB: Not very well, because we run into the problem of who does it. The whole process of reviewing is a problem that's deeper and more extensive than we can go into right now. If I were a critic of fiction and were asked to read and review a novel, I wouldn't need any special expertise, provided I knew something about fictional techniques and had some competence to judge whether this was a good novel or a bad novel—or in poetry, a good poem or a bad poem. Oscar Wilde once said, when he was a poorly paid young book critic, that one doesn't need to drink a whole bottle of wine to know whether the wine is good. This was when he used to write review after review after review and clearly hadn't read the books. But he may have been right that a page or two was all you needed to read, just as a sip of wine tells you if the wine's any good. That is not true with biography. A biography requires some real expertise in the period and in the person as well as in writing. Very few people who write just book criticism in general can deal with biographies out of their place and time.

I'm pleased when I see the expertise of a real biographer utilized in a book review. The new biography of Robert Lowell was just reviewed in the *New York Times Book Review* by Richard Ellmann. We know that's an authoritative book review. On the other hand, we get nonbiographers writing reviews of biographies, and such writers can be very suspicious of biography. To give you a recent example, which is just coincidence, Elizabeth Hardwick, who was married to Robert Lowell at one time, close upon the release of the Lowell book wrote a review for the *New York Times Book Review* of a biography of Katherine Anne Porter. She said something very nasty at the opening of the review—that biographers are "the quick in pursuit of the dead." Well, you know from that beginning that she is hostile to biography in general and she certainly doesn't want one written of herself. Although clearly she's going

to get one herself, one of these days.

DLB: You talked a bit earlier about the teaching of biography and the responsibilities you try to impress upon your students. Is biography being taught extensively?

WEINTRAUB: It's being taught more now than ever before. One of the reasons, I think, is that it's becoming more and more obvious that it's a special aspect of nonfiction writing. Also there is a market for it. The evidence becomes clear to students, especially advanced students, that there's a promising publishing market for biography, because, in the language of the market, biographies have a longer shelf life than fiction. Fiction is cleaned off the shelves in perhaps six weeks or thereabouts, but biographies are still marketable a year after publication. They get remaindered too; I'm not denying that—if one is not remaindered, one has never been published. But biographies stay on the shelves a lot longer.

The question confronting the teacher is, what can one teach a student about biography that is different from what one would teach a student of fiction writing or article writing? In some ways they're really the same. But I think we must stress the responsibilities to the genre of biography, the responsibilities to one's documentation, the need to define proportion and balance, to transport readers back to the time and place of the biography so that they can feel and sense what it was like then. That is in some ways like fiction, but one has to do more than merely convey a sense of authenticity; one has to *be* authentic. And there is the difference.

You do use graphic scenes and telling quotations if you can find them. More and more biographers are realizing that they can learn from fiction. Using fictional devices, you can begin in the middle and flash back, as I did in *Beardsley* and *Whistler*. But I get annoyed at people who try to use novelistic devices in the wrong way. For example, in the new biography of Winston Churchill, Ted Morgan begins with this line: "Spanked into life like the rest of us, Winston Leonard Spencer-Churchill was born on Monday, November 30, 1874, in Blenheim Palace." If it had been a traditional biography, it would have begun without the opening phrase: it would have read "Winston Leonard Spencer-Churchill was born on Monday, November 30, 1874, in Blenheim Palace"—which is a perfectly acceptable line, though it doesn't make one feel compelled to read on. But the first part of the sentence is entirely novelistic. We aren't all spanked into life, although some of us may need it. And I don't think Morgan was able to find the doctor or midwife who presided at that birth. One can attempt to teach students not to do this kind of thing, but it's hard when they read a commercially successful biography like this and see it done.

There's another kind of opening—I spend a lot of time with students on openings and closings of chapters of biographies—which I have an example of in front of me: "At the time of his birth on October 2, 1452, no man could plausibly have predicted for Richard Plantagenet the high and troubled destiny which was to lead him to the throne of England." This business of "no man could have predicted" is a very tired cliché. And we teach students in all kinds of writing to avoid clichés, to avoid tired language. We need to teach it in biography.

DLB: You've done some books that deal with more than one main figure, such as *Private Shaw and Public Shaw* and the collective biographies—*Four Rossettis*; *The Last Great Cause: The Intellectuals and the Spanish Civil War*; and *The London Yankees: Portraits of American Writers and Artists in England 1894-1914*. Would you comment on the advantages of collective biography?

WEINTRAUB: I think there is a special kind of drama available in collective biography that isn't available in another kind of biography. You have the interaction of people who share the billing. The interaction of lives is hardly new, but I think we are now realizing, more than ever, that we don't live in a social vacuum, that other people are deeply involved in our lives. They *share* our lives, for that matter. So where this is possible, I think the strategy works. Not every biography can be turned into a collective biography. There are some fine recent biographies that aren't, such as George Painter's elegant *Proust*, an English biography which may be one of the very best modern biographies. But Proust shared no life with anybody. He was a loner. And you can't have collective biography that way.

Four Rossettis dealt with a family in which there were four very creative children. There were rivalries; there were instances of cooperation; there was a good deal of interaction. I decided to use the "ten little Indians" method toward the end, because obviously they were going to die separately. I end with chapters labeled "Three Rossettis," "Two Rossettis," "One Rossetti" as the sisters and brothers die off. There's real drama to the collective biography where the interaction is profound or at least builds to a substantial level and then fades in this fashion.

I think the first example of collective biography I read was Robert Sherwood's *Roosevelt and Hopkins*—I may have been a teenager; I can't remember—and I was very impressed by the way a major figure was made to seem different because so much of his life had been dependent on the loyalty and the work of Harry Hopkins. *Roosevelt and Hopkins* was a new way of looking at biography, I think. And my own first experiment in this genre was *Private Shaw and Public Shaw*, where we have a major figure, Bernard Shaw, the dominant figure in English literature at the time Lawrence of Arabia, despite his notoriety, is trying to be an obscure private in the army. The interaction of the two of them was to me a dynamic kind of involvement that I thought was more dramatic than telling the story of either one separately.

What one has to avoid in collective biography, whether one deals with two people or four people or, as in *The London Yankees*, two dozen people, is what might be called the "one shoe-other shoe" approach. You know, you drop one shoe, then you drop the other shoe; you deal with one person, and then you say, "And on the other side of the nation . . ." and deal with another person. The figures really have to interact. You can't just tell the stories of separate people who happen to have some contact now and then. Collective biography is a relatively new way to look at people, but the subject matter must be responsive to this approach.

DLB: Are there other trends that you expect to play a larger part in biography in the near future?

WEINTRAUB: I think one trend in biography that has been rather recent—we can see it, in fact, just since the editor told me that lady librarians wouldn't buy *Beardsley* if we put in a few slightly off-color illustrations—is the increased openness that we find also in fiction, in films, and on the stage. The fact that censorship is not rearing its head in these areas has also affected biography, and it's going to continue to do so. We can now talk realistically about sex, as one example. There have been biographies in the past where one didn't know whether a person was a eunuch or not because there was such a reticence to talk about this. It doesn't mean that we should go novelistically into the bedroom and imagine what went on. But I think we can deal honestly with people's lives, and it may be that this openness will soon lead us to other kinds of openness. I'm not sure how far it can go. For example, how much do we need to talk about somebody's bathroom habits? Robert Caro's recent life of Lyn-

On/July 2?, 1903 Jonathan Sturges, Princeton '85, returned by hansom cab to Long's Hotel in New Bond

Street, London, where he lived. Crippled from birth, he could hardly walk

without a stick to support him, and the stick was always the silver-headed,

ebony one his friend Whistler had given him, after Sturges had admired the

four-foot ebony wand which was as much symbol of Whistler's bellicosity as the

butterfly signature to which the artist often added an anatomically incongruous sting.

Raised up on a folded blanket, with the glass top of the cab up and the

lower doors closed, his silk hat on his head and gloves in his hand, he looked

impressive and unbent. It was an overcast day, with a persistent drizzle, but

Sturges seemed not to notice. Nor did he seem ready to drag himself from the

cab when the driver pulled open the doors with his strap. After a pause Sturges

signalled the hotel porter, who came forward to the curb and helped down.

It was the first time anyone had seen him accept assistance, as he took the burly

porter's arm and hobbled into the hotel. he shifted a shaking hand to the arm of a friend,

who noticed that Sturges' coat was soaking wet and that under the sodden hat his

face was pale.

When they were settled in Sturges' rooms, he had a brandy and soda

brought to him; and after a sip or two he said, "It was dreadful; no one could

have imagined such a thing." Whistler had mourned, a few years before, when one of his

long-time adversaries died, that he hardly had a close enemy left in London. The

fact had been demonstrated that day at Chelsea old Church at Chiswick, where

Whistler was buried, Hardly a dozen friends were there, and several women--his

two sisters-in-law and a lady who kept in the background and was suspected to be

his loyal but cast-off mistress, Maud. There were no flowers: only a gilded

laurel wreath Whistler would have excoriated as in bad taste, and a primrose for

each to drop into the/open grave. When it came to Sturges' turn, after the

Revised typescript page for Whistler

don Johnson does. But the fading of censorship has been a very important factor in opening up biography so that it can be more authentic and tell more of the truth.

Sometimes telling the truth can be done diplomatically. One example was in the biography of Edward VII by Sir Philip Magnus. Magnus knew that Edward had had mistress after mistress. He couldn't tell that. It just wasn't possible at that time, and also the biography was authorized by the family. But he did want to say something about the coarser habits of King Edward, and he knew, among other things, that Edward ate gluttonously. He was a slob in a lot of ways, and Magnus wanted to deal with that. Finally he figured out a way. He wrote something like this: "Edward had a splendid appetite and never toyed with his food." The family thought that was fine. Now we can read between the lines and we know that Edward's "splendid appetite" and his never toying with his food probably meant that he ripped the stuff apart. We can do this sort of thing as biographers, and I think we have to learn that the dropping of censorship doesn't mean that we need to pander to the most prurient kinds of curiosity, and that we can deal honestly and diplomatically with the facts at hand without doing so.

DLB: Does writing biography affect the biographer emotionally?

WEINTRAUB: There's a line that I often quote to my students of biography. The story was told that when Arnold Bennett had finished a novel of his called *Lord Raingo*—not a very well-known one, though it was popular in the early 1920s—he told some friends of his who were visiting him that day, "I finished my book." And his mistress (the Dorothy Cheston whom I mentioned earlier) said, "Oh, how relieved and happy you must be now." Bennett replied, "On the contrary, I'm lonely and miserable and depressed. I've killed a friend." I think that's a point that must be made about biography. One's emotional involvement with the subject can get to be very profound. Sometimes too, because of this, it has to be self-monitored to prevent undue bias. One

finds oneself living vicariously with the subject—rejoicing, experiencing frustration, even mourning—and killing him off becomes like a death in one's family. I've killed a number of people off. And I've often felt real pain. I'm a murderer as a biographer. And I've felt, often for a long time afterward, the sense of loss. Not merely that the project is finished—in fact, when one does the killing-off, the project still has a long way to go. You have revision after revision, the reading of the proofs, and so on and on. But the research becomes something like the excitement of the chase. The work becomes exhilarating, living that person's life along with your own. You sometimes have to keep your subject, even a long-dead one, from trying to write his own life through the force of his character as it emerges from this cold and lifeless documentation you're working with. You know it's working when that happens, and yet at the same time you have to be careful not to let it run you. I'm sure that a novelist finds the same thing happening now and then. If he or she has really invented a lively figure, then the figure may take over. The novelist can, of course, put new events into the character's life, but the biographer cannot.

Sometimes the subject becomes boring. Then you have a problem. When I find a subject boring, I put the work away, either for a while or for good. Certainly if it bores me it will bore somebody else; I have the most reason of anyone to be interested and involved. So I try in my biographical practice to have more than one project going at a time. That way I can turn to something else while I give the problem-subject a fallow period. I'll return to it later, and if it works then, fine. If it doesn't come alive, it either remains in the desk drawer or I get rid of it altogether. If you don't have a number of unfinished projects, it probably means you have let work go out that shouldn't have gone out.

DLB: And are there any in your desk drawers?

WEINTRAUB: Yes. At least three. Perhaps their time will come.

—*Jean W. Ross*

"F. Scott Fitzgerald: St. Paul's Native Son and Distinguished American Writer"
University of Minnesota Conference, 29-31 October 1982

Donna Dacus and Diane Isaacs
University of Minnesota

In an event long overdue, the city of St. Paul finally honored its native son, F. Scott Fitzgerald, with a major scholarly conference. The idea for the conference began in the spring of 1981 when Diane Isaacs, an assistant professor at the University of Minnesota, contacted Donna Dacus, a program director at the University's Department of Conferences. A year and a half later, over the last weekend in October 1982, hundreds of scholars and area residents paid homage to Fitzgerald and his Minnesota roots by attending meetings, lectures, plays, and movies. The formal sponsors of the conference, which was entitled "F. Scott Fitzgerald: St. Paul's Native Son and Distinguished American Writer," were the University of Minnesota Department of Conferences and the St. Paul Public Libraries.

The conference itself was the capstone event in a month-long celebration. The St. Paul Public Libraries featured weekly presentations by local scholars whose efforts have encouraged a regional appreciation of Fitzgerald. A production by the Great North American History Theatre of Lance Belville's *Scott and Zelda: The Beautiful Fools* sold out its October run.

What helped to make the conference and these community events extraordinary was their firm grounding in Fitzgerald's sense of place. John Koblas's slide presentation, taken from his book *F. Scott Fitzgerald in Minnesota: His Homes and Haunts*, opened the conference activities. Professor Scott Donaldson followed, reading an excerpt from his forthcoming book which views Fitzgerald as "The Boy from St. Paul." Then conference participants attended a reception at the Commodore Hotel, where the Fitzgeralds lived in 1921.

The four primary attractions of the conference, which was sold out to more than three hundred attendees, were: Frances ("Scottie") Fitzgerald Smith, the author's only child; Matthew J. Bruccoli, editor and author of thirteen volumes on Fitzgerald including the biography *Some Sort of Epic Grandeur* (1981); Malcolm Cowley, the dean of American literary critics; and Nancy Mil-ford, author of the best-selling biography of Zelda Sayre Fitzgerald.

What many regarded as the highlight of the conference was a two-hour appearance by Cowley and Scottie Smith at the College of St. Thomas's O'Shaunessy auditorium. Cowley, who has known many major literary figures during the course of his distinguished career, delivered a paper on the subject of Fitzgerald and the romance of money, while Smith focused her remarks on remembrances of her father and mother. Perhaps most notable among these was her reply to a questioner who asked how it felt to be the daughter of such famous people. Smith replied that for many years she had come to regard her parents not as parents but as historical figures, and, as such, she discounted any particular effect of their fame on her. Nonetheless, she commented that speaking about her parents was "a great part-time job." Her candidness was complemented by the wit and acuity of Cowley's responses to requests for Fitzgerald anecdotes. The combination of two special personal perspectives created a sense of immediacy that evoked Fitzgerald's presence for the audience.

Another highlight of the conference was Prof. Matthew J. Bruccoli's presentation, "Fitzgerald: From St. Paul to the World." Bruccoli, Jefferies Professor of English at the University of South Carolina, discussed the bases for Fitzgerald's enduring stature. He asserted that Fitzgerald's talents as a writer did not diminish in Hollywood: that *The Last Tycoon*, rather than being a flawed fragment, was indeed evidence of a full artistic vision.

Zelda Sayre Fitzgerald and her impact on Fitzgerald's life and writing were not overlooked. Nancy Milford and Patricia Hampl, a St. Paul writer who introduced Milford, both examined the relationship between a writer and his material through their own experiences. Milford spoke intimately on the effect of shaping someone else's experience into literary biography and broadened her discussion to include Fitzgerald's fictional use of his relationship with Zelda. Such commentary con-

Front cover for the conference program

fronted a recurring issue in Fitzgerald criticism about who "owned" the material of their lives.

The biographical/literary interface raised other issues at the conference. The panel discussion on "Writers and Alcoholism" examined the relationship between the creative and the addictive personality from both therapeutic and literary modalities. It acknowledged that Fitzgerald and Hemingway were largely responsible for the promoting of the persona of the hard-drinking writer and that drinking had a destructive impact on both the Fitzgeralds and on their marriage. Daniel An-

dersen, president of the Hazelden Center (which developed the widely used Minnesota model for the treatment of alcoholism), characterized alcoholism and attitudes toward it, while writers Lewis Hyde and Hampl addressed the ambiguous connection between alcohol and the creative process. Dr. Martin Roth of the Program in American Studies at the University of Minnesota cited numerous instances to illustrate the substantial role drinking has in Fitzgerald's fiction. This event was cosponsored with the Loft, a center for literature and the arts located in Minneapolis.

Concurrent panel discussions supplemented these formal events. In small groups, participants could choose to approach Fitzgerald as a local personality or as a national literary figure. Topics ranged from the role of women in Fitzgerald's work, his short fiction, his influence on other authors, and influences on his own work, *The Great Gatsby*, *Tender Is the Night*, Fitzgerald's image in the local press, and personal reminiscences of those who knew him.

The conference accommodated multiple interests by also offering showings of films based on Fitzgerald's fiction: *The Great Gatsby*, *The Last Tycoon*, and *Bernice Bobs Her Hair*. An exhibit of Fitzgerald memorabilia included his flask and the paper dolls created by Zelda for her daughter.

As the concluding event, the creators of the conference staged a tour of the area around once-prestigious Summit Avenue. Principal conference speakers and organizers riding in classic cars led tour buses past places important in understanding Fitzgerald's experience of growing up in St. Paul.

Included on the tour were the homes of Marie Hersey, where in 1915 Fitzgerald met Ginevra King, and of Norris and Betty Ames Jackson, who had known Fitzgerald as a boy and later as a promising playwright. Other sites were the former St. Paul Academy building, where Fitzgerald attended school from 1908 to 1911; his birthplace; the houses where he lived and wrote, particularly 599 Summit Avenue, which has been designated as the place Fitzgerald completed *This Side of Paradise*, in the National Register of Historic Places; and the mansions which dominated Summit Avenue and symbolized St. Paul's wealthy social elite.

This procession ultimately made its way to the University Club, overlooking the Mississippi River and downtown St. Paul, where the young Fitzgerald attended many dances and social affairs. There conference participants concluded their experience of Fitzgerald's St. Paul with a brunch. Commenting on the success of the conference, Scottie Fitzgerald Smith stated: "I am sure my father would have been most impressed and *very* proud."

Malcolm Cowley, Donna Dacus, Matthew J. Bruccoli, Diane Isaacs, and Scottie Fitzgerald Smith

"Re-meeting of Old Friends": The Jack Kerouac Conference

Margaret A. Van Antwerp

From 23 July to 1 August 1982, an estimated 2,000 people gathered in Boulder, Colorado, to attend the Jack Kerouac Conference. The conference, an homage to Kerouac on the twenty-fifth anniversary of the publication of his novel *On the Road*, was sponsored by Boulder's Buddhist-oriented Naropa Institute (home of the Jack Kerouac School of Disembodied Poetics). Planning for the conference began in late 1981, at the suggestion of Naropa's dean, Judy Lief; poet Allen Ginsberg, one of the institute's founders, organized the meeting. According to Ginsberg, the conference—a "great delicious orgy of nostalgia"—was convened in part as a "re-meeting of old friends" from Beat Generation days. In Ginsberg's view, other equally important aims of the conference were to assess the legacy of "literary liberation" bequeathed by Kerouac and the Beats and to survey the Beat-inspired "consciousness-change in America during the last twenty-five years. We'll celebrate those culture changes and look at where we've been and where we can go from here in terms of opening up America's heart."

Kerouac's "tenderheartedness"—described by Ginsberg as an awareness of the "universal human vulnerability" to suffering and death—became a recurrent theme of the conference: "at this critical time when America officially is being dominated by competition and rivalry," Ginsberg asserted, "it's about time to have a discussion of the heart, a national discussion of the American heart," based, like Kerouac's vision of the United States, on "tenderheartedness and comradeship." Playing on the term *Lost Generation*, commonly applied to American writers living in Europe during the 1920s, participants at the conference dubbed themselves the "Found Generation." As Ginsberg explained: "We're using the 'Found Generation' term Kerouac coined in the early '60s when he said that, after the 'Lost' and 'Beat' generations, the next generation would be the 'Found' one. That notion makes sense today, when we're beginning to realize we've got to get ourselves straightened out in terms of nuclear arms if the earth is to survive."

Social and political concerns surfaced repeatedly, alongside aesthetic ones, in the conference's ten-day program of panel discussions, workshops, and poetry readings. Gregory Corso, a member of the original Beat group of the 1950s, addressed specifically the threat of global nuclear destruction in a reading of his long poem "The Day After Humankind." "Political Fallout of the Beat Generation" was the subject of one of the first panel discussions, featuring two more original Beat writers, Ginsberg and William S. Burroughs, as well as three others who became prominent as Beat descendants of the 1960s: Paul Krassner, Abbie Hoffman, and Timothy Leary. Summing up the farthest-reaching "political fallout" of the Beat movement, Burroughs pointed to Kerouac's importance as a catalyst of social change: "Art exerts a profound influence on the style of life. . . . Art tells us what we know and don't know. Certainly *On the Road* performed that function in 1957. There's no doubt that we're living in a freer America as a result of the Beat literary movement, which is an important part of the larger picture of cultural and political change in this country during the last forty years, when a four-letter word couldn't appear on the printed page, and minority rights were ridiculous." Burroughs's comments on censorship were elaborated at a later discussion, "Censorship and the Beats." For this session, Burroughs and Ginsberg were joined by three of their contemporaries, Michael McClure, Lawrence Ferlinghetti, and Jay Landesman, who, like them, had encountered problems with the censors during the 1950s. During this discussion, the speakers recalled the trials prompted by the publication of Ginsberg's *Howl and Other Poems* and Burroughs's *Naked Lunch*, and by the production of McClure's play *The Beard*. Ginsberg also warned listeners about the future, urging them to be aware of a "concerted campaign by the New Right to reimpose actual censorship on books" in the 1980s.

Other panels listed among the forty-six scheduled events on the conference program focused attention on "Kerouac and Women, The Beats and Women," "Kerouac's Biography," "Jack and Jazz," and "Kerouac, Catholicism, and Buddhism."

At one session, a writer's workshop, Ginsberg

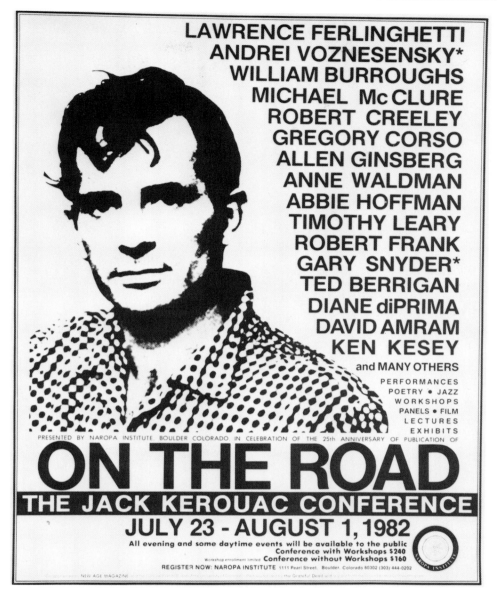

Poster announcing the Naropa Institute conference

read from Kerouac's guidelines for writing: "Scribble secret notebooks and wild typewritten pages"; "Be crazy. Write what you want, bottomless from the bottom of the mind." At another, jazz musician David Amram gave a concert with the help of Ginsberg, Landesman, and others. Sidelights of the conference included a day-long reading of *On the Road* by Kerouac fans, a showing of Robert Frank's Beat film *Pull My Daisy* (1958), which starred Corso, Ginsberg, and Peter Orlovsky, and an exhibit of manuscripts and photographs from the heyday of the Beats.

On the last day of the conference, a picnic was held for the members of "Camp Kerouac" (Abbie Hoffman's term). Merry Prankster Ken Kesey and his associate Ken Babbs, who had purportedly spent forty-three straight hours "on the road" to arrive at the conference, staged a Jack-Kerouac-Conference-version of a 1960s Be-In at the picnic. Events included the presentation of such prizes as the Jack Kerouac Look-alike Award (Jan Kerouac) and the Loudest Poet Award (Andy Clausen).

The following photographs were taken at the conference, the "re-meeting of old friends" that one observer described as "the Woodstock the intelligentsia never had."

Peter Orlovsky

Allen Ginsberg

Abbie Hoffman

Abbie Hoffman and William S. Burroughs

Anne Waldman and John Clellon Holmes

Michael McClure and Allen Ginsberg   *Lawrence Ferlinghetti*

Allen Ginsberg, John Clellon Holmes, Herbert Huncke, and William S. Burroughs

Joyce Johnson, Jan Kerouac, and Gregory Corso

Jack Micheline and artist Ken Krebbs

Allen Ginsberg

William S. Burroughs

Gregory Corso

Timothy Leary and John Clellon Holmes

Edie Parker, Jack Kerouac's first wife

Ken Kesey

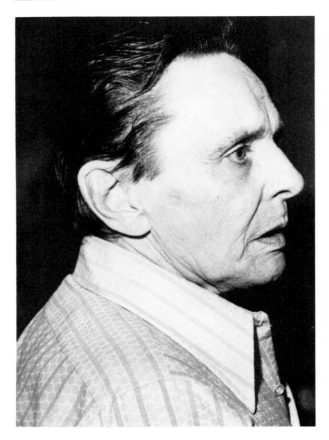

Herbert Huncke

Jan Kerouac

Ken Babbs

Peter Orlovsky, Timothy Leary, and Allen Ginsberg

Ken Babbs (driving), Ken Kesey (in glasses), and Jane Faigao (sitting on back of seat)

James Joyce Centenary: Dublin, 1982

Michael Groden
University of Western Ontario

Dublin; Wednesday, 16 June 1982; 2:30-3:30 P.M.. Among the many Dubliners out for a walk on a sunny summer afternoon are groups of Americans and other foreigners carrying copies of James Joyce's *Ulysses* and a surprisingly large number of people dressed in turn-of-the-century costumes. Pedestrians who move close enough to these costumed people can overhear such conversations as "Parnell's brother. There in the corner./Is that he?/Yes. That's John Howard, his brother, our city marshal" or "He's a cultured allroundman, Bloom is"—the first exchange referring to the city marshal from eighty years ago, the second remark to a fictional character. Spectators can also observe crowds gathering in front of the Ormond Hotel on the River Liffey, awaiting an event that turns out to be a procession of horse-drawn vehicles. Eventually, and for no apparent reason, the odd people and vehicles disappear, and the day's normal activities resume.

The occurrences were part of "O Rocks," a street theater reenactment of the "Wandering Rocks" episode of *Ulysses*. It was held on Bloomsday (16 June, the day on which *Ulysses* takes place) as one of the main events of the Eighth International James Joyce Symposium. Many of the spectators were among the over 500 Joyce scholars and enthusiasts from around the world who came to Dublin for the symposium; others were Dubliners who came out to see what was going on or who were simply out on the streets and got caught up in the activities. (Still others harassed the participants or ignored the whole thing.) The production of "O Rocks" captured the imagination of the city because of the event itself and the author of the book that inspired it. For many years Dublin has refused to celebrate or even to recognize the most famous novelist it has produced, but the 1982 symposium and the events surrounding it represented a belated Joycean homecoming.

Nineteen eighty-two was Joyce's centenary year—he was born on 2 February 1882 (and died on 13 January 1941)—and celebrations abounded. These activities included not only 500 people traveling to Dublin to talk about Joyce's works for six days but also conferences and festivals in Beirut; Hempstead, New York; Leeds; London; Newark, New Jersey; Puerto Rico; Purchase, New York;

Seville; Tokyo; Toronto; and the U.S.S.R. (Tbilisi State University); exhibits in Cork, New Haven, New York, and Trieste; many dramatic productions; marathon readings of the complete text of *Ulysses* on the Irish radio network and in London, Canada; musical compositions by John Cage ("Roaratorio: An Irish Circus on *Finnegans Wake*"), Anthony Burgess ("The Blooms of Dublin"), and Matyas Seiber ("Ulysses"); and a two-hour television biography produced by the Irish television network. On Bloomsday the government of Ireland issued a commemorative stamp in Joyce's honor. Many newspapers and magazines featured special articles on the birthday and on Bloomsday.

These activities focused on a novelist who wrote only four major prose works, all usually considered too difficult for general reading. Joyce has never been a popular novelist; many of his readers

Irish stamp commemorating the Joyce Centenary

60

are university professors and students, and there are no societies devoted to him like those for Jane Austen or Charles Dickens. But his readers are not found only in the academy, and even the university audience spreads far beyond English-speaking countries. As Joyce's works have become more and more a part of literary history, they have appealed freshly and strongly to successive generations of readers. The works are different from each other, and they attract readers for such varied reasons as their realism, humor, and difficulty, but their power has not diminished over the years. In 1959 Richard Ellmann began his biography of Joyce with words that remain true today: "We are still learning to be James Joyce's contemporaries, to understand our interpreter."

Joyce always insisted that readers accept and deal with his works on his own terms; he granted no concessions to conventional fictional expectations. Thus, *Dubliners*, his collection of fifteen short stories (written between 1904 and 1907 but not published until 1914), presents a series of grimly realistic pictures of life in turn-of-the-century Dublin. Joyce said that he wanted to present "a moral history of my country and I chose Dublin for the scene because that city seemed to me the centre of paralysis." The stories also subordinate matters of plot to those of character and images; they culminate not in climactic events but in moments of potential self-revelation, where a character discovers (or fails to discover) something about his or her life. Joyce called such moments "epiphanies." In *A Portrait of the Artist as a Young Man*, his first, semiautobiographical novel (written in several versions between 1904 and 1913, published in 1916), Joyce organized his account of the early years in the life of Stephen Dedalus around such moments of epiphany. (An incomplete earlier version of the novel, entitled "Stephen Hero," is structured like a conventional chronicle.) As we follow Stephen's growth from schoolboy to possible priest to university student to, finally, potential artist about to leave Ireland, highly evocative prose serves to cluster the reported incidents around crucial moments. Furthermore, in following the model of Gustave Flaubert, Joyce has "disappeared" from his work, filtering all the incidents and impressions through Stephen's consciousness, so that determining Joyce's attitudes toward his character, who in many ways represents his earlier self, becomes quite difficult. Indeed, the problem of how to react to Joyce's mixture of sympathy and irony toward Stephen Dedalus has always been one of the most vexing for readers and critics of the novel.

In *Ulysses* (written between 1914 and 1921, published on Joyce's fortieth birthday, 2 February 1922), Joyce continues the story of Stephen Dedalus, who is still a potential artist but who has now returned to Dublin after an unsuccessful stay in Paris. However, Stephen's story is now secondary to that of Leopold Bloom, a thirty-eight-year-old Dublin Jew. Bloom is an ordinary bourgeois citizen, a husband whose wife, Marion (Molly), is about to cuckold him later in the day, a father of a teenage daughter and a son who died ten years earlier, at the age of eleven days, an advertising canvasser, and a perpetual outsider because of his religion. The entire book takes place on one day, 16 June 1904. As in the earlier works, Joyce subordinates plot to other aspects of the fiction, and he introduces two startling devices here: a stream-of-consciousness method that gives the illusion of reproducing the characters' thought directly, and a running parallel between the book's characters and events and those of Homer's *Odyssey*. This parallel, never directly announced except in the book's title, has caused great debate ever since the book appeared: is Joyce comparing the ancient heroic world to the modern world in order to expose the "futility and anarchy which is contemporary history," as T. S. Eliot thought; to show that possibilities for heroism exist even today, although in different forms from those of past pages; or to suggest some mixture of these attitudes? Joyce further complicates *Ulysses* in the second half of the book by introducing a new style in each episode, so that one episode is narrated by a cynical Dublin barfly, another is filtered through the style of a Victorian sentimental novelist, and a third is written as a series of parodies of English prose writers from medieval to Victorian times. Thus, as *Ulysses* progresses, it concentrates less and less on its characters and more on its methods of presentation. Holding the book together is an element largely missing from the first two works, an exuberant comic spirit that can suggest the possibility of patterns recurring throughout history and can fill *Ulysses* with hilarious details.

Joyce's final prose work, *Finnegans Wake* (written between 1923 and 1939, published in 1939), carries some of the elements in *Ulysses* and the earlier works to a limit unmatched in literature before or since. In the background now is not Homer but an eighteenth-century Italian philosopher, Giambattista Vico, who presented a cyclical theory of history in which recurring patterns perpetually repeat themselves. Joyce created one such pattern: a family consisting of a middle-aged husband and father who has committed some sin or

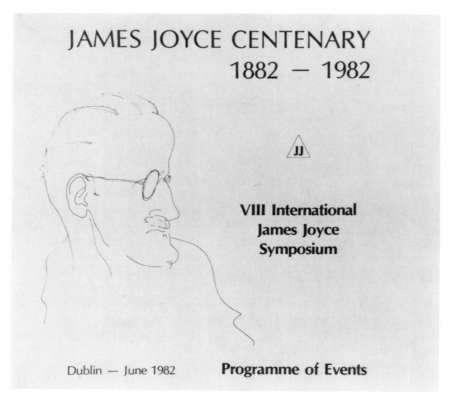

Front cover of program

crime for which he is now being punished; his critical but accepting wife; twin sons, constantly struggling with each other both to supplant the father and to win the tempting daughter; and the daughter, the desirable temptress. These five characters embody all of history—Humphrey Chimpden Earwicker, for example, represents all fathers, not only fathers of families but builders of all kinds (of monuments, societies, religions): God the Father, Abraham, Noah, Shakespeare, Parnell, Tim Finnegan. (For a chart listing many of these parallels, Adaline Glasheen supplied the witty title "Who is who when everybody is somebody else.") Furthermore, the language of *Finnegans Wake* embodies all of linguistic history as Joyce packs each word to the fullest possible extent through elaborate puns. Each word, like each character, has multiple meanings. Needless to say, much of the discussion of *Finnegans Wake* since its publication has dealt with the problem of its meanings on a literal level, and only recently have more complex interpretive and analytical problems begun to be considered.

In addition to these four prose works, Joyce published some poetry, a play, and some prose sketches and critical writings. The poetry, most of

which exists in two volumes, *Chamber Music* (1907, Joyce's first published book) and *Pomes Penyeach* (1927), is slight and of interest primarily because Joyce reveals a lyric, sentimental strain that is for the most part suppressed in the more ironic prose works. The play, *Exiles* (1915), is an exercise in realism in the style of Ibsen that deals with problems of jealousy and of freedom and possession between lovers, problems that Joyce went on to treat with more comic detachment in *Ulysses*. Joyce had difficulty getting the play produced (it was eventually produced in a German translation in Munich in 1919), but it has been revised several times in recent years, most notably in a production directed by Harold Pinter in 1971.

Joyce's prose works have been the subjects of countless interpretive and critical studies, a series that began almost simultaneously with their publication (before publication, in the case of *Ulysses* and *Finnegans Wake*). Joyce himself encouraged and aided some of the authors of the earliest studies; he played a significant role, for example, in the first two important book-length studies of *Ulysses* (opposing interpretations by Stuart Gilbert and Frank Budgen); in a collection of essays on *Finnegans Wake* (in 1929, when the book was only half-written) by such writers as Samuel Beckett, Budgen, Robert McAlmon, and William Carlos Williams; and in a 1939 biography by Herbert Gorman. Joyce felt that an author's greatness and importance could be measured by the number of studies he or she inspired, and by this standard he rests as one of the greatest writers who ever lived. He has been the subject of hundreds of books and thousands of articles; there have been four journals devoted exclusively to him; and eight international and many smaller conferences have been held to discuss his works. Predictably, the centenary year saw a surge in publishing activity as well as many conferences, with the culmination being the Eighth International James Joyce Symposium, held in Dublin from 13 to 19 June.

Since they began in 1967, the International Joyce Symposia have taken place in June; one day of the conference is always Bloomsday. The eight symposia held so far have taken place in cities in which Joyce lived: Dublin in 1967, 1969, 1971, 1977, and 1982; Trieste in 1973; Paris in 1975; and Zurich in 1979. The first few gatherings were very small, but the meetings have grown in size and length, and the organizers (members of the International James Joyce Foundation) have tried to accommodate everyone who wants a place on the program. Therefore, there are usually few formal, full-length papers; instead, the programs consist mainly of shorter papers, panel discussions, and workshops. The conferences tend to reflect the broad range of interests and approaches that characterizes Joyce studies.

The 1982 symposium—organized for the James Joyce Foundation by David Norris, Patrick J. Long, and Maurice Harmon of Ireland, and Bernard Benstock, Morris Beja, and Phillip Herring of the United States—consisted of lectures, panels and workshops, poetry readings, film screenings, exhibitions, unveilings of statues and plaques, receptions, a Bloomsday banquet, and the street theater presentation of "O Rocks." The public ceremonies testified to the official reacceptance of Joyce by his native city and country. For example, the president of Ireland unveiled a bust of Joyce in one of Dublin's parks, St. Stephen's Green; the Lord Mayor of Dublin presided over a ceremony renaming a bridge in Chapelizod as the Anna Livia Bridge (named for the wife in *Finnegans Wake*; the location is the Dublin suburb in which her family lives); and the city put up a plaque on the house where Joyce placed the birth of Leopold Bloom, the main character in *Ulysses*. (The plaque reads, "Here

in Joyce's Imagination/Was Born in May 1886/Leopold Bloom/Citizen, Husband, Father, Wanderer/Reincarnation of *Ulysses*.") Further signs of the enthusiasm with which the city embraced the rehabilitation were the many ancillary activities. There were several theater productions, including one-person readings of Joyce's works by Fionnula Flanagan, Patricia Levinton, Siobhan McKenna, and Eamon Morrissey. Also, there were exhibits on "James Joyce: Portrait of a Student" by the Newman House of University College, Dublin (Joyce's university), "These Young Men" at the National Library, an exhibit based on the "Scylla and Charybdis" episode of *Ulysses*, in which Stephen Dedalus gives a lecture on Shakespeare in the library to several skeptical listeners; "James Joyce in Trieste" by the Italian Cultural Institute; "The Ulysses Project" at Trinity College (paintings by Irish artists); and "Beirut in Dublin," an exhibit originally mounted at a centenary conference in Beirut in February. In the past, the Dublin newspapers sent only their humor columnist or resident satirist to cover the symposia, but this year the papers included many respectful articles during the course of the week.

The academic program consisted of four days of presentations. There were seven full-length lec-

James Joyce, 1904

tures, four by major critics (Richard Ellmann of Oxford University; Seamus Deane of University College, Dublin; Hugh Kenner of Johns Hopkins University; and A. Walton Litz of Princeton University) and special lectures by novelist Anthony Burgess, screenwriter Dennis Potter, and poet and critic William Empson. Richard Ellmann, Joyce's biographer, spoke on "Joyce's Hundredth Birthdays: Side and Front Views." Citing a remark Joyce made on 16 June 1924, the twentieth anniversary of the day on which *Ulysses* takes place, "Will anyone remember the date?," Ellmann emphasized Joyce's self-doubts throughout his career, especially doubts about his status as an Irish writer. The symposium itself, of course, served as one counter to those doubts, as did Ellmann's 1959 biography, a revised version of which appeared later in 1982. Ellmann talked about some of the new information he had uncovered in the intervening twenty years, including accounts of women who attracted Joyce in Locarno and Zurich and who served as models for characters in *Ulysses*. Seamus Deane, in a lecture called "'Masked with Matthew Arnold's Face': James Joyce and Liberalism," compared Arnold and Joyce and their attitudes toward Celticism, Irish nationalism, and various liberal movements of the late nineteenth and early twentieth centuries. In "Signs on a White Field," Hugh Kenner looked at three stories in *Dubliners* and at *Finnegans Wake* to see if paradigmatic stories might lie behind them as the *Odyssey* lies behind *Ulysses*. He argued that, as long as we do not consider it as *the* story" of *Finnegans Wake*, the events surrounding Rory O'Connor, a rebel shot by the Irish in 1922, might provide such a story. Finally, in *"Ulysses* and Its Audience," A. Walton Litz talked about ways in which our attitudes toward *Ulysses* have changed over the years (for example, it used to be fashionable to treat the book as a fixed, spatial image, whereas criticism now focuses more on the linear, temporal process of reading it) and suggested that the book has a way of forcing us to consider both approaches. Likewise, the old-fashioned concerns with mimetic realism and the structuralist and poststructuralist insistence on the work as a self-contained play of language both find support from the text. Litz argued that *Ulysses* is "simultaneously the most traditional and the most avant garde of all the great modernist works" and a book that resists "any theory that posits a special authority."

The bulk of the program consisted of more than sixty panels, workshops, and short paper sessions at which over 300 people spoke. The range of the panels' topics suggests the many different as-

pects of Joyce's works that interest his readers and critics. For example, readers have always responded strongly to Joyce's realism—his depiction of Dublin ("the centre of paralysis") and the frustrated lives of his characters, his treatment of the Catholic church, and his use of stream-of-consciousness techniques to portray the minds of his characters. Such realism was the source of much of the early controversy surrounding his writings (it inspired remarks on his "cloacal obsession," suggestions that he write a "treatise on drains," and descriptions of him as a "perverted lunatic who has made a specialty of the literature of the latrine"), but it was also the source of much of the enthusiasm for Joyce, then and now, including that of Ezra Pound, who tirelessly promoted Joyce's books and career. Recent criticism has been concerned less with the question of the crudity, or even the literal accuracy, of Joyce's realism (although an event like "O Rocks" was based on a study by Clive Hart demonstrating that the time scheme in Joyce's episode of simultaneous events was accurate) than with the relationship of the realistic details to the fictional narrative. In Dublin, panels looked at such topics as "Joyce's Ireland: Fact and Fiction," "Joyce and the City," "Joyce, Judaism, and Catholicism," "Joyce Subjective, Joyce Objective, Joyce Historical," and "Joyce, Psychoanalysis, and Irish Culture." At the Judaism and Catholicism panel, which was chaired by Marilyn Reizbaum of the University of Wisconsin, the main issue was the significance of Judaism in Joyce's work, especially the interdependence between Judaism and Catholicism. Judaism was seen as a source for much of what happens in *Ulysses* and *Finnegans Wake*, in terms of both realistic details and patterns of symbols and metaphors.

Another issue for criticism has been the problem of Joyce's attitude toward his characters and the events he describes: is he sympathetic or ironic toward the characters?; is his view of the events one of comic detachment or satirical pessimism? Critics facing these problems have offered arguments for all sides of the questions, while some recent approaches have suggested that a more balanced position, even one that sees Joyce as holding opposed opinions and refusing to endorse either one, is the most accurate one. Such issues were addressed by some Dublin panels, including those on "Indeterminacies in *Ulysses*" and Joyce's "Homer: A Duologue." At the Homer panel, Hugh Kenner and Fritz Senn discussed the problematical relationship between *Ulysses* and the *Odyssey*. When readers viewed the *Odyssey* as setting up a fixed standard of heroism, they could treat Joyce's characters as living up or failing to live up to that standard. But in a 1969 article, Kenner argued that the matter is much more complicated, since our view of the *Odyssey* can vary greatly depending on the translation we use. (Joyce read Homer only in translation.) At the panel, Senn suggested that we need to distinguish between a fixed Homeric text and a kind of diffused, sequential Homer, since the "Homer" we know is a combination of the original text and a series of refractions through translations. In fact, it was suggested the "influence" works in both directions, since we read Homer slightly differently because of Joyce. For example, we can now detect certain echoes of Leopold Bloom in the *Odyssey*. (This process of reverse influence is also suggested in Jorge Luis Borges's "Kafka and His Precursors.")

Another topic of concern from the start has been Joyce's various technical experimentations, including his use of epiphanies as structuring devices; the stream-of-consciousness techniques; the various narrative techniques, especially the ever-shifting methods in *Ulysses* and *Finnegans Wake*; and the complex wordplay in *Finnegans Wake*. The question of Joyce's narrative has been a prominent one recently; at the 1979 symposium in Zurich, the narrative of *Ulysses* was the subject of a panel that met for five different sessions. In Dublin, there was a panel on narrative in *A Portrait of the Artist as a Young Man* and two on narrative in *Finnegans Wake*. There were also sessions on "Joyce the Masterbilker: The Ar-

chitecture of *Finnegans Wake*" and on a "Linguistic Analysis of *Finnegans Wake*."

Other panels dealt with specific stories, episodes, or characters in Joyce's works: "The Dead" (the last and major story in *Dubliners*), the diary in *A Portrait of the Artist as a Young Man*, "W. B. Murphy" (a minor character in *Ulysses*; recent textual scholarship has determined, however, that his initials should be "D.B."), and "Butt and Taff" (an episode of *Finnegans Wake*). Three sessions dealt with recent books on Joyce in a format called "the living book review": several people reviewed the book in question and then the author responded to the comments. Panels also dealt with such Joycean topics as "Meals, Metabolism, and the Creative Process" (one episode of *Ulysses* is based on metabolic processes), "The Artist as Figure in Art," and "*Ulysses* and the Music-Hall." A few panels dealt with manuscripts and manuscript collections, a topic of recent interest because of the publication of manuscripts and an edition of *Ulysses* that is now in progress. One such panel surveyed some library collections, one dealt with the manuscript of Joyce's "Epiphanies" (a group of early prose sketches), and a workshop looked at a single *Finnegans Wake* notebook.

Two especially lively panels were concerned with Joyce and feminism, a relevant topic since women characters are prominent in Joyce's works as temptress, muse, mother, wife, virgin, and lover.

Martello Tower, where Joyce lived with Oliver St. John Gogarty in September 1904

"Style and Female Prose," chaired by Claudia Jannone of Worcester Polytechnic Institute, inquired into the existence of a "female" as distinct from a male or neutral prose style, especially in such passages as Molly Bloom's soliloquy at the end of *Ulysses* or Anna Livia Plurabelle's at the end of *Finnegans Wake*. One panelist, Elizabeth Flynn of Michigan Technological University, reported on journals that her students kept while they read *Ulysses* and was able to document some differences in the ways men and women responded to the book. (In terms of its difficulties, for example, men responded as if to a challenge, women as if to signs of their own inadequacies as readers.) Another panel, "Joyce and Feminism," chaired by Suzette Henke of the State University of New York at Binghamton, inspired a lively debate on Joyce's attitudes toward and depictions of the social structure in general, including attitudes toward women, politics, and social conditions.

Not surprisingly for an international symposium, several panels looked at Joyce in relation to other writers. Many of the subjects were English-language writers: W. B. Yeats, Ezra Pound, Virginia Woolf, Flann O'Brien, Samuel Beckett, and Thomas Pynchon. But others were not, suggesting the international nature of the influences on Joyce and his own influence and reputation; these subjects included Homer, Rabelais, Arno Schmidt, and Latin American writers, and there were papers on "Joyce Studies in China," "Joyce and the Arab World," "Joyce's Influence on Contemporary Catalan Narrative," "Africa and Africanisms in *Finnegans Wake*," and "The Translation of *Ulysses* into Korean." As another sign of Joyce's international audience, the eighty-two-year-old Argentinian writer Jorge Luis Borges delivered a moving toast in honor of Joyce at the Bloomsday Banquet.

Several panels dealt with Joyce in terms of recent critical theory. One looked at Joyce in relation to three twentieth-century European critics with whom he is not usually compared: Georg Lukacs, Walter Benjamin, and Mikhail Bakhtin. Another panel, a group of English and French poststructuralist critics, considered "Sirens Without Music," taking one of Joyce's most verbally playful passages, the "Sirens" episode of *Ulysses*, and playing their own word games with the text.

Finally, one of today's major Joycean scholarly activities was not discussed formally at this symposium, but it was presented at the 1979 Zurich conference and will be the centerpiece of the Ninth International Symposium in Frankfurt, Germany, in June 1984. Hans Walter Gabler of the University of Munich is nearing completion on a critical edition of *Ulysses* that will produce for the first time the text that Joyce wanted to appear. Every published edition of *Ulysses* contains thousands of errors; this edition sets out to eliminate those errors, not by comparing published texts but by recreating Joyce's processes of composition. The work is being done with computer assistance. The final text will be produced from a tape generated by the computer, so that the errors inevitably introduced by human compositors in traditional printing methods will be eliminated. Gabler brought to Dublin the five most recently completed episodes (bringing the total number of edited episodes to thirteen); the anticipated completion date for the edition is early 1984. Since it was assumed as recently as the mid-1970s that accurate texts of Joyce's works were not feasible in the near future (all the texts are in a very corrupt state), this edition of *Ulysses* will represent a major scholarly achievement. And it will be the highlight of the first of what will surely be many postcentenary Joyce symposia.

Ralph Waldo Emerson in 1982

Gay Wilson Allen
New York University

Ralph Waldo Emerson died in his home in Concord, Massachusetts, on 27 April 1882. It was appropriate, therefore, that observance of this centennial begin in the region where he lived and worked most of his life, in Concord, Cambridge (Harvard University), Boston, and Lexington, where he served as supply minister after he resigned as pastor of the Second Church in Boston. The actual date of Emerson's death was observed in the First Parish Church in Concord with addresses by Dr. Robert D. Richardson and Gay Wilson Allen. A program was also held in the Concord Free Library, and David Emerson, the poet's great-grandson, led a procession to Emerson's grave in Sleepy Hollow Cemetery. All of these observances and tributes emphasized Emerson's New England heritage and his early career in the Unitarian church, from which he revolted.

Although no other place in the United States paid so much attention to the anniversary of Emerson's death, critics and journalists discussed him from Boston to Los Angeles, not so much as a New Englander as a national literary figure. All of these recognized that his great reputation at the time of his death diminished during the following half century. David Warsh declared in the *Boston Globe* ("A Philosopher's Ups and Downs," 20 April 1982) that after his death he became "the philosopher *par excellence* of American business":

> bosses quoted him, workers read him, teachers cited him and his books made a small fortune for Boston publishers. The author of "Compensation" and "Self-Reliance" was as much a part of the folklore of American commerce as Henry Ford, Thomas Edison, Andrew Carnegie, who a couple of generations later would quote his words.

This reputation was bolstered at a Sunday evening program on 25 April in the Sanders Theatre at Harvard, when speeches were delivered by Woody Hayes, Elliot Richardson, Archibald Cox, Rhys Williams, David Emerson, and Dana Greeley. Hayes, the former Ohio State Unversity football coach, caught the headlines with his inspirational praise of Emerson as a morale builder. It was significant, too, that the distinguished speakers on this program were eminent in law and theology, rather than literature, though critics and biographers of Emerson such as Allen, Richardson, Joel Porte, and John McAleer participated in other programs.

As Warsh pointed out, "A wave of revisions of Emerson's reputation in the popular press hit broadside, starting in 1930 with a famous essay in *The Atlantic Monthly* by James Truslow Adams." Adams looked back upon his youthful admiration of Emerson as sophomoric and immature: "As the ordinary unimportant man, such as most of us are, reads Emerson, his self-esteem begins to glow and grow." Reading Emerson made them "drunk and drivelling." D. H. Lawrence in *Studies in Classic American Literature* (1923) improved upon this charge. To Emerson's saying he would like to treat all men as gods, Lawrence replied, "If you like, Waldo, but we've got to pay for it when you've made them feel that they are gods."

In the same vein, Quentin Anderson in *The*

Ralph Waldo Emerson at age 70

Imperial Self: an Essay Upon American Literature and Cultural History (1971) blamed Emerson's teaching of extreme self-reliance for a diminishing sense of community and social responsibility in the United States. Emerson has often, also, been accused of denying the existence of evil, and Robert Penn Warren, especially, has strongly rejected him for this reason. As Warsh says, "By the 1960s the diminished Emerson had become the established version, and by the 1970s he had become a villain."

However, as early as 1961 Roy Harvey Pearce in *The Continuity of American Poetry* had found Emerson's voice to be the strongest in preserving and perpetuating continuity in American poetry from Ann Bradstreet to Wallace Stevens, and seven years later Hyatt Waggoner in *American Poets: From the Puritans to the Present* made an even stronger plea for Emerson's historical importance. He was joined by Harold Bloom, who repeatedly called for a reevaluation of Emerson and a reversal in his reputation. Meanwhile the Harvard University Press began publication of a new edition of Emerson's *Journals and Notebooks* (fifteen volumes between 1960 and 1982) and Robert E. Spiller, Stephen E. Whicher, and Wallace E. Williams edited his unpublished

Emerson's grave in Concord, Massachusetts

Early Lectures (1966-1972). These editions provided new material for students, critics, and scholars. As a consequence, a rediscovery of Emerson was almost inevitable. Exactly when it began would be hard to say, but it was well under way by 1982. No new biography appeared in this year, though Allen's *Waldo Emerson, a Biography* (1981) was still being discussed, and a Penguin paperback edition was published in November 1982. This book also received the *Los Angeles Times* Award for the best biography of 1981, and the James Russell Lowell Prize of the Modern Language Association at the 1982 Convention.

Perhaps the most important publication in the centennial of Emerson's death was Joel Porte's selected edition of *Emerson in his Journals* for the Harvard University Press. Porte says in his preface that he did not intend "a Chrestomathy of choice passages" but a selection of passages "that tell us something about Emerson personally . . . entries that cast light on his doubts, dreams, fears, aspirations, quirks, social and intimate relations and the like. He was a great human character, not simply a dispenser of timeless wisdom in Yankee accents. . . ." Porte realized that Emerson must be rescued from the stereotypes which had obscured the real man who lived, wrote, and struggled through the tumultuous years of American geographical expansion to the Pacific Ocean, the divisive war with Mexico, the still more tragic divisive Civil War, and the industrialization which followed. Like everyone else, Emerson was profoundly affected by these events. His journals record how he struggled from day to day to understand them and himself.

It was Emerson the man that had been most distorted by his critics during his declining popularity. All of the negative traits which he himself, in his extreme self-criticism, had lamented, had been interpreted too literally and uncharitably: his emotional coldness, lack of sympathy for others, unsociability, and his distrust of institutions. He was so extremely conscientious that he was seldom satisfied with his own conduct, and especially regretted his deficient physical stamina. But a close examination of his record proves that these negative traits were exaggerated, or that by strenuous effort he overcame them to a considerable extent. It was not true that he gave little support to Abolition. Though he was slow to be fully aroused to the evils of slavery, throughout the 1840s and 1850s he gave some of the strongest antislavery speeches delivered by anyone.

As early as 1953 Stephen E. Whicher in *Free-*

Dust jacket

Dust jacket

dom and Fate: An Inner Life of Ralph Waldo Emerson had called attention to the "dark side" of Emerson's life. He lived much in "the House of Pain," to use Emerson's own phrase, and he was not a superficial optimist, as often thought. In fact, he fought a hard fight for his faith and courage in the face of doubt, failure, and personal suffering, and he experienced periods of pessimism. By 1982 the "inner life" had become better known, respected, and admired. The seeming contradictions between Emerson's "inner" and "outer" life led to more subtle analyses of his mind and art.

The most penetrating interpretation of Emerson published in 1982 was B. L. Packer's *Emerson's Fall: A New Interpretation of the Major Essays* (Continuum Publishing). Though Emerson rejected "original sin," he was well aware that modern man lived in a "fallen world." Was this condition the fault of his own character or of Nature? (To blame God would be to return to Calvinism.) Though Emerson's explanation of the "Fall" varied to some extent in *Nature*, in his lecture "The Protest," and in his essays on "Circles" and "Experience," in all of these he taught that the "Fall" is the consequence of "the self's ignorance or denial of its own divinity." And the "imperfections of the social and natural world" were not "Adamontine limitations," but periodic or enthropic forms of the soul. In simple words, Emerson believed that no social or natural evils are irremediable. As a substitute for the Biblical myths, "Emerson developed four fables or formulas for explaining the Fall in the years that begin with *Nature* and end with *Representative Men*." Packer calls these "interesting fables" of contraction and dislocation, ossification, and "reflection or self-consciousness." These "fables" she traces through Emerson's works between 1836 and 1849, with meticulous precision and close reasoning, while demonstrating the enormous complications in Emerson's thought and art. Some contradictions she cannot resolve, but no one who reads her book will ever again think Emerson simple or a superficial thinker. This book shows how far Emerson's reputation has risen since James Truslow Adams's attack.

The intellectual respect which Emerson had gained by 1982 is vividly illustrated in the collection of essays *Emerson: Prospect and Retrospect*, edited by Joel Porte (Harvard University Press). One of the mysteries in Emerson biography has always been his great admiration for his eccentric Aunt Mary Moody Emerson. Phyllis Cole shows why her religious ideas failed to influence her nephew. Kenneth Marc Harris finds that Emerson's concepts on na-

ture gradually changed from *Nature* (1836), when he regarded nature as spiritual, to the essay "Nature" (1844), when he accepted, in Harris's words, "our complete immersion in materialness." He even, according to Michael T. Gilmore, though "Disavowing . . . the commercial outlook of the times . . . purifies and sanctions an aggressive, 'capitalistic' ethos of mastery over nature." Joseph Jones also finds that in the poem "The Adirondacks" Emerson sides with "the improvers, the civilizers" against the wilderness preservationists, such as Thoreau.

On a more philosophical level, Robert D. Richardson, Jr., says in "Emerson on History " that he believed that "the mind common to the universe is disclosed to the individual through his own nature." Therefore, history "is the history of the mind common to all men." Jeffrey Steele also points out that Emerson found the source of action in the unconscious. The self developed by discovering "the secrets which preexisted in the closet of the mind." Michael Lopez compares Emerson's "philosophy of power" to Nietzsche's, but warns against trying to reduce his thought to formulas; it was an "unfolding of intuition, which was Emerson's definition of logic." Ronald Bush's essay is an amusing commentary on T. S. Eliot, who professed a sustained distaste for Emerson, but Bush has him "Singing the Emerson Blues" in 1933 when he gave an address at the Milton Academy. "With its overtones of spiritual as well as emotional fulfillment it reminds us of the Divinity School Address."

Further advances in Emerson scholarship were made in *Emerson Centenary Essays*, edited by Joel Myerson (Southern Illinois University Press). Here eleven authors explore problems and give answers based on the latest research. Evelyn Barish examines Emerson's mysterious eye affliction, lameness, and chest pains in 1825-1827 in the light of medical knowledge of both his time and ours. She concludes that his illnesses were all symptoms of early tuberculosis, which he conquered by psychological self-therapy. His hard-won victory explains his attitude toward illness in his writings. Jerome Loving explores Emerson's progression from Unitarian theology to his personal religion and philosophy. In two other essays Glenn M. Johnson and David Glenn explicate Emerson's dilemma over whether to depend upon intuition or craftsmanship in his writings. Both Richard Lee Francis and David W. Hill dissect Emerson's intellectual and emotional crises reflected in "Experience." In the penultimate essay Merton M. Sealts, Jr., shows that, in spite of Emerson's dislike of the classroom, he remained a teacher all his life.

In *Emerson, Whitman, and the American Muse* (University of North Carolina Press) Jerome Loving is less concerned with Emerson's influence on Whitman, which has already been investigated many times, than with their similarities, differences, and relations to the "American Muse." Though their social backgrounds were very different, Whitman and Emerson held similar ideas of Romanticism, Naturalism, and philosophical ideas of the 1850s. They shared many of the same attitudes toward nature, but, as Loving says, "To Emerson, the universe is the 'externalization of the soul,' but to Whitman, man is the condensation of the universe." In their earlier works both believed that the hero-poet and individual character would save society, but Emerson could not find "whole men" and settled for representative or partial men, and both finally came to feel that "self-reliance is now nothing if it is not institutionalized and called culture [Emerson] or personalism [Whitman]." Loving says that Emerson's essay on "Poetry and Imagination" anticipated Whitman's theme in "Passage to India." Emerson no longer preached that "poetry is faith." Its vision is now "part of religion."

Leonard Neufeldt's *The House of Emerson* (University of Nebraska Press) takes its title from Emerson's statement in *Nature* that "Every spirit builds itself a house, and beyond its house, a world, and beyond its world, a heaven." Neufeldt's book is a study of the world—and heaven—Emerson built. He finds this world described by different critics so various that it seems they are working from different texts. As a textual editor, Neufeldt has studied Emerson's manuscripts and the growth of individual works. He thinks that one reason for the variety of critical interpretations of Emerson is that they have been too partial in their selection of texts; they have not been sufficiently familiar with Emerson's total corpus. "Emerson is more complex and unlimited than any treatise on him has suggested."

Neufeldt's study of Emerson's "house" begins with his epistemology. In "Intellect" Emerson says, "All our progress is an unfolding, like the vegetable bud. You have first an instinct, then an opinion, then a knowledge." Thus thinking originates in the unconscious, and instinctive action generates consciousness. In Emerson's work, "We only open our senses, clear away as we can all obstruction from the fact, and suffer the intellect to see." Emerson's epistemology was, finally, based on faith, and he was unable to analyze it. In "Powers and Laws of Thought" Emerson describes what William James would later call "the Stream of Consciousness,"

using Emerson's metaphor: "endless flow of the stream" (though Neufeldt does not mention James). This observation that thought flows and metamorphoses profoundly affected Emerson's literary art. Neufeldt argues that the organizing principle of Emerson's prose is patterns and sequence of images and metaphors, which retain the fluidity of the author's mental experiences.

There is, after all, some justification for the appeal of Emerson to businessmen. In his earlier years Emerson was fascinated by machines and technology, and had great hopes that they would enrich American life. But his observations in England in 1848 raised doubts in his mind about industrialization and, like Henry Adams later, about mankind's acquiring too much power for its own good. "What a hell should we make of the world if we could do what we would!" However, he continued to hope that men would learn to use power for good and not for evil purposes. The danger is mindless use of power. And of course the danger has not decreased since Emerson wrote "Work and Days" (1867).

The primary objective of David Robinson in *Apostle of Culture: Emerson as Preacher and Lecturer* (University of Pennsylvania Press) is to present the "essential Emerson," which he believes most Emerson scholars have failed to do because they confine their interpretations to his printed works, largely ignoring his earlier sermons and the training in oratory out of which his literary works grew. He believes also that too much has been made of Emerson's revolt from Unitarianism and of his harsh criticism of the Church, beginning with the Divinity School Address. Robinson has been encouraged in this approach by a movement among some Unitarians to contradict, or even deny, the validity of Emerson's criticism. In other words, he misrepresented the Unitarians of his day. Robinson argues also that Emerson's unflattering self-analysis, "or despair at what he felt was personal failure," was probably more the result of the burden of self-improvement and unattainable spiritual perfection which Unitarianism had placed upon him than of actual personal failure. Whether Robinson is entirely right on this point or not, at least he does show that Emerson's goal of continual self-improvement, pursued throughout life, owed something to his Unitarian training. Though the Unitarians taught the divinity of the individual soul, it was an emerging divinity, needing constant cultivation. Emerson's doctrine of self-culture was Unitarian in origin. On the one hand, Unitarians taught "a process of culture based on intuition of the perfect," and on the other hand, "dissatisfaction with the imperfect." This distinction takes us "to the heart of the question of the optimism and pessimism of Emerson's thought." This background does, indeed, add a new dimension to Emerson's biography.

It is possible that Robinson goes a little too far in righting the neglect of Emerson's Unitarian background, for he finds the origin of nearly every major idea in Emerson's literary works in the sermons of Dr. William Ellery Channing, Henry Ware, Jr., Joseph Buckminster, or the sermons Emerson himself preached while a Unitarian minister. As Robinson sees it, there was no reason for Emerson to leave the Unitarian church to find freedom for his own self-development. The Unitarian church was neither as cold nor intolerant as he accused it of being. However, the fact remains that Emerson did find the pastorate uncongenial, and believed the Unitarian church (or any church) restricted his freedom.

The most monumental achievement in the field of Emerson scholarship in 1982 was the publication of Joel Myerson's *Ralph Waldo Emerson: A Descriptive Bibliography* (University of Pittsburgh Press). This work lists everything Emerson published through 1882 and posthumous editions, selections, and attributions through 1980. Myerson has personally examined everything he lists, thus guaranteeing the authenticity of this definitive bibliography.

The fifteenth volume of the Harvard edition of *The Journals and Miscellaneous Notebooks of Ralph Waldo Emerson*, edited by Linda Allardt and David W. Hill, also appeared in 1982. This volume covers 1860-1866, and another volume will be required to complete the edition, for Emerson continued to record some of his thoughts through 1876. Except for scattered memoranda, he wrote little during the last six years of his life, not even letters. It would have been appropriate if publication of this new edition of the *Journals* could have been completed in the centenary of Emerson's death, but with the decease of several of the editors and other problems, it is almost miraculous that fifteen volumes are now in print.

Near the end of 1982 Kent State University Press published a handsome two-volume edition of *The Letters of Ellen Tucker Emerson*, meticulously

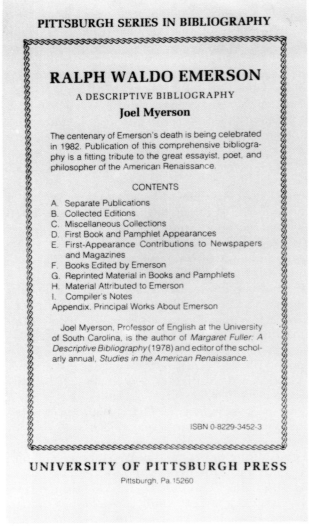

Promotional leaflet for the definitive bibliography of Emerson's works

edited by Edith E. W. Gregg, great-granddaughter of Emerson and president of the Ralph Waldo Emerson Memorial Association. These letters give intimate glimpses of Emerson's domestic life and reveal Concord as less provincial than Emerson's critics have thought. It was visited by many famous people and was in touch with the world. This edition contains a rich mine of information for future biographers and students of Emerson.

Literary Research Archives: The Humanities Research Center, University of Texas

Decherd Turner, Director

The Humanities Research Center of the University of Texas at Austin carries two distinct educational roles: first, to feed the advanced intellectual demands of the students and faculty of the university on whose grounds it is located; second, to service scholars from all over the world, many who yearly make trips to Austin to consult the materials housed in the Center. An even greater number use the mails to find the answers to their questions.

The Humanities Research Center (HRC) was founded by the late Harry Huntt Ransom whose vision and drive changed bibliographic geography. Reflecting his own discipline, the greatest strength of the HRC is in the fields of nineteenth- and twentieth-century American, British, and French literature. The present format of this resource is 9 million manuscripts, 800,000 rare books, 5 million photographs, an extensive theater arts collection, and 50,000 pieces of literary iconography.

The year of the founding of the HRC, 1957, was very late in bibliographic history, even by American standards. And to have repeated the established patterns of collecting would have been futile in any attempt to reach world rank. It was by unique definition of goal that Dr. Ransom broke the barrier of time and rank. What was this pattern?

Up to the time of HRC's emergence, collecting and criticism had been based for a century on the dominance of the first printed edition. And certainly no one still doubts the importance of the first printed edition. Quite clearly, however, in the fifties, it was apparent that literary criticism had run

The Humanities Research Center at the University of Texas, Austin

onto thin ground. The Ransom-HRC collecting pattern changed this by the basic assumption that the first printed edition was not really the beginning of the particular text's history, but it was the end. Rather, it was the prepublication materials which charted the real creative process: the author's notes, his many drafts, the finished draft, the galley proofs, corrected galley proofs, page proofs, corrected page proofs. In these were profiled the writer's development of the text, with its changes and rearrangements.

While some manuscripts had survived from earlier periods, this was the first massive attempt to save complete archival records of writers. The result was a new and large field for criticism and an immense amount of material to feed academic needs.

Books beget books, and the most fertile of book collections is the library of the working author. And so the search for the creative process has been pushed further at the Humanities Research Center by the acquisition of a number of writers' libraries, ranging from complete libraries of Evelyn Waugh, Erle Stanley Gardner, J. Frank Dobie, etc., to portions of the libraries of Ezra Pound and the Trieste Library of James Joyce (the source for *Ulysses*).

While there are hundreds of individual writers and literary figures represented in the manuscript holdings of HRC, the following British and American names represent some of the collections ranging in scale from "extensive" to "complete":

> James Agee, Maxwell Anderson, John Beecher, Elizabeth Bowen, Rupert Brooke, Roy Campbell, A. E. Coppard, Cid Corman, Gregory Corso, Thomas B. Costain, Edward Gordon Craig, Nancy Cunard, Edward Dahlberg, J. Frank Dobie, Arthur Conan Doyle, T. S. Eliot, William Faulkner, Eric Gill, Graham Greene, Radclyffe Hall, Lillian Hellman, Robinson Jeffers, Oliver LaFarge, D. H. Lawrence, T. E. Lawrence, John Lehman, Sinclair Lewis, Ludwig Lewisohn, Vachel Lindsay, Carson McCullers, Compton Mackenzie, Louis McNeice, John Masefield, Edgar Lee Masters, Somerset Maugham, Arthur Miller, Henry Miller, A. A. Milne, Jessica Mitford, Christopher Morley, Ogden Nash, George Sessions Perry, John Cowper Powys, Llewelyn Powys, Theodore Powys, J. B. Priestley, James Purdy, Siegfried Sassoon, Anne Sexton, George Bernard Shaw, Edith Sitwell, Osbert Sitwell, Sacheverell Sitwell, C. P. Snow, Stephen Spender, John Steinbeck, James Tate, Dylan Thomas, John Wain, Emery Walker, Irving Wallace, Hugh

Harry H. Ransom

Walpole, Alec Waugh, Jerome Weidman, Denton Welch, Edith Wharton, Tennessee Williams, William Butler Yeats, Louis Zukofsky.

It has been said that the Humanities Research Center has more materials for the study of nineteenth- and twentieth-century French literature than any other institution outside of the Bibliothèque nationale. And, indeed, with the mounting of the magnificent exhibition and publication of the catalogue in 1976 of the *Baudelaire to Beckett* exhibition of the Lake Collection, the right to the claim of major importance was securely established.

For example, the papers from the family archives of Henri de Toulouse-Lautrec consist of 386 holograph letters written by the artist, his mother, his grandmother, and other members of the immediate family and household, totaling 1,520 sides—together with a notebook and album of original drawings and sketches by Toulouse-Lautrec. This collection of letters, entirely unpublished except for fragments of about a half-dozen of them, is the richest of sources for an understanding of Toulouse-Lautrec's formative years. The insights they provide into the family life, the characters of the father and mother, their relationship with each other and with their son, enable us (in fact, compel us) to make a complete reappraisal of the effect of Toulouse-Lautrec's upbringing—in particular, his relationship with his mother—on his later behavior.

Such papers demonstrate the dramatic importance of archival collections. Some publications, before an examination of these papers, drew inaccurate conclusions concerning Toulouse-Lautrec.

Some other extensive archival holdings concerning French cultural figures are:

> Anouilh, Apollinaire, Baudelaire, Beckett, Breton, Celine, Cézanne, Char, Claudel, Cocteau, Colette, Debussy, Eluard, Gauguin, Genet, Gide, Edmond and Remy De Gourmont, Jarry, Larbaud, Mallarmé, Malraux, Matisse, Picasso, Proust, Renoir, Rimbaud, Sartre, Satie, Gertrude Stein, Tzara, Valery.

When visitors to the HRC discover that there is a major collection of photography on the sixth floor of the Harry Ransom Center, as well as a massive collection of theater arts on its seventh floor, they frequently ask: "What do photography and film have to do with the collection of nineteenth- and twentieth-century literary manuscripts?"

In the particular case of the HRC, the relationships among the literary manuscripts, photography, and theater arts collections are so profound and important as to form a unity rather than three distinct interests. Even the spatial arrangements as they now exist for the collections (literary manuscripts on the fifth floor, photography on the sixth floor, theater arts on the seventh floor) are symbolic of the ties that bind the three together: literary manuscripts forming the verbal roots, photography forming precise moments of visual arrest, and theater arts forming a combination of the two—verbal and visual.

With his enduring vision, Harry Huntt Ransom realized that, in building the HRC, an amassing of literary manuscripts would be a truncated treasure without the additions of photography and theater arts. From the time of the publication of Flaubert's *Madame Bovary* (1857), the visual element

has so pervaded the written word that indeed this facet is frequently spoken of now as "the camera eye" of fiction. As Joseph Conrad noted: "My task which I am trying to achieve is, by the power of the written word, to make you hear, to make you feel,—it is before all to make you *see*. That and no more, and it is everything." Joyce, Hemingway, and Faulkner, three of the greatest names in the literary pantheon, represent the supreme marriage of word and photograph by using the camera eye to unfold the development of character and plot bit by bit (verbal photograph by verbal photograph), demanding that the reader see the bump on the third finger or the beads of sweat on the doorkeeper's brow.

In pre-Flaubertian times, creative literature was basically a study of character, and action occurred only in relation to a defined character who dominated action (as opposed to the post-Flaubertian "camera eye" where action, piece by piece, creates the character). The story was usually controlled by a narrator's voice, with people and places not fully seen but more generally deduced from a few specific details—still within the control of an overall narrator. In post-Flaubertian literature, demands are made upon the reader to construct character out of a multiplicity of details—a thousand stills, as it were.

This revolutionary change in the style of the novel corresponds closely with the time periods of the literary manuscripts collected by the HRC. It is possible to think of a photography collection, separate and distinct from all other associations, in other institutions; it is possible to build and use a theater arts collection, separate and distinct, elsewhere; it is *impossible*, however, to think of the literary manuscript collection of the HRC existing in its fullest delineation without a supportive collection of photography and theater arts. The photography collection and the theater arts collection have many unique characteristics which are peculiar to their own media, yet their chief reason for being is that they are an integral part of the literary scene as viewed by the HRC.

A natural and supportive by-product of building the HRC collections is a strong collection of materials reflecting the many facets of the book arts. From the Gutenberg Bible, the first great printed book (1450-1455), through the revival of fine typography at the end of the last century, as most beautifully summarized by the William Morris Kelmscott *Chaucer* (1896), on to the production of the Pennyroyal *Alice* (1982), there has been a tradition of quality in production and beauty in design in

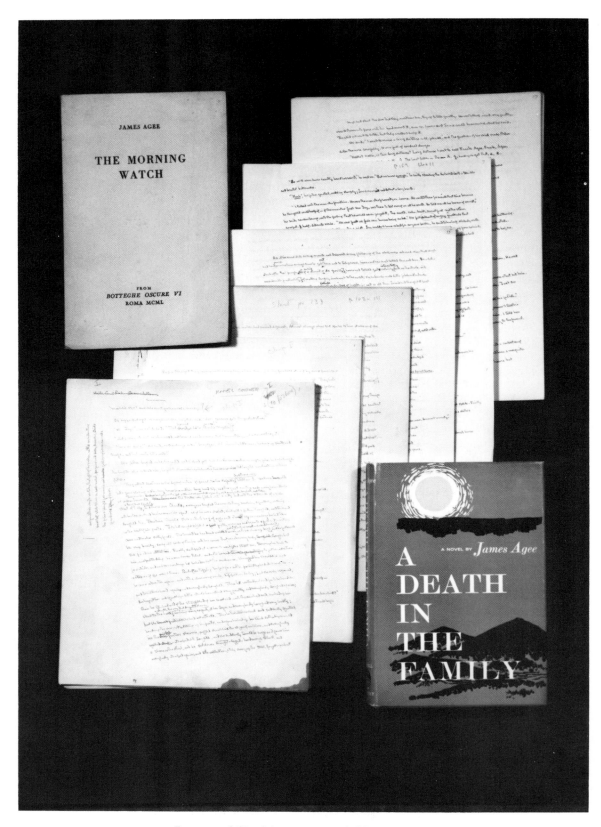

From an exhibit of the James Agee holdings at HRC

the book arts which defined the canons of taste as to what constitutes the finest qualities in the making of books.

A particular interest of the HRC is the field of bookbinding, with an emphasis in keeping with the strengths of the manuscript collections. That is, while HRC is interested in having, and indeed does have, many examples of classic historic bindings, the institution is primarily interested in the bindings of the twentieth century, beginning with the work of Pierre Legrain whose designs revolutionized the binding arts for our century. Legrain's great contribution to the philosophy of binding design was the insistence that design should be in harmony with the contents of the book, should reflect the nature and thrust of the words themselves.

This was a dramatic change. Earlier bindings had repeated established patterns of tooling which aimed for minimal decoration and perhaps to carry the coat of arms of the owner. There was no concern for the outer appearance of the bound book to reflect the contents. Pierre Legrain changed this. While his period of production was short (1919-1929), the amount of design work was immense, and his influence on subsequent binding arts was even greater. One of the prized possessions of the HRC is a collection of 162 Legrain drawings for his bindings.

What was started by Legrain was carried to its summit in the work of Paul Bonet, probably the greatest binding designer who ever lived. Bonet's first binding design was in 1925, and his inspiration was Pierre Legrain. But Bonet very early set his face against slavish imitation of Legrain, and as he came into worldwide prominence in the early 1930s, he tended more and more to reflect in his designs the work of the illustrator of the book rather than the text of the book. The French concern for the production of livres d'artiste naturally gave him an opportunity to range in design almost without limitation. A third generation of French binders reached its apex in the work of P. L. Martin. The binding arts continue to flourish in France today, and bindings from contemporary binding artists grace the HRC collections.

While the art of reliure (binding) is a distinctively French contribution, superb work is done elsewhere. In England today, the Designer Bookbinders, a group represented by such masters as Philip Smith, Sydney Cockerell, Bryan Maggs, and others, turn out in design and soundness of supportive work some of the finest bindings available.

The Manuscripts reading room at HRC

The same is true of the United States: Don Etherington, Lage Carlson, Gerard Charriere, and others have joined the international and Pierre Legrain-initiated tradition, thus making the twentieth century the greatest in the field of the binding arts.

A fundamental step in the academic process is the publication of the results of research. This responsibility to the world community of scholars lays a particular demand upon research libraries to inform the scholarly community as to holdings resulting in the publication of collection profiles and exhibition of materials. These are the communication routes of libraries.

The HRC mounted over 200 major exhibitions in its first twenty-five years, and these were memorialized by over 100 exhibition catalogues which analyzed in great detail the holdings represented by the exhibition subjects. On the occasion of its twenty-fifth anniversary (1982), the HRC had 110 publications on its "in print" list. The *Library Chronicle*, a quarterly publication of HRC, carries articles geared to inform the reader of the extent and quality of materials available in HRC collections.

The HRC has the greatest stake in conservation of any research library in the world. While the holdings of HRC are massive and diverse, it is the central collection of literary manuscripts of nineteenth- and twentieth-century American, British, and French writers which constitutes the chief base of HRC operations.

These come with built-in self-destruct quotients. Writers write on whatever is handy: wrapping paper, Big Chief tablets, scraps of cardboard, yellow second sheets. And thus it is that the HRC collection of modern manuscripts, the largest literary legacy of its type in any one place in the world, faces a relatively quick destruction unless the inroads of deterioration are turned back. The only salvation is the work of the conservation people.

The picture is made more complex in that the long-neglected process of proper housing and care—a worldwide phenomenon—brings at the same time the need for binding conservation, photographic conservation, and objets d'art conservation. Conservation is a link in the chain of that ongoing educational enterprise represented by research libraries such as HRC. A staff of twelve professionals with extensive laboratory facilities represents the beginning commitment of HRC to this tremendous task.

Why research libraries? Why an institution like the HRC? The answer is so obvious and so assumed that it has a tendency to slip out of focus, and other marginal reasons get inserted into conversation. The Humanities Research Center exists to furnish the raw materials for the continued growth of scholarship. Every new collection that comes within the examination of the HRC has to measure up to the fundamental inquiry: how can this material feed the gaping mouths of hungry scholars?

Scholarship exists within a historic framework. The work of each generation must be available for comparison and correction. If the basic materials themselves fall into decay and disappear, the way is opened to the beginning of a new Dark Age. Chemistry and time have presented this generation of academic institutions a challenge: to keep the intellectual stride going or to let it slack into nonexistence.

D. M. Thomas:
The Plagiarism Controversy

Lynn Felder

Donald Michael Thomas was born in Cornwall 27 January 1935. When he was twenty-four years old, after learning Russian in the army and taking a first in English at Oxford, Thomas decided to be a poet. Realizing that only the most established and revered poets actually made a living writing poetry, he reconciled himself to the life of a schoolmaster and eventually became head of the English department at Hereford College. When the college closed in 1979, the result of economic cutbacks by the British government, Thomas lived for a year on his severance pay and wrote his third novel, *The White Hotel*.

Its English publication in early 1981 met with mixed reviews and poor sales; about 700 copies were sold, bringing little more financial reward than his previous novels or his books of poetry and translation. After the American publication by Viking in January 1981, however, everything changed. By November 1982, *The White Hotel* had sold 85,000 copies in hardback, and over a million copies of the paperback Pocket Books edition were in print. The schoolmaster-poet was a best-selling author and an overnight celebrity.

In the midst of the best-seller hoopla surrounding the success of *The White Hotel*, Thomas received a transatlantic telephone call from American University, inviting him to teach for a semester. Flattered and perhaps nostalgic for his undergraduate days at Oxford, he accepted. In contrast to Oxford and to peaceful Hereford, where the doors are rarely bolted and the neighbors are neighborly, he found Washington, D.C., forbidding. His cell in a postdoctorate housing division had three locks on the door; he promptly lost the key to one. He was neither treated nor perceived as a human being, he says, but rather as " 'the successful author'—kind of revered. I felt I was becoming a 'grand old man.' " He fled American University after a week, leaving a note which expressed his fear of becoming "a media monster" instead of a teacher.

Shortly afterward, the monstrous media caught up with him. *The White Hotel*, called by *Newsweek* "Very likely the best novel to appear in 1981," is an unusually literary best-seller. It begins with a long erotic poem, uses as its structure a pastiche

Freudian case history, and climaxes in an actual historic event—the massacre at Babi Yar, as described by eyewitness Dina Provicheva in Anatoli Kuznetsov's book *Babi Yar*. Thomas credits both Freud and Kuznetsov on the acknowledgments page of *The White Hotel*. The acknowledgment, however, did not satisfy all readers.

In the 26 March 1982 issue of the *Times Literary Supplement* there appeared a letter from D. A. Kendrick, a London antiques dealer, accusing Thomas of willful plagiarism. Kendrick called part five of Thomas's novel "a superficially re-worked version of the historical accounts in *Babi Yar* of two people who (just) lived through the German occupation of the Ukraine." He provided, for comparison, passages from both *Babi Yar* and *The White Hotel* and set

D. M. Thomas

79

off an epistolary skirmish which raged for six weeks on the editorial page of the *TLS*.

On 2 April, Thomas defended himself and his book in a letter to the *TLS*:

> Sirs—I have declared my indebtedness in *The White Hotel* to the eye-witness account of *Babi Yar* both in formal acknowledgments and in innumerable interviews. Indeed, as a consequence of increased interest in Kuznetsov's *Babi Yar*, where Dina Provicheva's testimony appears, my American paperback publishers, Pocket Books, are reissuing it, and quoting my novel in its advertisements. *The White Hotel* is a synthesis of different visions and different voices; it asks only for readers with a sensibility to respond to it as a unity, and on the whole it has been fortunate in finding such readers.

A volley of letters followed. Emma Tennant questioned the appropriateness of an author's quoting verbatim from another book. Thomas countered that, in this case, imagination was no substitute for historical accuracy. David Frost expressed his concern for Thomas's "imaginative failure" at the point where he puts the documented words of Dina Provicheva into the mouth of his heroine, Lisa Erdman.

Early in his career as a poet, Thomas had written some verses inspired by the science-fiction stories of Ray Bradbury, Isaac Asimov, and others and had cited these writers in his acknowledgments. In his 16 April letter to the editor of the *TLS*, Jeffrey Grigson called this overscrupulous acknowledgment "admission of plagiarism in poetry."

Coming to Thomas's defense in a letter printed 23 April, Sylvia Kantaris concluded: "My admiration for *The White Hotel* is not without reservation, but I would defend it as a scrupulous attempt to explore the relationship between repression and brutality, a relationship which is itself composed of disparate elements, which looks different from different angles, at different times, and which Thomas approached accordingly."

Putting an end to the *TLS* battle, if not to the entire controversy surrounding his work, Thomas came to this conclusion in a letter printed 30 April: "I think the matter comes down to this: readers who admire *The White Hotel* think the letters attacking it silly; those who dislike the novel welcome the chance to say so, and are not going to be swayed by counter-arguments. I cannot imagine, therefore, that a prolonged correspondence is going to be fruitful; and I, at least, shall write no more."

Thomas enjoyed relative peace and quiet during the summer of 1982, appearing on talk shows, giving lectures and readings, and working on another novel. Then, in a review in the 26 September *New York Times Book Review*, Prof. Simon Karlinsky charged that in his collection of Pushkin translations, *The Bronze Horseman*, Thomas "adapted from, derived from, and heavily depended on" two previous translations. Referring to Walter Arndt's *Pushkin Threefold*, a book containing both literal prose translations and metrical translations along with the Russian text, Karlinsky claimed that "influence seems hardly the right term," citing similarities in the two translations.

Thomas denied extensive similarities, pointing out that "the Arndt translation and mine have exactly nine lines in common, out of 996. . . . If two Pushkin devotees set out independently to translate 'Tsar Sultan,' it would probably astonish them to find, in the end, that they had only nine lines in common. . . ."

Prof. John Fennell, author of *Pushkin*, another source on which Thomas is accused of having "depended" in *The Bronze Horseman*, also pointed out "striking similarities" between his prose translation and Thomas's verse. In answer, Thomas protested that "Reading Professor Fennell's book was partly instrumental in making me feel that, for certain poems, a verse translation should aim, above all, at directness and literal accuracy. My book acknowledges his influence and expresses my gratitude."

Translating poetry from one language to another is hard work. It is a task rarely undertaken for monetary gain; it is most often a labor of love. Thomas elaborates on this in a letter to the editor of the *New York Times Book Review* (24 October 1982):

> I read every English translation to be found in the Bodleian (Library), then set about my own. I was fired by love of Pushkin, not of his translators; and the joy of the labor was to try to express something of Pushkin . . . through my poetic voice. To have "depended upon" scholars' translations would have negated my whole reason for making the translations, and killed my pleasure.

In November 1982, as the debate over Pushkin began to flag, Carl R. Proffer, a professor of Russian literature at the University of Minnesota, accused Thomas of using many of the notes for Proffer's translation of *Anna Akhmatova: Selected Poems* "without acknowledgment, word for word" in Thomas's 1976 book-length translation of Akh-

Dust jacket for Thomas's controversial best-selling novel

matova's *Requiem and Poem Without a Hero.* He had brought a similar charge against Thomas four years ago, saying "Thomas's notes are nearly all derivative."

Thomas has chosen not to answer this latest allegation. Instead, he sums up his attitude toward the ongoing controversy which attends his work by serenely quoting Pushkin: "Receive with indifference both flattery and slander, / and do not argue with a fool."

Thomas has borne with equanimity the slings and arrows of critical and scholarly opinion—and of public opinion as well. A lady from Kansas, after reading his poetry, wrote to call him "the world's biggest pervert." A poet, a scholar, and a best-selling novelist, he draws fire from all quarters. He draws admiration as well, has won numerous awards, and has shown himself to be a writer of great vision, invention, and diversity, unaffected, by and large, by either flattery or slander.

Ion Trewin observed in his *Publishers Weekly* interview (27 March 1981) with Thomas, "He's not sure of what he wants to do now. He sees himself as a poet first, a novelist second." Thomas reinforces

this idea, saying, "it's a problem. Trying to be a juggler and keep two balls in the air is difficult enough, but to be a translator, too. . . . Then again, I can only write when the mood takes me, and when it does writing absorbs me totally." Of future publications Thomas predicts, "I know the critics will be breathing down my neck when my next novel is published, but that doesn't worry me. I simply carry on writing the best way I know how, and enjoy it."

D. M. Thomas lives in Hereford, England, with his first ex-wife, Maureen, and their two children. He is working on a fourth novel "about a contemporary Soviet poet. . . . about East and West, in people as well as in the world."

Books:

Personal and Possessive (London: Outposts, 1964);

Penguin Modern Poets, II, edited by Thomas, Peter Redgrove, and D. M. Black (London: Penguin, 1968);

Two Voices (London: Cape Goliard; New York: Grossman, 1968);

Logan Stone (London: Cape Goliard; New York: Grossman, 1971);

The Shaft (Gillingham, Kent: Arc, 1973);
Lilith-Prints (Cardiff: Second Aeon, 1974);
Symphony in Moscow (Richmond, Surrey: Keepsake Press, 1974);
Love and Other Deaths (London: Elek, 1975);
The Rock (Knotting, Bedfordshire: Sceptre Press, 1975);
Orpheus in Hell (Knotting, Bedfordshire: Sceptre Press, 1977);
The Honeymoon Voyage (London: Secker & Warburg, 1978);
The Flute Player (London: Gollancz, 1979; New York: Dutton, 1979);
The Birthstone (London: Gollancz, 1980);
The White Hotel (London: Gollancz, 1981; New York: Viking, 1981).

Other:
The Granite Kingdom: Poems of Cornwall, edited by Thomas (Truro, Cornwall: Barton, 1970);
Anna Akhmatova, *Requiem and Poem without a Hero*, translated by Thomas (London: Elek, 1976; Athens: Ohio University Press, 1976);
Akhmatova, *Way of All the Earth*, translated by Thomas (London: Secker & Warburg, 1979; Athens: Ohio University Press, 1980);
Alexander Pushkin, *The Bronze Horseman: Selected Poems of Alexander Pushkin*, translated by Thomas (New York: Viking, 1982).

References:
James Fenton, "Letter to the Editor," (London) *Times Literary Supplement*, 2 April 1982, p. 383;
David Frost, "Letter to the Editor," (London) *Times Literary Supplement*, 9 April 1982, p. 412;
Jeffrey Grigson, "Letter to the Editor," (London) *Times Literary Supplement*, 16 April 1982, p. 439;
Leslie Hazleton, "D. M. Thomas's War Against the Ordinary," *Esquire* (November 1982): 96-100;
Sylvia Kantaris, "Letter to the Editor," (London) *Times Literary Supplement*, 23 April 1982, p. 463;
Simon Karlinsky, "Pushkin Re-Englished," *New York Times Book Review*, 26 September 1982, p. 11;
D. A. Kendrick, "Letter to the Editor," (London) *Times Literary Supplement*, 26 March 1982, p. 355;
Edwin McDowell, "Behind the Bestsellers," *New York Times Book Review*, 86, 28 June 1981, p. 26;
McDowell, "New Allegations Made Against D. M. Thomas," *New York Times*, 12 November 1982, p. 24;
P. S. Prescott, "The Selling of a Novel," *Newsweek*, 99 (15 March 1982): 70;
Raymond Sokolov, "Doubting Thomas: The Plagiarism Flap," *Wall Street Journal*, 14 January 1983, p. 23;
Emma Tennant, "Letter to the Editor," (London) *Times Literary Supplement*, 9 April 1982, p. 412;
D. M. Thomas, "Letter to the Editor," (London) *Times Literary Supplement*, 2 April 1982, p. 383;
Thomas, "Letter to the Editor," (London) *Times Literary Supplement*, 30 April 1982, p. 487;
Thomas, "On Literary Celebrity," *New York Times Magazine*, 13 June 1982, pp. 24-29;
Thomas, "D. M. Thomas on His Pushkin (Letter to the Editor)," *New York Times Book Review*, 87, 24 October 1982, pp. 15ff.;
Ion Trewin, "Interview," *Publishers Weekly*, 219 (27 March 1981): 6-7.

A Transit of Poets and Others: American Biography in 1982

James H. Justus
Indiana University

The transit of American poets in our century has more often than not been spectacular. The natural arc of their passion—struggle, emergence, rise, and fall—is erratic and convulsed when we compare their careers with those of our nineteenth-century masters of the art. The tranquil and protracted years of the Cambridge versifiers are momentous when set beside the years and days of Emily Dickinson of Amherst; but even the most unconventional of those public poets, Walt Whitman, assumes the outlines of enormous fulfillment, an inevitability of renown, by the time the revered, much-photographed old poet comes to sketch the design for his imposing tomb at Camden. T. S. Eliot, Wallace Stevens, and William Carlos Williams fall into a similar pattern, in which recognition seems as inevitable as the private mastery of their art. The public trajectory of those poets who were born around the time of World War I and who came into their emotional maturity just prior to World War II is determined in large part by a private passion unlike their immediate predecessors': being "mad for poetry" becomes almost indistinguishable from the literal madness that dogged the private and public lives of Robert Lowell, John Berryman, Delmore Schwartz, Randall Jarrell, and, on both sides of the Atlantic, Dylan Thomas. If the seemingly serene accomplishments of Eliot and Yeats offered a younger generation a ready-made image of what ambition could amount to, the troubled ghost of Hart Crane, the incarcerated presence of Ezra Pound, and the academic accommodations to Theodore Roethke's sporadic derangements impinged more viscerally on the compulsions that began to shape their careers in the early 1940s.

The most stunning work in biography in 1982 deals with this generation. To read Ian Hamilton's life of Robert Lowell, John Haffenden's life of John Berryman, and Eileen Simpson's account of her associations with both of them is to come away from these careers stunned by the intensity of the poetic commitment in our time. We also follow these careers with guilty awe at the spectacle of these poets' sustained efforts to achieve aesthetic permanence out of personal instability, dislocation, and psychic fragility. Except for Hart Crane, no poets manage to tap the complexity of creativeness in both the manic effervescence of personality, convinced of its great gift, and the depressive fears and guilts with such singlemindedness as Lowell and Berryman, friends whose disabling larkiness so often belied their psychic desperation. What these biographies reveal is that such garden-variety obsessions as the oedipal attachment to the mother and the ambivalent rejection of the ambiguous father are something more than cases from an analyst's files—they are indeed gifts, but dearly paid for, that gave birth to, shaped and reshaped, and finally merged with the anguished art.

In *Robert Lowell: A Biography* (Random House), Ian Hamilton is particularly effective in tracing the acts of biography—marriage, remarriage, divorce, conversion, breakdown, recovery—in the acts of artistic creation. To cite just one example: the sixteen "Monteagle poems" completed by early spring 1943 are aesthetic responses to the moral act of baptism two years earlier; they are so marked, says Hamilton, by "high fever," an almost "deranged belligerence" in voice and diction that they become "hurled thunderbolts, instruments of grisly retribution." This is a poet as well as a biographer writing, but despite the overwrought description, the account of these transitional poems grows out of fact as well as artifact. In the course of a letter to Theodore Roethke in 1963 on the subject of "rivalry in poetry," Lowell writes of the "strange fact about the poets of roughly our age . . . that to write we seem to have to go at it with such single-minded intensity that we are always on the point of drowning." The elegiac tone edging this simple observation is repeated in his tribute to Berryman, whose death in 1972 reminded Lowell that "we had the same life,/ the generic one/ our generation offered. . . ."

John Haffenden's *The Life of John Berryman* (Routledge & Kegan Paul) is even more sadly engrossing than Hamilton's *Robert Lowell*. If this biographer is less critically astute in analyzing his subject's poetry, he is more clinically obsessed in analyzing the ailments of his subject. Haffenden begins early—with Berryman's anxieties over his physical stature, his poor eyesight, an attack of epilepsy (misdiagnosed), and an itchy scalp, all of which extend along with a gradual and frightening

Dust jacket

accrual of symptoms of mental collapse into the poet's full maturity. The best chapter in Haffenden's book, "Art and Adultery, 1947," perceptively links the poet's first adulterous liaison (with one "Lise") and a remarkable and frenzied outpouring of more than 100 sonnets spurred by guilt and passion alike. But the mysterious connections of mental states and creativity are not ordinarily pursued—merely the "self-consuming pattern of Berryman's days" calibrated in a succession of teaching appointments (that turn out badly about as often as they do well) and bouts of illness. Unlike Lowell, whose manic-depressive fluctuations could begin to be stabilized after 1967 with the discovery of lithium carbonate as a treatment, Berryman remains the case of an emotionally naked poet, deprived of the dubious emotional alternatives of the chemically dependent, who was forced to live out his own dictum: "We must travel in the direction of our fear."

A more intimate glimpse at that direction is found in the account of Berryman's first wife, Eileen Simpson, *Poets in Their Youth: A Memoir* (Random House), a book about Lowell's "generic" generation. Simpson's choice of epigraph is also a thesis

of sorts, but it is carried lightly but pertinently throughout—two lines from Wordsworth: "We poets in our youth begin in gladness;/ But thereof comes in the end despondency and madness." More personal than the clinical-minded Haffenden's biography, this reminiscence is not only a brilliant evocation of the generation of poets she knew intimately; it is judicious in its appraisal, affectionate in its selection of incident, evenhanded in its distribution of praise and blame, and superbly humane in its articulate, poignant rendering. Simpson's perspective on the writing of *Homage to Mistress Bradstreet* is one of the most harrowing accounts of the birth of a poem we are ever likely to read. Whereas we are wont to see the genesis of most poems as a creator's victory—over recalcitrant materials, trivial intrusions, domestic responsibilities, even mere inertia—we read this one of Berryman's as pure struggle, a poet's confrontation with his shadowy persona that is, alternately, subject, foe, and spectral lover, the aesthetic dispatching of which leaves a shattered psyche and a spent body. *Poets in Their Youth* is a signature of reluctant representativeness. As we read of the overlapping lives and books of Berryman, Lowell, Jarrell, R. P.

Dust jacket

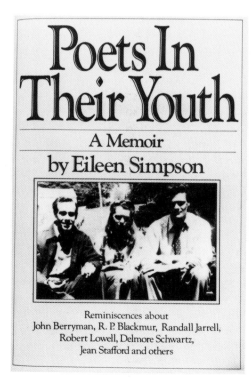

Dust jacket

Blackmur, and Delmore Schwartz, what we feel most is numbing recurrence: of manic highs; of depressive lows; of stable jobs and jobs unconsciously botched; of wives and lovers; of alliances of rivals; of projects planned, dropped, postponed, picked up, and finally driven to completion. In these poets the convergence of artist and artifact is so intense that to use a term like "confessional poets" seems ludicrously inadequate.

The emotional penalties of an art that willingly cannibalized life are what we most remember in the cases of these middle-generation poets. The other notable event in literary biography in 1982, Joan Givner's *Katherine Anne Porter: A Life* (Simon and Schuster), suggests another kind of penalty, another kind of victory. Porter's literary career has always seemed serene, well-paced, and leisurely—if a bit calculated—and the high moments of her life shape themselves into a pattern resembling a willed, consciously created scheme to participate in the large events of our time: Mexico during the Obregón Revolution, Greenwich Village during Prohibition, Boston during the Sacco-Vanzetti trial and execution, Germany during Hitler's rise, France just prior to the fall of Paris. Known for at least half

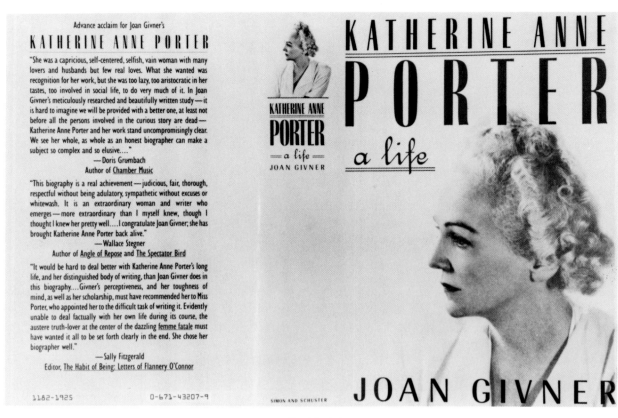

Dust jacket

of her ninety years as a "writer's writer," Porter gave to her life no less a chiseled precision than she gave to her art. "She edited the story of her life as she might have shaped one of her short stories," writes Givner; and that life, as it turns out, was as styled, as imaginatively fabricated as "Flowering Judas" and *Noon Wine*. The penalties for her transformations were a certain coldness (symbolized by the succession of her ill-chosen husbands and lovers), a tendency to use others for her career, self-torture, and harassment by personal demons. In congenial company, in making the very process of living artful, those demons were easily dispatched; but in private, working or trying to work, she battled them directly, exorcizing them by using them as the very conditions of her fictions. Quoting Porter, Givner sums up that effort as an attempt to "wangle the sprawling mass of . . . existence in this bloody world into some kind of shape." More often than not, Porter was uncommonly successful in wangling both life and the raw materials of art into memorable shapes. Givner's biography is a splendid recreation of the successive eras in which her subject lived and the remarkable and diverse talents with whom her life

intersected: Caroline Gordon, Allen Tate, Hart Crane, Josephine Herbst, Matthew Josephson, Glenway Wescott, Ford Madox Ford.

In the overlapping of literary generations perhaps no writer figures as prominently as Ford Madox Ford—friend, mentor, collaborator, and colleague in groups on both sides of the Atlantic. A sprightfully written but ultimately annoying book about such "colleagueship" is Nicholas Delbanco's *Group Portrait: Joseph Conrad, Stephen Crane, Ford Madox Ford, Henry James, and H. G. Wells* (William Morrow), one thesis of which is "that something in the place and period [South of London in 1900] caused talent to flourish as rarely before." The proposition goes unproved, but Delbanco does succeed in showing that the "galaxy of talents" in Sussex and Kent was more impressive finally than the more clamorously heralded Bloomsbury and Paris in the 1920s, those other notable examples of artistic clustering. But the significance of the "near daily contact" of these stellar figures never emerges— partly because Delbanco's calculated choice to write his account according to what he thinks is "impressionism" disallows any substantive exploration; his technique suggests Thomas Beer's *Stephen Crane* rather than John Berryman's *Stephen Crane*. Readers wanting a taste of the real thing might better turn to *Pound/Ford: The Story of a Literary Friendship* (Norton), the complete correspondence of the old man mad for writing and the young man mad to make it new, edited with precision and taste by Brita Lindberg-Seyersted.

Because, as Delbanco argues, "fiction-writing is a privacy made public," collaboration in whatever literary mode seems both rare and suspect. But the loose association of talents held together by a common cause—a club, a journal, an aesthetic or political movement—is almost as old as the republic. Three such accounts appeared in 1982. The first is a selection of letters that reveal the literary sensibility of an era as vividly as, but with more diverse perspectives than, recent collections of letters of the Nashville Fugitives: Mitzi Berger Hamovitch's *The Hound and Horn Letters* (University of Georgia Press). Although this fine journal under Lincoln Kirstein's editorship vacillated in its identity in the early 1930s, it published the work of Katherine Anne Porter, Ezra Pound, Gertrude Stein, and T. S.

Eliot; and for many it is often remembered as the "place" where the Henry James revival began—with a special number of provocative reassessments of James some eighteen years after his death. The Hamovitch volume is a fascinating compendium of opinions, literary commitments, and political persuasions—sound, testy, cranky, soothing, logical—from such figures as R. P. Blackmur, Allen Tate, Stephen Spender, E. E. Cummings, and Pound.

The other 1982 accounts of literary colleagueship concern two different kinds of theater which promoters and participants conceived of as "new." Jackson Bryer has edited and Travis Bogard has written introductions for *"The Theatre We Worked For": The Letters of Eugene O'Neill to Kenneth Macgowan* (Yale University Press), which documents the coming together, the collaborative success, and the eventual breakup of the gifted theater men known as the Triumvirate (O'Neill; Robert Edmond Jones, the designer; and Kenneth Macgowan, director-producer-critic). The apparent loss of Macgowan's letters to O'Neill prevents this from being a real correspondence, but many of the di-

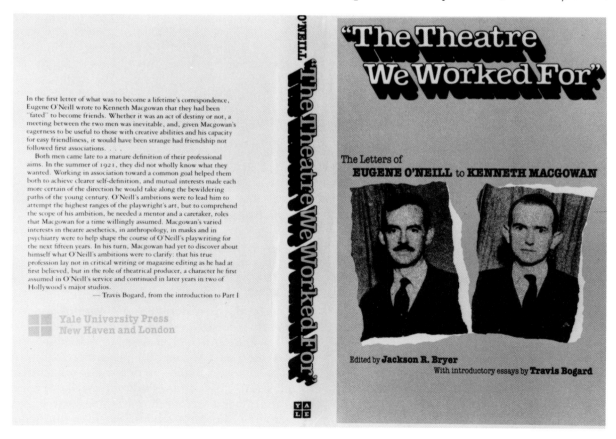

Dust jacket

rector's points of view at all stages of their association can be found in or inferred from the playwright's view; and Bryer has intelligently added occasional letters from others—Carlotta O'Neill, for example—that cast necessary light onto the tangled artistic and financial affairs of the trio. The reader comes away from this book, however, with the impression that even such imaginative colleagues as Macgowan and Jones were always several steps behind O'Neill—what Bogard calls his "extraordinary artistic courage" and the "energy of his libidinal imagination." But if the story of the Provincetown Players and the early days of the Theatre Guild is one of victory over staleness and convention, that of Hallie Flanagan's Federal Theatre is one of theatrical courage rejected by congressional fiat. Tony Buttitta and Barry Witham's *Uncle Sam Presents: A Memoir of the Federal Theatre 1935-1939* (University of Pennsylvania Press) is technically cultural history recounted by participants, but it provides valuable biographical profiles of Flanagan and her supporters in President Roosevelt's cabinet as well as her friends in the Federal Theatre Project itself, notably Pierre de Rohan of the *Federal Theatre Magazine*. Its four tumultuous years coincided with the promulgation of a drama far different from O'Neill's, and the Buttitta-Witham volume is rich in insights into the personalities and careers of other kinds of theatrical talents—Orson Welles, Marc Blitzstein, Will Geer, and Paul Green. Hemingway buffs will also want to note that the novelist's appearance at the Writers' Congress of the League of American Writers in 1937 is recorded here with none of the apologetics to be found in more conventional accounts.

The most fitting commemoration in 1982 of Emerson's death in 1882 is the completion of the vast editing and publishing enterprise of the past quarter of a century known as *The Journals and Miscellaneous Notebooks of Ralph Waldo Emerson*, the first volume of which appeared in 1960 under the supervision of the late William H. Gilman and the late Alfred Ferguson. Now bringing that impressive series to an impressive close—comprising in its totality something over three million words from eighty journals and seventy-four notebooks and diaries—is volume sixteen of the series (Harvard University Press), edited by Ronald A. Bosco and Glen M. Johnson, covering Emerson's final years from 1866 to 1882. Like its predecessors, this one is impeccably edited, and the editors have supplied a pertinent and succinct preface and generous ongoing informational notes. An appendix in volume sixteen provides a table showing precisely which of

Emerson's journals appear in the new Harvard edition. A readers' edition of *The Journals and Miscellaneous Notebooks* also coincides with the centenary of the poet's death: Joel Porte's *Emerson in His Journals* (Harvard University Press), a shrewd selection that gives a fair-minded representation of Emerson's wide-ranging moods, ideas, meditations, and pronouncements from the early years to the last; the next-to-the-last selection is drawn from an entry, probably in 1874, probing restlessly into the "secret of poetry" that resists full disclosure. The portrait that emerges under Porte's selecting hand is the one most of us now find most congenial—a man complex and ineradicably human, a husband, father, friend, poet, and man of letters in the world engaged in a struggle to attain emotional and intellectual equilibrium. The shadings in this Emerson are neither as light as those in Bliss Perry's *The Heart of Emerson's Journals* (1926), which this volume supplants, nor as dark as those in Stephen E. Whicher's *Freedom and Fate: An Inner Life of Ralph Waldo Emerson* (1953), the single most distinguished critical study of the author in our time. "I have been biased," writes Porte, "in favor of material that serves to bring Emerson most vividly to life," which practically means a necessary diminution of the "American Worthy" dispensing "timeless wisdom in Yankee accents," and a heightening of Emerson as observer and writer—"his keen eye for truth or folly, his penetrating wit, his verbal agility, his quotable apothegms." Here indeed Porte succeeds handsomely in presenting our most indispensable author in "all his moods and modes." Valuable in its own right is Edith E. W. Gregg's two-volume edition of *The Letters of Ellen Tucker Emerson* (Kent State University Press). Companion to and amanuensis for her father for nearly twenty years, the sharp-eyed and occasionally sharp-tongued Ellen maintained such a voluminous correspondence that these 1,400 pages project not just a narrow domestic perspective on a famous man but a major perspective on the entire social and cultural contexts of nineteenth-century New England. The editorial work is both perceptive and efficient.

In the past decade our image of Emerson's friend, Henry David Thoreau, has been perceptively shifting from the doughty individualist who, it is often said, became the practising Emersonian, to the more fallible, anxiety-ridden bachelor-intellectual. Thoreau may not necessarily be a warmer figure out of our literary past, but he is becoming more comprehendible. Even the dean of Thoreauvians, Walter Harding, in a 1982 paperback republication of the 1965 standard biography,

The Days of Henry Thoreau: A Biography (Dover), professes to be a convert to the view sometimes advanced of Thoreau as a latent homosexual, a fact that "helps to explain a number of curious facts about his life and facets of his personality"; indeed, Harding believes that the tension between his sexuality and the repressive attitudes of his society suggests "a possible source of some of his creativity." Because this new edition provides a new afterword and seven pages of notes keyed to the biography and corrects earlier typographical slips, it supersedes the older Knopf version. Thoreau's troubled response to his sexuality is only part of the *Dark Thoreau* (University of Nebraska Press) that Richard Bridgman emphasizes in his biographical study, but the image of false affirmation, evasion, and conflict behind a transcendentalized vision of the world that Thoreau projected is consistent with some revisionist notions. Although his special focus is on the revelatory implications of the writer's characteristic imagery (blood, dismemberment, putrifaction, excrement, copulation), Bridgman is perhaps overly cautious in drawing biographical conclusions.

At a time when a splendid new edition of the works of Mark Twain—complemented by another new edition of his letters and journals—is providing new insight into one of our most complex authors, it is disheartening to see the appearance of *The Selected Letters of Mark Twain* (Harper & Row), ineptly and capriciously edited by Charles Neider. This edition, apparently designed to appeal to the same public who buys such volumes as *The Family Mark Twain*, shows little advance over the old two-volume Paine edition of 1917 and betrays no evidence of how far bibliographical and textual practice have proceeded in the last two decades.

Reticence, omission, substitution, obfuscation: these are the perhaps necessary strategies that editors and biographers must adopt when dealing with recent literary figures whose lives impinged on others still living, but such discretion also inevitably insures another necessity: to rewrite the lives and reedit the raw materials that chronicle them at some future "safer" time. Some documents may be unrecoverable, such as Sylvia Plath's last journal that was destroyed by her husband, Ted Hughes, just after the poet's death. Another has been "lost." But the remaining *Journals of Sylvia Plath* (Dial), edited by Hughes and Frances McCullough, cover the period

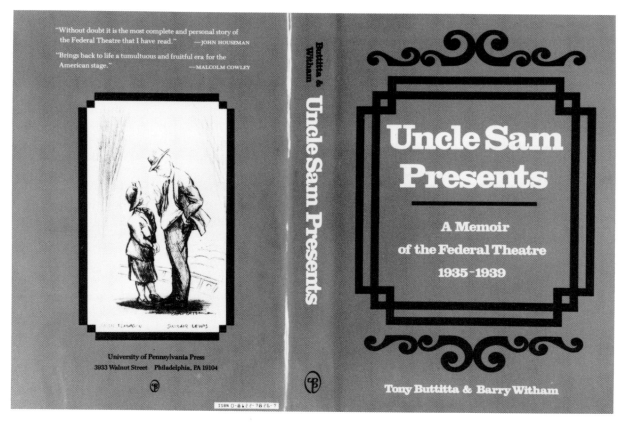

Dust jacket

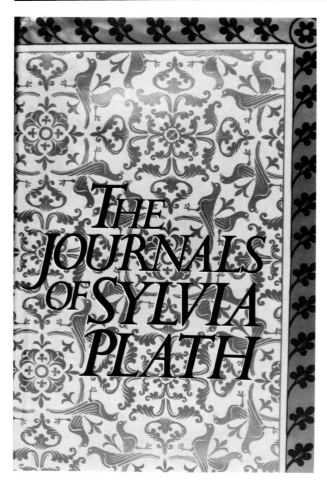

Dust jacket

from 1950 to 1962 and succeed, despite the cautious omissions, in depicting the enormous talent as well as the mercurial emotional sensibility of this distinctive poet.

Happily, detection and discovery rather than suppression and omission characterize another project of 1982. Theodore Dreiser's seven diaries, kept intermittently in Philadelphia, Greenwich Village, and elsewhere, have been edited in a handsomely designed volume by Adrianne D. Dudden, by Thomas P. Riggio, James L. W. West III, and Neda M. Westlake as the *American Diaries 1902-1926* (University of Pennsylvania Press). It includes all of the novelist's known diaries kept "while he was living or traveling in the United States," though no diaries are extant for the 1903-1916 period. The earliest begins at the urging of a doctor as a daily medical record, but Dreiser soon discovers the general therapeutic function of confession and meditation. Unlike Emerson's journals and Mark Twain's

diaries, Dreiser's are not repositories for literary projects, and for that reason are valuable corroboration for our view, gradually evolved over the years, of the novelist as a humorless loner, a man of vast energies solemnly marshaled, in the words of the editors, for "survival through creative work and intense participation in the life around him." From the beginning Dreiser's contemporary, Jack London, always offered a more exciting biographical base for the reading of his fiction; and as the subtitle of a new book announces, Joan D. Hedrick's *Solitary Comrade: Jack London and His Work* (University of North Carolina Press) is half criticism and half biography. It is especially fascinating for the explicit linkage of politics and sexuality and for the shrewd use that Hedrick makes of Charmian London's diary.

In 1979 Lewis Mumford's *My Works and Days: A Personal Chronicle* (Harcourt Brace Jovanovich) seemed disappointing as autobiography; with its curious melange of excerpts from previous works, personal letters, meditative observations on human nature, public addresses, and portraits of friends and intellectual acquaintances, it was more a self-anthologized collection of materials for an autobiography. A new volume, *Sketches from Life, the Autobiography of Lewis Mumford: The Early Years* (Dial), is precisely what the title announces. It begins with Mumford's memories as a child in New York City, where he was born in 1895, and includes an account of his German grandfather and ruminations on his mother's thwarted loves and his own, placed in the context of an otherwise comfortable domestic background, the surviving of which he seems to count a major achievement. For the literary scholar Mumford's segments on his association with the *Dial* and the talents connected with that influential journal—the happy age he designates as 1914 to 1929—will prove to be the value of this memoir. Bettina L. Knapp has provided what amounts to a kind of supplement to *Sketches from Life* with her edition of *Lewis Mumford/ David Liebovitz: Letters 1923-1968* (Whitson).

Two other volumes in 1982 contribute to the cultural history that the multitalented Mumford affected. *Writers and Friends* (Atlantic/ Little, Brown) is the second volume of Edward Weeks's memoirs (the first was *My Green Age*, 1974), which picks up in 1938 when Weeks assumes command of the *Atlantic*; the glimpses of writers great and near-great are rendered with style and generosity. Ida H. Washington is the author of *Dorothy Canfield Fisher: A Biography* (New England Press). This almost forgotten writer (1878-1958) was prolific, idealistic, genteel; by virtue of being a charter member of the board of the Book-of-the-Month Club alone, Fisher occupies a minor but firm place in the history of popular culture.

W. S. Merwin is the poet who also writes a plangent prose, and the most distinguished examples—his essays about his family that previously appeared in periodicals—have now been gathered together as *Unframed Originals: Recollections by W. S. Merwin* (Atheneum). His purpose in these six pieces is not a "chronological reconstruction, but a presentation of things that originally happened in sequence but now occur in the same moment in my mind, and so have become simultaneous, like flakes of snow that have fallen from different heights into the sea." The most affecting sketch details the last days of his mother, and the most brilliant is a lyrical meditation on "a particular hotel in Pittsburgh" evoked by a collection of yellow linen-textured postcards that subtly modulates into a tender memoir of his father.

The most unsettling of William Saroyan's five-foot shelf of books was the one entitled *Obituaries* (1978), a running memoir, alphabetically arranged, of friends, acquaintances, and near-acquaintances whose deaths were reported in California papers in 1976. It was also his final book. Now Aram Saroyan has written an extended obituary of his father, *Last Rites: The Death of William Saroyan* (William Morrow). Structured as a diary from 14 April to 5 May 1981, with a summary epilogue, the younger Saroyan chronicles both the "hate and brutal, hysterical anger" of the author's last days, when the father forbade his children's presence at his bedside, and the final reconciliation. A rambling memoir of life with and without father, with sporadic attempts to evaluate Saroyan's distinctive lyric proletarianism in Depression America, this volume with all its ambivalences will loom large in any future biography of the author of *The Human Comedy* and *The Time of Your Life*.

Some biographies, although somewhat peripheral to American literature, should nevertheless be noted. Virginia Gardner's *"Friend and Lover": The Life of Louise Bryant* (Horizon Press) is perhaps the first competent and objective account of the fluent journalist who with *Six Red Months in Russia* (1918) scooped by a year her friend John Reed and his more celebrated account of the Russian Revolution. But Gardner's ragged style and a penchant for piling up long quotations make the book appear to be an undigested source book more than a well-planned and effectively executed biography. Like her liberated contemporary, Katherine Anne Porter, Bryant freely improved her biography—her humdrum origins were imaginatively transformed into more socially auspicious ones—but unlike the more gifted writer, Bryant was deficient in self-control and in sustaining her newly fashioned (and often slippery) identity: by the age of forty-nine, with spectacular affairs and marriages behind her, she was dead.

P. G. Wodehouse, less than a decade after his death as a naturalized American citizen, still continues to charm biographers as well as a certain kind of reader. In 1981 David A. Jasen revised his *P. G. Wodehouse: A Portrait of a Master* (Continuum), his admiring biography of 1974, but not the fan-magazine quality of his prose. Now a more professional biographer, Frances Donaldson, has written a more straightforward life in *P. G. Wodehouse: A Biography* (Knopf). It is to be faulted for neither its style nor its clear, conscientious laying out of the facts. It will in fact be welcomed by both admirers of the humorist and those who look upon the admirers with puzzlement; Donaldson never quite interprets the facts in such a way that more detached readers might become less puzzled by the Wodehouse effect.

Finally to be noted is an invaluable reference work: *A Bibliography of American Autobiography, 1945-1980* (University of Wisconsin Press), edited by Mary Louise Briscoe. Fully annotated, this large listing supplements and updates Louis Kaplan's *A Bibliography of American Autobiographies* (Wisconsin, 1961), in which the cutoff date is 1945.

The Year in Drama

Howard Kissel

Declaring the death of the American theater has been a favorite pastime of critics for well over a century. Whenever someone begins making dire statements about the imminent demise of the theater, he can be put in his place by noting that in 1952, when Arthur Miller and Tennessee Williams were doing their strongest work, Brooks Atkinson lamented the decline of Broadway; in 1932, when Eugene O'Neill was in mid-career, Stark Young found little hope for the American theater; and in 1868 the anonymous author of a 700-page guide to New York City devoted only two of these pages to an assessment of its theater, concluding: "The era of sterling drama and talented actors is in the past, perhaps never to return."

Though boys do cry "Wolf!" needlessly, it must be remembered there are wolves in the forest; though one is mindful of the undue pessimism of one's predecessors, there are times when the situation is indeed bleak, and it is fruitless to pretend otherwise. But one wants to put as positive a face on things as possible, lest in fifty years one appear a fool. One can start by admitting that there is general impatience with conventional dramatic forms. When one attends revivals of well-made plays one hears audience members, in a phony kind of sophistication, complaining about the contrivances in the plot, overlooking the way harmless artifice contributes to the logical development of characters, the conscious build to an emotional climax, the sense of a crisis defined, met, and resolved. At one time these characteristics were expected of a play. It may well be that soon these expectations will look very old-fashioned. If so the early 1980s may be regarded as a time of innovation and discovery rather than one of decline.

For, looking over the plays that opened in New York in 1982, one's general impression is that structurally they owe little—perhaps too little—to the past. They are influenced less by classical theater than by the free-flowing forms of movies and television.

In the past a playwright was often confined to one stable set, which acted as a kind of discipline, limiting the number of characters and the kind of action but providing a focus and a clear milieu. Now playwrights—without any of the feeling of iconoclasm they might have had about such things a few decades ago—flash backward and forward as a matter of course, covering as much terrain, geographic or temporal, as they choose. A handful of actors may play dozens of parts, stressing versatility rather than one sustained and developed character. The usual result is a diffusion of emotional impact, though many of these plays, however much they avoid (perhaps evade) conventional forms, nevertheless resort to late nineteenth century devices to create some sort of climax—the plots ultimately hinge on some unexpected revelation to tie all the loose strands together.

Lean as the times are, there were a number of satisfying evenings of theater in 1982. The most acclaimed play of the year, David Hare's *Plenty*, first produced by Joseph Papp's New York Shakespeare Festival, then transferred to Broadway, is guilty of some of the above charges. It jumps backward and forward in time, showing isolated moments in its characters' lives rather than following their development sequentially. But each scene is so highly charged that one's emotional involvement is heightened, indicating that unconventional structures can engage as well as alienate audiences.

Plenty begins with a cold, alienating scene in 1962 as a caustic, hard woman tells her closest friend that her marriage to a witty, emotionally detached diplomat—whom we see sleeping on the floor—is at an end. Then we jump backward to the middle of World War II when the same woman is young and vital. She is engaged in undercover work in France and makes contact with the agent she has been assigned to meet. The electricity in this brief scene is intense and palpable. We then see the unsettled period just after the war when the heroine and the diplomat meet. We watch his career as it gathers energy, then falters, then falls apart completely. We watch her as the purposelessness and hypocrisy of the postwar world break her will and spirit. For most of the play the stage is in somber shades of black and gray; for the final scene the stage is flooded with brilliant sunlight—we are with the heroine in a French meadow the morning of the Liberation, a stunning contrast to the deterioration we have witnessed.

Again, Hare uses some of the same devices many of his contemporaries do, but he never evades his dramatic responsibilities—every scene has sharp

SCENES FROM
PLENTY

Top left: Kate Nelligan and Edward Herrmann. Top right: George N. Martin, Kate Nelligan, Ellen Parker, Ginny Yang, Conrad Yama and (standing) Edward Herrmann. Center left: Kate Nelligan and Bill Moor. Center right: Edward Herrmann, Kate Nelligan and George N. Martin. Bottom left: Edward Herrmann, Kate Nelligan and Ellen Parker. Bottom right: Kate Nelligan, Ellen Parker, Johann Carlo and Daniel Gerroll.

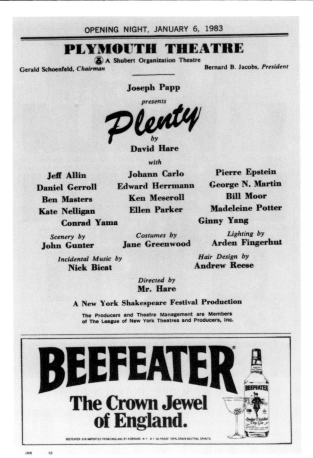

From the programm for Plenty

color, a rich sense of characters at moments of crisis. It doesn't matter that the technique is cinematic—a kind of montage—since it is so keenly realized. (Ultimately these distinctions between genres cease to matter: It was Eisenstein who pointed to a passage in *Oliver Twist* where Dickens, setting forth his theories of storytelling, outlined precisely the technique of montage Eisenstein advocated. As long as one is in masterful hands, structure matters less than content.) Most important, since the characters are all properly educated English people, Hare gives them something rarer than structure in our theater: language. Even rarer: wit.

Performed brilliantly under the author's direction, with Kate Nelligan and Edward Herrmann in the pivotal roles, *Plenty* demonstrates that none of what appears to be drawbacks in the contemporary dramatic imagination need be. The only mystery is why it took four years for the play to arrive on these shores from England.

A. R. Gurney's *The Dining Room*, first pre-

sented at Playwrights Horizons, then moved off Broadway, also demonstrates that episodic dramaturgy has great potential. *The Dining Room* is a beautiful, comic evocation of the well-ordered world of WASP America in the 1930s and 1940s, when its self-satisfaction and security were threatened by economic change, world politics, and "That Man in the White House."

The Dining Room is a series of vignettes in which familiar types appear and reappear in a succession of crises, some poignant, most extremely funny. It is, in effect, a collage in which a series of paper silhouettes, artfully repeated and placed, gives an impression of depth. The writing throughout is assured: this is a world Gurney obviously remembers with affection, though fondness has not dulled his analytical and satiric skills. As an exercise for six actors, *Dining Room* is virtuoso material. Even if the roles are stereotyped, they have to be performed as drama, not revue sketches. For underneath the often brittle comedy is the understanding that this is

Ann McDonough and John Shea in The Dining Room

a world just sensing its own fragility. This subtext redeems the play from ever being merely blackout numbers.

The most audacious of the significant plays of 1982 was John Guare's *Lydie Breeze*. Many of the characters in this play, set on Nantucket in 1895, are alumni of a New England utopian community, one of those characteristic expressions of America's conviction that its mission was to usher in the Messianic Age. The major result of this particular utopia was the dissemination of social disease, a rather extreme image for the effects of much American idealism but one suited to the wild mood of the play.

Guare has ventured into the grand, yearning style of the nineteenth century, its romantic melancholy, its tragic vision, without sacrificing the ironic sensibility of our own period. This is no small achievement. At first *Lydie Breeze* seems like an odd period piece, an artificial evocation of the past. But very quickly it becomes apparent that all the characters are haunted creatures. The past for them is not a place of solace or inspiration but an infection ravaging the present. In his own quirky, poetic idiom, Guare moves deftly from melodrama to comedy. The result is rather like O'Neill with

touches of Morrie Ryskind. The play was directed by Louis Malle, with whom Guare had worked on the film *Atlantic City*. The cast, which included Ben Cross, Josef Sommer, and Roberta Maxwell, brought Guare's baroque vision to life with intensity and bravura.

A related play, *Gardenia*, was presented a few months after *Lydie Breeze* at the Manhattan Theater Club. *Gardenia* shows Guare's understanding of the ways in which American life is cyclical. It is about young people living after a divisive war. Their idealistic dreams have been shattered and supplanted by banal commercial concerns. Guare might have been writing about the post-Vietnam era, but *Gardenia* is set in the wake of the Civil War and shows some of the same characters as *Lydie Breeze* twenty years younger. *Gardenia* lacks the audacity of its companion piece, though within its more conventional framework it offers its own dark poetry, which was realized beautifully by Sam Waterston, James Woods, Edward Herrmann, and JoBeth Williams, under the direction of Karel Reisz.

Another piece of dramatic audacity was David Mamet's *Edmond*, a series of short, pungent tableaux in which the title character, after leaving his wife, goes in search of sex in the seamier quarters of New York quite as earnestly, as naively as Everyman went in search of his salvation. *Edmond*, which often seems like a grotesque parody of a morality play, describes a world in which morality is tangential, in which there seem to be no moral feelings, only brutal, cruel ones, no concern for others, only selfishness and self-interest. Where conventional morality plays (or even moralistic ones) attempt to soothe or elevate, *Edmond* is a continuous assault on the audience until its final, oddly calm scene in which Edmond, convicted of murdering an actress he seduced, finds sexual communion and philosophic equanimity with his menacing black cellmate. Although the play has moments of comedy, the overall mood is chilling and haunting, almost in the manner of a Balthus canvas. The play was originally mounted at the Goodman Theater in Chicago under the direction of Greg Mosher, who seemed to have a perfect understanding of the playwright's intentions. It was transferred to the Provincetown Playhouse virtually intact. One could admire its theatrical ferocity without necessarily acceding to Mamet's stark vision.

Among significant American playwrights, none approaches his task in the strictest sense of the word more than Lanford Wilson. The word *playwright* is constructed, after all, like *shipwright* and hence implies a useful occupation rather than a

Ben Cross and Cynthia Nixon in Lydie Breeze

romantic, swashbuckling one. With admirable seriousness and ever deepening craft, Wilson has been documenting contemporary American life, fitting his engaging, troubling characters to the talents of the remarkable Circle Repertory Company, the city's major bastion of naturalistic theater.

In his latest work, *Angels Fall*, Wilson depicts a group of travelers stranded in a New Mexico church during a crisis precipitated by the mishandling of uranium. An art historian, convinced teaching is fraudulent, is on his way to a nearby psychiatric clinic with his wife, a former student. He once wrote condescendingly of a local artist who recently died. The artist's widow is leaving the area with her young lover, a promising, nervous tennis pro. A brooding young Indian doctor wants to leave off treating impoverished fellow Indians for a research position in San Francisco, much against the wishes of the

local priest. All these characters are on the verge of new chapters in their lives. The audience spends enough time with them to understand their hesitations, their ambitions, their limitations. As the play ends and they are allowed to move toward their new worlds, the audience sees the characters with charity, admiration, and probably greater realism than they will ever have themselves. Though it lacks the excitement of his recent *Fifth of July* and sometimes depends on Wilson's technical facility rather than genuine depth, *Angels Fall* shares with Wilson's best plays the clearheaded vision of *The Way We Live Now*.

Some of the most admired plays every season are those that appeal to the liberal sympathies of New York critics and theatergoers. Two interesting works fell under this heading last year—Athol Fugard's *Master Harold . . . and the Boys* and Harvey

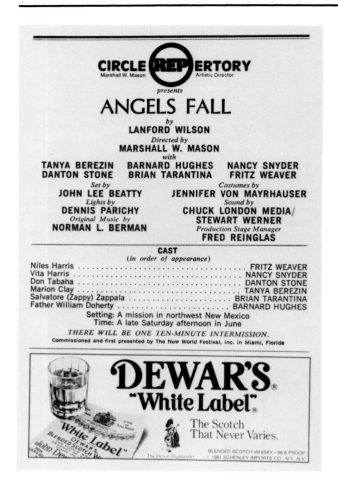

Program title page and cast list for Lanford Wilson's play about a group of travelers stranded in a New Mexico church

Feirstein's *Torch Song Trilogy.*

Fugard's play, set in a shabbily genteel South African tearoom, shows two black employees who entertain and nurture the white owners' spoiled adolescent son. After a slight provocation the condescension and insecurity just below the surface of the young white break through. By the end of the play his guilts and defensiveness have made him "mature" into a full-fledged member of his racist society. Deploring the racial problems of South Africa provides painless catharsis for American audiences, which may account for the self-righteous fervor this solid, if predictable, play arouses.

"International Stud," the first part of Harvey Feirstein's trilogy was written and performed by the author in 1979. It depicted the complicated, wild, funny, and sad life of a professional drag queen. It veered between drama and stand-up comedy, and when it opened critics admired Feirstein's frankness and candor in dealing with touchy subject matter,

though they had mixed feelings about its ultimate success as a play. A year later he introduced *Fugue in a Nursery,* which depicted the further adventures of his character on a country weekend with a current and former lover, the latter now married, his wife bringing a female voice into the otherwise male canon. Critics missed the abandon of the first play but found a growing admiration for Feirstein's craftsmanship. When a third play, "Widows and Children First," was added to these two, depicting the character as a victim of society (particularly as embodied in his stereotypical Jewish mother), the critics dropped their reservations about the first two works and expressed enthusiasm for the three pieces as a whole. In some ways the last of the plays is the shakiest, built as it is on stock Jewish mother jokes and sometimes shrill denunciations of society's attitudes toward homosexuality. Still the four-hour evening is full of vitality and wonderful humor and has at least one genuinely moving moment when the bitter young man explains his self-sufficiency as an outgrowth of his awareness that

Program title page for Athol Fugard's play about the maturation of a white South African man

Program title page for Harvey Fierstein's trilogy depicting the adventures of a drag queen

society is hostile to him and he can count only on himself. *Torch Song Trilogy* may be less significant as a play than as a turning point—its acceptance by straight as well as gay audiences indicates a new receptivity to sexual concerns that only a few years ago might have been regarded with discomfort or derision.

The Holocaust, which has received increasing attention in fiction and nonfiction books and cinema, is also making its way to the stage, seldom with conviction. The most publicized of the treatments was the late C. P. Taylor's *Good*, a moderate success in England, which received mixed reviews here. *Good* focuses on a Goethe scholar in Germany during the 1930s. Throughout the Nazi era his head is in the clouds. As great issues are being decided, he finds himself hearing music, largely kitschy, always beguiling and distracting. The first time he realizes what has happened is when he is in a position of authority in Auschwitz and hears the inmates' orchestra accompanying newcomers to their death. For many the play lacked a convincing center because the scholar was never "good" to begin with—he was morally flabby at the beginning of the play and became progressively flabbier. The only drama of interest was his betrayal of his Jewish friend, which hardly seemed shocking considering his lack of fiber.

Even less compelling was *Black Angel*, by Michael Cristofer, who won a Pulitzer Prize in 1976 for *The Shadow Box*. *Black Angel* is based on a true incident in which a Nazi officer, years after the war, decides to build a house in an area of France where, during the war, he had been responsible for the commission of atrocities. He is subjected to violence by masked French neighbors, not surprising in view of the nature of the atrocities. Toward the end of the play it is revealed that he was not present when the atrocities were committed, though, as officer in charge of the detail, he still took full responsibility for them. Cristofer ends the play denouncing those who took retribution on him, decrying hate in general, altogether too facile a conclusion for such a complicated case.

The most satisfying of the plays on this topic was Jean-Claude Grunberg's *The Workroom*, a series of scenes in a tiny Paris shop run by a Jewish survivor. A group of women sew cheap clothing under his supervision. Starting in the early aftermath of the war, we learn little by little where the women stood during the Vichy years. Their positions are always subtly delineated and Grunberg stresses the poignant humanity of each rather than their political stances. Two moving encounters hinge on an Auschwitz survivor—one in which, by the questions he asks and the answers she gives, we know that a woman who still believes her husband survived Auschwitz is deluding herself; another in which, without overt denunciation, we understand the survivor's contempt for the owner of the shop, who has aggrandized what he suffered hiding in the relative comfort of Paris. The French play, well translated, was performed with a marvelous sense of ensemble by a large cast.

It is obviously unfair to dispose of plays that have taken years of a writer's life and months of an actor's in a few sentences, but such brief mentions give a broader picture of the range of the year's offerings, not all of which require discursive treatment. Beth Henley, who won the Pulitzer Prize in 1981 for *Crimes of the Heart*, wrote another play juxtaposing comedy and death, *The Wake of Jamey Foster*, which disappointed her admirers because it seemed too facile a reworking of the same territory.

Jonathan Reynolds wrote an odd sandwich of a play, *Geniuses*, in which two acts of satire surround one of emotional discord and violence, ultimately unsatisfying despite the strength of individual moments. William Gibson tried to create a sequel to *The Miracle Worker*, *Monday After the Miracle*, following Helen Keller and her teacher Annie Sullivan into maturity, which, though absorbing and intelligent, lacked the direct impact of its predecessor.

Helene Hanff's *84 Charing Cross Road*, a winning correspondence between an impoverished American bibliophile and an old-fashioned London book dealer, was translated to the stage with surprising effectiveness, using only the original letters, no dialogue; a concern for fine bindings and dead authors has limited theatrical charm, though Ellen Burstyn and Joseph Maher made the characters enormously likable. There were strong reviews for the performances of Elizabeth Ashley, Geraldine Page, and Amanda Plummer in *Agnes of God*, an unconvincing play about the visions, erotic and

Program title page for John Pielmeier's play about the erotic visions of a young nun

Advertisement for Helene Hanff's epistolary play about the relationship between an American bibliophile and a British book dealer

otherwise, of a young nun. Hume Cronyn and Jessica Tandy received good reviews for their performances in a play coauthored by Cronyn, *Foxfire*, based on the book of that name, which sets down folk wisdom of the Appalachias. Cher and Robert Altman made shortlived Broadway debuts in an unmemorable, gimmicky play about small-town life, *Come Back to the Five and Dime, Jimmy Dean, Jimmy Dean*. Two Texas actors, Joe Sears and Jaston Williams, created an amusing spoof of the same milieu, its self-righteousness and bigotry, in *Greater Tuna*, in which they play the entire citizenry of Tuna, Texas, humanizing by their performances what might otherwise have been caricature. Murray Schisgal wrote two engaging one-acts with sexual overtones for Anne Jackson and Eli Wallach, *Twice Around the Park*. William Mastrosimone, whose 1980 *The Woolgatherers* showed a would-be seducer and his virginal prey finding chaste happiness together, treated similar material on a more violent level with a

Joe Sears and Jaston Williams in Greater Tuna

would-be rapist and his angry, savvy target—this time only the character of the rapist was treated with imagination, his would-be victim ultimately becoming more violent than he was and losing much of our sympathy.

At one time it would have seemed important to review the year's musicals along with the plays. Nowadays they seem worth noting only in passing. Yale musicologist Maury Yeston attempted to translate Federico Fellini's *8½* into a musical, *Nine*, and, though his score had riches, the show as a whole worked only because of the razzle-dazzle direction of Tommy Tune. *Cats*, an Andrew Lloyd-Webber score based on T. S. Eliot's *Old Possum's Book of Practical Cats*, won kudos as an extravaganza rather than for its dealing with the simple, eccentric material. There was general critical affection for an off Broadway adaptation of a Roger Corman comic scare flack, *Little Shop of Horrors*, and perhaps unnecessarily severe critical reaction to *A Doll's Life*, an attempt by Harold Prince, Betty Comden, Adolph Green, and Larry Grossman to find out what happens to Nora when she slams the door on Torvald at the end of Ibsen's *A Doll House*. The musical closed

after several weeks of previews and four performances at a loss of $4 million, an indication of the appalling cost of current Broadway musicals, which limits their ability to take risks or exercise any but the most commercial imagination. Once the focus of Broadway, musicals are now unwieldy dinosaurs plodding to oblivion.

The bleak critical estimate of the year's offerings was reflected in public response—by December 1982, the Broadway theater was experiencing its worst economic crisis in a decade. After a period of tremendous growth, only highly inflated ticket prices (forty-five dollars top for some musicals, thirty-five dollars for some straight plays) buoyed producers' outlooks.

Nineteen eighty-two was not without evenings of interest, but the number of dreary evenings far outweighed the satisfying ones. And there was little to offer encouragement for the future. Still no such gloominess should be allowed to pass without recalling that 1868 pundit convinced "the era of sterling drama . . . is in the past." The short view might be dark. The long view is beyond anyone's range.

The Year's Work in American Poetry

Brian Swann
Cooper Union

A word on method. I wrote to all the presses I could think of which publish poetry and asked them to send me copies of all the full-length books they'd published in 1982. The response was good. Probably ninety percent of the publishers responded, even if only to tell me they didn't publish poetry any more, or even if they misunderstood my letter and sent chapbooks, translations, or anthologies. Notable among the presses which didn't respond are those New York houses who this year published the grandiosely named National Poetry Series: Dutton; Harper and Row; Holt, Rinehart and Winston; Doubleday; and Random House.

I tried to review all the books I received through November starting with the so-called "small" presses (which should be changed to "literary" presses, since they publish a large proportion of the poetry in this country), then moving onto the university presses, which are increasing their poetry publications, and completing the review with the trade houses. There is no particular order in which I have chosen to discuss each book, but I have tried to allot the same (necessarily small) space to each. Frank O'Hara admonished the critic, "oh be droll, be jolly and be temperate!" I have aimed at temperance.

The first of the books from small presses is Allen Ginsberg's *Plutonian Ode and Other Poems, 1977-1980* (San Francisco: City Lights), described by Ginsberg as "lovelorn heart thumps . . . mantric rhymes . . . Zen bluegrass raunch . . . hot pants Skeltonic doggerel." These are sweet and sad poems, with plenty of anger still for his old enemies. The same themes are here, and the same heroes (Blake, Whitman, Reznikoff). There are poems on aging, but the same energy is there. The sixties are still alive and kicking in the eighties.

The Magician's Feastletters from Black Sparrow (Santa Barbara) is Diane Wakoski's thirty-eighth book of verse. Many of the poems are journallike, but the quotidian is transformed. Her plain language perfectly complements the episodes. There is a generosity, a willingness to share her life, an openness to experience. Wakoski's freshness and scope is a welcome contrast to much of the solipsistic poetry being written today.

Black Sparrow has also published William Everson's *Birth of a Poet* which, while not a book of poems, throws light on poetry. (Everson has published almost as many poetry books as Wakoski.) Subtitled "The Santa Cruz Meditations," the book consists of meditations around the theme of the poet's vocation: "taking a common subject . . . I began to meditate on it as I would on the Word of God."

William Bronk's *Life Supports: New and Collected Poems* (Berkeley: North Point Press) won the National Book Award in 1982. Bronk is not as well-known as he should be. His early poems are formal and reticent, glittering. Later poems continue the clarity and add a density of felt thought. Bronk is a poet of intelligence, even though "Anything we know is outside of rational expression." He knows "a whole world of inner knowledge"; is tough and resilient.

Graywolf Press (Port Townsend, Washington) has published two poetry volumes this year. James L. White's *The Salt Ecstasies* is his fourth book. These are poems of loss, alienation, loneliness in childhood, family, and love (mostly homosexual). Self-pity mars some of the poems, but on the whole the book works well. The best poems such as "Syphilis Prior to Penicillin" offer a view of horror in cool language.

Memory is Laura Jensen's sixth book. There are poems about her mother, childhood, nightmares at age five about the male creature. It is a book mostly about women, especially the poet's mother. The poems are quiet; their images work unobtrusively. There is a dreamlike, surrealist bent and complexity in the weave and drift.

Dragon Gate (Port Townsend, Washington) has published Richard Ronan's *Narratives From America*, sixteen poems, none short. Ronan stresses the story and the storyteller. There are multiple voices in a landscape of New England, Northern California, and, for the most part, the Midwest. He avoids autobiography on the whole, and there is a richness of incident and variety of occasion. The narrative flow makes it easier to overlook a certain flatness of diction.

Ithaca House (Ithaca, New York) sent three new volumes. Mary Gilliland's *Gathering Fire* is a first collection. Unfortunately, many of the poems are slight and lack sharp focus. While there are some pleasant poems of the natural scene ("Frost," "Coy Glen Again"), the language is not exciting, and there are too many clichés (e.g., "at the edge of dark").

Deborah Tall's second book, *Ninth Life*, has many poems set in Ireland. They are enjoyable for the most part but not memorable. Perhaps the rhythms of the poems in the book are too calm and stable. There is little sense of urgency. Certainly a number are too heavy in intent ("Our Garden"), and some are almost mawkish ("Anniversary").

The final book in this group is the best. Stephen Knauth's first collection, *Night Fishing On Irish Buffalo Creek*, is original and impressive. Knauth lives in North Carolina, and many of the best poems are set in that state ("From the Cherokee," "Viper Sunday"). The language gets a grip on things. There is a mythic consciousness as well as a feel for the here and now, as in "North Carolina Life Cycle," with its blend of pastoral and irony.

Toothpaste Press (West Branch, Iowa) published *Orders of the Retina* by Thomas M. Disch, who is well-known as a science-fiction writer. Sometimes the poems produce a strange effect: though they're strongly specific, they seem abstract. There are strong poems at the beginning, but the book tapers off somewhat. There are skillful "formal" poems as well as weaker, short "filler" poems. The best poems ("Delete Stars," "Bourgeois Idyll") are good-humored and precise.

Two books from Apple-wood Books (Cambridge, Massachusetts) are Miriam Levine's *The Graves of Delawanna* and William Corbett's *Runaway Pond*. Levine's book, her second, doesn't impress me, though the poems are competently written. The occasions slip away, "fog coat,/soft slag." Language is rarely pristine ("heavy with memory," "ancient trees," "the ghost of what you were"). Corbett's book is set in New England and is one journallike poem. Everything seems to get in, and the result is prosy—I am not sure why the book is written in lines of poetry. It is no more interesting than most journals, and certainly not the "lyric poem of astounding insight and beauty" the blurb announces.

Alice James Books (Cambridge, Massachusetts) is a poetry cooperative that publishes mainly women in the Boston area. *Backtalk*, by Robin Becker, is a curiously outward book, affable, calm even. The poems of childhood and young womanhood are quite well done. There are poems of women in love with other women, prose poems, and poem-letters. Jacqueline Frank's *No One Took a*

Country From Me is a posthumous work by a woman born in 1928 in France. There are poems of France during wartime, and poems about the poet's father, as well as love poems. While there is little here to stop the reader in his tracks, the poems are honest and unassumingly sufficient.

The Barnwood Cooperative (Daleville, Indiana) has published Donald W. Baker's *Formal Application*, a selection of poems from 1960 to 1980. There is nothing startling here, and often the reader is uncertain why a poem was written the way it was. Why the short to very short lines of "The Father, The Son," for instance? The problem of form is paramount. Perhaps this is because Baker feels more at home in the prose poem. The best poems are those in the final section, and those about teaching.

Barney Bush, the author of *Petroglyphs* (Greenfield Center, New York: Greenfield Review Press) is Shawnee/Cayuga. The reader is required to enter a different consciousness, learn a new history (assuming the reader is non-Native American). The contemporary and the mythic intertwine in these vivid poems. Bush's is a strong voice. As is Vivian Shipley's in *Jack Tales* (also Greenfield Review Press). In this, her first book, Shipley produces vivid impressions of people, mostly simple people. There are compassionate and direct poems about pregnancy, marriage, children. The poet's personality comes through clearly. There is no pretension and much openness.

W. S. DiPiero's *The First Hour* is a very handsome limited edition designed by Harry Duncan and published by the Abattoir Press (Omaha). DiPiero is best known as a translator from Italian, and many of these poems have Italian settings. Although abstractions in some of the poems form logjams, the best poems are precise and suggestive, richly observant. There are many people, and there is sensuous thought.

Hannah's Travel by Richard Speakes is the second volume in Ahsahta Press's (Boise, Idaho) series of Contemporary Poets of the American West. The book is written from the perspective of a mid-nineteenth century woman. There are some attractive poems ("Sara Discovers Her Hand"), but the whole is very uneven. It is simply unfair to Speakes to compare his poem with Berryman's *Homage to Mistress Bradstreet*, as William Matthews does in his introduction.

Too many poems are spoiled by overweighty (not to say abstruse) references in Frank Stewart's *The Open Water* (Point Reyes Station, California: Floating Island Publications). Who is going to check out "Thamyris losing at mild Dorion"? Too many poems lack pressure. The best, however, are simpler and face emotion directly ("The American Couple," "Train Window"). The poems get stronger as the collection progresses.

The Quarterly Review of Literature's Poetry Series (Princeton, New Jersey) is unusual in that it presents five books of poetry within one cover. This volume four features translations from Swedish and Polish as well as three volumes of poetry. *Alaya*, is a first book by a young woman—some of Jane Hirshfield's poems here were written in college. The poems are delicate, sometimes even slight. They stress quietude and simplicity. There are weak juvenilia ("Hunting Song"), but for the most part this is a promising debut. *Little Harbor*, Christopher Bursk's second collection, is very different. In his afterword, he says: "My poems are my way of approaching my father and the world of men he represented to me as a child—a world where good people in business and government sometimes make decisions that can endanger a planet." The

Front cover

"little harbor" is his own and his children's childhood. He sends ships from this harbor into the larger world, and the result is moving and committed poetry. The third collection is *Journeys Over Water*, by Marguerite Guzman Bouvard. "Trieste and its people are the landscape of my poetry," she writes in her afterword. A major figure is her grandmother, and the poems are filled with family. They are poems of memory and evocation. The book reads like lyric narrative, and the result is a satisfying whole.

Wind Over Ashes by Leonard Randolph is a very large book, and a good number of poems could have been omitted. There is too much sameness, and the book becomes predictable in content and attitude. Too many poems are just incidents recounted. The poet has a good heart, it seems, and he senses the real content of ordinary lives, but an editor at Carolina Wren Press (Chapel Hill, North Carolina) should have cut the book in half. Another book from the same press is Gene Fowler's *The Quiet Poems*, which are too quiet. Seldom does something rise from the page and demand attention. These are spaced-out poems, intangible, even when they're describing things as they happen.

One can cavil at some components of John Balaban's *Blue Mountain* (Greensboro, North Carolina: Unicorn Press). The tough-guy stance of the hitchhiking poems grates a little, and poems made up of a collection of vivid incidents seem excessive. But when incident is linked to charged theme, as in "Walking Down Into The Cebolla Canyon," the result is fine poetry. There are many poems as good as this one, and part two of the book, centered on "our war" in Asia, is very good indeed.

From the Diary of Peter Doyle by John Gill (Plainfield, Indiana: Alembic Press) contains as many prose poems as poems. The subjects are the usual stuff of poetry: loneliness, aging, passion. I liked poems such as "The Mercury Probes," ecological in a large sense: "the earth is alive." Also well done is the long title poem, a series of calamus songs (Doyle was Whitman's close friend).

The first of the New Rivers Press (St. Paul, Minnesota) books under review is James Bertolino's *Precinct Kali & The Gertrude Spicer Story*. Bertolino's effects baffle the intellect, and the poems draw on the authority of the rhythms for their results. The reader has to acquiesce, but he's not sure to what. A tongue-in-cheek anarchy rules, a deadpan humor. The book is full of probable improbabilities, attractive placebos for humdrum lives.

Robert Peters, poetry's roving reporter and gadfly, has written his twentieth book of poems, *The*

Picnic in the Snow: Ludwig of Bavaria. It is about "beauty, death, friendship, art, a disease, centered around one driven soul who happened to be king," according to the book's foreword. The king was ahead of his time, a visionary, Peters claims, and he draws on fact as well as imagination. There is variety in these poems, and the book has much of the scope of a novel, producing a similar pleasure.

Albert Goldbarth's *Faith* centers on the poet's Jewish heritage. It takes us from immigrant grandparents to Albert himself. There are long poems, short poems, pages of prose, serious and funny. Goldbarth has written many books, and this is one of his best.

From Red Hill Press (San Francisco) come two books: Paul Vangelisti's *Another You*, and Robert Crosson's *Geographies*. Both books are "experimental," but Vangelisti's is more concerned with language and linguistics; and part of his book consists of exhibit and performance poetry. Vangelisti uses visual resources (including a two-color "assemblage") and has a penchant for satire. Crosson's four sections are subtitled with the names of William James, Gertrude Stein, General Booth, and Charles Ives. Apart from a few references in the text, it is difficult to see the connection between text and name and to understand what is going on most of the time.

The dust jacket of Daniel Haberman's *The Furtive Wall* (New York: Art Directions Book Company) is covered with commendations. One is at a loss to explain the encomiums from Nemerov, Heaney, Davenport, and others. Ballads, shanties, and sonnets are all very well, but only if there's new wine in them. Versions of *The Greek Anthology* are no better. The language is stale—what are we to make of lines like "O wayfarer, pass softly by, indeed: Lest rouse the settled wasps of his lone sleep"? The whole book reeks of pastiche and artifice.

Michael Brownstein won the Frank O'Hara Award in 1969, and his *Oracle Night* sports an Ashbery blurb. Both of these facts orient us before we even open the book. The book is aleatory in drift and "pure" (that is, it approaches the condition of music and is short on "subject matter"). It calls for a lively imagination to follow the transformations, the dreamlike mutations. Another book from Sun & Moon Press (College Park, Maryland) is Douglas Messerli's *Dinner on the Lawn*. He uses Gertrude Stein's "I am inclined to believe there is no difference between clarity and confusion" as the epigraph. And then we are on our own. Messerli's is "language poetry," abstract, and a kind of shorthand to an unknown language. Readers should

try this book out for themselves and decide what is clarity, what is confusion, and what is both.

Three books from L'Epervier Press (Small Press Distributions, Berkeley, California) include collections by Floyce Alexander, Bruce Renner, and Jack Myers. Alexander's *Red Deer* consists of personal poems, but poems aware of a larger context. He says that "I write about a generation of orphans" whose adolescence has been betrayed by their fathers. His is the American nightmare, a wasteland human and social. Yet he has sympathy for the downtrodden and forgotten. Alexander is part Cherokee, and the American Indian crops up as a symbol of shattered society, as in the title poem, the best poem in the book, which is full of passion, anger, and despair.

I winced at the title of Renner's book: *Song Made Out Of A Pale Smoke*. It suggested wispiness, bloodlessness, the paleness of much of Mark Strand's poetry. When I turned the book over, I was not surprised to see a Strand blurb. The key words of this kind of poetry are "echo," "dark" (a favorite), and "dream." The favorite themes are emptiness, whiteness, solitude. They are all here. Such poetry floats by me.

I'm Amazed That You're Still Singing by Myers consists of love poems, poems of sexual stress, and poems about Jewishness and family as well as "Living Alone" (the subtitle of the fifth part). This is a generally pleasing book, even if not totally vivid.

Of the books published by university presses, the first is *Shadow Country* by the Laguna Pueblo scholar and poet Paula Gunn Allen (American Indian Studies Center, UCLA). The poems in this large book with a colorful centerfold painting are intense and intelligent. For once a blurb rings true: "This is a very large world, of abandoned pueblos and modern cities, dreams and deserts, loneliness and tribal consciousness, held together by the mind of a prophetic and arresting poet" (Adrienne Rich).

Edward Kamau Brathwaite's *Sun Poem* (Oxford University Press) may be my favorite of all the books under review. It is part of a trilogy (*Mother Poem* was first, exploring the female-dominated Barbadian landscape). *Sun Poem* explores the male history of Barbados as it passes from father to son. The tight structure is based on pun (sun/son), and sections are organized by colors of the rainbow. The inventive language, using dialect to create a genuine new sound and voice, is unique. The rich speech rhythms of the island stay in the mind. To retrieve and hand on, to collect and generate, this is the purpose of a marvelous book, energetic and original. Would there were American poets like

S H A D O W
C O U N T R Y

Paula Gunn Allen

Native American Series
American Indian Studies Center
University of California, Los Angeles

Front cover

Brathwaite!

The Flower Master by Medbh McGuckian (also Oxford) is the first book by a young Ulster poet. It is witty, but a little self-conscious and a little narcissistic. The subjects are not compelling, and the author is in love with taffeta phrases. Yet the effect is smooth and even elegant. The best poems (e.g., "Fossils") are graceful.

Barry Spacks's *Spacks Street: New and Selected Poems* (Johns Hopkins University Press) is disappointing. The poems are "formal" and come commended by the masters of form X. J. Kennedy and Richard Wilbur. But the poems are too often flip and light. The wit is heavy and closer to verse than poetry. Even the curse poem "Malediction" is leaden.

Wyatt Brunty's *The Times Between* (Johns Hopkins) is his first book. He writes free verse and formal verse; he runs to the self-conscious and allegoric—"This craft of putting fragile things aloft, / Of letting go and holding on at once" ("The Kite"). He is also sometimes too clever: "Out of the windless

house, / the still air stands, / nominal and aloof." When he lets the subjects speak for themselves the results can be impressive, as in "Channel Trout." When he doesn't, the ends of poems, striving for final significance, can clot ("The Floor").

Mary Kinzie's *The Threshold of the Year* won the annual Devins Award for Poetry. This prize for a first book brings with it publication by the University of Missouri Press. One is made to pay attention from the first poem, "Minor Landscapes." We become witness to "difficult dark passions." Kinzie uses rhymes, but, unlike Spacks, with a gnarled and difficult diction that impedes flow and makes a hard song. There are undercurrents here, almost a "metaphysical" texture and a serious wit. The subjects can be literary (Pope and Dryden appear) or involved with paintings. She reincarnates lost sensibilities in forcefully eloquent poems.

Kathy Callaway's *Heart of the Garfish* (University of Pittsburgh Press) is also a prizewinner, this time of the Agnes Lynch Starrett Prize—$1,000 and publication. There are family poems and poems of place. A sense of America comes over—Duluth, Anchorage. The Alaska poems are particularly good, detailed and felt. There are poems of travel all over the world and perhaps as a result of this travel an openness to experience.

Another first book is Bruce Guernsey's *January Thaw* (University of Pittsburgh Press). Guernsey writes with unpretentious, spare diction. Sometimes the poems are too predictable ("Louis B. Russell"), but there are precise poems on animals and things ("The Apple," "Toad") and activities ("Splitting Wood"). The poems often progress in imaginative and surprising ways, like a short story, and there is lucidity, even when the images or movements of a poem are surreal. There is a sense of the world's irony and mystery in these poems.

Another University of Pittsburgh book is Leonard Nathan's *Holding Patterns*, an urbane performance. Nathan is at home in short lyrics and long poems—"Meadow Foam" is a five-page tour de force of one sentence, and "Table Talk" is four pages. This is Nathan's eighth book of poems. It is meditative, sensuous, thoughtful.

Pittsburgh seems to publish more books of poetry than any other university press. The last book in this group is Richard Shelton's *Selected Poems, 1969-1981*. A generous selection makes for a large book (it collects from six previous volumes and adds some new poems). The early work has affinities with the Spanish surrealists and is marked by the loneliness shared by many American poets at that time. It is a poetry of shadows, paths, silence, departures, dead birds, and personifications. But the great theme is already there: the land of the American Southwest—Arizona in particular—its dreamscapes, landscapes, people. This is a collection that stays in the mind, a dark vision, one of much beauty.

The University of Alabama Press has begun its Alabama Poetry Series, publishing two books a year. The first book is Mary Ruefle's first collection, *Memling's Veil* (the other winner is my *The Middle of the Journey*). Ruefle's poetry is not easy to pin down, but the title poem is the key to her style and subjects. She steps out of the poem so the poems are curiously impersonal, "something/transparent goes on and on." The poems can be riddlelike, very demanding. And they can intrigue. A sense of joy pervades, even in loneliness. Ruefle's is an original new voice.

Louisiana State University Press publishes a lot of poetry and sent me five books brought out this year. *The Gymnast of Inertia* by William Hathaway is self-conscious. There are too many echoes of other poets and too many bad lines. The dying fall at the end of poems is irritating. Hathaway sees himself as a sensitive tough-guy. Good poems are spoiled with explanations ("The Poet Hunts Doves"). He tries to carry the day with plain talk or a "special" image, but the result is a strain. There is little of "the magic riddle in the poem," though the heart warms at a poem like "After an Evening of Robert Bly." One wishes that there were more poems like this.

Another Louisiana State Press book is Al Young's *The Blues Don't Change: New and Selected Poems*. "The whole circle of life / is ours for the jumping into," writes Young in a book of jazzy rhythms, poetry that dances and sings. This is a kind of antipoetry, poetry reborning (he uses an epigraph from the arch antipoet, Nicanor Parra). It is politically aware, yet, while seeing beyond the ego, is very involved with the sense of self. There is a kind of purity of language that makes you see and feel. There are satiric poems, poems of praise, boogies, and blues. It is a book full of people, open and generous, with scope.

Three other Louisiana State books are T. H. Hummer's *The Angelic Orders*, Dabney Stuart's *Common Ground*, and William Harmon's *One Long Poem*.

In Hummer's book, the father is a major figure. Poems draw on farm and country life, and we have strong imagery—a dead calf's legs tear off "like rubber boots pulled out of mud." Place is vital and rises before us distinctly. There is no romanticizing, and the people are expressively

Front cover

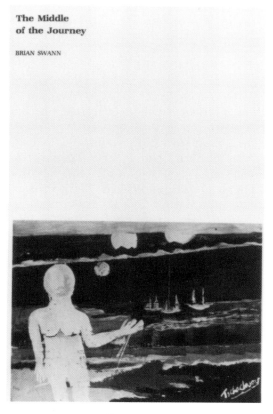

Front cover

portrayed. In this book we have real things and real events transformed by vision. Violence is accepted as part of life (even if sometimes the poet overindulges). There are some haunting poems ("Pointer," for example) in this collection of superior quality.

Stuart's book is philosophical about friendship, memory, change, identity. The diction doesn't startle or sparkle, but its quiet intensity leads one on. There is a thickness of texture, a texture of thought rather than a specificity of image. This is a modest but serious book: Stuart is "doing what I can to spread the word."

Harmon sees the world as one long poem. Once the reader gets over some abstraction of language and an enjambed syntax, these are interesting poems (it is questionable whether they make up the one long poem of the title, however). There is an abandon in the lines, a shrugging-off of images and attitudes. There is also a dark side, and poems take surprising turns.

The Associated Writing Programs have played an important role in persuading smaller university presses to publish the finalists of their annual competition. One of these finalists, published by the University Presses of Florida-Orlando, is Nicholas Rinaldi. His book is entitled *We Have Lost Our Fathers*. The poems are dreamlike but more like dream excerpts than fulfilling wholes (e.g., "Shadow of the Crow"). The poems don't do enough work and therefore are not very satisfying. He picks easy targets ("Musak") and doesn't reveal enough. One dulls on the surrealism; it's not amusing after a while. When he tries for profundity, Rinaldi comes up with things like "Scenes of violence, like great works of art,/make us pause."

John Frederick Nims's *Selected Poems* (University of Chicago Press) is made for readers with tired eyes. The print is large and clear. The poems start in the 1940s and are as "formal" as the most recent poems. In his introductory essay, Nims claims that by writing in form he is in touch with the laws of the universe. One might add that form is more fluid than he seems to realize, and there is more variety to it than he would admit into the universe. The poems are epigrammatical, aphoristic, condensed, and skillful. Nims is a witty master of form: " 'You say so, but will you be faithful? You men!' / But dear, I've been faithful again and again!" ("Protestation").

Lynn Luria-Sukenick's *Houdini, Houdini* (Cleveland State University Press) consists of factual and imaginary episodes from the life of Houdini, prose poems and poems. The book is not very interesting. We get little sense of Houdini, and the

poet just skates around the subject. This is a waste of a good subject.

Jane Flanders's *The Students of Snow* won the Juniper Prize from the University of Massachusetts Press. It's an elegant book, with unexpected corners. All things are alive and have something to say. Whether they're moss or wild asters, all are "related to the universe." One feels it's natural to talk to mountains—and to have streams talk back. This is a world of humor, a meaningful world, a world constantly being learned.

Poems of the Midwest predominate in Sonia Gernes's *Brief Lives* (University of Notre Dame Press), which won the Society of Midland Authors Poetry Book Award. It is a kind of *Spoon River* or *Local Lives*. It is a pleasant book of warm feelings, but the language is plain and some poems which are meant to be impressive, such as "The Commencement," which deals with a rite of passage, are rather obvious.

Another first collection by a young poet is Jordan Smith's *An Apology For Loving The Old Hymns* (Princeton University Press). He writes poems addressed to Edvard Munch and poems in the popular contemporary mode of the historical voice, in this case, Marina Tsvetayeva. He shows skill with the long poem (a poem by Strindberg to Siri), and, best of all, a long historical sequence in the voices of Walter Butler, Guy Johnson, and the great Mohawk chief Joseph Brant. Smith's poetry is ambitious, and this is a felicitous debut.

Two other Princeton books are Alicia Ostriker's *A Woman Under The Surface* and Phyllis Janowitz's *Visiting Rites*.

Ostriker's book is made up of candid poems from a feminist perspective ("feminist" in subject and treatment, not polemic). Here is woman as wife, mother, and creator. Some of the poems leave one with a sense of incompleteness, and others seem to have endings that are not strong enough. But these poems are open to growth and change; they are at home in the element of the water. So it is no surprise that the title poem is one of the best poems in the book, with "The Exchange" close behind.

Janowitz's volume contains poems that won just about every prize the Poetry Society of America awards. Hers is not a poetry of images but of accretion; it is a plain voice spiced with wit. A kind of domestic content pervades, and these are pleasant civilized poems, carrying authority in their careful speech rhythms.

Three volumes came from the University of Illinois Press: Jim Barnes's *The American Book of the Dead*, Frederick Morgan's *Northbook*, and Sydney

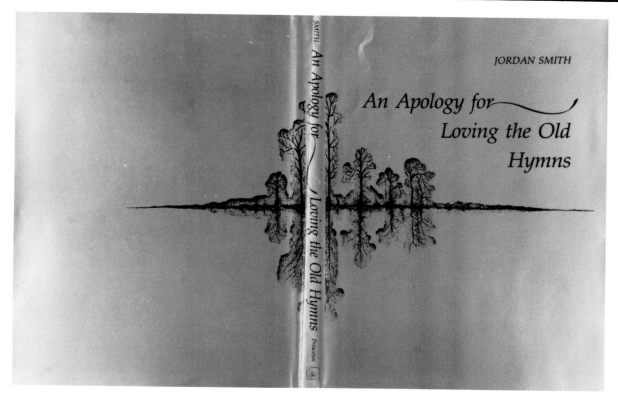

Dust jacket

Lea's *The Floating Candles*.

At first I feared that Barnes's title might swamp his book. But from the first poem the reader is engaged. Barnes writes about surviving, and he's tough-minded. Barnes writes from a Choctaw heritage, and his is a vision of America without compassion, without illusion. He writes of "Native American Poetry" that "you can believe it" since to get where it is "it had to walk through hell." We can believe Barnes too. This is a very fine collection.

Northbook is the fifth collection by the editor of the *Hudson Review*. The first section, which gives the book its title, draws on Norse mythology. The gnomic is taken up again in the third part, "Riddles and Evocations," and continues into the fourth, "Ten Dream Poems." This is not a easy book, and sometimes it is irritating, but the integrity and an engagement with the enigmatic aspects of our existence come through.

A full and rich New Hampshire landscape is integrated into the lives of the people in Lea's poems. The imagery is magical, and poems such as "The Feud" show a narrative gift. There are a variety of modes and moods—tough, gentle, ironic, affirmative. A poem like "Ghost Signs" lives up to its epigraph from Ortega y Gasset: "The mission of

thought is to construct archetypes." This is a savory abundant volume.

Gordon Osing describes his book *From The Boundary Waters* (Memphis State University Press) as "bread-and-butter-poetry." He's probably selling himself short since the poems, while dealing with everyday reality, lead to unusual places. The best poems, such as "Names, Love" are about things that have no names, and the poem sets about creating them. Such poems attract attention and give pleasure. This is a first collection of promise.

The Mohawk poet Maurice Kenny has written *Blackrobe* (Saranac Lake, New York: North Country Community College Press), in which he retells an episode from Mohawk history—the encounter with the Blackrobe (Jesuit) missionary Father Isaac Jogues in the seventeenth century. The conflicts begun then are traced to the present; and the book will be useful reading for a country still ethnocentric and largely ignorant of Indian reality, a country still blind "in the eye of cultural respect."

Among the poetry books published by the trade houses are several first books. "Finished enterprises of sensibility," says Robert Fitzgerald on the back of Katha Pollitt's first book, *Antarctic Traveller* (Knopf). Finished enterprises, however, have a way of appearing pale, and sensibility can turn in on itself. These are observer poems, "transparent as glass, thin air." There are five poems from Japanese paintings, and these seem to typify the book with their delicateness. The poems are rather removed, controlled, and not overfull of powerful emotion. Perhaps in her next book, Pollitt will go beyond the accomplishment of technique, beyond porcelain.

On Tour With Rita (Knopf) by Nicholas Christopher is another first book. It is almost flashy in its easy grace, inventive to the point of profligacy. It is a large book in the number of pages and in its scope—the whole middle section, the title poem, spans continents. Perhaps one should not complain, therefore, if in all this some of the poems are wispy and get blown away. Christopher's inventiveness is demonstrated in such poems as "Lord Byron in Paradise" and "Walt Whitman at the Reburial of Poe." At his worst he is showy and clever, but at his best he is a connoisseur of phrase and incident.

Also from Knopf is Brad Leithauser's *Hundred of Fireflies*, a first book. Although the book comes

Front cover

with praise from a battery of heavies, it is not really solid. Too often the poems are just pleasant bucolic description. There are also some downright bad poems ("Odd Carnivores" and "Astronomical Riddles"), and many lines are sheer prose (as in "Two Summer Jobs"). Some poems carry conviction, but as a collection it lacks resonance and resolution.

The tenth volume in Houghton Mifflin's New Poetry Series is Maria Flook's *Reckless Wedding*. It is a decent debut, though there is nothing thrilling. There are poems of her own and her daughter's childhood, love poems, and poems to her father. The book is satisfactory, if a little narrow in range.

Monolithos: Poems 1962-1982 (Knopf) is Jack Gilbert's first book since he won the Yale Series of Younger Poets Prize in 1962. Some of that first book is included here; the rest of the book is new. It is mostly autobiographical, but the more recent poems seem weaker than the early ones. The poems register the pain of separation, though many are self-pitying ("Mistrust of Bronze"). Clearly the poet suffers, and so one should not be too rough; the anguish is almost bare. But this is a disappointing collection. I was hoping for something better.

The poems in Mona Van Duyn's *Letters From a Father and Other Poems* are domestic. Balance and cycles (the last poem is entitled "First") characterize the book. A rich family life in the Midwest is lovingly portrayed. There is also a section of poems of place, from the Missouri Ozarks to Madrid. This is a pleasing and warm book from Atheneum.

Also from Atheneum is Stephen Dobyns's *The Balthus Poems*. This brief book, Dobyns's fifth, consists of thirty-two poems, each taking its title from a Balthus painting. The poems don't interpret; rather the paintings are used to create narrative poems "free from the lyrical first person voice" (author's introduction). In a sense the poems are dramatic interludes. Objectively passionate, they offer to know characters as in a drama. The poems create an aura of unreality, though they are concrete in detail.

Galway Kinnell's *Selected Poems* (Houghton Mifflin) is made up of thirty-five years of work, from 1946 to *Mortal Acts, Mortal Words*. This is a convenient selection from one of our leading poets. A weird light plays over the best of Kinnell's work; there is a haunting quality. The poems are precise, the images pure. His concern is not just with the self and family but with the lonely, lost, and dispossessed. The last poem, "Flying Home," is the most moving in the whole collection. We have been waiting for this fine book for a long time.

Candles in Babylon (New Directions) is Denise

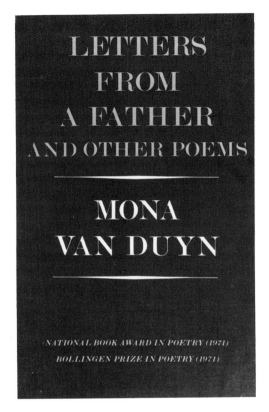

Front cover *Front cover*

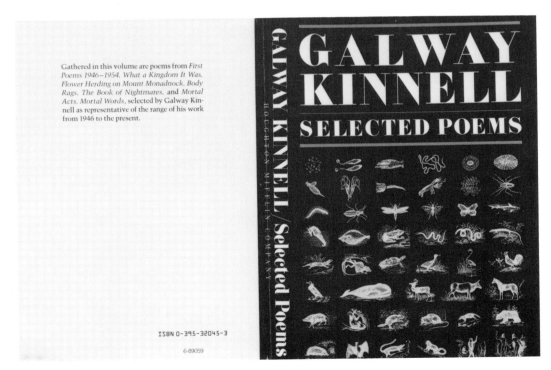

Dust jacket

Levertov's first book since 1978, and this too has been worth the wait. There is variety here, from the wry comic satire of "Pig Dreams" to antinuclear poems. The book ends with the impressive "Mass for the Day of St. Thomas Didymus." Levertov fuses mythic and social consciousness. There is a seriousness and heft to the lines, even if no corruscating imagery. The lines from "Williams: An Essay" might describe her own peculiar voice: "His theme / over and over: / the twang of plucked / catgut / from which struggles / music."

Allen Grossman's *Of The Great House* (New Directions) is ambitious and wide-ranging (it even necessitates a few pages of footnotes). It is not for the lazy mind. The great house is the world, the house of mind. There are ecstatic moments of intuitive poetry, and there are collagelike moments. The poems are not always easy to follow; they are demanding. And they are authorative.

The other John Frederick Nims book under review is his *The Kiss: A Jambalaya* (Houghton Mifflin). Again, the poems are tightly controlled and shaped, the statements concentrated and witty. Poems invoke Pound, Petrarch, and Catullus as well as blondes in bar booths. The sex and love poems give some trouble, and one, "Stewardess Falls from Plane," I found in dubious taste at best ("Unusual bird, unusual word for you? / Earth whistled, and you came. As all girls do"). Nims is a specialized taste, and he puts me off as much as he draws me in. There is something hyper, deliberately outré in expression. Phrases and rhythms seem too baroquely idiosyncratic, too active or truncated. At his best he elicits admiration, but I rankle at his straining for effect.

Ann Sexton's ten books are collected, together with seven uncollected poems and an excellent introduction by Maxine Kumin, in *Ann Sexton: The Complete Poems* (Houghton Mifflin). Sexton's frankness and vulnerability (as well as her toughness and resourcefulness) is brought home with renewed force by seeing so many poems in one place. Whether she is retelling Grimm's fairy tales or being directly autobiographical, Sexton portrays a woman at the extremes. She struck out alone, and

Front cover

Front cover

we all owe her a debt (as Kumin notes) for opening new ground.

The recent death of Muriel Rukeyser was a great loss, not just for poets but for all who care about human rights and human decency. *The Collected Poems of Muriel Rukeyser*, the first paperback edition put out by McGraw-Hill, draws on her twelve books of poetry to make what the poet calls in her introduction "a film strip of a life in poetry." The poetry is compassionate, frank, rich in human qualities. The sheer energy and strength of vision are amazing. If there is one book of poetry to buy this year, this is it.

Jim Harrison is the author of five novels as well as five books of poetry. *Selected Poems and New Poems* (Delacorte) is large and should make Harrison as well-known as he deserves to be, though his novels are better known to the public. One admires Harrison's largeness of scope and spirit, his grasp of the elemental, his absorption in the natural world. He is a passionate poet, a genuine American voice, one whose roots go deep into land and people.

Theodore Weiss for some time has been a master of the long poem, beginning with *Gunsight* in 1962. *Recoveries: A Poem* (Macmillan) continues this mastery. After a long and distinguished career, the poet begins again "to find his bearings, / world's spanned centuries," for "God's plenty crowds the fresco still"—the fresco which is Weiss's symbol for all art, for art and life. Weiss's language is hieratic, yet at the same time supple and demotic, which is to say his scope is large, his vision wide. This is a book of stamina and quality.

Linda Pastan's *PM/AM New and Selected Poems* (Norton) is drawn from four previous collections, with the addition of a section of new poems. The subjects are domestic, but with excursions into Monet's "Irises" and other works of art. The best poems surprise us by taking an ordinary subject ("At the Gynecologist's") and changing the temperature; the poem ends: "caught in these metal stirrups, / galloping towards death / with fingers of ether in my hair." It is good to have Pastan's poems in one place.

Also from Norton is A. R. Ammons's *Worldly Hopes*, rather a short book with many short poems, a large typeface, and plenty of space to move about in. This is Ammons's seventeenth book, and his voice is still unique. In his poems the specific becomes abstract, and what you thought you knew, you don't. But you know it another way. There is a gnomic force to the book, a concentration of matter (though some attempts at wise simplicity fail, as "Spruce Woods" does). There is humor and a kind

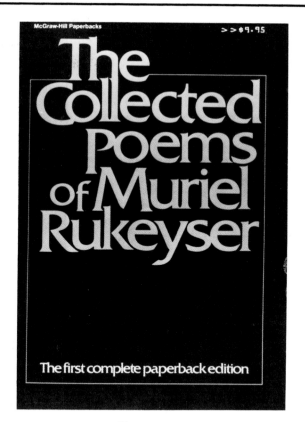

Front cover

Front cover

of looseness of the limbs ("I go about / to happenstance"). There is even an excursion into scatology ("Shit List"). This is vintage Ammons.

A generous selection from previous books (excluding *The Black Unicorn*) is Audre Lord's *Chosen Poems–Old and New* (Norton). Here we have a woman's life as mother and lover as well as a person of strong social and political commitment. There is a strong Black consciousness and a tough-mindedness ("I was born Black and without illusion"). The anger climaxes in "New York Head Shop and Museum." Lord's poetry is potent and true.

The poems in Donald Everett Axinn's *The Hawk's Dream* (Grove Press) have atmosphere but no real body, perhaps because of too much description and overuse of the first-person singular. The reader finds himself wishing the language were more special and winces at clichés like "your soul is on fire." The poems of place are well done, but this is only a moderately successful book.

Paul Mariani is author of the massive William Carlos Williams biography, and evidence of Williams is clear from the first poem with its young proletarian woman. The substantial poems are the longest—the title poem in particular, which uses autobiography to probe deep issues. The book is hard-hitting and rings true.

American Journal (Liveright) collects most of Robert Hayden's work since 1975. When Hayden died in 1980, we lost one of our leading Black poets. His brooding poems are historically based ("John Brown"), frightening ("Theory of Evil"), compassionate ("The Prisoners"). There are "Paul Lawrence Dunbar" and "Homage to Paul Robeson," as well as the excellent "Elegies for Paradise Valley," and poems set in Hayden's boyhood Detroit. This is Hayden's last book. It is also one of his finest.

The Year's Work in Fiction: A Survey

Dick Lochte

Nineteen eighty-two may not be remembered fondly by the publishers and booksellers who, throughout it, bemoaned the economic vagaries of the literary marketplace (cool in summer, lukewarm at Christmas). But it was a very good year for modern young women with problems, old men looking back over their lives, dynasties, an extraterrestrial, an emerging cave dweller, assorted secret agents and adventurers, mismatched lovers, and James A. Michener.

Its most significant literary event was the sudden and almost overpowering flowering of the woman writer. For example, of the five books nominated as best fiction by the National Book Critics Circle, four were by women—Anne Tyler's ninth novel, *Dinner at the Homesick Restaurant* (Knopf), a long, emotional look at a Baltimore family; Cynthia Ozick's *Levitation: Five Fictions* (Knopf); Alice Walker's *The Color Purple* (Harcourt Brace Jovanovich), the story of two black sisters told in letters spanning three decades; and Bobbie Ann Mason's *Shiloh and Other Stories* (Harper and Row), sixteen short pieces about blue-collar folks and their travails.

Additionally, Ann Beattie collected sixteen of her stories in *The Burning House* (Random House), Alice Adams brought out her second story collection, *To See You Again* (Knopf), Mary Lee Settle gave us the final book in her quintet about the West Virginia coal country, *The Killing Ground* (Farrar, Straus and Giroux), and Gloria Naylor introduced us to a group of troubled women in an urban development in *The Women of Brewster Place* (Viking). Joyce Carol Oates wittily treated the Victorian novel to feminist sensibilities in *A Bloodsmoor Romance* (Dutton). Anne Rice's penchant for unusual protagonists continued with *Cry To Heaven* (Knopf), about two castrati in Italy in the 1700s. And Rita Mae Brown delved into incest, miscegenation, and other steamy aspects of days gone by in Atlanta in *Southern Discomfort* (Harper and Row).

Though none of those lingered on best-seller lists, Jean M. Auel's sequel to *Clan of the Cave Bear*, *The Valley of Horses* (Crown) did, along with Elizabeth Forsythe Hailey's tale of college classmates, *Life Sentences* (Delacorte). And not to be overlooked was the popularity of three examples of the paperback romance craze that spilled over into hardcovers—Judith Krantz's *Mistral's Daughter* (Crown), Danielle Steel's *Crossings* (Delacorte), and, to a lesser degree, Shirley Conran's *Lace* (Simon and Schuster). The Krantz novel set a record of sorts. Though it carried a publication date of January 1983, it arrived at bookstores in October and on the best-seller lists in early November, shortly before it was reviewed. The mainly negative critiques did nothing to dampen reader enthusiasm.

One of the more curious displays of woman power was the publication of a sequel to a novel of a few seasons back. Titled *The Winners: Part II of Joyce Haber's The Users*, it was not actually written by Haber, but by Dominick Dunne. This did not result in any increase in quality: if anything, the book was even more depressingly sordid and witless than Part I. Another Dunne, John Gregory, published a considerably more serious, and in every way superior, novel, *Dutch Shea, Jr.* (Linden), about a criminal lawyer on a downward spiral. It was as good an example as any that, though outperformed, the male writer was not idle during the year.

Several veterans showed they could still spin a yarn. Irwin Shaw's *Acceptable Losses* (Arbor House), a thinking man's thriller, proved he had lost none of his narrative power. Saul Bellow's *The Dean's December* (Harper and Row), was popular with critics if not with a mass readership. Bernard Malamud told a charming fable, *God's Grace* (Farrar, Straus and Giroux), and John Cheever delivered a short, poignant paean to old age, *Oh What A Paradise It Seemed* (Knopf).

Kurt Vonnegut and Richard Brautigan, authors who have displayed a similarly whimsical approach and flippant style in *Deadeye Dick* and *So The Wind Won't Blow It All Away*, respectively, came up with first-person narrators who, as young men, altered their lives by playing with guns. Delacorte Press/Seymour Lawrence showed a certain amount of consistency by publishing both books. The always-entertaining Richard Condon enhanced his reputation with *Prizzi's Honor* (Coward, McCann and Geoghegan), a suspenseful satire about a contemporary Romeo and Juliet, Mafia-style; and Jimmy Breslin bulldozed through a tale of mismatched lovers in New York's troubled South Bronx, *Forsaking All Others* (Simon and Schuster).

Don DeLillo's *The Names* (Knopf) described the fate of an insurance risk analyst on the trail of a murder cult, and John Barth's *Sabbatical* (Putnam) presented a married couple, the male member of which had written an exposé of the CIA. But though both novels initially seemed to be thrillers, neither was designed to fulfill the expectations of fans of that genre.

That task was handled by Robert Ludlum's silly but apparently effective *The Parsifal Mosaic* (Random House), which was on best-seller lists more often than not in 1982. There was one week in June when *The Parsifal Mosaic* topped the *New York Times* hardcover list and Ludlum's *The Road To Gandolfo* (Bantam), the reprint of a novel published years ago under a pseudonym, led the paperback list. Ken Follett's *The Man From St. Petersburg* (Morrow) intrigued readers, as did John D. MacDonald's twentieth caper in the Travis McGee saga, *Cinnamon Skin* (Harper and Row). But the usually reliable Lawrence Sanders failed to satisfy his fans with *The Case of Lucy Bending* (Putnam), a departure from his usual criminal fare.

The "fictionalized" movie script, that dubious mixture of two media, seems to have lost most of its appeal for readers and, consequently, publishers, with one notable exception. The always unpredictable William Kotzwinkle reworked a film script and placed both *The E.T. Storybook* (Putnam) and *E.T.: The Extra-Terrestrial in His Adventure on Earth* (Berkeley) on hard- and soft-cover best-seller lists. Kotzwinkle was not quite so fortunate with his own creation, *Christmas At Fontaine's* (Putnam), an offbeat seasonal fable that was only fitfully amusing.

E.T. and other out-of-this-world film fodder probably helped to expand the frontier of the science-fiction genre to the point where Robert Heinlein was able to place *Friday* (Holt, Rinehart and Winston) on the lists. And two sequels followed suit: Isaac Asimov's *Foundation's Edge* (Doubleday) and Douglas Adams's *Life, The Universe and Everything: The Cosmic Conclusion to the Hitchhiker*.

This was, in fact, a year for sequels. Arthur C. Clarke's *2010: Odyssey Two* (Del Rey) transported us one decade past his previous story. And, getting more down to earth, Elia Kazan, in *The Anatolian* (Knopf), continued the adventures of his *America, America* hero Stavros Topouzoglou; Jeffrey Archer took us beyond *Kane & Abel* in *The Prodigal Daughter* (Linden); and John Updike, in *Bech Is Back* (Knopf), gave us seven more stories about the titular protagonist of *Bech: A Book*.

The collections by Cynthia Ozick, Bobbie Ann Mason, Ann Beattie, and Alice Adams were reminders that short fiction was plentiful in 1982. Other prominent examples included Bette Pesetsky's brief, punchy *Stories Up To A Point* (Knopf), Canadian Margaret Atwood's witty *Dancing Girls* (Simon and Schuster), and Joy Williams's *Taking Care* (Random House). And, not to be overlooked, there was *The Collected Stories of Isaac Bashevis Singer* (Farrar, Straus and Giroux).

In October, James A. Michener's *Space* (Random House) was successfully launched. With approximately five different plots explored along with the main story of a flight to the dark side of the moon, the novel couldn't have been more popular, even if it had been written by a woman.

Finally, the most discussed novelist of 1982 was Jerzy Kosinski. First, New York's weekly *Village Voice* accused him of being so overedited that the authorship of his books was in question. Then, several months later, the *New York Times* belatedly refuted the *Village Voice*'s claim and added a few asides regarding the weekly's political motivation in discrediting the author. All in all, it was a controversy that had more to do with newspaper editorializing than with book editing and, even with all the attending gossip and nattering, it apparently did nothing to add or to detract from the sales of Kosinski's new novel, *Pinball* (Bantam), which was not very good, regardless of who wrote it. Literary milestones should be made of sterner stuff.

Dust jacket

Dust jacket

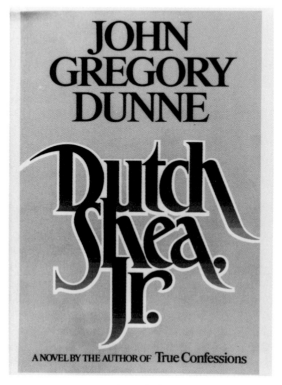

Dust jacket

Dust jacket

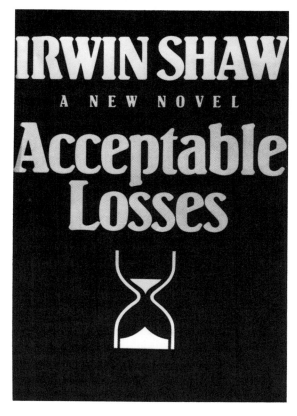

Dust jacket

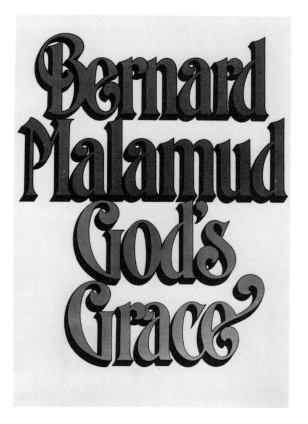

Dust jacket

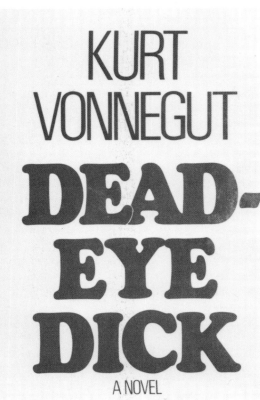

Dust jacket

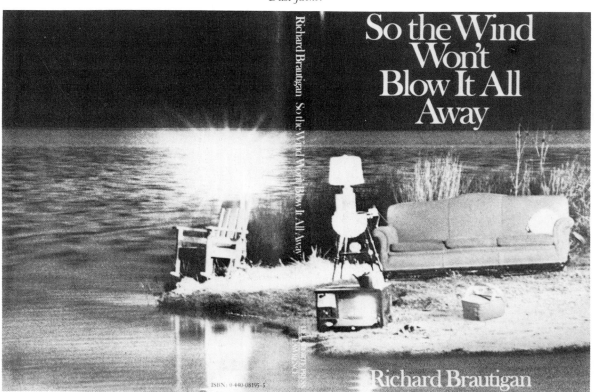

Dust jacket

Front cover

Dust jacket

Dust jacket

Dust jacket

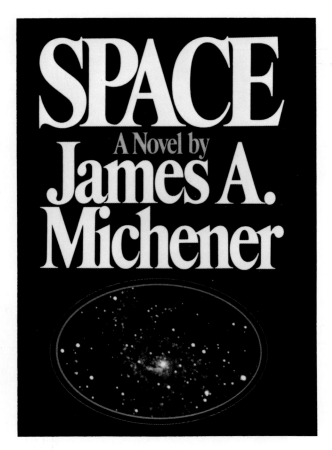

Dust jacket

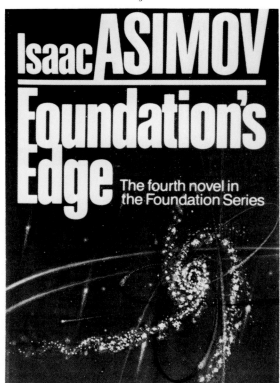

Dust jacket

UPDATED ENTRIES

Nelson Algren
(28 March 1909 - 9 May 1981)

James Hardin
University of South Carolina

See also the Algren entries in *DLB 9, American Novelists, 1910-1945*, and *DLB Yearbook: 1981*.

NEW BOOK: *Calhoun. Roman eines Verbrechens*, edited and translated by Carl Weissner (Frankfurt am Main: Zweitausendeins, 1981).

The English working title of Algren's post-humously published novel was "The Devil's Stocking," by which is meant a stocking made inside out, one that has no useful function. Algren's title is an allusion to the protagonist Ruby Calhoun, a black boxer who is convicted on three counts of murder just at a point when his career appears to be ready to take off. But the manuscript title is ironically appropriate to the book itself and ultimately to the author, who liked to think of himself as an outsider. And the way the book came into being says a lot about its author.

It all started in 1974 as an article for *Esquire* magazine. By then Rubin "Hurricane" Carter had already served seven years in a New Jersey prison for a triple murder committed in a Paterson bar. The conviction of Carter and his alleged accomplice, John Artis, was largely based on the evidence of two witnesses, who now had denied their earlier testimony identifying the two blacks who robbed the bar. The New Jersey Supreme Court ruled that there would have to be a second trial. Expectations were that the two would be found not guilty, and there was premature talk of a damage suit. The case attracted the attention of the press and of celebrities such as Bob Dylan, who performed in a benefit concert to raise money for the defendants' legal expenses.

Before the beginning of the second trial, Algren came into contact with Fred Hogan, a former policeman who now worked in the public defender's office. Hogan's contacts with the key witnesses and his knowledge of questionable evidence used in the case had convinced him that the wrong men had been convicted, and it was his persistence that eventually caused the two key witnesses to change their story. He persuaded them that they could not now be charged with perjury owing to the time elapsed since the first trial. Algren became

fascinated—the word "obsessed" is perhaps not too strong—with the case and went so far as to move from Chicago to Paterson, New Jersey. He even tried, unsuccessfully, to rent a room over the bar where the murders had taken place. He visited Carter in the penitentiary, read Carter's autobiography ("The Sixteenth Round"), and read the transcripts of the original trial. When the second trial began, Algren was in the courtroom every day.

But Carter was a loser a second time. Two circumstances were decisive: Carter refused—against his attorney's advice—to take the stand in his own defense, knowing that his previous criminal record would be revealed to the jury, and one of the two "eyewitnesses" changed his story again. Carter and Artis were found guilty a second time. The story no longer appealed to the editors of *Esquire*, who had reckoned with a different outcome. The article appeared to be stillborn.

Nelson Algren

121

But Algren was not about to drop the story. He was not just speaking of Norman Mailer when he said that he did not know of a single writer who did not believe himself to be a boxer. The two small boxing gloves tattooed on his right arm were a clue to his nature. He thought of himself as a fighter, a reporter who championed the rights of the outsiders, the guys who reminded him of the phrase he had picked up from a prostitute, "the devil's stocking." He once said that he lived from writing, but that he didn't particularly care for writers, that he wasn't interested in Marcel Proust but liked the company of boxers, whores, and crooks. The social milieu of the case appealed to Algren, not merely the opportunity to expose an injustice.

Algren rewrote the *Esquire* piece in the style of a documentary report, but the magazine was no longer interested. At this point he decided to work the material into a novel. While Algren claimed that the book is not about Rubin Carter, that it deals with a man named Ruby Calhoun who is sentenced to life imprisonment, it is difficult to take the statement seriously. All the figures of the novel have or had their counterparts in real life, among them Algren himself. It is a world of prostitutes, gangsters, jaded barkeeps—the fringes of society—but it also describes the brief rise in the fortunes of the title figure and gives a glimpse of the life that might have been, of the loser who was on the way to the big time.

As a work of fiction, *Calhoun* is an excellent example of unpretentious reportage. The conversations have the ring of authenticity. It is an honest, hard-nosed piece of writing. The action of the novel is gripping. How could it be otherwise given the actual events that inspired the book? But one wonders why these events had to be put into fictional form. Since most of the work is patently based on fact, it could be argued that a "documentary"—Algren's original plan—would have been more effective, more disquieting.

It is something of a curiosity that the first edition of *Calhoun* should be a German translation. The novel was declined by American publishers on the grounds that Algren demanded, in their view, an exorbitant advance. The copyright page provides only this information about the original manuscript: "Die deutsche Ausgabe folgt dem Originalmanuskript in der Fassung vom Oktober 1980." [The German edition follows the original manuscript in the version of October 1980.] There was a printing of 5,000 copies in October 1981 and a printing of another 5,000 copies January 1982. Algren's unmannered style has survived translation into German very well, although the translator has

Roman
eines Verbrechens

CALHOUN

Herausgegeben und übersetzt
von Carl Weissner

Zweitausendeins

Title page for Algren's last book, first published in German after being rejected by American publishers

naturally not caught all the subtle nuances of "streetalk" used by most of the novel's figures.

The novel has aroused some interest in the German Federal Republic and is seen as literary documentation of pervasive racism and exploitation of blacks in the United States. A young German writer, Wolf Wondratschek, who visited Algren and obviously admired his social engagement, writes in his foreword to the novel that "Der Justizirrtum im Falle 'Hurricane' Carter diente Algren als letzte Abrechnung mit Amerika. . . . Anklagen will der Roman die andauernde rassistische Gewalttaetigkeit weisser Geschworenengerichte gegen farbige Angeklagte." [The breach of justice in the case of "Hurricane" Carter served Algren as his last reckoning with America. . . . The novel aims to pillory the persistent racist violence of white juries against colored defendants.] Wondratschek has overstated the case (the courts are not lily-white as he seems to imply), and does Algren's *Calhoun* a disservice.

Saul Bellow
(10 June 1915-   )

Keith Opdahl
DePauw University

See also the Bellow entries in *DLB 2, American Novelists Since World War II*, and *DLB Documentary Series 3*.

NEW BOOK: *The Dean's December* (New York: Harper & Row, 1982; London: Secker & Warburg, 1982).

Since he won the Nobel Prize in 1976, Saul Bellow has led a quiet life. His long and public court battle with his third wife is settled. His marriage to Alexandra Ionescu Tulcea, a professor of mathematics at Northwestern University, is, by all accounts, successful. He lives with his wife in a large apartment overlooking Lake Michigan, and three times a week he travels the Outer Drive to the University of Chicago, where he teaches as a member of the Committee on Social Thought.

A serene life for a sixty-seven-year-old novelist enjoying the fruits of his long labor? Not at all— Bellow has used his honored and orderly life as a podium from which to challenge and scold his country. His latest novel, *The Dean's December* (1982), is nothing less than an indictment of American society—on all levels. The blacks in our cities are in truth doomed, Bellow says; the whites show only a cruel indifference. Public officials are guilty of hypocrisy, and those unofficial public figures who have the opportunity to study the problem, our journalists and experts and professors, are guilty of jargon and cant. "Many American writers cross the bar in their 60's and 70's," Bellow has said, "and

Saul Bellow

123

become Grand Old Men, gurus or bonzes of the Robert Frost variety. This is how society eases us out." Who could retire a writer who takes on his whole culture? Bellow's concern for America is deep, but his tone is anything but grandfatherly.

The novelist delivers his views in a book that seems at first to be vintage Bellow. His pages spring to life with the precision that is his finest talent. The face of a corpse, Bellow writes, "had the only-just-subtracted expression" of the dead. Winter dusk in Rumania is notable for the light: "Brown darkness took over the pavements, and then came back again from the pavements more thickly and isolated the street lamps. They were feebly yellow in the impure melancholy winter effluence. Air-sadness, Corde called this." Such description takes place in a context that is now Bellow's most characteristic mode, as an intelligent (but fumbling) protagonist has the leisure to reflect upon a shocking event in the past, providing not only the drama of a mind in action but a fascinating exercise in perspective.

When one thinks about the novel after reading it, moreover, he is again impressed, for Bellow's intention is ambitious and his story promising. Albert Corde, a dean of students at a Chicago college, has accompanied his sensible astronomer wife, Minna, to Bucharest, where her mother lies ill in a hospital. There petty Communist officials make it difficult for Minna to visit the dying woman, a Communist official now fallen from grace, and finally permit her only one visit—she must choose the time. Corde's wife must suffer the ordeal of her mother dying alone, without her daughter at her bedside.

As Minna hurries about the city seeking help, Albert Corde passes the time in a chilly apartment remembering the problems he had left behind in Chicago. He had published a set of articles in *Harper's* on the black underclass of the city and had insisted upon the prosecution of two blacks for the murder of a white student. In both instances he has rocked the boat in a way administrators dare not do. He has alienated whites by reminding them of the millions of people they have abandoned. He has alienated the blacks by insisting that however victimized they may be, they must be responsible for their actions. The blacks are "startled souls," Bellow told an interviewer. "They cannot be reasoned with or talked to about anything."

To the liberal, Corde sounds suspiciously racist. To the conservative, he stirs up muddy waters. And to his provost in the university, Corde has violated academic decorum: how dare he wade into a messy social issue? Doesn't he realize that he is an officer of the university? To everyone else Corde is an aesthete, arguing that the problem is one of perception, since people have learned to evade the truth, shutting off experience. Like the nineteenth-century realistic novelists, to whom Bellow has confessed a debt, Corde believes that facing the truth can be a rare (and perhaps heroic) accomplishment. His articles (like the novel itself) are meant "to recover the world that is buried under the debris of false description or nonexperience."

What Bellow manages to do is provide several different sources of narrative interest. As the reader awaits the outcome of Minna's struggle to visit her mother, he also awaits the outcome of the trial in Chicago (Had the white student sought kinky sex? Had he asked for trouble?) and the effect of his articles on Corde's career. His job hangs by a thread. The novel moves from Rumania to Chicago, sometimes in Corde's memory and at other times in his articles or letters sent him from America. In the two cities, the style of administrators, the ways of death and the kinds of parties (a Rumanian tea and a high-rise celebration of a dog's birthday), the dome of the crematorium and that of the telescope at Mount Palomar, California—in all these ways the novel sets contrasts that reveal and dramatize each society. The Communist society is cold and harsh, as dreary administrators parcel out pain. The capitalistic society is hot and chaotic, as the slums whirl out of control. In both countries good people struggle to be decent. Rumanian women support one another, remembering the old European culture, while black heroes such as Rufus Ridpath, a prison warden, and Toby Winthrop, the founder of a drug rehabilitation center, struggle to stop the people from brutalizing themselves and one another. And lest these issues flag, Corde's articles in *Harper's* (which Bellow excerpts in the novel) provide riveting accounts of the underclass and the officials who work with it.

And yet, much as one appreciates Bellow's fine style and excellent ideas, the novel is a disappointment to read—or so many reviewers felt, as they wrote their mixed reviews. Those who called the book a success confessed that it was a near thing. Everything depends on the protagonist, said Robert Towers in the *New York Times Book Review*: does Corde work as a character? Yes. "Sentence by sentence, page by page, Saul Bellow is simply the best writer that we have." Other reviewers objected that Corde does not have the independent existence of Bellow's other protagonists—he is clearly a spokesman for Bellow. Many critics gave Bellow high marks for struggling with this difficult but crucial subject. Some readers, most notably David Evanier in the *National Review*, were put off by Bellow's subject. Didn't he realize it was stale? Hadn't he read the book of Job, asked another: didn't he realize that suffering we will always have with us? Others complained with more justice that the book is too grim (to read it is like hitting yourself over the head with a hammer, said one) or too talky or too full of scolding. Those who praised it were exhilarated, however, much as one might be by a cold shower: "He gives Corde's thoughts such palpable immediacy, such convincing shifts in tone," wrote Dean Flower in the *Hudson Review*, "that sometimes one can only revel in Bellow's gifts."

It seems true that Bellow is somewhat careless in his writing. He creates wooden dialogue at times, forgetting that a literal transcription of talk does not work in fiction. His characters can be thin and his plot does creak. All of this is true, on occasion, and so is the sparseness of Corde's character and the large amount of talk in the book. Bellow doesn't make his fiction any more attractive, moreover, by including a host of creeps and bullies he himself does not like.

And yet all of Bellow's novels have had flaws that have with time dwindled in importance. *The Dean's December* is a mixed novel but is really decent and skillful. It may, like *Mr. Sammler's Planet*, be the best book possible given the subject and the climate, and critics will probably come to see it as a solid and ambitious effort. How many others have dared to tackle this difficult but central fact of our nation?

One may appreciate the novel for the language, or for the play of ideas, as Corde spars with the public defenders and scientists concerned over lead poisoning. One may appreciate Bellow's moral seriousness and his instinct for what is crucial to the future of our society. But *The Dean's December* is interesting too in terms of its aesthetic, for while it is true that Bellow drops certain niceties for the sake of his content, it is also true that he finds a way to write about an incredibly difficult subject. How can a wealthy and cultured white get into the experience of a desolate people? How can a novelist today cope with such an awesome and incendiary subject? How can he immerse himself in it and yet not drown? Bellow might have done better to complete the journalistic book on Chicago he had earlier planned, doing for the blacks what he did for the Mideast in *To Jerusalem and Back*, but one suspects that he realized that fiction written in a certain way could give him the perspective that was very much required.

He required such a perspective, it is clear, for

Dust jacket for Bellow's 1982 novel, regarded by reviewers as a wholesale indictment of American society

he has always been affected by a vision of suffering masses and a murderous humanity—the social reality here matches an intense, imaginative one. To place Corde in his stocking feet 6,000 miles from Chicago, surrounded by women attempting to minister to the dying, gave a personal and domestic perspective from which to view Chicago. What many reviewers found to be defects, in other words, are actually Bellow's means of providing distance: his use of Corde's articles, his shift from scene to scene, his use of Corde's memory and his conversations all permit him to move close in, as he does, looking hard at prisons and public housing and the county hospital, and yet permit him to pull back too, to avoid drowning in the natural and intense emotions of outrage and fear. Corde in Chicago became a partisan, entering the fray. He had to. In Rumania, indulging in a great deal of talk, he can wonder about larger causes and attempt to do justice to all parties. How do people solve problems if not by talk? The reader gets in this novel both a close look at the reality (albeit from the outside) and a distant look from which to seek the larger solution. Bellow invents a form that permits him to move from one scale to the other at will.

Bellow was probably disappointed that the reviews of his novel did not stimulate more discussion about the underclass. And yet he must know that books work quietly. If most reviewers had mixed feelings about *The Dean's December*, no one doubted that Bellow is a fine and even a great writer. No one announced that he is washed up, which is pretty good for a sixty-seven-year-old Nobel Prize-winner. John Updike found many things wrong with *The Dean's December*, but he also provided an almost definitive appreciation of Bellow's gift: "He is not just a very good writer," Updike wrote in the *New Yorker*, "he is one of the rare writers who when we read them feel to be taking mimesis a layer or two deeper than it has gone before. His lavish, rippling notations of persons, furniture, habiliments, and vistas awaken us to what is truly there." And that, of course, as Corde says, is all that any novelist could hope to do.

Periodical Publications:
"Nobel Lecture," *American Scholar*, 46 (Summer 1977): 316-325;
"A Silver Dish," *New Yorker*, 54 (25 September 1978): 40-62;
"Him with His Foot in His Mouth," *Atlantic*, 250 (November 1982): 115-144.

References:
Mark Harris, *Drumlin Woodchuck* (Athens, Ga.: University of Georgia Press, 1980);
Chirantan Kulshrestha, *Saul Bellow: The Problem of Affirmation* (New Delhi: Arnold-Heinemann, 1978);
Frank D. McConnell, *Four Postwar American Novelists* (Chicago: University of Chicago Press, 1977);
Modern Fiction Studies, special Bellow issue, 25 (Spring 1979);
Stanley Trachtenberg, ed., *Critical Essays on Saul Bellow* (Boston: G. K. Hall, 1979).

John Cheever
(27 May 1912-18 June 1982)

James O'Hara
Pennsylvania State University at York

See also the Cheever entries in *DLB 2, American Novelists Since World War II*, and *DLB Yearbook 1980*.

NEW BOOK: *Oh What a Paradise It Seems* (New York: Knopf, 1982).

The death of John Cheever on 18 June 1982 ended one of the more remarkable careers in American literature. Cheever was seventy when he finally lost a protracted battle against cancer. He had been writing for more than fifty years, the last seven of which amounted to a brilliant comeback.

He was buried near his parents, Frederick and Mary Cheever, in Norwell, Massachusetts. At a memorial service in Ossining, New York (the Cheevers' home for over twenty years), his friend Saul Bellow praised his constant struggle for self-revelation, calling him a writer who put "human essence in the first place," ahead of social distinctions. "There are writers whose last novels are like the first," Bellow observed; "John Cheever was a writer of a different sort altogether." At the funeral service in Norwell, John Updike, a friend with whom he toured the Soviet Union in 1964, characterized Cheever as a "teller of tales of purity."

Cheever's final work, a short novel titled *Oh What a Paradise It Seems*, appeared in early 1982. Its narrator suggests that the story is "to be read in bed in an old house on a rainy night. The dogs are asleep and the saddle horses—Dombey and Trey—can be heard in their stalls across the dirt road beyond the orchard." But this pleasantly pastoral beginning is deliberately misleading. The story centers on a small ecological crusade led by Lemuel Sears, an older businessman who one day discovers that Beasley's Pond, his favorite skating spot, is being senselessly contaminated by garbage dumping. Sears, an executive with a firm that produces "cerbical" (computer) chips and afflicted by most of the psychological shortcomings of a typical middle-

American male, is an unlikely hero. His antagonists are an organization of faceless mobsters, well-financed and ruthless, and through most of the story it seems certain that Sears is destined to fail. The desecration of the pond, which represents the innocent vitality of his past, almost crushes him before he is stirred to action: "It was a blow. Nearly a third of it had already been despoiled and on his right he saw the shell of a ten-year-old automobile and a little closer to him a dead dog." Cheever, who loved to work technical variations on narrative point of view, momentarily departs from Sears's perspective to analyze the social import of the scene: "Here was the discharge of a society that was inclined to nomadism without having lessened its passion for portables."

The conduct of the crusade is interrupted by Sears's affair with a beautiful real estate agent named Renée, whom he accidentally encounters in a line of bank customers. His infatuation with her is purely physical at first, but he is subsequently drawn

John Cheever

to her by a mysterious behavior pattern that he is never able to understand. As their sexual relationship becomes more intimate and mutually gratifying, their social life remains severely inhibited by Renée's schedule of commitments to speak before many gatherings in New York-area churches on a subject that she refuses to discuss with Sears and that is never identified for the reader. Her diffidence concerning an obviously major part of her life, although happily tolerated at first by her admiring lover, underscores the casual nature of their affair. Before long it ends with Renée's abrupt departure for the Midwest, ostensibly to visit her daughter. In the meantime Sears has found consolation for her capricious treatment of him in a homosexual liaison with Eduardo, an elevator operator in Renée's apartment building. The fact that Sears has been driven to what seems to him a perverse extreme sends him to a psychiatrist's office. In a typically Cheeverian plot twist, the doctor also turns out to be homosexual. Like Farragut, the hero of Cheever's earlier novel *Falconer*, in the end Sears simply stops fighting his newly discovered impulse toward male love, and he and Eduardo take off for a fishing vacation near the Canadian wilderness.

Among the episodes recounting Sears's personal joys and sorrows, Cheever intersperses other segments describing the daily life of Betsy Logan, a suburban housewife and ultimately Sears's most effective ally in the fight to save Beasley's Pond. Betsy, the mother of two small children, lives next door to the man chosen by the mob to supervise the trashing of the pond. Her instinctive dislike for him and his family disposes her to take her first halting steps in the direction of ecological extremism, by simply observing her neighbor's activities.

Another important character (but one given scant development) is Horace Chisolm, an environmentalist selected to study Beasley's Pond by Sears's law firm. Improbably, the paths of Chisolm and Betsy Logan converge when the Logans, returning from a day at the beach, absentmindedly deposit their infant son at a highway exit. Chisolm discovers the child shortly afterward, and he and the Logans become fast friends. Their happiness is short-lived, however. Chisolm and Sears attend a public meeting on the dumping issue, only to find that it has been rigged by the forces behind the contamination. The mayor harangues the environmentalists and their cause in the name of American enterprise; Chisolm's request for a delay in the proceedings is refused. Moments after leaving the town hall, he is run down and killed by an automobile, in a contract murder arranged by the polluters.

Although Chisolm's murderers are never brought to justice, the pond is finally saved by the fanaticism of Betsy Logan. "Sad and vengeful" because of her friend's death, she takes it upon herself to fight the corrupt system that killed him. In a narrative turn unusual even for Cheever, she poisons a bottle of Teriyaki sauce at a local supermarket and threatens further poisoning on a large scale unless the dumping is stopped. Her plan works all too well; a local family is hospitalized (they eventually recover), and the attendant publicity guarantees the desired outcome. With Sears in the vanguard, the pond is restored to its former health.

The ethical ambiguity of this resolution never seems to occur to Cheever or his characters. It is not, of course, the responsibility of the storyteller to defend or denigrate the behavior of his creations, but there can be little doubt that at the conclusion of *Oh What a Paradise It Seems*, the reader is supposed to feel as entirely satisfied as Sears himself does. As in most of Cheever's fiction, good has triumphed in the face of adversity. In this case, however, that triumph has been accomplished by a heroine whose unscrupulous Machiavellianism mirrors the evil of the story's villains.

Critical reaction to the novella's appearance was not much concerned with moral problems and marked a continuation of the favorable treatment given Cheever's work since the appearance of *Falconer* in 1977. Some reviewers combined their judgments of the story with retrospective comments on Cheever's past work. Partly because of its length (100 pages), the book was not received as a major accomplishment by the reviewers, but Cheever himself was again accorded the warm praise that had sometimes been denied him in the past. John Leonard compared him favorably with Chekhov in the *New York Times*, and Cheever was commended by Paul Gray of *Time* (1 March 1982) for not trying to surpass himself after bringing forth *Falconer* and *The Stories of John Cheever* (1978). Gray labeled the novella a "coda" working final variations on characters and subjects seen in earlier work. He also felt the book would have had to be longer to make the points that contemporary life is not being constantly degraded and that the present is informed by the rituals of the past. He is certainly right in observing that Cheever returned to earlier preoccupations in *Oh What a Paradise It Seems*. The book's title, in fact, may be an echo from the third chapter of *The Wapshot Scandal*, where Coverly Wapshot is visited in the middle of the night by the ghost of his father, Leander. When Coverly calls out to Leander's spirit, it seems to disappear, and Coverly imagines that his father has returned for a final, momentary glimpse of the earth and its pleasures: "he had wanted no less than any youth to chase the nymphs. Over hill and dale. Now you see them; now you don't. The world a paradise, a paradise!" And in the lusty vigor of his maturity, Lemuel Sears is strikingly similar to the Leander of the first half of *The Wapshot Chronicle*. In the latter half of Cheever's first novel, Leander is worn down and defeated by business failure and the merciless women in his life; in that sense Sears's experience is notably different from his forerunner's. Yet while Sears is both a successful businessman and an ecological crusader, his affair with Renée establishes an interesting connection with Cheever's prototype of a father figure. Both of them are unable to truly love and understand women—perhaps to the same extent that both are fully capable of loving and appreciating the outdoors. (One of Leander's favorite pastimes was ice-skating on St. Botolph's Parson's Pond.)

Another thematic connection between the first novel and *Oh What a Paradise It Seems* can be found in Sears's troubled affection for Eduardo, which may have its roots in Coverly Wapshot's youthful brush with homosexuality. That experience leaves Coverly puzzled and worried; in the mid-fifties, Cheever was not yet willing to acquiesce in the notion that none of love's manifestations is evil in itself.

Robert Adams, reviewing the novella for the *New York Review of Books* (29 April 1982), concluded that Cheever had "done more to create spacious and lively harmony than one would have thought possible in a small room" but also noted the tendency of characters in that room to be somewhat vague and slippery. Writing for *New Republic* (31 March 1982), Ann Hulbert evenhandedly credited Cheever for his desire to experiment with viewpoint and to ring changes on established themes but like Adams faulted the book's lack of convincing characterization: "Renee, Sears's enigmatic amour, has soft lips and secrets, and next to no other notable qualities; the elevator man . . . with whom Sears also has a brief, bizarre affair, is a phantom presence as well." Hulbert also found Sears himself to be insufficiently developed; in her reading he "never becomes a soul lit from within by a memory of love."

In trying to classify the story's form more precisely than the term *novella* can manage, John Updike in the *New Yorker* (5 April 1982) called it "an ecological romance," "a parable and a tall tale." More than other critics, Updike was able to see a

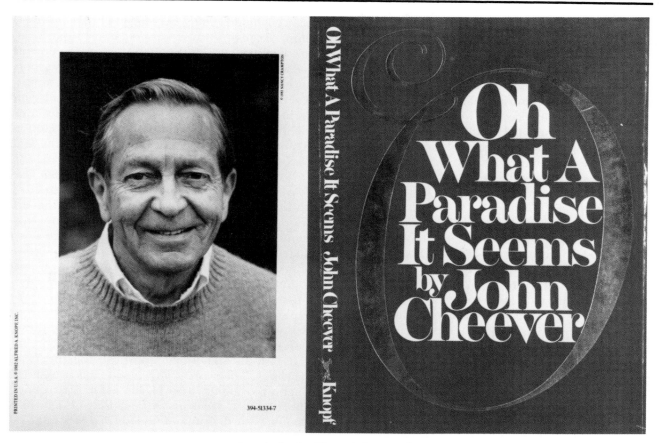

Dust jacket for Cheever's last novel

prophetic quality in the story—one that might reasonably be expected from a seasoned master nearing seventy: "Ever more boldly the celebrant of the grand poetry of life, Cheever, once a taut and mordant chronicler of urban and suburban disappointments, now speaks in the cranky, granular, impulsive, confessional style of our native wise men and exhorters since Emerson." In his friend's targeting of corruption, Updike saw Cheever picking up a familiar thread: the concurrent belief in purity and sensitivity to evil that permeates so much of serious American literature, extending back at least to Hawthorne.

Toward the end of his life Cheever was not reluctant to discuss the influence of New England's traditional values on his early life and, by extension, his work. He told Eleanor Munro in a *Ms.* interview (April 1977) that he had grown up in the "twilight of Athenian New England, but even so late in time, New England families shared a strong sense of what was practical in the establishment. In marriage, or personal display. . . . The role, so far as appear-

ances go, of the sons, the daughter, the husband." He did not feel, he said, that deviations from those norms proved the community of shared values terribly hypocritical. Yet he also confided to John Hersey not long afterward (December 1977) that "the darkness—the capacity for darkness that was cherished by New England—certainly colored our lives." And in his essay "What Happened," he said his aim as a writer was to record a "moderation" of the harsh Puritanism of some of his relatives.

Cheever's literary career began at the age of seventeen, when he found that he could rework the experience of his own life into art. He turned his dismissal from Thayer Academy into a short story, "Expelled," which would have been considered a virtuoso performance for a more mature stylist. It was published by *New Republic* in 1930. Unfortunately this initial success was not sustained. The Depression had arrived, and during the thirties Cheever led a lean existence, first in Boston, then in New York City. He occasionally worked on book synopses for MGM studios. Some of his stories were published, at irregular intervals, in *Collier's*, *Atlantic Monthly*, and *New Republic*.

Cheever married Mary Winternitz, daughter of the dean of Yale Medical School, on 22 March 1941. The marriage would last until his death, and although it was not always a placid arrangement for either husband or wife (she would pursue career interests in teaching and writing, and her husband would jokingly claim that scarcely a week passed without the possibility of divorce being raised), the couple raised three children who became successful, and it can be said that family life was one of the stabilizing forces in Cheever's life.

His career might be divided into three major phases. The first extends from 1930 to 1953 (including a four-year stretch of service in the army during World War II) and was a time of scant but steadily growing recognition. Cheever's output during this period consisted entirely of short stories, thirty of which were collected during the war and published in a volume called *The Way Some People Live* (1943). These are primarily brief, tentative pieces, some of which ("The Brothers," "The Law of the Jungle") draw on Cheever's early family life and in that sense look forward to his later work. While most of these youthful efforts are now thought of mainly in terms of historical value, it was in the middle of this period that Cheever began his association with the *New Yorker*. Starting in 1940 and continuing through the publication of over 120 stories (a record surpassed only by John O'Hara), this connection was to both enhance his reputation and expose him to considerable criticism as the "quintessential" writer of the *New Yorker* genre. He rejected the idea; as he told his daughter Susan, "I never wrote for *The New Yorker* and I never stopped writing for *The New Yorker*—they bought my stories" (*Newsweek*, 14 March 1977). In his preface to *The Stories of John Cheever*, however, he recalled his years with Harold Ross and the *New Yorker* staff fondly. Ross in particular, he said, "taught one . . . that decorum is a mode of speech, as profound and connotative as any other, differing not in content but in syntax and imagery."

As late as 1953, when he had already started to work on *The Wapshot Chronicle*, Cheever was publicly expressing his preference for the short story as opposed to the novel: "The novel seems artificial to me. . . . The short story is determined by moving about from place to place, by the interrupted event. The vigorous Nineteenth Century novel is based on parish life and lack of communications." That apparently disdainful view of longer fiction can, of course, be charged to personal doubts about his own

chances of succeeding in a form he had yet to attempt. But the attitude was not simply superficial; ultimately Cheever's reputation may depend as much on the achievements of a dozen or so short stories as on the undeniable merits of the novels. Several of them are arguably classics already, including "The Enormous Radio," "The Season of Divorce," "O Youth and Beauty," "The Housebreaker of Shady Hill," "The Brigadier and the Golf Widow," and "The Swimmer."

A second collection, *The Enormous Radio and Other Stories*, appeared in 1953 and marks the end of Cheever's first phase of artistic growth, the developmental years. Its contents, although not uniformly excellent, feature characters who are more sharply delineated, situations that are more dramatically realized than those of the previous volume. The title story, for example, is a rich combination of urban realism and fantasy carefully exploited to unmask the hypocrisy of its main characters, a New York couple suddenly afflicted with more reality than they can handle.

Critical and public approval, together with growing confidence in his own powers, naturally led Cheever to attempt a novel. The effort was a taxing one, however. *The Wapshot Chronicle* (1957), which examines the decline and renewal of a New England family unmistakably patterned on his own, appeared four years into his "middle" period. It was seen as structurally weak by critic Maxwell Geismar, but its sharp social satire and wonderful characterization of St. Botolph's Wapshot clan were enough to earn it the National Book Award. Subsequent critics of *The Wapshot Chronicle* and its sequel, *The Wapshot Scandal* (1964), have been more willing to take them on their own terms, as experiments in novel form by one whose distrust of conventional plot structure ran very deep. "I don't work with plots," Cheever told Annette Grant in an interview for *Paris Review* (Fall 1976); "I work with intuition, apprehension, dreams, concepts. Characters and events come simultaneously to me." *The Wapshot Chronicle* constantly shifts focus from the lives and loves of Moses and Coverly to the misadventures of their father, Leander, and back again. In *The Wapshot Scandal*, awarded the Howells Medal in 1965, Cheever imposed a tighter narrative control, trimming potentially extraneous material in order to develop the complex marital situations of the Wapshot brothers. Robert Morace has detected a more subtle, and probably more significant, change in tone between the first and second Wapshot novels; both celebrate life, but the world that informs *The Wapshot Scandal* is one where "it has become harder to see that there is anything worth celebrating." The otherwise tenacious Moses, worn down by his wife's adultery, has become an alcoholic; Coverly struggles to survive and live decently in the midst of America's technological jungle. Coverly's unquenchable vitality makes for a hopeful ending—a Christmas dinner that brings the novel full circle—but the unhappiness of Moses strikes a discordant note that Cheever's insistent optimism could not soften. In an existentially bleak postscript, the narrator promises never to return to St. Botolph's.

In the seven years between his first two novels, two more books of short stories appeared. *The Housebreaker of Shady Hill* (1958) established Cheever's credentials as one of the best chroniclers of suburban ills and pleasures this country has produced, if not the best. His comic detachment from the foibles of his characters is self-assured, and he is able to establish story lines that, on objective consideration, seem absurd. Yet he balances his detachment with an apparent concern for people like Johnny Hake, Francis Weed, and Marcie Flint, who find themselves trapped in a life-style so given over to outward appearances that it leaves them unprepared for a real crisis. Cheever's suburban protagonists, men and women, are outwardly normal people who stumble into a problem (drinking, infidelity, the loss of a job) and are then compelled to watch the edifice of normality crumble around them. They are usually able to make a partial recovery, but in the process of self-discovery they often suffer intense humiliation. Cheever, however, refuses to scoff at them, and they are generally pulled back from the edge of the abyss with a few shreds of dignity intact.

Some People, Places and Things That Will Not Appear in My Next Novel (1961) ranged as far as Italy for its story settings. Cheever had made use of a National Institute of Arts and Letters grant in 1956 to spend a year abroad and brought back with him a store of information that he would continue to use in his work until the end of his career. In terms of his later work the item of greatest interest in this collection is "A Miscellany of Characters That Will Not Appear." It is highly innovative, working fictional pieces into a mosaic of literary criticism on fashionable trends in fiction. The authorial voice inveighs against "alcoholics, scarifying descriptions of the American landscape, and fat parts for Marlon Brando." These are juxtaposed against "the perfumes of life: sea water, the smoke of burning hemlock, and the breasts of women." The thematic preferences are so obviously Cheever's own that the essay reads like a manifesto; but if that is the case, it

was one from which Cheever would eventually depart.

The Brigadier and the Golf Widow appeared the same year as *The Wapshot Scandal* and mirrors its predominantly pessimistic tone. By this time it was becoming more difficult for Cheever to rescue his characters from their own destructiveness. The title story, set against a backdrop of nuclear holocaust, and "The Swimmer," in which Neddy Merrill swims his way home through his neighbors' backyard pools only to arrive at a deserted house, are chillingly representative of the anthology's somber mood. Lynne Waldeland has rightly noted an evolution in Cheever's treatment of the changes occurring in American society in the early sixties; like one of his own creations, perhaps, he was forced to confront realities that could not be easily ignored or disposed of with old-fashioned good cheer.

Alcohol, drug addiction, and other forms of personal disintegration were becoming increasingly prevalent facts of life in Cheever's fiction, and this is nowhere truer than in *Bullet Park* (1969). The novel's antihero, Eliot Nailles, becomes an addict after trying and failing simply to be an average, workaday commuter, and to cope with the shortcomings of his wife and son. Another gradually converging plot line concerns the wanderings of Paul Hammer, a madman who at story's end threatens to immolate the Nailles's son in a locked church. Nailles saves his son at the last minute, but once again the conclusion seems almost forced, a superimposition of grace by the author. The larger world of *Bullet Park* is a place where things have gone badly awry. Hammer's illness is exacerbated by drinking, a neurotic wife, and a social environment that is indifferent to psychic depredation. Nailles is finally unable to translate his heroism into self-assurance and remains an addict.

Although Cheever could be blithely indifferent to criticism, he was stunned and embittered by the rough treatment given *Bullet Park*. Benjamin DeMott, who attacked the novel's "lax composition" in the *New York Times Book Review*, was seen by Cheever as a bellwether for other reviewers. In a familiar pattern, later critics (including John Gardner) would disagree and find Cheever's design and accomplishment in this novel to be significant. But in the meantime Cheever's life went into a tailspin. As he later told Annette Grant, "I ruined my left leg in a skiing accident and ended up so broke that I took out working papers for my youngest son. It was simply a question of journalistic bad luck [the *Times* review] and an over-estimation of my powers." He turned increasingly to alcohol for solace, and his physical condition deteriorated until he suffered a near-fatal heart attack in 1972.

The long downward slide seemed temporarily halted with the appearance of *The World of Apples* in 1973. The old narrative vigor and love of playful experimentation were once again in evidence, but a careful reading of pieces like "The Fourth Alarm," "Artemis, the Honest Well Digger," and the title story reveals an almost obsessive concern with pornography and scatology. There are occasional bright spots in the stories, and Asa Bascomb, the central character of the title story, may be a hopeful foreshadowing of the artist Cheever wanted to become if he could shake off the demons besetting him. But the predominant tone is one of depressing darkness.

Cheever would later admit to considering suicide during this period: "I felt my life and career were over. I wanted to end it" (*New York Times*, 19 June 1982). He accepted appointments as writer in residence, first at the University of Iowa (1974) and then at Boston University (1975), but he was not able to halt his emotional decline. During the worst part of it, in Boston, he began work on a new novel set in a prison. To John Hersey he described his condition at this point as being "drunk and drugged much of the time, putting hats on the statuary on Commonwealth Avenue. . . ." Finally in 1975, at the insistence of his family, he entered a rehabilitation program at the Smithers Clinic in New York. The second phase of Cheever's career was coming to a close. It had been a long and very productive one, but success had been attained at a tremendous personal cost. To all intents and purposes, it had nearly finished him.

Almost miraculously, however, Cheever's medical treatment marked the beginning of a creative regeneration. After a month at Smithers he was well enough to be released. He felt he had achieved a personal victory and was ready to take up where he had left off on his new novel. The third phase of his career had started. Within a year, he had completed *Falconer* (1977), an immediate critical success. The story drew heavily on the experience of a teaching assignment he had accepted at Sing Sing in the early seventies and may also have benefited from his own forced confinement during his recovery. Farragut, the hero, is a genteel, upper-class intellectual, imprisoned at forty-eight for the murder of his brother. He struggles to find his way in a world he could never have imagined and then stages a convincing comeback from self-pity and drug use to regain a sense of self-worth that transcends the squalor around him. His long, some-

times painful, emotional journey is made possible by a brief affair with a younger prisoner, Jody, who challenges the conventional values that Farragut continues to honor but also sets a pattern for survival by planning and executing a clever escape. After an interval of tortuous backsliding from the path to psychological regeneration, Farragut follows Jody's example; he escapes in a dead prisoner's burial shroud.

Cheever had led a fairly private life until the publication of *Falconer*. That was to change radically after he became the subject of a 14 March 1977 *Newsweek* cover story; over the following years he gave several lengthy interviews, some of them on television, and candidly discussed his life and work. His public fame grew with the publication of *The Stories of John Cheever* in 1978. The book won several major awards, including the Pulitzer Prize. Three of the stories were adapted for public television in late 1979, and subsequently Cheever himself wrote a light satiric drama for the same network. In the midst of all the publicity, he conducted himself as an elder statesman of letters, fielding questions and answering letters from admirers and students of his work with a graceful, witty generosity. And despite the distractions of celebrity status, he managed to stay close to his craft by working on *Oh What a Paradise It Seems*. As Saul Bellow realized, this final effort marks yet another departure into fresh subject matter, even though it examines familiar themes. Cheever was not content to end where he had begun.

In his life and in his art, Cheever had learned the necessity of tempering discipline with compassion. He had seen the human failings so skillfully anatomized in his fiction rise up to haunt himself and his family but had successfully charted a course through them to recovery that stands as a tribute to his own indomitable spirit and the patience of those who loved him. And instead of allowing his personal attitudes to harden into fixed formulas, he had demonstrated a willingness to change his mind and extend himself while staying true to his basic sense of decency.

References:
Robert M. Adams, "Chance-taker," *New York Review of Books* (29 April 1982): 8;
Benjamin DeMott, "A Grand Gatherum of Some Late Twentieth Century Weirdos," *New York Times Book Review*, 27 April 1969, pp. 1, 40-41;
John Gardner, "Witchcraft in *Bullet Park*," *New York Times Book Review*, 24 October 1971, pp. 2, 24;
Annette Grant, "The Art of Fiction LXII: John

Cheever," *Paris Review*, 17 (Fall 1976): 39-66;

Paul Gray, "Coda," *Time*, 119 (1 March 1982): 85;

John Hersey, "John Cheever, Boy and Man," *New York Times Book Review*, 26 March 1978, pp. 3, 31-32;

Ann Hulbert, "Lonely Nomads," *New Republic*, 186 (31 March 1982): 42-45;

Michiko Kakutani, "John Cheever Dead at 70," *New York Times*, 19 June 1982, pp. 1, 17;

John Leonard, "Cheever Country," *New York Times Book Review*, 7 March 1982, pp. 1, 25-26;

Paul Montgomery, "Friends and Colleagues Recall Cheever," *New York Times*, 24 June 1982, IV: 23;

Eleanor Munro, "Not only I the narrator, but I John Cheever," *Ms.*, 5 (April 1977): 74-77, 105;

"Updike Hails Cheever For His Tales of Purity," *New York Times*, 23 June 1982, II: 11;

John Updike, "On Such a Beautiful Green Little Planet," *New Yorker* (5 April 1982): 189-193;

Lynne Waldeland, *John Cheever* (Boston: Twayne, 1979).

Peter De Vries
(27 February 1910 -   )

Jean W. Ross

See also the De Vries entry in *DLB 6, American Novelists Since World War II*, Second Series.

NEW BOOKS: *Consenting Adults, or The Duchess Will Be Furious* (New York: Little, Brown, 1980; London: Gollancz, 1981);
Sauce for the Goose (New York: Little, Brown, 1981; London: Gollancz, 1982).

With the publication of *Consenting Adults, or The Duchess Will Be Furious*, his nineteenth book and a 1980 Book-of-the-Month Club Christmas dividend, Peter De Vries told Lewis Grossberger for *People* magazine, "My secret ambition is to sell a million copies of every book . . . and then also have a small, select cult of aficionados who look down on my mass audience."

De Vries lives in Westport, Connecticut, as he has for more than thirty years, with his wife, the writer Katinka Loeser. He continues to work for the *New Yorker* (a job he has had since 1944), going into New York City twice a week to serve as a cartoon editor. And he writes daily, never at a loss for something to satirize or the words with which to do it. "I write when I'm inspired," he told Grossberger, "and I see to it that I'm inspired at nine o'clock every morning."

In 1982 De Vries was elected to the American Academy of Arts and Letters. Though humorists in the Academy have not been numerous, the genre has been respectably represented by Mark Twain, Joel Chandler Harris, E. B. White, and S. J. Perel-

Peter De Vries

man. And James Thurber, De Vries noted of his early mentor at the *New Yorker*, "the greatest humorist since Twain, would certainly have been in ahead of everyone else. Thurber declined membership, I think, because he didn't want to get into the institute before White." Commenting on his own election the day after it occurred, De Vries told Herbert Mitgang of the *New York Times*, "I have always been strongly opposed to official honors and establishment laurels—what Emerson called 'the mercuries of approbation'—but, overnight, I have become less hidebound."

Consenting Adults gives us the philosophical and sexual adventures of Ted Peachum of the Chicago suburb of Pocock. For reasons that seem good, Ted wants to "flee the family hearth at the earliest possible moment." He tells us at once, "For as long as I can remember, my father hibernated." Near the end of fall every year, "he would stuff himself on lots of good greasy food, like potato pancakes and pork butts, give us all a bear hug, and shuffle off to bed for the winter." During this time, Ted's mother ran the family furniture-moving business, in which Ted helped. "She could back a truck into a parking spot herself with emasculating skill, though I wished there weren't so often a Camel cigarette hanging from her lip as she leaned out of the cab to do so."

To rise above all this, Ted learns big words, studies philosophy (until he becomes a "self-pitying stoic" and has a nervous breakdown), and cultivates the friendship of the d'Amboise family. Mrs. d'Amboise decides at once that Ted must someday marry her sensitive daughter Columbine, who is about ten—six years younger than Ted—as the story opens. While he waits to see ("Who knew what this prepubescent reed would be five or seven years hence?"), Ted indulges in an affair with brewery heiress Snooky von Sickle, whom he loses when she marries his best friend, Ambrose d'Amboise, but regains when he later joins the pair in a ménage à trois. He also lusts after Kathy Arpeggio, a liberated woman who has become a police officer. Perhaps his greatest sexual adventure, however, is a love affair with the Peppermint Sisters, a set of show-business triplets he meets in a hotel on alternate Saturdays.

By the time this ménage à quatre is in process, Ted is living in New York and acting in soap operas, though he continues to move furniture part-time. When he hears that Columbine (now twenty-one and a fashion model) has been rejected by her fiancé and is hospitalized with anorexia nervosa, he hurries back home. He finds his parents well, both having affairs: "With both of them happily fooling around, their marriage seemed secure, at least for the time being. My mother said my father 'stayed up till all months.' " Columbine is down to eighty-nine pounds, but Ted manages to fatten her up and persuades her to marry him, after which they settle in New York.

One of the best characters in *Consenting Adults* is the Prophet, a smelly Pocock crank in a homemade toga who preaches to any crowd he can gather. Though he rages with all the Old Testament vehemence of an Elijah, his harangues are up-to-the-minute: "But the Lord will say, 'Screw your portfolios. . . . the day is not far off, verily is at hand, when the dollar won't be worth a plugged nickel. It's on the skids right now in Zurich, Paris and Tokyo. So get your ass in gear,' saith the Lord, 'and hurry down to my house, fall on your knees, and there ask forgiveness. Maybe we can work something out. . . .' "

De Vries's work usually provokes mixed critical response, and *Consenting Adults* elicited its share of unfavorable reviews. In *Time* (21 July 1980), R. Z. Sheppard commented, "The plot is meager, the characters wear thin too quickly, the gags are often laid out as if for a garage sale. . . ." "Everything in De Vries is grist for a giggle," Rhoda Koenig wrote in *Saturday Review* (July 1980). "But shouldn't a novel at least hint at a heart?"

On the other hand, the book was lauded by Christopher Cerf (*New York Times Book Review*, 17 August 1980) and Peter S. Prescott (*Newsweek*, 1 September 1980). "Many, I suspect, will find 'Consenting Adults' a book they can—and will—put down," Cerf wrote. "But they will almost surely pick it up again, refreshed and ready to enjoy more magic from one of the true masters of humorous style the past half-century has produced." Prescott, noting that a furniture mover (Stan Waltz) narrated an earlier De Vries novel, *Let Me Count the Ways* (1965), compared the two novels and placed *Let Me Count the Ways* in "De Vries' Middle Period in which his books, funny as they were, ran to fat, didacticism and the search for God. . . ." *Consenting Adults*, he concludes, "shows De Vries performing close to peak efficiency. His story may end sentimentally, but his stories are not what one remembers: his aphorisms and his inventive way with a character are. Moreover, De Vries manages to be both witty and funny at the same time. These two qualities are often mistaken for each other, but few writers have been able to manage both."

An earlier criticism of De Vries's novels was that his female characters tended to be mere foils for the men, as William R. Higgins noted in *Dictio-*

nary of Literary Biography, volume six. In *Sauce for the Goose* (1981), De Vries writes from a woman's point of view for the first time. The novel's central character, Daisy Dobbin, is hired by radical feminist Bobsy Diesel of *Femme* magazine to do an exposé of sexual harassment in the offices of *Metropole* magazine. With the help of coconspirator and childhood friend Effie Sniffen, Daisy infiltrates *Metropole* as a typist. Unfortunately for the journalistic expectations of *Femme*, she quickly falls in love with Dirk Dolfin, the handsome head of the conglomerate that owns *Metropole*, and finds herself "sleeping with the boss without first having put the masculine integrity to the test: by waiting to see, that is, whether inducements such as a promotion or a raise would have been venally dangled before her. . . . That was the reverse of the coin of harassment. . . ." (The only sexual harassment Daisy gets, in fact, is from Bobsy Diesel.) Daisy's liaison with Dirk causes further inconvenience by drawing her into a rivalry with Effie, who has her mind made up to marry Dirk as soon as her divorce has become

Dust jacket for De Vries's twentieth book (1981), his first novel written from a woman's point of view

final. After much intrigue, the article is salvaged, though in a different form, Daisy and Effie fight it out at a fancy brunch (in a swimming pool brawl that nearly causes Dirk to drown), and Daisy marries Dirk and gets *Metropole* as a wedding present.

Sauce for the Goose includes a good assortment of De Vries characters. Daisy is credible. Like Ted Peachum, she is embarrassed by her parents, "the couple with a horse's name who were seen strolling at five-thirty into restaurants where the posh crowd didn't eat until half-past six . . . and who emerged an hour later fondling toothpicks." Mr. Dobbin limps from "a war wound contracted on the way to a Selective Service examination." Dirk Dolfin retains, in varying degrees, traces of his original Dutch speech and an interest in theology; during romantic interludes with Daisy, he whispers things like "Mine grandfather, the dominie, was a supralapsarian." He develops a taste for the music of a jazz cornetist he calls Big Spiderbecke.

Bobsy Diesel is not bad looking, but she dresses like a stevedore, smokes panatelas, and provokes this observation: "Promiscuity has a way of driving standards up, since everyone will have acquired a broad background of experience from which to judge palatability and performance, and the Diesel was so unsatisfactory in bed that she became known among local wags as the *Lay Misérable*." In another of the many literary allusions in the book, a quite minor character, a tall Englishman named Schrubsole, leaves the brunch early, explaining to his uncomprehending hostess that he has "premises to keep . . . and miles to mow before I sleep."

Sauce for the Goose did not receive strong reviews. Anna Shapiro called it "a quick two-step that makes for bright light reading" (*Saturday Review*, September 1981). In the *New York Times Book Review* (20 September 1981), Peter Andrews acknowledged the novel's skimpy plot and the author's tendency to overkill with verbal gags. But he says that "even a weak Peter De Vries novel is fun to read" and compliments De Vries for writing about sex with restraint when he is not treating it humorously.

Whitney Balliett, in his long treatment of the novel in the *New Yorker* (19 October 1981), gave the best advice to De Vries readers and critics: "Peter De Vries' novels should be regarded not as free-floating literary creations so much as clever fronts from behind which he broadcasts his unerring puns, malapropisms, hyperbole, metaphors, parodies, slapstick, mimicry, and one-liners. What should be judged is not the book . . . but the voice emanating from it. It is a manic voice, capable of countless timbres, inflections, and speeds, and it is just as sharp and funny and inventive as it was thirty years ago."

De Vries is philosophical about reviews, recognizing, as he told Sybil S. Steinberg in *Publishers Weekly* (16 October 1981), that responses to humor are personal. And, says Steinberg, "De Vries remains something of a national humorist laureate, his sophisticated satires having skewered pretensions, illuminated idiosyncracies and fondly mocked the mating game for over four decades."

References:

Lewis Grossberger, "Pages," *People*, 14 (29 September 1980): 41-42;

Herbert Mitgang, "American Academy Selects Four Members," *New York Times*, 2 December 1982;

Sybil S. Steinberg, "PW Interviews Peter De Vries," *Publishers Weekly* (16 October 1981): 6-8;

James Wolcott, "Naughty Old Men," *Harper's*, 265 (October 1982): 60-63.

AN INTERVIEW
with PETER DE VRIES

DLB: In his *New York Times* article about your recent election to the American Academy of Arts and Letters, Herbert Mitgang called you a "confessed humorist," a rather funny description in itself.

DE VRIES: That's humor on Mitgang's part, like calling someone a confessed card-carrying Communist—a little semantic twist. But I guess you'd have to call me that; what I aim for is to amuse. Always rather a tall order, you know.

DLB: Did you set out from the beginning to make people laugh?

DE VRIES: Yes, although I have played hooky from that intention and written a few overtly serious books. I can't remember not wanting, as a child, to amuse people. I'm sure there are tedious psychological explanations for a tot's wanting virtually from the cradle to keep kith and kin in stitches, but there it is.

DLB: One of your fictional characters might ask if it's harder for a humorist to be taken seriously. Is it?

DE VRIES: I think probably it is, yes. But at the same time election to a fifty-member academy might be taken as giving the lie to that. Being "taken seriously" may have two meanings. It can mean, are you taken seriously as a humorist, or is the work regarded as serious. I take Mel Brooks seriously as a humorist. But if you mean to ask, is the sense of human validity underlying your humor recognized, that's another thing. I don't think the comic and the serious can be separated in talking about human reality, any more than you can separate hydrogen and oxygen and still be talking about water. They're inseparably one.

One of my favorite remarks about all that is a comment of Robert Frost's in his introduction to Edward Arlington Robinson's *King Jasper*: "If it is with outer seriousness, it must be with inner humor. If it is with outer humor, it must be with inner seriousness." Obviously some of our best serious writers have humor. I was asked one time at a college, in one of those after-lecture question periods where they hope to barbecue you, who the greatest living humorist was and I said William Faulkner. The students were quiet for a few minutes while they got their jaws back up. But it's true. Nobody's been funnier than Faulkner is in stories like "Lo!" and "The Bear Hunt," and passages in nearly all the novels. "Lo!" is my nomination for the greatest American comic short story.

DLB: You've created so many memorable characters that I can't narrow them down to one or two personal favorites. Are there any you think of as best, or most memorable?

DE VRIES: I think Mrs. Wallop would be one of the best, and McGland, in *Reuben, Reuben*. He's finally a tragic figure, but he's very funny because his attitude is one of sardonic amusement with the world, however tragic it is—there's an example of what I mean about the inseparability of the tragic and comic in human reality. By the way, they've just finished making a movie out of that part of the book. I'm interested in seeing how it turns out. That was based on Dylan Thomas; there's no point in my denying it any longer.

DLB: Do a lot of revision and rewriting go into those very funny lines that seem to pop so easily out of your characters' mouths?

DE VRIES: Yes, though sometimes a line is absolutely inevitable. A one-liner *should* be inevitable, or there's something wrong.

DLB: The many literary allusions and parodies in your work give you away as a long-time reading addict. Are there contemporary novelists whose work you especially enjoy?

DE VRIES: Anthony Powell and Elizabeth Bowen. And Kingsley Amis. The final test is whether one rereads a writer. I cut my eyeteeth on Thurber, Ring Lardner, and Mark Twain. They have to be counted among my favorites. Also Fitzgerald and Faulkner. I like Faulkner's use of rhetoric, even when it spills over into self-parody, as it often does. Not even the dithyrambic jags in *The Wild Palms* are too much for me, who as a high-school adolescent would overdose on De Quincey. Certainly an odd first enthusiasm for a humorist. Odd.

DLB: Do you and your wife [Katinka Loeser] try your work out on each other?

DE VRIES: Yes, we do. She shows me work in the gestation period more than I do her; she doesn't mind having things looked at while they're still in the oven. I usually wait and show her the finished product to see what she thinks of it. We have a good partnership that way. We respect each other's work. I think in some ways she's a better writer than I am. She has a growing following all around the country; you can tell that by the reviews of *A Thousand Pardons* as they come in.

DLB: Would you comment on your long association with the *New Yorker*, its significance in your writing?

DE VRIES: It's been a great school for me. Meeting their standards has helped me discipline and hone my work, in particular to purge it of an element I might call the bane of comedy, which is facetiousness. It's the old Charlie Chaplin principle (at least it's been attributed to him), as true for writers as for actors and comedians: If what you're doing is funny, don't be funny doing it.

Which gets us back to where we started about the indissoluble union of the ludicrous and the grave.

—*Jean W. Ross*

James Dickey
(2 February 1923-   )

Donald J. Greiner
University of South Carolina

See also the Dickey entry in *DLB 5, American Poets Since World War II.*

NEW BOOKS AND PAMPHLETS: *The Water-Bug's Mittens/Ezra Pound: What We Can Use* (Columbia, S.C. & Bloomfield Hills, Mich.: Bruccoli Clark, 1980)—350 numbered copies, signed;
Scion (Deerfield, Mass.: Deerfield Press, 1980)—300 copies, signed;
The Eagle's Mile (Columbia, S.C. & Bloomfield Hills, Mich.: Bruccoli Clark, 1981)—trade edition and 250 numbered copies, signed;
The Early Motion: Drowning with Others and Helmets (Middletown, Conn.: Wesleyan University Press, 1981);
Falling, May Day Sermon, and Other Poems (Middletown, Conn.: Wesleyan University Press, 1981);
The Starry Place Between the Antlers: Why I Live in South Carolina (Columbia, S.C. & Bloomfield Hills, Mich.: Bruccoli Clark, 1981)—trade edition and 500 numbered copies, signed;
How To Enjoy Poetry (New York: International Paper Company, 1982);
Puella (Garden City: Doubleday, 1982);
Night Hurdling: Poems, Essays, Conversations, Commencements, and Afterwords (Columbia, S.C. & Bloomfield Hills, Mich.: Bruccoli Clark, 1983);
Four Seasons: False Youth (Dallas: Pressworks, 1983).

Followers of contemporary American literature recognize the man immediately: the sheer size,

James and Deborah Dickey

the back-slung guitar, the unusual hats, the ready smile. Even those who rarely read poetry can readily spot the poet. They have, they will eagerly tell you, read about him in *People*, seen him on the "Today Show," and watched him in the movie *Deliverance*. James Dickey is a presence to be reckoned with. But those who care about art, about man's need to create, about—as it were—the cultural health of the nation, recognize more than the distinctive face. Identifying the personality, they respond beyond the guitar and the hats. They hear a well-defined literary voice, acknowledge a quality of mind, and seek out the work of a master poet. For a writer who sold his first poem for $28.50 and who made $114 on his first book, James Dickey has walked a long mile—all the way to a distinguished place among America's literary giants.

He belongs there. Carping about the image cannot detract from the achievement. The con-

sciously calculated, larger-than-life reputation has accomplished its goal of focusing the public's attention on writers and writing. When Dickey sidesteps the spotlight, the poetry is always there. He explains, "I don't carry literary grudges . . . but American poets are like crabs in a bucket. When one crawls up, the others try to pull him down. I just pay them no mind and go about my business. . . . I've attracted attention. . . . The poet is like a doctor. At least he has the illusion he's a party to something important. He is engaging an important part of people's bodies—their emotions, their states of mind, their spirits. . . . That's why poetry is vital."

The vitality of both the man and his art has rewarded readers for more than twenty years now. Always accessible, generous with his time, Dickey gives a great deal of himself to students and strangers. Part of his willingness to talk at odd hours about strange topics stems from his refusal to write on schedule. Rarely inspired, he says, and inevitably working slowly, he notes that most interruptions do not rattle him because he has learned to compartmentalize his time: "I'm fortunate I learned to write in the service, on troop trains, at stoplights. I would write a little when I could, then come back to it when I could. . . . My work is like a process of refining low-grade ore. . . . I don't think I should turn loose a poem until I've given it a long and honorable fight. At the point at which I can't think of a change for the better I let a poem go."

Although poetry is always the central attraction, criticism is a challenging sidelight. Dickey excels at both. A contemporary personification of Emerson's "Man Thinking," he has written widely and penetratingly about authors and their art. A recent example is the lecture on Ezra Pound that he delivered at the University of Idaho on 26 April 1979, which was published as *The Water-Bug's Mittens/Ezra Pound: What We Can Use* (1980). His essay on the eclectic shaper of modernism is a tribute to an attitude that Whitman began and Dickey admires: The poet as great embracer, as creating man eager to experience all. Everything fuels the imagination's fire.

Dickey finds four Ezra Pounds as he strips aside the myths to pin down the useful, the Pound who helps all readers as they glance over their shoulders at the vital past before stepping forward toward the uncharted future. He admits that Pound's presence remains pervasive. Pound the wrongheaded propagandist of economics and politics is dismissed. But not the Pound of ideas. Dickey acknowledges the poet who discovered and rediscovered men, places, and things, and who then invited the reader to join him on a tour of the always-shimmering yet all-but-unrecoverable past.

Of equal value is Dickey's "complex-associating Pound," the Pound who simultaneously stuns the reader with a bewildering "cross-fertilization of languages, cultures, writers" and opens up the reader to what Dickey calls "the shock of possibility." Some of the *Cantos* may be stupefying and foolish because they lack "the true human encounter," but many show Pound "catching an observable or imaginable part of the world in fresh, clean language." Pound the imagist, however, is the most useful. A keen-eyed observer, he urged a joining of "mind, thing observed, and thing remembered." His insistence on seeing, on spotting the water-bug's mittens, is, writes Dickey, "the best tool he has put in our hands."

Dickey's insights make Pound accessible to us. As much a celebration of an angle of vision as hom-

age to a man, his remarks on Pound sing the vitality of the exploring mind. Opening up Pound for the reader, Dickey also reveals himself as a sympathetic, wide-ranging thinker. The essay illustrates a side of Dickey that his friends admire and his public ignores: the poet as critic. To remain interested—that is traditionally the challenge to successful authors. Always sharp-minded and plainspoken, Dickey brings to his criticism the sensibility of the artist and the energy of the athlete. It is an invigorating combination, a union that persuades the reader to note not only the ideas offered but also the way they are expressed.

This side of Dickey is not new, of course. From *The Suspect in Poetry* (1964) and *Babel to Byzantium* (1968) to *Self-Interviews* (1970) and *Sorties* (1971), he has committed himself to a lively exchange of ideas. The guitar-playing, Southern-drawling, wide-brimmed hat-wearing Dickey is for show, but the thinking, debating, creating Dickey is for real. He does not hesitate to tell the reader what he thinks.

Those interested in Dickey's opinions and comments will be able to explore them in more depth in *Night Hurdling: Poems, Essays, Conversations, Commencements, and Afterwords* (1983). Dickey's first miscellany since *Sorties*, the new volume includes statements on poetry and observations on topics as various as shell roads, movies, and courage. The heart of the book, however, will be a section titled "Writers and Beholders" in which Dickey writes about the famous—Jack London—and the not-so-famous—Thomas Boyd—with the perspicacity one has come to expect.

Part of his sensitivity derives from observing nature. Dickey is no pre-Darwinian, Romantic wanderer through hills and dales. Ever the twentieth-century man, he steps off the trail and confronts nonhuman otherness. Solace and peace are rarely the issues: "You see, my orientation toward nature, towards the woods and trees and mountains, is not at all that of someone like Thoreau, who felt himself an intimate and knowledgeable part of nature. I'm a person of the generation who goes into the woods and sees a wild river, and to me it's a kind of vision of the ultimate strangeness."

This is why his essay *How to Enjoy Poetry* (1982) is important. Addressed not to the academic specialist but to the average reader, the essay is another illustration of Dickey's campaign to promote the centrality of poetry, the necessity for art. One need not be a poet to respond to nature's "ultimate strangeness." Beginning with the ageless question "What is poetry?," Dickey answers, "Poetry makes possible the deepest kind of personal possession of the world." Like Whitman and Pound before him, he urges mankind to open its eyes and plunge into experience with memory and emotion, into what Dickey calls "the *now* of your own existence and the endless mystery of it . . . a handful of gravel is a good place to start." Indeed it is. Dickey the poet, Dickey the critic, Dickey the ever-responding witness of his world bends, picks up a stone, and hands it across the page by way of words. Life itself is the issue. One must react.

One of Dickey's most delightful reactions is *The Starry Place Between the Antlers: Why I Live in South Carolina* (1981). Originally published in *Esquire* (April 1981), this short essay illustrates his sense of visionary strangeness when confronted with nonhuman otherness. A stunning combination of stars and sea and mountains, flowers and snakes and deer draws him to South Carolina. Sitting on a dock or in a walled garden, he feels "radiation—quanta—of pure Good, of uncontaminated metaphysical well-being, coming inward on me with the full force of the way things are—at least are, here: *de rerum natura* from every brick."

The sentiments as well as the wording are vintage Dickey. Looking at the essay closely, initiated readers everywhere would call his name. But distinctive style does not mean repetitive vision. Changes and new directions equal growth. To those who argue that his various writing projects dull the edge of his poetry, Dickey responds, "No way! People will second-guess you endlessly. Picasso never allowed himself to be trapped in a single style. I think ideas can cross-fertilize; for instance, my dramatic visual sense has been considerably sharpened by my film writing. That's good. . . . It's just that my viewpoint on my writing is constantly changing and that's the way it should be, new energy coming from one thing and going into another."

The energy of the canon is a highlight of his art. One looks back over the earlier volumes and marvels at the change perceived, the growth displayed. The reissue of his first success encourages such an examination, and Dickey himself has taken a look. His new preface to *The Early Motion: Drowning with Others and Helmets* (1981) focuses on an element of the poetry that most readers of Dickey recognize: the difference in sound between the first books and the later volumes. Edging toward a goal of sound over sense in *Drowning with Others* (1962), he developed what he describes in the preface as a "night-rhythm," an anapestic urging that satisfies a gut need for "unassailable rhythmic authority." One may experience this pulse beat in poets as vari-

ous and as variously good as Poe, Swinburne, Kipling, and Robert Service. Not the meanings of the poets but the surges of their sound convinced Dickey to bring his own nightmares and metaphors to a union with this most elemental rhythm.

Helmets (1964) is equally distinctive. Longer poems emphasizing narrative begin to appear. Although he explains in the preface that he still stressed the night-rhythm of sound before sense, Dickey also notes that the poems in *Helmets* value story, the narrative movement that one associates with, say, "Drinking from a Helmet."

The preface to the reissue of *Falling, May Day Sermon, and Other Poems* (1981) is just as revealing. A succinct essay on the rationale for the prosody in such long poems as "Falling," the preface refers to a time when Dickey played "a game of metaphysical Scrabble." He remembers his first efforts to write poetry as like glancing at a little light that sneaked at intermittent places from behind an imagined solid wall of words. From arranging cut-out words on cardboard to typing directly on the paper, he gradually formulated the page-wide line composed of short internal units that is the hallmark of his most recognizable verse. The changes readily discernible in *Puella* (1982) are alterations of the page-wide line, for rather than work with walls of words in his most recent collection, Dickey experiments with arrangements of balance "analogous to the balance given to the trunk of a tree by its limbs." Linguistically, *Puella* is as different from *Buckdancer's Choice* (1965) as *Buckdancer's Choice* is from *Drowning with Others*. Word clusters linked by alliteration and assonance result in lines more closely packed, and thus *Puella* has phrases that could not have appeared in the earlier poetry.

Dickey's insistence on growth guarantees the development of his art. Mere change is not the issue: "The make-or-break point, especially in poetry, that tells you when you're entering something distinctive or not, is not just at the point when you say, 'This is very good.' And it is not at the point when you say, 'This is not only good, but it is also interesting and imaginative.' No. The watershed point is when you can say, 'This is not only good, not only interesting and imaginative, and only I could have said this. This has the Dickey feel to it that no imitator can manage.' " Such a statement is not the preening of the ego. It is practicing what one preaches, thrusting oneself into the world and then asking, what do I think of that?

As Dickey says, "it is a fatal flaw among American writers that they tend to repeat what's been successful for them and what people expect of

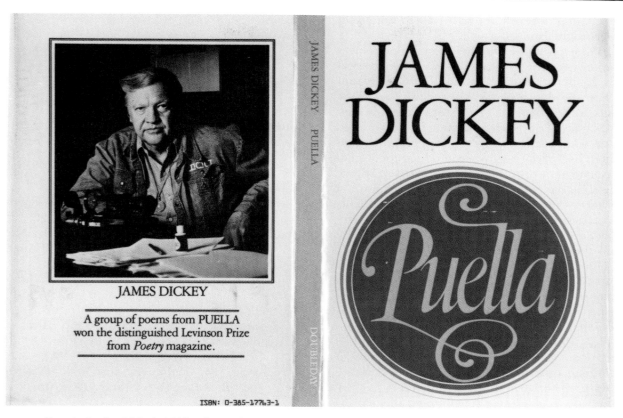

Dust jacket for Dickey's 1982 volume of poetry dedicated to his wife, Deborah: "her girlhood, male-imagined"

them. I don't want to do the same things. I've written all of the poems in the vein of 'The Heaven of Animals' and 'Falling' that I'm ever going to write; now must come something else. . . . I want to open up poetry more, open up vast new areas of experience. But it won't be like anything I've ever done before." How right he was when he made that statement in 1979, for *Puella* is different. Paul Zweig correctly notes that Dickey is one of the few American writers "whose imagination rides the edge of violence." Significantly, the ride slows down in *Puella*. Reflection and meditation set the tone, and the volume suggests a delicate stretching toward beauty through the mists of the real. Dickey's fascination with risk is still an issue, but in *Puella* the risk is not only in the technique but also in the exchange of subject matter from masculine energy to female sensibility. The distinctively charged Dickey style is softened. Beauty rather than force abides.

Still, his muse is both dramatic and metaphysical. Dedicated to his wife Deborah as "her girlhood, male-imagined," *Puella* (Latin for *girl*) explores another realm of otherness just as strange to a man as a heaven of animals or a shark's parlor. Adjusting

his sights from the alluring invitations of nature, Dickey focuses on a mystery equally enticing: femaleness. The unfamiliar voyage to femininity is, he suggests, a journey that all men must take. Dickey takes it joyfully. In so doing he not only pays homage to his wife but also bows to the eternal rib that developed into Lilith, Eve, Helen, and the girl next door.

Like all voyages that matter, this one begins with the imagination. The question he raises is not just what is woman but also what lives did his wife live before he met her. The answers are lovingly expressed as Dickey mixes myth and reality to envision his spouse encountering her adolescence, beginning her relationship with nature, and accepting her initiation into fantasy.

An epigraph from Rilke suggests the blessing of fate in their meeting: "I know, I know it was necessary for us to have things of this kind, which acquiesced in everything." Have them they do, as the imagination's strength introduces the real poet to the mythical girl in such a way as to make their subsequent marriage inevitable: "A woman's live playing of the universe/ As inner light, stands clear,/ And is, where I last was" ("Deborah, Moon, Mirror, Right Hand Rising").

These poems extend the dramatic monologue as Dickey encourages his visionary woman to speak about dollhouses, horses, and rain—especially rain, as when she describes "gravity's slow/ Secretional slashes on this house." The silent listener to these monologues is, of course, the poet, but it is also the reader who peers over the poet's shoulder and through his special lens to see and hear the woman respond to her world. The ultimate listener is finally life itself in the many guises that are the triumph of the Dickey canon. Describing a cycle of experience that carries the girl from childhood concerns into nature's energies and beyond, Dickey ends this voyage of the male imagination with a summons from the all-encompassing other. Life has heard the woman. Now it beckons her from the far side of "the flexing swamp" with "primal instructions" and "invention unending" ("Summons"). But the poet knows that the instructions and invention are also the girl's. Primal energy swirls through all women. The poet can only listen—and imagine—as nonhuman otherness in the guise of the swamp embraces the otherness of womanhood in the form of the wife to guarantee renewal and the affirmation of tomorrow.

Puella is the change of pace in the Dickey canon promised by the transitional collection *The Strength of Fields* (1979). Years will pass before one can say with certainty that individual poems in *Puella* equal the accomplishment of "The Performance," "The Heaven of Animals," "The Firebombing," "The Fiend," and "Falling." But comparison of selected titles is not the point. *Puella* is a volume of interlocking poems meant to be read together. Indeed, the entire collection is one poem. What matters, then, is not the excellence or lack thereof of individual poems but the achievement of the whole.

That achievement should be measured by the new direction that *Puella* signals for Dickey's writing. Taker of risks, seeker of growth, Dickey refuses to repeat performances already accomplished, poems already acclaimed. Applause is finally not enough. The public personality will remain, of course, because it calls attention to the poems. Yet Dickey also knows that not the artist but the art counts. Established writer and pursuer of the untried, he has entered with *Puella* a phase of his career where beginnings are once again possible, where prosody promises possibilities, where past success urges future development, and where beauty, strangely, both relieves and renews.

Other:

Introduction to *The Call of the Wild, White Fang, and Other Stories*, by Jack London (New York: Penguin, 1981), pp. 7-16;

"Why Men Drive," *Playboy Guide* (Spring/ Summer 1982): 58-61.

Interview:

L. Elizabeth Beattie, "James Dickey Rides Again," *Carolina Lifestyle* (May 1982): 43-46.

References:

David McCullough, "Eye on Books," *Book-of-the-Month Club News* (Spring 1979): 24, 26;

Dannye Romine, "Bad Boy Writer Provides More Pastry, Less Puff," *Charlotte Observer*, 2 August 1981, E1, E6;

William W. Starr, "Assignment Books," *Columbia* (S.C.) *State Magazine*, 30 March 1980, p. 10;

Starr, "James Dickey," *Columbia* (S.C.) *State Magazine*, 23 September 1979, pp. 10-11;

Chris Tucker, "An Interview with James Dickey," *Lone Star Book Review* (December 1979): 5, 25;

Paul Zweig, "Bel Canto, American-Style," *New York Times Book Review*, 6 January 1980, pp. 6, 17.

AN INTERVIEW ───────────
                    with JAMES DICKEY

DLB: Your forthcoming volume, *Night Hurdling*, is really the first collection that you have done. You have published volumes made up of shorter pieces before, but they were all of a kind. *Night Hurdling* is the first time that you have assembled a variety of forms and types of work. What made you decide to do it now?

DICKEY: It seemed to me that I had enough different kinds—enough essays and enough literary criticism and enough odd forms, like graduation addresses and various interviews with various periodicals and people and so on—to make an interesting collection. As I said in the introduction, the main point of interest for a reader would be that the selections are all forms of my own particular reactive mechanism to things, and if readers are interested in anything of mine—poetry or novels or screenplays or essays or whatever the form—they might be interested in this. If they're not interested in my opinions, they wouldn't be interested in the book. If they *are*, they would.

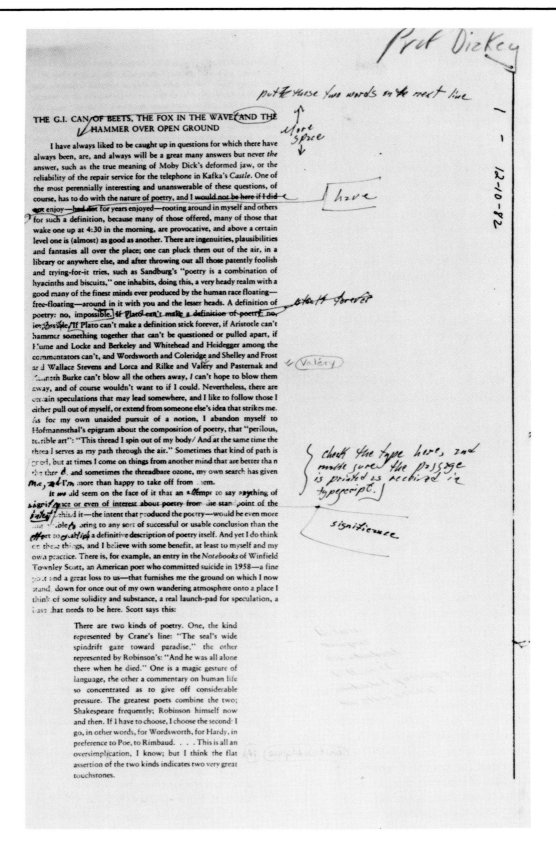

Page from Dickey's corrected proofs for Night Hurdling

DLB: Is *Night Hurdling* something more than an occasion to put together all of these things? Does the volume, as a volume, add up to anything? Does it make its own statement?

DICKEY: Well, I think so. A book of this sort can't be themed as one would theme a book which is written around a simple central point, with various commentaries on a central position that was predetermined. But one hopes, in a collection of this sort, that the thrust of a personality will be felt by the reader, even though the pieces have been collected from different sources and written and spoken over a long period of time, and for many diverse occasions. One would hope that the thrust of a personality would come through. Whether the personality itself is valuable is a question that I'm not able to answer.

DLB: Are there any pieces included in *Night Hurdling* that you are particularly happy to rescue from inaccessibility?

DICKEY: Surely; some more than others, surely. The essay about blowgun hunting for snakes—the one called "The Enemy From Eden"—I'm very happy to have in a book form. It was originally in a gift-book format, and it's been out of print for some time. I'm glad to have it generally available. Norman Mailer suggested that I collect it in some kind of way, and I asked him what type of book it should be in, and he said, "Any book, as long as it's available as the same piece." This is the book that "The Enemy From Eden" is finally appearing in. You don't have to dig back through the library and the back files of *Esquire* to find it.

DLB: You have included commencement addresses in *Night Hurdling*. Do you have any special feeling about the commencement address, and why it is important to preserve them?

DICKEY: Yes, I think it is important. The commencement address is one of the most fragile forms of all, and the most perishable; the most likely to get lost in the general darkness that immediately begins to gather around any sort of utterance that we think is appropriate to a specific occasion. Richard Wilbur has pointed out that the commencement address is an extremely difficult literary form, and very demanding in its need for appropriateness. The hazard of the graduation address is that the things of permanent value will not get said and that hot air will be the main property of the discourse. Well,

these are very real hazards, and I think the form demands that you try to transcend them and say what you have to say or think you have to say, hoping that it will be of some sort of permanent value to people. One of my addresses, the one I did at Wesleyan University in Macon, has to do with a very topical kind of subject—which was more urgent then maybe than it is now, but is to some extent topical now as well—was on the assignment of guilt to other people because they don't agree with you politically or on certain public issues, such as the Vietnam War. It's to the eternal shame of some members of my generation that they seem to believe—either covertly or, in some cases, overtly—that poetry is simply a form of propaganda. In other words: if you don't agree with us on the Vietnam War, no matter what our opinion is (most of these people I'm talking about were against it), then we're going to shoot your poetry down in reviews as often as we can. This is a sad, weak, and cowardly position for people to take, I think: the assumption of virtue by yourself, and the corresponding assignment of guilt to other people who either don't agree with you politically or are in some sort of literary rivalry with you, and making the political issue either the main issue of a discussion of a writer's literary efforts or deliberately leaving it unsaid but still the main basis for attacking your literary work. This is an unfortunate practice, but it went on all the time, and to a certain extent still exists.

DLB: You are known in the trade as a generous interview and a good interview; that is to say, you make yourself available for interviews and you obviously try hard to give the interviewer something that he can use. You have long since passed the point in your career where you need free publicity, but yet you go on giving a great deal of your time to anybody who shows up on your doorstep with a tape recorder. What purpose do you see your interviews as serving? Are you contributing to the eventual biography of James Dickey, piece by piece, in these interviews?

DICKEY: No, I don't think so. I don't have that in mind, at least not consciously. I don't really want a biography. I did some sort of cursory research on literary people's biographies and found three major literary figures who refused to authorize biographies. One of them was Matthew Arnold, another was T. S. Eliot, and a third was W. H. Auden. I don't forbid it—and I suppose eventually that there might be some possibility that there will be a biography written—but I don't encourage it either. I don't have any official designatee, such as Frost had Lawrance Thompson. I'd just rather let the work speak for itself; but one's talk and opinions are part of one's work as well, it seems to me. And lately there have been some extreme statements made about the value of interviews. Norman Mailer and I—sort of half jokingly—once asserted to each other that the interview is the real literary form of our time because more real stuff gets said there, and it's less considered and more spontaneous and therefore truer to a specific person or to a specific issue than a written and edited account of his opinions could be. I don't know if I would go so far as to maintain that opinion in all seriousness, but I do think that the spontaneity of an interview can lead to valuable insights some of the time—with certain interviewers and certain interviewees—and that these might not ever get around to being made available in any other way. I think that a person should get everything that he has or wants to say in front of anybody who wants to listen to it. This assumption inevitably makes for some repetitiousness, because the interviewers tend to ask the same questions and the interviewee has the same answers, or roughly the same answers, to the same questions. But after a person does that a certain amount, he starts looking for different answers to the same questions, and a new aspect of the original subject comes into play, all from the need to avoid one's reliable stock answer. The interview is a variation on the Socratic Method, I guess: a question-and-answer attempt to get at the truth of something. Although maybe truth is not what you want to get either, but something that could be useful to the imagination in some way—something revealing.

DLB: Except for the three poems included in *Night Hurdling*, it is all prose. You are obviously a born poet. Nonetheless, you have written and published more than your share of prose. Do you consciously approach a prose job in some way different from the way you feel when you're writing poetry?

DICKEY: Well, yes, there's inevitably going to have to be some differences, although there are also some very great similarities. The kind of poetry I write takes off from a rhythmical premise. A good deal of the time I start with some kind of rhythm that doesn't have anything to it *but* rhythm. It has a *sound*, a sound or a sequence of sounds. And then the subject—I have initially only the vaguest notion of the subject—will sort of come out of that. As nearly as I can tell, this practice has no parallel in the way I write prose. When I write a review of, say, a

book of poems or someone's work, like the piece I did on Robert Penn Warren, I start out with an opinion about the work, and I try to articulate that. It's an opinion which I more or less already have as soon as I've finished reading the work in question. I have a definite position on it, and the prose work is an attempt to articulate that as best I can, when possible quoting from the work itself to back up the points that I'm making. But that's quite a different process from working out of a rhythm into a sequence of images and actions, as I do when I'm working on a poem. The form is different, the approach is different, and the possibilities are different, and above all the kind of concentration that I try to get into poetry would be detrimental to a prose piece, because the essential thing in the latter is discourse. It's not revelation by a juxtaposition of words in a rhythmical pattern, as poetry is; it's the development of an idea and a presentation of a sequence of thought which is directed to some subject which is previously present instead of discovered in the process of the writing.

DLB: You recently had a birthday (2 February 1983) which the University of South Carolina marked with an extended James Dickey festival, which brought distinguished critics and scholars to talk about your achievement. What's left?

DICKEY: Everything is left. At the age of sixty I feel that, through a great many vicissitudes and false starts and trials and errors and much frustration, I have finally arrived at the beginning. Now it takes me both longer to write something and not as long: I realize that's a paradox! I know now, though, after a good many years, when I'm into a subject that has potential for me, or not. I know now when I've got into a subject and a treatment of it that's right for me; in other words, that I haven't just got a piece of it, but have got something like the whole thing in view or just under the surface somewhere. I can tell when it's there. I spent so many years looking for it when it really wasn't there, or trying to will it into existence. It's the difference between making something—getting something—and discovering something. It's very largely a matter of intuition, but it's an intuition that develops with a great deal of trial and error, and I feel that when I write now, I have a better mode or means of choosing things than I used to have.

DLB: You don't agree, then, with James Gould Cozzens's complaint that the hell of writing is that the better you get at it the harder it becomes?

DICKEY: Well, yes, I do. But you have more confidence because you know you're not wasting—at least I feel like I'm not wasting—your substance in trying to evolve something that was never capable of evolving to begin with. I spent most of my early years trying to make poems work which never had the possibility of working, the potential for coming to something. And I've now learned to say of a subject, I might get a piece of this, but I can't get fully enough into it to do it the kind of justice that I particularly and uniquely can do to a subject, so I won't try it. *This* one, though, I *feel* it; the thing is there for me; it's potential. Not for me in the sense of being potential for any poet (either a good poet or a bad poet or a mediocre), but for *me*, being the poet that I am, for better or worse: this is *mine*; it will become part of the kind of thing that I do best.

DLB: Are there compensations for a poet, for a writer, in getting older?

DICKEY: I think so. If I could maintain a reasonable level of health, I think this is the best age that I've ever had. It's a far better youth than the one I had! If I can remain ambulatory and perceptive for a reasonable time, I'll try to write the things I think are possible for me to write; I'll give it the best shot I can anyway.

DLB: Most people who keep track of what's going on in the literary world are aware that you're nearing completion of a big novel with the working title of "Alnilam." This is your first novel in fourteen or fifteen years. Why have you returned to the novel form?

DICKEY: It's something I want to do. I'm not one of those people who are prolific about novelistic ideas. I remember reading some letters of Hart Crane when he was just a boy, eighteen, nineteen years old. He wanted to write a novel, and he tried for a while, but in the end he went back to writing poems. He said, "I just finally have to admit that I don't have the kind of mind that thinks up plots." I could see what he meant immediately, because I don't either; but to a limited extent, I guess, I suppose I do, after all. One or two or three ideas for a novel will come to a writer like myself in a lifetime. *Deliverance* was one of them, and this is another one, although it's a much more complicated book than *Deliverance* is. It's about the early days of the air force—back in the days when it was part of the U.S. Air Corps, the Army Air Corps—and that *is* a long ways back. It

takes place in the early part of 1943. My difficulty with it is to know when to research the material and when just to remember or imagine. I went through the first draft of the book deliberately not looking up any aircraft specifications or any tables of organization for training-command bases, or any of those things. I just went with what I either remembered or figured out or imagined, and then went back and checked. I don't want the book to be overwhelmed with technical jargon and data about the air force doings. That could be boring. A book I read in connection with this, or reread, was John Hersey's novel *The War Lover*, which is about B-17's. I'm a great admirer of that book, but it has a defect that I don't want mine to have; this is the constant bombardment of the reader with the technical paraphernalia of the aircraft itself. That's interesting in a way, and John Hersey is a demon researcher; he knows what he's talking about, but all the information gets in the way of the narrative to a degree that I don't think is working for it. On the other hand, with the premier writer about the air, I suppose of all time, Antoine de Saint-Exupéry, you don't have even the slightest idea of what kind of airplane he's flying, most of the time. He says nothing about throttle settings; he says nothing about fuel consumption; he says nothing about any of the instrument flying at all. What he tries to give you is the sensation of flight itself, which is much more what I want to try for. The Bible says, "The letter killeth, but the spirit giveth life." I'm trying to get close to the spirit. What I really want to try to do in "Alnilam" is to write about the air itself. That's the element that we're in, you know, and it's maybe more dramatic to write about than water and the mysterious creatures that live in it, even Moby Dick. Air is more fundamental than water. When we fly in it, we enter a new kind of existence. I don't want to talk away the book now, but it's about flight and about the human body taking off the ground into the element of the air, and into its particular mystiques. Saint-Exupéry is a good writer, maybe a great writer in some ways, but he does not have—even *he* does not have—the air thing really right. John Hersey's *The War Lover*—these, of course, are not the only two examples—has got part of it right, especially the air-war hysteria of technique and procedure, but there's still an area that has not been touched on yet, and that's what I want to try to get into. It's not done yet, but I'm closer than I was.

DLB: If you were promised that you would have time to write three more books—and only three—

what would those three books be?

DICKEY: I'd like to finish "Alnilam," and if I had a lot of time and if "Alnilam" comes off, not in a way that pleases the public or the critics or anything like that, but in a way that pleases me, then I would like to write another novel, a sequel to it, called "Crux." The star Alnilam is in the middle of the northern winter constellation, Orion; and Crux, the Southern Cross, is south of the equator. I would like to write about the night air war in the Pacific. "Al-nilam" first, definitely, and then "Crux," maybe. And definitely as much poetry as I can write, according to my standards. And I think the book of poems I would really like to write would also be about the air: would be a suite of poems about bodily flight in things like engineless vehicles like soaring-craft or sailplanes or hang gliders: anything in which the human body on its own is in the element of air. I plan to call the poems "Peace-Raids," or at least right now I do.

John Gardner
(21 July 1933 - 14 September 1982)

Carol A. MacCurdy

See also the Gardner entry in *DLB 2, American Novelists Since World War II.*

NEW BOOKS: *On Moral Fiction* (New York: Basic Books, 1978);
Poems (Northridge, Cal.: Lord John Press, 1978);
Rumpelstiltskin (Dallas: New London Press, 1979);
Frankenstein (Dallas: New London Press, 1979);
William Wilson (Dallas: New London Press, 1979);
Vlemk the Box-Painter (Northridge, Cal.: Lord John Press, 1979);
Death and the Maiden (Dallas: New London Press, 1979);
Freddy's Book (New York: Knopf, 1980; London: Secker & Warburg, 1981);
The Temptation Game (Dallas: New London Press, 1980);
The Art of Living and Other Stories (New York: Knopf, 1981);
Mickelsson's Ghosts (New York: Knopf, 1982; London: Secker & Warburg, 1982).

John Gardner's approach to fiction was always messianic. "Fiction is the only religion I have," he once told Stephen Singular. "If I don't teach and get my point across to younger writers, I will burn in hell for a thousand years." Gardner made this statement with his characteristic sense of humor and acknowledgment of obsessive behavior. "It's as if God put me on earth to write." Indeed this prodigious writer spent most of his forty-nine years

John Gardner

writing. In the afterword to John Howell's bibliography of his works, Gardner reflects on his writing habits with an apologetic note: "That embarrasses me now, reminds me how much of my life, from childhood upward, I've spent cheating my employers and loved-ones to write fiction. Why did it seem so important? I wonder. Even when I was a child, writing under a tractor parked at the far end of some back lot when I was supposed to be plowing or dragging, and then in graduate school, writing all night, skipping classes to write by day, pretending I was studying, convincing my poor wife that I was worked to the bone by classes and my teaching assistantship—terrible page after page, stories, poems, novels—what madness it seems! Well, that is how I've spent my life. It could have been worse, I suppose. As my friend Lennis Dunlap once said to me, 'Cheer up, it could've been heroin.' "

In *John Gardner: A Bibliographical Profile* (1980), John Howell lists over thirty published "books, pamphlets, and broadsides; over one hundred stories, poems, articles, essays, and reviews; and over one hundred interviews." In the following two years his output did not diminish; he completed two more novels, *Freddy's Book* (1980) and *Mickelsson's Ghosts* (1982); a volume of short stories, *The Art of Living and Other Stories* (1981); and edited two books, *MSS: A Retrospective* (1980) and *The Best American Short Stories 1982*. Although Gardner worked at an incredible pace and left an impressive canon, his accidental death on 14 September 1982 ended his literary career prematurely. As was usual practice for Gardner, he had many works in progress. He also left two children—his son, Joel (born 31 December 1959), and daughter, Lucy (born 3 January 1962), writer of two published novels.

As the 1976 winner of the National Book Critics Circle Award for *October Light* (1976), author of three best-selling novels (*The Sunlight Dialogues*, 1972, *Nickel Mountain*, 1973, and *October Light*), and frequent college lecturer on the state of contemporary fiction, Gardner was a prominent literary figure. Easily recognizable with his white, shoulder-length hair, ever-present church warden pipe, and black leather jacket, he taught at several universities, including Oberlin, San Francisco State, Southern Illinois, Skidmore, Bennington, and Northwestern. Early in his career he taught medieval English literature but later focused on creative-writing courses. He spent at least three summers at Bread Loaf in Vermont. In 1977 he accepted a position as writer in residence at George Mason University and made, according to a friend, "something like his twentieth move in twenty-five years." The last school with which Gardner was associated was the State University of New York at Binghamton. Joining its English faculty in the fall of 1978, he returned to an area of the country near where he was born (Batavia, New York).

In many ways, the publication of *October Light* in 1976 was the highlight of Gardner's literary career. This novel not only garnered the National Book Critics Circle Award for fiction but also marked Gardner's biggest commercial success. The years following 1976, however, proved more difficult—both professionally and personally. A few months before winning the award Gardner and his wife of twenty-three years separated. Later, in 1977, doctors discovered and removed a cancer of the colon. Regularly tested for a cancer recurrence, he began to "feel pressed for time" and desired only time for reading and writing. Renting a large century-old house in Lanesboro, Pennsylvania, he moved in with Liz Rosenberg, a young writer whom he married in February 1980. His books *In the Suicide Mountains* (1977), *On Moral Fiction* (1978), and *Mickelsson's Ghosts* are all dedicated to her. Yet this marriage too ended in divorce. In fact, his fatal motorcycle accident came only four days before the twice-divorced Gardner planned to marry Susan Thornton, whom he had met at a writers' conference.

Gardner's professional problems also began in 1977. Following the publication of his biography, *The Life and Times of Chaucer* (1977), he was accused of "borrowing passages" from other Chaucerian scholars. The controversy even sparked an article in *Newsweek* (10 April 1978) entitled "Did John Gardner Paraphrase or Plagiarize?" He admitted to "paraphrasing" and remained somewhat defensive of the charge throughout his career. His post-1977 novels acknowledge sources and influences in an effort to fend off any further charges.

The publication of Gardner's critical manifesto *On Moral Fiction* generated an even more far-reaching controversy. His asserted purpose in this book is to analyze "what has gone wrong" in recent years with fiction—to explain why "most art these days is either trivial or false." Prior to its publication other contemporary writers were alerted to Gardner's assessments of their work because several of the book's essays were excerpted in literary journals (the title essay won the Pushcart Prize). Gardner further fanned the controversy over his criticism of contemporary fiction by reading papers on the subject at various universities. He also appeared on the "Dick Cavett Show"(PBS, 16 May 1978) to explain his position.

Early drafts of this book began evolving as early as 1965, before Gardner himself had published fiction. Society's need for truly moral art was a major concern for Gardner, and one he felt a great conviction in espousing. He begins his book with the claim that "art is essentially and primarily moral—that is, life-giving." He is careful to clarify that, by the word *moral*, he does not mean didactic, for "didacticism and true art are immiscible." To Gardner "true art is moral" because it "clarifies life, establishes models of human action, casts nets toward the future, carefully judges our right and wrong directions, celebrates and mourns. It does not rant. It does not sneer or giggle in the face of death, it invents prayers and weapons. It designs visions worth trying to make fact. It does not whimper or cower or throw up its hands and bat its lashes. It does not make hope contingent on acceptance of some religious theory. It strikes like lightning, or *is* lightning; whichever."

Gardner finds fault with postmodernist writers "who disparage the pursuit of truth" and refers to them as "a gang of absurdist and jubilant nihilists." To explain why "our serious fiction is not much good," he points to the writers' emphasis on technique over truth. Such "performance" artists call attention to their fiction's linguistic fabric or to what Gardner calls "texture." The reason writers occupy themselves with surface is "that we tend to feel we have nothing to say. . . .Texture is our refuge, the one thing we know we're good at." Therefore, he explains, "Fiction as pure language (texture over structure) is *in*," and writers who are concerned with pursuing truth, goodness, and beauty are "old-fashioned." The end result of focusing on language, Gardner argues, is a lack of communication: "linguistic opacity suggests indifference to the needs and wishes of the reader and to whatever ideas may be buried underneath all that brush."

To illustrate his theory, Gardner comments on many of his fellow novelists. As a particular example of a writer who concentrates on "language for its own sake," he selects his friend William Gass, who is "the best of the lot." But he also lists J. P. Donleavy, James Purdy, Stanley Elkin, and John Barth as "more in love, on principle, with the sound of words—or with newfangledness—than with creating fictional worlds."

Even those authors who are interested in ideas and arguments too often turn to outrage or propaganda, according to Gardner. Such a "fierce ethic," he says, is not "rooted in love," a requirement of truly great art. Gardner states, "Despite the labors of academic artists and those sophisticates who are embarrassed by emotion, it seems all but self-evident that it is for the pleasure of exercising our capacity to love that we pick up a book at all." For Gardner morality and love are inextricably bound. Artists, therefore, who assert only causes, those who have no love of character but only of style, and those who approach the world with cynical detachment are doomed to short literary lives.

As examples, Gardner points to the meanness of Robert Coover, the "fashionable pain" of Joan Didion, the "chicanery" of E. L. Doctorow, the "limitation" of Donald Barthelme, and the "winking mugging despair" of Thomas Pynchon. He cites John Fowles as a novelist with true compassion for his characters and their problems, and he expresses disappointment with Norman Mailer, Kurt Vonnegut, and Joseph Heller, for none of them "cares enough about his characters to use them as anything but examples in a forced proof." Acknowledging at least their interest in truth-telling, he labels them as "essentially transcribers of the moods of their time."

For Gardner the morality of art is not a matter of "message" or doctrine but is a "process." "The writer discovers, works out, and tests his ideas in the process of writing. Thus at its best fiction is . . . a way of thinking, a philosophical method." Art's morality springs from this "process" which clarifies life and opposes chaos. Gardner warns, "Discursive thought is not fiction's most efficient tool." For this reason he faults Saul Bellow. His "novels come off in the end as sprawling works of advice, not art." "At heart" Bellow is, according to Gardner, "an essayist disguised as a writer of fiction."

Gardner's annoyance with the present state of the arts comes from his firm belief that art affects the way people behave. "Life follows art." In his view society is cynical and debased because its art is, not the other way around: "if we celebrate bad values in our arts, we're going to have a bad society." In this rather angry book Gardner sends out a cry for fiction that will bolster life, not undermine its value. To Gardner the literary artist is the conscious guardian of society; his message to the reader is clear: "Since bad art has a harmful effect on society, it should never go unchallenged."

Gardner got the literary gunfight he wanted. Many prominent novelists fired back. In a *New York Times Magazine* article entitled "The Sound and the Fury Over Fiction," Stephen Singular quoted sev-

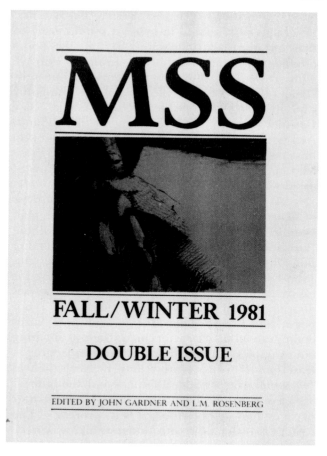

Front cover for the first issue of the literary journal founded,
copublished, and coedited by Gardner

eral writers' responses:

> John Updike—" 'Moral' is such a moot word.
> Surely, morality in fiction is accuracy and
> truth. The world has changed, and in a sense
> we are all heirs to despair. Better to face this
> and tell the truth, however dismal, than to do
> whatever life-enhancing thing he was pro-
> posing. . . . I thought he was awfully cavalier
> with Bellow."

> Joseph Heller—"Gardner is a pretentious
> young man, talks a lot and has little of intelli-
> gence to say. He writes dull novels and dull
> carping criticism."

> Norman Mailer—"No comment. We'll meet
> in heaven."

One of the most blistering reactions came from
John Barth: "There's something very self-serving
about his argument. He's making a shrill pitch to the
literary right wing that wants to repudiate all of
modernism and jump back into the arms of their
19th-century literary grandfathers. Gardner's own
later novels do this and are applauded, of course.
He's banging his betters over the head with ter-
minology and, when the smoke clears, nobody is left
in the room but Mr. Gardner himself."

Many reviewers found the book to be an ar-
rogant recitation of pronouncements in which
Gardner magisterially dismisses other writers for
the purpose of offering an extended apologia for
his own writing. Gardner's combativeness, his
"bombastic exaggerations," according to Thomas
LeClair in *Saturday Review*, simply "reveal a writer ill
at ease with himself." Gardner's argument does
seem to be defensive, for he puts most other current
writers on the other side of his moral fence. In an
Atlantic Monthly interview he says that "hardly anybody belongs with me" and then explains, "Very few
people believe in fiction as exploration, as understanding."

Gardner's view of the artist as moral agent
places him on old-fashioned, time-tested ground
and aligns him with Tolstoy. His call for "moral
fiction" appeals to disgruntled readers and critics
alike who find current fiction too remote from their
experience and devoid of sincere emotions. Although Gardner fired up some literary tempers, he
also found a sympathetic audience. Julian Moynahan, for example, in the *New York Times Book Review*
admits that, despite Gardner's "righteousness," "it's
a positive pleasure to see various fashionable gloom
spreaders and doomsday peddlers get it in the
neck." In *Contemporary Literature* Thomas LeClair
criticizes Gardner's "pride" and "militantly imaginative" readings of recent fiction but finds it "still a
necessary book. . . . its earnest force requires even
the reader who resists it page by page to examine his
assumptions about fiction and because no other
writer . . . has reminded us recently that art is by
and for human beings." LeClair concludes that the
book "does not collapse through its many weaknesses because, ultimately, Gardner sides with great
art. . . ."

Following the publication of *On Moral Fiction*,
Gardner continued to demonstrate his versatility as
a writer and his wide-ranging creative interests by
writing poetry, opera libretti, children's tales, and
radio plays. A small volume of his verse, entitled
Poems, was published in 1978. A broadside of the
poem "Nicholas Vergette 1923-1974" coincided
with the publication of *Poems*. Gardner first read the
poem at a memorial service held for his friend
Nicholas Vergette in Carbondale, Illinois, on 28

February 1974. The New London Press published three of his opera libretti—*Rumpelstiltskin* (1979), *Frankenstein* (1979), and *William Wilson* (1979). Gardner had a passion for opera and saw his *Rumpelstiltskin* performed by the Opera Company of Philadelphia. Gardner also began writing radio plays in 1979 and won the Armstrong Prize for *The Temptation Game* (1980).

Gardner's next novel, *Freddy's Book*, came out in 1980. It resembles in structure the widely praised *October Light*, since it too is composed of a novel within a novel. Beginning with "Freddy," a sixty-page prologue, the novel introduces Prof. Jack Winesap, a "psycho-historian." Guest-lecturing at the University of Wisconsin (on "The Psycho-politics of the Late Welsh Fairytale: Fee, Fie, Foe—Revolution"), Winesap meets a strange old historian, Professor Agaard, at a reception. While Winesap holds forth on "the popular appeal of monstrosity," Agaard begins to twitch nervously and says, "I have a son who's a monster." Although the admission leads to a rather awkward conversation, Winesap later accepts an invitation to the man's house. Arriving at the isolated, run-down estate in a blizzard, Winesap becomes snowed in for the night. After a suspenseful delay, Agaard takes his visitor upstairs to meet his "monster" son. A painfully shy, obese, eight-foot-tall adolescent, Freddy exiles himself in a locked room which keeps the mocking world at bay. For two years he has been working on a book. A "fan" of Winesap's writing, Freddy sneaks down during the night to the visitor's room and deposits his book, called "Freddy's Book."

"Freddy's Book" is the tale "King Gustav and the Devil." A fablelike retelling of historical events in sixteenth-century Scandinavia, his story traces the rise to power of young Gustav Vasa (an authentic historical figure). After the Stockholm massacre of 1520, this new young leader emerges, and with the help of both his giant, country-bred cousin Lars-Goren and of the protean Devil who whispers in men's ears, he becomes King Gustavus I of Sweden. In the process he makes an ally and then an enemy of Bishop Brask, an intellectual cleric and cynical kingmaker.

Although Gustav is the king of Sweden, Lars-Goren is the hero of the story. This simple knight's only fear is the Devil, and toward the story's end King Gustav sends his comrade Lars-Goren and Bishop Brask to Lapland to kill the Devil. Suspecting treachery brought on by his own injustices, Gustav betrays his friend by sending men out to kill him. In flight Lars-Goren and Bishop Brask ride to the northern-most tip of the world through an arc-

tic snowscape that obscures all form. In a powerful final scene they scale the Devil as if he were an ice-encrusted mountain:

> Even to Hans Brask it was a strange business, a kind of miracle. He had meant to cry out from despair, as usual, and he had reason enough: he was beyond pain, numb to the heart; yet what he felt was the wild excitement of a child or an animal. He would not be fooled by it. He was a sick old man, and he knew there was no chance of getting back from here alive. Bishop, man-of-God, whatever, he had no faith in God. As surely as he knew he was alive he knew God was dead or had never existed. What was this euphoria but an animal pleasure in existence at the margin—the joy of the antelope when the tiger leaps? Yet the joy was real enough. Absurdly, for all his philosophy, he was glad to be alive and dying. . . . "This is poetry, this is love and religion!" he thought. He crawled closer to Lars-Goren, filled with excitement, almost laughing, though no sound came out and his cheeks were all ice from his tears.

Euphoric in the face of Lars-Goren's brave actions, Brask simultaneously mocks him: "What a stupid fool you are, Lars-Goren! You know as well as I do that all this means nothing!" Lars-Goren, nevertheless, succeeds in killing the Devil with his knife of bone. The mission is accomplished and Lars-Goren can return to his country home. Back in the city of Stockholm, however, the future appears anything but heroic. Gustav looks out from his window as "darkness fell. There was no light anywhere, except for the yellow light of cities."

The ending seems to suggest that evil cannot be conquered; that the Devil as dragon has been killed, but that he remains a human condition—"the evil is life itself." Because the novel's close seems to substantiate fatalism, some critics point to the discrepancy between *Freddy's Book* and the moral values Gardner advocates in *On Moral Fiction*. Yet Lars-Goren's individual triumph over his personal nemesis seems life-affirming. As he rides toward his impossible quest and the confrontation with what he fears most, he identifies his fear as "the chaos" that is "in myself, as in everything around me." He then acts with the double knowledge that the Devil cannot be killed and that his striking out at evil is a necessity. Although Gardner laments civilization's moral failure, he embraces human aspiration for magnificence.

After the publication of *On Moral Fiction*, critics tended to assess Gardner's fiction in the light of his critical theory. Many critics alienated by his argument were eager to attack *Freddy's Book*; others were eager to defend it. Many reviewers found the book's provocative opening the most entertaining part and wished, as Paul Gray expressed in *Time*, that he had provided "the other half of the framing tale." Pointing to the artificiality of the two-part structure, some critics accused Gardner of building Barthian funhouses for no purpose, a practice which *On Moral Fiction* criticizes.

An association between the book's two parts does, however, seem evident, with freakish Freddy transforming himself into the heroic Lars-Goren. As artist rather than misfit, Freddy is equipped to fight the hostile forces of the outside world. In the *Saturday Review* LeClair explains that Freddy's composing himself into Lars-Goren is an attempt to heal his wound—"his difference from others, the country-boy feeling of not being good enough." LeClair goes a step further in suggesting that "Gardner 'lives with' an analogous, perhaps quite similar wound—the sense of being a literary misfit," which "is quite explicitly suggested by the prologue." If LeClair's theory is correct, then Gardner's self-portrait as a writer may be partly responsible for the book's main flaw—his interjection of ideas at the expense of the story and its characters. At one point Lars-Goren and Brask become, in LeClair's phrase, "mouths on horseback," with one championing moral fiction and the other elegant rhetoric.

In the *New York Times Book Review* John Romano suggests that Gardner's two consuming interests—one, his love of "the fabulous, the en-

New York Times Book Review, *10 October 1982*

chanted" and the other, his philosophical commitment to a "moral scheme"—often work at cross-purposes. Romano explains: "Gardner's particular brand of morality, with its characteristic stress on strength of will, turns out to be incompatible in practice with the softer charms of storytelling. Gardner's problem, then, is that he is unwilling, on principle, to indulge the fabulistic for its own sake. In just the same way, he won't allow himself simply to revel in those Chinese-box structures that so strongly attract him." Romano implies that Gardner struggles against his own gifts and "is a better modernist than he knows."

Gardner followed *Freddy's Book* with a collection of ten stories—his first since *The King's Indian* (1974)—entitled *The Art of Living and Other Stories.* Half the stories were published earlier in various journals and magazines. All the stories explore the relationship between art and life. For example, in "Nimran," dedicated to William Gass, a famous orchestra conductor meets a dying girl, who later goes to his stirring concert. Gardner's theme of art's transcending powers unites these stories. In a 1974 *New Fiction* interview he explained his approach to art: "Blake says a wonderful thing: 'I look upon the dark satanic mills; I shake my head; they vanish.' That's it. That's right. You *redeem* the world by acts of imagination. . . ." Unfortunately, in this short-story collection oftentimes the theme relating to art overpowers the simple story.

The short story "Redemption" is a truly fine one that carries much personal significance for its author. Originally published in the *Atlantic Monthly*, it was later chosen for *The Best American Short Stories 1978.* Based on the death of Gardner's younger brother, the story opens: "One day in April—a clear, blue day when there were crocuses in bloom—Jack Hawthorne ran over and killed his brother, David. Even at the last moment he could have prevented his brother's death by slamming on the tractor brakes, easily in reach for all the shortness of his legs; but he was unable to think, or, rather, thought unclearly, and so watched it happen, as he would again and again watch it happen in his mind, with nearly undiminished intensity and clarity, all his life." The accident described in the story took place when Gardner was almost twelve and his brother seven. Although the death shook the family, no one blamed John Gardner; his mother insisted, "only God could have stopped that tractor, and he doesn't work that way." Jack Hawthorne struggles with his belief that he could have prevented the death, and the story traces his resulting grief, rage, and guilt. Just as Gardner did,

Jack begins playing the French horn and goes to Rochester's Eastman School of Music for lessons. Jack seeks redemption through art, yet learns from his crusty old Russian teacher, who survived the Bolshevik slaughter, that he must also plunge back into "the herd" of humanity.

The experience of writing the story proved cathartic for Gardner. In a 1979 *Paris Review* interview he described how, before he wrote "Redemption," he "always, regularly, everyday" used "to have four or five flashes of that accident. I'd be driving down the highway and I couldn't see what was coming because I'd have a memory flash. I haven't had it once since I wrote the story. You really do ground your nightmares, you *name* them. When you write a story, you have to play that image, no matter how painful, over and over until you've got all the sharp details so you know exactly how to put it down on paper. By the time you've run your mind through it a hundred times, relentlessly worked every tic of your terror, it's lost its power over you. That's what bibliotherapy is all about, I guess."

"Redemption" was praised for its pure power and its lack of self-conscious pyrotechnics. In a 1977 interview with Henry Allen, Gardner explains that he purposely shunned some of his early writing bravura, "I spent a lot of time evading the dark center of things by, usually, technical tricks." In "Redemption," however, "for once the techniques aren't showing. That's the important thing. I have spent all my life so far developing more and more techniques. . . . What I want to do now is start using them. And that's the moment when you change from a kind of good writer with a very serious mind and set of emotions into a really major writer. And whether or not I can make that transition, I don't know." He goes on to suggest that he is at the beginning of the transition and that he wants "to write great fiction."

Gardner obviously had ambitions for his next novel, *Mickelsson's Ghosts*, a lengthy work, and one that resembles *The Sunlight Dialogues* (1972) with its immense cast and labyrinthine story. At the center of this ambitious novel is Peter Mickelsson, a mid-fiftyish philosophy professor who teaches at the State University of New York in Binghamton. The novel of over 600 pages is an immersion into the emotional, intellectual, and psychic life of this beleaguered professor and his surrounding world. Separated, but not yet divorced, from an embittered, money-hungry wife, worried about his terrorist son who is fighting the nuclear-power industry, and unable to write, teach, or pay his bills, Mickelsson is in the grips of a terrible life crisis.

"Once the most orderly of men, a philosopher almost obsessively devoted to precision and neatness (despite his love of Nietzsche), distrustful if not downright disdainful of passion," he has lost control of himself and his world.

In an effort to simplify his life, Mickelsson buys an old farmhouse outside of the depressed town of Susquehanna, Pennsylvania, and devotes himself to restoring the old house in a massive self-renewal project. Drinking and brooding as he works, he discovers that his Eden is more like hell. From the locals he learns his sanctuary is not only haunted but was also the former residence of Joseph Smith, the Mormon prophet, and scene of a murder. Almost immediately bizarre events begin to happen. His house is ransacked, unlit trucks barrel down the dark mountain highway, mysterious burnt-out patches appear in the landscape, and rumors of unsolved murders, witchcraft, and UFO landings whisper through the community. These mysterious omens culminate in Mickelsson's house with the ghosts' eventual appearance—an old man with no teeth and an angry-looking woman. Trying to maintain his equilibrium, Mickelsson shares his house with the knowledge of their horror—his ghosts are an incestuous brother and sister who killed their child and eventually each other.

Interwoven with this Gothic story line are Mickelsson's academic escapades in Binghamton. Commuting into this otherworld of academia, he faces his seemingly affable colleagues who are murderously competitive, his students—among them a possibly suicidal young man who looks to him for salvation—and a beautiful sociology professor, Jessica Stark, who is the victim of a campaign to oust her. Mickelsson is in love with this elegant Jewish widow, but becomes shamelessly obsessed with a teenage prostitute named Donnie, who lives in a Susquehanna tenement. When the teenager becomes pregnant and tells Mickelsson the baby is his, the antiabortionist professor robs a man to pay Donnie to have the baby. During the robbery, the man (a former bank thief) is stricken with a heart attack, and Mickelsson watches him die. Under suspicion for murder, he hides out in his house only to learn that Donnie has escaped with the money and had an abortion. This crisis, along with the events at school and the presence of the ghosts, pushes him more deeply into self-loathing and despair.

Near the end when madness threatens, a violent crisis precipitates his eventual redemption. A Mormon fanatic (actually a member of the secret society known as Sons of Dan, which pursues apostate saints to their death) bangs on Mickelsson's door bearing arms. Threatening Mickelsson's life, the fanatic commands him to tear apart his newly renovated rooms piece by piece in order to uncover a church scandal that is hidden in the walls. As Mickelsson dismantles his entire house, tearing out the fresh plaster, the ending of the novel moves toward the apocalyptic. Saved from murderous destruction at the very last, Mickelsson is finally able to reach out for affirmation—his love for Jessica.

Many of Gardner's lifelong preoccupations are evidenced in *Mickelsson's Ghosts*, especially his philosophical bent and moral vision. The reader of this novel can hear Gardner's voice from *On Moral Fiction*. The author clearly cares about his central character—perhaps too much. He lovingly describes every mood, nervous habit, or intellectual query of Mickelsson's. Always a lover of ideas, Gardner has difficulty maintaining his distance from his central character, especially as the novel progresses. In the *Saturday Review*, Robert Harris suggests that "too often Mickelsson is a garrulous spokesman for Gardner" and that, even though the author "may chastise Mickelsson for what he does," he is too "taken with Mickelsson's thought-processes (because they are so much his own)." Examples of such excesses occur when Gardner relates not only Mickelsson's philosophical conversations with his friends but also entire class discussions from his Philosophy 108 course.

Throughout his career Gardner referred to himself as a "philosophical novelist." In a *Paris Review* interview he explained that "when I write a piece of fiction I select my characters and settings and so on because they have a bearing, at least to me, on the old unanswerable philosophical questions. And as I spin out the action, I'm always very concerned with springing discoveries. But at the same time I'm concerned—and finally *more* concerned—with what the discoveries do to the character who makes them, and to the people around him." Benjamin DeMott points out in the *New York Times Book Review* that all of Gardner's novels to an extent are "the story of somebody's intellectual life" and that *Mickelsson's Ghosts*, in particular, demonstrates Gardner's engagement in the "genuinely challenging philosophical theme" of "the mind's endless—and doomed—hunt for self-knowledge." Indeed, Gardner envelops the reader in Mickelsson's agonizing musings about life and offers him no other perspective. This feeling of entrapment suggests Mickelsson's own intellectual imprisonment. Gardner once commented to Ed Christian in a *Prairie Schooner* interview that "the real prison is the prison of the intellect. We're locked into logical systems, unwilling to have faith in the things that count, like love." Gardner's last novel, like many of his others, traces his central character's movement from such ordered restrictions toward a renewed faith in life's potentiality.

Gardner's hopes for this ambitious novel went unrealized, for the reviews were largely negative, some hostile. James Wolcott in *Esquire* called it "a whopping piece of academic bullslinging." In the *New York Review of Books*, Robert Towers offered a more evenhanded criticism of the novel: "My objection, of course, is not to the presence of significant ideas in a novel or to a protagonist who is an academic philosopher; rather, it is the indiscriminate, underdramatized parade of the ideas that makes this reader quail—that, and the verbal self-intoxication of the philosopher-protagonist."

Throughout his career Gardner's propensity for philosophical argumentation brought him criticism, and perhaps *Mickelsson's Ghosts* suffers the most from this inclination, making it all the more unfortunate that this novel is his last. Before his fatal accident Gardner was reportedly "badly hurt" at the poor reviews and blamed them on a critical backlash resulting from *On Moral Fiction*.

His last contribution to American letters is *The Best American Short Stories 1982*, which he edited. This collection, selected and introduced by Gardner, provides a clear statement of his artistic vision. In his selection he passes over many well-known writers, such as John Updike, Donald Barthelme, and Ann Beattie as well as most *New Yorker* pieces, in favor of many newcomers whose works appear in literary reviews, quarterlies, and little magazines. Acknowledging in the ten-page introduction that literary choice is mainly a matter of taste, he selected works that convey "a new seriousness"—not by chronicling manners or politics but by engaging "in serious personal concern."

Gardner's untiring commitment to the state of the art of fiction cannot be questioned. Even though his outspoken opinions alienated some critics and fellow novelists, his intellectual energy and devotion to fiction will be missed. His messianic voice is responsible for much of the literary discussion on the direction of contemporary fiction. His critical voice will be missed, but his fiction will be a greater loss. Even though his career was cut short, he left an impressive canon. Most impressive are his novels, which are inventive, witty, and extraordinarily varied. Many critics consider *Grendel* (1971) a modern classic, *The Sunlight Dialogues* an epic of the 1970's, and *October Light* a dazzling piece of Americana. Explaining his commitment to art, Gardner told

Stephen Singular, "It's made my life, and it made my life when I was a kid. . . . Art has filled my life with joy and I want everybody to know the kind of joy I know—"

Other:

MSS: A Retrospective, edited by Gardner and L. M. Rosenberg (Dallas: New London Press, 1980);

John M. Howell, *John Gardner: A Bibliographical Profile*, afterword by Gardner (Carbondale: Southern Illinois University Press, 1980);

John Gardner: Critical Perspectives, edited by Robert A. Morace and Kathryn Van Spanckeren, afterword by Gardner (Carbondale: Southern Illinois University Press, 1982);

The Best American Short Stories 1982, edited by Gardner and Shannon Ravenel, with an introduction by Gardner (Boston: Houghton Mifflin, 1982).

Periodical Publications:

FICTION:

"The Music Lover," *Antaeus: Special Fiction Issue*, edited by Daniel Halpern, no. 13-14 (Spring-Summer 1974): 176-182;

"Trumpeter," *Esquire*, 86 (December 1976): 114-116, 182;

"Redemption," *Atlantic Monthly*, 239 (May 1977): 48-50, 55-56, 58-59;

"Stillness," *Hudson Review*, 30 (Winter 1977-1978): 549-559;

"Nimran," *Atlantic Monthly*, 244 (September 1979): 39-48;

"Come on Back," *Atlantic Monthly*, 24 (March 1981): 52.

NONFICTION:

"The Way We Write Now," *New York Times Book Review*, 9 July 1972, pp. 2, 32-33;

"Moral Fiction," *Hudson Review*, 29 (Winter 1976-1977): 497-512;

"The Quest for the Philosophical Novel," review of *Lancelot* by Walker Percy, *New York Review of Books*, 20 February 1977, pp. 1, 16, 20;

"The Idea of Moral Criticism," *Western Humanities Review*, 31 (Spring 1977): 97-109;

"Death by Art; or, 'Some Men Kill You with a Six-Gun, Some Men with a Pen,' " *Critical Inquiry*, 3 (Summer 1977): 741-771;

"Moral Fiction," *Saturday Review*, 5 (1 April 1978): 29-30, 32-33;

"A Novel of Evil," review of *Sophie's Choice* by William Styron, *New York Times Book Review*, 27 May 1979, pp. 1, 16-17;

"What Johnny can't read," *Saturday Review*, 7 (1 March 1980): 35-37.

Interviews:

Joe David Bellamy, *The New Fiction: Interviews with Innovative American Writers* (Urbana: University of Illinois Press, 1974);

Don Edwards and Carol Polsgrove, "A Conversation with John Gardner," *Atlantic Monthly*, 239 (May 1977): 43-47;

Henry Allen, "John Gardner: 'I'm One of the Really Great Writers,' " *Washington Post Magazine*, 6 November 1977, pp. 22-23, 28, 33, 37;

C. E. Frazer Clark, Jr., *Conversations with Writers I* (Detroit: Bruccoli Clark/ Gale, 1977);

Marshall L. Harvey, "Where Philosophy and Fiction Meet: An Interview with John Gardner," *Chicago Review*, 29 (Spring 1978): 73-87;

Daniel Laskin, "Challenging the Literary Naysayers," *Horizon*, 21 (July 1978): 32-36;

Thomas LeClair, "William Gass and John Gardner: A Debate on Fiction," *New Republic*, 180 (10 March 1979): 25, 28-33;

Paul F. Ferguson, John R. Maier, Frank McConnell, and Sara Matthieson, "John Gardner: The Art of Fiction LXXIII," *Paris Review*, 21 (Spring 1979): 36-74;

Joyce Renwick and Howard Smith, "Last of the Radio Heroes," *Horizon*, 22 (July 1979): 67-71;

Stephen Singular, "The Sound and the Fury Over Fiction," *New York Times Magazine*, 8 July 1979, pp. 13-15, 34, 36-39;

Ed Christian, "An Interview with John Gardner," *Prairie Schooner*, 54 (Winter 1980-1981): 70-93;

Alan Burns and Charles Sugnet, *The Imagination on Trial: British and American Writers Discuss Their Working Methods* (London: Allison & Busby, 1981).

References:

Benjamin DeMott, "A Philosophical Novel of Academe," *New York Times Book Review*, 20 June 1982, pp. 1, 26-27;

W. P. Fitzpatrick, "John Gardner and the Defense of Fiction," *Midwest Quarterly*, 20 (Summer 1979): 405-415.

Paul Gray, "Devil's Due," *Time*, 155 (31 March 1980): 82;

Robert Harris, "What's So Moral About John Gardner's Fiction?," *Saturday Review*, 9 (June 1982): 70-71;

John M. Howell, *John Gardner: A Bibliographical Pro-*

file (Carbondale: Southern Illinois University Press, 1980);

Thomas LeClair, "The Clatter of Moral Fiction," *Saturday Review*, 7 (29 March 1980): 53-54;

LeClair, "Moral Criticism," *Contemporary Literature*, 20 (Autumn 1979): 509-512;

Larry McCaffery, "The Gass-Gardner Debate: Showdown on Main Street," *Literary Review*, 23 (Fall 1979): 134-144;

Robert A. Morace and Kathryn Van Spanckeren, eds., *John Gardner: Critical Perspectives* (Carbondale: Southern Illinois University Press, 1982);

Julian Moynahan, "Moral Fictions," *New York Times Book Review*, 17 May 1981, pp. 7, 27-28;

John Romano, "A Moralist's Fable," *New York Times Book Review*, 23 March 1980, pp. 1, 26-27;

Roger Sale, "Banging on the Table," *New York Times Book Review*, 16 April 1978, pp. 10-11;

Elizabeth Spencer, "Experiment is Out, Concern is In," *New York Times Book Review*, 21 November 1982, pp. 7, 49;

Robert Towers, "So Big," *New York Review of Books*, 24 June 1982, pp. 17-18;

James Wolcott, "Core Curriculum," *Esquire*, 97 (June 1982): 134, 136.

TRIBUTES TO JOHN GARDNER

From DAVE SMITH

Several years ago I was in New York to receive an award from the American Academy and Institute of Arts and Letters, under the big tent where a gala party was going on, the writers feasting on food and gossip, laughing, behaving as writers do when they are gathered in public. I stood off to the edge, knowing only a few of these people and feeling overwhelmed by it all. Suddenly Joyce Carol Oates stood beside me. I'd met her once but did not know her. Now we were chatting. I don't remember what this very pleasant woman had to say or what I might have said, except I remember the subject was John Gardner. I do recall that Joyce Oates said it was a shame how Gardner turned on all his friends. This was chilling to me since I had reason to think myself Gardner's friend and especially since I was going to take up a Visiting Professor job at SUNY-Binghamton, a job which John and I both hoped would turn into a permanent position. We had both said we hoped to have the chance to teach together. I hoped that because I admired John as a teacher and as a writer.

I met John at the Bread Loaf Writers' Conference in 1975. He asked one night if it was true that I, a Fellow in Poetry, had a novel in manuscript. I said I did. He asked to read it. I demurred and he persisted. In the end he read that unfinished book and he encouraged me to finish it. He did not otherwise respond to the book, but that was enough. Because of his faith, I finished it and published it. I will not recite the names of those who had a similar experience with John, but it would be a long and impressive list.

While I was Director of Creative Writing at the University of Utah I had John come and do a residency. He was unstinting in the attention he gave our students, graduates and undergraduates alike. And he told some of them that they were wasting their time. Others he praised. One fellow was told that he was either misguided or evil. John could respond to a student with the same passion and conviction that he might feel in responding to internationally famous writers. The message for the students was unequivocal: they were going to be taken seriously as writers and had better, therefore, put in the time and effort and thought that art demanded. Or else John would let them know. I remember that my daughter called him *the man who came on the airplane* since he stayed with us, he read to her, he argued aesthetics, he pranced, and in the middle of dinner, music, anything at all, up he would bound and disappear. Soon I'd hear him at my typewriter, banging it as fast as it would go. Nothing stopped John from writing.

Perhaps that is what is most clear in my mind of the man I will never be able to imagine not out there, about to call, about to write a cryptic note. He couldn't, wouldn't stop writing. It was obsessive, compulsive, endless to him. We never really had a long conversation, not even during the year we worked together at Binghamton. After a few minutes a kind of glaze came over John and anyone could tell that his mind was writing. Had there been a typewriter within arm's reach he couldn't have resisted it. Doubtless a lot of John's work is dull, pretentious, needlessly thick. Much of his *Moral Fiction* is suspicious and inconsistent. John regretted that book, although I don't think he ever said so in public. And for a man who loved the sound, the many sounds, of language as John did, he always seemed to me to have a wooden ear for poetry. He wrote a piece about my poems and I am eternally grateful for it, but I think it is superficial and shows a real lack of understanding about what poetry is. I am saying all this because I know that John valued above all else honesty in what one said about writing.

That's a curious assertion for several reasons. John was, I have often thought, a curious and compulsive liar. He lied about everything. I never saw him do this in malice or do it to hurt anyone. I have not in my life met a person gentler and readier to feel for another than the person John Gardner was. Yet he liked to recreate the world. He seemed to feel it was just there, in all of its forms and dimensions and varieties, waiting for him to alter it, to set it right. So with friend or colleague he was ever willing to say an absolutely outrageous thing—just to see if people would believe it. Usually they did. I always did. But John didn't lie about books or writers. He said what he thought, bluntly and without regard for the fact that his subject might be a lifelong friend. He seemed to expect the same treatment in return and seemed bemused, even bewildered, when old friends weren't friends any longer.

I don't really know what it required emotionally to be a student of John's, a sustained, prolonged student, but I suspect it exacted a heavy price. This was also true of being his friend, at least for me. John loved me and I loved him. I have no doubt whatsoever about this. Yet I found him unable, on the whole, to show his affection in the most ordinary ways. He was very difficult to talk to unless one kept to his subjects, his enthusiasms. When I went to Binghamton, John encouraged me to live in Pennsylvania, where he lived, some 28 miles from school. Because of his encouragement, I bought a Harley-Davidson motorcycle. He and I and a mutual friend, the playwright Jan Quackenbush, used to ride through those country roads that prowled through the Endless Mountains. We were, he once said, the Mild Bunch. On the bikes we didn't have to talk. If I can say it without grinning, we communed. Others have told me John rode his bike irresponsibly. He seemed to me to ride like an old maid, slowly, with enormous caution, though he once tried to convince me he had been a member of the original Hell's Angels. To be John's friend you had to put up with a solemn, rarely laughing, very serious man of narrow interests and compulsive character. Perhaps it is best to say he was incredibly ambitious. But it had better be added that he was ambitious for words, art, and to a degree that I have known in no other man. Because of this, if you were his friend, he made you a better, more conscientious writer than you would have been otherwise.

What or who was John Gardner? Like any man of complexity and depth and dreams, he is all those people in his novels, plays, poems, allegories, and studies. He was a boy who wanted to think through all the secrets and a man who saw that there was no "hole in the bag" as William Carlos Williams said. I think he never got over being a Christian, though he once told me when I asked him about this that he was the last worshipper of Zeus. He was a farmer who didn't farm. Once I asked him if he thought much about home, where it was for him, what it was. His response was quick and testy. Nowhere was home. Anywhere was the same and would do. Yet here he was on a rocky thirty acres of Pennsylvania countryside, close enough to make the frequent drive to his parents's place in Batavia, New York, a place not very unlike his own. He was a musician. Once I saw him leap up in the middle of a conversation, turn my stereo on very loud, and argue with someone's performance of a composition that had been playing so low I hadn't heard it. He was a loving father, proud of his children, worried about them. When he'd come to Utah that week, his marriage to Joan was ending and the children were heavy with him. My children and I watched him sob as he tried to say what he thought was happening.

Among all these John Gardners were the others, the drunk—occasional and sometimes sustained—the boor with his idealistic arguments, the savage reviewers, the self-styled bard, the con artist who let himself be portrayed by *Washington Post* journalists as a windbag who called himself the world's greatest novelist. In a second *Post* essay about him, I could see him thinking up whoppers one after another and the journalist, either young or stupid, put it all down. I roared with belly laughs as I read, as I thought of all those who knew John reading this piece. He was also the man who had beaten colonic cancer. He bore this bravely, very bravely. Yet I remember that I hadn't heard from him in several years when I got a Christmas card. Its return address was Johns Hopkins University Hospital. The card said "Merry Christmas. I have cancer but I'm fine." When I visited John in the somewhat seedy Baltimore apartment where he was recuperating, he told me that his young wife was a student of John Barth's. For a man who was as prolix as the winds at Buffalo, John could say a lot with great economy. Perhaps that is why I think his best books are *Grendel*, *The King's Indian*, and *October Light*. And despite its terrible shortcomings, I admire *Moral Fiction*. The John Gardner I knew was

many men, but he was first of all a writer.

When I decided not to remain at SUNY-Binghamton, though I had been offered a handsome and tenured position, I asked John to come to my office and I told him. We were both a little teary. I gave him a lot of blather about my reasons and he listened patiently. I don't think that, until that moment, I realized how much he wanted me there, how much I was his friend, how much he cared about me as a writer. Suddenly he told me he knew that I was leaving for a reason I could not discuss with him—or could not well express—the need to go home, to see if my home in the South was in fact still there. I don't remember what he said, only that he knew what was going on in me as well or better than I did. He knew more than anyone else around him. He really was one of those people on whom nothing is lost.

I've said all this to say that John was for me nothing less than one of the few friends a man makes in a lifetime. Joyce Carol Oates spoke to me of his turning on people, not in malice but in that tone of voice you use when you have seen or thought something sad and inescapable, something you wish you didn't feel or know welling up inside. I've said that John had narrow interests. He hated sports. My son was playing a last Little League game on the day before we moved from Pennsylvania. It was raining and the game was played nearly 25 miles from John's house. Yet suddenly beside me in the stands there he was. We'd said our goodbyes, we'd made our promises to write letters, to meet from time to time. But he'd ridden his Harley in that rain, left his writing, to sit with me and say almost nothing. We'd become that kind of friends. We didn't have much to say and we didn't have much need to talk. Before the game ended, I saw him growing restless. I said it was almost over and he might as well go home. I didn't really want him to but I knew he had to go. We stood and embraced. John always hugged me. This was the last hug, though. I talked to him on the telephone once when he called to say he had heard about a job I might want. After that I never saw or heard from him again. As far as I am able to tell, John Gardner was one of those gifted, difficult, wonderfully special people who are so alive they change everyone around them. I admired him, respected him, argued with him, disappointed him, defended him, and most of all I loved him. I didn't go to his funeral because I couldn't bear the proof of his absence. Probably I ought to have spent these words on the words, the books he made, but I couldn't bear to do that either. When I look at them I hear John saying, through a cloud of pipe smoke, "I hear you've been writing a novel." And then there's just a long silence.

From GUY DAVENPORT

Thirty years ago John Gardner was one of a group of students and faculty at Washington University in St. Louis who met on Friday afternoons in my and Leonard Peters's office to explicate Pound's *Cantos*. After which we all had dinner together, and those of us who also constituted The Corelli Society went back to the office to play very simple pieces of Baroque music in a very amateurish way on recorders and guitars. I don't remember John at these latter sessions. Fine ear that he had, and great lover of music that he was, I rather think he discreetly stayed away. But in the Pound explications he was one of our most rigorous annotators.

The day John was killed on his awful, big motorcycle, I was coming out of the anesthesia from a minor operation when Bonnie Jean told me that she'd heard on the radio he was dead. There was an extra measure of grief in the news for me, because I'd seen him recently and did not like the last memory I was to have of him alive. He was at the University of Kentucky debating William Gass in the amorphous and quicksilvery matter of Moral Fiction. Both debaters managed to be raucous and silly, and I said to John afterwards that he must give up this road show. "I know," he said with a pained smile.

It was outrageous of me to say such a thing. I said it before I thought, and I hope he saw how spontaneously I had spoken. But that was not our last exchange. More recently he'd called for one of his long phone conversations. The reason he'd called was to report with glee that he had got the name of the road past his country house legally changed to Samuel Taylor Coleridge Road. This (and all the rest of his characteristically eclectic conversation that evening) is a far better last memory than my admonishing him for wasting his time on the lecture circuit, where his exuberance got away from him all too often and he sounded cranky, querulous, and a bit dotty. He could never disguise how sweet a person he was, whose generosity made him singularly unfit for scoring points in a formal debate.

John Gardner is a phenomenon in American writing. His range of subjects, his inventiveness, his energy were astounding, and we had all begun to take them for granted. Scholar, poet, novelist, critic, folklorist, musician, teacher—Lord knows what else. He once explained solemnly to me that he was not any of these things: he was, he insisted, a philosopher. All artists are philosophers. The duty of the artist is to make people live better lives. It was as simple as that. One could stay at the typewriter quite a long time pursuing this idea through John's work, uncovering surprise after surprise. How, for instance, do his operas with Joseph Baber, the atonal *Frankenstein* and the Rossini-like *Rumpelstiltskin*, change our lives? There are athletic workouts for our moral sense in *Grendel* and *The Sunlight Dialogues*. What philosophy underlies this prodigy of tale-telling, of robust scholarship? I don't know. All I can see is a wind of energy, most musical and refreshing, that blew now this way, now that.

There was much of the traditional American writer in John. He reminded me most of Hawthorne in his love of myth and folktale, and in his ability to bring the deep past forward into our time. He did this with great skill as a storyteller, master of narrative that he was, and with a sense of awe. His root idea of literature was that of communal discourse, of moral example, of understanding that knit people together rather than tore them apart in discord.

As his life comes to be known, we will have occasion to be surprised by the extent of his generosity, the helping hand he proffered to fellow writers, to artists and composers. His humility was saintly, his energy boundless. I had seen him face death and walk away triumphant over cancer. I had followed his successes with delight. His death was all the more terrible in that it came when he was at the height of his creative powers, when he had the sense of having begun again after a time of trouble and renovation. It was like hearing, if we were all back in the times John loved and could summon with such authority, that Beowulf had fallen from a stumbling horse and broken his neck. There were dragons he had yet to fight. There was, decidedly, more of his song yet to be heard.

From LARRY WOIWODE

It would be difficult to estimate the number of people that John Gardner pulled up out of a low place, as it were, and back on their feet during his lifetime as teacher, editor, critic, essayist, advocate, poet, children's writer, short-story writer, and, of course, novelist. He was a troubadour moving at the outlying lines of American writing. There was a look of a medieval artisan or page or jongleur about him and he had the medieval era, and a good many other eras, too, under his belt. He was one of the best-read of contemporary writers and spoke out of the distance of his historical perspective. He didn't follow the contours of established opinion, and never fell under the thrall of modishness.

That outlying line where he moved and made himself an available target seems destined to become, as he has predicted, the new wave in American fiction, or the returning one, since it represents fiction of the sort that continues to last: fiction which presses its narrative forward with the rhythms of storytelling, which is rooted in human relationships, and which derives its power from the seriousness (not solemnness) of its concern for the moral values that over the centuries have come to represent the "truth"—this truth being the only enduring standard by which we can live and measure our lives or our affirmations of life itself. He was a practitioner of such fiction and an ardent spokesman and advocate for it. There is a concerned, corporeal warmth and a bulking, breathing aura behind all of his prose; more than any contemporary writer, perhaps, he conveyed in his writing a tactile *presence*. This very presence made his sudden death hit with even more impact. The extent of that impact is just beginning to be felt among those who care about the condition of contemporary writing. And one thinks, in the backwash, less of the loss of promise, which one feels, than of the breadth and scope and variety of John Gardner's living accomplishment.

From *JOHN JAKES*

Millions admired John Gardner's talent; I am among them. But I admired two other qualities just as much or more—because they are generally even rarer than talent.

John took his work seriously, but not himself. This is in contrast to many other writers I've met who, if invited to a party in a grand ballroom and asked to bring their egos, as well as themselves, could scarcely squeeze both into the available space. Certainly there would be no room for so much as one other guest.

John was not that kind. When we first met—and two writers of more dissimilar background, bent, and ability you could not find—we sparred for a few minutes, before a book-and-author dinner at a

Pittsburgh department store, he in his bike leathers and long silver hair, me in my banker's pinstripe three-piece and crew cut (some friends call it my "FBI period"); we were getting the measure of one another, and we soon fell to talking like colleagues who had known, understood, and liked one another for years. We got rousingly tanked later that night in the bar of the local Hilton, which is where I discovered that John had concerns as ordinary as mine: flight schedules next day; advances paid; agents (if any) who could be trusted. It was friendly and unpretentious and grand—unlike a couple of weeks I spent on a cruise ship, imprisoned in a small universe with a writer of smaller talent who perpetually referred to himself in the royal we. John's nature proved the old adage that—many times, anyway—the bigger they are, the nicer they are.

Second—and crucial—he shared his humanity and his immense talent through the teaching to which he was dedicated. There may be other benchmarks of a great writer—which I believe John was—but I know of few more reliable benchmarks of a great human being.

From *LIZ ROSENBERG*

He was the brightest, the swiftest, the sweetest and the wisest soul I ever knew.

From *BERNARD ROSENTHAL*

John Gardner gave his students the gift of his commitment to them. He earned their affection and respect, and they will honor him through the years by the prose and the poetry they give to others.

From *W. V. SPANOS*

John Gardner lived and wrote in the rift between life and death. I know he wouldn't have liked my putting it that way, because the word "rift" is a crucial term in Heidegger's philosophical rhetoric—and he didn't like it. For Heidegger, in his mind, was an obscurantist. I can still hear him saying to me—patiently, generously, but with no less exasperation, as he did so often, whenever I tried to suggest that his books were explosions triggered by his living collision with death—"Bill, Bill, Bill, you're a wonderful philosopher, but you don't know a god-damned thing about literature." John never converted me away from Heidegger—nor did he cure me of my language. Nor, finally, despite his messianic efforts, did he really want to. Because, in the end, it would have meant closing the rift. And John knew, whatever he thought about such language, that the abysmal space between living and dying was where the dreadful mystery—all the crazy, and rich, possibilities of earth and heaven—resides.

John's critics pontificated relentlessly that his writing was too old-fashioned, too simplified, too constrained by worn-out moral and literary values. On the contrary, he was always in the midst, always *there—Da-sein*—in the ineffable realm of the wonderful, a word he often invoked to exclaim about things of this earth—the accidents of our occasion—that for most of us, because we refuse to risk them, go on being ordinary, familiar, and safe. It was the nameless monsters who exist in the awful rift he passionately—exorbitantly—loved, and, so, interrogated, both in his life and his writing, with a courage and generous ferocity that few other writers in our time have been capable of: " 'Poor Grendel's had an accident,' I whispered. *'So may you all.'* "

I had just finished reading an essay on *Moby-Dick* before some students and teachers of the Comparative Literature Department and was engaged in an intense and exhilarating defense of my admiration of Melville's errant art when Berny Rosenthal interrupted and took me aside to break the news of John's fatal accident. Later in the evening, after the initial shock, the grief, the outrage at the monstrous absurdity of John's untimely death had subsided, I broke into the calendar book I keep to record the routine of my academic life.

> John Gardner is dead
> He had a rage to die.
> He lived on this dreadful earth
> As if each day was always already
> the last day
> He lived in a way
> that few of us dare to.

In the last two years or so, I was privileged to become John's friend. During this too-short time, we talked a lot about philosophers, writers, their thought, their books—or, more accurately, we brawled over them, since it was usually deep into the night, after having drunk too much, when these conversations occurred. We disagreed violently on virtually everything. But way down—in the rift, where alone such things can happen—we met and, I think, learned to love each other. I have thought much about how this wonderful meeting could have

happened between two such different minds. I'm still baffled by the mystery. What I do know is that it had something to do with what I can only call his rage to die. My hopelessly academic rhetoric—"*It's stupid!*" he would cry—can't say it. But maybe the language of a writer who made the same astonishingly wonderful mistakes he did *can*, a writer, come to think of it, who was a monstrous exception to the mutually exclusive canons we thought we adhered to—

> Know ye, now, Bulkington? Glimpses do ye seem to see of that mortally intolerable truth; that all deep, earnest thinking is but the intrepid effort of the soul to keep the open independence of her sea; while the wildest winds of heaven and earth conspire to cast her on the treacherous, slavish shore?
> But as in landlessness alone resides the highest truth, shoreless, indefinite as God—so, better is it to perish in that howling infinite, than be ingloriously dashed upon the lee, even if that were safety! For worm-like, then, oh! who would craven crawl to land! Terrors of the terrible! is all this agony so vain? Take heart, take heart, O Bulkington! Bear thee grimly, demigod! Up from the spray of thy ocean-perishing—straight up, leaps thy apotheosis!

(Written for the memorial service sponsored by the English Department, State University of New York at Binghamton.)

From DAVID COWART

John Gardner led what may prove the crucial counterattack on the hand-wringing negativism of his age. His philosophy can be compared to that of T. E. Lawrence contemplating a hopeless military situation: "There could be no honor in a sure success, but much might be wrested from a sure defeat." If Lawrence's Turks be taken as a metaphor for the general existential situation, then the observation suggests the terms of Gardner's heroic refusal to despair. While most of his contemporaries struck postures of modish pessimism about the prospects for an embattled humanity, Gardner insisted that the twentieth century might yet prove an age of promise if only artists would do their job—which he construed not as documenting bleak existential truths but as reimagining reality so persuasively as to effect a reordering of that reality.

Before his death at the age of forty-nine (like

Lawrence he perished in a motorcycle accident), Gardner produced an impressive body of imaginative and critical work; in both quantity and quality his novels, stories, plays, poems, and criticism would suffice to establish the reputations of two or three lesser writers. He joked about his prodigious output when he saw it catalogued in John Howell's book-length bibliography: "I feel pleasure and then alarm, rolling my eyes toward the ceiling, asking God, '*Is it enough?*'" In a sentence like this one—its characteristically tardy participials masquerading as offhandedness, disguising control—one hears the voice that, through remarkable feats of ventriloquism, became in turn the voices of Agathon, of Jonathan Upchurch, of Professor Winesap. Grendel, too, eyes heaven and speaks in tardy participials: "'Waaah!' I cry, with another quick, nasty glance at the sky, mournfully observing the way it is, bitterly remembering the way it was . . . ."

Grendel, archetypal brother-murderer, must have haunted Gardner, who never quite forgave himself for his own brother's death under the wheels of a tractor he was driving. But the author exorcised more than a personal guilt in *Grendel*: he made the monster a brilliant parody of the contemporary, nay-saying literary artist that he attacked frontally in *On Moral Fiction*. Though he allows Grendel to parade the Eternal No with wit, charm, and genius, Gardner continually undercuts him, continually hints at the inadequacy of the monster's world picture and artistic credo. Gardner's real spokesman in the book is the Shaper, an artist capable of transforming an aimless, inchoate moment in human history into an age of purpose and promise.

Like the Shaper, Gardner knew that "real art creates myths a society can live instead of die by. . . ." He pointed out that much of the century's art has been jejune, self-indulgent, and nihilistic. It has embraced a kind of negative didacticism aptly summed up in Beckett's weary assessment of the span from womb to tomb: "They give birth astride a grave, the light gleams an instant, then it's night once more." But Gardner, though he understood perfectly well the grim metaphysics of the human condition, never stopped insisting that the modern temper could be altered positively by enlightened artists. The heroes of Gardner's fiction, then, are *real* heroes, figures of daring who face the impossible challenge and prove—as T. E. Lawrence did—that one can prevail against overwhelming odds. His exemplars include Beowulf and the Shaper in *Grendel*, Chief Clumly in *The Sunlight Dialogues*, the title characters in "John Napper Sailing Through the Universe" and "The Temptation

of St. Ivo," and Lars-Goren Bergquist in *Freddy's Book*. These characters triumph over the darkness in a variety of forms. So did Gardner.

From BARRY TARGAN

For whatever other of his many accomplishments John might be remembered, it is his commitment to teaching that his colleagues and students will keep in mind longest because that is where he bore most directly upon us: not simply what he knew and communicated, but the model he provided, the *idea* that he vivified. This is the monument, this memory, that I think he would most have cherished.

From JOHN VERNON

As a novelist, John Gardner was the poet of upstate New York. He seemed to have grown out of this landscape, out of its small backwoods half abandoned towns, out of its rocks and hills. Physically, he resembled a tree stump, but he had more energy than people three times his size. He could dress like a farmer or an aristocrat, depending on his mood (he called himself half bohemian, half upstate Republican). He was one of those people for whom sleep is a distraction, someone who apparently knew in advance he was living on borrowed time. I've seen him fall asleep at poetry readings and wake up refreshed and grinning, applauding warmly, ready for another twenty-four hours. He taught, lived, and wrote like someone possessed, driven—to teach, live, and write. He was also one of our finest novelists. A generous, tactful, awkward, good, brilliant, demonic man. A private man who needed to be surrounded by people. A manic talker. Like Merton Bliss in *The Sunlight Dialogues*, the last of the New York State liars, and like all liars, a person obsessed with the truth.

From JOANNA HIGGINS

John understood—perhaps more than we ourselves did—our crazy desire to write. We would come to him—some of us pulling up stakes and traveling cross country to do so, line up outside his office, clutching our manuscripts, our hands damp, maybe, our faces flushed, and then his door would open and there he'd be, saying yes, he would read our stories, yes he had the time, *Come in!* He made time not only for his own students, of whom there were quite a few each semester, but also for writers from the community and the region: people with other jobs, people without jobs, people a day's drive away. He never seemed out of sorts when, later, we grew bold and pestered him for more and more of his time. His patience with us, his incredible energy and stamina became legendary, a model. He had a craftsman's faith (and mulish singlemindedness) that a piece of writing would come right in the end—if we revised enough (but not too much), if we lavished enough time on it. He taught us technique, but above all he taught us the art of revision: seeing again, seeing further, seeing more. After talking over a manuscript with him, we'd return to our desks lighthearted and fortified, for it was all so amazingly clear: cut out that pushy rhetoric, fix the motivation, develop that scene, sharpen this image, make the flaccid taut. We may have suspected that somehow, somewhere (he'd spot it!) we'd screw up again, but so what? There'd be another draft and another and another—who could know how many?—until at last we'd *do it*. And sometimes we did. Because he had faith in the process of writing—that long journey—and faith in us, we learned to have faith in ourselves. Only the greatest teachers are able to impart *that*.

From CHARLES JOHNSON

Novelist John Gardner was, I am convinced, the Muhammad Ali of American literature—a noisy, bellicose writer, yes, and one seldom guilty of false humility, but also a genuine heavyweight when it came to literary invention and moral vision: the man, we must admit, who made contemporary fiction interesting again for people who care about the positive relationship between literature and life. No writer, to my knowledge, has worked harder for excellence—thirty years, writing for seventy-two hours at a stretch—and certainly no contemporary novelist has given more of himself in the service of fiction and his fellow craftsmen. To be sure, *On Moral Fiction* has faults, as Gardner knew, but it is a courageous essay that stands alone, in my opinion, among modern literary manifestoes in its argument for artistic responsibility, love, and a concern for the welfare of those who follow us as essential ingredients in any fictional interpretation of the world. Always he argued the primacy of "character," the fair treatment of people and their feelings, as the basis of great literature and, I should add, the foundation of morality. It is not an argument but rather

an ancient faith in man that Gardner gave us, and no philosopher, however cynical he may be, can deny the nobility of this vision.

Nor can anyone deny Gardner's contributions, as an innovative craftsman, to fiction. His place as a "philosophical novelist" is, I believe, important (though he never saw himself as an original philosopher), but more important is the literary strategy that fused theory and technique in his many tales and novels: namely, Gardner's appropriation of such classical forms as the architechtonic novel (*Sunlight Dialogues*), pastoral (*Nickel Mountain*), and the epic (*Jason and Medeia*) because these ancient vehicles are so rich, by virtue of their having been in circulation for centuries, that they possess the authority and objectivity (or intersubjectivity) lacking in the "interior," subjective fiction that Gardner so disliked. Often, he called this "genre-crossing," as in his finest invention, the novel-within-the-novel in *October Light*, and what it demanded of him was a deep understanding of fictional genres, their genesis and structure, and the philosophy of form. Form as meaning. Classical forms as vehicles infused with dignity, an affirmative worldview, and a timeless sense of value. His novels and stories, then, are gifts that offered us the achievements of the past—artistic and metaphysical—as models for the future. We shall never see the like of this man, this sort of global talent, this sort of generosity in an artist, in our lifetimes again.

From RON HANSEN

John Gardner was a gifted, loving, very intelligent man who delighted in everything that was positive, hopeful, aspiring, and deep. He was, to all who knew him, an encouraging teacher, generous colleague, and genuine friend who helped and provoked us with his thought, pleased and profoundly moved us with the genius of his art, inspired us by his example and his extraordinary humanity.

From PAULETTE HACKMAN

In 1981, when John Gardner, with his wife and coeditor L. M. Rosenberg, reestablished *MSS*, a literary magazine that published the first short stories by Joyce Carol Oates, William Gass, and John Hawkes while he was its founder and editor in the early 1960s, a press release was sent out over the wire services. Picked up by newspapers all over the country, the small news item announced that John

Gardner intended to publish the work of unknown writers, that his magazine was dedicated to providing an outlet for writers who could not—or would not—write for the commercial market.

The response was immediate and predictable. Manuscripts poured in from hamlets in rural Kentucky, Maine, and New Mexico, from apartments in the middle of vast urban areas, from English departments in small colleges and large universities, from overseas embassies and military bases, from Japan, Italy, and Australia. Often, the news item that had prompted the submission accompanied the manuscript, as if the writer feared seeming presumptuous.

In the spring of 1982, three of us screened fiction. Our job was to ferret out the best work for John. When a story distinguished itself, I scribbled a "To John" on the envelope, and, after collecting about a half-dozen manuscripts at a time, delivered them to his office down the hall. If he was there, working with a student, he would pause for a moment and thumb through the pile for familiar names. Usually there weren't any. "Good, good," he'd say approvingly and thank me for the work.

Having studied with John—each of us hard at work on our own fiction—we were well acquainted with his standards. We knew what bothered him and what bored him. But, since his tastes were broad, what pleased him was sometimes a surprise. If pinned down, he would say, "Bring me something that will delight me."

Out of the manuscripts we passed on, we might later see a familiar name and title come back from the typesetter as a galley for the next issue. We knew that John must have found a problem with the other stories and that he had returned the manuscripts to the authors. We each worked independently, covering our designated responsibilities; no one had time to spare for structured editorial meetings.

The spring had been a fertile time. I had sent John more than a dozen stories to read. So had the other assistant editors. The academic year ended. John was once again working out of his home, writing fiction and participating in a local theater group, or on the road giving lectures and readings, the money from which underwrote some of the magazine's expenses. Two of us continued to pick up the mail at the office and bring manuscripts home to read.

In July, John and I met at a diner near his home in Pennsylvania for the purpose of discussing a trip I was taking to promote the magazine. During a quick lunch break, our business taken care of, I decided to use the opportunity to find out if my literary judgment was measuring up to his standards. I was curious about the fate of a couple of writers whose work I had taken a special interest in.

I sprung the question abruptly. I asked if he had had the chance to read any of the stories I had given him back in May. I inquired about one author in particular whom I had encouraged to send more work—work that John now had.

"What story was that?" he asked, gathering up the pieces of his sandwich.

I couldn't remember the title. I had only a hazy recollection of the plot and the setting. I regretted my question; I had acted on impulse. Not only was my information incomplete, but now it seemed that my behavior had been rude. I had put him on the spot and perhaps it seemed like I was accusing him of negligence.

Before I could find a diplomatic way to change the subject, he said, "Oh, I know the one you mean."

He offered a quick summary of the plot to establish the story I was asking about.

It was coming back to me.

He took another bite of his sandwich. He looked distracted. "The trouble with Nina . . ." he said. Then he proceeded to explain the weakness of a character, a secondary character but one whom the writer had placed in a pivotal role for the conflict in the story. He talked on about Nina, as if he knew her and the writer had not quite captured her complexity, as if she deserved better treatment and the writer had been too lazy.

The story that I thought he had neglected or forgotten came alive while he spoke. He interrupted himself then, as he often did when he became passionately involved in the logic of a certain story, and said, "But, I'm going to write all of this in a letter to her."

The author of that story was someone whom John had never met and never would. She was one of those unknown writers whom he, in fact, did not know—but whose efforts he felt obligated to respond to and encourage.

from HEATHER MCHUGH

I knew him best as teacher and talker (in which capacities he was tirelessly available and characteristically dogmatic). He was no doxophobe: he had and held opinions. His generosity lay in his eagerness to share them.

John Irving
(2 March 1942-   )

Hugh M. Ruppersburg
University of Georgia

See also the Irving entry in *DLB 6, American Novelists Since World War II*, Second Series.

NEW BOOK: *The Hotel New Hampshire* (New York: Dutton, 1981; London: Cape, 1981).

Expectations for John Irving's fifth novel, *The Hotel New Hampshire*, ran extremely high. *The World According to Garp* (1978) has been enormously popular, especially in the Pocket Books paperback edition, and has made Irving a celebrity, a status he has never wanted or sought. The production of a movie based on *The World According to Garp*, along with press reports about Irving's work on the fifth

book and plans for a sixth, encouraged anticipation surrounding the new novel's appearance. Although not scheduled for official release until the end of September 1981, *The Hotel New Hampshire* appeared in major bookstores several weeks earlier and began selling briskly. By the end of the year it had sold 372,000 hardback copies and was the second best-selling book for 1981. In fact, by the end of 1981 it had surpassed its predecessor in hardback sales by nearly 300,000 copies. In November 1982 the Pocket Books edition remained at the top of the paperback best-seller lists.

The reasons for the immediate financial success of Irving's fifth novel may also explain its mixed

John Irving

critical reception. *The World According to Garp* made Irving a literary lion whom many reviewers were ready, even eager, to slay. In particular they wanted to discover whether *The Hotel New Hampshire* could measure up artistically to its predecessor, whether the remarkable narrative of T. S. Garp's life had been a fluke. Sooner or later practically every review got around to comparing the two books, usually to the new one's disadvantage. The *New Yorker* reviewer opined: "there seem to be fewer clever stories and charming sentences this time, and more arbitrary disasters, and more time for the reader to wonder whether punny names and furry animals ever (except in tall tales) make unbearable sorrow bearable." The *New York Times Book Review* adjudged the novel obsessed with cruel violence and marred by bad writing. Benjamin DeMott concluded his relatively favorable notice in the *Saturday Review* by objecting to the "preoccupation with rape," to "a certain frailty in the book's emotional life. . . . Grief at the loss of a parent or child disappears from the page almost before its weight can be imagined," and to intellectual shallowness: "for me, [Irving's] frequent allusion to F. Scott Fitzgerald only underlines the fact that the example of the writer's moral penetration has been missed. Irving's work brings to mind lesser heroes—J. D. Salinger, Kurt Vonnegut, the Beatles."

Of course, judging a book by comparing it to others that its author has written is at best a questionable practice. All Irving's novels resemble one another generally in theme, setting, and character. In narrative method, however, they differ considerably. It would be difficult to find two books more distinctly different in structure than Irving's *The Water-Method Man* and *The 158-Pound Marriage*. To expect *The Hotel New Hampshire* to satisfy the same criteria which *The World According to Garp* satisfied for so many readers is to demand that it be nothing more than a sequel. Although it is more closely related to its immediate predecessor than to any of Irving's other books, we still must recognize *The Hotel New Hampshire* as a work with its own artistic integrity, whatever its weaknesses.

The Hotel New Hampshire chronicles the lives and deaths of the Winslow Berry family over a span of more than forty years. The father is Win Berry, an English teacher at a second-rate preparatory school in New Hampshire. His wife, Mary, is remarkable for her indulgence of her husband's starry-eyed schemes and her children's eccentricities. Their oldest child is Frank, who as an adolescent is a morose and self-centered homosexual abused by friends and siblings alike. Next comes Franny, a brusquely spoken young woman who is gang-raped by prep-school football players, has an affair with a woman dressed in a bear costume, and finally becomes a famous actress. Younger than she is John Berry, the narrator and least unusual family member (he justifies his telling of the story by explaining that "it's up to me—the middle child, and the least opinionated—to set the record straight, or nearly straight"). His younger sister, Lilly, abhors violence and writes a best-selling autobiography. Egg, the youngest, loves to dress up in costumes. Iowa Bob, Win's father, coaches Dairy School's perennially losing football team.

The variety of characters extends beyond the Berry family: there is Freud, for instance, an Austrian Jew who sells a dancing bear to Win and twenty years later invites Win to help run his hotel in Vienna; or Junior Jones, a black football player whose sister was raped and who is thus attracted to Franny; or Screaming Annie, the prostitute whose orgasmic screams echo through the halls of the second Hotel New Hampshire; or the Austrian terrorist obsessed with *The Great Gatsby* and *Moby-Dick*.

The World According to Garp drew its power from an intricately woven plot and a variety of memorable characters. Wealth of human character is the central quality of *The Hotel New Hampshire*. Although a few dramatic conflicts do develop (in the plan of terrorists to blow up the Vienna Opera House, in John's incestuous attraction to Franny), *The Hotel New Hampshire* essentially lacks a formal plot. It focuses on no fundamental conflict or problem. Indeed, it does not even conclude in any real sense; it simply ends after the narrator describes the adult lives of the Berry children (a method more successfully applied in *The World According to Garp*). Instead, the novel centers on the shifting fortunes of the Berry family as they are affected by diversely capricious and usually violent influences.

In the first chapter, a kind of preface to the novel, John Berry recounts his parents' marriage and the early lives of their children. Win and Mary meet one idyllic summer while working at a resort hotel (the Arbuthnot-by-the-Sea). Win spends the first years of their marriage trooping around the country with the dancing bear (named "State O' Maine"), earning tuition for a Harvard education while Mary stays at home and raises their children. The rest of the book falls into three general sections, each relating one of Win's attempts to run a resort hotel—the dream which he resigns from Dairy School to pursue. He opens the first Hotel New Hampshire in an abandoned female seminary near

Dust jacket for Irving's fifth novel, which sold 372,000 copies in 1981

Dairy School. The second is located in the Gasthaus Freud, a run-down Viennese hotel owned by the old man who sold Win the dancing bear. Most of the narrative occurs in these two settings. The final two chapters bring the novel to a finish by relating the adult fates of the Berry children and describing the third Hotel New Hampshire, established in the same seaside resort where Win and Mary first met.

Many of the events in this chronicle are whimsically funny, and, in fact, a mood of fantasy pervades the novel. This mood can be at least partially attributed to the narrator John, who romanticizes his parents and seems incapable of thinking critically of his family. Yet fantasy and the unrealistic lie at the heart of this novel, which Benjamin DeMott has compared to a fairy tale, "the only literary form that has ever satisfactorily tamed the horrible." Nightmarish and terrible violence fills the book, yet a no-less-evident humor usually accompanies it. Various family members suffer grim fates: Iowa Bob dies of fright when he discovers the family dog, dead and stuffed, in John's closet; Mary and Egg perish in a plane crash; a terrorist's bomb blinds Win; Franny is gang-raped; Lilly stops growing by the age of twelve and later kills herself. Yet the

Berrys endure and move beyond these catastrophes, content to remember the past but not to dwell in it. Moreover, John's description of these events never makes them quite as horrible as we might expect. John views these calamities as little worse than unfortunate episodes from past history, though they have a clearly painful impact on others in his family. The effects of rape plague Franny for years, while violence so traumatizes Lilly that, John implies, she stops growing in protest. Though his characteristic lack of realism might account for his anesthetized attitude toward violence, his refusal to distinguish tragedy from comedy seems fundamental to the book's view of modern life. "Everything is a fairy tale," he suggests, an opinion he shares with Lilly and which shapes his entire narration.

Like Frank and Franny, John survives. But the various disasters which befall the Berry clan make it difficult not to see in this book a grimly pessimistic vision of modern life: the Berrys are innocents. Win, John, Lilly, and Egg are naifs. They do not knowingly hurt other people and usually have the best of intentions. They hardly deserve what happens to them. Like *The World According to Garp, The*

Hotel New Hampshire depicts modern life as punctured by indifferent misfortune, capricious violence, pain, and inhumanity which afflict deserving and undeserving without distinction. John emphasizes the necessity of enduring life's misfortunes by repeating the two Berry family mottoes which embody the novel's theme: "Sorrow floats"—implying the inevitability of dire misfortune—and "You have to keep passing the open windows"—with which the family warns one another against despair and its ultimate consequence, suicide. The stoic optimism of the concluding chapters rests upon the survival of Frank, Franny, and John. They come through and continue to look to the future. Frank enjoys a successful career as a literary agent. Franny marries Junior Jones and prospers as an actress. John marries the woman who once dressed as a bear. When the novel ends they are awaiting the birth of Franny's child, whom they will raise—another generation of Berrys. Life continues, whether for good or bad. Love, family, and the company of friends provide happiness and the will to survive. Yet the optimism at the end of *The Hotel New Hampshire* seems more shallow, less certain, than in *The World According to Garp*, as if Irving himself feels unsure of life's value in the modern world.

The lively array of characters redeems *The Hotel New Hampshire* from several serious failings. Foremost among them is a fizzling momentum in the last hundred pages. Throughout the novel John foreshadows some climax concerning the Austrian terrorists as well as Franny's desire for revenge against Chipper Dove, one of the football players who raped her. The terrorists meet a rather spectacular end: one commits suicide, Win clubs another to death with a baseball bat, and a third is blown to bits in an explosion. Franny gets her revenge, however, in a cruel and embarrassingly silly "play" which she, John, and Susie concoct: they lure Chipper Dove to Franny's New York apartment and convince him he is about to be raped by a bear. Terrified, he wets his pants. They all laugh and let him go. Dove's rape of Franny was vicious and horrible, yet his crime does not seem to justify even the pretense of similar behavior from his victim and her friends. The marathon lovemaking session between John and Franny, which frees them of their desire for each other, likewise seems a gratuitous consummation of the feelings they have grappled with throughout the novel.

Finally, *The Hotel New Hampshire* tends to patronize certain social issues primarily related to the feminist movement. In both this novel and *The*

World According to Garp, Irving suggests the need for a rigid code of ethics governing behavior in a sexually liberated world. He accepts homosexuality, transsexuality, cohabitation without marriage, and premarital sex as natural aspects of life. Yet he rejects such by-products of the sexual revolution as wife-swapping, adultery, and sexual aggression in any form, all of which cause victimization, pain, and emotional anguish. Rape is the worst sexual crime of all, the ultimate act of violent dehumanization. In *The World According to Garp*, Ellen James symbolized the terrible effects of rape and sexual extremism. Franny Berry plays a similar role, though she suffers less and is a more fully developed character. Yet Irving's insistence on a moral and humane sexual liberation occasionally leads to certain weaknesses in his latest book. He awkwardly interrupts his narrative, for instance, with several digressions on the treatment of rape victims. He also strains so obviously to treat without bias Frank's homosexuality and Franny's lesbian affair that the novel occasionally adopts a patronizing tone. His portrayal of Junior Jones, in many ways the most memorable character in the novel, may suffer from a similar patronization. On the other hand, the violence which some reviewers have criticized as excessive seems an essential element of the novel's portrayal of modern life. Violence in Irving's fiction pales in comparison with the murder, rape, terrorism, inhumanity, and general peril of the "real" world. The Berrys may suffer inordinately more than the average American family, but for that very reason they provide a genuine symbol of the texture of contemporary life.

John Berry ends his chronicle with a poignant summation of the novel's concern with family, dreams and fantasy, violence, and modern life: "So we dream on. Thus we invent our lives. We give ourselves a sainted mother; we make our father a hero; and someone's older brother, and someone's older sister—they become our heroes, too. We invent what we love, and what we fear. . . . We dream on and on: the best hotel, the perfect family, the resort life. And our dreams escape us almost as vividly as we can imagine them." Despite its loss of momentum, its occasional excesses and indulgent patronizations, *The Hotel New Hampshire* justifies the lyricism of the final paragraph. Not a perfect book, it is still a good one, and it offers every promise that John Irving will remain an important force in American literature during the 1980s.

Interviews:

A. P. Sanoff, "Humans are a Violent Species—we

always have been," *US News and World Report*, 91 (26 October 1981): 70-71;

V. Monroe, "Talking With John Irving," *Redbook*, 158 (November 1981): 12ff.;

L. McCaffery, "Interview with John Irving," *Contemporary Literature*, 23 (Winter 1982): 1-18.

References:

R. Dahlin, "World of Film according to Irving—and a bit about New Hampshire as well," 220 (7 August 1981): 34-35ff.;

J. Epstein, "Why John Irving is So Popular," *Commentary*, 73 (June 1982): 59-63;

S. Haller, "John Irving's Bizarre World," *Saturday*

Review, 8 (September 1981): 30-32;

M. Priestley, "Structure in the Worlds of John Irving," *Critique*, 23, no. 1 (1981): 82-96;

R. Z. Sheppard, "Life into Art," *Time*, 118 (31 August 1981): 46-51;

J. M. Wall, "Passing the Open Window: John Irving's New Novel," *Christian Century*, 98 (7 October 1981): 986-988;

R. West, "John Irving's World After 'Garp,' " *New York*, 14 (17 August 1981): 29-32;

E. B. Wymard, "New Version of the Midas Touch: Daniel Martin and the World According to Garp," *Modern Fiction Studies*, 27 (Summer 1981): 284-286.

Jerzy Kosinski

(14 June 1933-)

Sally Johns
University of South Carolina

See also the Kosinski entry in *DLB 2, American Novelists Since World War II.*

NEW BOOKS: *Passion Play* (New York: St. Martin's, 1979; London: M. Joseph, 1980);

Pinball (New York: Bantam, 1982; London: M. Joseph, 1982).

By 1978 Jerzy Kosinski enjoyed a reasonably comfortable and secure reputation on the American literary scene. Although his most recent works had hardly been met with wide acclaim, they had not seriously eclipsed the impact of his first novel, *The Painted Bird* (1965), and *Steps* (1968), winner of the 1969 National Book Award. From 1968 to 1972 he had held faculty positions at Wesleyan, Princeton, and Yale universities. His two-year term as president of the American Center of P.E.N. (1973-1975) had solidly established him as a tireless defender of individual and artistic freedom against a variety of totalitarian forces. Coupled with these impressive credentials was an electric personality that—underscored by the bizarre and tragic events of his early life—made for a public figure of enormous appeal. Four years later, his reputation as a novelist had not increased (both *Passion Play*, 1979, and *Pinball*, 1982, were met with negative critical responses), but in other realms his star had soared.

The 1979 film *Being There*, which he had adapted from his 1971 novel, was both a critical and a popular success (winning for Peter Sellers an Academy Award nomination for his performance in the leading role, for Melvyn Douglas a best supporting actor award, and for Kosinski a British best screenplay award). Kosinski himself ventured into acting in the 1981 film *Reds*, and his performance as the Bolshevik Zinoviev startled film critics, who acclaimed his talent in this unexpected arena. Always a passionate antitotalitarian spokesman, he continued to work for the release of imprisoned writers and joined American labor leaders in making public statements in support of Polish Solidarity. Counting among his close friends diplomats and fashion designers, he was a favorite guest both at elegant dinner parties and on television talk shows: he had become a celebrity. Then, in the summer of 1982, he found himself at the center of the year's biggest literary brouhaha, the dust of which has not yet settled.

The uproar erupted with the publication of an article in the 22 June 1982 *Village Voice* by Geoffrey Stokes and Eliot Fremont-Smith. Playing on the title of Kosinski's first novel, they entitled the piece "Jerzy Kosinski's Tainted Words," and in it they provide support for two charges that challenge his "ethics and his very role as an author": first, that

Kosinski has not written his books alone, and, second, that he has had a concealed relationship with the CIA. There is little equivocation in their tone:

> For almost 10 years now, Jerzy Kosinski has been treating his art as though it were just another commodity, a widget to be assembled by anonymous hired hands.
>
> He evidently grew used to this mode of work during the late 1950s when, under the pen name of Joseph Novak, he published the first of two anti-Communist tracts in which the Central Intelligence Agency apparently played a clandestine role. It is perhaps this dirty little secret that explains the fast shuffle of autobiographical tales making up the Kosinski myth.

Stokes and Fremont-Smith's initial point of departure is a lengthy cover feature by Barbara Gelb in the 21 February 1982 *New York Times Magazine*. Upon publication, the laudatory "Being Jerzy Kosinski" may have raised a few staid eyebrows because of its cover photograph (Kosinski in polo garb, minus a shirt), its space devoted to some of his pranks (hiding under a desk to tickle the ankle of a diplomat, "hoping to be taken for a tarantula"), or its tone, which borders on the sentimental. However, paean though it be, the piece is mostly based on often-repeated anecdotes and information already familiar to those who know his works and their acknowledged autobiographical nature; it is a comprehensive and highly readable compilation, but little in it could be regarded as groundbreaking or controversial.

Beginning by citing discrepancies between incidents in the Gelb profile and other published accounts of the same episodes, Stokes and Fremont-Smith systematically build a case for Kosinski's lack of credibility: "The net effect is that almost *nothing* he says can be relied on; *everything* must be checked." By recounting information gathered from interviews with both Kosinski and his former hired assistants, they contend that the assistance he has received on his books goes beyond the level of editing into the realm of composition itself. Among their claims are that he "probably" wrote *The Painted Bird* in Polish (and gave no credit to the women he hired to translate it into English) and that *The Future Is Ours, Comrade: Conversations with the Russians* (1960) was "apparently" funded—and very likely edited as well—by the CIA. Their conclusion is to fault Kosinski most of all for his "wall of denials," his "lies"—or, as Fremont-Smith is quoted in a subsequent *Publishers Weekly* editorial, "The point is

that Kosinski has always insisted it was all him. Basically the story is that it isn't all him."

The controversy was refueled by a lengthy defense of Kosinski by John Corry, "A Case History: 17 Years of Ideological Attack on a Cultural Target," beginning on the first page of the Arts and Leisure section of the 7 November 1982 *New York Times*. In 6,000-plus words, Corry presents a highly detailed account of Communist Poland's response over the years to a writer who permanently left that country in 1957 to live in the United States. Corry reiterates Kosinski's accomplishments—emphasizing his highly praised efforts as president of the American Center of P.E.N.—and provides information that seems to refute certain details of the *Village Voice* story. But the bulk of the article is devoted to chronicling the history of Kosinski's denunciation by the Communist press in Eastern Europe. Corry enumerates charges of plagiarism (directed toward both *The Painted Bird* and *Being There*), contending that they have been in evidence for many years, but they have been recognizable—and thus dismissed—as pro-Communist propaganda. He is careful, however, not to dismiss past charges lightly; painstakingly he recounts the details of the charges and with equal exactitude refutes them. He is also careful to note that the Polish press, in 1966, was among "the first to suggest that hidden forces operated behind the publication of *The Painted Bird*." (One of the most interesting points he brings to light is that *The Painted Bird* has never been translated into Polish; thus the majority of its widespread denunciation in Poland cannot have been based on firsthand evaluation.) While Corry maintains that "the burden of the [*Village Voice*] article was to discredit Mr. Kosinski," his essay is not a direct refutation. However, by presenting Kosinski as a long-term ideological target, the article's cumulative effect is the suggestion that the *Village Voice* story was at least influenced by this history of propaganda and rumors.

Corry's *Times* defense of Kosinski sparked instant response—and the response was more to the length and detail of the defense than to its accuracy or effectiveness; few journalists even dealt with the question of whether or not Kosinski had been vindicated. Many writers expressed surprise and even embarrassment that a newspaper as powerful as the *New York Times* would devote so much space to one side of such a controversy—especially after having run a lengthy story on the same writer only nine months previously. There were accusations of patronage by those who noted that Arthur Gelb, deputy managing editor of the *Times*, his wife, Barbara

*Jerzy Kosinski was the subject of a literary and political feud fought in some of the nation's leading newspapers and magazines,
including the* New York Times *and* New York *magazine*

Gelb (author of the previous *Times* piece), and the newspaper's executive editor, A. M. Rosenthal, are all close friends of Kosinski. More than one journalist maintained that the story had been reassigned to Corry after the first writer had been unable to refute Stokes and Fremont-Smith's assertions. There was even the suggestion that the Kosinski controversy might be evidence of a brewing ideological battle in the American print media. Kosinski had criticized the American Writers Congress, sponsored by the *Nation*, expressing fear that (according to Corry) it was being "politically exploited." The *Nation* described the congress as "unabashedly and even exuberantly progressive"; the *New Republic* said it was "an entirely political undertaking. The principal characteristic of the participants was a virulent hatred of the country for which [it] was named." John F. Baker in a *Publishers Weekly* editorial, "Kosinski—And Beyond," suggested that "at a time when the *Times* seems to be growing increasingly conservative in tone," there is a danger to its readers if "the kinds of attitudes embodied in the Kosinski story were to become more firmly rooted."

Despite the literary row created by the attack and defense, the question of authorship at this point remains unresolved—and even overlooked—in the midst of the heat generated by the fact that the defense appeared in the *New York Times*. As Charles Kaiser points out in *Newsweek*, "Neither the *Voice* nor the *Times* provided conclusive evidence." The whole episode has, according to the Corry article, taken its toll on Kosinski. He finds himself in more than one double bind, and some of them are not without his own making. One area is his efforts as a proponent of ideological freedom. Even Stokes and Fremont-Smith find "his work for human rights . . . unassailable," but the damage is incontrovertible. Says Kosinski: "My anti-Communism now becomes nothing but payment for a supposed association with the CIA."

As Corry writes in his *Times* article, "Mr. Kosinski's predicament is not helped by the literary genre in which he writes, or by his apparent predilection for the demimondaine." Indeed, in light of the *Village Voice* accusations, some of Barbara Gelb's statements in her highly complimentary piece might even be read as damaging: "In [his novels], he is . . . a man with a highly idiosyncratic moral code." "The need to become someone he was not became a habit." "He is secretive about many things, and often he contradicts himself, possibly by design—another form of trick or test, to catch you

out, part of his social experimenting." His eccentricities and social experimenting—including "living every moment of his life in fear of the knock on the door"—seem to have backfired. After the appearance of the *Village Voice* story, Corry reports, *Les Nouvelles Littéraires* in Paris queried, "Why do you always carry arms? Why the dozens of false identities? Why the tear gas bombs in your car? Whom are you afraid of Jerzy Kosinski?" That he has real reason to fear (other than justifiable psychic scars left by his childhood during the Holocaust) is implausible, but the public persona he has fostered is more likely to advance the mystique and intrigue than to squelch rumors and discourage speculation.

In his "Uncivil Liberties" column in the 11 December 1982 *Nation*, Calvin Trillin facetiously proposes that Kosinski himself planted the idea that he does not write his own books. "Have you read the reviews of his last few books? . . . the black plague got a more respectful reception. . . . This way, Kosinski gets paid for the books and someone else gets blamed for writing them." Whether or not the *Village Voice* charges will be borne out remains to be seen, but Trillin's assessment of Kosinski's recent works' critical reception is accurate. Writers throughout history have survived charges as serious as plagiarism (and those against Kosinski fall short of this extreme), but the area of literary accomplishment is one in which he has suffered, and the decline took place before the question of authorship entered the picture.

Published in 1979, *Passion Play* focuses on Fabian, an "existential cowboy" who roves the country in a mobile VanHome in search of beautiful women and polo players. Critics found in it many of the elements that characterized his early critical successes, *The Painted Bird* and *Steps*, but without the artistry, thus reducing it, in the words of the London *Times Literary Supplement*'s Valentine Cunningham, to "a set of bloodied obsessions." The *New York Times Book Review* noted "some virtuoso writing about sex and horsemanship that is sometimes fun to read . . . but too often the tone is leaden and arbitrary." According to Cunningham's assessment, "Kosinski's dazzling flighted bursts of rhetoric can press on the dizzying limits of any thesaurus of violence or sex; they can also plummet into the awful metaphorical banalities of quite ordinary pornography." Despite unfavorable reviews of the novel, Gelb reports that Kosinski is working on a screenplay adaptation of *Passion Play*.

Pinball, published in early 1982 and reviewed before the appearance of the June *Village Voice* story, fared little better with the critics. Joining what has become almost a chorus of respondents to Kosinski's novels, Joshua Gilder in *Saturday Review* found the book "nothing more than a pornographic thriller." A once-famous composer now in decline (Domostroy) is hired by a beautiful and sexy young Julliard student (Andrea) to uncover the identity of Goddard, a fabulously successful rock star who has managed to produce record albums from what appears to be a vacuum: neither his fans nor even his recording company has one bit of information about who he is. The first half of the novel focuses on Domostroy and Andrea's scheme for forcing Goddard to reveal himself, and—after he has been identified to the reader midway through—the perspective alternates between the pursuers and the object of their search. Goddard is actually Jimmy Osten, a casual acquaintance of Domostroy, the son of a classical record executive to whom rock music is anathema. (Ironically, the son's earnings are secretly keeping the father's business afloat.) The novel dovetails toward a less than satisfactory resolution as the pair come closer and closer to unraveling the mystery of Goddard, and Osten comes closer and closer to discovering the identity of the woman he knows is pursuing him. Violence is

the result: Andrea (along with three other people) is killed. In the end, Domostroy assures Osten that he will not reveal Goddard's identity.

A major concern of Kosinski's is the relationships between the artist, his art, and his audience. In some ways, Osten/Goddard seems to have achieved the ideal state: his music is accepted on its own merits, without a public persona of the artist to either add to or detract from it. (In the case of Goddard, however, the very lack of the artist's identity *is* a public persona that heightens the impact of his works upon their audience.) Critics were not impressed with Kosinski's handling of the theme. Lester Bangs in *Village Voice* maintained that "Kosinski is muzzling around after some Big Statement on how celebrityhood destroys artists, but he never makes it . . . because the plot is ludicrous, the characters (especially the women) unbelievable cartoons, and the dialogue leaden and melodramatic. . . ." Echoing the notion that the theme is nonserious, *Saturday Review*'s Gilder also faults the novelist for "purple" prose and "adolescent" imagery. Adam Mars-Jones in the London *Times Literary Supplement* found *Pinball* "as flaky and mechanical as the game that gives it its title." *Time*'s Stefan Kanfer refused to be totally negative, maintaining

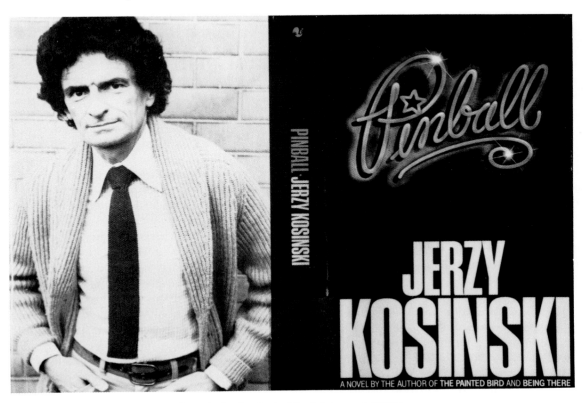

Dust jacket for Kosinski's eighth novel (1982)

that, despite its excesses, "*Pinball* has its payoffs." Yet he concluded that the novel is an inconsistent work "that, in the end, can only prompt admirers to respond: 'What a premise!' 'What talent!' 'What a waste!'"

In his review of *Pinball* in the *New York Times Book Review*, Benjamin DeMott most accurately pinpoints the reason for the decline of a writer whose second novel won the National Book Award a decade and a half ago but whose recent works have achieved less and less success:

> *The Painted Bird* and *Steps*, Mr. Kosinski's first two novels, were memorable partly because the grotesque, brilliantly lit scenes of fury and coupling in their pages seemed rooted in an objective time and place—a primitive world with laws of its own, grim, necessitous, somewhat independent of the author's sensitivity. But in his more recent work, blood-cruelty and beating have had the character of personal choice—items selected from the great bazaar of Possibility merely because his taste so directs.

Kosinski's work for humanitarian causes is a testament to his commitment to individual freedom. His early novels won him acclaim, and his successful forays into the medium of film—both as writer and actor—show promise. His almost phenomenal survival skills thus far would indicate that he will withstand ideological attacks. However, his recent fiction is, as DeMott says, "a descent into self-indulgent laxness."

References:

Paul Bruss, *Victims: Textual Strategies in Recent American Fiction* (Lewisburg: Bucknell University Press, 1981), pp. 167-227;

John Corry, "A Case History: 17 Years of Ideological Attack on a Cultural Target," *New York Times*, 7 November 1982, II: 1, 28-29;

Barbara Gelb, "Being Jerzy Kosinski," *New York Times Magazine*, 21 February 1982, pp. 42-58;

Charles Kaiser, "Friends at the Top of the Times," *Newsweek* (22 November 1982): 125-126;

Norman Lavers, *Jerzy Kosinski* (Boston: Twayne, 1982);

Geoffrey Stokes and Eliot Fremont-Smith, "Jerzy Kosinski's Tainted Words," *Village Voice*, 22 June 1982, pp. 1, 41, 42-43.

Archibald MacLeish
(7 May 1892-20 April 1982)

Ashley Brown
University of South Carolina

See also the MacLeish entries in *DLB 4, American Writers in Paris, 1920-1939* and *DLB 7, Twentieth-Century American Dramatists*.

NEW BOOK: *Letters of Archibald MacLeish, 1907 to 1982*, edited by R. H. Winnick (Boston: Houghton Mifflin, 1983).

When he died last year as he was approaching his ninetieth birthday, Archibald MacLeish was the dean of American poets. He had outlived his literary contemporaries—Hemingway and Dos Passos, Cummings and Tate, and the others—and he continued to write prose and poetry almost to the end. But one could not quite think of him during these last years as a grand old man of letters from another time; he was very intent on living in the present generation, and in conversation he easily struck up an acquaintanceship with persons sixty years younger than himself. Few men have grown old so gracefully.

Perhaps MacLeish's generous optimism was partly accounted for by the circumstances of his youth. He was born to wealthy parents in Glencoe, Illinois, near Chicago; they provided him with the best education at the Hotchkiss School, Yale, and Harvard Law School, where he stood at the head of his class. His talents were such that he could easily have had a distinguished career in the legal profession, and indeed he was a member of a firm in Boston for three years before he committed himself to the literary life of the 1920s. By this time, 1923, he had a wife and two children. He had been writing verse since his undergraduate days, but only at this point could he take it seriously, and now he approached it as he would any profession. From 1923 to 1928 he lived abroad, mostly in Paris, where he quickly became a part of the expatriate group that included Hemingway, Fitzgerald, Dos Passos, and the painter Gerald Murphy. He seems at this time to have been closer to the novelists than the poets in his generation.

His friendship with Murphy is rather instructive. Murphy, four years older, had also gone to Hotchkiss and Yale and was supported by his father's prosperity. Between 1922 and 1929 he produced a few paintings which are now considered among the most remarkable work done by Americans during that period. But Murphy and his wife were more devoted to the art of living well, and in the end he had to return to New York to head the family business that he once had shunned. He simply lacked the drive that MacLeish brought to the profession of poetry. Many years later, in 1964, it was MacLeish who gave one of Murphy's paintings to the Museum of Modern Art in order that Murphy, dying of cancer, might have the satisfaction of knowing that his work was represented there. In 1974 MacLeish wrote the foreword to the catalog of the Murphy exhibition at the museum and, with

Archibald MacLeish

characteristic modesty, omitted his part in this episode.

MacLeish was a prolific poet after his late start; between 1924 and 1928 he had published four books: *The Happy Marriage* (1924), *The Pot of Earth* (1925), *Streets in the Moon* (1926), and *The Hamlet of A. MacLeish* (1928). He also rapidly assimilated some of the characteristic poetic procedures of the 1920s, notably those of Eliot. *The Pot of Earth*, for instance, moves back through *The Waste Land* to Frazer's *The Golden Bough* for its mythical properties and its structure; its three sections, entitled "The Sowing of the Wild Corn," "The Shallow Grass," and "The Carrion Spring," indicate very clearly its source. Perhaps this would not matter so much, but at almost every turn of the poem MacLeish apprehends the subject by way of Eliot's rhythms:

> Come, I will conduct you
> By seven doors into a closed tomb.
> I will show you the mystery of mysteries.
> I will show you the body of the dead god
> bringing forth
> The corn. I will show you the reaped ear
> Sprouting.

One might say here that MacLeish lacked the dramatic sense that Eliot had even in short poems but which he showed to greatest advantage in *The Waste Land*, where the many voices are so keenly differentiated. In MacLeish's poem there is only one voice. This is also the case in his most ambitious poem of the period, "The Hamlet of A. MacLeish," which uses Shakespeare's *Hamlet* as a kind of scaffolding for a personal rumination of twenty-nine pages.

Ezra Pound was a more useful source. The classical sections of the early *Cantos* soon led to an elegiac mode of verse which was MacLeish's most characteristic, as in "American Letter" (1930), dedicated to Gerald Murphy:

> The tossing of
> Pines is the low sound. In the wind's running
> The wild carrots smell of the burning sun.
> Why should I think of the dolphins at Capo di
> Mele?
> Why should I see in my mind the taut sail
> And the hill over St. Tropez and your hand
> on the tiller?

The refinement of sensory impressions as they occur to a civilized mind: this is the basis for MacLeish's style at its best, and the style in turn is the expression of his refined humanism, which can be

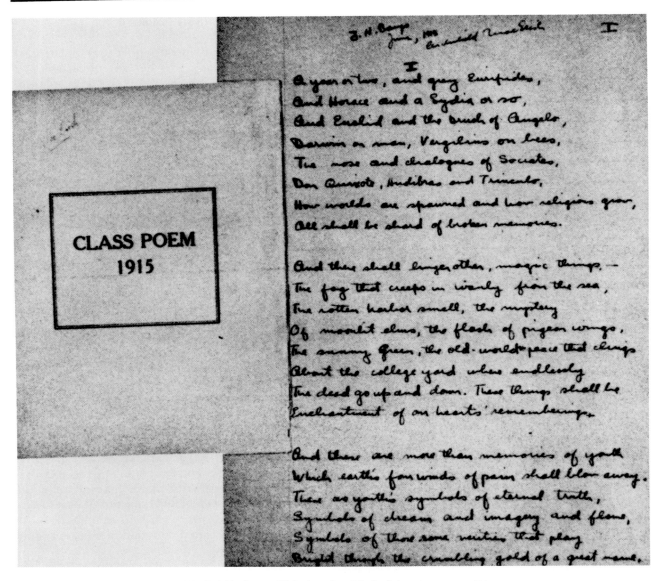

MacLeish's first published work, with the fair-copy manuscript

very attractive. This is evident in what, for many readers, is his finest poem, "You, Andrew Marvell" (1930). Very likely MacLeish's admiration for Marvell's "To His Coy Mistress" (1681) started with Eliot's famous essay, but no matter; he transmuted the idea of "deserts of vast eternity" into a metaphor which perfectly governs the poem; the circular movement of the poem approximates the rotation of the planet. Allen Tate soon imitated the form of "You, Andrew Marvell" in "The Traveller" (dedicated to MacLeish) and tried to give the subject a metaphysical dimension, but his poem is not as successful.

In 1928 the MacLeishes returned from France and bought a house near Conway, Massachusetts. This was to be home for the rest of his life. Back in the United States he was frequently engaged with public issues, just as he nearly always occupied a post that brought him into contact with influential persons. In 1929 his Yale classmate Henry R. Luce, the publisher of *Time*, put him on the editorial staff of his new business magazine, *Fortune*. This is where he spent the years of the Depression, ironically perhaps, since his political position was rather to the left of *Fortune*'s. Indeed one poem from this period, "Frescoes for Mr. Rockefeller's City" (1933), seems distinctly at odds with what *Fortune* and Luce represented.

The major work of the early 1930s is *Conquistador*, written between 1928 and 1931 and published in 1932 with great success; it was awarded the Pulitzer Prize. This small epic of the conquest of Mexico by the Spanish in the sixteenth century was based, as MacLeish says in an introductory note, "upon my own experience of the route and the country by foot and mule-back in the winter of 1929 and differs from that of the historians." The result was a poem in modified terza rima, told from the point of view of Bernal Diaz del Castillo, who wrote the actual historical account that is the main source for this event. Bernal Diaz is not a man of action so much as a civilized observer, who in a sense stands for the poet. *Conquistador* will probably remain MacLeish's best-known work; its perfection of style, essentially elegiac, seems right for the subject. Some would say that it is the style of the *Cantos* diluted for a large audience, but it succeeds in much the same way that the opening pages of *A Farewell to Arms* succeed.

MacLeish moved more directly into public life as the Depression decade drew to its close. As chairman of the League of American Writers, he headed an anti-Fascist organization whose main concern was the course of the civil war in Spain. (At this point he was associated with his old friends Hemingway and Dos Passos.) Likewise his verse took more social forms, as he experimented with work in radio, ballet, and drama. *Panic* (1935), *The Fall of the City* (1937), and *Air Raid* (1938) were verse plays that had a considerable popularity in their day, but their documentary interest has scarcely survived. In 1939 MacLeish received an honorary degree from Harvard (he was probably the first poet of his generation to be honored in this way), and President Roosevelt appointed him Librarian of Congress. As a high government official, he was now in a position to exercise a certain power, especially in the matter of literary culture, and here his actions were sometimes inconsistent.

MacLeish arrived in Washington as World War II broke out. Committed to the anti-Fascist cause, he now felt that the democracies of the West, including the United States, were desperately threatened by Hitler, and it was the duty of writers to rally the public against the enemy. His feelings on this matter were so intense that in the following year, 1940, he published a prose manifesto called *The Irresponsibles*, an indictment of his fellow writers and scholars who "freed themselves of the personal responsibility associated with personal choice. They

emerged free, pure, and single into the antiseptic air of objectivity. And by that sublimation of the mind they prepared the mind's disaster." Needless to say, the American literary community, including many of MacLeish's friends, resented this public attack on their private motives, and inevitably there were reactions. A distinguished critic, Morton Dauwen Zabel, published a quite damaging essay on MacLeish's fluctuating literary and political opinions ("The Poet on Capitol Hill") in the *Partisan Review* in 1941. And in 1943 Tate openly attacked MacLeish and Van Wyck Brooks in a brilliant verse satire, "Ode to Our Young Pro-Consuls of the Air." It was evident that as MacLeish's official and popular reputation grew, he was becoming suspect in the literary circles where he once had friends.

But at the same time MacLeish's real services to the republic of letters were quietly but effectively being carried out. After the collapse of France in 1940, he managed to secure a post at the Library of Congress for the great French poet St.-John Perse (Alexis Saint Léger Léger), whom he had known in Paris. It is not too much to say that he thus made possible the remarkable second part of Perse's career, which took place in the United States during and after the war. It was MacLeish who established the post of Consultant on Poetry in English at the Library—a position that was to be held by a poet for one year. Tate was the first to occupy it in 1943; he was followed by Robert Penn Warren; and by now at least twenty American poets of the first rank have moved in and out of Washington for a year's residence in a mainly honorary position. The poet at the Library has become our temporary laureate. MacLeish likewise used his influence on behalf of Pound, who was confined at St. Elizabeth's Hospital in 1945 following his indictment for treason. Pound was not released until 1958, during the Eisenhower administration, but MacLeish, with his thorough knowledge of the legal issues involved, had been dealing with government officials for years.

MacLeish's official career in Washington ended with the war; by this time, 1945, he was an Assistant Secretary of State, in which position he helped draft the constitution for the United Nations Educational, Scientific, and Cultural Organization (UNESCO). Then he was appointed Boylston Professor of Rhetoric at Harvard in 1949, where he stayed until 1962, teaching another generation of poets. He came back to another kind of literary prominence with his *Collected Poems 1917-1952*, which was awarded the Pulitzer Prize, the Bollingen Prize, and the National Book Award in 1953. His greatest success came with *J.B.*, a verse drama about a twentieth-century Job, which was produced in 1958 and had a surprisingly long run on Broadway. The merits of this play have been much debated, by theologians as well as literary critics, but in retrospect it seems part of an enterprise—the postwar revival of poetic drama—from which much was expected but of which little remains.

As he grew older, MacLeish tended to identify himself with the later Yeats; the title of one book, *"The Wild Old Wicked Man" and Other Poems* (1968) made that clear. He liked to quote Yeats's lines: "Whatever flames upon the night / Man's own resinous heart has fed." He admired Yeats's involvement with the world and ranked him with Perse and Pablo Neruda and George Seferis. These poets, all Nobel laureates, were statesmen as well, and they tended to think in large heroic terms. Most of them, one might add, came from relatively small countries of which they could be representative. Could any American poet be representative of so sprawling and complicated a nation? MacLeish would have liked to think so; the evidence of American literary history seems to be otherwise. But he maintained a dignified ideal of the poet at every stage, and one must respect it even if one finds it difficult to believe in.

A TRIBUTE ————————————
from DANIEL J. BOORSTIN

Archibald MacLeish was the poet laureate of democracy. He had an uncanny feeling for the main currents of our national life, a talent for reminding us of how they flowed out of our past, and a prophetic vision of where they could flow in our future. With a remarkable capacity for growth himself, he dared boldly to shift the focus and style of his poems from his first publications in the 1920s until his latest in the 1980s. Celebrating the adventurous spirit of the American past, he saw the menaces to democracy from without and within. Poet, playwright, essayist, he was a responsible and effective public servant—as Librarian of Congress, as Assistant Secretary of State in wartime, and as inspiring teacher. With a remarkable practical sense, as ninth Librarian of Congress, he undertook a reorganization of the Library to meet the challenges of World War II and the post-war world. His administration widened the services of the Library of the Congress, to scholars, and to the nation's libraries. He will speak the fears and hopes of the nation to future students of our history in a clear, unforgettable voice. He remains a paragon of the American man of letters. His warmth and vivid cheerful spirit will be missed by all of us who knew him.

A TRIBUTE ————————————
from JAMES DICKEY

Archibald MacLeish is one of the few American poets who ever had a *sound*, in the sense that a jazz musician or singer is said to have one. MacLeish's is sinewy, masculine, melancholy, strong and haunting; his verse has always made me think of the kind that Hemingway would have written, if he had been skilled in poetic technique. The same male melancholy and longing is here, the resigned strength, the defeated unforgettable melody. The best of MacLeish is undeniably his, in the only way that matters.

Kenneth Rexroth

(22 December 1905-6 June 1982)

Kenneth Rexroth died in his home in Montecito, California, on 6 June 1982. See also the Rexroth entry in *DLB 16, The Beats: Literary Bohemians in Postwar America.*

A TRIBUTE

from MORGAN GIBSON

Toward the end of World War II, when I discovered a couple of passages anthologized from Kenneth Rexroth's *The Homestead Called Damascus*, I was astonished by his vision of the creative process of the universe, extending from the molten core of the earth through eons of evolution revealed by the geological ladder of fossils, culminating in the union of lovers lying under the turning stars, and all passionately realized in lyric poetry. I had found nothing like this, no comparable comprehension of natural process, in Eliot, Yeats, Pound, Stevens, and other great modernists. Teachers in my high school, and later in college and graduate school, ignored Rexroth, but I eventually learned that he had been,

Kenneth Rexroth

at the time of my discovery, a conscientious objector working in a mental hospital—seriously injured by a violent patient—and a leader of the West Coast avant-garde: a libertarian revolutionary, an innovative abstract painter, a brilliant translator from a half dozen languages, an erudite critic, and a philosophical poet.

The work of Eliot, Joyce, and others had inspired me to be a writer; but I could not be their kind of writer—an impersonal creator concealed by personae. The personality of Rexroth, on the other hand, came through his poems directly: they clearly projected his voice, long before I heard him read his poems, and I felt that I was in his presence long before I met him. Every book of his intrigued me, revealing his adventurous life and fertile mind. His poetry made more sense of life, of my own experience and the condition of the world, than the work of his contemporaries—though I admired them for other reasons. He had somehow brought scientific thought, which most modern poets had shunned, into poetry that was intensely personal; and it was also morally prophetic in its denunciations of the injustices of modern life ("August 22, 1939," for example, one of his many poems written on anniversaries of the execution of the anarchists Sacco and Vanzetti). I also found many extraordinary poems of ecstatic love ("When We with Sappho" and "The Thin Edge of Your Pride," for example), and calm contemplative nature poems (such as "Towards an Organic Philosophy")—an amazing intellectual and emotional range. As we began corresponding in the late 1950s, and became friends for two decades, meeting frequently in California, the midwest, and later in Japan, I found him fiercely opinionated, but always a true friend and more often wise than wrong in an age of absurdity. He offered, in speech and writing, a liberating, enlightening world vision that seemed to me badly needed in the "century of horror," as he called it.

The center of Rexroth's stormy life was quiet contemplation. He seemed to have done everything, to have met everyone of importance, to have read all of the great books and many minor ones, to have fought the good fights (nonviolently)—but all of this creative activity seemed to circulate around a calm center of light. Oceanic, ecstatic illuminations of the oneness of all beings had brought him an early sense of mission as philosophical artist and poet. These mystical experiences permeate his work, from *Homestead* (1920-1925, but not published as a whole long poem until 1957, concerning two brothers' quest for salvation) through *The Love Poems of Marichiko* (1978, a sequence of Tantric ecstasy written in Japan, his last great work). He told about early visionary experiences in *An Autobiographical Novel* (1966)—a work comparable to Yeats's *Autobiographies* in revealing the growth of a poet's mind: a sense of heavenly peace came over him when his mother died, and again when he nearly became a monk in an Anglo-Catholic monastery in New York state. Such experiences defy description or explanation, but he never stopped philosophizing about them and their meaning, and in doing so he absorbed and interpreted major religious, philosophical, and literary traditions, Asian and Western, for our own age.

Like the Hebrew prophets he had an uncompromising commitment to justice and found in Martin Buber's I-Thou a key to interpersonal love. From Jesus and Christian saints and mystics he derived his understanding of the communion of beings and the universal community of love. He considered himself an Anglo-Catholic, but he was ecumenical enough to absorb Asian wisdom from Vedanta, Taoism, and Buddhism in its major forms—Theravada, Mahayana, and Tantra—channeled especially through his five visits to Japan from 1967 on, though Japanese and Chinese influences are apparent in his poetry from its beginnings. Like a man of the Renaissance, he brought to modern American poetry a sense of classical reason, centered on humanity; and his humanism accepted modern revolutionary thought from Marx more than from the Marxists (he thought that Leninists had betrayed Marx), and from anarchists and pacifists. Nor were these ideas only in his head, for he had been active in the Industrial Workers of the World, the John Reed Clubs, and the San Francisco Libertarian Circle, always advancing his communal personalism in opposition to the injustices of capitalism and totalitarianism of left and right. Revolutionary and conservative, worldly and spiritual, Asian and western ideas from traditions that may seem irreconcilable were uniquely harmonized in Rexroth's world view as expressed in his philosophical poetry and essays. His commitment to the liberation of the person in community with all beings offers a way out of the alienating technological crisis of the postmodern world, for his work revives the intrinsic values of living, loving, and being.

Rexroth insisted that poetry is fundamentally vision, and vision is not hallucination but loving

consciousness of persons in communion with all beings. He thought of poetry as a kind of living speech, person to person, a sacrament recreating community, rather than impersonal artifice. So his most characteristic mode of writing became direct address in normal syntax—a mode that he called "natural numbers" (the title of his collection of 1963) and employed in most of his translations (except for modern French poetry), most of his shorter poems, and in three long poems—*The Phoenix and the Tortoise* (1944, his Christian meditation on World War II and the collapse of civilizations), *The Dragon and the Unicorn* (1952, his anarchist travel poem centered on Cold War Europe), and *The Heart's Garden, The Garden's Heart* (1967, a poem of Zen realization in Japan). "Natural numbers" are written, for the most part, in carefully modulated syllabic prosody, in which great attention has been directed to enhancing the melodies and rhythms of speech. This mode evolved into the vigorous dramatic verse of *Beyond the Mountains*, the tetralogy about the collapse of classical Greek civilization, and our own, influenced by Japanese *Nōh*, premiered by the Living Theater, and published as a whole in 1951. He worked in other modes as well. Throughout his career he defended the revolution of the word, the creation of a new syntax of the mind, but most of his work in the cubist-objectivist mode was done before World War II: most notably, "Prolegomena to a Theodicy," the long poem culminating in a Dantean vision, written between 1925 and 1927 and published in Louis Zukofsky's *An "Objectivists" Anthology* in 1932, then reprinted with changes in *The Art of Worldly Wisdom* in 1949, with shorter cubist poems written mostly during the 1920s. Cubist poems written mostly during the 1930s comprise about half of *In What Hour* (his first book, published in 1940). As a youth in the early 1920s he had written *Homestead* in the symbolist mode, influenced by Eliot before he realized the reactionary nature of Eliot's poetry: he delayed publication of the whole poem until 1957 and never wrote in this mode again. Even in his symbolist and cubist poems there are many lines of "natural numbers," and this dominant style was exactly right for the many public readings that Rexroth gave all over the world, often with jazz accompaniment (some on commercial recordings), and later with Chinese and Japanese music. In fact, he and Kenneth Patchen pioneered in public performances of poetry long before most poets attempted them.

Rexroth published thirty-five books of poetry, of which thirteen are translations from Japanese and Chinese (including two volumes of women poets of Japan and China), Greek and Latin, French and Spanish. Virtually all of his poetry, excluding most of the translations and plays, can be found in *The Collected Shorter Poems* (1967), *The Collected Longer Poems* (including five of them, 1968), *New Poems* (1974), and *The Morning Star* (1979—containing three previously published sequences written in Japan: *The Silver Swan*, *On Flower Wreath Hill*, and *The Love Poems of Marichiko*). As for translations, he made the work of such poets as Pierre Reverdy, Martial, Sappho, Tu Fu, Li Ch'ing Chao, *Manyoshu* poets, Yosano Akiko, and Shiraishi Kazuko available in lively English versions. Japanese poets and critics have especially admired his translations, his comprehension of Japanese culture, and its absorption into his poetry and thought. His understanding of the cultures of both Japan and China seems more reliable than that of Pound or any other poet in English excepting Arthur Waley and Gary Snyder. His translations make the original poet seem vitally present in the poem—no doubt because of his practice of communing with dead poets in imaginary conversations. He called translation "an act of sympathy," rather than thinking of it as literal rendering. So translation was an essential activity in his vision of world community.

His vision is brilliantly articulated and expanded in his essays as well. His knowledge was vast and his judgment keen. His "Classics Revisited" column in *Saturday Review* introduced many readers to great books of the world (widening the scope of the Hutchins-Adler conception) and offered fresh insights to those familiar with them. In *American Poetry in the Twentieth Century* (1971), he analyzed literary interactions among various communities such as the Indian, Negro, Jewish, German, French, Chinese, Japanese, Spanish, Protestant and Catholic English, New England Transcendentalists, Southern Agrarians, the Midwest Renaissance, and the West Coast Renaissance (in which he was a founder), for example, and imagist, cubist, Marxist, and Beat movements. His social criticism, often mingling with his literary interpretations, reached its apex in his longest scholarly study, *Communalism: from Its Origins to the Twentieth Century* (1974), in which he surveyed and evaluated the history of utopian thought and experimentation from the Neolithic village to hippie communes of the 1960s. In all, he produced eight books of essays and seven editions of others' work with his introductions (notably, *The Selected Poems of D. H. Lawrence*, 1947; *The New British Poets: An Anthology*, 1949; and *The Buddhist Writings of Lafcadio Hearn*, 1977).

As a leader of the international avant-garde for six decades, Rexroth had an incalculable influence on literature and thought. Some critics have tried to ignore or play down his achievement, perhaps because he relentlessly battled New York and academic intellectuals of right and left. Some critics have praised one aspect of his work while neglecting his whole achievement, calling him a major nature poet, or love poet, or protest poet, or translator, or West Coast poet, or critic, without understanding his whole world view. Since my first book on him (*Kenneth Rexroth*, 1972), critical attention to him has increased in Japan and the United States, culminating in *For Rexroth*, a *Festschrift*-anthology edited by Geoffrey Gardner in 1980, Japanese journals dedicated to him in 1982, and a forthcoming issue of *Sagetrieb* and a *Festschrift* about his accomplishments. Experts in a half dozen languages need to evaluate his translations. Literary theorists and philosophers need to evaluate his poetics of vision and theory of community and communication. We need to understand how he functioned in various movements—the Industrial Workers of the World, the Objectivists, the San Francisco Libertarian Circle and Poetry Renaissance, for example. The crude label "Godfather of the Beats" needs to be rejected, for he roundly criticized the Beats for corrupting basic values soon after he introduced Allen Ginsberg and *Howl* at the famous Six Gallery reading in 1955. The issue is complex, for he continued to praise certain aspects of the work of Ginsberg, Ferlinghetti, McClure, and others, while denouncing the Beat movement. Similarly, he both encouraged and condemned aspects of the Counter Culture of the 1960s—opposing drugs, violence, and mindless music. Experts in painting and music need to evaluate his work in these forms and their relationship to his poetry: his visual and verbal cubism is now being studied, for instance. My *World Vision of Kenneth Rexroth* has just been completed, but much more needs to be done on his philosophical synthesis of diverse traditions. Rexroth deserves to be understood and evaluated in relation to other visionary poets such as Isaiah, Dante, Milton, Seami (the writer of Japanese *Nōh* plays), Blake, Whitman, and Yeats.

It would be a mistake, however, to leave the impression that Rexroth can be appreciated only by intellectuals. He is not usually obscure, and most of his poems and translations convey a sense of life so directly that they are popular. The elegies for his mother (Delia) and first wife (Andrée); the sequence for his daughters called "The Lights in the

Sky Are Stars"; his most powerful protest poem, "Thou Shalt Not Kill: a Memorial for Dylan Thomas"; and his many poems of mountain climbing, in which he told his life among wildlife under the stars, have endeared him to many readers, even those who do not understand or agree with his ideas. His world vision sprang from perennial experiences of love and loss, natural wonders and realizations that everyone can find celebrated in his poetry. It is in such common experiences that Rexroth, like other great poets, found universal value and conveyed it to us.

A TRIBUTE ————————————
from LAWRENCE FERLINGHETTI

Kenneth Rexroth was the *gad*father of the Beat Generation.

A TRIBUTE ————————————
from JAMES LAUGHLIN

With the death of Kenneth Rexroth last June we have lost one of the best poets this country ever had, in any age. And we have lost a brilliant, iconoclastic critic, who dealt not only with literature but with all aspects of culture, including the social, and a translator of the first order. Personally, I have lost a best friend of thirty years who taught me more than anyone except Ezra Pound—who, by the way, Kenneth detested for his political views.

During his lifetime, Rexroth never received the popular and academic recognition which his work deserved. As an autodidact of enormous learning he took a dim view of professors who had reactionary tastes. When he was invited to give readings at colleges, nothing amused him more than to bait his hosts. Naturally they did not take such tactics very well and few of them assigned his books to their classes for study. Thus many students knew him only from a few poems in anthologies. He also alienated the literary establishment by his attacks on it in reviews and articles. As a result, I think, he never won one of the major poetry prizes, though I believe he did have two Guggenheim Fellowships and of course the Copernicus Award of

The Academy of American Poets in 1975. But a good light cannot be hidden forever under a bushel, and I am confident that ten years from now Rexroth's books will be part of the standard curriculum in American Literature and that he will have a wide following among "common readers."

I think that it is his poetry which will speak best for him. The early poems, in which it might be said that he was trying to make poetry do what Cubist painting did, are sometimes tedious, but when he hit his true vein, a poetry of nature mixed with contemplation and philosophy, it was magnificent. Read "The Signature of All Things." You will never forget it. Written on one of his camping trips in the Sierra Nevadas, it, how shall I put it, pulls everything in human life together. It is all there, all the things we cherish, all our aspirations, and over it all a kind of Buddhist calm.

His two personal narrative poems, "The Phoenix and the Tortoise" and "The Dragon and the Unicorn"—one might call them travelogues of the soul—are both instructive and highly entertaining. KR had a sense of humour. He was also one of the great raconteurs. I shall never forget those evenings in the book-filled rooms of his apartment in Scott Street in the black section of San Francisco where the young writers would gather for the best show in town—Kenneth's stories. In a long life, lived all over America and Europe, he had known everybody and all the amusing or illuminating things about them and their work.

His translations of Japanese and Chinese poetry are perennial best-sellers on the New Directions list, different in their style but as fine as Pound's *Cathay*. He began them by working from Judith Gautier's French versions, but he was such a good linguist that he had soon mastered the basic Oriental characters and was working direct from them. He even "translated" the work of a Japanese poet named Marichiko, whom I took to be completely authentic until he confessed, under pressure, that Marichiko was really KR. His translations from the French of Pierre Reverdy are first rate, and his version from the Italian of Leopardi's "L'Infinito" is, in my opinion, as good as the original.

A great man has gone from the American literary scene. We will not see his like again. But we have his books, and they will be with us for a long time.

(Poetry Pilot, December 1982)

Philip Roth
(19 March 1933-   )

Jeffrey Helterman
University of South Carolina

See also the Roth entry in *DLB 2, American Novelists Since World War II*.

NEW BOOKS: *The Ghost Writer* (New York: Farrar, Straus & Giroux, 1979; London: Cape, 1979);
A Philip Roth Reader (New York: Farrar, Straus & Giroux, 1981; London: Cape, 1981);
Zuckerman Unbound (New York: Farrar, Straus & Giroux, 1981; London: Cape, 1981).

Nathan Zuckerman, the hero of Philip Roth's 1979 novel, *The Ghost Writer*, finds two possible courses open to the great novelist. He can either retire from the literary and social community and devote himself totally to his art like the master E. I. Lonoff, or he can become like the literary lion Felix Abravanel—sleek with adulation, wealth, and beautiful mistresses. In *The Ghost Writer*, Zuckerman chooses Lonoff's way. Many critics have speculated on the similarity of Lonoff to Bernard Malamud (and to a lesser extent, Malamud's own master, I. B. Singer) and of Abravanel's similarity to Saul Bellow and/or Norman Mailer. None of these identifications are completely off the mark (Lonoff as Malamud is particularly valid), but in fact the Jewish-American novelist closest to both Lonoff and Abravanel is Roth himself. He has trod the path of self-imposed exile and lived the life of celebrity and continues to do both. So, in fact, will Zuckerman.

Since 1976, Roth has spent part of the year living in isolation from the literary community on his country estate in Connecticut. Much of the rest of the year is spent in the artistic world of London and the Continent. In both lives, his constant companion is British actress Claire Bloom. In Connecticut, he writes under a watchful portrait of his own literary master, Franz Kafka, and on the Continent he works with and edits the heirs to Kafka—central European novelists like the Czech Milan Kundera. He also teaches sporadically at the University of Pennsylvania. All this indicates how far Roth has come from his roots in lower-middle-class Newark, and yet, in some ways he has not come very far at all.

Zuckerman has also come a long way from Newark. Already a character in two short stories

(presented in full) by Peter Tarnapol, himself a character in Roth's novel *My Life as a Man*, Zuckerman is also the hero of Roth's latest novel, *Zuckerman Unbound* (1981), where he tries the Abravanel path of celebrity. Though the characterization is not entirely consistent in these three incarnations, Zuckerman, a surrogate for Roth (though not an autobiographical figure), tells us a great deal about the life of a novelist at different points in his career.

In each case, Zuckerman's fate concerns itself with the way art impinges on life and life does the same to art. Of this issue Roth has said, "My obsession for the last seven or eight years has been the uses to which literature has been put in this country. The writer in his isolation publishes a book, the book goes out into the world and the strangest things begin to happen." In both novels, Zuckerman has written a work which has gone out into the world only to offend Zuckerman's family, friends, and neighbors. In *The Ghost Writer*, it is a short story not unlike Roth's "Defender of the Faith" or "Ep-

Philip Roth

183

tein" (both about obnoxious Jews).

In *The Ghost Writer*, Zuckerman goes off to the Berkshires, hoping to find a spiritual father in Lonoff, a painstaking creator of brilliant parables in the style of Russian masters like Anton Chekhov and Isaak Babel. Zuckerman seeks a surrogate father because his own father, a well-meaning, loving podiatrist, has refused to see the aesthetic virtues in Zuckerman's story "Higher Education," which uses an old family quarrel to show grasping, greedy Jews. Though the ambience of Lonoff's fiction is Jewish American, the issue he raises of the conflict of art and life is Jamesian. Consequently, the stories of Henry James are among the significant literary ghosts that inhabit the novel.

The primary analogues are two of James's stories, "The Lesson of the Master" and "The Middle Years." In "The Lesson of the Master," a young writer named Paul Overt seeks out his literary hero, Henry St. George, only to find him looking disappointingly like a "lucky stockbroker." St. George is artistically exhausted and advises Overt not to waste his energies by falling in love with and marrying

Dust jacket for Roth's 1979 novel about the Jewish writer Nathan Zuckerman in search of a spiritual and literary ideal

Marian Fancourt, a beautiful young woman of their mutual acquaintance. Life—the business of being a husband and father—drains the artist. Better to leave life behind and create the perfect work of art. Overt follows his master's lesson, goes off to write his novel (we never know if it is great) and returns to find that St. George's wife has died and that St. George is about to marry Marian himself. Only then does Overt realize the terrible price he has paid for his art.

Like James's young hero, Zuckerman is rather disappointed in his first meeting with the master. Lonoff seems discontent not only with his life but with his art. The pursuit of perfection has become for him an act of verbal juggling. "I turn sentences around," says Lonoff. "That's my life." Lonoff's wife, ironically named Hope, is at the point of leaving him. She is tired of having to provide the atmosphere of passive perfection in which the pursuit of literary perfection is to thrive. Furthermore, she has to compete for his meager affections with Amy Bellette, a former student who sees in Lonoff both a love object and a father figure. Like Marian Fancourt in "The Lesson of the Master," Amy becomes the focal point of the conflicting ideals of master and pupil.

In "The Middle Years," Dr. Hugh, a young physician and literary enthusiast, meets his favorite novelist, Dencombe, the author of *The Middle Years*. In pursuing the dying Dencombe and his art, the doctor neglects his only patient, a wealthy countess who had planned to leave him her fortune. Ultimately, his choice of Dencombe costs him his fortune, but he accepts the consequences with equanimity. "I chose to accept, whatever they might be, the consequences of my infatuation," he tells Dencombe. "It's your own fault if I can't get your things out of my head."

Like Dr. Hugh, Zuckerman is ready to give up everything—success, life, home—for the chance to live Lonoff's life of art. Ironically, Zuckerman is standing on Lonoff's copy of the stories of Henry James (so he can listen at the ceiling to the conversation in the room above), when he overhears Amy Bellette offer herself to Lonoff. The great man rejects her advances and can satisfy her only by doing an imitation of Jimmy Durante. When a Jewish artist is reduced to doing a vaudeville routine, and of a big-nosed Italian at that, he has turned his life into mockery for the sake of his art. Zuckerman is sanguine about this folly, however, and sees Lonoff's performance as "mad, heroic restraint."

The thought of Amy Bellette has sent Zuckerman reeling, however, and in an imaginative tour de force, he gives the exotic young woman a past. Zuckerman convinces himself that Amy Bellette is none other than Anne Frank, whose diary made her Saint Anne of the Holocaust. Zuckerman posits that Anne Frank survived in the confusion at the end of the war, but decided that the impact of her story—the message that her family died because they were Jews, even though they thought of themselves as Dutch—would be lost if she were no longer a martyr. Roth is at his best in creating this fictional continuation of Anne Frank's life.

Zuckerman soon cheapens his dream. He sees Bellette/Frank as the way out of his conflicts at home, out of his father's insistence that he is betraying his race, out of the ridiculous questions of Judge Leopold Wapter, Newark's most illustrious Jewish citizen. Judge Wapter has sent him a questionnaire which includes such leading questions as "Do you practice Judaism? If so, how? If not, what credentials qualify you for writing about Jewish life for national magazines?," "What in your character makes you associate so much of life's ugliness with Jewish people?," and "Can you honestly say there is anything in your short story that would not warm the heart of a Julius Streicher or a Joseph Goebbels?"

Well, Zuckerman has the answer for philistines like Wapter. He will marry Anne Frank. Let Judge Wapter question that! He can picture the moment when he announces his engagement to his parents. " 'Nathan, is she Jewish?' 'Yes, she is.' 'But who is she?' 'Anne Frank.' " The moment would be a triumph no doubt, but this imagined victory is simply beating Wapter at his own game. Wapter invokes the ghosts of the Holocaust to damn Zuckerman, and Zuckerman, just as unthinkingly, uses those same ghosts to call down a blessing on his own head. His "marriage" to St. Anne Frank would make it impossible for Wapter to condemn him, but Zuckerman has not really countered the charges leveled against him in the questionnaire. Wapter, after all, is saying that literature matters in the real world. His sensibility may be coarse and his morality superficial, but his objections will not be whisked away simply by waving an icon in front of them.

In the end, both Zuckerman and Lonoff lose Amy. Zuckerman's "Has anyone ever told you you look like Anne Frank?" is just as hollow as it sounds, and Amy ignores his attempt at flirtation. Amy also refuses to accept Lonoff from his wife's hands. Hope's warning ("She can be ready to begin boring you as soon as I'm out the door . . . and get everything ready to make you happy and then see the

look on your stone face when you come in at night and sit down at the table") may have some influence on her leaving, but his rejection of Amy on the night before seems to be the major reason. Hope also walks out on Lonoff, and he goes out into the snow in pursuit of his Hope. It seems like Lonoff's wife will return, but nothing will change. Zuckerman will probably treat the marriage with more sanctity than it deserves and praise Hope as a saint. If he writes the story, Zuckerman will call it "Married to Tolstoy."

If the life of the hermit is perilous, so is the life of the literary celebrity. In *Zuckerman Unbound*, Roth deals with the tribulations brought to Nathan Zuckerman by the success of his notorious novel *Carnovsky*. The situation is based in some measure on Roth's phenomenal success and attendant problems following the publication of *Portnoy's Complaint*. Nathan Zuckerman suffers under the watchful eye of brahmin money managers, English custom tailors, and even an aging ingenue, who happens to be Fidel Castro's mistress. None of these minor demons, however, can compare with Zuckerman's personal dybbuk, a former quiz-show contestant named Alvin Pepler.

Pepler is modeled in part upon Teddy Nadler, the postal clerk with a photographic memory who won thousands of dollars before the scandals closed the big-money quiz shows in the late fifties. Like the real-life Nadler, Roth's Pepler catches facts like flypaper. Unlike Nadler, Pepler is a Jew and a landsman of Zuckerman's from his old Newark neighborhood. When Pepler first latches on to him, Zuckerman sees him merely as one of the annoying appurtenances of fame, those talentless would-be writers who come waving manuscripts in the famous author's face.

Pepler is more; he is Zuckerman's alter ego. If the novelist locked in his study is the spirit of the imagination, then Pepler with his undigested information is his polar opposite, the man of fact . . . and both dwell on the edges of the real world. Zuckerman wonders if either of them lives *dans le vrai*, in reality.

One of the possibilities that Zuckerman has to face is that Pepler is just as real as he is, or less optimistically, that he is as unreal as Pepler. Pepler even was for three weeks a celebrity as great as Zuckerman when he was the quiz-show champion. At first, Pepler just seems to want what most people want from celebrated writers—help with a manuscript, advice about publishing, and criticism— criticism that, of course, will go unheard.

Little by little, Zuckerman attributes all sorts of

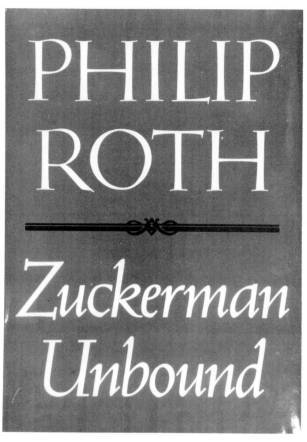

Dust jacket for Roth's 1981 novel, in which Zuckerman indulges himself in literary celebrity

powers to Pepler and his facts. This becomes particularly striking once Pepler turns against him. Pepler first approaches Zuckerman as his redeemer, the man who can tell the world how the quiz show's producers (both Jews) refused to let him remain champion because the American television audience would not be happy with a Jewish champion. The fix was on. And in a reverse of the mythology of the scandals, Pepler was the first to cheat . . . by agreeing to lose in exchange for promises of a career in television—promises which were later broken.

When Zuckerman shows no interest in his cause, Pepler turns accuser—first charging Zuckerman with anti-Semitism and then with a greater crime among writers, plagiarism. Pepler accuses Zuckerman not of stealing his manuscript but of stealing his life. He has taken Pepler's personality and put it between the covers of a book called *Carnovsky* instead of *Pepler*. Zuckerman has achieved what most writers long for, a reader who identifies completely with one of his characters. Instead of cheering Zuckerman up, Pepler's total involvement makes the author's life a horror. Pepler haunts him, lies to him, bullies him, and then sends him a semen-soaked handkerchief (Zuckerman's handkerchief, which Pepler had stolen), proof-positive that the masturbating hero of *Carnovsky* is really Pepler. Not even Othello had so much trouble with his own handkerchief.

One of the many paradoxes of the novel is that the fact-catcher Pepler leads a fictional life, while Zuckerman's life is mired in facts. Pepler invents an entire Broadway production company working on the musical version of the "Alvin Pepler Story," while Zuckerman finds that the only thing he still has in common with his last ex-wife is the Xerox machine in their bathroom.

Celebrity in America brings out more than screwball fans; it brings out honest-to-God crazies. Zuckerman has achieved a measure of fame smaller than John and Robert Kennedy and Martin Luther King, Jr., but he has his own threatening phone calls. In this case, the caller threatens to kidnap Zuckerman's mother. Is it Pepler? An unknown crank? Or just paranoia? Zuckerman never finds out. What he does find out is that books do not confine themselves to the study, but make their way into the real world and have consequences there. Zuckerman tells the threatening caller that he has been watching too many bad movies to which his tormentor replies, "Could be, Zuck. Haw, haw, haw. Also real life." In a world where Jack Ruby murders the murderer of a president before a live television audience, the boundaries of life and art have been curiously blurred. The Kennedy assassinations have long held a fascination for Roth, and a friend of his has said, "Long before the Kennedys were assassinated, he'd been waiting for the bullet."

Carnovsky, then, does not bring harm to his mother, but it does destroy Zuckerman's last day with his father. His father had seen the book as mercilessly satiric of his family, and there is the expected talk that the book has killed him. The old man has been paralyzed by a stroke, but manages to mouth a last word that seems to be "bastard!" and seems to be aimed at Zuckerman. At least, it seems so to Zuckerman. Zuckerman's brother, a dentist (the fate of Jewish boys who cannot make it as doctors) and a man who wanted a life in the theater but settled for the conventional and the ordinary, tries to convince Zuckerman that their father could not have said that as his last word to his son. Zuckerman is not convinced. If this rejection is the price he must pay for his art, so be it.

The novel's title refers to Zuckerman's freeing himself from all the bonds that tie one to life. Each untying is done at the cost of terrible pain, but there is no other way. Zuckerman ends his relationship with his father, discovers he no longer can stand the spiritual dishonesty of his smiling brother or the honest virtue of his ex-wife, and loses his mistress to Fidel Castro. In a scene as wrenching as the death of his father, Zuckerman returns to his old neighborhood in Newark, the source of most of his fiction, only to find it a burnt-out slum. When Zuckerman has unbound himself from this last tie, the past, he is free. The book does not speculate on what Zuckerman will do with this freedom. Only Roth's next book will tell if he is unbound like Zuckerman.

Interviews:
James Atlas, "A Visit With Philip Roth," *New York Times Book Review*, 2 September 1979, p. 1;

Alain Finkielkraut, "The Ghosts of Roth," *Esquire*, 96 (September 1981): 92-97.

References:
Leslie Field, "Philip Roth: Days of Whine and Moses," *Studies in American Jewish Literature*, 5, no. 2 (1979): 11-14;

Alice Kaminsky, "Philip Roth's Professor Kepesh and the 'Reality Principle,'" *Denver Quarterly*, 13, no. 2 (1978): 41-54;

Bernice Kliman, "Women in Roth's Fiction," *Nassau Review*, 3, no. 4 (1978): 75-88;

Judith Lee, "Flights of Fancy," *Chicago Review*, 31, no. 4 (1980): 46-52;

Saul Maloff, "The Uses of Adversity," *Commonweal*, 106 (19 November 1979): 628-631;

Bernard F. Rodgers, Jr., *Philip Roth* (Boston: Twayne, 1978).

Anne Tyler
(25 October 1941-   )

Sarah English
Meredith College

See also the Tyler entry in *DLB 6, American Novelists Since World War II*, Second Series.

NEW BOOK: *Dinner at the Homesick Restaurant* (New York: Knopf, 1982).

Anne Tyler is a private person and a private writer. She does not go on television talk shows, give lectures, teach courses, or write screenplays. Instead, during the past eighteen years she has brought up two children, now in their teens, and written nine novels, as well as short stories and essays. The novels are about private life—childhood, love, marriage, parenthood, families. In spite of her now impressive body of work, her fiction has received little academic analysis. That absence of attention is puzzling, since Tyler is a serious, gifted, prolific writer whose fiction has been consistently admired by important critics and fellow novelists.

Tyler's work does not fit neatly into any critical categories. It is not, in the first place, "difficult." Her novels are always polished and entertaining and quite often funny, but they offer little arcane material for critics to explain: no religious allusions (most of her characters are cheerfully unreligious), no multiple endings or allusions to the *nouveau roman*, no existentialism, little fashionable alienation. Her novels are straightforward and rarely experimental in form. Although Tyler writes that she considers herself a Southerner—she grew up in the South and now lives in Baltimore, where most of her recent fiction is set—her work does not fit easily into the category of Southern literature either. Like the great Southern writers, she is centrally occupied with the survival of the past in the present, but for her the past is not moonlight-and-magnolias romance or miscegenation or incest or racism or violence (black people play mostly peripheral roles in her fiction). The past in her work is never antebellum; the furthest back she has gone, in *Searching for Caleb*, is Baltimore in the 1880s. Instead, in Tyler's work the past is one's mother, grandmother, and aunts, who uphold certain genteel standards of behavior: a lady does not wear overalls; one should always send a bread-and-butter note after visiting; a lady should not expect to support herself. And,

Anne Tyler

although Tyler is a writer and a woman, one cannot imagine her work fitting comfortably in most women's studies courses. She does indeed write about subjects that matter to women: romantic love and the way it tends to get lost or just not noticed in most marriages, marriage itself, and motherhood—a central theme of her most recent novel, *Dinner at the Homesick Restaurant* (1982). Nonetheless, in spite of her insight into women and their lives, Tyler's perspective is not feminist. She does not protest against the institution of marriage. In her fiction husbands and wives are equally powerful in creating or helpless in averting the muddle or their lives. Indeed, her males tend to be more romantic—and thus less effective and more vulnerable—than her women.

Dinner at the Homesick Restaurant, Tyler's ninth novel, was enthusiastically praised by important reviewers and moved quickly to the *New York Times* best-seller list. In it she explores the themes that have always been central in her fiction, but with a

new depth and resonance and psychological insight.

The plot of *Dinner at the Homesick Restaurant* is deceptively simple. When Pearl, the protagonist, is thirty and beginning to think of herself as an old maid, she meets Beck Tull at the Charity Baptist Church and marries him after a short courtship. During the first twenty years of their marriage, they move frequently—he is a traveling salesman, often away, and forever seeking "a chance of promotion, or richer territory"—and have three children, Cody, Ezra, and Jenny. Then, one Sunday night in 1944, Beck tells Pearl that he does not want to be married anymore, packs, and leaves the family, giving her no explanation for his action and never returning to see his children. Convinced that Beck will return, Pearl tells the children that he is traveling on business, and eventually, driven by financial necessity, she takes a job as cashier at Sweeney Brothers Grocery and Fine Produce. After Pearl is left to raise her children alone, she becomes a tense, even frightening, mother, a victim to rages in which she berates and even strikes her children. The worst scenes tend to occur at the dinner table. Cody remembers a typical one:

> Pearl threw the spoon in his face. "You upstart," she said. She rose and slapped him across the cheek. "You wretch, you ugly horror." She grabbed one of Jenny's braids and yanked it so Jenny was pulled off her chair. "Stupid clod," she said to Ezra, and she took the bowl of peas and brought it down on his head. It didn't break, but peas flew everywhere. Ezra cowered, shielding his head with his arms. "Parasites," she told them. "I wish you'd all die, and let me go free. I wish I'd find you dead in your beds."

Nonetheless the family survives, as families do, and the children become in their own ways successful adults: Cody an efficiency consultant, a "time-study man" and a traveler like his father; Ezra the owner of the Homesick Restaurant, where the food "is made with love"; Jenny a pediatrician who at the end of the novel is happily married to a third husband, bringing up seven children from his and her former marriages. Pearl dies in the last chapter of the novel, and her family reassembles for her funeral—including, at last, Beck Tull, whom Ezra has invited. When they all gather around the dinner table at the Homesick Restaurant, Beck looks at the group and says complacently, "It looks like this is one of those great big, jolly, noisy, rambling . . . why, *families!*" The Tulls have prevailed.

Thus summarized, the plot of *Dinner at the*

Homesick Restaurant is that of most lives, since most families are not perfect and most people survive anyhow. As John Updike commented in the *New Yorker* (5 April 1982), "The Tulls, in short, present a not untypical American family history, marred by abandonment and scattering but redeemed by a certain persisting loyalty and, after early privation, respectable success." However, Tyler's vision of family life here is more somber than in her early work. If *Searching for Caleb* was what Updike called "genetic comedy," *Dinner at the Homesick Restaurant* "deepens into the tragedy of closeness, of familial limitations that work upon us like Greek fates and condemn us to lives of surrender and secret fury." The narrow and embittered past remains alive in Pearl Tull and her children, for all their efforts to escape or transcend it. Pearl muses:

> She wondered if her children blamed her for something. Sitting close at family gatherings (with the spouses and offspring slightly apart, nonmembers forever), they tended to recall only poverty and loneliness—toys she couldn't afford for them, parties where they weren't invited. Cody, in particular, referred continually to Pearl's short temper, displaying it against a background of stunned, childish faces so sad and bewildered that Pearl herself hardly recognized them. Honestly, she thought, wasn't there some statute of limitations here?

The answer to Pearl's question is no. In Tyler's earlier novels, many characters do manage to leave their constricting family roles: Elizabeth Abbott of *The Clock Winder*, who imagines "a federal law ordering everybody to switch parents at a certain age. . . . There would be a gigantic migration of children across the country, all cutting the old tangled threads and picking up new ones when they found the right niche, free forever of other people's notions about them," and who lives out that dream, becoming for the family she marries into calm, capable, nurturing; Justine and Duncan Peck of *Searching for Caleb*, who become travelers and bohemians, the antithesis of "Peckness"; and Morgan Gower of *Morgan's Passing*, who impersonates doctors, shoe-repairmen, magicians, puppeteers, taking and discarding roles at will. In *Dinner at the Homesick Restaurant* there are no such charming eccentrics, and, for the first time since Tyler's first novel, no artists (unless we count Ezra as a cook), with their special powers of making and seeing things anew. Well into adulthood, Pearl Tull's children reenact the roles of their childhood, resem-

bling their parents even as they strive to be different, to compensate.

Thus Cody and Ezra, as adults, remain locked in their roles of bad son and good son. Cody, who was a difficult baby, feels all his life that his mother loves Ezra better than him and takes his revenge on Ezra accordingly. As a child, he plants pornography and liquor bottles in Ezra's bed; "He hid Ezra's left sneaker, his arithmetic homework, his baseball mitt, his fountain pen, and his favorite sweater. He shut Ezra's cat in the linen cupboard. He took Ezra's bamboo whistle to school and put it in the jacket of Josiah Payson, Ezra's best friend." As an adult, he steals Ezra's fiancée, "a weasel-faced little redhead" and the only woman Ezra ever loves, marries her himself, has one son, and believes that she (like his mother) still loves Ezra better and even that the boy is not his. A traveler like his father, Cody takes his wife and son with him on his assignments—he remembers what it was like to be left behind—but he is not there for Pearl's last illness and is out of reach on a hunting trip when she finally dies. Pearl "never intended to foster one of those good son/bad son arrangements, but what can you do when one son is consistently good and the other consistently bad? What can the sons do, even?" Ezra, Pearl's good son, lives with her as an adult, nurses her through her last illness, and makes the Homesick Restaurant into an establishment where the diners feel loved and cherished. (Pearl's dinners were typically Spam and canned vegetables; Cody remembers her as "a nonfeeder, if there ever was one.") Ezra plans family dinners at his restaurant throughout the book, but the family always fights and someone always walks out; they never get past the appetizer. Jenny (always on a diet, a noneater) marries twice unsuccessfully and, when her second husband has deserted her and their daughter in the middle of her internship, finds herself slapping her child as her own mother did and thinks despairingly, "Was this what it came to—that you could never escape? Were certain things doomed to continue, generation after generation?" Ironically, this time it is Pearl who rescues her, Pearl who nurses her through a breakdown and cares for the child, Pearl who is a more loving grandmother than she was a mother. Even in her third marriage when, as a mother and a pediatrician, Jenny plays the role of Lady Bountiful, she remains a bit distant, wary of feelings, hers and others'. Tyler shows the old patterns continuing even in the third generation: Jenny's daughter develops anorexia, and Cody's son, Luke, who is very much like his Uncle Ezra, becomes convinced that Ezra is his real father and runs away from home.

2nd draft

I. SOMETHING YOU SHOULD KNOW

While Pearl Tull was dying, a funny thought occurred to her. It twitched her lips and rustled her breath, and she felt her son lean forward from where he kept watch by her bed. "Get..." she told him. "You should have got..."

You should have got an extra mother, was what she meant to say; the way we started extra children after the first child fell so ill. Cody, that was; the oldest boy. Not Ezra here beside her bed but Cody the troublemaker — a difficult baby, born late in her life. They had decided on no more. Then he developed croup. This was in 1931, when croup was something serious. She'd been frantic. Over his crib she had draped a flannel sheet, and she set out skillets, saucepans, buckets full of water that she'd heated on the stove. She lifted the flannel sheet to catch the steam. The baby's breathing was choked and rough, like something pulled through tightly packed gravel. Toward morning, his skin was blazing and his hair was plastered stiffly to his temples. When he slept. Pearl's head sagged in the rocking chair and she slept too, fingers still gripping the ivory metal crib rail. Beck was away on business — came home when the worst was over, Cody toddling around again with nothing worse than a runny nose and a loose, unalarming cough that Beck didn't even notice. I want some more children, Pearl told him. He acted surprised, though pleased.

the croup: if Cody died, what would she have left? Their little rented house, fixed up so carefully and pathetically; the nursery with its Mother Goose theme; and her husband, of course, but he was so busy with the Tanner Corporation, away from home more often than not, and even when home always fretting over business: who was on the rise and who was on the skids, who had spread damaging rumors behind his back, what chance he had of being let go now that times were so hard.

"I don't know why I thought one little boy would suffice," said Pearl. But it wasn't as simple as she had supposed. The second child was Ezra, so sweet and clumsy it could break your heart. She was more endangered than ever. It would have been best to stop at Cody. You never learn, though. After Ezra came Jenny, the girl — such fun to dress, to fix her hair in different styles. Girls were a kind of luxury, Pearl felt. But she couldn't give Jenny up, either. What she had now was not one loss to fear but three. Still, she thought, it had seemed a good idea once upon a time: spare children, like spare tires, or those extra lisle stockings they used to package free with each pair.

"You should have arranged for a second-string mother, Ezra," she said. Or she meant to say. "How short-sighted of you." But evidently she failed to form the words, for she heard him sit back again without comment and turn a page of his magazine.

She had not seen Ezra clearly since the spring of '75, four and a half years ago, when she first started losing her vision. She'd had a little trouble with blurring. She went

Page from the manuscript for Dinner at the Homesick Restaurant *(1982)*

There is no statute of limitations in this novel.

Pearl's family is successful, and it is scarred. More clearly than in any of her previous novels, Tyler seems to be saying that that is the nature of all families. Pearl, like Mrs. Emerson in *The Clock Winder* and Charlotte in *Earthly Possessions*, thinks wistfully that other families must know the secret of happiness:

> Often, like a child peering over the fence at someone else's party, she gazes wistfully at other families and wonders what their secret is. They seem so close. Is it that they're more religious? Or stricter, or more lenient? Could it be the fact that they participate in sports? Read books together? Have some common hobby? Recently, she overheard a neighbor woman discussing her plans for Independence Day: her family was having a picnic. Every member—child or grownup—was cooking his or her specialty. Those who were too little to cook were in charge of the paper plates.
> Pearl felt such a wave of longing that her knees went weak.

Tyler, though, hints that there are no such happy, perfect families in a way that is both funny and sad: Luke, when he hitchhikes away from home, steps into a different kind of family pain with each person who picks him up. His first ride is with a truck driver who lost his first baby to crib death and, though he had three other children, "lost the knack of getting attached." Luke's second ride is with a recently divorced man and his son who are "looking up Daddy's old girlfriends." His third ride is with a woman who tells him that her adolescent daughter hates her; she drives the beltway around Washington every day until she can find her daughter's past self and her own, the selves that once liked each other. The happy family is a myth, says Tyler, even as she recognizes its power to torment—and recognizes the bedrock of family love. For, of course, once Luke's parents realize he is gone, they are frantic with worry and come home to Pearl and Ezra's house to fetch him back, where the Tull family has a pleasant reunion for once, with no ceremonial dinner.

Dinner at the Homesick Restaurant makes a plainer, more powerful, and darker statement about the nature of family life than Tyler's previous novels. The Tulls are not as charming as the families of *Searching for Caleb* and *Morgan's Passing*. The humor that has been so much a part of Tyler's distinctive vision of the world is still here: in the sign

Dust jacket for Tyler's best-selling ninth novel (1982)

in Jenny's office that reads "DR. TULL IS NOT A TOY"; in Jenny as a grown woman, capable, laughing at problems, relentlessly antipsychological; and even in the slender pretexts for quarrels that break up the family dinners. But the humor in this novel is characteristically somewhat black, as in Cody's boyhood tricks on Ezra and the riders who pick up Luke.

Another important way in which *Dinner at the Homesick Restaurant* differs from Tyler's earlier work is the narrative technique. This novel is more complex in point of view than anything else she has written, except *Celestial Navigation*—also a rather dark novel. The latest book begins with Pearl's thoughts and memories on her deathbed, and then moves from present to past and back again, giving up in succession the viewpoints of Cody, Ezra, Jenny, Luke, and finally, in the last chapter, even Beck. Each chapter has a character as center, and each, as

John Updike notes, is "rounded like a short story." Tyler's narrative technique allows her to juxtapose past and present and thus to convey the vision—that she has always had—of the past not as a continuum but as layers of still, vivid memories. The wealth of points of view also allows Tyler to show more fully than ever the essential subjectivity of the past. Cody and Jenny remember Pearl as a witch; Ezra remembers her as a source of strength and security. Cody remembers his wife's leaving home to go to Ezra; Luke knows she was going to go back to her parents. Beck saw the son he abandoned as strong, carefree, successful; Cody saw himself as abandoned to his mother's clutches. Every character's vision of the past is different. Their memories mostly focus on pain, but there was also, Tyler insists, joy. Dying, Pearl asks Ezra to describe all her old photographs and read her journals out loud; she is clearly looking for something specific that she finds when Ezra reads this passage:

> Early this morning, I went out behind the house to weed. Was kneeling in the dirt by the stable with my pinafore a mess and the perspiration rolling down my back, wiped my face on my sleeve, reached for the trowel, and all at once thought, Why I believe that at just this moment I am absolutely happy.
>
> The Bedloe girl's piano scales were floating out her window, and a bottle fly was buzzing in the grass, and I saw that I was kneeling on such a beautiful green little planet. I don't care what else might come about. I have had this moment. It belongs to me.

Dinner at the Homesick Restaurant says that we all have had such moments. Like all of Tyler's work, it is about both the mystery of human individuality and inescapable claims of everyday chores, family life, that keep us from looking at the mystery very hard or long. What Tyler gives us, in Beck Tull's words, is "the grayness; grayness of things; half-right-and-half-wrongness of things. Everything tangled, mingled, not perfect any more."

Perhaps because of the continuity of theme in Tyler's work—she has written about several different kinds of families, but families are always her subject—the main critical controversy surrounding her work is whether or not she is developing as a writer. Her harsher critics say that she is not, that she mines the same territory again and again, writes the same novel over and over. Such accusations were made, predictably enough, by some reviewers of *Dinner at the Homesick Restaurant*. James Wolcott's

Esquire review (April 1982) advised Tyler "to take a holiday from chronicling domestic strife in Baltimore and let her mind go carelessly ballooning off into the blue. Unexplored vistas are needed to rejuvenate Anne Tyler's novels; her last two novels are so suffocatingly cozy that her characters seem hammered into their lives, sealed off against the elements." In a *Village Voice* review entitled "Anne Tyler's Arrested Development" (30 March 1982), Vivian Gornick wrote that "Tyler mythicizes the inability to give up the family, and because she does her novels do not achieve depth." Even Gornick, though, finds *Dinner at the Homesick Restaurant* the best of Tyler's novels. And other critics have found this novel to represent a breakthrough, a genuine advance in her development as a writer. Benjamin DeMott, in the *New York Times Book Review* (14 March 1982), argued that the novel "edges deep into truth that's simultaneously (and interdependently) psychological, moral and formal—deeper than many living novelists of serious reputation, deeper than Miss Tyler herself has gone before. It is a border crossing." John Updike, long a champion of Tyler's fiction, also found *Dinner at the Homesick Restaurant* to be a breakthrough, both in sophistication of narrative technique and depth of insight.

Quarreling with Tyler for writing about families is, after all, a bit like condemning Jane Austen for writing about courtship and marriage. The preoccupations of Tyler's fiction are central to our lives. Now in *Dinner at the Homesick Restaurant* she has written her most serious exploration of her subject to date. One way of measuring her growth as a writer is to compare *Dinner at the Homesick Restaurant* to her first novel, *If Morning Ever Comes*. The two are deceptively similar in subject. *If Morning Ever Comes* is about a family whose father has deserted it; the central character, Ben Joe Hawkes, is like Cody and Ezra in his worried, compulsive involvement with his mother and sisters, even after he has supposedly left home and become an adult. Ben Joe is also like Jenny in the way he leaps into marriage: after three dates he proposes to a girl, saying, "Don't be mad any more. You come with me on the train tomorrow and we'll be married in New York when we get there. You want to? Just pack a bag and Jeremy will be our best man. . . . Oh hell, who wants to go away and leave you with the dishes?" The differences between the two books, though, are as interesting as the similarities. *If Morning Ever Comes* covers Ben Joe's six-day visit home; the action of *Dinner at the Homesick Restaurant* takes place over fifty years. *If Morning Ever Comes* is told entirely from the point of view of a young man in his early twenties; *Dinner at the Homesick Restaurant* has many points of view, from Pearl in her eighties to Luke at thirteen. *If Morning Ever Comes* is a comedy: the Hawkes family is happy, and their lives go on, cheerfully unscarred by the father's desertion. *Dinner at the Homesick Restaurant* explores the psychological consequences of such a loss. Tyler's preoccupations have not changed; what have changed are the depth and range and complexity of her writing.

For eighteen years Anne Tyler's novels have been consistently polished, consistently entertaining, consistently both serious and funny, and they have developed in range and depth. It is time for critics to stop worrying about the direction her work is taking and to look seriously at what she has accomplished. As Benjamin DeMott wrote in the *New York Times Book Review* (14 March 1982), "What one wants to do finishing such a work as *Dinner at the Homesick Restaurant* is maintain balance, keep things intact for a stretch, stay under the spell as long as feasible. The before and after are immaterial; nothing counts except the knowledge, solid and serene, that's all at once breathing in the room. We're speaking, obviously, about an extremely beautiful book."

Periodical Publications:
FICTION:
"The Country Cook," *Harper's* (March 1982): 54-62.
NONFICTION:
"Trouble in the Boys' Club," *New Republic* (30 July 1977): 16-19;
"Please Don't Call It Persia," *New York Times Book Review*, 18 February 1979, pp. 3, 34-36;
"Visit with Eudora Welty," *New York Times Book Review*, 2 November 1980, pp. 33-34;
"All in the Family: *A Mother and Two Daughters* by Gail Godwin," *New Republic* (17 February 1982): 39-40.

References:
Benjamin DeMott, "Funny, Wise and True," *New York Times Book Review*, 14 March 1982, pp. 1, 14;
Vivian Gornick, "Anne Tyler's Arrested Development," *Village Voice*, 30 March 1982, pp. 40-41;
John Updike, "On Such a Beautiful Green Little Planet," *New Yorker* (5 April 1982): 189-197;
James Wolcott, "Strange New World," *Esquire* (April 1982): 123-124.

AN INTERVIEW ————————
with ANNE TYLER

The following interview was conducted in writing; the interviewer mailed the questions, and Anne Tyler wrote answers to them on 10 July 1982.

DLB: Are there any contemporary writers whose books matter to you? Who are they?

TYLER: Gabriel García Márquez's books matter to me immensely; I read Joyce Carol Oates with awe; I am continually on the lookout for something new by Eudora Welty. And I find it heartening that so many young, previously unpublished writers can enthrall me.

DLB: Is there any new biographical information about you we should know? How old are your children now? Did raising them ever interfere with your writing? How did you cope with it all?

TYLER: I've never felt my real life had that much to do with my writing life. My children are fourteen and sixteen. Their infancy did interrupt my work for a few years—or made me shift my working time to evening, which is the same as interrupting it since I can't think past 3 p.m.

Generally, I cope with interruptions like school vacations, mono, etc., by giving in gracefully—I make no attempt to work under such conditions.

DLB: I've heard that you don't give guest lectures, seminars, or readings because you want to keep free to work. Do you have any other ways of protecting your time?

TYLER: My main reason for doing little in public is that it's not what I'm good at—but yes, it also protects my working time. As I get older, I've learned to say "no" more and more—and I get happier and happier.

DLB: I'm interested in the way families in your fiction tend to divide into two extremes: great big noisy ones where something is always happening and small ones where the parents are middle-aged and there is only one child who never quite fits in anywhere. What was your childhood like? Did you ever know anyone who ran away from home?

TYLER: There was nothing very unusual about my family life, but I did spend much of my older childhood and adolescence as a semi-outsider—a Northerner, commune-reared, looking wistfully at large Southern families around me.

No, I never knew anyone who ran away from home.

DLB: One thing in your novels I think critics have not commented on enough is the humor. A lot of it seems "black," or mixed with violence; I'm thinking of the scenes in *The Clock Winder* when Elizabeth and Timothy kill the turkey and when Timothy shoots himself, and the terrible/funny tricks Cody plays on Ezra as a child. Where does that humor come from?

TYLER: The humor comes from the appalling realization I keep having that even the largest and most tragic events have their quirky little funny details underneath.

DLB: Since *The Clock Winder* it seems to me that the points of view in your novels have become increasingly complex. Your first three books looked at the world mostly through the eyes of young people, but since then you have used the viewpoints of middle-aged and old people, and now in *Dinner at the Homesick Restaurant* three generations including Pearl on her deathbed. Do you have any ideas about why this expansion in points of view happened?

TYLER: I've waited ever since adolescence for the authority to speak from a more seasoned age, and finally I'm there.

DLB: Do you think that *Dinner at the Homesick Restaurant* is more somber in tone than your earlier novels?

TYLER: Yes, *Dinner* is more somber—not because it reflects any change in my viewpoint, though. I think what I was doing was saying, "Well, all right, I've joked around about families long enough; let me

tell you now what I really believe about them."

DLB: In the *New York Times Book Review* Benjamin DeMott wrote that *Dinner at the Homesick Restaurant* teaches us: "If we pause too long in the comtemplation of a former self, studying some lesson or other, we run the risk of forgetting how to take our present selves for granted. And down that road there's a risk of starting to treat life as a mystery instead of the way smart people treat it—as a set of done and undone errands. No way, says Jenny—clearly one of us." These two perspectives—romantic-life-as-mystery, which usually involves the character's wanting himself to be *seen* as a mystery, and anti-romantic—seem to inform your work. Do you identify more strongly with one perspective or the other?

TYLER: I suspect that I just have fun dealing with the tension between the two perspectives, without necessarily favoring one over the other.

DLB: Are you working on another novel now? Do you show or discuss work in progress?

TYLER: Yes, but it's going slowly for a couple of reasons—first because it's now my daughter's summer vacation; second because I poured out so much in the last book that I'm having trouble refueling.

I am superstitious about discussing a book-in-progress with anyone at all, even my husband, so I'll pass on discussing what it's about.

DLB: What do you think of the critical reception of your fiction?

TYLER: I try to think as little as possible about critical reception, since the only way I can happily write a book is to pretend that no one but me will ever read it.

—Sarah English

John Updike

(18 March 1932-   )

Donald J. Greiner
University of South Carolina

See also the Updike entries in *DLB 2, American Novelists Since World War II*; *DLB 5, American Poets Since World War II*; *DLB Yearbook: 1980*; and *DLB Documentary Series*, volume 3.

NEW BOOKS: *People One Knows: Interviews with Insufficiently Famous Americans* (Northridge, Cal.: Lord John Press, 1980), 300 numbered copies, signed;
Hawthorne's Creed (New York: Targ Editions, 1981), 250 numbered copies, signed;
Rabbit Is Rich (New York: Knopf, 1981);
Invasion of the Book Envelopes (Concord, N.H.: Ewert, 1981), 125 copies for private distribution;
Bech Is Back (New York: Knopf, 1982);
The Beloved (Northridge, Cal.: Lord John Press, 1982), 300 numbered copies, signed;
Spring Trio (Winston-Salem: Palaemon Press, 1982), 150 numbered copies, signed.

The period of 1981-1982 was a homecoming of sorts for John Updike. Already celebrated as America's premier living man of letters, he took the opportunity at the turn of the decade not to imagine new major characters but to reacquaint himself with old ones. Harry "Rabbit" Angstrom and Henry Bech, two stalwarts of the Updike canon, returned after an absence of ten years to confront the specters of advancing age and declining potency. No longer young and vigorous, they turn the corner and find mortality beckoning from the far side of the alleyway. Yet their trials are Updike's triumph: *Rabbit Is Rich* (1981) won the Pulitzer Prize, the National Book Critics Circle Award, and an American Book Award.

None of the applause came easily. Like Henry Bech, a novelist cursed with writer's block, Updike understands the invitation to avoid the typewriter, but unlike Bech, he knows that he must confront the blank page: "It's always a push to get up the stairs, to sit down and go to work. You'd rather do almost anything, read the paper again, write some letters, play with your old dust jackets, any number of things you'd rather do than tackle that empty page, because what you do on the page is you, your ticket

John Updike

to all the good luck you've enjoyed." Yet, despite the hesitation, he climbs the stairs.

Updike is applauded; Bech is back; and Rabbit is rich. Angstrom wants money for the security it promises. He last surfaced ten years ago when, in *Rabbit Redux* (1971), he and his wife, Janice, scampered back to each other to fall asleep in a motel room. He first appeared ten years before that when, in *Rabbit, Run* (1960), he scurried from family and friends, crammed ash trays and stasis, in search of grace and fluidity. Grace in all its guises still eludes him in *Rabbit Is Rich*, and fluidity seems lost in an expanding waistline and bank account, but Rabbit is alive and well and moderately rich.

The three Rabbit novels are Updike's Barchester chronicles, for, like Anthony Trollope, Updike uses fiction to choreograph the social dance of an age. Each Rabbit novel records the tone of a decade. *Rabbit Is Rich* is about the 1970s, and the rainbow that Harry chases in the 1950s and 1960s has shrunk as the American dream goes sour with the bad taste of middle age and aimless youth.

Farmland turns to shopping malls; overflowing garbage cans stand by unsuccessful plywood restaurants; and people reel from a combination of less energy and higher prices. Now forty-six years old and gaining, Rabbit does not blame anyone for *Skylab*'s falling or Exxon's greed, but death leers from the horizon, and he is afraid of running out of gas. When he looks over his shoulder at the glory of early fame too easily won on the basketball court and thinks of himself as "king of the lot" and "the star and spear point" of the flourishing Toyota dealership his family owns, we know that he has not changed much from the man in the earlier novels whose value system was defined in terms of athletic prowess.

But he has changed some: golf has replaced basketball, and he rumbles rather than runs with a forty-two-inch waist and a tendency to avoid mirrors when he used to love reflections of himself.

Still, Rabbit is rich in the ironic sense of being able to afford cashews instead of peanuts. Life is sweet. For the first time in twenty-five years he is happy to be alive, even happy with his marriage to Janice. Deserted by Harry in the first Rabbit novel and deserting him in the second, Janice fits snugly into a middle-age routine, plays tennis at the country club, and, says Rabbit, "never looked sharper." She still drinks too much, and she rarely serves meals on time, but she finally enjoys sex and even manages now and then to stand up to her husband.

Despite Janice, golf, and money, Rabbit needs to run, not as fast and not as far, but somewhere. He muses on "the entire squeezed and cut-down shape of his life," and he realizes that middle age is upon him, a time when dreams decline to awareness of limits and stomachs take on a noticeable sag. The strained jollity of the country club set, "the kind of crowd that will do a marriage in if you let it," makes him uneasy, but his flight in this novel is not as urgent as it is in *Rabbit, Run* and thus not as poignant. He knows that he is a "soft and a broad target."

Aiming at the target is his son Nelson,

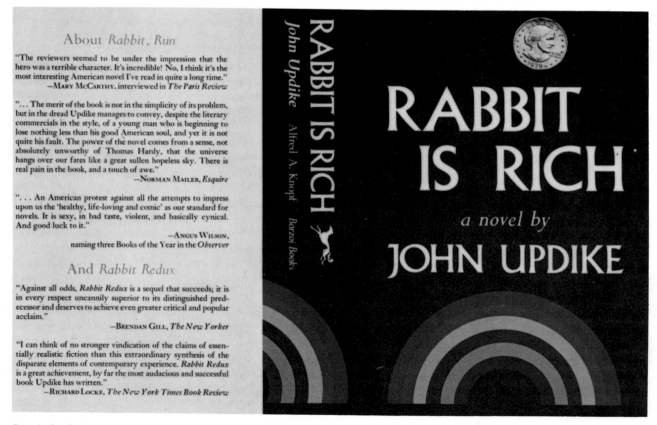

Dust jacket for Updike's third novel about Harry Angstrom, Rabbit Is Rich *(1981), which won the American Book Award, the Pulitzer Prize, and the National Book Critics Circle Award*

twenty-two years old, a surly college dropout, and, in Rabbit's eyes, "humpbacked and mean, a rat going out to be drowned." Hitchhiking home to a hurry-up marriage to a pregnant secretary, Nelson wants a job at Rabbit's Toyota dealership. Updike sketches the father-son tension with superb detail so that the reader understands Rabbit's lament: "How can you respect the world when you see it's being run by a bunch of kids turned old?" But that old bunch was once Rabbit's bunch, and Nelson will be right behind them. He is tired of being young, but he doesn't know how to grow up. Nelson lacks fluidity and grace. Sympathy for his fear of being trapped is not easy because, unlike his father, he has no intuitive sense of joy, no yearning. His wife is correct: he is a spoiled bully. Nelson runs but without Rabbit's faith; the son runs from while the father runs toward.

Later, Rabbit "glimpses the truth that to be rich is to be robbed, to be rich is to be poor." In part he means spiritually poor, though he would not say it that way, so he and Janice break from his mother-in-law and buy their own home. Maybe his rainbow is in the suburbs. He still longs for a world without ruts, but God has become a "raisin lost under the car seat." In the earlier novels, Rabbit runs toward transcendence, toward what he calls "it," but now he has only a vacation in the Caribbean to rejuvenate him. There, engaged in wife-swapping where he once pursued life's rhythm, he even misses his dream girl when he is paired with his second choice. Sex is part of Rabbit's scampering, his questing, as Updike established twenty years ago.

Rabbit returns home to find his son drifted back to college but his granddaughter born. The birth calms him for a moment, soothes his undefined sense of unsettledness, but he knows that it is also a giant step toward extinction: "What you lose as you age is witnesses." Mortality looms beyond the middle years.

It is sad to think of death setting its snare for Rabbit Angstrom, because after two decades and three long novels he has joined the pantheon of American literary heroes. Yet a glimpse of final defeat is the price to be paid for membership in that exclusive club. Like Natty Bumppo, Ahab, Huck Finn, Gatsby, Ike McCaslin, Holden Caulfield, and many others before him, Harry is learning that no matter how far he runs in space, he cannot outrace time.

Henry Bech has all but stopped running. In *Bech Is Back* (1982), Henry returns to the literary scene with a new wife and a new novel, but his old

bewilderment is still intact. His former mistress knows that the book is lousy, but the ad-fed public adores it anyway. Henry suspects that her judgment is correct; yet after suffering through a silence lasting more than a decade, he wonders how he can reject the royalties and the fanfare, since he has poured enough sex and violence into his latest novel to guarantee a best-seller all but created by media hype. Silence, he reasons, offers only limited rewards.

Bech is Updike's favorite writer, a character who promises to have the longevity of Rabbit in the Updike canon and who allows Updike the opportunity to work out the frustrations that inevitably trap the successful artist in America. When last seen in *Bech: A Book* (1970), Bech had published enough fiction to shape a reputation with the intelligentsia, had fallen into the hell of writer's block that, ironically, increased his reputation, and had emerged as a kind of artifact that Uncle Sam paraded around the globe to fulfill various cultural exchanges. Bech is Updike's joke on himself. More to the point, he is also Updike's joke on the discouraging hoopla with which Americans surround their authors in order to worship not the writing but the writer.

The laughs begin on the first page of *Bech: A Book*. There Updike reveals a letter to himself from Bech in which Bech says with his ego showing, "Well, if you must commit the artistic indecency of writing about a writer, better I suppose about me than about you." The laughs continued through the 1970s when Updike kept up the charade of Henry Bech as real author by publishing bogus interviews between Bech and himself in the *New York Times*.

Yet there is a serious tone to the laughter. The jokes about Bech may illustrate the appalling way America treats her authors, but Updike is just as concerned with the fate that dooms so many American writers to lesser and lesser achievement. While the royalty checks jump to six figures and the talk show appearances multiply, the quality of the writing diminishes. In 1974 Updike said in a speech entitled "Why Write?": *To remain interested—of* American novelists, only Henry James continued in old age to advance his art."

How right he is—but only up to a point. Those who care about American fiction may now place Updike's name beside James's. The point is not that he rivals James but that unlike Hawthorne and Melville, unlike Twain and Hemingway, unlike, arguably, even Faulkner, Updike has continued to advance his art. The hoopla dogs him too, as his picture on a recent cover of *Time* (18 October 1982) and his appearances on the talk shows illustrate, but

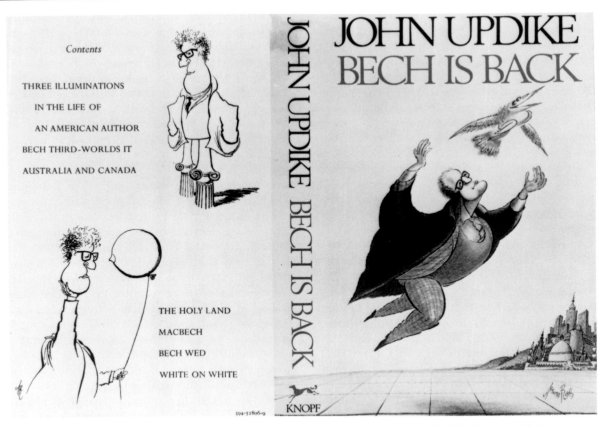

Dust jacket for Updike's second book (1982) about Henry Bech, a writer ruined by literary celebrity

at age fifty he has published twenty-six major books, most of them distinguished and all of them interesting. What other practicing American writer has pursued his art with such rigorous devotion to poetry, short stories, essays, drama, and fiction? What other American writer combines lyrical prose with such wide-ranging knowledge? What other American writer speaks so eloquently about domestic trauma, crises of belief, suburban tension, and the darkening road of middle age? The answer is no one except John Updike. Apprenticing himself in his early twenties to the long tradition of the man of letters, Updike stands tall in his early fifties as a dominant figure of contemporary literature.

Henry Bech is not so lucky. In *Bech Is Back* irony irritates his life. Even enduring reputation smarts: "Though Henry Bech, the author, in his middle years had all but ceased to write, his books continued, as if ironically, to live, to cast shuddering shadows toward the center of his life, where that thing called his reputation cowered." This sentence begins the book, and one thinks immediately of Bech's fellow author J.D. Salinger. But Salinger's

silence seems noble. Rejecting the show biz of big-time publishing, he may be writing his books only for himself. Bech's silence is more demeaning. Languishing in the success of his first novel, he is paralyzed by an old-fashioned writer's block. Silent before his public for almost fifteen years, Bech has become, to his dismay, a kind of myth.

But silence does not mean invisibility. If Americans cannot recognize true artists, they are proficient at worshiping stars. Rather than let Henry suffer privately from his inability to write, they send him around the world again to give speeches on "The Cultural Situation of the American Writer" and inadvertently to act the patsy to third-world audiences who use literature for political ends.

Henry's travels are the slowest part of *Bech Is Back*, but the entire book is a delight. Rebounding, for example, from the disillusion of meeting an avid collector who hoards Bech's novels for their potential value on the rare book market, Henry agrees for a price to sign his name to 28,500 of his books. Transported to a balmy island for the chore and ministered to by his mistress, Bech confronts a stunning silence: He cannot even write his own name.

When he finally does dodge the spotlight for a moment and inches his way toward true literary recognition, he is selected for, of all things, the Melville Medal, "awarded every five years to that American author who has maintained the most meaningful silence."

This kind of humor sparkles throughout *Bech Is Back*. Success, it seems, is unavoidable. Marrying his mistress's sister and moving to her family home in Ossining, he gives in to his wife's nudges to free his blocked inspiration with pep talks, changes the working title of his novel in progress from *Think Big* to *Easy Money*, and accepts the degradation of advertising's stranglehold on literature when Madison Avenue turns the book into a best-seller. "Bech is back," scream the hucksters, but, Henry and Updike muse, at what cost? Lionized as the latest rage, surrounded by New York's prettiest at a gaudy white-on-white party, he closes with a word that typifies the entire experience: "unclean."

For all Bech's troubles, however, one hopes that he will rebound again in ten years or so. For Updike has more to say about the paradox that afflicts writers: their craving for applause and their need for privacy. The conflict between easy money and noble silence is deadly to American artists. Rather than pontificate about this cultural trap in ponderous essays, Updike uses sharp wit and beautiful prose to create a memorable character who lives the dilemma.

Henry Bech may not be an author of lyrical grace and enduring fame.

But John Updike surely is.

Other:

Introduction to *Lectures on Literature* by Vladimir Nabokov (New York: Harcourt Brace Jovanovich/Bruccoli Clark, 1980), pp. xvii-xxvii.

Periodical Publications:

"Frontiersmen," *New Yorker* (8 September 1980): 106-114;

"The Last of Barthes," *New Yorker* (22 September 1980): 151-157;

"Still of Some Use," *New Yorker* (6 October 1980): 52-54;

"The Book of Laughter and Forgetting," *New York Times Book Review*, 30 November 1980, pp. 7, 74, 76, 78;

"An Earlier Day," *New Yorker* (15 December 1980): 162-170;

"An Armful of Field Flowers," *New Yorker* (29 December 1980): 69-72;

"Faibe Italiane," *New Yorker* (23 February 1981): 120-126;

"On Hawthorne's Mind," *New York Review of Books*, 19 March 1981, pp. 41-42;

"Worlds and Worlds," *New Yorker* (23 March 1981): 148-157;

"The Lovely Troubled Daughters of Our Old Crowd," *New Yorker* (6 April 1981): 38-39;

"Venezuela for Visitors," *New Yorker* (11 May 1981): 34-35;

"Fresh from the Forties," *New Yorker* (8 June 1981): 148-156;

"Happy on Nono Despite Odosha," *New Yorker* (29 June 1981): 98-100;

"Pygmalion," *Atlantic Monthly* (July 1981), p. 27;

"Hem Battles the Pack; Wins, Loses," *New Yorker* (13 July 1981): 96-106;

"Invasion of the Book Envelopes," *New Yorker* (20 July 1981): 33;

"Readers and Writers," *New Yorker* (3 August 1981): 90-93;

"Penumbrae," *New Yorker* (14 September 1981): 45;

"Updike on Updike," *New York Times Book Review*, 27 September 1981, pp. 1, 34-35;

"Rabbit Is Rich," *Playboy* (September 1981): 111ff.;

"The Long and Reluctant Stasis of Wan-li," *New Yorker* (5 October 1981): 182-191;

"The Fancy-Forger Takes the Lectern," *New Yorker* (2 November 1981): 183-188;

"The City," *New Yorker* (16 November 1981): 53-62;

"Two Late Arrivals, Featuring Resilient Females," *New Yorker* (14 December 1981): 200-209;

"Learn a Trade," *New Yorker* (28 December 1981): 42-44;

"No Dearth of Death," *New Yorker* (11 January 1982): 92-95;

"Killing," *Playboy* (January 1982): 102ff.;

"Private Lives, Public Tantrums," *World Tennis* (January 1982): 40;

"Toppling Towers Seen by a Whirling Soul," *New Yorker* (22 February 1982):120-128;

"On Such a Beautiful Green Little Planet," *New Yorker* (5 April 1982): 189-197;

"Gathering the Poets of Faith," *New York Times Book Review*, 11 April 1982, pp. 1, 18;

"A Mild 'Complaint,' " *New Yorker* (19 April 1982): 39;

"Reflections: Melville's Withdrawal," *New Yorker* (10 May 1982): 120-147;

"Borges Warmed Over," *New Yorker* (24 May 1982): 126-133;

"Deaths of Distant Friends," *New Yorker* (7 June 1982): 34-36;

"The Squeeze Is On," *New Yorker* (14 June 1982): 129-134;

"India Going On," *New Yorker* (16 August 1982): 84-89;

"More Stately Mansions," *Esquire* (October 1982): 142-157;

"Cohn's Doom," *New Yorker* (8 November 1982): 167-170.

Reference:

Paul Gray, "Perennial Promises, Kept," *Time* (18 October 1982): 72-81.

NEW ENTRIES

Ann Arensberg

(21 February 1937-   )

Diane Scholl
Luther College

BOOK: *Sister Wolf* (New York: Knopf, 1980; London: Sidgwick & Jackson, 1981).

Ann Arensberg is the author of several short stories, among them "Art History" and "Group Sex," which were included in O. Henry Awards collections, and of the novel *Sister Wolf*, published by Knopf in 1980.

Born in Pittsburgh, Pennsylvania, in 1937, Arensberg spent part of her childhood in Havana, Cuba, and later received her undergraduate education at Radcliffe College. Subsequently she earned her master's degree at Harvard University. At present she lives with her husband, Richard Grossman, the editor and author, in Salisbury, Connecticut, and in New York City. They are the parents of three daughters.

Arensberg's first novel is a chilling story of tormented love and jealousy. In *Sister Wolf* she has created an odd combination of elegance and primitive passion. Marit Deym is the central character, the daughter of displaced Hungarian aristocrats with a historic Magyar lineage and a mania for building massive and ornate structures. Left alone in young adulthood to occupy her parents' estate in the Berkshires, Marit wins the community's permission to begin a sanctuary for endangered species on her grounds.

She restlessly awaits a delivery van of wolves as the novel opens. For Marit animals are easier to understand and far more predictable than are humans:

> Marit loved wolves more than any other animal because they were the most reclusive and least valued. They tallied with her image of herself, but she did not try to scale them to her size. They were creatures and she was human, and she cherished the difference more than any likeness. When she was close to the wolves, she would learn what they could teach her: loyalty, endurance, stoicism, and courage, the traits that made them symbols of survival.

Marit is a virtual outcast in her semirural community, once a fashionable resort. She needs intimacy with very few humans, preferring to lavish her love on animals. Her woman friend Lola Brevard, social secretary to a local society matron, provides her with companionship and a refuge from unremitting loneliness. Their friendship is often close and amiable; although Lola is a lesbian, they do not share sexual intimacies. Marit admits to a need for a relationship with a man, and when startled Gabriel Frankman is driven to her door by his fear of her wolves, her impetuous, rather inexplicable lovemaking with him begins.

Gabriel teaches creative writing at Meyerling Community for the Unsighted, a progressive, benevolent institution for blind children which adjoins Marit's 150 acres. He has spent years of his life in an effort to control his temper and to assume a

203

self-sacrificing role, since a boyhood accident involving his injury to a playmate reduced him to shame and self-loathing. Later, his youthful affair with a brilliant but childlike scholar came to a tragic end when the young woman was run over in heavy traffic following an argument. Repentant for his not altogether unjustified criticism of the fey and incompetent Francesca, Gabriel has come to teach the blind in Niles, Massachusetts, in order to be close to her grave, which he visits daily.

Gabriel wears his love like a badge; because it is so very visible, it often fails to accomplish what his idealistic ambitions intend. In his effort to console his students and to convince them that their blindness is a gift, he often errs. His artless probing of their private emotions is often ill-timed. Although he manages to be a special friend to a young girl, Aimée, troubled by terrifying nightmares, his love is studied and self-conscious.

In contrast to Gabriel's love, Marit believes her desire for him to be primitive lust, a frank yet abashed physical need that leaves her diminished in his presence. Gabriel's often painstaking concern for others is the opposite of her mistrust of humans, the lesson of her harsh experience:

> What power she had to help her animals came from love untrammeled by suspicion, the kind of love that does not seek its own advantage or negotiate for favorable terms. With human beings her insight foundered in mistrust. When animals bared their fangs, they were enraged; in humans a show of teeth was called a smile. A freak of weather could make an animal erratic, or a tumor pressing in upon the brain; but human actions were always uncertain and perplexing, especially the actions of the people whom she wished to love.

The blind, the handicapped, only inspire her with uneasiness. Driven to distracted jealousy by Gabriel's story of his love affair with Francesca, she desecrates the woman's grave in a paroxysm of anger and grief which she is powerless to control. Again without obvious justification she is embittered over Gabriel's attentions to the blind, dream-tormented Aimée. In pursuit of an armed man she sees in her sanctuary, Marit spends a night in her wilderness enclosure, during which she finds Aimée stumbling through a waking nightmare of unfamiliar obstacles. Marit, driven by her jealousy and her senseless mistrust of the handicapped, does not help the girl back to Meyerling; she lets Aimée fall into a pond and leaves the girl to drown.

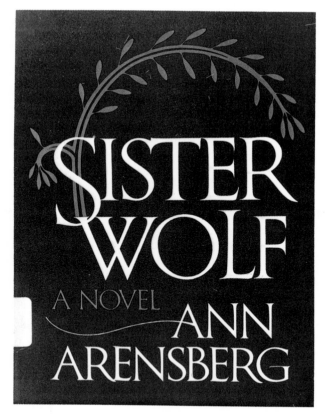

Dust jacket for Arensberg's 1980 novel, "a Gothic Passion play with animalistic overtones"

When Aimée's body is recovered, turtles have gnawed small holes in her face and limbs. Mistaking the work of the turtles for the savagery of the wolves, the townspeople descend on Marit's preserve with weapons. Marit is shot to death when she runs to save her beloved wolf, Swan. The wolves surround her in death, "taking precedence over any human kin."

Clearly Marit Deym is "Sister Wolf," acknowledging a love for animals which transcends her love for unpredictable people. Her avoidance of the human community for its petty vices and hypocrisies is not altogether well founded or acceptable in her. Lola Brevard, although she is a loyal friend to Marit, in her ruthless seduction of young athletic society girls, her callous withdrawal of affection when she is bored and restless, knows a diminished and self-serving kind of love in her human relationships too. In apparent contrast, the novel presents us with Gabriel's self-conscious denial of himself in his concern for others; perhaps the irony in his love is that he is also serving himself, in his overwhelming obsession with his own goodness and compassion.

Although *Sister Wolf* is not obviously a Christian novel, the iconography of the church is present throughout its course, in the epigraph which tells the story of St. Francis's peace pact made with Brother Wolf, and in the allusions to St. Sebastian, St. Peter, and St. Teresa. The Christian view of love is felt throughout the novel in the glaring omission of a just and honestly compassionate love displayed by the characters. Yet the need to love is powerful in most of them, as is evidenced by the blind boy who tells Marit that he keeps rabbits in spite of the scratches they inflict on his arms.

Called a "modern Gothic Passion play with animalistic overtones" by Jean Strouse in *Newsweek* (20 October 1980), *Sister Wolf* is a novel which suggests an allegorical reading in its depiction of the stark and elemental conflicts aroused by human passions. "Marit and Gabriel follow their self-destructive paths to a dénouement that leaves you wondering whether the meek will inherit the earth or throw it to the wolves," Strouse wrote. Clearly more than a cautionary tale, *Sister Wolf* causes the reader to consider the tangled web of human emotions and desires in its full complexity; one's tendency is to judge Marit in the end, but also to think ruefully of the difficulties implicit in human relationships.

Reviewers have been quick to note the fairy-tale qualities of the novel and its resemblance to folklore and legend. The Gothic elements threaten to get out of hand. "Imagine *Northanger Abbey* rewritten by Mrs. Radcliffe and you will have some idea of the problems raised by *Sister Wolf*. . . . Is it,

one wonders, an analysis of the over-heated Gothic imagination, or is it the only slightly abashed product of such? Ms. Arensberg's prose seems equally undecided, veering hectically between passages of acute psychological perceptiveness and sketches of pruriently heightened narrative where the only *frisson* induced is one of embarrassment," asserted Paul Taylor in the London *Times Literary Supplement* (3 April 1981). The fairy-tale elements are exploited to enable Arensberg "to arrive at significances which her story has not earned," Taylor claimed.

Yet Taylor acknowledged the author's "genuine insight into the workings of obsession," and it is for its startling originality that *Sister Wolf* is often praised. Ella Leffland wrote in the *New York Times Book Review* (28 December 1980) of Arensberg: "In Marit Deym she has created a character who combines extravagance and strangeness with something more commonly, and in the best sense, human. What reverberates is an oddly invigorating clang, a jolt of harsh, unyielding purity." In the unlikely combination of the strange and the recognizably human is the best of fiction to be found, and Arensberg's first novel is deserving of attention.

Other:
"Art History," in *Prize Stories, O. Henry Awards* (Garden City: Doubleday, 1975);
"Group Sex," in *Prize Stories, O. Henry Awards* (Garden City: Doubleday, 1980).

Ann Beattie
(8 September 1947-)

David M. Taylor
Livingston University

BOOKS: *Chilly Scenes of Winter* (Garden City: Doubleday, 1976);
Distortions (Garden City: Doubleday, 1976);
Secrets and Surprises (New York: Random House, 1978; London: Hamilton, 1979);
Falling in Place (New York: Random House, 1980; London: Secker & Warburg, 1981);
The Burning House (New York: Random House, 1982).

Ann Beattie was twenty-one when on 15 August 1969 the first wave of what would grow to a throng of over 300,000 youths began to trickle onto a 600-acre pastoral site at Bethel, New York, to attend a three-day folk and rock music festival that had been billed as the Woodstock Music and Art Fair and Aquarian Exposition. The energized crowd joined Joan Baez in "We Shall Overcome" and eagerly awaited the arrival of other such greats as Janis Joplin, Jimi Hendrix, and the Grateful Dead. As the event progressed, reporters would describe the multitude as amiable in spite of the traffic jams, the food and water shortages, and the occasional bad trips from a circulating batch of second-grade acid. Elsewhere on 15 August, President Richard Nixon was reconsidering a scheduled second major withdrawal of American troops from Vietnam in light of increased enemy aggression; demands were being made for an autopsy on the body of Mary Jo Kopechne, who had drowned on Chappaquiddick Island less than a month earlier; and the *New York Times* ran a feature story on a special summer course in guerrilla warfare being offered at Scarsdale High School.

Woodstock was to become a symbol of the children of the Age of Aquarius, the iconoclastic youth of the 1960s who enumerated the failings of their fathers and abjured convention in favor of ostensibly more promising avenues of fulfillment. Ann Beattie was, involuntarily, to become identified as a chronicler of the postlapsarian counterculture, what James N. Baker calls Beattie's "own lost generation: the committed young people of the late '60s who ten years later have found themselves demoralized by society's code of ordinariness, which they have tentatively begun to embrace." Her

Ann Beattie

characters are generally educated middle-class WASPs who live in New Hampshire, Vermont, Connecticut, Maine, or New York. Their earlier idealism has eroded in the face of the bleak prospects of the 1970s, and they are often between jobs or trapped in boring jobs. They live in old houses, drive aging automobiles, smoke marijuana, and listen to music. Most of all, they suffer—from indirection, indecision, angst. Their personal landscapes are cluttered with ex-spouses and ex-lovers and often with less promising could-be or would-be lovers. They live with a foot in the past, holding Gatsby dreams, but despite their characteristic egocentricity, they are surprisingly congenial and often even generous to a fault. Their anomie imparts to Beattie's fiction a slow-motion effect, 33-rpm characters operating in a 45-rpm world.

Beattie begrudgingly acknowledges the merits of reviewers' arguments that she speaks for the youth of the 1960s. "It is certainly true that people I write about are essentially my age," she tells Joyce Maynard in the *New York Times Book Review*, "and so they were a certain age in the 60's and had certain common experiences and tend to listen to the same kind of music and get stoned and wear the same kind of clothes." Beattie has explained that much of her material arises from observation of her friends, and although the resulting characters are said to be composites, a friend who felt the identification a little too obvious in a *New Yorker* story once flung that copy of the magazine across the room. In discussing her first novel, *Chilly Scenes of Winter* (1976), with Bob Miner in the *Village Voice*, Beattie admits that "I *was* going out of my way in the novel to say something about the 60's having passed," explaining that the anomie of its characters "just seems to me to be an attitude that most of my friends and most of the people I know have. They all feel sort of let down, either by not having involved themselves more in the '60s now that the '70s are so dreadful, or else by having involved themselves very much to no avail." Despite such concessions, Beattie has with increasing fervor struggled against being reduced to a cultic voice. "I usually think it's very irritating when people talk to me about . . . being the writer of the '70s about the lost '60s kind of stuff," she says to Maggie Lewis in the *Christian Science Monitor*. "I keep protesting that's a horribly reductive approach to my work." She insists upon the value of her writing beyond sociological record, telling Maynard that if readers choose to take the counterculture "as a stepping stone for what I'm writing about, well, it's there. . . . but what I've always hoped for is that somebody will then start talking more about the meat and bones of what I'm writing about." The counterculture skin is indeed thick, particularly in the earlier works, but the reader who flays period eccentricities finds universal concerns: the fragility and vacillation of human interrelationships, the search for self-identification, the burdens of alienation from society.

Beattie is more James than Hemingway in her method of collecting material. She tells Maynard, "I was watching the 1960's on my parents' television. I wasn't out getting gassed every day. I never took acid." She admits that she is "much more interested in alienation than I personally feel alienated." Her father was a retired HEW administrator, and Beattie was raised in Washington, D.C. She earned a B.A. in English at American University in 1969 and an M.A. at the University of Connecticut in 1970,

afterward entering the Ph.D. program, but she stopped short of the degree. In Connecticut she met and later married David Gates, a musician who, *People* reports, also works for *Newsweek*, writing responses to letters from readers. She left Connecticut for Charlottesville, where she taught at the University of Virginia until 1977, when she accepted the position of Briggs-Copeland Lecturer in English at Harvard. She later returned to Virginia for a brief stay as visiting writer. She left Harvard, she explains to Mary Vespa in *People*, "without ever meeting the head of the English department. . . . I did not feel important at Harvard." With a Guggenheim grant of $10,000, Beattie returned to Connecticut, where she lived in an old house in the suburbs of West Redding until she moved to New York in 1980. She has received several other awards, including an award of excellence from the American Academy and Institute of Arts and Letters in 1980.

Beattie speaks of her literary achievement almost casually, sidesteps membership in literary circles, and thwarts the portrait of writer as oracle. Maggie Lewis comments that Beattie, attired in "Adidas, army surplus fatigue pants, and T-shirt," looks out of place in New York's Algonquin lounge, "that dark brown wood-panelled literary preserve haunted since the Thurber and Ross days by denizens of the New Yorker." Maynard describes a more natural habitat, the Connecticut house: "Inside this house there are objects enough to set up a shop on Columbus Avenue: comfortable, unmatched second-hand furniture and antiques, good Oriental rugs and a giant cardboard Land O'Lakes Butter sign. There are books along the walls, except where there are records: rock, blues, soul, jazz, country. Clusters of photographs from the 20's, a large head of Richard Nixon and a formal framed portrait of L.B.J., Lady Bird, Luci and Lynda, hand tinted. There are tiny celluloid baby dolls, a tin kangaroo wind-up toy, shells, a set of toy appliances still in the box, labeled 'My Dream Kitchen.' A 1940's dust-bowl kind of dress hangs from the ceiling with a bulldog face mask attached and a long scarf draped around the neck." Beattie reports a fondness for wearing her husband's clothes when she writes and says she produces her works in brief, intense bursts of creative energy, often writing eighteen hours a day, with lengthy intervals between works. "What I do most is *not* write," she says in *People*.

Beattie explains that she more or less wandered into writing fiction, partially out of the frustration she felt about the handling of literature in graduate courses. "I never had a burning ambition to become a writer," she says to Michiko Kakutani in the *New York Times Book Review*. "I started writing because I was bored with graduate school—in some kind of attempt to care about literature again, I guess I started writing it. Years ago when I might have done something else, I just didn't pursue it, and now I don't know what else to call myself except a writer." When asked by Lewis if she had been in a hurry to have her work published, Beattie replies, "I was in a big hurry not to be impoverished, and I was in a big hurry to get out of graduate school, and I was in a big hurry never to teach again. Writing was just sort of a process of elimination. I don't have tremendous skills in a tremendous number of areas. I never really set out to be a writer. I just sort of backed into it." While at the University of Connecticut, Beattie placed short stories in several publications, including the *Western Humanities Review* and the *Texas Quarterly*. Some twenty submissions, however, were rejected by the *New Yorker* before "A Platonic Relationship" was published in the 8 April 1974 issue. She has since become a regular contributor to the *New Yorker*; J. D. O'Hara, to whom *Falling in Place* (1980) is dedicated, has called her, in the *New York Times Book Review*, "the best new writer to come down that particular pike since Donald Barthelme."

Beattie's fiction has been both panned and praised for its form. Her works characteristically depend upon voluminous detail that establishes mood rather than upon well-planned linear plot. As Jack Beatty observes in the *New Republic*, Beattie, "along with her characters, . . . seems to be stalling, marking time, trying to figure out what to do next." Beattie freely admits that she writes blindly, explaining to Lewis that "when I sit down to write something it's very true that I only know the first line or I only know one tiny part of some tiny event. I don't even know how that will turn out in the story. . . . I really don't have ideas—that is, discussable, bandyable-about ideas that you can point to." Some readers find the accumulation of detail without careful plotting boring and irritating. However, as Daniel Zitin perceptively notes in a review of *The Burning House* (1982), "The structural weakness of her stories emphasizes her themes. There is little action. . . . She is less interested in narrative, in the unfolding of events, than she is in states of being, moments, immobility." The anomie of Beattie's characters is reinforced by the indirection of plot. "My stories are a lot about chaos," she tells Miner, " . . . and many of the simple flat statements that I bring together are usually non sequiturs—or bordering on being non sequiturs—which reinforces the chaos." The lack of well-planned complication

and climax can understandably lead to difficulty with denouement. "I get into a lot of trouble with endings," Beattie explains to Maynard. "They either come to me or they don't." She adds that she has written one novel that was never published—was "a total loss"—because after 400 pages, she "still had no idea what the ending was." (Both *Chilly Scenes of Winter* and *Falling in Place* have been criticized for unrealistically "happy" endings.) It is not unexpected that a writer who says her stories offer no answers because she doesn't believe there are any answers to offer would shy from neatly resolved conflicts. Thomas Griffith maintains in the *Atlantic Monthly* that the absence of such neat resolutions accounts for Beattie's *New Yorker* audience: "*New Yorker* fiction, . . . in its rejection of moralizing and pat endings, has stayed true to [Harold] Ross. Nothing is ever summed up, or brought to an end; a moment passes and is wryly commented upon. It is a fictional approximation of value-free science."

Many readers agree that Beattie's method is more successful in the short story than in the prolonged format of the novel, where the volume of detail can become tedious and the lack of structure frustrating. Commenting on *Chilly Scenes of Winter* in the *New England Review*, Blanche H. Gelfant writes that "Beattie is more exciting, more creative with *nothing*, as a short story writer than as a novelist," explaining that "the short story will be sustained by trivia; a sudden revelation of the significance they have hidden . . . will surprise and satisfy. But the novel becomes monotonous when insignificant details multiply and recur." Pearl K. Bell, writing for *Commentary*, applies the same reasoning to *Falling in Place*: "While . . . wads of dissociated irrelevance have sometimes worked in Ann Beattie's short stories, they become unendurably monotonous in a novel unless the purposeless inertia is disrupted by some decisive action." She grants that such a "decisive action" occurs in *Falling in Place*, the accidental shooting of a teenage girl by her younger brother, but objects that it does not occur until the novel is half over, and it results in no meaningful change in the lives of the characters.

Beattie's style is decidedly "unliterary." She writes in straightforward, unadorned sentences in which metaphor is surprising because of its rarity. A passage from *Chilly Scenes of Winter* is representative: "The rain has stopped. Charles turns on the radio. Elvis Presley is singing 'Loving You.' Elvis Presley is forty. Charles turns off the radio. Susan wipes tears out of her eyes." Beattie tells Miner, "I write in those flat simple sentences because that's the way I think. I don't mean to do it as a technique.

Dust jacket for Beattie's second novel, which Richard Locke called the most impressive American novel of the spring 1980 publishing season

It might just be that I am incapable of breaking through to the complexities underlying all that sort of simple statement you find in my work." Several critics have observed that upon initial confrontation, the style appears tedious, but that the tedium dissipates as the characters establish themselves because, as Bell observes, "Beattie's austerely unadorned, uninflected, all but catatonic prose is the exact language of these lost souls. . . . the medium becomes the message; she slyly affects the uncritical neutrality of a tape recorder, never signaling us to notice how ingenious and canny a device of literary style this is."

Beattie's debut in book form was impressive with Doubleday's simultaneous publication of *Chilly Scenes of Winter* and her first short story collection, *Distortions*, on 13 August 1976. The novel was offered as a Book-of-the-Month Club alternate. The protagonist of *Chilly Scenes of Winter*, Charles, is a study in paralysis. His only articulated desire is to regain his lover Laura, who has returned to her husband, her stepdaughter, and her A-frame, yet he makes minimal effort to effect a reconciliation,

partially from fear of rebuff. Instead, he wafts along with his *idée fixe*, finding some solace in the companionship of his friend Sam, and being plagued by the psychic intrusions of relatives, friends, and acquaintances—each with his own nebulous yearning. Charles's hypochondriacal mother seeks relief through alcohol, movie magazines, laxatives, and excessive bathing. His stepfather, Pete, reminiscent of Carson McCullers's Biff in his maternal desire for children and of Nathanael West's Homer in his ineffectual attempts at communication, looks to the trappings of Middle America—dance lessons, BankAmericard, and a Honda Civic with a good Turtle Wax shine. Charles's ex-lover Pamela tries lesbianism. Sam is perhaps the most engaging, yet the most aimless, character in the novel. A Phi Beta Kappa with abandoned plans for law school, Sam is an unemployed clothing salesman whose nostalgic longing for his dog, dead at eight, parallels Charles's longing for Laura throughout the work. (Dogs, dead or alive, appear often in Beattie's fiction, sometimes almost achieving human status because their condition so closely mirrors that of the characters. Beattie has often been photographed with her own dog, Rufus, a part collie, part huskie that is erroneously listed as her son in *Who's Who in America*.)

Set in a large unidentified city, which John Updike speculates in the *New Yorker* is Washington, D. C., the novel takes place during the 1974-1975 Christmas and New Year season, a time which accentuates the unhappiness of the characters. Reminders of the lost 1960s seem omnipresent for Charles and Sam. The seemingly ubiquitous music from radio or stereo serves to remind the two that Janis Joplin and Brian Jones are dead, that even Jim Morrison's *widow* is dead. The lyrics are often poignantly appropriate to the situation, but Beattie has said she uses whatever songs happen to be playing as she writes. Serving as foil to Sam and Charles, who turns twenty-seven during the novel, is Charles's nineteen-year-old sister, Susan. Charles is scandalized by Susan's lack of reverence for what he considers the glorious past: "What a generation. Never heard of Amy Vanderbilt. Never heard of Dale Carnegie. And you think Woodstock was a drag." Charles's rosy coloring of the 1960s is grounded in large part, it seems, in vicarious experience. "I almost went to Woodstock," he says. "I wish I had gone to Woodstock."

Beattie's portrait of Charles is keenly insightful. Updike comments that "she succeeds in showing love from the male point of view, not in its well-publicized sexual dimension but in the pastel spectrum of nostalgia, daydream, and sentimental longing." Charles's yearning for the past is accompanied by a paranoia about the present. He is near hysteria when around policemen, uneasily checks his pockets for cash at the grocery store checkout, and is haunted by thoughts of inoperable melanoma. Charles longs for the safety of childhood, where he thinks his withdrawal would be more acceptable. He would like Susan to be his mother rather than his sister. Then he could sit in her lap—"he could curl up and shut his eyes, and everyone would think he was being good, instead of bad." Susan, at times wisely mature in contrast to her brother, calls Charles an egomaniac: "You deliberately make yourself suffer all the time because then you can be aware of *yourself*."

Despite the wretched condition of her protagonist, Beattie escapes sentimentality in *Chilly Scenes of Winter* through humor, mostly black humor arising from the idiosyncratic life-styles of her characters and the inclusion of such things as a Dewars profile of Richard Nixon. And the novel ends, unrealistically to some readers, on an upbeat. Sam adopts a new dog, and Charles and Laura reconcile. But Sam's new dog is a "terrible genetic mistake," a mixture of dachshund and cocker spaniel, and the reader must wonder if Charles and Laura's reunion is not folie à deux. Responding to Maynard's observation that her two novels "have surprisingly hopeful endings—considering the bleakness of the characters' situations earlier in the books," Beattie says, "If you had the facts of the story, maybe so, but if you had the cumulative effect of the material that's gone before, it should somewhat alter your unmitigated joy in finding out the characters are going off together." She adds that the reader should understand by the end of *Chilly Scenes of Winter* that Charles is "a strange enough character and that they're mismatched enough that the rest of their life clearly isn't going to be easy." J. D. O'Hara cautions that the novel's statement does not evolve from the love affair. The work's major theme, he observes, "is not waiting for an answer or Laura or love, but waiting itself, wistful anticipation, life unfulfilled and yearning."

The ending of *Chilly Scenes of Winter* became even more problematic in Joan Micklin Silver's film adaptation of the novel, entitled *Head Over Heels*. The movie's conclusion even exceeds Hollywood's usual penchant for happy endings. Co-starring John Heard and Mary Beth Hurt, *Head Over Heels* opened in New York in the fall of 1979 and was withdrawn after five weeks. Beattie, who appears in a cameo role as a waitress in the film, has said the

title "sounded as if Fred Astaire should be dancing across the credits." The movie was rereleased in 1982 with the original title and an edited ending.

Beattie's second published novel, *Falling in Place*, followed four years after *Chilly Scenes of Winter* and was written, Beattie says, in seven weeks at the cost of two burnt-out typewriters. The novel reflects something of a departure from Beattie's usual method, perhaps a conscious effort on the author's part to refute her assignment as a spokesman of the counterculture and to deal with earlier criticism of structure. She broadens her repertoire of characters and provides a definite climax—a "decisive action" as Pearl K. Bell calls it. The changes did not go unnoted by critics. Comparing the novel with the earlier fiction, Richard Locke says in the *New York Times Book Review* that *Falling in Place* is "like going from gray televison to full-color movies" and labels it "the most impressive American novel of the season."

The setting, the black humor, the accumulation of detail, even the theme of *Falling in Place* are familiar to readers of the earlier works, but Beattie offers a greater variety of perspectives. The novel is set in Connecticut and New York during the summer of 1979, the time firmly established through saturation of the familiar Beattie detail: Skylab is

Dust jacket for Beattie's third collection of stories (1982)

falling, Blondie is singing "Heart of Glass" on the radio, Sally Field is starring in *Norma Rae*. There are centers of action, one of which involves the deteriorating family of forty-year-old advertising man John Knapp. John escapes his suburban Connecticut home and his lifeless marriage to Louise during the week, when he lives with his mother in Rye, New York, and commutes to his office in Manhattan. There he finds a haven in the cramped Columbus Avenue apartment of his twenty-five-year-old mistress, Nina, a clerk at Lord and Taylor who is often surrounded by pot-smoking friends. Back in New Haven, Louise mourns over her dead dog and attempts to cope with her loneliness through her friendship with a staunch women's liberationist. The Knapps' fifteen-year-old daughter, Mary, maintains a running feud with her obese ten-year-old brother, John Joel, apotheosizes Peter Frampton, and generally illustrates the unpleasant aspects of adolescence. John Joel occupies himself with hating his sister and with his single, last-resort friendship with a twelve-year-old miscreant named Parker, who finds entertainment in such things as punching holes in his mother's diaphragm. The youngest Knapp child, Brandt, lives with John's alcoholic mother in Rye.

Another center of action is found in Mary Knapp's summer-school English teacher, Cynthia Forrest. A doctoral student at Yale, Cynthia is plagued by her unappreciative students and her uncertain relationship with her lover, Peter Spangle. Beattie accommodates this host of characters plus a number of peripheral characters through a cinematic method, with numerous, often abrupt, shifts in scene. There is an attempt to connect the different sets of characters toward the end of the novel. The reader discovers that Peter Spangle is Nina's former lover, and the two rendezvous with John and Cynthia waiting in the wings. The action climaxes when John Joel, under Parker's guidance, points what he soon discovers to be a loaded gun at Mary and pulls the trigger. The incident is the coup de grace for John's failed marriage, prompting him to confront his wife with the possibility of divorce in order to commit himself to Nina. *Falling in Place* ends with the same type of fragile, tentative happiness found with Charles and Laura. John and Nina are together, and Cynthia and Spangle are together, but there's little basis for optimistic predictions about the future.

The critical consensus appears to be that Ann Beattie's talents are better realized in the short story than in the novel, and she has happily been prolific in that genre, publishing three sizable collections in

six years: *Distortions* (1976), *Secrets and Surprises* (1978), and *The Burning House* (1982). Most of the collected stories first appeared in the *New Yorker*. Given the indirection of the typical Beattie character and the subsequent monotonal plot, the stories in collection, as Baker observes, "tend to blur," yet certain stories, such as "Friends" in *Secrets and Surprises*, stand out in their achievement. The characters in the last two collections are less grotesque than those in *Distortions*, but the difference lies primarily in Beattie's maturing artistry—her growing ability to deal more subtly with the nuances of her characters' lives. Margaret Atwood's observations in the *New York Times Book Review* on the stories in *The Burning House* are applicable as well to those in *Distortions* and *Secrets and Surprises*: "These people are on maintenance doses, getting from one day to the next, like a climber seizing the next rung on the ladder without having any idea of where he's going or wants to go. . . . These are stories not of suspense but of suspension." James Baker's comments in *Newsweek* on *Secrets and Surprises* also describe the stories in the other two collections: "Reading Ann Beattie's short stories is like reading reports of bad weather ahead. Beattie tells us how things stand with her unhappy characters, yet gives them little to do but endure the prospect of more rain."

Television Script:
"Weekend," WNET, New York, 20 April 1982.

Interviews:
Bob Miner, "Ann Beattie: 'I Write Best When I Am Sick,' " *Village Voice*, 9 August 1976, pp. 33-34;
Maggie Lewis, "The Sixties: Where Are They Now? Novelist Ann Beattie Knows," *Christian Science Monitor*, 23 October 1979, pp. B6-B10;
Joyce Maynard, "Visiting Ann Beattie," *New York Times Book Review*, 11 May 1980, pp. 1, 39-41.

References:
James Atlas, "How 'Chilly Scenes' was Rescued," *New York Times*, 10 October 1982, pp. 15, 25;
Margaret Atwood, "Stories From the American Front," *New York Times Book Review*, 26 September 1982, pp. 1, 34;
James Baker, "Lost Generation," *Newsweek* (22 January 1979): 76;
Whitney Balliett, "Closeups," *New Yorker* (9 June 1980): 148, 150, 154;
Jack Beatty, "*Falling in Place*," *New Republic* (7 June 1980): 34-36;
Pearl K. Bell, "Literary Waifs," *Commentary*, 67 (February 1979): 67-71;

Bell, "Marge Piercy and Ann Beattie," *Commentary*, 70 (July 1980): 59-61;

Anatole Broyard, "Books of the Times: *Secrets and Surprises*," *New York Times*, 3 January 1979, p. C17;

Broyard, "Kicking and Falling," *New York Times*, 25 September 1982, p. 16;

Broyard, "The Shock of Unrecognition," *New York Times*, 24 August 1976, p. 27;

Walter Clemons, "Secret Societies," *Newsweek* (5 May 1980): 86-88;

Blanche H. Gelfant, "Ann Beattie's Magic Slate *or* The End of the Sixties," *New England Review*, 1 (1979): 374-384;

John Gerlach, "Through 'The Octascope': A View of Ann Beattie," *Studies in Short Fiction*, 17 (Fall 1980): 489-494;

Gail Godwin, "Sufferers From Smug Despair," *New York Times Book Review*, 14 January 1979, p. 14;

Thomas Griffith, "Rejoice If You Can," *Atlantic Monthly*, 246 (September 1980): 28-29;

Ann Hulbert, "*Falling in Place*," *Saturday Review*, 7 (June 1980): 82;

Hulbert, "*Secrets and Surprises*," *New Republic* (20 January 1979): 34-36;

Margo Jefferson, "Going Down the Drain," *Newsweek* (23 August 1976): 76;

Michiko Kakutani, "Portrait of the Artist as a First Novelist," *New York Times Book Review*, 8 June 1980, pp. 7, 38;

Annie Leibovitz, "Ann Beattie," *Vogue*, 170 (July 1980): 148-151, 193-194;

John Leonard, "Books of the Times: *Falling in Place*," *New York Times*, 2 May 1980, p. C25;

Maggie Lewis, "Bleak Lives Vividly Painted," *Christian Science Monitor*, 4 June 1980, p. 17;

Richard Locke, "Keeping Cool," *New York Times Book Review*, 11 May 1980, pp. 1, 38-39;

G. E. Murray, "Secrets and Surprises," *Saturday Review* (20 January 1979): 65;

John J. O'Connor, "TV: Ann Beattie Story on 'American Playhouse,' " *New York Times*, 20 April 1982, p. C14;

J. D. O'Hara, "*Chilly Scenes of Winter, Distortions*," *New York Times Book Review*, 15 August 1976, pp. 14, 18;

John Romano, "Ann Beattie & the 60's," *Commentary*, 63 (February 1977): 62-64;

R. Z. Sheppard, "A Summer of Discontent," *Time* (12 May 1980): 79;

John Updike, "Seeresses," *New Yorker* (29 November 1976): 164ff.;

Mary Vespa, "Once a Cub Among Literary Bears, Ann Beattie Finds Her Career Falling in Place," *People* (16 June 1980): 67-68;

Paul Wilner, "For the '60s, With Love and Squalor," *Village Voice*, 9 August 1976, pp. 33-34;

Daniel Zitin, "Fixed and Unchangeable," *Nation* (30 October 1982): 441-442.

Gregory Benford
(30 January 1941-   )

Mark J. Lidman
University of South Carolina at Sumter

BOOKS: *Deeper Than the Darkness* (New York: Ace, 1970); republished as *The Stars in Shroud* (New York: Putnam's, 1978; London: Gollancz, 1979);

Jupiter Project (Nashville: Nelson, 1975; London: Sphere, 1982);

If the Stars Are Gods, by Benford and Gordon Eklund (New York: Putnam's, 1977; London: Gollancz, 1978);

In the Ocean of Night (New York: Dial/James Wade, 1977; London: Sidgwick & Jackson, 1978);

Find the Changeling, by Benford and Eklund (New York: Dell, 1980; London: Sphere, 1982);

Timescape (New York: Simon & Schuster, 1980; London: Gollancz, 1980).

A distinguished scientist, Gregory Benford is acutely aware of modern society's fascination with technology, but his novels also stress the negative aspects of living in a technological age. His works about alien contact have an appeal that is widespread in the 1980s, and his works which deal with science show us that we must learn to live intelligently in a technological world.

Gregory Benford

An identical twin, Gregory Benford was born in Mobile, Alabama, in 1941 to James and Mary Benford. His father's decision to remain in the army after World War II enabled him to see much of the world. The Benfords lived in Japan, Atlanta, Germany, and Texas before Gregory went to the University of Oklahoma to study physics. He graduated in 1963 and was a Woodrow Wilson Fellow in 1963-1964. Benford then received his M.S. in physics in 1965 and his Ph.D. in theoretical physics from the University of California at San Diego in 1967. An avid science fiction reader before he became a writer, Benford for several years edited a fan magazine (or fanzine) called *Void*. Among his coeditors were science fiction luminaries Terry Carr and Ted White. Benford's first published story, "Stand-in" (1965), won second place in a contest organized by the *Magazine of Fantasy and Science Fiction* and promised a bright future for its author.

Benford's achievements in physics perhaps overshadow his accomplishments as an author, although his careers complement each other. His novels are characterized by thoughtful composition and scientific expertise, and his work experience lends authenticity to his perspective on science. He worked as a research assistant at the University of California at San Diego from 1964 to 1967 and at the Lawrence Radiation Laboratory in Livermore, California, from 1969 to 1971, following a two-year postdoctoral fellowship there from 1967 to 1969. Since 1971 he has been a physics professor at the University of California, Irvine. He lives at Laguna Beach with his wife, Joan, and their children, Alyson and Mark.

In addition to his novels, Benford has written research papers on plasma physics, astrophysics, and solid-state physics and has contributed articles to *Smithsonian* and *Natural History*. He has received grants from the Office of Naval Research, the National Science Foundation, and the Army Research Organization. He belongs to the Royal Astronomical Society, the International Astronomical Union, and the American Physical Society. Benford's background in science has led him to what David N. Samuelson calls "an agnostic position" regarding aliens and man's first encounter with them, his favorite theme. Recognizing both the statistical probability that there are intelligent aliens and the improbability that man has met them, Benford focuses on the desire for contact in the realm of human imagination—both for its artistic and scientific potential. He views science fiction as an attempt to incorporate the landscape of modern science into human scales, including theology.

Benford's treatment of the alien theme has evolved through his writings. His afterword to "And the Sea Like Mirrors" in 1972 suggested dimensions of the alien theme in his later fiction:

> The alien doesn't have to be some extraterrestrial life form. Every person on this planet is undergoing a continuous encounter with the incredibly strange world our technology is creating for us just around the corner. It is alien. We have to come to terms with it. So we adjust, we change, we accept. And often we don't know what price we have had to pay.

But early in his career, Benford's treatment of the alien was rather melodramatic, as two 1971 stories indicate. In "Battleground" the enemy alien is depicted as a gigantic man-eating insect which travels in time; in "Star Crossing," polyp aliens reproduce by budding. However, even at this early point in his career, Benford was intrigued by the alienness of mankind. The Quarn, the alien enemy in his first novel, can be regarded as a distorted mirror of the human condition and not merely as "the enemy."

Deeper Than the Darkness (1970), rewritten as *The Stars in Shroud* (1978), concerns the villainous Quarn who try to spread a psychic disease among members of earth's far-flung space empire by disrupting the human sense of community. Humans prevail in this psychological war, but the victory is at best Pyrrhic for the forces of individualism. For Benford this novel seems to represent the first step in the evolution of the alien theme in his fiction.

In his later novels the human hero is also an alien, an outcast from his own society. This idea is made clear in two works which vaulted Benford into prominence among science fiction writers. *If the Stars Are Gods* (1977), written with Gordon Eklund, and *In the Ocean of Night* (1977) represent an extension of and, at the same time, a reaction against the use of aliens in other science fiction. In Benford's fiction, the term "alien" need not apply only to extraterrestrial beings. Humans themselves can be "alienated" or outcast from their own societies, and Benford often draws parallels between human and extraterrestrial aliens.

If the Stars Are Gods, an expansion of the 1974 Nebula Award-winning novelette, centers on Bradley Reynolds, astronaut and alien seeker, who finds himself "doubly alienated." Ill at ease with other men, he has devoted his life to questing for the impossible; now preferring to work alone, he has been chosen to contact Jonathon and Richard, two giraffelike beings from a distant planet who have come to "worship" our sun. Since climactic changes threaten their planet, they seek a benevolent new world. Reynolds finds himself identifying more and more with the aliens, which estranges him further from humankind. While American scientists explain the complex climate changes in terms of astrophysics, the aliens explain the phenomena in religious, even mystical, terms, and Reynolds tries to establish contact with the sun in a mystical way as well. At the end, Reynolds wants to accompany Jonathon and Richard, who refuse to allow him on their ship. Like Swift's Houyhnhnms, the aliens are incapable of lying, so it seems, and the whole of *If the Stars Are Gods* may recall *Gulliver's Travels*, but its protagonist is a middle-aged man trying to discover himself; he is not a butt of satire.

The protagonist of *In the Ocean of Night*, Nigel Walmsley, is the only British astronaut in the American program, which makes him somewhat "alien":

> Now, when he spoke amid these flat American voices, he heard his father's smooth vowels. Angina and emphysema had stolen these two blended figures from him, finally, but here in this alien land he felt them closer than before.

Moreover, Nigel is continually second-guessed by a paranoiac American bureaucracy which feels itself threatened by the New Sons of God, a popular but irrational religious movement, and by new

economic rivals, such as Brazil and China. The novel's first part, set in 1999, centers on Nigel's refusal to destroy an alien spacecraft originally thought to be merely an asteroid. In another treatment of the rather well-worn "national security versus potential scientific knowledge" dilemma, Nigel agrees to destroy the craft but is scorned by many for his initial refusal. In the book's second part, set fifteen years later, the world has not forgotten Nigel's earlier refusal, but his unique experience with alien contact makes him more qualified to contact another ship, J-27, or "the Snark," as Nigel calls it. This strange ship takes over the body of Nigel's lover at the moment of her death; later, the craft uses Nigel's own senses to explore the earth's environment. At the end of part two, the Snark meets Nigel in space and educates him about the realities of the universe:

> He would pass through that lens. All would pass. But for the moment:
>
> The Snark   feels the booming
> pulse
>
> unfolds the rocks
> before him
>
> carves the dry air
>
> smacks boots into
> yielding earth—
>
> seeing
>
> tasting
>
> opening.
>
> Eases him into the warming world.
>
> Pins him loving to the day
>
> —EversLubkinShirleyHufmanAlexandriaAlexandria—
>
> Thinking of them, knowing he will return to that world someday, a weight slips from him and he rolls and basks and floats in these familiar waters of the desert.
>   EversHufmanShirley—
>
> Alien, they are, his brothers.
>
> So alien.

One of the lessons which the Snark imparts to Nigel

3

Lydia carefully unpatches the chemsampler from her arm. There

are
~~were~~ other tubes and wires; they all came off pretty easily. The

lights   violet,
medmon ~~lit~~ up with warnings: ~~blue,~~ red, orange, oscillating pink.

thinks. She lets a tremor of excitement almost
Rather pretty, Lydia ~~thought,~~ ~~letting the feeling wind seep through~~
like lust sweep through
her with a heady energy.

is getting together her personal effects
She ~~was pulling on a blouse~~ when Dr Reiss comes bustling in.
"Hey, hey,
What's this I hear?" he ~~said~~ says with a compressed kind of joviality.
no. Just no."
"Frank," she ~~said~~ says flatly. And ~~left~~ leaves it at that. They had
gone
~~been~~ through all the stages already and she thinks he owes her some-
A Death therapy.
thing better than this false bouyancy. She had been through the

stages with Frank, and with Rita, the therapist. Rejection of the

news, followed by an apparent acceptance. Then a sudden point where

the bottom dropped out of that and she fell into the first real

depression. ~~A~~fter ~~that~~ward, a slow working uphill until a calmness
returned. She had felt expansive. She had wanted to gobble up the

world, travel everywhere and read everything, and see everyone she

had ever known, and relive what she could. But the interferon

therapy required that she stay nearby, and by then her energy was
predictable
trickling away. So she had entered the last depression with a

Page from the first draft for the story "Cadenza"

is that the alien need not be an organism: the aliens here are machines which outlive and supplant organic forms like ourselves.

Following a two-page transitional Part Three, the novel's consciousness temporarily shifts to Mr. Ichino who represents an older, ascetic version of what Nigel could become. Ichino questions bureaucrat George Evers who puts national security interests over the potential scientific knowledge that contacting aliens could bring. Now Nigel goes into space to meet the Snark, with orders to destroy it if it seems dangerous. When Evers takes command and fires Nigel's missiles at the vessel, the Snark refuses to detonate them, knowing that Nigel too would be killed by the blast in spite of the government's assurances to the contrary. Instead, the Snark merely accelerates out of danger, maintaining contact with the astronaut, telling him that the stars are populated by machines, descendants of extinct organic cultures. This numbing realization is alleviated a bit by the Snark somewhat enviously equating human laughter with immortality: "Machine societies cannot respond to your strange mixture of minds coupled with glands."

The remainder of the novel concerns a third alien confrontation as Nigel and a crew go to the moon to investigate the wreck of a craft in Mare Marginis. By now the bureaucracy has been infiltrated by New Sons who want to block information that might damage man's mythological self-portrait. At the same time, when he meets Peter Graves, a wealthy adventurer who has devoted his life to "trapping the unusual and finding the elusive," Ichino independently confirms the ancient alien contact with the fabled Northwest creature Bigfoot. Apparently the alien ship had affected human evolution, but the wreck resulted in the arrested development of the humanoid Bigfoot half a million years earlier. When Ichino discovers Bigfoot's essence, he destroys the film Graves had taken of the creatures because he empathizes with their desire to be left alone. At the end Graves is killed as his helicopter is shot out of the sky by a Bigfoot using a strange weapon given to his ancestors by the alien creature.

The character of Nigel Walmsley makes *In the Ocean of Night* an advance over Benford's earlier works, for the protagonist is an adventurer but also a scientist who understands the implications of his discoveries. By equating the aliens with the future, Benford argues that alien contact and artificial intelligence would destroy man's anthropocentric world view. As a physicist, Benford knows how science can familiarize man with the unknown by

Dust jacket for Benford's fourth novel (1977), a reaction against the use of aliens in science fiction

using terms like myth, religion, art, and science.

The two positions—science and humanism—conflict in "Nooncoming" (1978). Brian works for the High Hopes agency, which uses people as computers in order to save money. He yearns for a return to the old ways of materialism while at the same time perceiving his humanist friend Joanna's values as somehow new and threatening. The irony of the story is that she is the one who evokes the ideals of the American past. At the end, not surprisingly, Brian chooses computers over compassion. Such a choice reflects one of the dangers of a technological age, a theme which appears in slightly variant forms in Benford's other fiction. The callousness of mankind is one of the themes of *In the Ocean of Night*; in Benford's latest novel, *Timescape* (1980), callousness and insensitivity to nature and humanity threatens to end man's existence.

In *Timescape*, Benford shows how science can solve the very problems it creates. The novel depicts a future world where the decay of the ocean prompts an ecological crisis and accounts for deaths

216

through an unusual form of food poisoning. Nowhere is the fusion of Benford the scientist and Benford the novelist more evident than in this novel which won the Australian Ditmar Award and the John W. Campbell Award for fiction in 1981. Alienation from the threatening world which technology could create is a major concern in Benford's work, and mankind in 1998 has created that kind of world for himself. What makes the novel's premise work is the author's acceptance of the existence of the tachyon, a hypothetical faster-than-light particle which seems to permit time travel and even a new manner of looking at causality as a loop rather than as a chain of events. Thus British scientists in 1998 are able to transmit messages to a lab in La Jolla, California, in 1962 and 1963, with the hope that the past can prevent certain aspects of the future from occurring.

Timescape succeeds on several levels, not the least of which is its nostalgic evocation of California life in the early 1960s. But all the horrors of the decade are not altered: the assassination of President Kennedy is recounted with vivid accuracy near the novel's end, and a sense of impending doom permeates all facets of life in 1998. The culprit here is not nuclear war but ecological collapse; otherwise well-to-do Britishers must eat canned goods and guard their property from squatters who try to steal from their more affluent neighbors. To avert their miserable present, scientists in 1998 try to contact a point and a place in the 1960s. They send enough of a message to begin research, but not enough to solve the problem entirely, avoiding a paradox. For if the world of 1962 could solve the problem, the problem would not exist in 1998, and that world would never send the message. This problem at the root of *Timescape* prevents the sort of outright time travel in which characters trying to change history cause whatever they are trying to prevent.

These technical aspects do not diminish the novel's human drama. Its hero, Gordon Bernstein, is the victim of ridicule and perhaps professional jealousy; but he continues with the experiment to the detriment of his career at the university, his relationship with Penny, and the career of Albert Cooper, a promising graduate student. Once the experiment is made public, Bernstein is assaulted by all sorts of crackpots, and overexposure by the media damages his professional credibility. Bernstein believes in what he is doing, but his attempts are not met with approval by the scientific community until the novel's end. Events at the end of the novel indicate that the future was changed. In 1974 Bernstein is presented the Enrico Fermi

Award for his endeavors by President William Scranton, former Pennsylvania governor who won the election of 1968 when history was altered. The world of 1998 would be a better place because of the transmissions from British scientists in that year.

What Benford wants to show in *Timescape* is how science works. Because of its two settings—one in the past, one in the future—the reader is able to see that he knows the answers while the scientists, especially Bernstein, do not. The "sociology of scientists" is best conveyed by descriptive passages within the novel whereby major characters observe their environment. Benford emphasizes character much more than other writers in his genre, and his use of descriptive passages to delineate character is unusual among science fiction writers. While at Cambridge, Gregory Markham takes a walk and, in a passage reminiscent of Stephen Dedalus's musings in James Joyce's *A Portrait of the Artist as a Young Man*, ponders upon theoretical physics. In it, as in Joyce's work, the syntax of the sentence blends with the content to reveal how a theoretical physicist thinks and looks at the world.

> The equations were mute. If Renfrew succeeded, how would the things around them change? Markham had a sudden, sinking vision of a world in which the ocean bloom simply had not happened. He and Renfrew and Peterson would emerge from the Cav to find that no one knew what they were babbling about. *Ocean Bloom? We solved that ages ago.* So they would be madmen, a curious trio sharing a common delusion. Yet to be consistent, the equations said that sending the message *couldn't* have too great an effect. It couldn't cut off the very reason for sending the tachyons in the first place. So there had to be some self-consistent picture, in which Renfrew still got his initial idea, and approached the World Council, and yet. . . .

Timescape is Benford's most autobiographical novel. Bernstein is modeled on an electromagnetics professor with whom Benford studied in San Diego, and the lecture given on the day of Kennedy's assassination is the same lecture Benford heard as a student. The twins who question Bernstein near the end of the novel are Gregory Benford and his twin brother, James. The author has lived everywhere the novel is set and has experienced much of what the characters experience.

The novels and stories of Gregory Benford blend technology as a poetic with thoughtful storytelling. His forthcoming book, "Across the Sea

Dust jacket for the rewritten and retitled hardcover edition of Benford's first novel (1978)

of Suns," is a sequel to *In the Ocean of Night*; another Benford novel in progress, "Against Infinity," promises to be the first science fiction novel written from the philosophical viewpoint of the South. The novel, essentially concerned with hunting, contains what Benford considers to be cultural attitudes of the South—an antagonism toward urban life, for example—but it promises to be more than just Faulkner with a philosophical twist. As Benford moves further away from the melodramatic elements which characterized some of his earlier fiction, he gives a sophisticated fusion of humanistic themes and scientific expertise, all too rare in the science fiction genre.

Other:
"What Did You Do Last Year?," by Benford and Gordon Eklund, in *Universe 6*, edited by Terry Carr (New York: Popular Library, 1976);
"Nooncoming," in *Universe 8*, edited by Carr (Garden City: Doubleday, 1978);
"Time Shards," in *Universe 9*, edited by Carr (Garden City: Doubleday, 1979);
"Aliens and Knowability," in *Bridges to Science Fiction* (Carbondale & Edwardsville: Southern Illinois University Press, 1981).

Reference:
David N. Samuelson, "From Aliens to Alienation: Gregory Benford's Variations on a Theme," *Foundations*, 14 (Winter 1977-78): 5-19.

Doris Betts

(4 June 1932-   )

Jean W. Ross

BOOKS: *The Gentle Insurrection* (New York: Putnam's, 1954; London: Gollancz, 1955);
Tall Houses in Winter (New York: Putnam's, 1957; London: Gollancz, 1958);
The Scarlet Thread (New York: Harper & Row, 1964);
The Astronomer and Other Stories (New York: Harper & Row, 1966);
The River to Pickle Beach (New York: Harper & Row, 1972);
Beasts of the Southern Wild and Other Stories (New York: Harper & Row, 1973);
Heading West (New York: Knopf, 1981).

Doris Betts's fiction grows directly out of the North Carolina surroundings and Calvinistic influences of her childhood; her voice is earthy, compassionate, and country-smart. Since her college years, Betts has written steadily and had professional acclaim: she won the 1953 *Mademoiselle* College Fiction Contest for her short story "Mr. Shawn and Father Scott" and the 1954 University of North Carolina-G. P. Putnam Award for her first short-story collection, *The Gentle Insurrection* (1954). Her third collection, *Beasts of the Southern Wild and Other Stories* (1973), was a National Book Award finalist. Public recognition, however, has been elusive. With

Doris Betts

219

the recent publication of *Heading West* (1981), a February 1982 Book-of-the-Month Club selection, her novels now outnumber her short-story collections four to three.

Betts was born in Statesville, North Carolina, to William Elmore Waugh (who worked at the local cotton mill) and Mary Ellen Freeze Waugh. She has described her family as close to the land and strictly religious (Associate Reformed Presbyterian). The Bible stories she read early and eagerly became a shaping influence in her writing; she has noted that their rhythms and their concreteness can provide "a great sense of the flesh, and the blood, and the same material which I see about me, and about which I have written extensively." The public library, which substituted for a baby-sitter while her mother did the week's shopping on Saturdays, offered further education: "It didn't take me long to realize that you could cut through the employees' bathroom and get to the adult section."

Betts attended public schools in Statesville and worked at a series of part-time jobs, including a position on the *Statesville Daily Record* from 1946 to 1950. When she graduated from high school, in 1950, she was a stringer for UPI and several area papers. Through the help of some of the *Greensboro News* staff, she was able to get a job with the news bureau at UNC-Greensboro (at that time a women's college) and attended college there until 1953. She attended the University of North Carolina-Chapel Hill in 1954.

In 1952, Betts married Lowry Matthew Betts, an attorney. The following year was notable not only for her winning the *Mademoiselle* College Fiction Contest but also for the birth of the Betts's first child, Doris LewEllyn. Two more children followed: David Lowry in 1954 and Erskine Moore II in 1960. Through the 1950s, during which her first two books were published, Betts continued to do newspaper work, remaining in her UPI job until 1954, reporting for area papers, and writing a daily column for the *Sanford Daily Herald* in 1957-1958. From 1958 to 1960 she served on the editorial board of the *North Carolina Democrat* and in 1960 became a full-time editor for the *Sanford News Leader*.

Betts originally considered herself a short-story writer rather than a novelist. In a 1969 interview (published in *Kite-Flying and Other Irrational Acts*, 1972), she told George Wolfe, "One of the most obvious things to be said about the short story as a form is that it seems to *stop* time, to gather it together, to make it dense and glowing." Her stories have appeared in such popular magazines as *Redbook*, *Ms.*, and *Saturday Evening Post*, as well as little

magazines and campus publications. The short stories that make up *The Gentle Insurrection* treat some of the everyday concerns that dominate her subsequent fiction: growing up, growing old, relationships between family members and associates, racial tensions, and, most of all, death, as its approach is perceived by the dying and as it is dealt with by the living who must observe.

In "A Sense of Humor," ten-year-old Evie tries to make some sense of her uncle's death and explain it to her younger brother Mark. As they peer into the coffin while the adults are out of the room, Evie assures Mark that Uncle John is "just asleep." Through the afternoon of the approaching funeral, the children listen to the grownups reminiscing about John and exclaiming over his sudden death. Evie remembers the tricks he played: "hiding in the dark places at night, and then leaping out at her—screaming—until she ran down the long carpet with her stomach soggy from fear. . . . the lizards he had hidden in Mark's box and the buzzer in his hand and the flower that squirted salt water." After the funeral, Evie's mother explains that the coffin was put in the ground and covered up with dirt. Lying in the dark later, Evie begins to giggle as she reasons that this joke is on Uncle John. "When he wakes up tonight, he can't get out," she explains to Mark. "He can't ever get out again, that's all. Isn't that funny?" Both children fall asleep smiling.

In "The Sword" and "The End of Henry Fribble," impending death causes men to examine family relationships and find them wanting. A happier story, "The Very Old Are Beautiful," presents a character portrait of a strong-willed old woman whose death comes about with as much order as she had imposed on the events of life. Betts deftly describes Mama Bower as having "a self-respect that somehow stopped short of being pride; it is a hard distinction to draw—that thin line where self-confidence reaches the point of diminishing returns." Underlying all the stories is a recognition of the essential loneliness of individuals and the tensions produced by the passage of time—the frequent friction between youth and age, modern and traditional values, religious belief and loss of faith.

Betts's first novel, *Tall Houses in Winter* (1957), won the Historical Book Club of North Carolina's Sir Walter Raleigh Award for Fiction but failed to attract general critical or public notice. She described it as a story "about love and responsibility" in which the protagonist Ryan Godwin "must learn to accept the world as he finds it; he must learn to change it when he can." Ryan has violated tradition by rejecting his family's religion, rejecting his father's plan for his life in becoming a teacher rather than a businessman, leaving his Southern hometown to live and work in New England, and falling in love with Jessica Godwin, the wife of his brother Avery. Ryan and Jessica's affair, carried on mainly during holidays and school vacations when Ryan returned to Stoneville, ended when Jessica and Avery were killed in an automobile accident, not quite two years after Jessica had given birth to a son, Fen, who may or may not have been fathered by Ryan. This is all told in retrospect after Ryan returns to Stoneville when he learns that he has cancer and must decide whether to undergo surgery that could save his life. The real question is whether or not he has anything to live for. After confronting the past and its most vivid present reminder, twelve-year-old Fen, he decides to make every effort to live.

A second novel, *The Scarlet Thread* (1964), was written with the assistance of a Guggenheim Fellowship. It is set in a rural North Carolina piedmont community that becomes the site of a cotton mill. The action takes place from 1897 to 1912 and centers on the family of Sam Allen, a storekeeper who eventually becomes owner of the mill. Each of the three major sections of the book focuses on one of the three Allen children while covering a period of time in the community's history; a fourth section serves as a 1920 postscript. This novel also received the Sir Walter Raleigh Award but little further attention. It deserves to be read, however, for its careful structure, effective characterization, and its depiction of the corrupting effects of the mill on the community.

The Scarlet Thread was followed in 1966 by *The Astronomer and Other Stories*. The title story was started as a novel under the same Guggenheim Fellowship that aided *The Scarlet Thread* but turned out to be a novella and one of Betts's finest works. It is about Horton Beam, who retires at sixty-five from his job as a weaver at the Corey Knitting Mill, receives the customary wristwatch with "WELL DONE!" engraved on it, and goes home to the house he has occupied alone since his wife died years earlier.

Although he plans to do "nothing whatsoever" with his time, he immediately becomes interested in astronomy when he opens a book that had belonged to one of his sons (both dead now also) and begins to read "When I Heard the Learn'd Astronomer. . . ." He goes to the library for books on the stars, checking them out under the name Walt Whitman, and begins to call himself privately the Astronomer. Astronomy, Mr. Beam feels, will not disrupt the

deliberate solitude that has characterized his life, even when his wife and children were alive. "You buy a dog, now," he explains later, "you get involved in the thing, try to read its mind, decide the animal loves you. Decide you love it back. . . . The stars are just out there. Facts."

But Mr. Beam's careful solitude is disrupted by the appearance of Fred Ridge, a stranger who persuades Mr. Beam to take him in as a roomer and the following day brings in a young woman whom he introduces as his wife. Reluctant at first to allow them to stay, Mr. Beam gives in. It is apparent at once that there is a conflict between Fred and the woman Eva. As the days go on, Mr. Beam has more contact with Eva and learns that she has run away from her husband and two small children, whom she misses and feels guilty about leaving, to be with Fred, and that she is pregnant with Fred's child. Coincidentally, Mr. Beam's hobby has led him to read mythology, a mistake: "He had allowed for only fact and observation. Now these were being pressed into the mold of old and human stories; and when he watched the distant constellations drift westward he began to see quarrels and loving and

Dust jacket for Betts's second collection of stories (1966)

sudden death." He realizes that his life has become bound up with the young couple living uneasily together in his house—and that he loves Eva.

A concern with order in "The Astronomer" is expressed through several motifs, the first being astronomy itself, the formation of constellations and the use of stars as directional guides. The telling of time is another. After Fred and Eva move in with Mr. Beam, "as soon as each began giving any attention to the other, a pattern and schedule developed." To go to his second job, "Fred Ridge left the house at twilight and every night the Astronomer woke at 3:15 A.M. and heard him coming home. He knew suddenly how clocks—and pocket watches, and wrist watches—had first been invented. Three people living together in some cave had been enough to start it." Maps are a third motif. "Everything turns into a map for Fred," Eva explains to Mr. Beam. "There's just one way to travel, one shortest, easiest highway. The widest, blackest line on the paper." Later, after reading about Theseus and the labyrinth, Mr. Beam muses: "I want to know whether life is really a map, where you follow the trails marked out for you, or whether it's a labyrinth."

A sense of unrest leads Eva to create further moral disorder for herself. She begins sneaking away from the house at night to frequent Fisher Street, a rough part of town, where she slips into prostitution and eventually has a near-fatal abortion. Convalescing under the constant care of Mr. Beam, she voraciously reads all the religious books he can bring her, searching for some absolution from her guilt. In the end she decides to return to her husband and try to make things right again.

Arguing with Mr. Beam, who feels Eva has not thought it through logically (and badly wants her to stay), she shouts, "No more of this clear direction, thought-through, plain road. Nosir, you and Fred go right off on it! Me, I'll think about *all* the roads at once. And what I'd be like if I happened to be on them." Fred accepts her leaving, when it finally happens, and Mr. Beam, "sixty-five and retired, in this house of thunderous silence," runs out back to look at the stars, where "Pegasus was galloping over the east" and "from near Capella a small torch skidded down the sky."

Seven short stories accompany the novella in this collection. "The Spies in the Herb House" and "All That Glisters Isn't Gold" are two charming and frankly autobiographical stories of childhood. Both excel in evoking the ambience of a small, unprosperous town and its characters. In the second story, the tension between the religious and the secular is present in Miss Carrie, whose house smelled like "cold, leftover biscuits," and her twenty-three-year-old nephew Granville, "who had gone off to the university in Chapel Hill and learned to be an atheist." "Clarissa and the Depths" is a good example of Betts's sympathetic handling of black characters and, again, the friction between age and youth, the old and the new orders. The fragility of the human ego is exemplified in fifty-eight-year-old Wink Thomas of "Careful, Sharp Eggs Underfoot," a story with a slight feeling of surreality about it, in which humor and pathos are very closely woven.

In 1966 Betts began a teaching career at the University of North Carolina at Chapel Hill, work she clearly relishes. Now Alumni Distinguished Professor of English (since 1980) and Chairman of the Faculty, she has taught literature and creative writing courses and edited university publications. She credits the university for widening the scope of her activities, having also been a visiting lecturer at Duke, taught an extension course at the University of California-Davis, and worked on the staffs of writers' conferences. From 1978 through 1981 she served on the Literature Panel of the National Endowment for the Arts, acting as chairman in 1980-1981.

The Astronomer and Other Stories was followed in 1972 by Betts's third novel, *The River to Pickle Beach*. It is set in a fictional North Carolina beach community where Jack and Bebe Sellars have moved, in spite of Jack's misgivings, to manage some beach houses and trailers. Both in their forties, Jack and Bebe have a warm, close relationship. They are opposites: she is impractical and romantic, a daydreamer whose perceptions are shaped primarily by the frothy movies she has seen; he is rational, realistic, wary. As a boy, he witnessed his mother murder his father, wading out into the Katsewa River with an ax over her shoulder to where the drunken man was washing himself. Jack's recurrent nightmare of the scene acts as a motif in the story's movement toward violence. It is set in the turbulent summer of 1968, the year Robert Kennedy and Martin Luther King, Jr., were murdered.

The couple's peace is disturbed by Mickey McCane, an old army buddy of Jack's who brazenly pursues Bebe. Tormented by his strong prejudices and his sexual inadequacy with his wife, McCane becomes increasingly frustrated by his unsuccessful attempts to seduce Bebe. The "Pinheads," a retarded woman and her retarded child who are vacationing at the beach in the care of a nurse, become the target of his anger, which finally erupts in the act of violence that provides the novel's climax.

The River to Pickle Beach brought Betts favorable notice in the *New York Times Book Review* for her prose and her portrayals of Jack and Bebe Sellars. Some of the secondary characters are also quite credibly portrayed and serve to exemplify polarities in the national turmoil of the time: Foley Dickinson, a young university dropout on his way to the Democratic National Convention, is a foil for Willis Buncombe, a bigoted local storekeeper. One of the book's best sections is the interlude when Bebe goes home to visit her family in Greenway, the mill town where she grew up. While she is there, she joins her relatives and other townspeople in the cemetery cleaning at the Mount Hebron churchyard, an annual ceremony that involves scrubbing gravestones, weeding, planting, hymnsinging, picnicking, and general socializing. A long pine table is spread with the food everyone has brought, mostly Southern specialties: "fried chicken, ham biscuits, potato salad, chess tarts, many sandwiches, deviled eggs, candied yams, a dozen cakes and pies . . . pulled mints . . . jelly roll, grated sweet potato pudding." At the end of the table three washtubs contain lemonade, tea, and a block of ice with a pick. Bebe and her mother look at the work that has been done

that morning: "Daddy's grave seemed splotched with the new plants. Sticks and weeds had been piled up near the pond. Morrisons a hundred years gone now had their boxwoods pruned. Around the headstones had sprung up petunias and yellow marigolds and iris with their spears slashed back. Some of the stones were still wet from a Borax scrubbing."

Just as mealtime finally arrives and "like magicians the women began whipping their hands over the table, jerking off foil and wax paper, slicing desserts and thrusting spoons into bowls," a scream alerts the crowd that one of the children is drowning in the pond. He is rescued and rushed off to the hospital. "Everyone was talking softly now, wandering up the hillside, outside the wall, far away from the tombstones. Hardly noticing what they did, awed children filled their cardboard plates and ate, stared at the quiet pond while their jaws were grinding. . . . A honeybee still struggled in a bowl of beet juice. Nobody mentioned it, or ate a beet. They tended to cluster in families."

In *Beasts of the Southern Wild and Other Stories,* her third collection, Betts continues to demonstrate her concern with everyday characters and emo-

Dust jacket for Betts's third collection of stories, shortlisted in 1973 for the National Book Award

tions, but in "Hitchhiker" and the novella "Benson Watts Is Dead and in Virginia," she takes her characters into life beyond death, "a logical extension of things that interest me most in fiction . . . mortality and time." She creates strong characters in Violet Karl of "The Ugliest Pilgrim," who is traveling by bus from her Southern mountain home to a faith healer in Oklahoma, where she expects to trade the ugliness of her ax-scarred face for the smooth looks of a movie star, and the widow Wanda Quincey in "The Glory of His Nostrils," who falls in love and goes north with the abortionist Dr. Benjamin.

In "Still Life with Fruit" Gwen Gower endures the routine humiliations of childbirth in a hospital while already experiencing the emotional ambivalence of motherhood. In a story of great tenderness, "The Mother-in-Law," a wife imagines herself once again a child, invisibly observing the dying woman of forty whose son she will one day marry, then follows the family, including herself and her children, up into her fortieth year. Her kinship with the mother-in-law she never knew is felt not only in her love for the woman's son Philip but also in her caring for Ross, the son who was born intelligent but with physical defects. Michael Mewshaw found Betts "unbeatable" in this story: "Here her style finds its perfect theme and structure."

The title story presents a skillful balancing of reality and fantasy in the drab life but rich imaginings of Carol Walsh, a high-school English teacher married to a bigoted upholsterer. Carol's fantasy, which becomes increasingly predominant over the interspersed scenes of her real life, takes place in a future time in which a revolution has resulted in a new social order with blacks ruling over an enslaved white population. Long imprisoned with other women, Carol is taken away by Sam Porter, now provost at New Africa University, which Carol had attended under its old name. At Porter's luxurious and civilized town house, she is elegantly clothed and fed. She spends her evenings after dinner reading aloud to Porter. When Carol finally becomes Porter's mistress the fantasy is interrupted briefly by the sexual attention of her real husband. She returns in her mind to Porter, who comforts her and asks the name of the intruder who has "raped" her and whom, with Carol's complicity, he will hunt down and kill.

Beasts of the Southern Wild got Betts not only her third Sir Walter Raleigh Award but also the nomination for the National Book Award and some highly favorable reviews. Michael Mewshaw wrote in the *New York Times Book Review* (28 October 1973),

"Although liberally laced with elements of the Southern gothic, the grotesque, black humor, surrealism and fantasy, the writing escapes categorization and remains very much an index of one woman's intriguing mind. . . ." Doris Grumbach, in the *New Republic* (10 November 1973), commented on Betts's "accurate, biting style, the simplicity of the narrative structures, the richness of their implications" in dealing with "living suffering persons caught in sometimes ordinary situations . . . which her subtle, rapid prose renders distinctive and memorable."

Heading West is Betts's most ambitious novel to date, venturing far from the Southern settings of her previous novels into what she calls the "psychological landscape" of the Grand Canyon, and much farther than before into the psychology of her characters. Its main character (the word *heroine* is appropriate) is Nancy Finch, a thirtyish, unmarried librarian in a small North Carolina town. All of her adult life she has lived at home and cared

Dust jacket for Betts's fourth novel (1981), which, she says, represents her attempt to change from a short story writer to a novelist

for her mother and her younger brother, who is epileptic and slightly retarded. "Some days their dependence ate her alive."

Vacationing in the mountains with her sister and sister's husband, Nancy is kidnapped by a man who calls himself Dwight Anderson. As his victim, heading west, Nancy tries on several occasions to escape but seems to muff other opportunities. It becomes obvious to the reader, and to Nancy, that she is what one reviewer calls a willing victim in this situation, as she has been a willing victim of her family. Once she decides in earnest that she is ready to escape, Nancy begins to do so, taking the step that leads to her descent into the Grand Canyon, with Dwight in pursuit, for the final confrontation that only one of them can survive. It is Nancy who survives, though barely, through the help of her new friend Chan Thatcher. Recuperating at Chan's home in nearby Valle, Nancy meets and falls in love with Chan's son. This gives her the impetus and courage for the last leg of her escape to freedom—the trip back to North Carolina to come to terms with her family and her own sense of responsibility.

Heading West has had very favorable reviews. Beth Gutcheon (*New York Times Book Review*, 17 January 1982) comments on Betts's technique: "Just as the horizontal progress of the Colorado River cuts vertically through stratum after stratum of rock in the canyon that is the central image of the novel, she tells a story that is taut and linear and compelling while simultaneously she cuts through layer after layer of different kinds of meaning." Because of this density, which probes the moral, social, and psychological implications of the action, "the pleasures of 'Heading West' are infinitely more subtle, complex and memorable than being scared in your armchair."

Heading West is coming out in paperback, and there is talk of a movie. In the meantime, Doris Betts continues to teach, to enjoy some quiet time at her home in the country near Chapel Hill, where she lives with her husband, and to hone her considerable writing talent—this time on a fifth novel, a long family chronicle in which she will use falconry as a central metaphor in exploring the decline of religion in American life.

Periodical Publications:
"Writers in Glass Houses," *Writer*, 88 (February 1975): 9-11;
"Bringing Down the House," *Redbook* (August 1979): 43, 103, 105-108;

"The Agony of the Mothers," *Life*, 4 (April 1981): 68ff.

References:
Elizabeth Evans, "Negro Characters in the Fiction of Doris Betts," *Critique*, no. 2, 17 (1975): 59-76;
George Wolfe, "The Unique Voice: Doris Betts," in *Kite-Flying and Other Irrational Acts*, edited by John Carr (Baton Rouge: Louisiana State University Press, 1972), pp. 149-173.

AN INTERVIEW
with DORIS BETTS

DLB: In the past you have considered yourself more a short-story writer than a novelist. Does this fourth novel, *Heading West*, change your mind?

BETTS: It would probably be more accurate to say *Heading West* represents my *attempt* to change. The short story, like the lyric poem, may be the form of youth, when you still believe in the revelation and the isolated moment, and you do believe that people can change in twenty-four-hour periods. As you get older you can't help seeing that the more things change, the more they stay the same, just the way your grandmother told you. I think that causes you to get interested in longer structures. I think I am still a more natural short-story writer, but trying to learn to be a novelist. It is harder for me.

DLB: You have said you spent more time on *Heading West* than on the earlier novels. Was it harder to write?

BETTS: Yes, I guess so, because it is a more complicated book. I like it better. I think it is more successful as a novel than they are. It seems to me that one of the problems in changing from short-story writer to novelist is that you tend as a story writer to make each chapter like a little bitty story, and then they're like beads on a string. Also, if you're a natural novelist, you really work on a larger linear scale, and I think I have done better at getting larger this time—not as large as I want to grow, but larger.

DLB: Then you are pleased with *Heading West*?

BETTS: Oh no. I think if you ever write something you're pleased with, then you can quit. And I hope still to be displeased when the last trump sounds. I take very seriously that you do need to have some feeling of progress, that, relative to the last prose you wrote, you have grown somewhat. Otherwise, there wouldn't be a carrot out there to keep extending for; you'd get disheartened. But the minute you have the slightest feeling that you've done what you've set out to do, you're in bad trouble.

DLB: Your descriptions of the Grand Canyon make me feel as if I were there, though I have never seen it. Did you actually do some writing in the Canyon?

BETTS: I did some jotting, but not too much, because I was carrying a limited amount of stuff on a raft—I had one notebook, I think, and a pen. I brought back maps and pictures and so on, all of which were unsatisfactory. But in a funny way, if you know too much, if you know too many facts, you lose the impact that reality has on you. It's not so much the facts as a wordless response that the Grand Canyon elicits. I did go back and check (an old journalist's habit), and I take facts seriously because they do turn symbolic. By now I own a pretty good library on the Grand Canyon, because it will be a long time before I get back.

DLB: What are the possibilities of a movie based on *Heading West*?

BETTS: There has been a movie offer, which, last I heard, my agent had turned down—I strangled on the phone and asked him who he thought I was. But he didn't think the terms satisfactory. I'd be happy to take a smile and a dime! One of my stories, "The Ugliest Pilgrim," has been filmed now by the American Film Institute as "Violet," and has won an Academy Award. I've seen a videotape, and when I can look at it as a film that I know nothing about, it seems very well done. The original story is very subjective, hard to translate to film; so they omitted the subjective aspect. In a way that makes all my pores slam shut, but I realize their technical problem. There are things film can do better than words, but there are subtler things words can do better than pictures. Viewing this film confirmed for me that we do indeed need both. Film does not supplant literature. It is something else. Something good, too, but something else.

DLB: I know you consider becoming a teacher at the University of North Carolina at Chapel Hill one of the best things that ever happened to you, but aren't there some frustrations because of the inferior sec-

ondary education many young people are coming to college with?

BETTS: What I find most frustrating is that they're not doing the one good thing I did for myself—which was to live in the library. They're not reading. They have a fast, breezy, oral-type writing, which can be lively and accurate for now but is inadequate for the experience they're going to want to convey in five years. They have not read enough—and the bright ones know it. It's rare that I get a student who has read one tenth of what I had read by the time I was in tenth grade. At that age, sixteen, you don't even know what you're learning; you're just sponging up, but it turns out to be your real education. This reduced reading is serious, a cultural problem—our whole society recognizes it now. And perhaps writing and serious reading will become a specialty, something for the elite, like opera. That possibility grieves me when I think of how hard-won literacy was for the masses, and realize that in any other century I would be out in the fields, unlettered, unawakened.

DLB: You served from 1978 through 1981 on the Literature Panel of the National Endowment for the Arts. At the American Writers Conference held in New York in October 1981, you defended the work of the NEA. Would you like to comment on that?

BETTS: Well, the NEA has a hard job; it's doomed to ingratitude. Every year it's going to make more people angry than it helps, and some of the criticisms against it may even be justified. But on its panels and staff I have seen so many earnest, idealistic, hardworking people who have tried to make the literature program fair as well as artistic that I will defend it, warts and all. I can't prove that it has produced a golden renaissance of letters, but we don't even know its failures and successes yet. Nobody thought at the time that the WPA [Work Projects Administration, 1935-1943] writers were accomplishing much. From my own contact with many young writers, I honestly have been impressed. I have now read writers from all over the country, and their level of technical competency is extremely high. Of course the combination of technical competency and magnificent content will always be rare, in any century, with financial help or without. But I think there are more enormously talented writers out there than I once thought. Luck, publishing outlets, timing, stubbornness—

these play a part in who gives up and who keeps growing.

DLB: You have criticized antirational writing that assumes "that there is never a point at which the reason and the intellect act upon these experiences." Do you think that trend is on its way out now?

BETTS: In fact, I think the wave undulates. After I made that statement, we got into extremely cerebral fiction. We got into John Barth and Donald Barthelme and Thomas Pynchon, all of whom I admire. There was a full decade of abstract fiction by writers writing for other writers and playing games with technique. Now the trend is moving back (I hate to say this, it sounds so conservative) toward the

nineteenth-century novel. This is a natural undulation of the wave, a wish to capture microcosms instead of just having the isolated ego looking at his navel. A reaction. In the popular taste, that's why people have liked Michener and *The Thorn Birds*, the kind of fiction that literary writers viewed with contempt. I now see even their return to it, partly because women writers are on the ascendency, and women do write about family or neighborhood as microcosm. Part may just reflect the general conservative back-to-basics trend that everywhere in our 1980s culture is a reaction to the 1960s. These things wax and wane. We're probably in for ten years of bad family chronicles. I'm sorry to admit I am working on a family chronicle, by what I originally thought was independent choice.

—*Jean W. Ross*

Philip Booth
(8 October 1925 -   )

Gary Margolis
Middlebury College

BOOKS: *Letter from a Distant Land* (New York: Viking, 1957);
The Islanders (New York: Viking, 1961);
Weathers and Edges (New York: Viking, 1966);
Margins (New York: Viking, 1970);
Available Light (New York & Harmondsworth, U.K.: Viking, 1974);
Before Sleep (New York: Penguin, 1980).

Born in Hanover, New Hampshire, the son of Edmund Booth, a professor at Dartmouth College, and Jeanette Hooke, and raised in that college community, Philip Booth was educated at Dartmouth (A.B., 1948) and Columbia University (M.A., 1949). He says, "If my father taught me respect for words, my mother's imagination intuitively made real to me the world words reach for." After, as he says, "frustrated pilot training in 1944-1945" in the air force, he married Margaret Tillman in 1946 and returned to Dartmouth, "to read rather than ski, to find myself as more than a faculty son." Booth and his wife have three daughters.

Booth initially taught in New England, at Bowdoin (1949), Dartmouth (1954), and Wellesley

(1954-1961), before taking his present position (part-time since 1975) of professor of English and poet-in-residence at Syracuse University. He has received the Bess Hokin Prize from *Poetry* magazine (1955), the Lamont Poetry Selection Award (1956), the *Saturday Review* Prize (1957), Guggenheim Fellowships (1958 and 1965), the Emily Clark Balch Prize (*Virginia Quarterly Review*, 1964), a National Institute of Arts and Letters grant (1967), a Rockefeller Fellowship (1968), the Theodore Roethke Prize (*Poetry Northwest*, 1970), and a National Endowment for the Arts grant (1980). He divides his time between Syracuse and Castine, Maine, the site of the 130-year-old family house where his maternal grandparents lived. He is a member of the Castine Yacht Club and was its commodore in 1963. In addition to his six books, his poems have appeared widely and continuously in national magazines and anthologies.

In *Letter from a Distant Land* (1957), his first volume, Booth finds his reasons for writing poems. Nature presents herself in ways he can see, feel, and shape into poetic forms. Relying on the structure of meter and rhyme to frame his vision, in the winter beauty of "North," he says, "Between what will be and was, rime / whites the foothill night and flowers / The rushes stilled in black millpond ice." Just as rhyme attaches sound to sound, Booth searches for the parallel relationship between self and nature, to ground himself in what he knows and to go beyond himself. In "Sunday Climb" seeing and imagining "the riding hawk," he says, "I barely escape / wishing myself a hawk's pure shape,. . . And I / climb both as killer and as prey." In nature—the sea, woods, birds, and weather—Booth locates himself in landscapes he trusts, and therefore, as he says in "Instruction in the Art," "can praise, but not prize."

Yet the reader may be sometimes uneasy that something disturbing is too easily lost or concealed by these forms. Nature seems to exist in Booth's early poems as an easier way of expanding the self. In "Heron" he writes, "I saw the herring flash / and drop. And the dash of lesser wings in the barren / marsh flew through my flesh." It is for the mind alone and even the cranky surprises in language, occasionally without natural images, that, in later poems, he confronts survival and transcendence. In *Letter from a Distant Land*, Booth's less successful poems rely on the Adam and Eve story or trips into the city in which his mastered forms carry too much weight, where the subjects are insulated by their poetic structures.

His love for nature is matched by love for his wife and daughters, and the lyric forms serve his

expressed tenderness in "The Seiners," "First Lesson," "Polaris," "Design," "North," and most beautifully in the pair "The Wilding" and "Nightsong."

However sure of himself in his observations, in his reliance on the literary past, Booth shows he can doubt in these early poems. There are sleeping problems ("The Long Night"), problems with sleep itself as a balm, and problems with trusting what nature means, however much he celebrates it. At the end of "Chart 1203," Booth says, "He knows the chart is not the sea." He even is troubled with words themselves as in "The Wilding": "Words are a ruin / no animals heed, so kiss / me to silence: This wood is for you." The tension between order and chaos, or more personally, how the mind works and what to expect of it, Booth realizes in repeating lines in "The Margin": "where, cast away, I wake from numb surprise, a chance perfection makes my wonder wise."

Letter from a Distant Land is grounded in its longest poem, which gives the volume its title. Here, sufficiently "distant" from Thoreau to speak to and past him, Booth acknowledges how many ways he is "in between": "I am half-way, I tell you." The form of this poem lets him musically express himself in a longer line these thoughts and feelings need. The poet is in between traditions, wars, the destruction of the landscape ("Machines as murderous / as mad bulls gore the land") and his desire to praise the past and restore it. It is difficult to stay halfway. Booth knows this when, in the poem's last lines, he says, "I walk this good March morning out / to say my strange love in a distant land." In later work he explores the strangeness this first book intimates.

In *The Islanders* (1961), his second book, Booth lets himself become unsettled; he reaches out and in, through forms he mastered in *Letter from a Distant Land*, and more fully into a personally revealing and disturbing landscape—the coast and characters of Maine. He risks the repetition of past accomplishments, yet uses them to establish and experiment with the three- and four-beat lines conducive to his images and representative of local speech. He chooses the coastal island and sleep as central images and, thus, metaphors. Sleep is the common balm which contains creativity and nightmare. The island, similarly, is safety, yet often danger. In many of these poems he uses the idioms of the sea and sailing to explore language. The book's explanatory notes serve as a guide to verify his subjects and to capture the reader's interest.

Poems in section one turn inward. In "The Counter Shadow" and "Convoy," Booth analyzes human identity, asking: Who am I? Are one's alter egos true others or part of oneself? In our encounter with nature, do we reflect it? In "Was a Man," a hung-over character, shaving, knocks down a mirror "facing/himself almost intact, /in his final terror hung / the wrong face back." Booth's rewarding obsession with location continues to emerge, not only as a sailor in foggy or poorly mapped seas but as contemplative man anywhere. In "Nebraska, USA," he says, "They [immigrants] settle in the furrowing / of their first view, not knowing where they're lost." In these flatlands and fields, perspective and vision are difficult and danger hard to predict; thus the need for "no place to go but underground," in and back to oneself.

Booth engages contemporary political issues in "Grit" and "The Tower"—native Americans in the first and nuclear power plants in the second. His eerie image making can be upsetting—"The interval / of each warning light / and how, just / at dawn, the strange / orange glow / on top will go / out, with something / suspended, like lazing snow / in the morning air"; however, sometimes within that flat and ironic tone, too much of the feeling these poems encourage is withheld. In his careful poetry, how emotion emerges is as important a problem for Booth as encountering the relationship between seeing, imagining, and being ("Night Notes on an Old Dream").

Booth casts *The Islanders* most disturbing poem, "If it Comes," in the book's successful three-beat lines which allow thought, image, line break and syntax to mingle and stand alone. The speaker addresses a "you" (self, reader, specific other) which adds to the poem's haunting elements of invader, night, and sleep itself. He leaves uncertain what the dangerous "it" is, "if for / once, you have enough warning, enough to break / out, from what pass as dreams, / you will wake, / if it comes, / near morning."

Preceded by "The Line" ("but once you leave / it clear astern you'll know what you have crossed"), the book's concluding thirteen poems move back into the Maine coast and people. These poems work better when they engage the picture, persons, and Booth's imagination on their own terms—not when the natural facts of the sea carry more symbolic weight than they can bear. "Matinicus," though, sheds its light like a Wyeth painting.

In this collection's title poem, "The Islanders," we are led to believe we know who and where we are—fishermen using the islands to gauge our positions. Yet Booth lets us wonderfully drift among Maine's islands, the sea's mirages of them, and what the mind needs to make of this confusion: "yet

harbored knowing it was real; / and fished, like us, offshore, as if it were." Like rural New England for Robert Frost, coastal Maine holds some of the same attachment and desperation for Philip Booth. The sea is there to watch, ride, and listen to. Its people require it to live. Their lives make a history and language from it.

Teaching in Syracuse part of the year, living in Maine for the rest, Booth's dual residences and allegiances emerge in his third book, *Weathers and Edges* (1966); here he treads water to keep afloat. Many of the poems are cast in three-line stanzas with some end and internal rhyme, some, like "Dear Isle," more formally, others in blank verse. Booth's alienation from urban life, changes from childhood, and the necessary complications of his adult perception are represented, with the uneasiness of weather. His style must accommodate these changes in order to more accurately present his thought and feeling. He recognizes this dilemma when he says in "Cleaning Out the Garage": "I try to sweep out the useless stuff I still / cherish . . . what I / mean to leave here: how to let go what won't do." Again he pulls himself back, and is pulled back, to Maine's sea world; in those poems, his precise language matches his knowledge and speculation.

Facing reality for Booth is knowing when he can choose and when he cannot, that is, when he can locate himself. In the music and mystery of "A Refusal of Still Perfections," the speaker says in reference to his farm by the sea: "I know I can never live there. / Never for pasture, mortgage the river / or pawn dark hopes to insure pure sleep." Being where he wants to be is tied to the comfort and healing of uninterrupted sleep. The problem of living in Maine and New York, between past and future, memory and hope, emerges in the narrative of "Deer Isle." Driving home after work, he stops to watch six browsing does which remind him of a buck he encountered on an island. The memory is dangerous because of the reality it forces him to confront. Is he happy where he is? What does he truly need? This is too much on which to focus, and the poem ends, "I looked my way clear / tramping the gas / toward nowhere / but where home was. My wife understood. / If I didn't go now, I never would." Here Booth is finding his position and the risks locating himself entails. In "Voyages," referring to the snail and himself, he says "snails / bring the tide in, hulls / on their own horizon: bound / as I am to the very edge." The challenge exists in living with this paradox and, for Booth as poet, in transforming it into what he can see and write. In the book's penultimate poem, "Tenants' Harbor," he says, "The world / is wherever we quiet to hear it."

Booth addresses questions of identity, not only who he is but with what and whom he wishes to identify. Often it is the nature of coastal Maine or its residents in which he chooses to discover himself. In "Denying the Day's Mile," the speaker in anger and despair says, "I can't / even stand my neighbors, / or free myself when I go / to bed with no love left." Regretting his need to judge and other lost intentions, he says in the poem's last lines, "but tonight I'm not even / myself: where I haven't been / is already yesterday." Uncharacteristically and wonderfully, in "Heart of Darkness," Booth's character speaks to the poem directly for revelation and security, for some good sleep. "Lost as we / are, with no choice of nightmares left, but only stakes higher than Kurtz / could dream of, what / we need is the poem."

Poetry often is meditation, and for Booth the relationship between meditation and sleep is important. In "Small Dance," the speaker allows his attention to wander with a cat interested and uninterested in his pipe smoke. The poem unwinds in the structure of its unrhymed couplets, through its story and speculation, to its own open conclusions: "Neither of us understands// but something we could not resolve / had, for a moment, smoke to wreath it." Some of the crises of these poems, their repetitions and familiar sentiments, mixed with new intuitions and experiments, are necessary antecedents for the development of his later work.

Selecting poems from his previous books, a poet underlines his most important concerns while, at the same time, suggesting themes he wishes to carry with him for pleasure and further exploration—poems with which he wants to be identified and through which he creates a more dynamic identity. In his fourth book, *Margins* (1970), Booth selects those poems which resonate his significant ideas and images and adds eighteen new poems that intensify and expand his concerns and poetic styles.

Section one's choices confirm the questions that interest and happily confuse Booth: How do our relationship and encounter with nature create our sense of self? How is identity a function of place and interaction between perception and dreaming? How do we use our experience of night, nature, and, by extension, death to know ourselves? How do we turn seeing into vision? And how can we trust imagination to add to our senses of meaning and security? These are questions for any poet, yet particularly for Booth in the characters, landscapes, and psychology that inhabit his poetry. He em-

bodies them in lines from the new poems. In "Native to Valleys" he says, "I wake to a mirror of hardwood, / facing myself in the shape of familiar hills." And in "Lives from an Orchard Once Surveyed by Thoreau": "The orchard quiets; I sip / at its silence, letting the nectar change me." He expresses the self's uncertainty in "Crosstones": "And now I'm not even / myself, with nobody left to tell what I / came to, or how I got here, or where it was." In "To Chekhov" Booth opens and lets go of himself when he says, "There is much about myself / I do not believe; much about the river, / and every mountain behind it, / I cannot yet love." He touches this tone again in "Supposition with Qualification," in reference to feelings and events: "only to let it / balance in its own light, to let light fall where it would." Judgment becomes temporarily suspended.

Booth's selection in section two takes these themes deeper to the dynamic margin that possesses his work. Coastal Maine is his place to live; he lets himself use it and be used by it to reveal more of himself, to let his mind turn in and out. Marine and rural nature, his two homes, are places he retreats to for information and meditation, so he can return to his family and the outer world. Places and conditions sometimes merge. Memory, dream, perception, and imagination create their own magic and voice. In "Night Notes on an Old Dream" he says, "night's snowbirds rise; / and I count them, white and moonstruck, climbing beyond Orion to the moon / behind my eyes." And in "Crows," observing the special actions of the feeding birds, he is taken over, although he says the opposite: "So. April. The crows in possession." Because his themes include nature and human feeling, they must contemplate the relationship between the temporary and permanent, and how, in facing ourselves, we create possibility from what is possible. In "The Misery of Mechanics," Booth in angry resignation says, "—his mechanic's eye sees that the parts are all there: //it is, in fact, already jacked up. / But nothing that he can fix."

In section three the poet moves into the particulars of his Maine locality, yet, by securing this ground, he feels its trembling; he is forced to exist within the context of change. Coast weather, tides, time, and death create the circumstances in which he must love, attach, and gain conviction. However much he wants to hold on or, in the deepest sense, remain, he says in "Cleaning Out the Garage," "I mean to leave here: how to let go what won't do." In "Triple Exposure," Booth's ability to create empathy, by identifying with an injured gull, allows him to look into the self and still live with the human wish for transcendence, "trying to free himself from himself."

In the last section, Booth explores the margins on which he finds himself. He realizes that in this world the points of contact and revelation are indeed these edges. Tides, island, rock, and coast house, stars, gulls, and even debris are the occurrences by which he creates his vision. They are points at which uncertainty can be felt and observed, where memory and hope anchor reality. Even the mind is margin to itself, characterized in the book's last poem, "The Stranding": "When I put my eyes up to / the eyes of my skull and / look in through both eyes / at once. . . ." Booth's selections and additions give *Margins* an identity beyond the individual poems.

In an interview, commenting on the creation of "Dreamscape," a poem in his fifth book, *Available Light* (1974), Booth says, "This apparently small poem is more likely to be shaded out by new growth than to thrust up through old. But it might seed some strong new roots." In it the speaker says, "I am asleep. / I cannot explain it. I do not / want to explain it." This is a striking book in which past and future often merge into a vibrating present. Nature and dream are combined in Booth's distinctive voice. He speaks through a personality that is both personal and abstract; his language creates and invites the contemplation of mystery—for example, in "The Way Tide Comes," when he says, "There's nothing left, nothing to add, / for which the tide will not account. . . . We have / to follow it all the way out." Some of these poems define their subjects ("A Number of Ways of Looking at It," "Like a Woman," "It is Being") and, when the poems quietly invoke their "its," the abstractions include the reader as their subjects.

How Booth came to construct this book, without sections, with its variety of line lengths, without traditional forms, may have been a matter of personal need or wish. Yet the book's insistence on letting dream, image, and voice speak for themselves suggests that the poetry itself, within the context of Booth's life and vocation as poet, truly found its own shape. He says, "Writing writing, I try only to get back, down, and out to what the world of the poem may come to." In this direct encounter with what is seen, dreamed, and imagined, language does not represent the world but rather becomes it. In addition to the poem's subject, the associative richness of words creates its own, original meaning, as in "This Dream": "The sun / has come back from nowhere, / and brought with it incalcula-

ble light. / This morning will not go away." This is what happens when these poems succeed. When they falter, as this risk necessitates, abstraction can obscure feeling and meaning. One of Booth's challenges is to let the poem move to its own conclusion, while at the same time anchoring its natural and psychological mysteries in identifiable feelings.

Booth tells us his poet's role in "Dark": "This is the pure time.// Nobody but me is awake. / Not in this house. Nobody / anywhere that I know// But everyone I imagine." In the book's longest and last poem, "Lives," Booth again shows his locations in memory and image, in a self-consciousness that includes the idea and experience of nothing and in voices that speak. "The chickadee in the hackmatack whistles his calling across / the marsh, a small solace / where we skate / filled / with an absence. / Who knows what we did to help? Who / knows what we did to help? Who / knows, ever, how to give what's due?" *Available Light* is the opening that Booth, in the middle of his life, needed to take his readers further.

In his sixth volume, *Before Sleep* (1980)—a book of mid-life apprehension and celebration—

Dust jacket for Booth's fifth volume of poetry (1974)

Booth is provocative in his experiments. He uses a variety of line lengths and line breaks, a complexity of subjects and characters, in order to isolate his psychological themes and personal landscapes. The poems are separated and integrated with eighteen pieces called "Night Notes," small inventive streams that flow around the idea, the experience, and the word "nothing." These poems captivate and challenge the reader to explore the mysteries of the book's title. Booth contemplates the multiple meanings of "before sleep": before we fall asleep—that dreamy, evocative state; before we die—how we accumulate our lives in order to die; and, in its largest developmental sense, before there ever was sleep for mankind—a time or condition when we were always awake. Staying awake has the potential for enlightenment and nightmare. When we see too much as either poet or healer, we could tragically be included with the suicide of a psychiatrist in his "Night Note" "Ord kept asking": "Maybe / he couldn't stand / all he knew / . . . . A man / sits all day / on the edge of nothing / after a while he / gets numb and falls in." Or we can take our seeing as a condition of experience, as he says in "Eaton's Boatyard": "a life given to / how today feels: / to make of what's here / what has to be made / to make do."

At this point in his writing, Booth has the pleasure and capacity to look back and ahead and to express his immediate and existential anxiety. In "Falling Apart" he says, "I lean / in a lot of directions, / all without compass." And later in "Fog," rowing out between islands, he speaks, "I sit facing backwards, pulling myself slowly, toward the life I'm still trying to get at." In elegizing the deaths of Hannah Arendt, his friend Robert Lowell, and his father, Booth sees where he is in his own life, preceding his own death. Mourning is one way to confirm himself. In "Recall," remembering and identifying with his dead father, Booth writes, "I own to it now: / the way I have to reclaim what I've left, / the way I need to get myself back." Creating a hold, he knows he must also let go; in the book's last poem, "The House in the Trees," he mourns himself, this fact of life: "before it could ever be done / he would have finally, to leave it."

As in the best of his work, Booth appreciates who and what he loves. In "Soundings," thinking of his wife he says, "You, going gray, have grown new, you've touched me / to learn to see how you feel." In "Building Her," working wood into a boat: "The hull will / take to sea the way the tree knew wind." And in the book's last "Night Note": "I have to / to feel for the planet: nowhere better, with nothing to lose, than here / to give thanks / life takes place."

Again, as in previous books, these poems sometimes miss when they avoid an emotional connection to their subject without reason as to why feeling needs to be denied, or where Booth chooses to keep his poems small in their ambition and with a concomitant loss of evocative language. Occasionally criticized in his early work as being imitative of Frost, over the years Booth has come to be reviewed very positively. On *Before Sleep* Paul Breslin, in the *New York Times*, says, "Not many poets could get the voices right, yet compress so much meaning into a few colloquial words."

This book's most exciting and successful experiment comes in its "Night Notes," an extension of language and existential theme Booth began in *Available Light*. In these pieces he lets language uncover its own richness, its own intellectual, humorous, and dramatic consequences. By talking about "nothing" in its variety of forms, Booth permits the reader to experience and contemplate the dynamic relationship between meaning and no meaning, within the sequence of life and death. In one piece, a nurse speaks to her patient: "Don't worry, *she said*, you're going to / to be all right. Nothing / is going to happen. / I know, Noam said, it already has."

Other:

The Dark Island, edited by Booth (Lunenberg, Vt.: Stinehour Press, 1960);

Syracuse Poems, edited by Booth (Syracuse, N.Y.: Syracuse University Department of English, 1965, 1970, 1973, 1978);

"Dreamscape," in *Fifty Contemporary Poets: The Creative Process*, edited by Alberta T. Hunter (New York: McKay, 1977), pp. 54-57.

Papers:

Booth's manuscripts are located at the State University of New York, Buffalo; the Humanities Research Center, University of Texas, Austin; and Dartmouth College, Hanover, New Hampshire.

Susan Cheever
(31 July 1943-)

Susan Currier
California Polytechnic State University

BOOKS: *Looking for Work* (New York: Simon & Schuster, 1979; London: Weidenfeld & Nicolson, 1980);

A Handsome Man (New York: Simon & Schuster, 1981; London: Weidenfeld & Nicolson, 1981);

The Cage (Boston: Houghton Mifflin, 1982).

Susan Cheever, oldest child and only daughter of author John Cheever, "never wanted to be a writer." After graduating from college, she became first a teacher and then a wife, instead. But in 1979, after a four-year stint at *Newsweek*, she published her first novel, *Looking for Work*. Her second, *A Handsome Man*, appeared a year and a half later. A third, *The Cage*, was published in 1982 and a fourth, "Elizabeth Cole," is scheduled for publication in 1983. Meanwhile, she is collaborating with her husband Calvin Tomkins on a fifth and different work, a "comic lark of a novel." Cheever's characters, themes, and settings are drawn from upper-middle-class New York literary society. Her protagonists are contemporary young women struggling to confirm their identities in work and love. Reviewers compliment Cheever's craft, but they criticize her characterizations—her shallow conceptions of Salley Gardens "looking for work" and of Hannah Bart securing "a handsome man." Susan Cheever seems likely to remain a writer whether she ever wanted to be one or not. How important a writer she becomes may well depend on whether she can discover material on which to exercise her wit and style.

Born in New York City in 1943, Cheever grew up first on the Upper East Side and later in the suburbs. Of her childhood, she recalls that she was fat and unpopular and that her father was more accessible than most fathers since he worked at home. He was free to teach her sports, to take her shopping, to go for a walk, to drive her to school. He was not yet rich or famous, and, unlike her heroine in *Looking for Work*, Susan Cheever does not recall many literary celebrities, occasions, or conversations from her formative years: "My parents didn't know many book people. . . . I met Ralph Ellison,

and Irwin Shaw gave me a birthday present once, but that's about it."

As an adolescent, Cheever attended the Masters School in Dobbs Ferry, New York, where she played sports miserably and failed to gain acceptance into the literary club. After prep school she went to Brown, and after college she taught English at the Rocky Mountain School in Colorado. In 1967 she married Robert Cowley, editor at Random House and offspring of another author, Malcolm Cowley. During their marriage Cheever worked successively as an editor for a fashion magazine in London, as a writer for the *Tarrytown Daily News*, and as a free-lance writer in both San Francisco and New York while she followed Cowley's job changes. After their divorce eight years later, Cheever went to work as a writer for *Newsweek*, to which she contributed an extensive interview with her father, "A Duet of Cheevers," in March 1977. By 1978 Cheever had tired of her *Newsweek* job: "I had been a writer at *Newsweek* for four years dealing with other people's facts and I was chomping at the bit to write something of my own." She quit to travel to France and write with Calvin Tomkins, who became her second husband.

Cheever disclaims any paternal influence on her decision to become a writer. The impulse was her own, "although having him as a father gave me one huge advantage. I never thought of fiction as being something untouchable. I didn't approach writing a novel thinking 'I have to have a great gift.'" But to the heroines in her novels fathers are more important than mothers, and in her own autobiographical remarks John Cheever figures much more prominently than her mother, Mary. The biographical sketch with which Susan Cheever introduces her *Newsweek* interview with her father culminates in a powerful sequence of images of her father writing, a sequence which seems to order her own past:

> After he married my mother, Mary, in 1941, he wrote in their one-room apartment in Chelsea. Later, when he was living on the Upper East Side, he wrote in a windowless storage space in the basement of our apartment house. In the morning he put on his one suit, went down in the elevator with other men on their way to work, took off the suit, hung it up and wrote in his boxer shorts. At lunchtime he would put on the suit and come back upstairs.
>
> In 1951, we moved to the suburbs . . . and he wrote in the guest room of the little-house-on-a-big-estate where we lived. In 1956, when we went to Rome for a year, he worked on the ormolu dining-room table of our flat. In 1961, we moved to the house in Ossining, where he wrote *Bullet Park* in the maid's room off the kitchen, *The World of Apples* in the second-floor bedroom I left when I got married and, last year, *Falconer* in my brother Ben's old bedroom at the top of the house.

First novels tend to be autobiographical, and it is easy to construe Cheever's first book, *Looking for Work* (1979), as more memoir than fiction. Its heroine, Salley Gardens, is privileged. Her father is the Regius Professor of Comparative Literature at Columbia University. During the winter she studies French or ballet in the city; during the summer she

rides in Connecticut or sails off Nantucket. Ralph Ellison and Robert Penn Warren frequent her living room. At a party that includes Leonard Bernstein and the Arthur Millers, Yevtushenko singles her out: "But I had no idea you would be so beautiful." Both Philip Roth and John Cheever attend the celebration of her marriage to Jason Gardens, an editor for *American Magazine* and son of another Columbia professor. When she tires of her marriage, Salley begins "looking for work." Before she is divorced, she falls in love with a sculptor. After she is divorced, she leaves the sculptor so she can become a writer. One free-lance assignment for the *Village Voice* leads quickly to a permanent position at *Newsweek*.

But by Cheever's own admission, the roster of famous names is fictional and so is the character of Salley Gardens, even if some of the events in her life are not: "Oh, she's not me at all . . . Of course we all write about what we know, but we're very different women. She's very passive—I call her a dip, which isn't flattering. And I'm very impatient, intolerant, aggressive, bossy, managerial and take charge." Salley Gardens certainly is passive—pathologically so. External forces determine her feelings ("We were very much in love, everybody said so") as well as her fate ("The search for a [wedding] dress took on a lonely momentum of its own. In the beginning, I didn't even want to get married. But soon, all I cared about was being one of those white and gleaming light-hearted butterfly brides-to-be"). After the ceremony, which "isn't for the bride and groom" but rather "for their family and friends," Salley and Jason retire like "lost children . . . curled against each other for warmth."

Like children, both compile "private lists of angers and disappointments," and both require more than either can give. Jason is weaker than Salley, but Salley is blinder than Jason: "It's certainly not Jason's fault that I am such a fool. Nor that I thought at first his craziness was so romantic, or that if two people loved each other nothing else mattered. It's enough for Jason just to keep himself together at all, just to get through life without bringing the disaster he sees everywhere down on his handsome head. He can barely get by, and he certainly can't afford to take chances." Even as Salley exposes her errors of judgment in the past, she reveals herself as unreliable narrator in the present. The author means her to be taken seriously, but Salley Gardens betrays her readers and herself now just as she did Jason and herself in the past.

First, she attitudinizes about her growing up. After a long account of French and ballet classes, of

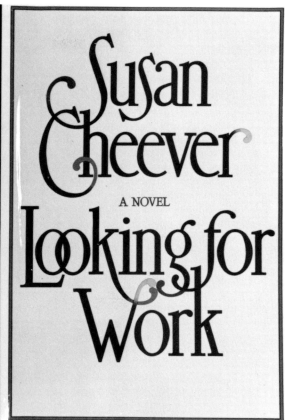

Dust jacket for Cheever's first novel (1979) about a woman who tires of marriage and begins looking for work

a spacious home with "grand views of the East River," of academic guests who welcomed her into their "conclaves," she remarks unconvincingly: "Well, with that kind of background you might suppose I would have the sense to think twice about marrying into another academic family." Her only complaint is that some of the guests in "worn-out tweeds" could not shuttle as gracefully as her parents "between proper society and the world of the intellectual elite." A few pages later, with reference to her marriage, Salley claims, "But the decision eluded me, and in the end I had to trick my wary self into that final joining." Salley's self is not wary. This novel is about "looking for work." At its beginning Salley Gardens quits work for love. She spends the rest of the novel trying to quit love for work.

Second, Salley contradicts her own self-analyses even as she postures. Describing her tension following her divorce and her means of discharging that tension, Salley remarks: "Sometimes people say I am driven, and they are right. But thank God no one ever gets to see the driver. He doesn't drive safely. He doesn't stop or start or slow down. When he is at the wheel I am out of control. And he is a man." What are we to make of this male daredevil? What relation has he to the Salley who cooks for her friend Mike Abrams because "he is good to hug, and safe"? Or to the Salley who wakes in a sweat "imagining a strange man . . . his face obscenely smiling in anticipation of my screams"? Or to the Salley who purchases amenities to ease inner pain, who wanders "through the stores in the look, leap, plunge, retreat pattern of the shopper bird"? These are all the versions of Salley in the chapter which culminates with the race-car driver. None of them seems driven by a daredevil. Nor does the Salley who takes leave at the close of the novel with one last rhetorical affectation: "There are plenty of times now when I don't think I'll ever get married, or have children. . . . Or ever love again at all, really. I'm not very tough, if you must know, but that's a secret." Why does Salley Gardens suddenly sound like Holden Caulfield at twice his age? She may have landed a job at *Newsweek*, but she has not found her voice or herself.

If Salley Gardens's character is a problem,

Susan Cheever's style is not. Her sentences in *Looking for Work* are clean and spare, wry and witty, "the kind of prose that sounds effortless but is bone-breaking to write." Adroit one-liners such as Salley's "I walked proudly along on Max's leash" liven the narrative. So do Cheever's (and in these examples, Salley's) abrupt transitions from Jason or the world to herself:

> And I wonder sometimes if you [Jason] are feeling that horrible knotting in the stomach, that rock in the guts, that is there when you know that someone you love is slowly leaving you. . . . Because you know, oh you know with a bone-chilling certainty, oh you never know anything quite so well as you know when someone you love is slowly leaving you.
> But where will I go?

> How can it work anyway, this money business between men and women? Why do some people pay for other people if not in return for services rendered? Charity is no longer saintly either. Is marriage just another exercise in acquisition. . . . Is courtship just another hype? You've got me.
> And so has Jason for that matter. Really, I tell myself in the depths of this funk, I don't have much of a choice anyway. I can find someone else to support me. I can shut up and cook. I can go on trying to find a job that will enable me to support myself.

Cheever is, perhaps, best at description. Most notable throughout *Looking for Work* is the soft-focus lens scene, set to Handel's *Water Music*, in which Jason and Salley make lyrical love to one another on the Nantucket beach. They walk, picnic, dig clams, cook chowder. They seem an advertisement for an expensive liquor or automobile. They seem a media vision. But they are not themselves, for Cheever has artfully overlaid the detail of their activities with the filmy fantasy that controls them. The range and control of language in *Looking for Work* are unusual in a first novel.

A Handsome Man (1981) is about looking for love. Its heroine is Hannah Bart, a divorced, thirty-two-year-old public relations employee in a publishing house, who falls in love with Sam Noble, the divorced fifty-year-old aristocratic president of another publishing house. The germ of the story seems to have been an episode in *Looking for Work*, another soft-focus lens scene—in the Carlyle hotel with white wine and Bobby Short playing "As Time Goes By" and an elegant writer inviting Salley to Ireland and romance. Salley and her writer get no

farther than the Carlyle. But, a book later, Hannah and Sam make the proposed journey to Ireland, along with Sam's estranged son, Travis, who jealously sabotages some of its intended romance.

Hannah has urged that Travis be invited. Indeed, she has gambled on endearing herself to Sam by reconciling the two. But she competes with Travis much as if she were another of Sam's children. Finally, she is not very different from Salley Gardens, and it is difficult to understand her appeal for Sam. She is supposed to represent a healthy change after a long string of Sam's Pippas, Biancas, and Angelicas, beautiful women by night but "harridans" by day, women who wished "to get him, to trap him and tie him down, to make him as weak as they were." Hannah plays tennis well, and she drags Sam up a cliff for an ocean view near Sligo, but she also trots along on Sam's leash much as Salley does on Max's—until in a moment of pique, she abandons herself to a passionate encounter with Travis. Hannah is forgiven, and Travis is exiled. Travis is not a very likable fellow, but Hannah earns his parting remark: "You guys are supposed to be so damn smart. Please, after this, could you just leave me alone?"

In the end, Sam rewards Hannah for her meddling by breaking down before her, the woman from whom he has "learned" so much, and by marrying her. Hannah Bart, like Salley Gardens, does not seem to earn her fortunes. In the epilogue Travis runs races all over New England until he finishes the Boston Marathon and is cured of his need for a father: " 'Oh, my dad took off years ago,' Travis said. He shrugged his silver shoulders to show that he didn't mind any more. 'I haven't seen him since I was a kid.' "

Ireland is not wasted on the descriptive talents of Susan Cheever. Sequences of Irish history and legend as well as scenes of Irish coast, country, and town relieve repetitive passages of eating, sleeping, quarreling, and changing clothes. Cheever covers the road from Shannon to Galway to Donegal to Letterkenny with authentic and telling detail. She introduces Irish farmers, schoolboys, priests, publicans, schoolteachers, telephone operators, British soldiers, and international aristocrats. Most notable is the trio's trip across the border to Northern Ireland, to Derry, where Sam bullies Hannah and Travis into a tense introduction to war and war zones.

In addition to her descriptive abilities, in these two books Susan Cheever demonstrates an ear for dialogue and, in *A Handsome Man*, an unobtrusive facility with point of view. That work depends almost entirely upon the shifting dynamics between Hannah, Sam, and Travis. Cheever moves the reader smoothly from one character's mind and feelings to another's, though Hannah's remains the dominant perspective.

The critics nearly all agree that Susan Cheever writes well. But they are divided about the final merit of her first two books. There is nothing wrong with her subjects. Women in search of love and work are inexhaustible themes. Certainly others deal with them at far greater length. Yet Cheever does not fully develop these themes or the characters she intends to carry them. An *Atlantic* review (January 1980) of *Looking for Work* suggested an apt metaphor:

> In a way, readers looking for a novel of any sort will be disappointed; this book is better thought of in some other category; think of it as a lunch, a basic forty-three-dollar lunch in a little East Side restaurant with an old friend who has been through a lot.

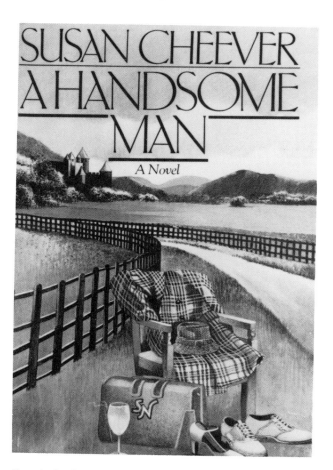

Dust jacket for Cheever's second novel (1981) about a woman looking for love

A *New Republic* review (16 May 1981) of *A Handsome Man* echoed this judgment:

> *A Handsome Man* should not have been a novel: it would have worked better as a short story, a vignette, or even an excursus within a vignette. Cheever's writing is adequate but, except for brief passages where she captures a mood or a thought with telling precision, the book is exceedingly dull. Nothing happens. It is like a faded color photograph: a brief moment of reality is accurately reproduced, but there is no movement or excitement.

After two books, Cheever at least needed to get past Salley Gardens and Hannah Bart, for the quality of both *Looking for Work* and *A Handsome Man* seems compromised by Cheever's lack of distance from her own protagonists. One senses that she is these characters, even though she claims she is not and that a new perspective would permit her to outgrow them.

In *The Cage* (1982), her third novel, Cheever achieves a more mature vision. This book is about "female possessiveness and male passivity in an upper-middle-class couple who also suffer from the loss of the past—a past when their class led much more comfortable, more secure lives than they can hope for now."

No youthful protagonist in search of either love or work animates this novel. It is a more tightly structured book than the first two, with a darker vision of a middle-aged couple trapped in mutual disappointment and destruction. Julia Bristol, who tends a suburban home, and Billy Bristol, who writes cover stories for a New York magazine, alternate chapters of their separate lives for the first half of the novel. Infrequent enactments of one or another of the failed rituals of their relationship punctuate these chapters, underscoring ever more emphatically the futility of their marriage and the mute disability of both its partners. Julia and Billy do better not to try to reach one another: "He looked into her face and for a moment they gazed blindly at each other, locked away, like two people who have seen in the distance their forgotten dreams, and remembered."

Billy Bristol literally becomes "locked away" in the second half of *The Cage*. On vacation at their summer home in New Hampshire, a relic of an elegant past in which Julia figured as a princess, Billy devotes himself to refurbishing empty animal cages which once housed his late father-in-law's menagerie. Billy surrenders himself to this manual labor

87

of his skin. He imagined his own pallid, deeply lined face;
he could feel the criss-cross of tiny sore red capillaries in
his eyes under the lights. His teeth ached and an eye muscle
beat an involuntary rhythm under his right lid. He hated Walter.

"Good, good job," Walter said. "I think you have it." He
flashed his teeth at Bristol and slapped the top of his maho-
gany desk with his palm. Bristol smiled back. He loved Walter.

"Just a~~x~~ few things...." Walter put his head back down to
read and began flipping through the pages. He hated Walter.

"The lead still isn't quite right. It's good, this human
interest stuff, but we don't want to ~~give it so much~~ have it
so up front." Walter was thinking about Herbert Rose. "Try
to mix the facts in sooner," he said, as he drew a red line
across the first page of Bristol's story. "I think the rest
will just drop in the basket for you."

"Okay."

"Let Larry edit it tomorrow. I'll see it again the final
version."

As Walter tightened the knot of his tie, took his summer-
weight silk blazer from behind the door of his secretary's
cubicle, and switched off the lights, Bristol turned and trudged
back down the hall. ~~The end was in sight.~~ Walter had passed
the story down to Larry and this meant that he was basically
satisfied and didn't expect big problems. The end was in sight.
Words and phrases bounced around like manic ping-pon balls in
Bristol's head as he eased his soreness back into his office

Page from a draft of The Cage. *"Since I write 10-12 drafts, my pages tend to be depressingly neat," Cheever commented.*

with "the reassuring sense that the work of men had gone on for hundreds and thousands of years and would continue for hundreds and thousands more." But the cage symbolizes the pernicious hold of an irrecoverable past upon both Julia and himself as well as the trap of his guilt and resentment toward Julia. Perception is relative, and at first it is Billy who sees Julia as captive of the cage: "As he turned, he saw her watching him from the other side of the bars and grille-work. All that wild iron had the effect of giving her a surreal quality, as if she were a woman in a picture, or an example of an endangered breed living out her life in captivity." But it is Julia who turns and pockets the key, trapping Billy at his faithful labors in her father's cage.

Two days and nights later, Billy negotiates his own escape and emerges from the cage transformed into "a free man." He correctly assesses that "her desperate feminine shrewdness" can no longer hurt him, but he does not allow for instincts more profound than shrewdness. Unknown to Billy, Julia has risen in the same dawn to shoot the deer which trample the "neat, fertile rows" of the old gardens near the cage. Brute beasts with no regard for the order and elegance of the old estate, they deserve "the bloody humiliation of having their bodies tied to the fenders of the hunters' big gas-guzzling cars." As Billy hikes across the property from the cage to the road in the shadowy dawn, Julia takes accurate aim and fires.

Billy is the best developed of Cheever's characters so far, and the entire work presents greater depth of vision and less adolescent egoism than Cheever's first two novels. The same clean style, adroit one-liners, and strong description are evident throughout—the same soft-focus lens that showed Jason and Salley Gardens on vacation at the beach is now trained just as effectively on Julia

Bristol's childhood in that gracious, irreproachable past which steadily consumes the present. But although it preserves the strengths of Cheever's first two books and eliminates some of their flaws (it can by no account be reduced to "a forty-three-dollar lunch . . . with an old friend who has been through a lot"), *The Cage*, like *Looking for Work* and *A Handsome Man*, is still another short story instead of a novel.

Susan Cheever is such a new writer that critics might be more appropriately curious than evaluative. She is, so far, a minor story writer, but she will soon publish a more ambitious novel. This year's "Elizabeth Cole" will be "a long book about New York City and coming of age [t]here." Cheever's model is Rastignac in Paris from *The Wild Ass's Skin*. Under Balzac's influence, she may successfully fit her ready style and technique to a broader complexity of life.

Other:
"A Duet of Cheevers," *Newsweek*, 89 (14 March 1977): 69-70.

References:
Dominique Browning, "Cheever's House of Cards," *Esquire* (January 1980): 84-85;
Randy Sue Coborn, "Susan Cheever: Her Father's Daughter," *Washington Star*, 10 February 1980, C7-8;
Georgia Jones, "Cheever isn't 'Looking for Work,'" *Los Angeles Herald Examiner*, 28 January 1980, C5-6;
Judy Klemesbud, "Susan Cheever Followed Father's Lead, After All," *New York Times*, 15 January 1980, III: 17;
Cheryl Rivers, "Working it out," *Commonweal* (4 July 1980): 410-411.

John Crowley
(1 December 1942-   )

Mark J. Lidman
University of South Carolina at Sumter

BOOKS: *The Deep* (Garden City: Doubleday, 1975;
London: New English Library, 1977);
Beasts (Garden City: Doubleday, 1976);
Engine Summer (Garden City: Doubleday, 1979;
London: Gollancz, 1980);
Little, Big (New York: Bantam, 1981; London: Gol-
lancz, 1982).

Called "a leader of the 1970s generation of
science fiction writers," John Crowley has been recognized as a writer who makes full use of numerous
generic conventions. Most of his writings utilize science fiction, fantasy, and history, although his more
recent works seem to be a bit more realistic and less
related to the realms of fantasy and literary convention.

The son of Dr. Joseph and Patience Crowley,
John Crowley was born 1 December 1942 in
Presque Isle, Maine, and spent his youth in Vermont and later in Kentucky, where he dabbled in
writing quatrains which he called "my first introduction to hack writing." In high school his interests
changed from classical archaeology to theater, and
he continued to write. Crowley attended Indiana
University, earning a B.A. degree in 1964, majoring
in English and minoring in photography. He acted
in a few plays, worked on a film with his roommate,
and considered becoming a poet. He claims he
abandoned the idea because "I had no calling. I
really believe that you need a vocation to be a poet
just as you do to be a priest. I was a fair versifier, but
there's a big difference between poetry and verse.
You can learn to be a versifier, you can't learn to be a
poet."

After graduation, Crowley went to New York
to work as an assistant to a fashion photographer. At
this time he began writing documentary films, a
sideline which he still pursues. During this period
he was also employed as a proofreader for the telephone directory. This job, which he has called his
favorite, introduced him to "other weirdos and
dropouts," some of whom are still his friends.

Crowley claims that "My life (as that of most
writers) is uneventful and sedentary. A distillation
of its important occasions will be found (disguised
or reinvented) in my two books (*The Deep* and

John Crowley

Beasts); and as I am a writer, my opinions on other
subjects are (or should be) without interest." But the
unusual seems to nurture his creative spark. "Writing really demands that you be a bit different from
everyone else, and in a way that strikes people as
peculiar. I've always been a little odd myself. Generally, the inside of peoples' heads matches the outside. In my case, that's not true."

It would be difficult to match the inside of
Crowley's head with his literary output, for his four
novels share few similarities. He is equally adept at
dealing with past, present, and future through
fantasy or realism. His first literary effort, "Learning to Live With It," "a meditation on the human
race," found no publisher, but the fact that he had
completed a manuscript spurred Crowley to rewrite
an unfinished history novel he had begun in 1963

while at Indiana University. This novel became *The Deep* (1975) and raised the hope that Crowley might be a major voice in science fiction in the future.

The Deep describes a flat disc resting on a pillar that extends an unimaginable distance into the surrounding deep of outer space. On this disc are played out complex feudal conflicts controlled by the Leviathan who had brought humans to a new habitat. *The Deep* is told from multiple points of view, but the chief one seems to be that of the Visitor, a damaged android who has been sent to record events. As the novel progresses, the Visitor becomes the Secretary and finally the Recorder, and as the Leviathan explains the mysteries of creation to him, he recalls his identity and his purpose.

Despite its futuristic extraterrestrial setting, *The Deep* is principally the historical romance about the Wars of the Roses that Crowley had begun as an undergraduate. But the turbulent English civil wars have been reconstructed into a memorable fantasy. The clashing houses of Lancaster and York have become the novel's Blacks and Reds, and Warwick "the Kingmaker" appears as Redhand. Characters not directly involved in the wars include the Grays (a brotherhood of learned men who make judgments and arbitrate between factions) and the Just (a faction armed with guns which fights against the landowning Protectors). *The Deep* was "an extremely impressive debut" for Crowley, who seemed to be aware of the appeal in the mixture of genres. He admits having been led to pursue science fiction because "I could write the sort of book I wanted and still get published. In science fiction, as long as everything takes place on another planet or in the future you can write what you like."

Following the success of his first published novel, Crowley put together some ideas he had harbored since high school—the image of a lion smoking a cigarette in a café, the notion of a wild dog pack roaming Central Park, and Paolo Soleri's science of archology which proposed that mankind move into huge buildings that could become self-contained cities to prevent the earth's further destruction. These ideas are set forth in *Beasts* (1976), Crowley's favorably received second novel, which demonstrates his ability to incorporate standard science fiction and fantasy themes into a larger literary tradition. The novel includes such divergent threads as the legend of Reynard the fox and the theme of genetic engineering. At times the novel's episodic nature resembles that of a collection of animal stories, but unifying the work is the ubiquitous Union of Social Engineering, a pseudo-government trying to restore order in the war-ravaged America of the future.

Much of the action of *Beasts* centers on the human-lion hybrids, or leos, who are joined by Sweets, a genetically altered dog, and Meric Landseer, a documentary filmmaker. Perhaps the most enigmatic of the beasts is Reynard, a sterile, sexless fox who orchestrates much of the novel's action, even after his death. Reynard reappears at the end to the surprise of all, a clone of his original self, to aid the new society which he has helped to rebuild.

Beasts comments on the pitfall of genetic engineering and science "gone wrong," suggesting frightening possibilities. The beasts of the title are, not surprisingly, quite human in some ways. Sweets and the wild dogs in his pack turn to the leos because they feel that animals should follow the king of beasts and not man. The novel points out that "beasts are not less than men, less ingenious in expression, less complex in personality, but as complete; as feeling, as capable of overmastering sorrow, hurt, rage, love."

Beasts was followed by *Engine Summer* (1979), a rewrite of the rejected "Learning to Live With It." With the publication of this novel, Crowley went beyond the science-fiction genre "into the hilly country on the borderline of literature," and the book received an American Book Award nomination. Crowley set *Engine Summer* in the distant future and cast it in the form of an interview between an unidentified human and the novel's hero, Rush That Speaks. Rush seeks sainthood, wishing to become one who tells his life story in such a way as to make it meaningful to all humanity, and his story mentions superhighways, organ transplants, birth control, word puzzles, even a Howard Johnson's motel whose ruins function as Service City. The continent's population has been reduced to a handful of people who live in self-absorbed, isolated communities following the Storm, an unspecified disaster, most likely a war. Crowley has returned to some of his earlier themes (Soleri's archology, animal transformations) while at the same time criticizing contemporary American culture. He names the city where the mysterious "angels" live Laputa, an apparent allusion to *Gulliver's Travels*, another multifaceted work that resisted simple classification.

In his most recent novel, however, Crowley appears to be moving in a different direction. *Little, Big* (1981) is a complex tale, longer than his three previous novels combined, which traces five generations of the family of John Drinkwater, an eccentric Victorian architect. In *Little, Big* we see Crowley's facility at working in the past, present, and the

4   Insnar'd in flowers, I fall on grass.
                              —Marvell

A Suit of   All on a Summer morning ~~he~~ *Smoky* dressed
Trumans   himself to wed, in a white suit of yellowed
                    linen or alpaca that his father had said belonged
                    to Harry Truman; there were the initials on
                    the inside pocket, HST; ~~who else's could they~~
                    ~~be~~; it was only ~~a short while ago~~ when he came
                    to consider it for a wedding suit that he
                    realized
                    ~~thought~~ that the initials could *upon in* stand ~~for somebody~~
                    ~~else~~, and ~~realized~~ that his father had ~~perpetuated~~
                                                                   kept up a
                    a joke *his* through his whole life and then ~~beyond~~, *probably as it*
                    ~~it~~ without cracking a smile. ~~Beneath the~~
                    ~~suit Smoky wore a pastel shirt, and as he~~
                    ~~proof. It was like him though; and there was~~
                    ~~the remote possibility that he had thought it~~
                    ~~was Harry's suit.~~ The sensation was not
                    unknown to him. He *had* wondered if his education
                    weren't ~~the~~ some kind of posthumous ~~joke~~ (revenge *him*
                    on his betraying mother?) and though Smoky
                    could take a joke, he did just now as he shot
                    his cuffs at himself in the bathroom mirror
                    feel a little at a loss and wish his father had
                    given him some man-to-man advice on
                    wedding behavior. Barnable hated weddings
                    and funerals and christenings, and whenever
                    ~~possible~~ one seemed ~~too~~ imminent would pack
                    socks, books, dogs and son and move on; Smoky
                    had been to Franz *Mouse's* wedding reception and danced
                    with the starry-eyed bride, who made him a
                    surprising suggestion; ~~that he never knew how to~~
                                                    didn't know
                    ~~action go about picking up;~~ but that was a
                    Mouse wedding after all and the couple were
                    ~~separated~~ already; He knew there must be
                    a Ring; he ~~he~~ patted his pocket where he had it;

Page from the manuscript for Little, Big

future, for the novel spans the whole of the twentieth century.

The novel opens with Smoky Barnable traveling to Edgewood, the Drinkwater estate, to marry Alice Dale Drinkwater, or Daily Alice, as she is known. Edgewood is built to hold an orrery, a clockwork model of the universe, but it also serves as a secret place where the real world intersects with fairyland. Smoky, the novel's center of consciousness, spends much energy trying to repair the broken orrery, which serves as symbol for the fragmented universe, but he learns that the orrery runs Edgewood itself.

Smoky is only one of a number of memorable characters in *Little, Big*. Russell Eigenblick becomes president of the United States, but he is in reality the reincarnation of the Holy Roman Emperor Frederick Barbarossa. Smoky's son Auberon, a scriptwriter for a soap opera, turns his program into another version of his family history. He has a love affair with Sylvie, a Puerto Rican girl whose childhood nickname, Titania, reminds us that we are not too far removed from Shakespeare's forest in *A Midsummer-Night's Dream*, another fairy world where overlapping patterns of life intersect. From the outset, when John Drinkwater marries Violet Bramble because she has access to the fairy world, *Little, Big* introduces its readers to a seemingly unending procession of gnomes, fairies, sibyls, and the like.

"To me the fairies represent the sense we all have that there's a story being told about us—that there's a larger meaning or a plot to life," Crowley comments. To Crowley, who "brooded over" the novel for a decade, *Little, Big* is "a tale within a tale, a series of paradoxes that, like Chinese boxes, are nested within one another." Within his rather realistic family chronicle are interlaced the fairy myth and the tale which is a paradigm of life itself. Before Smoky can die in peace, he fixes the orrery and sets the universe aright. As the locust tree sighs "our revels are now ended," we respond imaginatively to echoes of Prospero's enchanted island, another world within a world.

Publishers Weekly noted that Crowley "brings wit, worldly wisdom and a wild imaginative gift to each excursion" in the novel. In the *Washington Post Book World* (4 October 1981), John Clute praised the "calm, unremitting clarity" of Crowley's style in his "dense, marvelous, magic-realist family chronicle." *Little, Big* has solidified Crowley's reputation both within and without the realm of science fiction. It garnered for its creator the World Fantasy Award in

Dust jacket for Crowley's fourth novel (1981), which he describes as "a series of paradoxes that, like Chinese boxes, are nested within one another"

1981 as well as a prestigious Hugo Award nomination.

John Crowley currently lives in Northampton, Massachusetts, and is writing films as well as novels. His most recent films include the PBS documentary *No Place to Hide*, a frightening look at the bombshelter phenomenon of the 1950s, and *America Lost and Found*, a documentary about American life in the 1930s, which won an award at the American Film Festival in 1982. In addition, he is working on a fifth novel which he expects to complete by 1984 or 1985, a long historical fantasy dealing with a contemporary historian investigating Renaissance magic. The settings of his novel in progress and *Little, Big* indicate the direction his work is taking, a movement toward realism and away from the obvious realms of fantasy. While his work remains enigmatic, it appears that Crowley has secured an audience for years to come.

Other:
"Where Spirits Got Them Home," in *Shadows*, edited by Charles Grant (Garden City: Doubleday, 1977);
"Green Child," in *Elsewhere*, edited by Terri Windling and M. A. Arnold (New York: Ace, 1981).

Reference:
Eileen Kuperschmid, "John Crowley: The Story's the Thing," *Berkshire Sampler* (13 September 1981): 4-5.

Martha Gellhorn
(November 1908-   )

Jacqueline E. Orsagh
Tri-State University

BOOKS: *What Mad Pursuit* (New York: Stokes, 1934);
The Trouble I've Seen (London: Putnam's, 1936; New York: Morrow, 1936);
A Stricken Field (New York: Duell, Sloan & Pearce, 1940; London: Cape, 1942);
The Heart of Another (New York: Scribners, 1941; London: Home & Van Thal, 1946);
Liana (New York: Scribners, 1944; London: Home & Van Thal, 1944);
The Wine of Astonishment (New York: Scribners, 1948);
The Honeyed Peace: Stories (Garden City: Doubleday, 1953; London: Deutsch, 1954);
Two By Two (New York: Simon & Schuster, 1958; London: Longmans, Green, 1958);
The Face of War (New York: Simon & Schuster, 1959; London: Hart-Davis, 1959);
His Own Man (New York: Simon & Schuster, 1961);
Pretty Tales for Tired People (New York: Simon & Schuster, 1965; London: M. Joseph, 1965);
Vietnam: A New Kind of War (Manchester, U.K.: Manchester Guardian & Evening News, 1966);
The Lowest Trees Have Tops (London: M. Joseph, 1967; New York: Dodd, Mead, 1969);
Travels With Myself and Another (London: Allen Lane, 1978; New York: Dodd, Mead, 1979);
The Weather in Africa (New York: Dodd, Mead, 1980).

Many children believe they can do everything, that nothing can stop them, that nothing should. Martha Gellhorn never outgrew that belief nor her ambition to write nor her dream to see the world. Her family enjoyed a tradition of service and re- form long before she was born in November 1908 in St. Louis. Her maternal grandmother, an influential woman in nineteenth-century St. Louis society, agitated for an eight-hour workday for servants and organized a school for domestics which treated their work scientifically and won for them community respect. Her father, George Gellhorn, earned his M.D. in Germany but sailed around the world to satisfy the wanderlust he eventually passed on to his daughter before settling down in St. Louis to an exemplary medical career. Edna Fischel was an early suffragette and, according to her daughter, Martha, "almost invented" the League of Women Voters. Perhaps it was Martha Gellhorn's personal motivation shaped by her family's philosophy—"Ich Dien" (I Serve)—which set the course for her life.

Her ambition and her refusal to heed obstacles brought her face to face with some of the giants of the twentieth century. In addition to her husbands Ernest Hemingway and Thomas Matthews, her friends included H. G. Wells, Granville Hicks, Archibald MacLeish, John Dos Passos, Irwin Shaw, and Leonard Bernstein. She encountered the Nazis in Berlin in 1934, debated the relief system of the New Deal with Franklin and Eleanor Roosevelt, witnessed the early maneuverings of Mao Tse-tung and Chiang Kai-shek in China in 1941, traveled with the 82nd Airborne in Holland and Germany, talked to the first Russians occupying Berlin, and numbered among her friends Adlai Stevenson and John F. Kennedy.

In 1937, during the Spanish Civil War, she went into Spain with only a knapsack and fifty dollars. Gellhorn's passport to the history of her century was an article on Madrid that Ernest Hemingway and Herbert Matthews had persuaded her to send to *Collier's* in 1937. Gellhorn worked herself into the traditionally male-dominated profession of war correspondent. In the seven wars that she covered as a foreign correspondent for American and British magazines, Gellhorn endured shellings and bombings and risked torture and disease; in fact, she thrived on the intensified life she experienced as history shaped itself before her.

In the 1940s her ambition and sense of duty (she saw journalism then as a "guiding light," a beacon of truth) drove her back to war. She stowed away on a hospital ship—from which she viewed the invasion of Normandy—then escaped the consequent incarceration, and covered the war in Italy and France and accompanied the Allied forces to Arnhem and the Battle of the Bulge. When Vietnam was too controversial a subject for American magazines to cover accurately, Gellhorn traveled across Europe and Asia at her own expense and published her accounts in British newspapers.

Her magazine career, which began in 1929 with an article on Rudy Vallee in the *New Republic*, matured as her writing pace increased. While her aim was always to enlist support for the oppressed—the poor in America's Depression, the Republicans in Madrid, the refugees in Czechoslovakia, the Jews in Dachau—Gellhorn learned quickly to concentrate paragraphs into a few carefully selected details. Rather than philosophize about the horrors of war, she used powerful images: a mother crossing the street with her son, unaware that he had died with the last shellburst.

Gellhorn wrote her journalism primarily for others; her fiction she wrote mainly for herself. It is not that she did not care if others read her stories, for she cared passionately, but she had more time to develop and create in her fiction and there she could work out her own vision of the world. Her early drive to become a writer, which began well before the batch of poetry she sent to Carl Sandburg when she was fourteen, would never have been satisfied with reporting.

Gellhorn's first novel was published in 1934. *What Mad Pursuit* derives from her three years at Bryn Mawr, her leaving college to become a cub reporter with the *Albany Times-Union*, and her involvement with the pacifistic youth movement in Europe. The main problem in this novel lies in the reordering of fact into fiction. She is too close to her material, and her protagonist, a beautiful blond idealistic reporter, is a transparent characterization of the author. Yet while the style is overenthusiastic, the book holds the reader's attention. Gellhorn's lifelong concerns—justice, responsible action, a heightened sense of living, fulfillment of the independent woman—provide depth and interest.

Gellhorn's early fiction relied too heavily on her journalistic techniques. Stemming from her experiences as a relief investigator for the Federal Emergency Relief Administration, *The Trouble I've Seen* (1936) impresses one as a vivid collection of case studies of the unemployed. Gellhorn wanted to depict the mental and physical suffering of middle-class Americans who suddenly confront a reality which allows them no means for maintaining their homes, paying their doctors' bills, or even feeding their children. The prose is hard, clean, and honest. Like the articles Gellhorn later wrote on the Nuremburg and Eichmann trials, her second book stands as a graphic report and important lesson. It lacks the density of major fiction.

Gellhorn had similar difficulties with *A Stricken Field* (1940), a novel about the misery of the refugees in Czechoslovakia between the time of the Munich Pact and the Anschluss. A story within a story, the book depicts both the suffering of two Communist Germans, Rita and Peter, and the help given them by Mary Douglas, an American war correspondent. It is the correspondent, however, who is the novel's focal point, and therein lies Gellhorn's difficulty. Young, idealistic, with "fine legs," and recently from Spain, Douglas possesses Gellhorn's looks and ideas, past and present. The reader recognizes Douglas as Gellhorn, and when the author enlists sympathy and support for her romantic heroine, it is as if she asks these things for herself. In addition, Douglas is too good; she is the ideal of responsible action, combining, as do the refugees, all that is noble and brave. Apparently, Gellhorn's determination to reveal the extent of the Czechoslovakian tragedy loosens her artistic con-

trol. Not only do her characters remain types in *A Stricken Field*, but she crowds her pages with too many details and scenes.

Of the three books published in the early 1940s, *A Stricken Field* was the least impressive but received the most attention from the critics. This was due in part to her distinguishing herself earlier that year as the first correspondent in Russian-bombed Finland and in part to her connection with Ernest Hemingway—whom she married in 1940 and to whom she dedicated her novel. While *A Stricken Field*, *The Heart of Another* (1941), and *Liana* (1944) were only lukewarmly received, Gellhorn's journalism of the same period enjoyed enthusiastic approval, and her articles were often featured as *Collier's* cover stories.

Gellhorn with her first husband, Ernest Hemingway, whom she married in 1940

The transformation of her journalism into fiction was a painfully slow and frustrating task for Gellhorn, and she hated the critics who pronounced that she was a better journalist than novelist. But it was not until 1943 and the publication of *Liana* that Gellhorn finally rid her work of that autobiographical figure who had dominated her novels. The characters had remained caricatures: noble and base, oppressed and oppressor. Although these works bear the authenticating stamp of Gellhorn's journalistic detail, they are not good fiction.

With "Luigi's Place" and "Last Train From Garmisch," the more mature stories in *The Heart of Another*, Gellhorn began to formulate her own philosophy and invest her fiction with a richness beyond provocative plot and graphic detail. She shifted in her fiction from an emphasis on the external to an absorption with the internal. Gellhorn concentrated on the individual's struggle to find happiness and purpose in a world that seemed to deny both. She recognized, as is perhaps most evident in "Miami-New York," a short story from her 1953 volume, *The Honeyed Peace*, the great emptiness in the lives of most modern men and women. Bolstered by her long-standing family tradition, Gellhorn believed that one must attempt to bridge the existential gulf with personal relationships and responsible actions. To isolate oneself, Gellhorn began to imply in her fiction, is both self-condemning and criminal.

Gellhorn's fiction culminates in *The Wine of Astonishment* (1948), a complex book which focuses on man's self-imposed isolation. Jacob Levy, who shares the spotlight with Lieutenant Colonel Smithers in this World War II novel, is a nonpracticing Jew whose philosophy is to "get along and not have any trouble." He resents the awkwardness his heritage causes him and thanks fate that his being a high school football star cleared the way for him in St. Louis. His dream is to escape at the war's end to a Thoreauvian existence in the Smokies; his Jewishness seems always to interfere with his life plans for, as he believes, "a Jew had to earn being left alone."

Smithers, pleased to have no Jews in his battalion, is upset when his injured driver is replaced by a soldier named Levy. As the private and the CO endure heavy combat, including the advance into Luxembourg where the battalion suffers sixty-five percent casualties, their time together fosters a particular affinity of understanding and respect. That relationship deepens as they consider their great fortune in driving away from war to Luxembourg City and to the arms of Kathe and Dotty, whom they joyfully love. Because the comfort and

warmth of their women is all they look forward to in the idiocy in which they live, Levy and Smithers are emotionally devastated to discover their women are gone. Yet Gellhorn refuses to exploit the separation of the lovers and treats the incident matter-of-factly. She means to show that war ruins people's lives; what little hope and solace Levy and Smithers have is removed by chance. Smithers, whom we suspect has buried his bigotry, proves in the end to have made an exception of Levy rather than change his mind about Jews: " 'you'd never think Levy was a Jew,' Lieutenant Colonel Smithers interrupted. 'I swear I forgot all about it. . . . there wasn't a thing like a Jew about Levy. I don't know how many times I said to my officers that Levy was a real white man.' "

In the same way that Smithers returns to his earlier bigotry, the plot returns to the initial incident, only this time Levy is hospitalized after an auto accident and Smithers must again find a driver. This cyclical structure is Gellhorn's reminder that nothing really changes. Peace comes, and men return to their old lives. Old allies become new enemies; old enemies are forgiven and become new allies. Another war with its share of lost and ruined lives will be followed by another uncertain peace. War, Gellhorn implies, is the pattern that is man. Only the character of Jacob Levy departs from the cyclical concept, but it is in his development that Gellhorn is most interested, and it is in this linear structure that the thrust of the book lies. After peace comes "in the most unspectacular way, after lunch over the radio," Levy drives off to be by himself and chances upon Dachau. There the brutality of the Nazis falls upon Levy as it had upon Gellhorn. Everywhere are walking skeletons and piles of dead bodies, hair and clothing carefully removed; everywhere the gagging smell of burnt flesh. As the doctors and prisoners tell their atrocious tales, Levy excoriates both that apathy that kept him from knowing the truth and the Germans who allowed Hitler to execute his plans. Even if the Nazis shot you, Levy reasons with new resolve, "that was when you had to get shot." If you did not, "you were the filth the way the S.S. guards were." Jacob Levy transcends his self-preserving escapism and, in the novel's extraordinary climax, becomes one of those whom Gellhorn labels the "gallant minority," the people who oppose evil wherever they see it. He perceives that he alone is responsible for his actions and that those actions give his life what meaning it has.

In *The Wine of Astonishment* Gellhorn takes the best from her journalism: her delicate timing, her

Dust jacket for Gellhorn's third collection of stories, 1958

(1958), and *Pretty Tales for Tired People* (1965) reveal the craft of the mature artist. The detail is spare but poignant; the characters are human beings who impress us simultaneously with their ordinariness and singularity. Ever present are the tension and depth essential to good writing.

In these later books, as in all of Gellhorn's fiction and journalism, her themes are similar: justice, the crush of poverty and war on the psyche, the growth which springs from pain and near devastation, and the necessity for purpose in one's life. There is no art for art's sake for Gellhorn although she writes painstakingly and constantly experiments with form. There is no dialogue in the entire fifty pages of "The Clever One" (*Pretty Tales for Tired People*). She has always been interested in how something is said, but her writing must *say* something. In *The Lowest Trees Have Tops* (1967), a fantasy novel through which Gellhorn escaped the mental horrors of Vietnam, the American residents of the utopian Mexican community are refugees from

Dust jacket for Gellhorn's 1967 fantasy novel about Americans who flee to a utopian Mexican community to escape McCarthyism

capacity for selecting the perfect detail, and her ability to impart immediacy. Levy's discovery that responsible action and service to others gives purpose to life is Gellhorn's personal philosophy. But here her artistic weaving of material and distancing of the autobiographical enhance the story. Levy impresses not as a conventional hero but as a man.

The depth which Gellhorn had sought in her fiction was clearly achieved in *The Wine of Astonishment*. The critics were impressed and surprised that a woman could write of a soldier's reaction to war with such keen insights and some linked her book with Norman Mailer's *The Naked and the Dead* as the best of the year.

Although Gellhorn's journalism maintained a recognized level of excellence to the point where, in 1959, several of her war articles were selected for the much-acclaimed *The Face of War*, her fiction was not as consistently praised nor as praiseworthy. *His Own Man* (1961), however, and those stories which Gellhorn collected in *The Honeyed Peace*, *Two By Two*

Full Circle
(10/12/80)

At the ~~advanced~~ age of nineteen, which was ~~considered~~ young in those days, I first set foot on this scepter'd isle this England and thought it blissful mainly because no grown-ups were along. There had been a chaperoned summer in France and a family summer in Germany but now at last, in the company of another pink-cheeked buxom maiden, I was free: travel by whim, the only way ~~to go~~ for pleasure then as now. With ~~incredible good sense~~ surprising good sense, my chum and I made straight for Cornwall and rented bikes, ~~puffed and pushed upwards, sailed donwards over the countryside.~~ We had no plans. (over). We It is too long ago to remember much except this, a memory ~~I know is true but~~ that I find unbelievable: hot golden sun day after day.

We discovered ~~Beyond that,~~ cream teas and a new ~~way to live~~ type of dwelling, called bed-and-breakfast ~~are major memories. It~~ The village, the scenery were ~~small as pretty and tiny and cosy and sweet; a perfectly olde worlde, an adorable doll's~~ as fine country ~~house in my mind.~~ We proceeded to London and stayed at the Regent Palace for two days, seeing ourselves in our wide cotton skirts and sleeveless tops, bare legs and sneakers, as women of the world in a rather louche ~~pleasure~~ setting, as if on a stationary Orient Express. We went to the ballet, high up, and from that eeyrie, watched "L'Après Midi d'un Faune" and ~~saw~~ the Great Leap. For most of my life I was sure I had seen Nijinsky until it was borne in upon me that he was ~~long~~ long before. mad and dead. No other ballet ever ~~again~~ moved me so deeply; ~~the rest of~~ otherwise London was ~~without~~ not ~~exciting.~~ alluring. ~~interest.~~ love I did not ~~like~~ love cities and do not ~~like~~ love cities.

~~The reason I have lived longer in London than in any one~~ other

---

First page of the revised typescript for an article Gellhorn wrote for the periodical In Britain

McCarthyism. And even in this, Gellhorn's lightest work, her preoccupation with justice is obvious.

By some definitions Gellhorn is a loner. She divorced Hemingway in 1945 and her ten-year marriage to Thomas Matthews ended in divorce in 1963. Gellhorn became a single parent in 1949, adopting her son, Sandy, from an Italian orphanage. When the United States refused hospitality to her alien son, Gellhorn settled for a time in Cuernavaca, Mexico. She deliberately has few possessions and has changed residences and countries every few years. She lives in her spartan London flat, writing fiction and sending supportive letters to other writers. In 1978, she had published *Travels With Myself and Another*, which describes the lives of artists in Moscow, the depressed lives of the Chinese, and the French prisons in Surinam; but it also shows us the woman who dared flout Russian regulations and smuggle orange marmalade and Yehudi Menuhin records to Nadia Mandelshtam, who journeyed across the mud-drenched Chinese interior on tiny horses (so tiny Hemingway carried his), and who sailed the Caribbean dodging typhoons and German submarines in a potato boat.

Martha Gellhorn wanted to see the world. She wanted to write. But neither goal would have satisfied her had she not believed she was in some way serving others. Her journalism, which functions at its best as a kind of conscience, and her fiction, which provides a provocative reflection of humanity and reveals the crucial difference between keeping busy and living, serve both author and reader.

Periodical Publications:
"Only the Shells Whine," *Collier's*, 100 (17 July 1937): 64;
"Arabs of Palestine," *Atlantic*, 208 (October 1961): 45-65;
"Eichmann and the Private Conscience," *Atlantic*, 209 (February 1962): 52-59;
"The Indomitable Losers: Spain Revisited," *New York*, 9 (2 February 1976): 42.

References:
Carlos Baker, *Ernest Hemingway: A Life Story* (New York: Scribners, 1969);
Thomas S. Matthews, *O My America! Notes on a Trip* (New York: Simon & Schuster, 1962);
Jacqueline Orsagh, "A Critical Biography of Martha Gellhorn," Ph.D. dissertation, Michigan State University, 1978.

Peter Gent
(23 August 1942-   )

Michael Adams
Louisiana State University

BOOKS: *North Dallas Forty* (New York: Morrow, 1973; London: M. Joseph, 1974);
Texas Celebrity Turkey Trot (New York: Morrow, 1978).

Famous as a football-star-turned-novelist, Peter Gent is more than just another ex-jock who has made good, more than just another insider telling tales out of the locker room. He is a writer with a journalist's awareness of the significance of details, a satirist's eye for absurdities, and a moralist's sense of the trivialities of contemporary American life. With his two novels, *North Dallas Forty* (1973) and *Texas Celebrity Turkey Trot* (1978), Gent is perhaps the most perceptive chronicler of America's favorite form of violence.

Gent was born and raised in Bangor, Michigan, the son of Charles Edward and Elizabeth Katherine Davis Gent. His father worked on a railway mail car and then as a rural mail carrier before retiring after thirty years of postal work. His mother worked in the high school principal's office. Gent was an all-state football player at Bangor High but played only basketball at Michigan State, being voted most valuable player on the team two of his three seasons. The six-foot-four-inch Gent refused to play football at Michigan State because "I just heard too many bad reports from guys on the football team." He says that Coach Duffy Daugherty once offered him a starting position one week be-

Peter Gent

fore a season started: "I figured Duffy was either lying to me or screwing the guy who was playing the position." Gent's suspicions about the motives and morality not only of coaches but of anyone in positions of power and influence are at the center of his two novels.

After graduating with honors from Michigan State in 1964 (he majored in communcations arts but did most of his course work in history and religion), Gent was signed as a free agent by the Dallas Cowboys, who in the 1960s took on several basketball and track athletes and converted them into football players. Gent was a pass receiver for the Cowboys for five years, enjoying his best season statistically in 1966 when he caught twenty-seven passes for an average gain of 17.6 yards, although he says he was a "better player" in 1967 and 1968. His career was severely hampered by injuries: he broke his right leg and ankle and had surgery on his right knee three times. Traded to the New York Giants in 1969, Gent was released during the exhibition season after being assured by Coach Allie Sherman that he had made the team.

Like Mabry Jenkins, the protagonist of *Texas Celebrity Turkey Trot*, Gent tried to maintain his

"celebrityhood" as a disc jockey but did not succeed, and he also failed a sportscasting audition. "Being out of football was shocking," Gent says, "and it took me a while to learn how to handle it." He eventually turned to writing, and his first novel, *North Dallas Forty*, sold 54,000 hardcover copies. "I made more money from that book than I ever made from football," says Gent, whose highest salary with the Cowboys was $17,000. Gent lives with his wife, Jo Ellen Walton Gent, whom he married in 1969, and their children, Holly and Carter, in Wimberly, Texas, near Austin.

North Dallas Forty covers eight days in the life of Dallas receiver Phil Elliott, a part-time player with a lot of talent but with what B. A., the head coach, considers a bad attitude. Elliott seems to have a better relationship with the team's star player, quarterback Seth Maxwell, but Maxwell never quite stands up for his friend the way he should and betrays him in the end when Elliott is kicked out of professional football, supposedly for smoking marijuana. The novel focuses on Elliott's relationships with teammates, coaches, management, fans, and the women in his life. Divorced, Elliott has had a longtime affair with Joanne Remington, but she is engaged to the team owner's brother because he can afford to give her the life to which she has grown accustomed. During these eight days, Elliott meets and falls in love with Charlotte Caulder, who seems to be the woman he has been searching for, but in the novel's powerful conclusion, she is murdered by a rejected suitor.

North Dallas Forty (the title refers to the forty players on the team) appeared at a time when several former professional football players, encouraged by the political climate of the time, were writing exposés of the inhumanity, hypocrisy, and enforced conformity of life in the National Football League. Yet while the St. Louis Cardinals' Dave Meggyesy in *Out of Their League* (1970) and the Oakland Raiders' Chip Oliver in *High for the Game* (1971) chose nonfiction as a means of telling their stories, Gent has more freedom to criticize the system through fiction. Part of his purpose is to expose the impersonality, pettiness, and stupidity of coaches and management and to show how the players use and abuse drugs and sex.

The pain the athletes are expected to endure while playing is discussed in almost every scene: "They say you should quit when you still hurt on Sunday from last Sunday. I wasn't sure I wasn't still hurting from exhibition season." Because they are professionals, the players must perform regardless of their injuries and are often forced to take painkillers which increase the possibility of further and permanent injuries. As Gent presents things, it is only a logical extension for players to go from taking medication when they need it to taking it all the time, from taking legal painkillers to taking illegal ones: "I was high on something all the time—codeine, booze, grass, fear; in fact, I doubt that during a season I was ever in a normal state of mind, if there is such a thing as normal. After the season I went through withdrawal, sweating and walking most of the night for weeks, not really calming down until mid-March." The players use sex in the same way as a release for the accumulation of energy, tension, and frustration.

Just as much a problem as pain is the mentality of the coaches and management. Elliott admires the intelligence of B. A. but is angered by his manipulations and evasions of responsibility: "It was B. A.'s philosophy to point out only mistakes, as we were 'paid to make great plays.' He also felt the team 'deserved to know who was letting them down' in the course of a game." Management is as much concerned that a player conform as perform. Thomas Richardson, a talented running back, seldom plays because he refuses to give in to the system: "he refused to deal in anything but profoundly

relevant and personal terms. He insisted that management meet him on a man-to-man basis. Not even the most confident of football general managers or head coaches is willing to meet an angry 225-pound black on a man-to-man basis." The most devastating part of management's insistence upon seeing the players not as individuals but as property is that those in power feel free to distort reality: "Like so many people, they weren't concerned with the truth. They wanted an arrangement of facts that coincided with their present needs and wishes. And because they were powerful, it was relatively easy for them to rearrange the stuff of daily experience to correspond with their current views and desires. Once they rearranged it all, they attacked the situation with a moral zeal and believed they were doing the right and just thing."

Elliott cannot forgive those in power for destroying something he loves—the pleasure of playing football: "There is a basic reality where it is just me and the job to be done, the game and all its skills. And the reward wasn't what other people thought or how much they paid me but how I felt at the moment I was exhibiting my special skill. How I felt about me. That's what's true. That's what I loved. All the rest is just a matter of opinion." Gent sums up all these points in a moving scene in which O. W. Meadows, a gigantic lineman, spews his feelings out to an assistant coach: "Every time I try and call it a business you say it's a game and every time I say it should be a game you call it a business. You and B. A. and the rest want us to be eleven total strangers out there thinkin' we was a team."

Gent is concerned with much more than just telling the inside story of professional football in *North Dallas Forty*. Depicting violence, racism, materialism, conflicting attitudes toward success and failure, and the inability of the individual to stand up to the organization, the novel is as much about politics as sports. Gent uses urban Texas as a symbol of everything bland and unfeeling about America, of what has gone wrong with the American Dream: "It was the afternoon rush hour and I was going against the grain of the traffic escaping north to the suburbs. I passed miles of glazed eyes, tight jaws, and hands tensely gripped on steering wheels, people rushing home, dazedly thankful that the world had held together for another day." Elliott can escape this fate through football, which he sees as an art form when it is played as it should be, and through love, but both are taken away from him. Gent presents a savage indictment of a society seemingly determined to destroy itself.

Reviewers were generally enthusiastic about *North Dallas Forty*. *Newsweek*'s Pete Axthelm wrote

Dust jacket for Gent's second novel (1978), in which an ex-athlete struggles to adjust to life without football

the book: 'If they had that much sex constantly, how did they have the energy to suit up for the Sunday game?' " Gent's excesses are perhaps the result of his zeal in presenting a side of football most fans are unaware of or reluctant to acknowledge.

Gent received credit for writing the screenplay for the film version of *North Dallas Forty* (1979) with director Ted Kotcheff and producer Frank Yablans. According to Gent, "I was on the set writing the scenes as we shot them." He was fired by Yablans four times during the shooting, but Kotcheff and star Nick Nolte "would get me back. I finally just went. The shooting was almost done." Gent praises Nolte, Kotcheff, and cinematographer Paul Lohmann for being "tireless workers who also took the time to read and understand the novel." Their efforts produced results "that often exceeded what I had hoped." Nolte called Gent after he had seen the final edited version of the film: " 'We got about eighty percent,' he said, and I think he's right. Eighty percent is Damn Good." According to Gent, "the problem in the film is the inability to resolve the relationship between Phil and Charlotte fully." He had difficulty convincing his publisher to accept the novel's violent ending, and the movie studio refused to agree to it. A critical and box-office success, the movie plays up the comic aspects of the story while downplaying the social criticisms. Nevertheless, it is still the most honest treatment of American sports on the screen, with the possible exception of Michael Ritchie and James Salter's *Downhill Racer* (1969).

Although the protagonist of *Texas Celebrity Turkey Trot* is once again a professional football player, Gent's main concern is satirizing American materialism, vulgarity, and obsession with the trivial. Mabry Jenkins, a thirty-year-old defensive back, feels he is having the best of his nine training camps with Dallas and plans to play five more years. Unlike Phil Elliott, the disciplined, "coachable" Jenkins is no rebel. He cannot afford to be because he needs football badly: "I love the competition and the adrenaline highs—the high of living on the edge matched against equally intense men desperate to live on the edge, scratching and digging for your place right on the brink. You feel and taste more on one Sunday afternoon than most people do in a lifetime and you don't have to wait years to find out if you are doing a good job." After Jenkins injures his knee, however, he no longer fits into Dallas's plans and is forced to retire to avoid the "embarrassment" of waivers: "I began to feel old. I never thought I'd feel old at thirty. Jesus, was I sad." The rest of the novel deals with his bumbling efforts to adjust to life without football, all the time expecting

that the "unassuming bits of philosophy, complemented by some remarkable satire and self-mockery, produce the best moments in a book that has many good ones." He called Gent "a writer so talented that he seems certain, with a few more efforts, to make us forget that he ever happened to catch passes for a living." In the *New York Times Book Review*, Dick Schaap praised Gent for proving "his case without preaching, without sermonizing, almost without judging. He balances shock with humor, irony with warmth, detail with insight, and ends up with a book that easily transcends its subject matter."

Schaap pointed out that the weakest part of the novel is, ironically, the account of Elliott's last game when Gent becomes less a novelist than a reporter. Reviewers also complained about the overemphasis on drugs and sex. In *Sports in America*, James Michener observed that Gent's "unrelieved emphasis on brutality, venality, drugs and sex sometimes seems unreal. My comment on finishing the entire National Football League to collapse "of its own weight without the necessary ingredient of Mabry Jenkins and his amazing discipline."

The athletes in *Texas Celebrity Turkey Trot*, because they are allowed to live out their fantasies, feel somewhat estranged from nonathletes who have to find substitutes for the glory and excitement the athletes experience all the time. As an ex-athlete, Jenkins is in a kind of limbo: "I had to come back. I hadn't finished dreaming." By hanging out with the wealthy and the famous—a television actor, a country-and-western singer, a rodeo star, an ex-astronaut, a beauty queen, and assorted Texas millionaires—he hopes to find some purpose in his life.

Those who think they are always right just because they are rich are a frequent target of Gent's satire. These characters go around saying, "Every nation has responsibilities to support the world market system," and wearing sweatshirts proclaiming, "The Third World Sucks." One Texan wants the government to turn amateur athletics over to the corporations so that the United States can kick "the holy bejesus out of the East Germans."

Gent presents the pursuit of wealth as necessitating a person's giving up most of his humanity and a good deal of his sanity. The quest for fame results in events such as the Midland/Odessa Battle of the Celebrity Sexes Golf Tournament and Charity Telethon, whose participants are obsessed with self-promotion. Jenkins's desperate need for recognition induces him to do whatever is necessary to get back into the limelight to which he has become addicted. The triviality of "celebrityhood" becomes even clearer when Jenkins, after failing as a country-and-western disc jockey, becomes a hero for helping to nab a robber when he is only trying to get out of the crook's way. The novel ends with Jenkins's return to pro football and the fantasy life he can control: "Outside, I find life hard—nothing is ever resolved, and everybody's paranoid from watching each other on television. We all get too much feedback on life."

Although much of Gent's satire is hilarious, his targets are usually such easy ones that the result is less substantial than it should be. The trivialization of American life through the mindless pursuit of celebrity status is an excellent subject for satire, but Gent's approach is not as hard-hitting as it could have been. And as with *North Dallas Forty*, *Texas Celebrity Turkey Trot* has several annoying minor problems; one is that the time is vague. American involvement in Vietnam has apparently recently ended, but other topical references place the events later in the 1970s. Finally, because Mabry Jenkins is not the victim of a system as Phil Elliott is, he is not interesting or sympathetic enough.

Peter Gent's novels in progress include "The Franchise," the history of a professional football team from its inception to its first Super Bowl, and "The Espantosa War," a historical detective story set in the San Antonio area. Gent, who has also written some twenty articles about sports subjects for periodicals such as *Sport, Rolling Stone,* and *Esquire,* is a promising writer because of his wicked sense of humor, his ability to juggle large casts of characters, and his insight into what is rotting away at America's soul. He could make a career of writing about sports and Texas in the same way that Joseph Wambaugh, to whom he has been compared, writes about police and Los Angeles, but one hopes he will not limit himself to these subjects.

Screenplay:
North Dallas Forty, by Gent, Ted Kotcheff, and Frank Yablans, Paramount, 1979.

Periodical Publications:
"North Hollywood Forty," *Esquire,* 94 (September 1980): 36ff.;
"Snake Attack," *Rolling Stone,* 11 December 1980, pp. 46-48, 64-65;
"Is Mickey Mantle Safe At Home?," *Esquire,* 95 (March 1981): 54-61, 63.

Interview:
Kelso F. Sutton, "Letter from the Publisher," *Sports Illustrated,* 49 (31 July 1978): 4.

Reference:
James Michener, *Sports in America* (New York: Random House, 1976), pp. 14-15.

Stephen Goodwin
(20 October 1943-)

Bernice Werner White
Southwestern at Memphis

BOOKS: *Kin* (New York: Harper & Row, 1975); *The Blood of Paradise* (New York: Dutton/Henry Robbins, 1979).

Stephen Goodwin was born 20 October 1943 in Pennsylvania, to Claudius Lee Goodwin and Jeannette Francis Levy. When he "was a wee little thing," the family moved to Brewton, Alabama, where his grandfather Horace Levy was, as Goodwin said, "a carpetbagger—he owned textile mills and exploited, alas, the inexpensive female labor in the area." Goodwin attended Portsmouth Priory, a Catholic boarding school in Rhode Island—an experience that he says "probably had more to do with [his] development than Harvard did."

Goodwin earned his A.B. in English from Harvard University (1965) and an M.A. from the University of Virginia (1969), where he studied under Peter Taylor, to whom Goodwin believes he owes "a great deal." From 1966 to 1968 he served in the United States Army, assigned to "cushy duty as a stenographer in a NATO HQ" in Germany. From 1969 to 1973 he was an instructor in English at Washington and Lee University; from 1973 to 1978 he held the position of assistant professor at Bryn Mawr. Concurrently, he served as fiction editor of *Shenandoah* (1972-1973) and as an editor of *Southern Voices* (1974). He married Lucia Collier Stanton on 16 June 1964; their daughter, Eliza, was born on 3 March 1972. After a year of teaching at the University of Virginia, Goodwin moved to George Mason University (the state university in northern Virginia) in Fairfax, where he directed the writing program. Now divorced, Goodwin lives and works in Washington, D.C., but he still owns the house that he built in the mountains and that he still considers home despite five years of city living.

Although Goodwin thinks of himself as a Southerner and although his fiction is frequently set in the South, his concerns are not limited to that or any region. Taken as a group, his short stories suggest the same concern that their author saw in *The Collected Stories* of his graduate instructor Peter Taylor: the "characters are up against ... circumstance, particularly the terrifying circumstance of their own preoccupations." For example, in "The

Lizard of Conques" (1971), one of the more literary and the most haunting of his short pieces, Goodwin portrays a graduate student/playwright, Gregory Geraud, who toys with the fears and fixations of another student. Geraud is an obnoxious young man who is jolted out of his cruelty when a brown lizard's fall from a church wall teaches him a degree of humility and gives him some understanding of his failure as a self-aware human being. In "Spring Correspondence" (1971), a middle-aged man married to an apparently unsympathetic woman is surprised by his desire for a younger woman, awakens to a glorious spring day, and discovers in a letter from his father intimations of a mortality to which he cannot respond. At the close, Martin returns to his preoccupations with his marriage and the gloom of middle age: "He took up the pen and added a single sentence to the letter: *This morning, Sunday, I cried.* The statement was a fact that seemed to finish and cancel the opening paragraph [describing the spring day]. For several minutes Martin stared at the correspondence which no one else ever need see." The wordplay touches the reader with surprise and pity.

In "Sole Surviving Son" (1970), the best sustained of the earlier stories, Goodwin uses his army experience to explore not only the preoccupations of Arthur N. Waldo (a volunteer in the army who has a scheme for discharge) but also the nation's need to examine the values it professes. While waiting for his release on the grounds that he is his mother's only support, Arthur is assigned to the "Doomsday Machine," an automatic typewriter programmed to print death notices. As men he knows depart for Vietnam, Arthur puts his own name on all the letters the machine prints that day. The result is his removal from the detail and his being designated a "mental defective." Finally released, he returns to the Midwest on a train named "Manifest Destiny" and reports at the end that "The best I can do . . . is tell [people] my own name and try to learn theirs . . . that seems to be all I can do, but it's something." Arthur's dehumanizing experience requires the reader to question and challenge the nation's preoccupations with war and victory and the price at which they come: the literal and spiritual deaths of too many young men.

Goodwin's first novel, *Kin* (1975), draws in part upon the author's experience and opinion of the army and in part upon his acquaintance with and understanding of the South and the workings of prejudice. The title is the name of a character, Arthur Kin, an ex-soldier whom Parker Livingston invites to his mother's home in Ewell ("EE-well"), Alabama, in September 1968—without informing Mrs. Livingston that Arthur is black. The title is also a pointer: the word *kin*, as James Boatwright noted in his brief review (*Shenandoah*, Winter 1975), derives ultimately from the Greek "to be born." The novel is about race, family, and blood relationships. Parker has a preoccupation with those connections that have influenced his life: his confusion over his father's life and suicide and his own inability, thus far, to confront the fact he has illegitimate kin—his father's son by a black woman. "Philip Livingston was as imperfectly conceived [by Parker] as a character in a dream, so that Parker believed himself less the issue of an individual father, the chromosomal sum of a particular union between that man and his mother, than the get of a racial principle." The observation sets the tone for the

novel, which examines racism and kinship in multiple ways. There is a fracas in which Arthur is in mortal danger; an official investigation follows, for which Parker writes a lengthy deposition that examines not only the event but the nature of prejudice. There is family strife between Parker, his mother, and his mother's lover, and between Parker and his sister, Amsy—partly because of her familiarity with Arthur. Parker's main difficulty in writing the statement lies in the truth that he must tell about himself. When three "good ol' boys" threaten Arthur, he flees. Parker betrays him, and when the shooting stops, Parker believes Arthur is dead, but Arthur is faking to save himself. Once Parker has confessed his betrayal of Arthur, he writes:

> I know I can't be acquitted, freed, or even pleased by anyone else's guilt. . . . I honestly don't know any longer if I want the case to come to trial. It should. . . .
>
> Here we are again, the difference between justice and law. And all we need to do to accomplish justice, to extinguish that desire, is change history. Well, I don't believe that any longer; I think it's a question of how we inhabit our history. If we can't overcome it, we can at least gain possession of our lives within it. And we *have* to do that; otherwise we are subject not just to those murderous desires but to the griefs they engender, to sorrows that increase, to despair.

If Parker's preoccupation with his past governs the novel up to the completion of the deposition, the position he takes in his confession dominates the close of the novel. Before finishing the document, Parker becomes involved in a crisis in his half-brother's family and finds himself face to face with Esther, his father's mistress: "he didn't have to think to know that his sight of Esther was the accusation and judgment he had sought since returning home. Not related to him by blood, kin only through the lost and maddened Andrew [Parker's half-brother], Esther spoke for the wreckage of family, for love unhoused and forbidden to continue." Later, attempting to explain Philip, Esther, Andrew, and Arthur to his sister, Parker discovers that the ghosts that have haunted him have disappeared and that, although he cannot verbalize his new understanding of kin and love to Amsy, he has gained possession of the perplexing events of the past and has learned from his anguish over his father and the confusion of the entire family's life that "grief is love freed of object."

Through the complications of Parker's situation, Goodwin says several things: from Parker's deposition it is clear that the author understands the necessity of coming to grips with the past—familial, national, racial—so that the individual can overcome grief, sorrow, and despair and give all his energies to love for others. From the familial situation comes the message that love—especially when it takes the compulsive, unthinking form it assumed in Philip Livingston—is not a unifying, nurturing, humanizing force: "love freed from object," such as Parker begins to experience with his mother and sister at the novel's close, is the best kind for the future of the human race. If Parker had not petulantly invited Arthur Kin to Ewell, he would never have learned that truth.

Goodwin's examination of racism and love does not offer easy answers or imitable patterns of behavior. It is a personal, rigorous study that, as Boatwright observed, yields up "insights and revelations as blunt and solid as iron" and as difficult to forget as a blow to the head.

Of the two stories that come between *Kin* and *The Blood of Paradise* (1979), "God's Spies" (1975) is the more interesting. Once again Goodwin presents a person trying to deal with his own preoccupations: Todd Stewart Hart is not a likable man, but he has the ability to mock his attitudes and posturings. He almost disarms the reader by admitting immediately that his story has a "hack" plot: married man with wife and daughter thinks he is in love with Ingrid, a younger woman. She becomes pregnant and has an abortion; he returns to his life, but with a recognition of something lost. In the course of telling his tale, Todd quotes Shakespeare frequently but self-mockingly: "this ex-drama student who quotes only the most obvious passages of Shakespeare." The title comes from *King Lear* and appears as Todd comments about his life: "happiness requires a gift for banality. . . . If only we could take upon us 'the mystery of things, as if we were God's spies'—but Lear always wanted too much from Cordelia"—just as Todd wants too much from everyone.

Preoccupied as he is with sex, Todd can also judge his "modern" attitude. He describes his first time in bed with Ingrid in a mocking, gritty tone and in telling, homely images: "Orgasm was experienced by all—a cheap little orgasm like something that might have come out of a cereal box. . . . what was grim and mean was our conspiracy to pass it off as something better. At least we didn't congratulate ourselves afterward; we separated cleanly like a stick of firewood that has just been split."

At the close of the affair with Ingrid, the story

Dust jacket for Goodwin's second novel (1979), which takes its title from a poem by Wallace Stevens: "Shall our blood fail? Or shall it come to be / The blood of paradise?"

becomes more serious and heavy-handed. Ingrid tells Todd, "You have what you always had," and Todd muses: "she was not entirely right: I do still have [my wife] and Victoria [the daughter], a house and a job. That same banality, but I have lost the gift for it. Found out, by God's spies: are they other than the blind sperm lashing their way toward the ovum to imprint upon it the chromosomal legend? And the mystery of things is not how we love but how we keep ourselves from it." He thinks of Victoria and Desdemona's willow song and concludes, "While there are men like me in the world, I cannot put off the day when she will need that song, any more than I can put off the day when she, like her mother [whose father is dying], will come to watch by my bed."

The mysteries of love, sex, and death explored in "God's Spies" are not resolved by Todd. That the same mysteries—and others—are central to Goodwin's second novel, *The Blood of Paradise*, suggests that the author still had not resolved them, but the novel takes them farther and looks into them more deeply than the story did. The book takes its title from Wallace Stevens's poem "Sunday Morning," lines 39-41: "Shall our blood fail? Or shall it come to be / The blood of paradise? And shall the earth / Seem all of paradise that we shall know?" In the "paradise" of earthly life in Goodwin's Virginia mountains, there is a great deal of blood, both animal and human: the blood that accompanies birth and death; menstrual flow; the unseen blood from an abortion. It is almost as if bleeding and dying were the price of whatever earthly paradise Goodwin's characters may attain.

The novel is the story of Anna, Steadman, and their young daughter,Maggie, as they move from city to country, to a relatively solitary life among different kinds of people from those they knew. There are deep problems for each partner: Anna is afraid of everything; Steadman has to establish his own identity, to work out who he is after having grown up in the shadow of his maternal grandfather (about whom he has written a novel, *The Making of a Mountain*, apparently one attempt at coming to terms with his questions).

The critical response to the novel suggests some disagreement over Goodwin's main concern: Julian Moynahan, in the *New York Times Book Review* (24 June 1979), stated that "The substance . . . is [the] effort at regeneration" that each of the characters undergoes. One can only agree with the reviewer that "it is far from clear . . . that the effort succeeds," since Anna and Steadman separate and are only tentatively moving back toward each other as the novel closes. The notice in the *Virginia Quarterly Review* (Autumn 1979) suggested that *The Blood of Paradise* might stand as an example for any writers who emerge from "the back-to-nature movement of the sixties and seventies:" this judgment makes the Steadmans' move to the mountains of Virginia, where Goodwin himself lived for a time, a major component of their story.

It is likely that most readers will understand *The Blood of Paradise* primarily as a novel that deals with love, as M. A. Haynes indicated in the *Library Journal* review (15 May 1979). In many ways, the characters have to learn the same things about love that the Livingstons and their kin have to learn in the earlier novel: love must be free and selfless; it must not seek to convert another being to its own notions, as when Steadman seems to want to convert the timid, fearful Anna to his blustery, gutsy (but as yet unexamined) view of life. Love must attempt to understand the other's feelings, which Steadman isn't willing to do until Anna has left and he has had to confront himself.

Anna's twin sister, Kay, a brittle, cruel, and tormented woman, comes for a visit and plants seeds of suspicion in the couple's already complicated relationship. There are temptations for Steadman in the group at a nearby commune, Xanaduc. Ultimately, Steadman and Peggy, young, rich, and spoiled, spend two nights in Steadman's empty house. The encounter is intensely ironic and messy in comparison with the "no mess" abortion Anna has just undergone without Steadman's knowledge. There is a brief reconciliation between Anna and her husband, but she has clearly lost the little happiness and security she had gained on the farm. Matters become further exacerbated when Anna learns about Peggy and Steadman from another member of the commune. When Kay is killed in a wreck on the twins' birthday, Anna understands that her sister is a suicide and, after accusing Steadman of sexual relationships with both Kay and Peggy, announces that she is leaving—still without having told him about the abortion.

But after some months of separation, communication begins again—or perhaps for the first time—between Anna and her husband. They agree to talk in person because "*We're no good on the phone*." As the first year in the farmhouse draws to a close, Steadman realizes that he has changed and is still changing: as he grasps the meaning of his experiences, he weeps over his memory of his daughter's birth and over the lambing at the neighboring farm. Finally Anna tells Steadman about the abortion; then, acknowledging the importance of time to inventing their life together, she reveals that she is returning to him.

While it is true that the problems of love dominate the novel, it is also the case that communication figures as a primary concern. The evidence is fragmentary but persuasive: Anna, Steadman, and Maggie have private word games and contorted phrases that they use among themselves. They discuss Waylon Jennings as "The Great Wailin' "; "rabid foxes" become "rabbit foxes"; "pharaohs," "fairy-o's"; "oohs and ahs," "oozes and awes." In a neighbor's vocabulary, "llamas" are "yammers" and "ornament" becomes "ointment"—language that Anna understands immediately with her sensitive nature. When Kay arrives, she cannot talk to the locals; Anna, who once shared a private language of colors with Kay, can no longer communicate easily with her twin. Indeed, in the midst of trying to speak to Kay, Anna observes that "ordinary language" has "more to do with—reality" than any other kind of communication can have. Her new connection with reality is part of Anna's learning to be less afraid.

I felt very queasy.

I'd been doodling while I listened, ~~doodling~~, and now ~~I wrote~~ *my row of dollar signs*
was rounded off off with a pair of words, ~~very queasy~~, *Glory be.* The conversation — a monologue, really — got
~~very~~ sticky. ~~I knew I should break in—I should~~ *break in,* but *I*
honestly didn't know what to say. The man on the phone ~~as assured~~

AMO 1 ~~It the~~ *closed and* and ~~then~~ ~~stopped~~ *altogether.* "You ~~are~~ still there?"
the man on the phone asked nervously. "I guess you hadn't heard that
                                                                    he caught it."

Last month I got a phone call from a man who graduated from Bolton

Abbey a few years after I did. He had lived in Fortune House, where I

was a prefect, ~~but~~ When I drew a blank on his name, he said he'd been

in Nino *Von* ~~Van~~Lear's class. Did I remember Nino? *No one forgot Nino.* ~~who didn't?~~ I was
on the edge of ~~going to~~ *asking* ~~whatever became~~
~~tempted to ask him what had become~~ of Nino, but *my caller* ~~he~~ pressed on, so hearty

and nostalgic an~~d~~ ~~smarmy~~ that I ~~had no doubt~~ *was sure* he was *raising money for the school.* ~~a fund-raiser, and~~

~~I expected to be asked for money.~~ He spoke of Father Augustine, the
                        in the tones of awe and reverence usually associated with the
Master of Fortune House, ~~with the reverence~~ ~~ordinarily reserved for the~~
~~The conversation — a monologue, really — got very sticky. I didn't want to ask, you see.~~
dead. ~~and Father Augustine was dead, as it happened.~~ He'd keeled

over back in April. ~~my caller assumed that I'd heard,~~ ~~but~~ My ties to
                                                            heard.
Bolton are long and loose, and I hadn't. ~~Anyway, they were wondering ——~~ →

you could ~~his~~ *the* relief when ~~at last the conversation became official~~
                in his voice he made the request
and he no longer ~~had to~~ speak *up* for himself -- if I'd write something
                                        short
for the alumni newsletter, a ~~little~~ tribute, just a few lines. They

were asking other boys who'd been close to him, and they wanted

something personal, it didn't have to be long, just whatever I remembered
                                                                    assured us,
best about him. Father Augustine was such a great character, he ~~said~~,
          it   *be*
that ~~I~~ shouldn't ~~have~~ any trouble at all.
    It wasn't.
And I didn't. ~~Oh, I understood~~ ~~what they wanted~~ *perfectly what they*
~~Oh, I understood perfectly that the time had come~~
wanted ~~out~~ *knew exactly who they were, and*
~~to add Father Augustine to the Bolton mythology, and~~ **I** wrote an appropriate

parable in which Father Augustine appeared strong and good and wise.

He was the soccer coach when I went to Bolton, and I was the goalie, and

he used to test me in the net with shots that were soft at first, soft and

straight, but got harder and nastier with each kick. He never tried to

*So he told me that Father Augustine had died just the
way he would have wanted, ~~in this proudmost~~ of a
heart-attack as he was leaving the dining ~~out of~~ on to
the beach, and they were wondering — you could hear*

Communication is also at stake when Steadman's writing is the subject. Anna is not entirely sympathetic to her husband's work: "His stories struck her as efforts to charm. She never quite believed them. They were too smooth, too neat, didn't have edges. Because she'd had to say something about them, she told Steadman that the language was beautiful, and she meant it, but she was aware that this compliment was insufficient to him. He had not asked her to read any of his novel"—presumably the story of his grandfather. Later, when Steadman has written a piece based on a local family, he and Anna disagree about it, but by this time the situation is complicated to an almost unbearable degree by the probability of Anna's unwanted pregnancy. The increasing silence between husband and wife is aggravated as her "whimwhams" begin, and she moves toward her lonely decision to have an abortion.

As Steadman's affair with Peggy develops, he muses about how and why people speak to each other in "love" situations: "Talk, talk, talk—that was probably the greatest delight a love conferred. . . . this loosening of the tongue, this dusting off and revising of the biography, this invention and presentation of a fictive self." But "a fictive self" and "Talk, talk, talk" are superficial, not real, up to this point in the Anna-Steadman relationship. The ability really to speak to each other that develops at the close is only a beginning for the process of inventing a life for themselves.

The Blood of Paradise is a complex novel, dealing with many themes: the return-to-the-land; modern sexuality; family interactions; personal fears; the hazy edges of human existence and connection where intuition and dreams seem both to grow out of and form reality; the discovery of the important elements of life—"love and work"; the meaning of life and death as the characters experience the births and deaths of humans and animals. Goodwin handles the intricacy of his story, as the *New Yorker* notice (25 June 1979) put it, "with grace and precision," "subtly" outlining the struggles, hopes, dreams, and achievements of his people.

Goodwin's characters and their preoccupations are compelling in themselves; their creator's use of imagistic language frequently heightens the reader's engagement in the story. As already noted, wordplay underscores the communication motif in *The Blood of Paradise*. But the apposite use of literary allusions in "The Lizard of Conques" and in "God's Spies" may give a too-literary cast to the stories.

In the fall of 1981, Goodwin was at work "on a series of long stories" and on a novel, "Luther Pie, American," which "is set in Washington. . . . its hero, Mr. Pie, is a lapsed journalist." Goodwin has described one of the stories, "Amo, Amas, Amat," as "more like a Taylor story than anything I've ever done." At present, Goodwin is again working in fiction, having just completed a play entitled "The Night Lennon Died."

Critical estimates of Stephen Goodwin's work are sparse: they do not examine his achievements with topic, plot, and language, and they are not at all helpful in indicating the author's direction. His treatment of his most frequent topics—love, sex, and the intricacies of human relationships—is thoughtful and colored with just enough irony to persuade the reader that the author is honest and fair in his assessment of human behavior. The conclusions Goodwin has drawn thus far are tentative, even cautious, but relatively optimistic, suggesting that love is possible between human beings, but it is not easy to achieve; that understanding of the self, past and present, is a necessary corollary to the full experience of life. Stephen Goodwin has the potential for development and significance.

Periodical Publications:
FICTION:
"Veteran's Evening Song," *Shenandoah*, 20 (Summer 1969): 28-41;
"Children and Cannibals," *Sewanee Review*, 78 (Spring 1970): 269-284;
"Sole Surviving Son," *Shenandoah*, 22 (Autumn 1970): 17-46; reprinted in *Best Little Magazine Fiction 1971*, edited by Curt Johnson (New York: New York University Press, 1972);
"Spring Correspondence," *Shenandoah*, 22 (Spring 1971): 3-12;
"The Lizard of Conques," *Georgia Review*, 25 (Fall 1971): 343-363;
"Papa Silverstone," *Shenandoah*, 25 (Fall 1973): 29-40;
"God's Spies," *Shenandoah*, 26 (Summer 1975): 33-49;
"His Heart," *Shenandoah*, 28 (Fall 1976): 3-14;
"Sire and Pup," *Shenandoah*, 30 (Fall 1978): 21-43—chapter 3 of *The Blood of Paradise*.
NON-FICTION:
"Life Studies," review of *The Collected Stories of Peter Taylor*, *Shenandoah*, 21 (Winter 1970): 100-102;
"An Interview with Peter Taylor," *Shenandoah*, 24 (1973): 3-20;
"Like Nothing Else in Tennessee," *Shenandoah*, special Peter Taylor issue, 28 (Winter 1977): 53-58;

"Sugar Time in Virginia," *Blair and Ketchum's Country Journal* (March 1979): 48-50;

"On the Divide," *Blair and Ketchum's Country Journal* (May 1980): 61-67;

"The Art of Getting Lost," *Blair and Ketchum's Country Journal* (September 1980): 106-111;

"Hubbert's Curve," *Blair and Ketchum's Country Journal* (November 1980): 56-61.

Arthur Hailey
(5 April 1920-   )

Winifred Farrant Bevilacqua
University of Turin, Italy

SELECTED BOOKS: *Flight Into Danger*, by Hailey and John Castle (London: Souvenir, 1958); republished as *Runway Zero-Eight* (Garden City: Doubleday, 1959);

The Final Diagnosis (Garden City: Doubleday, 1959; London: M. Joseph/ Souvenir, 1960);

In High Places (Garden City: Doubleday, 1962; London: M. Joseph/ Souvenir, 1962);

Hotel (Garden City: Doubleday, 1965; London: M. Joseph/ Souvenir, 1965);

Airport (Garden City: Doubleday, 1968; London: M. Joseph/ Souvenir, 1968);

Wheels (Garden City: Doubleday, 1971; London: M. Joseph/ Souvenir, 1972);

The Moneychangers (Garden City: Doubleday, 1975; London: M. Joseph, 1975);

Overload (Garden City: Doubleday, 1979; London: M. Joseph/ Souvenir, 1979).

Arthur Hailey

Arthur Hailey, Canadian citizen, is the author of *Airport* and other novels which have won popular acclaim because they elucidate clearly and simply some of the complex machinery of contemporary society and satisfy in melodramatic fashion the average reader's desire for a well-packaged and entertaining story. He was born in Luton, England, the only child of George and Elsie Wright Hailey. Upon leaving school at the age of fourteen, he worked as an office boy for a real estate broker and then as a clerk for the Conservative party. At the outbreak of World War II he joined the Royal Air Force, serving as a pilot in the Middle and Far East and reaching the rank of flight lieutenant. After the war he was editor of the RAF publication *Air Clues* until 1947, when he immigrated to Canada, where he sold real estate for a short while before obtaining employment with the Maclean-Hunter Publishing Company in Toronto, first as a staff member and

then, from 1949 to 1953, as editor of the trade magazine *Bus and Truck Transport*. On the strength of this experience, he became manager of sales promotion and advertising for the trucking firm Canadian Trailmobile Ltd. Although he had always been interested in writing and had had several stories printed in such periodicals as *London Opinion* and *Punch*, it was not until 1956 that, encouraged by the successful production of his play *Flight Into*

Danger by the Canadian Broadcasting Corporation, he decided to experiment with a writing career. That same year, to have more time for writing without losing the security of a regular income, he quit his job and set up his own advertising agency, with Canadian Trailmobile as his major client. In 1958, having sold all of the television scripts he had written, he felt able to devote himself solely to his literary vocation and gave up his agency. Hailey has six children, three by his first marriage to Joan Fishwick from 1944 to 1950 and three by Sheila Dunlop, whom he married in 1951. He lived in and around Toronto until 1965, then spent several years in Napa Valley, California, and finally moved to the Bahamas, where he now resides.

Notable for their sustained suspense, fast pace, and broad audience appeal, his television dramas, produced by Canadian and British networks as well as by such American showcase theaters as the U. S. Steel Hour, NBC Matinee Theater, Playhouse 90, and Studio One, generally center on a crisis that reveals an unsuspected heroism in the ordinary people involved. *Flight Into Danger* (produced in 1956), which appears in several anthologies of the best plays from the golden age of live television, was adapted into a movie in 1957, and from this film emerged a novel (published in 1958) by Hailey and John Castle (a pseudonym for Ronald Charles Payne and John William Garrod). The story is about a flight from Winnipeg to Vancouver during which many of the passengers and both pilots are incapacitated by botulism from an in-flight meal. The protagonist, an ex-wartime pilot who has only flown single-engine fighter planes, takes over in the cockpit and, despite a thickening fog and the tension of knowing that some of the people aboard are near death from the food poisoning, bravely and with the help of instructions radioed in from the control tower of the Vancouver airport, succeeds in bringing the plane to its destination. Both the play and movie versions are well-executed exercises in suspense; but the novel, though retaining the same tension, lacks in-depth characterizations. Among his other teleplays that are credible because of sound technical details are *Time Lock* (1956), later adapted for the screen, which tells the story of a child trapped in a bank vault; *Course for Collision* (1957), about the near collision over the North Pole of a Soviet bomber with a plane carrying the president of the United States; and *Death Minus One* (1959), in which a V2 bomb gets activated after lying undetected for twelve years in the rubble of a World War II ruin in London.

Hailey's strongest television play, however,

Dust jacket for Hailey's fourth novel (1968), which dramatizes the operation of a metropolitan airport

was *No Deadly Medicine* (1956), which was produced by Studio One and received two Emmy Awards, one for the author and one for the leading actor, Lee J. Cobb. It dramatizes the relentless intellectual, moral, and physical demands which modern medicine makes on the physician in the story of an aging hospital pathologist who reluctantly agrees to be replaced by a younger doctor after errors made in his department have caused serious problems and one unnecessary death. Hailey later transformed the play into the novel *The Final Diagnosis* (1959) by expanding the central story line with many detailed descriptions of medical and surgical procedures and hospital administration and by adding subplots about the crisscrossing relationships of a dozen characters. The sales of the book totaled five million copies, and in 1961 it was made into the movie *The Young Doctors*, which starred Fredric March.

In his next novel, *In High Places* (1962), the

prospect of an imminent war with the Soviet Union leads the Canadian prime minister to initiate negotiations with the American president aimed at incorporating Canada into the United States. Discussions about this delicate matter, which is left unresolved in the book, almost flounder under an angry public protest against the Canadian government's insensitive handling of a young stowaway trapped by bureaucracy on a ship in Vancouver and under a bitter struggle between the prime minister's party and the opposition because of old scandals. Much attention is also paid to the private lives of the characters, who engage in all sorts of chicanery and love affairs. Loosely organized and redundant, the book never achieves a high point, but its controversial themes contributed to its popularity in Canada.

Sharing the same strengths and weaknesses and quite similar in content and form, Hailey's subsequent internationally best-selling novels—*Hotel*, *Airport*, *Wheels*, *The Moneychangers*, and *Overload*—are based on a wealth of accurate information gathered during a year of exhaustive preliminary research and written according to a highly successful formula which blends fact with fiction. Each of these books deals with a major modern institution that inevitably affects the lives of ordinary people and focuses on it during an emergency or turning point in policy that threatens to disrupt its complex

mechanism. From this crisis emerge the largely melodramatic plots and subplots about the personal and professional lives of the many characters, who are frequently placed in situations which evoke extreme emotions and are sometimes menaced with a terrible fate before receiving their appropriate rewards and punishments. To further appeal to the widest possible audience, the cast of characters always includes representatives from different social groups and figures whose involvement in the central institution ranges from the top to the lower levels of employment and responsibility. The protagonists are for the most part interchangeable from book to book and easily identifiable as villains obsessed with wealth and power or as heroes and heroines who realize or come to know the primacy of loving relationships and personal integrity over success. All are seen from the outside and characterized in such bold strokes that they qualify as types rather than individuals. The narratives are generally fast-moving, and every novel is structured to offer regularly recurring crescendos through an alternation of episodes about the characters' problems with other episodes that contain lectures, debates, and informed asides about technical matters, and that discuss how the institution operates. As the author provides his many-layered, behind-the-scenes look at the institution, he makes some nega-

Dust jacket for Hailey's fifth novel (1971), a sympathetic exposé of the auto industry

263

tive observations about it. Although his books are often described as being more like muckraking journalism than popular fiction, his criticism is actually not far-reaching. He either limits himself to presenting problems without looking forward to their elimination or reaffirms the essential validity of the institution through the injection of conservative values in a manner that is structurally weak and at odds with the character values established earlier. Similarly, he exploits such pressing social issues as racial discrimination, poverty, and pollution for their timely interest but never makes them part of a sweeping critique of the dominant social, economic, and political order.

In spite of Hailey's reluctance to deal profoundly with complex issues, his oversimplified picture of life, his slighting of literary artistry in favor of literary mechanics, his enthusiasm for his subject, and his energy as a storyteller are evidently sufficient to carry his books for his readers. Indeed, his novels are very skillful manipulations of the highly successful formulaic type of fiction which John Cawelti has termed the contemporary social melodrama since they synthesize "the archetype of melodrama with a carefully and elaborately developed social setting in such a way as to combine the emotional satisfactions of melodrama with the interest inherent in a detailed, intimate, and realistic analysis of major social or historical phenomena."

Hotel (1965) fits this pattern neatly, for it contains the better part of an introductory course in hotel management, has characters who arouse uncomplicated feelings of sympathy or condemnation in the reader, features a medley of story lines, unfolds episodically, and has various small and large climaxes. Set at the St. Gregory, a gracious old luxury hotel in New Orleans, the action begins on Monday and ends on Friday of a week in October 1964. Around the possible sale of the hotel to a ruthless tycoon, who wishes to transform it into a standardized Hilton-type establishment, rotate diverse, event-filled stories of people staying or working at the hotel. The long-delayed resolutions of some of these plots occur in the closing pages when the author puts a few crucial characters into a defective elevator and has it plunge to disaster. Likewise, only at the very end is the central dilemma resolved when an eccentric millionaire turns up and decides to buy the St. Gregory, thus allowing it to carry on its old traditions. Although little more than a contrivance of heterogeneous humanity and a matching of slightly related plots, *Hotel* stayed on the best-seller lists for over a year and in 1967 was

made into a popular motion picture.

Hailey solidified his reputation as a leading popular novelist with *Airport* (1968), in which he explores confidently and with interest the inner workings of a big-city airport, devises several gripping crises, and offers glimpses into the private frustrations, failures, and triumphs of his characters, most of them airport personnel. The action takes place during a blizzard, when every man, machine, and function go wrong: a disabled Boeing 707 is stuck in the snow blocking a needed runway and causing emergencies in the air; a psychotic is determined to blow up the plane he is on for the insurance; a depressed air traffic controller is contemplating suicide because of guilt feelings about a crash that was his fault; a stewardess and her pilot lover argue over her pregnancy; and a group of local citizens protesting about the noise the airport creates demand to speak to the general manager just as his wife is telling him that she wants a divorce. The concise dramatizations of the many difficulties the airport manager and the other characters have in coping with the crises are intended to create sustained excitement and tension, while the human-interest stories are aimed at suggesting the hidden drama of everyday life. The readers' curiosity about airports is satisfied by generally well-integrated bits of reliable information about airport procedures and about the handling of planes from the cockpit to the control tower. Detractors objected to the prefabrication of the novel, to its unbelievable coincidences, and to the stereotypical quality of its characterizations—faults which did not prevent it from becoming a prodigious best-seller nor its 1970 film version from being a hit.

Hailey's following novel, *Wheels* (1971), offers both an exposé of and a salute to the auto industry. The key plot element is the preparation by a major company of a radically new car model, the success or failure of which will help determine whether the company will continue to manufacture only large cars or produce smaller, fuel efficient models as well. The proliferating subplots deal with all aspects of the planning, making, and selling of cars, with criminality in the plant, and with the lives of numerous characters. Throughout, the author criticizes the industry for its lack of social conscience about safety, pollution, and hard-core unemployment; but in typical fashion at the end he negates his criticism by having one of his heroes declaim: "a good deal was wrong with the auto industry, but there was a great deal more that, overwhelmingly, was right. The miracle of the modern automobile was not that it sometimes failed, but that it mostly didn't; not that it was costly, but that—for the marvels of design and engineering that it embodied—it cost so little; not that it cluttered highways and polluted air, but that it gave free men and women what, through history, they had mostly craved—a personal mobility." Written entirely in short, discontinuous scenes, *Wheels* lacks the drama of *Airport* and is further weakened by the author's compulsion to set down everything he has learned about cars by having the characters tell it to one another.

In his next two books, Hailey uses his method of novel writing and his stock characters and situations with even less inventiveness and freshness. In *The Moneychangers* (1975), a kaleidoscopic view of the banking industry, along with treating the many grave problems and decisions facing the First Mercantile American Bank and offering strategically located dissertations that explain in detail a myriad of banking practices, he gratifies aficionados of romance, pathos, suspense, and violence with a modest amount of sex, several visits to an insane asylum, a suicide, a chase scene, and the horrible torture and mutilation of one of the characters. The novel sold very well and was rendered into a popular television mini-series; but, as Peter Andrews observed in the *New York Times Book Review* (18 May 1975), its protagonists are uniformly like "bores at a cocktail party you forget the second they disappear and have to be reintroduced when they reappear" while its technical data give "less information than a well-constructed Sunday piece in a newspaper." Hailey's latest novel, *Overload* (1979), is essentially a debate between an executive in the public utilities industry (who foresees severe electrical shortages unless the industry is given more financing and the right to build coal-burning and nuclear power plants) and two antagonists, one the leader of an activist group that accuses the electric company of piling up profits at the expense of the consumer and the other a former atomic scientist and prominent ecologist who is aware of the energy crisis but also concerned about the long-range effects of certain alternative fuels on the environment. Had these serious and timely issues been presented in a balanced manner, the book might have been intellectually engaging and stimulating, but unfortunately the author very obviously supports the industry executive's point of view and ridicules the other two. The banality of the novel is increased by a heavy reliance on cliche situations, maudlin character interactions, and an overabundance of sex and violence.

After announcing his retirement in 1979, Hailey began writing a novel about the pharmaceutical industry in 1982. "It is a constantly

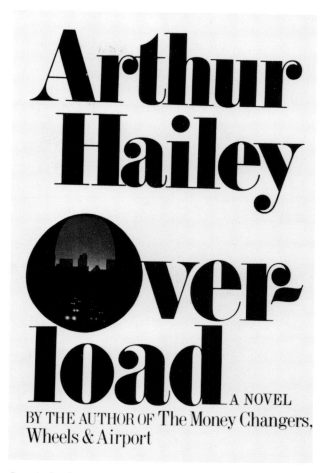

Dust jacket for Hailey's seventh novel (1979), which focuses on the responsibilities of an electric company executive

changing industry of tremendous promise, really a life-and-death industry for many people," he told *Publishers Weekly*. Completion of the untitled novel is projected for 1984, and Hailey has received from Doubleday a guarantee of $1,750,000.

Hailey has enjoyed a wide readership and suffered critical attack for essentially the same reasons. Knowing which subjects are of topical interest and universal appeal and how to investigate them without calling into question conventional values and attitudes, he has succeeded in producing slick narratives that are engrossing only on a first reading. Most likely, in the future he will be considered just another popular novelist of interest primarily to social and cultural historians.

Television Script:
No Deadly Medicine, Studio One, 1956.

References:

John Cawelti, "The Best-Selling Social Melodrama," in his *Adventure, Mystery, and Romance: Formula Stories as Art and Popular Culture* (Chicago: University of Chicago Press, 1976), pp. 260-295;

John Sutherland, "The Novels of Arthur Hailey," in his *Bestsellers: Popular Fiction of the 1970s* (London: Routledge & Kegan Paul, 1981), pp. 47-58.

Jim Harrison
(11 December 1937-   )

Robert E. Burkholder
Pennsylvania State University/Wilkes-Barre

BOOKS: *Plain Song* (New York: Norton, 1965);
Walking (Cambridge, Mass.: Pym-Randall, 1967);
Locations (New York: Norton, 1968);
Outlyer and Ghazals (New York: Simon & Schuster, 1971);
Wolf: A False Memoir (New York: Simon & Schuster, 1971);
A Good Day to Die (New York: Simon & Schuster, 1973);
Letters to Yesinin (Fremont, Mich.: Sumac Press, 1973);
Farmer (New York: Viking, 1976);
Returning to Earth (Ithaca, N.Y.: Ithaca House Press, 1977);
Legends of the Fall (New York: Delacorte/ Seymour Lawrence, 1979);
The Man Who Gave Up His Name (New York: Delacorte/ Seymour Lawrence, 1979);
Revenge (New York: Delacorte/ Seymour Lawrence, 1979);
Warlock (New York: Delacorte/ Seymour Lawrence, 1981);
Selected & New Poems 1961-1981 (New York: Delacorte/ Seymour Lawrence, 1982).

Jim Harrison is a poet, novelist, critic, outdoorsman, and nature writer, but in Harrison's case, the appellation "poet" supersedes and includes all the other literary roles he has chosen for himself. Because he began his career as a poet and because he is still searching for the most suitable form to embody his bleak message of man's misuse of the earth and his displacement in contemporary America, Harrison is still a poet who now happens to work largely in the genre of prose fiction. Because he continues his formal experiments—using his own variations of the ghazal and suite structures

Jim Harrison

in his poetry and trying his hand at the memoir, in *Wolf: A False Memoir* (1971), the novella, in *Legends of the Fall* (1979), and even the thriller, in *A Good Day to Die* (1973) and *Warlock* (1981)—Harrison remains something of a critical conundrum. He and his work have often been the victims of analogies that fail to give him his due as one of the most original writers at work today. His work as both poet and fiction writer and the theme of violence that threads through his work have caused some to view him as a midwestern James Dickey; his northern Michigan boyhood and an occasional terseness of style have called forth the obvious comparisons with Hemingway; and his personal associations with writers such as Richard Brautigan and Thomas McGuane have led to comparisons and implications of influence. Certainly, Jim Harrison is at work within a tradition that might plausibly include the work of all the writers just mentioned; however, to emphasize the possible effect of literary precursors and friends at the expense of the one constant perceivable in his work—his love for experiment—does a disservice to a writer who approaches each new task with considerable inventiveness.

Harrison was born in Grayling, Michigan, on 11 December 1937 to Winfield Sprague Harrison, a farmer, and Norma Walgren Harrison. He would later draw heavily on the occupation of his father, the Scandinavian heritage of his mother, and his own rural upbringing as subject matter for his work. In a 1972 *Detroit Magazine* interview, Harrison stated that it was the boredom of middle-class life and the "romantic conviction" that being a writer "was an attractive way to live" that decided him, at age twelve, to become a writer: "Middle class life seemed to me then to be very remote and boring and meaningless. . . . It still does." However, his career was postponed until after receiving bachelor's and master's degrees from Michigan State University in 1960 and 1964. In October 1960 Harrison married Linda King. They have two daughters, Jamie Louise and Anna Severin, and live in northern Michigan. Harrison, who principally supports himself and his family with his writing, has tried his hand at teaching, notably at the State University of New York at Stony Brook in the late 1960s, but he makes it clear why he found such a position untenable and returned to a farm in Michigan: "When you're a writer in a university, you're a freak, sort of a town clown. I feel much less isolated from people here [on the farm] than at a university." The success of Harrison's first volumes of poetry also resulted in a certain amount of freedom, and he ultimately received a grant from the National Endowment for the Arts (1968-1969) and a Guggenheim Fellowship (1969-1970) to enable him to write full time. In describing himself, Harrison once said that he was a "Zennist," but now, with some of the wryness that characterizes his latest novel, *Warlock*, he refers to himself as "an international white trash sports fop." However, while the value of self-contemplation so important to Zen is apparent in much of Harrison's work, there is little evidence of sports foppery in any of the poems or fictions, all of which admirably bear the burden of an important and serious message.

Harrison's first substantial literary success was with his poetry, in volumes that appeared between 1965 and 1978: *Plain Song* (1965), *Locations* (1968), *Outlyer and Ghazals* (1971), *Letters to Yesinin* (1973), and *Returning to Earth* (1977). Poetry from all these volumes is represented in Harrison's *Selected & New Poems 1961-1981*, published in the fall of 1982.

Much of what Harrison has attempted in his poetry has a direct bearing on his fiction. For example, one of his major poetic subjects is the vanishing wilderness and his ecological concerns; these concerns reappear many times in Harrison's fiction. Because of his preoccupation with nature, there is also much of the romantic poet in Harrison, although it should not be assumed that this romanticism is in any way anachronistic or affected. As Harrison's fiction makes evident, he is obsessed with the place of the romantic in an antiromantic age, and many of his fictional protagonists are assigned the task of working out that dilemma.

Another characteristic of Harrison's poetry is experimentation with form. He is essentially a lyric poet, writing almost exclusively in free verse, a form that allows him room to examine poetic topics of extreme breadth or of minute focus. Harrison has, however, demonstrated an ability to adapt his verse style to more formal patterns of his own invention, specifically the suite and the ghazal. In *Locations* Harrison experimented with the suite form for the first time. As a poetic form, the suite, as Harrison conceives of it, owes a great deal to its musical counterpart, which is a musical composition consisting of several movements in the same key; Harrison's suites are also made up of a number of "movements" or image clusters, each in the "same key" or devoted to expanding the same topic by offering a variety of imagistic perspectives. The ghazal is a more venerable form that originated with the Arabs and was perfected by the Persians, notably Hafiz, to whom some 500 ghazals are attributed. In his "Notes on Ghazals" in *Outlyer and Ghazals*, Harrison states that "Even Goethe and Schlegel wrote ghazals," and he notes that Adrienne Rich has been successful with the form. However, Harrison has abandoned most of the strict metrical and structural rules of the form to write poems that are a series of couplets "not related by reason or logic and their only continuity is made by a metaphorical jump." The ghazal, then, is actually a more condensed version of the suite that allows Harrison the opportunity to build ostensibly unrelated couplet components into whole poems on a single theme. Harrison is a poet concerned with providing for his reader wave after wave of images and sensual detail without logic or narrative links, and this goal accounts perhaps for the general critical misunderstanding of his fiction, which attacks the senses in much the same manner as the poetry but is often denounced for being formless or lacking in narrative logic.

Ironically, what has been the critical bane of

Harrison's fiction has been commended by review-ers as one of his strengths as a poet. In reviewing *Locations* for *Poetry* (February 1971), Lisel Mueller congratulated him for breaking syntactical rules "to maintain a constant flow of shifting images," and she suggested that he may be one of the last of the truly great American poets. M. L. Rosenthal dubbed Harrison "one of our finest young poets" in the *New York Times Book Review* (18 July 1971), and argued that his often "exquisitely beautiful" poetry is indeed "worth loving, hating, and fighting over" because it is "a subjective mirror of our American days and needs"; and in the *Saturday Review* (18 December 1971), James Whitehead stated that at his best, Harrison "is right there with James Dickey and Hugo and Huff and Roethke." Hayden Carruth, in his review of *Returning to Earth* in *Harper's* magazine (June 1978) accurately summed up the primary quality of Harrison's poetry, while also suggesting how it is related to his fiction: "It is hard-boiled poetry, some of the best of its kind, and one is not surprised to know that Harrison has written very tough novels and many magazine pieces about sports and outdoor life. His poetic vision is at the heart of it all. To stay alive now is primitivism. And that is the hard best we can know."

Harrison's most recently published work, *Selected & New Poems 1961-1981*, provides the op-portunity for an overview of both the continuity of theme in his poetry and his dedication to experi-ment. This work contains selections from his five previously published collections and twenty new poems which suggest that Harrison remains com-mitted to his use of nature as the principal source for the substance of his poetry. His style remains unaffected, even in works such as "A Redolence for Nims" and "Birthday"—poems intended to mark the occasion of Harrison's fortieth birthday that transcend their self-serving purpose through the use of powerful imagery and understatement. These new poems range in tone from despair and pessimism to the wryly perverse "Weeping," whose speaker is so "tickled pink with life" that he is unable to stop laughing. To make himself weep, he must imagine the deaths of his wife and daughters, thoughts so shattering that he resolves in the poem's ironic last line that he must die with them. Harrison also demonstrates his continued commitment to formal experiment by including two ghazals—"The Chatham Ghazal," and "Marriage Ghazal"—among his new work. In a review of *Selected & New Poems* in the *New York Times Book Review* (12 December 1981), Richard Tillinghast cited the apparent lack of

"feeling for form, rhythm, pacing and develop-ment" in Harrison's poetry, but he praised his "vivid and colorful language," and pointed out perhaps the most engaging quality in all these poems—the underlying presence of the poet himself: "Behind the words one always feels the presence of a pas-sionate, exuberant man who is at the same time possessed of a quick, subtle intelligence and a deeply questioning attitude toward life."

Wolf: A False Memoir was Harrison's first sortie with fictional forms and, as one might expect, he used the opportunity to experiment with two prose subgenres, the memoir and the romance. Obvi-ously, *Wolf* is a "false" memoir because it is a work of fiction, but Harrison also means to suggest by his subtitle that this memoir will paradoxically be truer than those chronological, fact-bound narratives usually called memoirs, since, as the writer of an admittedly false memoir, he is free to invent characters and situations that better illustrate the truth as he perceives it. Harrison also states, through his narrator, Swanson, that *Wolf* is a "ro-mance"; and the traditional concepts of romance and the romantic hero are concerns of Harrison in each of his books. In *Wolf*, however, Harrison ar-gues that in terms of the modern world the tradi-tional concept of romance, which is inextricably caught up with the mystery and wildness of the woods, is really antiromance: "There is no romance in the woods in opposition to what fools insist. The romance is in progress, change, the removing of the face of the earth to install another face." Therefore, we must view this "false memoir" as the story of Swanson's progress, the removing of one face for another; but, we must also ask, progress toward or away from what?

Swanson's journey is an experiment in self-discovery and reconciliation. Joyce Carol Oates has suggested that "*Wolf* is a novel of initiation that comes to no end." It is, however, clear that this tale is rather an anti-initiation novel or, at best, an "unini-tiation" novel, since Swanson's primary goal in this false memoir is to come to grips with the person he has become after his initiation into the decadence and corruption of modern America.

This uninitiation takes place in the Huron Mountains of northern Michigan, where Swanson has come, in Thoreau's words, "to front the facts of life" by distancing himself from the civilization-gone-haywire that has corrupted him and, through isolation in the wilderness, to attempt to find him-self. The process is obviously one of conscious de-privation, but Swanson's thoughts repeatedly return to his life in the West, Boston, and New York City, and to sex, alcohol, cigarettes, and all of the "civilized" things and attitudes he has forsworn in an effort to find himself. Swanson sets out to see a wolf in the wild, but despite promising signs he does not. Perhaps the wolf does not exist, and even if it is out there somewhere, it does not exist in Swanson's experience. The wolf metaphor functions as a clue to Swanson's progress in his narrative, for he goes to the Huron Mountains also to discover the wolf within himself, the elemental or basic man, and he ends up settling for an acceptance of the complexities that contribute to his personality. Unlike Thoreau in *Walden*, when Swanson leaves the woods it is not with a sense of optimism about the future but with an affirmation of the value of the past, including his own personal history: "My interests are anachronistic—fishing, forests, alcohol, food, art, in that order." To emphasize this commitment to the past, Harrison ends the novel with Swanson promising himself to saddle-soap the harness his grandfather used for his team of Belgian horses to "bring it back to useless life." Of course, to Swanson the act of renewing the harness is anything but useless, since it represents his commitment to his own past. Like Swanson's other interests, the revivified harness will be an anachronism, a symbol of what he would call his antiromantic attitude.

Wolf was greeted with generally negative reviews that recognized Harrison's promise. Joyce Carol Oates, writing in the *Partisan Review* (Summer 1972), called it a novel of initiation, but she also suggested that it was an initiation for Harrison as well by claiming that it is "the kind of diarylike work many writers must publish before they can write their first significant books." H. L. Van Brunt, in the *Saturday Review* (25 December 1971), found humor and energy to be the saving graces in *Wolf*, a novel with a protagonist whose "rages against life as it is and people as they are come to sound like the long howl of a mangy timber wolf unable to run with the pack—or perhaps merely unwilling to tolerate anyone's company except his own."

Harrison's second novel, *A Good Day to Die*, is an experiment with another literary form, the adventure tale. The unnamed narrator of this story is searching for adventure and romance in an essentially antiromantic age, the late 1960s. His odyssey begins when he meets Tim, a physically and emotionally scarred veteran of Vietnam, in a bar in Key West. Together the two decide to blow up a dam on the Colorado River at the Grand Canyon, so they pool their resources and head to Valdosta, Georgia,

to pick up Tim's girl friend, Sylvia. Much of the novel is concerned with the ménage à trois that develops as this trio travels cross-country: Tim desires drugs, alcohol, and an occasional whore; Sylvia desires Tim; and the narrator is most often poised precariously between his desire for Sylvia and a rather altruistic desire to make Sylvia happy by making Tim a more suitable lover for her. The narrator fails miserably on both counts. He is, after all, essentially different from Sylvia and Tim: they are children of the 1950s corrupted by the realities of the 1960s, whereas the narrator is an intellectual who understands history and who knows there is no turning back, neither through drugs, as Tim attempts, nor through Sylvia's fantasies of middle-class happiness. When the trio arrives at the Grand Canyon and discovers that there is no dam, they head for the North Fork of the Clearwater River in Idaho, where they do succeed in blowing up a dam. However, when Tim tries to save a cow from being destroyed in the explosion, he is killed—one last, chilling absurdity in the mock-commando operation that, with the narrator and Tim in war paint, has overtones of *The Adventures of Huckleberry Finn*. The results, however, are deadly serious: at the end of the novel Tim is dead; any hope of Sylvia's bourgeois dream of happiness is destroyed with Tim, and she is left in despair; the narrator realizes that he, too, will never find his place. In fulfillment of the novel's epigraph from Rilke—"Each torpid turn of this world bears such disinherited children to whom neither what's been, nor what is coming, belongs"—the narrator bears the full weight of the knowledge that his entire generation is disinherited.

Harrison expands the form of the adventure tale into a novel that becomes a search for meaning or place in a nihilistic world. In *A Good Day to Die* he manages to juxtapose the world of the Vietnam War, environmental disasters, and drug dependence with a simpler time, represented in part by the narrator's desire to fish unpolluted streams and his respect for Native American cultures. But the narrator is obviously displaced, just as Tim and Sylvia are: he has deserted his family, is a borderline alcoholic, and despite having no income he is burdened with expensive tastes. Throughout the novel, the narrator believes that his chance to find a place is dependent upon Sylvia's acceptance of him as her lover; but the last lines of the novel suggest that he finally realizes that to choose life with Sylvia would be to mislead her cruelly into believing that her fantasies of happy fulfillment are real and the horrors of being one of a disinherited generation are not: "Someone should take care of her but if I had any qualities of mercy left, any perceptions of what I was on earth however dim and stupid, I knew it couldn't be me."

Critics were generally divided on the value of Harrison's attempt to deal with the crises of the 1960s in America in *A Good Day to Die*. In the *Library Journal* (15 September 1973) Patrick Fanning admitted that the "guerilla morality" of the novel is hardly enough to meet the ecological and spiritual dilemmas to America. Sara Blackburn, reviewing the novel for the *New York Times Book Review* (9 September 1973), stated that Harrison ruins "an excellent narrative" with "super-machismo a-man's-a-man stuff," concluding that *A Good Day to Die* "is an adolescent book by a talented writer" who should know better than to preach a "me-burned-out-Tarzan dogma." These views are in sharp contrast to those of an anonymous reviewer in *Choice* (February 1974), who calls *A Good Day to Die* a "fine novel" that "furnishes an engrossing and terrifying experience," and especially of William Crawford Woods in the *Washington Post Bookworld* (9 September 1973), who admitted that both *Wolf* and *A Good Day to Die* are failures as novels, but only because both books "triumph as poetry, diatribe and personal memoir."

Concern about the disappearing wilderness and the conflict between the past and present receive a reprise in Harrison's third novel, *Farmer* (1976). Like Swanson in *Wolf*, the protagonist of *Farmer*, Joseph, has reached a turning point in his life, a time to assess where he has been and where he is going, and also like Swanson, Joseph is motivated by his profound dissatisfaction with the status quo. He is forty-three years old, unmarried, and occupies his time as a halfhearted farmer, enthusiastic hunter and woodsman, and a teacher in a two-room school in northern Michigan.

As the narrative begins, Joseph divides his attention among his farm chores, his schoolwork, his hunting and fishing expeditions with Dr. Evans, an old family friend, and uninspired sex with Rosalee, a fellow teacher who is the widow of his best friend, Orin. Everything that Joseph does is done out of habit rather than interest, but the impending closing of his school by a hostile school board, the death of his mother, Rosalee's desire for marriage, and his affair with one of his students force Joseph to weigh what he wants for himself with the reality of who he is. What Joseph discovers is that life has jilted him, made him a prisoner of circumstance and habit, when he really wants to be an adventurer. The two

dominant aspects of Joseph's personality, the farmer and the poet (he is an admirer of Keats and Whitman), are represented by Joseph's two loves—Rosalee, whom he has known since childhood, and Catherine, a winsome student whom Joseph associates with the exciting world beyond his experience: "She was from the outside world and this clearly interested him no matter how dangerous the situation was." It is exactly this sort of danger that Joseph most desires. He is attracted both to the familiar, as represented by Dr. Evans, Rosalee, and his attachment to the farm and the surrounding forests, and simultaneously he is drawn toward the unknown, as evidenced by his affair with Catherine, his longing to live by the sea, and his obvious envy of Orin, a fighter pilot killed in the Korean War. *Farmer* is a study of Joseph's resolution of these conflicting desires, and the battle itself seems to make his malaise worse: "It seemed that he had lost all of the spirit that he had maintained so steadily for many years, that he had become a sack of willess meat and guts and bone like everyone else he scorned."

At the novel's end, Joseph, on a trip to Chicago with his senior students, including Catherine, is forced by circumstances to make a conscious choice. Given the opportunity to make love to Catherine and thereby choose the exciting life he imagines she represents, Joseph finds instead that more than anything he wants to talk to Rosalee. A final image of Rosalee suggests the novel's opening, dreamlike sketch, which pictures Joseph and Rosalee honeymooning in an Atlantic coast town. Thus *Farmer* closes as it began, with Joseph reconciled to his old identity and committed to married life with Rosalee; the narrative itself becomes justification for and an explanation of the brief sketch that prefaces it. In terms of that sketch, Joseph's craving for the mystery and adventure that lie beyond his experience, which in the novel are so often symbolized by the sea, is also tailored to fit his acceptance of himself, for he is glimpsed in the honeymoon scene prodding at the ocean with his walking stick as though it were a familiar clod of dirt on the farm; and he is described as feeling the same "raptness" for the ocean as "he felt for the northern lights as a child." No longer is the sea a symbol of strangeness; it is rather something to be associated with the wonders of a childhood spent on a farm in northern Michigan.

Some reviews of *Farmer*, like that by Webster Schott in the *New York Times Book Review* (10 October 1976), suggested that the novel is evidence that Harrison is maturing as a writer of fiction, but others were more critical, choosing to ignore the poetic qualities of the work to concentrate on its failure as traditional fiction. An anonymous reviewer in the *New Yorker* (30 August 1976) characterized *Farmer* as "vapid and stale." In the *Library Journal* (15 June 1976), L. W. Griffin stated that it was "simple, largely without suspense, its end predicted at its beginning," and while Parkman Howe, in the *Christian Science Monitor* (27 January 1977), found the "descriptive passages" and the "relentless coming on of seasons in upstate Michigan" to be strengths in *Farmer*, he dismissed the book because "Harrison manages little ironic distance: Joseph's tribulations are treated with teenage seriousness."

Legends of the Fall is a dramatic departure from Harrison's other fictional work. In fact, following his experimental bent, *Legends of the Fall* is not a novel at all but a collection of three novellas—"Revenge," "The Man Who Gave Up His Name," and "Legends of the Fall"—that appear to be startlingly different but are actually closely related through the recurring themes of obsession, revenge, and violence. Up to this point in his career, Harrison had written relatively short novels that allowed him to capitalize upon his skills as a poet, a gift for compression, and the ability to find what is often the shockingly apt image or phrase, while at the same time providing the opportunity for structural experimentation. Additional fictional compression of form demanded that Harrison force his talent into new areas that would create greater focus and further emphasize his skill as an accomplished poet.

In "Revenge," Cochran, an American pilot, is severely beaten and abandoned in the desert to die because he has made love to the wife of a Mexican gangster. Cochran is found by peons and nursed back to health at an isolated mission, where through his months of recuperation he can think of nothing but accomplishing his revenge on the gangster, Tibey, and reclaiming his lost love, Miryea. Tibey, too, is set on revenge, not only in attempting to kill Cochran but also in abusing Miryea, his own wife—by forcing her into prostitution, addicting her to heroin, and finally committing her to an asylum for the terminally insane. It is clear that Harrison wishes to emphasize that as the two men, who are really obsessed artists of a sort, work to meet the formal demands of their revenge, they forget their humanity and the suffering Miryea. By the time Tibey and Cochran end their childish game simply by forgiving each other, it is too late for Miryea, who dies. The eternal guilt we are told the two men will bear seems paltry compensation for

Miryea's horrible death, and the Sicilian adage that serves as an epigraph to this tale—"Revenge is a dish better served cold"—takes on new significance.

The second of the novellas, "The Man Who Gave Up His Name," is a brief and peaceful interlude between two dramatically violent tales, but the reader should not be fooled into believing that it is not a story of obsession, for Nordstrom, the hero of this piece, is a lost soul like Swanson in *Wolf* and Joseph in *Farmer*, whose sole outlet for the frustrations of midlife is dancing alone. Like the protagonists of those earlier novels, Nordstrom, once a young, successful junior executive with Standard Oil of California, attempts to discover the basics of living so that he can establish his true identity. The narrator of this tale tells us that Nordstrom's "arduous study of reality" aimed at discovery of the true necessities has made him "a trifle goofy"; Nordstrom, in one of the diary entries that dot the narrative, asks rather plaintively, "Why should I want to know the strange when I am ignorant of the familiar?" Nevertheless, he abandons what he chooses to call "normal" life and sets about his elemental search, symbolically looking up "earth, fire, water, and air" in the *Encyclopaedia Britannica*, giving vent to all of his animal urges, and dancing alone. He ends the tale with life truly reduced to its essentials, breathing and sensation: "Just breathing on the bed in the moonlight seemed quite enough for the moment. First you breathed in, then out, and so on. It was easy if you tried to keep calm." In the story's epilogue, Nordstrom has taken a menial job in a seafood restaurant in Florida, a life-style that allows him to live essentially, but the final image of him dancing "alone to the jukebox" in a bar "until four thirty in the morning when everyone had to leave" implies that despite giving up one identity (or name) for a less complex one, the midlife frustrations continue to plague him.

The novella "Legends of the Fall" is yet another departure for Harrison, for it is a historically based fiction set in Montana in the early decades of the twentieth century. The hero of the tale is Tristan Ludlow, one of three sons of a U.S. Cavalry engineer and a Boston socialite. As the story opens, the three brothers—Samuel, the youngest and most innocent; Alfred, the oldest and most priggish; and Tristan—are riding from Choteau, Montana, to Calgary in 1914 to enlist in World War I. Upon reaching Europe, Alfred is wounded and Samuel is killed. Tristan, after learning of Samuel's death and recovering his body, damns God for the irrationality of his brother's death, and from this point in the narrative Tristan is Harrison's principal

30.

believed on certain matters. For his seventh birthday

he had been given the twelve volume Book House, edited

by Olive Beaupre Miller, who had assured her young

readers that "the world is so full of a number of things.

I'm sure we should all be happy as kings." Approaching

age forty-three, it would still be difficult to convince

him that a Norse girl didn't ride a polar bear on a

long journey, or that Odin didn't exist on some rainy

northern Taiga, dressed in reindeer skins and warmed by

a huge fire fed on human marrow with the music of the

cries of the dying floating across a misty lake. Merlin

was real and so was Arthur; in the twelfth century Japan

there was a madman who painted pictures of mountains

and rivers by dipping his hair in ink and whipping his

head over the paper. Sometimes he painted with live

chickens. Why wouldn't certain ghosts live at the bottoms

of lakes and express themselves through the voice of a

loon? In his eleventh year Nordstrom shot a crow and

Henry, an Ojibway indian who worked as a carpenter for

his father when he wasn't drunk, wouldn't speak to him

for months, after telling Nordstrom that any fool "knows

that a crow is not a crow." ·By fall Henry had become

pacified and that early winter for a Christmas present he

built Nordstrom a small rowboat out of white pine. Late

From the setting copy for Harrison's novella "The Man Who Gave Up His Name," published in Legends of the Fall focus. Tristan, who is in fact driven temporarily insane by the death of Samuel, is eventually sent to Paris to recover and is discharged from the army. From there he travels to the home of his paternal grandfather in Cornwall, England, where he becomes a hand on the schooner his grandfather captains. When he arrives back in the United States, Tristan marries the patrician Susannah, second cousin to his mother, in Boston. Within months, Tristan is off again, this time on a six-year voyage around the world. In the course of his voyage he and Susannah are divorced, and when he returns to Montana he marries Isabel Two, the half-breed daughter of his father's foreman, Roscoe Decker. After seven years of peace, Isabel Two is accidentally shot and killed by federal officers who intercept Tristan and his party enroute from Great Falls to Choteau because they had learned he was transporting ten cases of illegal whiskey. The loss of his wife leads Tristan to become an outlaw (Harrison is careful to distinguish between the romantic "outlaw" and the less savory "gangster") and he gets involved in a rum-running operation in northern California, the territory controlled by a Seattle-based mob called the "Irish Gang." Tristan outsmarts the gang, but they come looking for him. He kills two gang members in Saratoga, New York, and a third gangster is shotgunned by the enfeebled Colonel Ludlow in Montana. The reader is informed early in the story that Tristan does not die until December 1977, when he is found in the Alberta wilderness beside the carcass of a deer he was in the act of skinning. Harrison's epilogue describes the fates of the other members of the Ludlow family and their graves near Choteau, but as if to emphasize Tristan's romantic isolation, we are told that "Always alone, apart, somehow solitary, Tristan is buried in Alberta."

"Legends of the Fall" is one of Harrison's more strongly plotted fictions. It is in fact reminiscent of *A Good Day to Die* as an example of Harrison's ability to weave a thrilling and suspenseful story, but in Tristan Ludlow there is another permutation of the romantic hero, this time in even more traditional dress. Tristan is the noble savage, the offspring of a civilized English engineer and a Brahmin socialite, who is raised in the Montana wilderness by One Stab, a Cheyenne warrior, and one cannot help but feel that Harrison's tale of Tristan, which might ostensibly seem to be purely an adventure yarn, is an environmental statement that laments the extinction of a species, whether it be the true romantic hero like Tristan or the passenger pigeon. In any case, Tristan is the spiritual grandfather of Swanson, Joseph, Nordstrom, Johnny Lundgren of *Warlock*, and the other protagonists of Harrison's fiction because he is the elemental man who has successfully fronted the facts of life. Indeed, Tristan is what so many of the other characters yearn to be but cannot—at least not in an age that defines romance as the rape of the land in the name of progress.

Reviews of *Legends of the Fall* were generally more positive than reviews of earlier novels, perhaps in recognition of Harrison's mastery of the shorter fictional form of the novella or maybe because he was finally receiving some acceptance. In *Bestsellers* (September 1979), Anne V. Kish wrote that these are "three good stories each with a neat epilogue that adds a sense of completeness to the story, each involving fascinating rare characters whose singlemindedness, if not their particular brand of grace under pressure, is to be admired." An anonymous reviewer in the *New Yorker* (30 July 1979) even hailed Harrison as one of the best writers of his generation, as well as one of the few "not to have been drawn into navel-gazing introspection," and in the *New York Times Book Review* (17 June 1979), Vance Bourjaily found all three novellas to be "absorbing," but he singled out "The Man Who Gave Up His Name" for special praise. However, many of the complaints registered against previous work surfaced in reviews of *Legends of the Fall*. In the *Atlantic Monthly* (September 1979), an anonymous reviewer characterized Harrison's style as consisting of "taut lines of prose" that "eventually reel in only small, bland truths," and writing in the *Nation* (7 July 1979), Keith Opdahl denounced Harrison's work as "the pure, raw, *macho* daydream": "Has Harrison seen too many gangster movies, too many Westerns, too much TV? He seems to *believe* all this, though I would guess that he is either doing movie scenarios, attempting to tap the great American Dream Machine, . . . or has trained himself as a poet to be too honest, too direct to soften these American fantasies. They are not after all so very different from Grimm's fairy tales. The bad guys must be destroyed. The good guy provides a catharsis of self-pity and resentment."

Johnny Lundgren of *Warlock* is the latest Harrison hero to be subjected to the throes of identity crisis, but this time Harrison makes the confusion more dramatic by supplying the hero with two identities. Lundgren is an out-of-work foundation executive and "Keatsian romanticist" with a beautiful wife, Diana, and a passion for gourmet cooking. According to Lundgren, "Warlock" is the nickname given him by a gay scoutmaster when he was still a

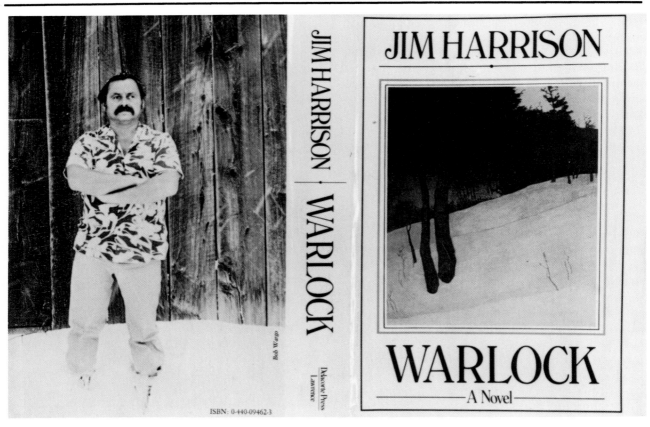

Dust jacket for Harrison's 1981 novel about an out-of-work executive offered the opportunity to live out his romantic fantasies

"morose youngster," but that nickname serves also to characterize the private-detective persona Lundgren assumes when, nearly halfway through the novel, he, like many of Harrison's other protagonists, is nearly swallowed by his own fantasies. Lundgren's desire for change is apparent early in the narrative, when he draws up a list of rules for self-improvement, in the manner of Ben Franklin; however, when the opportunity for change finally arrives, all rules are forgotten. After considerable soul-searching and boredom as a house husband, Lundgren is offered the chance to become a troubleshooter for the eccentric and lecherous Dr. Rabun, Harrison's clever caricature of the mad scientist. Lundgren becomes completely entrapped by his pseudodetective identity and, at one point, announces, "Let's face it, my life is changed," but after a trip to Florida to spy on Rabun's wife and son, a narrow escape from gangsters hired to murder Lundgren after he commits adultery with the don's temporarily paralyzed wife, and the eventual discovery that Rabun himself is a crook whom the Internal Revenue Service has been watching for

years, Lundgren learns that his job as Rabun's troubleshooter is merely a ruse to get him out of town so that Rabun can enjoy the beautiful Diana unhindered by her clumsy husband. Lundgren assists the State Police and the IRS in their capture of Rabun, whom Diana later describes as "a Hugh Hefner of the sciences." Diana and Lundgren reconcile, and Lundgren decides to send Diana to medical school, but the final scene suggests that for Lundgren little has really changed. He refuses to doubt that a noise he hears in the woods is Pan playing his pipes, just as he would undoubtedly refuse to deny that he is still Warlock, the detective alter ego that has caused him so much trouble. Lundgren, the diehard romantic, clings to his fantasies, even if he has to ignore reality to do so.

Once again, the reviewers tended to focus on Harrison's purported inability to create conventional fiction without recognizing the importance of his experimentation. In the *Saturday Review* (October 1981), John Buckley argued that *Warlock* might have been better as a novella: "It's flawed in its timing, taking forever to start then no time to end. There is rich irony in that ending, but it is less conclusion than punch line." Writing in the *New York Times Book Review* (22 November 1981), John D. Casey pointed out Harrison's debt to John D. MacDonald and suggested a parallel between Lundgren and Thomas Berger's Carlo Reinhart; despite the pleasures Casey found in *Warlock*, he too complained of "its unevenness of pacing."

Certainly the key to understanding Harrison's work is acknowledging that he is principally a poet and an experimentalist. To approach his novels with the expectations one would bring to traditional, realistic fiction is to do a disservice to Harrison and his work that will undoubtedly result in misinterpretation of the work and misapprehension of his value as a writer. He creates novels that are poetic experiments, which may not supply the needs of those who want conventionalities; however, Harrison's work does fulfill the demands John Barth has suggested for postmodernist fiction in his essay on "The Literature of Replenishment": "My ideal postmodernist author neither merely repudiates nor imitates either his twentieth-century modernist parents or his nineteenth-century premodernist grandparents. He has the first half of our century under his belt, but not on his back. Without lapsing into moral or artistic simplism, shoddy craftsmanship, Madison Avenue venality, or either false or real naivete, he nevertheless aspires to a fiction more democratic in its appeal than such late-modernist novels (by my definition and in my judgment) as Beckett's *Stories and Texts for Nothing* or Nabokov's *Pale Fire*. He may not hope to reach and move the devotees of James Michener and Irving Wallace—not to mention the lobotomized mass-media illiterates. But he *should* hope to reach and delight, at least part of the time, beyond the circle of what Mann used to call the Early Christians: professional devotees of high art." Harrison offers the challenges for those "professional devotees of high art" who wish to examine his poems and fictions, but he also offers interesting characters and good stories for those who do not. He is a relatively unknown major writer whose career has not yet peaked.

Periodical Publications:

"Plaster Trout in Worm Heaven," *Sports Illustrated*, 34 (10 May 1971): 70-72ff;

"Grim Reapers of the Land's Bounty," *Sports Illustrated*, 35 (11 October 1971): 38-40ff;

"To Each His Own Chills and Thrills," *Sports Illustrated*, 36 (7 February 1972): 30-34;

"Old, Faithful and Mysterious," *Sports Illustrated*, 36 (14 February 1972): 68-72ff;

Review of *All My Friends are Going to be Strangers*, by Larry McMurtry, *New York Times Book Review*, 19 March 1972, pp. 5ff;

"Where the Chase is the Song of the Hound and the Horn," *Sports Illustrated*, 36 (20 March 1972): 64-69ff;

"Machine with Two Pistons," *Sports Illustrated*, 39 (27 August 1973): 36-38ff;

"Guiding Light in the Keys," *Sports Illustrated*, 39 (3 December 1973): 78-81ff;

"Fishing," *Sports Illustrated*, 41 (14 October 1974): 98ff;

"Marching to a Different Drummer," *Sports Illustrated*, 41 (4 November 1974): 38-40ff;

"Not at All Like Up Home in Michigan," *Sports Illustrated*, 45 (25 October 1976): 54-56ff;

"Ten Thousand Octobers," *Nation*, 227 (16 September 1978): 250-251.

Interview:

Eric Siegel, "A New Voice from the North Country: Portrait of the Prodigal Poet Who Came Home to Michigan," *Detroit (Free Press) Magazine*, 16 April 1972, pp. 19-20.

AN INTERVIEW
with JIM HARRISON

DLB: The writer of the preceding essay calls you "still a poet who happens to work largely in the genre of prose fiction." With the publication of *Selected & New Poems 1961-1981*, do you think of yourself more as a poet lately, or do you think of yourself in categories at all?

HARRISON: I don't think of myself in categories much. I used to, but it became too schizoid. The last time I really thought about it was seven years ago. I was writing articles for *Sports Illustrated* and *Esquire* and also doing screenplays and writing poems and writing novels. I was a quadrischizoid. At that time I decided, like a lot of people do, that everything I did was an individual piece. That was a mental convenience. Since I want to make a living as a writer, I usually end up doing a lot of things. As far as poetry versus prose is concerned, I never think of the obvious formal differences, which are almost artificial. I do both with the same kind of interest and, I hope, vigor.

DLB: You've experimented with form in both your poetry and your prose works. Does a piece of work sometimes originate with form—the wish to work in a certain form—rather than with an idea for a story or poem?

HARRISON: Not really. I never start with an idea anyway; I usually start, even on a novel, with a collection of sensations and images. A form is a convenience that emerges out of what I have to say rather than something I impose on the material. Like the ghazals years ago: ghazals are a kind of lyric explosion, and I discovered that form that hadn't been used much for four or five hundred years.

DLB: The business of form emerging from the material reminds me that almost every time you write a novel, some critic or other thinks it should have been a novella, and when you write a novella, somebody is sure to say it should have been a novel.

HARRISON: Uh-huh. I don't care. I have at last broken myself from reading reviews, unless I need a boost and I read something by a big supporter—which I don't have a lot of, but I do have some good ones in England. If Bernard Levin does a piece on me, I read it, because I know it's going to be interesting. I've explained to my secretary, who gets upset, because she has to read the reviews: a critic is in the same position as a sports announcer, somebody like Howard Cosell: he has to talk in great detail about something he's not very intimate with. Or even better, like all the Frenchmen who talk about being in the Resistance. If you believe every Frenchman who claims he was in the Resistance, there had to be millions and millions of them. In truth there were only a couple of handsful. There's one more comparison: a critic is like certain Hollywood actors who have led us to believe they were in the armed services but in fact weren't, like John Wayne—he never served a day, but you'd have thought he was out there killing for his country all his life.

DLB: You mentioned to *Contemporary Authors* the "super-exhilarated sense of verbal humor" you get in writing poetry. Is it the same with writing fiction?

HARRISON: Sometimes. It depends. In reference to writing poetry, a poet named Wang Wei said a thousand years before our Lord that no one knew what caused the opening and closing of the door. You can feel very dumpy and forlorn, then write well and get exhilarated. I don't believe it when people say they write poetry very coldly. It's a mannerism they adopt to protect themselves.

DLB: As more of your work is published, do you find it harder to maintain the privacy that means so much to you?

HARRISON: Sure. I've got a big sign in my driveway here that says, "Do not stop here without calling. This means *you*." And now I've got a cabin in the Upper Peninsula where I spend part of the year. It's five miles from the nearest neighbor. The sign there says, "Do not stop without calling." There's no phone, so nobody can call. Plus I have some Airedale dogs, and shotguns.

DLB: Are you doing any screenplays now?

HARRISON: I just started work on a film project with Jeanne Moreau, the French actress. She heard of me through the French translations of my novels, which are all coming out there now. I'll do it partly because I saw *Jules and Jim* a dozen times, and partly because I just took six months off to work on my newest novel, and then I went broke, so now I have to do a couple of screen things to get solvent. But I don't mind. I'm at the age where I just assume I'm working most of the time. You get sort of distantly professional, and you still know how superior a way of life this is to being around a college, where all the people are the same, as they are in certain communities in the United States—Beverly Hills, Aspen, Palm Beach, the Upper East Side of New York, places like that.

DLB: How do you feel about current poetry and fiction here?

HARRISON: They're thoroughly balkanized. I was writing to my friend Tom McGuane the other day that more now than ever, critically speaking, the United States is like that Steinberg cartoon that shows the skyline of New York, behind which you see the huge Mississippi, and beyond that, Hollywood. In other words, if you're writing out of the Midwest, it's very easy to get ignored. People in New York are very busy, and they don't believe you exist unless they see you. I don't mind it to a certain extent, because obviously I've been able to make a living out of writing. But New York has become a microcosm of Hollywood. Hollywood moguls refer to everyone between the two coasts as "flyovers." They say, "Will this play in Kansas? Will the flyovers like it?" And this is getting to be more and more the fungoid, self-congratulatory nature of the Eastern literary establishment.

—*Jean W. Ross*

Harrison with his daughter Anna

Shirley Hazzard
(30 January 1931-   )

Carol A. MacCurdy
University of Southwestern Louisiana

BOOKS: *Cliffs of Fall and Other Stories* (New York: Knopf, 1963; London: Macmillan, 1963);
The Evening of the Holiday (New York: Knopf, 1966; London: Macmillan, 1966);
People in Glass Houses: Portraits from Organization Life (New York: Knopf, 1967; London: Macmillan, 1967);
The Bay of Noon (Boston: Little, Brown, 1970; London: Macmillan, 1970);
Defeat of an Ideal: A Study of the Self-Destruction of the United Nations (Boston: Little, Brown, 1973; London: Macmillan, 1973);
The Transit of Venus (New York: Viking, 1980; London: Macmillan, 1980).

Shirley Hazzard

An elegant prose stylist who beautifully elucidates the interior lives of her characters as well as their external landscapes, Shirley Hazzard has authored six books, numerous articles, and several essays. First working with the short-story form, this Australian-born writer has won first prize from the O. Henry Short Story Awards and regularly contributes to the *New Yorker*. Her first book, *Cliffs of Fall and Other Stories* (1963), is a collection of short stories, but she has subsequently concentrated on writing longer fiction: *The Evening of the Holiday* (1966), a short novel; *People in Glass Houses: Portraits from Organization Life* (1967), a collection of interrelated stories; and *The Bay of Noon* (1970), a novel nominated for the National Book Award. Parts of all of her fiction have continued to appear in the *New Yorker* as short stories. Her one nonfiction work, *Defeat of an Ideal: A Study of the Self-Destruction of the United Nations* (1973), concerns another of her interests—the work of the United Nations. All of her books have been well received by the critics, but none has earned such widespread recognition as *The Transit of Venus* (1980), winner of the National Book Critics Circle Award and the masterwork of her canon.

Born the daughter of a diplomat in Sydney, Australia, on 30 January 1931, Hazzard was educated at Queenwood School until age sixteen, when she accompanied her parents to Hong Kong, where her father was on government assignment. With no further formal education, she began her official career working for British Intelligence in Hong Kong. From 1949 to 1951 she worked for the United Kingdom High Commissioner's Office in Wellington, New Zealand, before joining the United Nations Secretariat in New York in 1952. For ten years she served at United Nations headquarters, concentrating mainly on the economic and social problems of underdeveloped countries. One of her ten years was spent on field assignment in Italy following the 1956 Suez crisis. In 1961 she resigned to devote full time to writing, and at the end of the following year she married Francis Steegmuller, a biographer and critic. The two of them make their home in both New York City and Capri.

Having lived in Australia, New Zealand, the

Far East, the United States, and Italy, Hazzard chooses a variety of worldwide locales for her fiction and brings to each work an authenticity of place so unerring that setting seems to be the fount of her creativity. Her short stories range in location from America to Switzerland, from England to Italy, but both of her early novels focus on Italy, a country that elicits from her imagination a depth of mystery and beauty. So keenly sensitive to place, she makes her settings part of her characters' experiences, thus using landscape much like a poet by suggesting it is emblematic of inner realities.

Hazzard brings to her writing a strong sense of not only place but language. In an interview with Michiko Kakutani, she says, "Language is the meaning. You want it to be as true as you can make it, and that has to do with the balance of sentences and the weight of sound." To achieve this intricate balance, she wanders about her New York apartment running phrases through her mind because, as she explains in a *New York Times Book Review* article, "For me, the ear has an essential role in literary meaning." Each page of *The Transit of Venus* went through twenty to thirty drafts, and the novel took seven years to complete. For this careful stylist, writing is an agonizing process that requires constant scrutiny and revision in order to achieve the beautifully sculptured prose for which she is known. Looking toward her next novel, she says not too optimistically, "The only thing that gets easier is that you recognize the states of despair you pass through as a writer and you realize that if you can persist, you'll probably get through. Writing has lots of real joy in it, but it's also a life sentence to hard labor."

Hazzard's creative talent is evident in her first book. Of the ten collected stories, nine appeared originally in the *New Yorker* with one in *Mademoiselle*. The main subject of the volume is love. From the opening story ("The Party"), which presents the spiteful dialogue of two lovers, to the concluding piece ("The Worst Moment of the Day"), in which a marriage has lapsed into conventional emptiness, the central theme is the supreme necessity of love and the inability to express one's longings. Emotions springing from passion, loneliness, and pain remain suppressed and create an emotional climate of regret and grieving.

The men and women in the stories differ in their approach to love, and most often the women, vulnerable to this difference, accept love's strictures and experience its inevitable pain. In one of the longest stories, "A Place in the Country," the heroine Nettie is passionately in love with Clem, the middle-aged husband of her cousin May. Once May finds out, Nettie prepares herself for Clem's rational explanation for their breakup:

> But ideas don't supplant feelings, she thought; rather, they prepare us for, sustain us in our feelings. If I understand why I am to be hurt, then, does that really mean that it will hurt me less? I know that I risked—invited—this, wounded May. I have disturbed the balance. There is balance in life, but not fairness. The seasons, the universe give an impression of concord, but it is order, not harmony; consistency, not sympathy. We suffer because our demands are unreasonable or disorderly. But if reason is inescapable, so is humanity. We are human beings, not rational ones.

In his *Meanjin* article on Hazzard, John Colmer explains that this idea of Nettie's "that there is a balance but no fairness, and the related idea that the claims of humanity are prior to the demands of reason, inform all Shirley Hazzard's fiction."

Hazzard brings to these love stories a dispassionate reason that underscores through her detachment the intensity of these moments of crisis. Antisentimental in her accounts of love, she renders dramatic situations with controlled sensitivity that relies on dialogue, reportage of gesture, and what Don Wolfe in the *Saturday Review* refers to as a "deft characterizing abstraction." Abstaining from imagery and description, she instead offers a simple statement of penetrating psychological insight: "He could not have been more embarrassed had he found her praying," "as aloof as curiosity would allow," and "in her face poetry and reason met without the customary signs of struggle." This ability to express her characters' inner worlds in a few lines of lucid, periodic prose is a strength that graces all of her fiction.

Reviewers were quick to praise this new artist's stylistic gift. In the *New Statesman*, Brigid Brophy described Hazzard as "an outstanding, gifted, expert writer, who knows the precisely most economical point at which to make the incision. . . ." Although Don Wolfe noted the writer's tendency to use introspection indiscriminately and too abruptly, he nevertheless thought the richness of her stylistic resources boded well for her future work. Only Stanley Kauffmann in the *New York Times Book Review* dismissed her, saying that the net result of her book "is not to move us, only to demonstrate that she is well-bred."

Hazzard's first novel, *The Evening of the Holi-*

day, which originally appeared in the *New Yorker*, is a short, polished work that demonstrates her feeling for words, acute perception of scene, and shrewd handling of a familiar theme. This slight but poetically rendered story set in Northern Italy describes the summer love affair between a cultivated English woman and a middle-aged Italian architect separated from his wife. Sophie is half Italian, a fact which surprises Tancredi since he decides on their first meeting that she is "the archetypal English woman." Although she is drawn to his Italian homeland, her varying responses to and expectations of his native country underscore the difference between them. Despite their inherent disparity, the two move carefully from an idle curiosity to a sexual intensity.

When Sophie finally agrees to rendezvous with Tancredi in Florence, she makes her decision on the day of the town festival, which celebrates an ancient battle, not a victory because the opposing side won. The holiday crowds coming in celebration trap her, and she has to fight her way through in a scene whose urgency marks the novel's climax. Her panic at the fear of separation foreshadows the real loss when they subsequently part, thus suggesting the title—"the evening of the holiday."

Although on the surface the plot seems slight and clichéd or the stuff of sentimental romance, the book's charm arises, according to the reviewer in *Time* magazine, from "the fact that the reader never quite discovers how author Hazzard makes a small masterpiece out of such unlikely material. Partly it is because her prose is so understated that it forces the reader to become uncommonly attentive." The *Saturday Review* critic Patricia MacManus makes much the same point when she says that "the primary interest of this brief tale is the artistry with which the love affair is limned." The novel's artistry prompted the National Institute of Arts and Letters to grant the author an Award in Literature in 1966.

From this rather wistful first novel, Hazzard turned the following year to a satirical work. Dissimilar in tone and seemingly unrelated to her other fiction, *People in Glass Houses: Portraits from Organization Life* satirizes the horrors of a rigidified corporate life. Based on her ten years' work for the United Nations, this book is a series of sketches, all of which first appeared in the *New Yorker*, which focus on the bureaucracy of bureaucracies, the United Nations. Although the author never names the U.N. but refers to it simply as the Organization, the reader never doubts the identity of the tall glass structure standing on the bank of Manhattan's East River as a monument to international good works.

Hazzard carefully exposes the impotence of this idealistic behemoth by focusing on the deficiencies of the organizational men and women. "The Organization had bred, out of a staff recruited from its hundred member nations, a peculiarly anonymous variety of public official, of recognizable aspect and manners." Taking up an individual employee of the Organization, each section or chapter comically depicts the ennui of the modern bureaucrat—the secretaries, personnel people, section heads, and committee members—all of whom keep files bursting, memoranda flying, cafeteria trays moving, and jargon thriving. Clearly each character's difficulty is functioning as an individual in the organizational maze, for the ideal worker "must walk the middle path—a man of middle years and middle brow was wanted, a man not burdened with significant characteristics." As Alan Cheuse points out in the *Nation*, "those who are supposed to be aiding the people of the world are all in need of assistance to the arid and depressed areas of their own souls and underdeveloped hearts."

Hazzard further suggests the dehumanizing effect of the Organization by showing what it has done to language. Words are no longer carriers of truth but are instruments of perversion and deception. In one scene the Department of Aid to the Less Technically Oriented meets to hear progress reports from field workers to underdeveloped countries. During a dazzling slide show accompanied by a barrage of words, one worker describes his mission: "This was the deplorable condition of the area when I arrived. Low level of overall production, cottage industries static for centuries, poor communications with neighbouring towns, no telegraph or telephone system, partial electrification, dissemination of information by shepherd's rumour, little or no interest in national or international events. In short, minimal adjustment to contemporary requirements, and incomplete utilization of resources." Throughout the book Hazzard's style mocks the official banalities and pompous jargon as targets for her satire. She even closes the book with a bureaucratic letter that could serve as a model of official obfuscation.

Despite the clever stylistic play, *People in Glass Houses: Portraits from Organization Life* lacks the subtlety of Hazzard's other fiction. In the *New York Times Book Review*, Frederic Raphael points out that "the ironic compassion she showed earlier is missing" and that "the irony has turned to steeliness, compassion to derision." This harsher tone suggests the author's real need to write about her experiences in the U.N. and her closeness to the material. Seven years later she tried again to grapple with her

The Story of Miss Sadie Graine

The instant his new secretary was introduced to him, Demetropoulos knew it would
not do. He looked at Miss Sadie Graine and, even as he smiled and shook her hand, he
knew that it would not do. It was his first day at the Organization and, although his
appointment was a lofty one, he did not wish to begin with a complaint. But the next day,
or the following one at latest, he would ask for a different secretary. For Miss Graine
would never do.

Miss Sadie Graine was a tiny woman. She was barely five feet tall. Her features
and bones were bird-like, her head tightly feathered in grey. She was an angular little
creature, sharp of nose, eye and tongue, but her lips were her most remarkable characteristic, being in repose (if that is the word) no more than a small straight line. People
meeting Miss Graine for the first time were apt to exclaim afterwards, "But the mouth.
My God, the mouth."

It had not always been so. Miss Sadie Graine had been a baby once, pink and plump
like so many others, gurgling approval of the very world that was later to fall so low in
her esteem. There existed, in fact, a childhood photograph from which little Sadie gazed forth
with eyes large and luminous. These eyes, taking in less and less, had diminished
into their present dimensions. It is not the purpose here to study the causes for pre shrinkage.
Causes there were, for Miss Sadie Graine's story, like all lives, was a tale of truth and consequences. Miss Graine's story will rather be told in the
form, old-fashioned as it may be, of her effect on others.

Her initial effect on Mr. Demetropoulos has been described. Ajax Demetropoulos
was a Greek, and it gave him a pang to see what had become of this woman of the western
world. Had the certain faces of male colleagues been pointed out to him as correspondingly
ravaged, he would have replied that, in the case of a woman, a more aesthetically pleasing
article had been despoiled. He was well disposed towards women. He was prepared to find
beauty in almost any
woman, and it depressed him when, as in the case of Sadie Graine, he was thwarted. It must
not be thought, however, that Mr. Demetropoulos recoiled from Miss Graine merely for her
lack of good looks: he was not a profound man, but equally he was not superficial, and his glance penetrated at least into the upper
sub-strata of Miss Graine's nature. His own nature, stripped of its
meridional pretentions, was
an easy-going one, and he knew that he could not stand it.

experiences, but this time in a nonfiction work. *Defeat of an Ideal: A Study of the Self-Destruction of the United Nations* is the author's documented conviction that the U.N. objectives are indispensable but failing within its current structure. Concentrating on the office of the Secretariat where she worked, the author provides an exposé of the violations of the ideals that led to the U.N.'s creation and that have caused its paralysis. Her purpose is to demonstrate why the U.N. should be abolished and replaced by an organization that would more faithfully carry out its original tasks. In various articles since this book's publication, she has continued to express her views on the U.N. and its failings.

Hazzard's satirical treatment of the U.N. in *People in Glass Houses* deals with a subject and uses a style so apparently different from her other fiction that when her next novel, *The Bay of Noon*, was published, R. G. Geering commented on the seeming discrepancy: "At first glance *People in Glass Houses* seems to show another side of Shirley Hazzard's talent—the writer of love stories turned satirist, except that a feature of her previous books is the cool, probing sympathy she brings to her analysis of characters in and out of love. In summary *The Evening of the Holiday* and *The Bay of Noon* might be made to sound like the conventional woman novelist's stories of romantic love set in historical, picture-book Italy; in fact their detachment and the quality of their perception and style make them much like the love stories of, say, Turgenev, in his elegiac mood." Rather than a radical departure from *People in Glass Houses*, *The Bay of Noon*, with its exploration of love's paradox, is a demonstration of the author's ability to fuse the satirical and romantic elements.

Jenny, the heroine of this love story, narrates her search for self from a twelve- or fifteen-year perspective in order to understand the significance of the past. A victim of the war as a child, she was exiled to South Africa only to return later to England and her brother, whom she loves deeply but finds in the hands of a grasping wife. Suffering from a sense of dislocation and deprivation, she says, "Of true homesickness—the longing for the habitual—I suffered little, for I had never acquired or been provided with familiar things; mine, from childhood, had been an existence improvised among the unfamiliar." With the insecurity of not belonging, the young woman accepts a job as a NATO translator in Naples, where she has a letter of introduction to Gioconda, an Italian novelist in her early thirties. This young woman emanates a self-assurance and grace that come only from a

completion of suffering, and, as such, she appeals to the estranged Jenny. The two central male characters are the flamboyant and egocentric Gianni, Gioconda's older lover who is caught in an unhappy but indissoluble Italian marriage, and Justin, a witty Scottish biologist who toys at love with Jenny. The story evolves from the quite natural attachments of these people into inadvertent betrayals.

In despair over her life with Gianni, Gioconda runs off to Spain with Justin. For consolation, Jenny and Gianni fall into each other's arms for a few days. From such a loss of innocence, Jenny finds love for Gianni's human frailties, gives up her worship of Gioconda, and, through love's disenchantment, salvages a more complete understanding of life's transience. Near the end she says, "The outcome of such a crossing is immaterial. One can only discover what has already come into existence. Equipped to search, we justify ourselves by ranging as far afield as possible, in order to render a plausible account, to be able to say, 'I looked everywhere.' But it is not by such journeys as these that one approaches home."

Years later the now-married Jenny, along with her English solicitor husband, returns to Italy, the place where she began to live, not observe. Thinking about her year in Naples and her identification with it, she realizes that "there now existed at last a place that could be missed. . . . Some part of me would always be coming, now, from this. Like the dye they had injected into my veins, the country coloured my essence, illuminated the reaction to everything else. Here, literally, I had come to my senses." Thus Naples gives Jenny her sense of life, and is, according to Elizabeth Dalton in *Bookworld*, the main agent of her transformation. The special ambience of this city with its splendors and miseries permeates the novel as the author succeeds in making the setting a physical experience that interacts with the characters and the reader as well. Like the settings in most of Hazzard's fiction, Naples serves not as a background for action but as another character in the story.

Nominated for a National Book Award, *The Bay of Noon* garnered critical praise for its sophisticated evocation of place and economy of style. Although Robert Long suggested in the *Saturday Review* that "Ms. Hazzard's book is carried, perhaps too exclusively, by her highly sophisticated manner," most critics welcomed a novel that relied on the importance of craft. Fearing that the book was "unfashionable" in these "trend-driven days," L. E. Sissman in the *New Yorker* heralded the author for telling a recognizable story and "using all the arsenal of perception, sensitivity, and diction she can command." Likewise, in the *New York Times Book Review*, Robie Macauley says, "Shirley Hazzard is a writer who has caught none of the fashionable fever, and *The Bay of Noon* is one of those rare novels that tries to address itself to the reader's intelligence rather than his nightmares."

Granted a Guggenheim fellowship in 1974 and writing exclusively for seven years, Hazzard worked painstakingly on her next book, which is considerably longer and more complex than her previous works. A vibrant, poetic novel, *The Transit of Venus* extends the author's talent and confirms her artistry. In this book she covers some fifty years (1930s-1980s) and five continents while telling a carefully constructed story through an omniscient narrator. Against this large world she carefully brings six pivotal characters into focus; the two central characters are a pair of beautiful orphaned sisters from Australia. Using her native land for the first time in her fiction, Hazzard expresses in a single passage the significance of mother country to these two well-bred sisters, Grace and Caro: "To appear without gloves, or in other ways suggest the flesh, to so much as show unguarded love, was to be pitchforked into brutish, bottomless Australia, all the way back to primitive man. Refinement was a frail construction continually dashed by waves of a raw, reminding humanity."

Fleeing this primitive homeland, the sisters in their early twenties immigrate to England. Once there Grace quickly falls into a conventional marriage with Christian Thrale, a prototypical government bureaucrat. "Those peering into the oven of his career would report, 'Christian is rising' as if he were a cake or a loaf of bread." Independent and darkly beautiful, Caro reaches for more and in the process takes over the story. Caro is Venus and Hazzard follows her fateful transit from an incomplete to a full comprehension of love.

Three men in the novel fall in love with Caro because "there was the everlasting, irritating and alluring impression that she addressed herself to an objective beyond the small, egoistic drama of their own desires." The first, Ted Tice, a young astronomer, develops and lives with an unrequited yet indestructible love that will last throughout his life. The second is Caro's passion, Paul Ivory, a cruelly brilliant and attractive playwright, who cynically marries into British aristocracy rather than permit Caro power over his emotions or hidden secrets. "It had not occurred to Paul that Caro's influence might increase with her submission. Or that she would remain intelligent." The third is Adam Vail, a wealthy American of decency and substance, whom

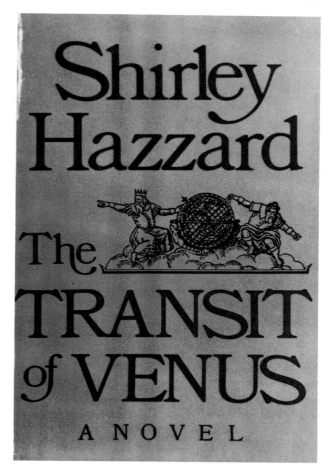

Dust jacket for Hazzard's third novel (1980), winner of the National Book Critics Circle Award

Caro marries in reconciliation to her loss and lives with in New York. His generosity of spirit revives her, and after his premature death, she reaches a newfound strength that readies her for her postponed conjunction with Ted Tice—a rendezvous that never takes place. Her final flight is doomed, with tragedy the result.

With its reliance on coincidence, renunciation, retribution, and doom, *The Transit of Venus* evokes an aura of tragedy. Preoccupied with what she calls "the grinding mills of the gods," Hazzard possesses a truly tragic imagination. Most reviewers of the book were quick to comment on this element of her artistic vision. In fact, the novel's seemingly inexorable events reminded many of Thomas Hardy, to whom Hazzard pays homage in the novel through allusions. In the *New York Times Book Review*, Gail Godwin suggested that this "family saga" was "reminiscent of Greek tragedy," but regardless of the comparison, the book does emanate a sense of doom and an "implied acceptance of larger patterns beyond an individual's fate."

Much of this tragic overview comes from the omniscient narrator's voice and what Godwin calls the author's "godlike grammar." Indeed, her immaculate style ironically comments on the indefiniteness of life by offering an elegantly removed detachment. As Webster Schott says in *Bookworld*, the "human movement" in *The Transit of Venus* is "seen from near the highest level art achieves. Shirley Hazzard's novel seems to me almost without flaw. Aphoristic and iridescent, her language turns paragraphs into events. Her perceptions of gesture, voice, attitude bespeak an omniscient understanding of human personality. The story she tells is, for the most part, so usual as to sound irrelevant. What she brings to it is virtually everything that story alone cannot tell about human lives." In agreement, Godwin summarizes her review: "This is a novel in which you are given the rooms of country houses, the interiors of people's minds *and* the vast sweep of stars as seen from the philosophical masthead, and that's a lot in one novel." This award-winning novel thus verifies Hazzard's artful mastery of style, character, and place, and moreover demonstrates her ability to present a more extensive world view.

With the publication of *The Transit of Venus*, Shirley Hazzard not only received her usual rhapsodic reviews, but she also began to gather a larger reading audience. Perhaps because of the recognition from winning the National Book Critics Circle Award, this novel made it to the best-seller list and became a Book-of-the-Month Club alternate. Always praised for writing well-crafted fiction, Hazzard struggles with the label of being "too coolly elegant" or "unfashionable." Even so, her fiction is compared to that of Thomas Hardy and Henry James because of her tragic vision and refined style. With a growing reading public she may prove that honest craftsmanship, delicate perceptions of character and place, and eternal themes that strike the commonality of the heart are fashionable and have a place in contemporary literature.

Periodical Publications:
FICTION:
"Sir Cecil's Ride," *New Yorker*, 50 (17 June 1974): 30-36;
"A Long Story Short," *New Yorker*, 52 (26 July 1976): 30-40, 45;
"Letter From Australia," *New Yorker*, 52 (7 January 1977): 32-37;
"A Crush on Doctor Dance," *New Yorker*, 53 (26 September 1977): 36-44;

"Something You'll Remember Always," *New Yorker*, 55 (17 September 1979): 40-49;
"She Will Make You Very Happy," *New Yorker*, 55 (26 November 1979): 43-44.
NONFICTION:
"League of Frightened Men," *New Republic*, 182 (19 January 1980): 17-20;
"UNhelpful," *New Republic*, 182 (12 April 1980): 10;
"UN Silence," *New Republic*, 183 (20 September 1980): 20-21;
"We Need Silence to Find Out What We Think," *New York Times Book Review*, 14 November 1982, pp. 11, 28-29.

References:
Patricia Blake, "Star-Crossed," review of *The Transit of Venus*, *Time*, 116 (14 July 1980): 54-56;
Brigid Brophy, "A Sight of Intriguers: 'Cliffs of Fall,' " *New Statesman*, 66 (25 October 1963): 578-579;
Eugene Chesnick, "Chance's Encounters," review of *The Transit of Venus*, *Nation*, 230 (24 May 1980): 633-634;
Alan Cheuse, review of *People in Glass Houses*, *Nation*, 206 (8 January 1968): 59;
John Colmer, "Patterns and Preoccupations of Love: The Novels of Shirley Hazzard," *Meanjin*, 29 (Summer 1970): 461-467;
Elizabeth Dalton, "See Naples and Grow Up," review of *The Bay of Noon*, *Bookworld*, 3 May 1970, p. 6;
"Elusive Echo," review of *The Evening of the Holiday*, *Time*, 87 (14 January 1966): 92;
R. G. Geering, *Recent Fiction* (London: Oxford University Press, 1973);
Gail Godwin, "A Novel of Intersecting Lives," review of *The Transit of Venus*, *New York Times Book Review* (16 March 1980): 7, 16-17;
Robert Granat, "Organization Cake," review of *People in Glass Houses*, *Bookworld*, 5 November 1967, p. 10;
Michiko Kakutani, "Behind the Best Sellers," *New York Times Book Review*, 11 May 1980, p. 46;
Stanley Kauffmann, "Violence Amid Gentility," review of *Cliffs of Fall and Other Stories*, *New York Times Book Review*, 10 November 1963, p. 4;
Laurence Lafore, "A Nightingale Sang at Last," review of *The Evening of the Holiday*, *New York Times Book Review*, 9 January 1966, p. 5;
Robert Long, review of *The Bay of Noon*, *Saturday Review*, 53 (11 April 1970): 37;
Robie Macauley, "The Bay of Noon," *New York Times Book Review*, 5 April 1970, pp. 4-5;
Patricia MacManus, "Depth-Soundings of Love,"

review of *The Evening of the Holiday*, *Saturday Review*, 49 (8 January 1966): 87;

Herbert Mitgang, "Concerned Novelists," *New York Times Book Review*, 9 March 1980, p. 35;

Frederic Raphael, "Coming Out Wrong," review of *People in Glass Houses*, *New York Times Book Review*, 15 October 1967, p. 5;

Webster Schott, "Journey with Love and Chance," review of *The Transit of Venus*, *Bookworld*, 9 March 1980, pp. 1, 9;

Robert Sellick, "Shirley Hazzard: Dislocation and Continuity," *Australian Literary Studies*, 9 (October 1979): 182-188;

L. E. Sissman, "Craft," review of *The Bay of Noon*, *New Yorker*, 46 (13 June 1970): 117;

Frances Taliaferro, "Death and Love," review of *The Transit of Venus*, *Harper's*, 260 (February 1980): 84-85;

Don Wolfe, "Lessons from the Lovelorn," review of *Cliffs of Fall and Other Stories*, *Saturday Review*, 46 (28 December 1963): 38.

AN INTERVIEW

with SHIRLEY HAZZARD

DLB: *The Transit of Venus* has brought you wider recognition than your previous books. How do you feel about the attention that has come along with it?

HAZZARD: Of course it's pleasant that one has more readers. And one's vanity is always vulnerable to gratification, I suppose. I have many letters, and it's both humbling and heartening to realize how many readers there are who bring to a book the sort of feeling one hoped for. But the interruptions have burgeoned, and the burden of correspondence has become enormous. That's a peripheral complaint, or at least a cursory one, but it's not unreal. I've answered literally thousands of letters since that novel came out, and I don't know quite what to do about it. These things are rather difficult. We go away to an island in the Mediterranean with no telephone some months of the year, but even so a great deal of interruption finds us out. People can't quite believe that you want solitude.

DLB: When *The Transit of Venus* was published, you told a *New York Times* reporter that you only wanted to write novels now. Does that mean we won't have any more of your short stories?

HAZZARD: I meant that I don't want to write arti-

cles and reviews; and particularly that I don't want to write political articles, although I still sometimes do so. I only write one kind of political article—about the United Nations, where I worked for ten years. I see that almost nobody else in the press will treat the United Nations with adult reality, so I have kept on doing that.

It's true that I only want to write novels at present; and I find that, although I have ideas for short stories, in some way they seem to be swallowed up in a novel. I miss writing stories and would certainly always want to have the possibility of writing them again. It's a form I enjoy and a very intense and good form of fiction. I'm not moving away from short stories in my heart, so to speak.

DLB: In addition to the articles you've just mentioned, *People in Glass Houses* and *Defeat of an Ideal* grew out of your work with the United Nations. Since you left there at the beginning of 1962 to write full-time, have you missed the diplomatic life in any way, despite its frustrations and imperfections?

HAZZARD: Good heavens, no! It's a constant wonder to me that I stood it as long as I did. My father was in the diplomatic life, and I should have known better. I joined the United Nations when I was twenty years old. As many people did in the early years of the U.N., I joined in a spirit of idealism and from a desire to do something useful. I don't think I did one useful thing in my entire time there, nothing that I can look back on and feel that it was necessary or helpful to anybody—except of course the things one was doing against the organization's wishes, to sustain the original principles of the U.N., which the administration seemed determined to abolish, and which *have* in fact been abolished. When I allow myself the distraction of feeling strongly about it, I think that if there were a war—God forbid—and if we survived it, there would immediately be a public outcry for a different kind of organism for international conciliation. I don't see why we should wait for a war in order to change things. The United Nations should be rethought right now. All other institutions that are found wanting—through change or decay, or fundamental unresponsiveness to the public need—are openly questioned, dissolved, and reconstituted; except this one, which has failed us on every count and far more profoundly than the public realizes. The present travesty of the United Nations idea prevents the formation of a rational organism adapted to the terrible new dimensions of the world crisis.

I didn't understand these matters easily or

quickly. I'm amazed at the ignorance and naiveté with which I worked there in the first years. However, I know it now and have had ever more occasion to understand the U.N. failure since I published *Defeat of an Ideal* ten years ago. That book brought an inundation of letters from concerned persons who have no other "outlet" for their U.N. knowledge except myself. These are not people expressing personal grievance. They are thinking men and women who may still work for the organization, or who have left it, or have been associated with it temporarily as consultants. And they all ask, Why doesn't the public know, why isn't the public aroused? Usually, I can do little more for them than share their anxiety—but even this is a development, for in my own day there was no informed person to turn to outside the United Nations. Columbia University has agreed to provide a repository for the mass of papers I've accumulated in this way, and I'm beginning to get together my innumerable documents concerning the United Nations.

The experience of writing about the United Nations has brought a number of revelations. One starts out, I think, in such matters with some expectation of stimulating reforms. In a case where the vested interests—not only huge material interests, but questions of vanity and self-esteem—are as strong as they are at the United Nations, and where the press is generally negligent, exposure does not generate reform. Roy Jenkins, the British politician, once wrote of Joseph McCarthy that exposure did not touch McCarthy because he showed no shame; Jenkins said, "Exposure is at least fifty per cent subjective." Thus I have had to see the United Nations deteriorate tragically while at the same time watching it expand into an ever more wasteful hypertrophy, more and more removed from the world's realities, and less and less accessible to truth. I have come to understand that, from my own point of view, it is important simply to record the truth.

The inability to have these matters treated in the press, and so to engage the public before it is too late, has itself become part of the U.N. story, part of history.

DLB: Did you actually begin writing or thinking about writing early in your life?

HAZZARD: When I was a child, eleven or twelve years old, my sister and I used to write stories and even "novels." Many children, especially I think young girls, do that—when they read a lot, as I did. But few such children go on to become writers; and I therefore don't think early "writing" is necessarily

indicative. There's no real way of knowing why one person becomes a writer and others don't. For years after childhood and adolescence I didn't really write anything. During my United Nations years, friends would tell me that I ought to be a writer. In a way, that confirmed my feeling that I should not try to write, because I understood that people tend to say such things without considering the real meaning of the word "talent." In the end, having in this way disbelieved in the possibility, I have to say there must be a compulsion. If one's destiny is to write, one will apparently set to work whatever the impediments. I'm not clear why I began to write—although I can trace certain circumstances that combined to make it more likely. Once I started, I realized it was the only thing I wanted to do. I began to write about 1960 when I was still at the United Nations, and it was through writing that I was able to leave bureaucracy at last. I lived from my own earnings, and—when I made a little money from my writing—I thought I would support myself from my work. And so I left, and lived happily ever after.

DLB: There are many references in both your fiction and your nonfiction to painting. Is it a special interest of yours?

HAZZARD: I've loved painting all my mature life. I had little encouragement to be interested in visual art or receptive to beauty in nature when I was a child. My parents had little pleasure in painting, and in Australia at that time there was virtually no exposure to works of art. This interest was another thing that was latent. The visual content of my books is of course quite conscious. When I was in England for a time I began to go to museums and be aware of painting in a more realized way, to know a little about painters. When I first came to New York and was working at the United Nations I went regularly to museums. These changes occurred because of the possibility of seeing beautiful pictures and also through coming to know people who cared for such things. After I went to live in Italy, in 1956, visual pleasure became an indivisible part of my existence, my consciousness.

DLB: You've said that it's easier to write in Capri than in New York. Why so?

HAZZARD: I should say, it varies. It used to be that when I went to Italy—in the years I was living in Tuscany—I found it very difficult to write, for the usual given reasons: it's too beautiful, there are too many distractions of a supreme aesthetic kind.

Chekhov said that living in Italy gave courage, for it is the one country in which art is truly supreme. Of course that's true; but the power of art in Italy is at the same time intimidating to a living writer who must continually question the quality of contemporary work. And then Italy, even now, relieves one of *burdens* towards art: it seems sufficient, there, to develop one's pleasure in art. It was obvious to me at one time that I wrote more easily in New York, which is a city *about* work; and I used to have a great deal of privacy in New York—being somewhat housebound, too, in the winter. There are many interesting things to do, of course, but those are, ideally at least, a stimulus to writing rather than distractions.

But in the last few years I find the pattern has changed quite a bit. The city has intensified. Now when we come back from Italy, we're both, for some days and even weeks, a bit aghast at the difficulties of living here. It has grown more inhuman, more irrational. Buildings are higher and higher and higher, more and more concentrated. There's a feeling of urgency in the streets. One negotiates one's body as if it were a car; you practically feel you should wear signals. It's inevitable that this overcrowding has detrimental effects. Along with that one has the troubles that all larger cities suffer from, and, everywhere, the overpowering fears of the nuclear age. These mount up in one's mind and give New York a distraction of its own that makes itself felt even when you're quietly in your room. One must establish some equanimity to be able to explore one's mind, one's imagination; and that's a harder struggle now than it was.

DLB: Is there work in progress that you'd like to talk about?

HAZZARD: I'm working on a novel, but from superstition I don't like to tell the plot. I find that meaning tends to seep out of one's ideas as one discusses them, as far as manuscripts are concerned. I hope it will be finished in a year or two.

—*Jean W. Ross*

Marcy Heidish
(22 April 1947-   )

Diane Scholl
Luther College

BOOKS: *A Woman Called Moses* (Boston: Houghton Mifflin, 1976);
Witnesses (Boston: Houghton Mifflin, 1980).

Marcy Moran Heidish was born on 22 April 1947 in New York City. She received her B.A. from Vassar College in 1969 and her M.A. from Catholic University of America in 1972. She also attended American University from 1970 to 1972. At present she resides in Arlington, Virginia. Heidish is the author of two major historical novels, *A Woman Called Moses* (1976) and *Witnesses* (1980). A member of Washington Independent Writers and Washington Women's Network, she is a frequent contributor to Washington area newspapers. She was awarded a National Endowment for the Arts creative writing fellowship in 1980 and is presently working on a fictionalized biography of Annie Oakley, which is nearing publication. She values her privacy and prefers to work undisturbed by publicity.

Heidish shows careful research in her historical novels. She uses her scholarship in order to present in accurate detail the lives of two singular women, products of their social and cultural contexts, who still transcend the limitations imposed on women by the prevailing codes of their times. Harriet Tubman and Anne Hutchinson emerge as memorable, richly drawn models of female initiative and enterprise.

A Woman Called Moses first appeared in *Redbook* in February 1976. It is a novel based on the life of Harriet Tubman, a slave born on Maryland's eastern shore in about 1820, who led more than 300 slaves to freedom in nineteen daring raids during the late 1840s and 1850s. The legendary Tubman, known as "Moses," which became her code name, felt called by God to deliver her people from the torments of slavery in order to start new lives in Canada.

A work of fiction, *A Woman Called Moses* relies on historical documentation. Though little in the way of primary sources can be found on the life of Harriet Tubman, the author uses several important nineteenth-century sources, imaginatively recreating Tubman's life when the sources conflict or provide too sketchy a picture of her mission. Heidish relies on two nineteenth-century biographies of Tubman by Sarah H. Bradford; also used are letters and speeches dictated by Tubman, who remained illiterate to the end of her life. Slave narratives furnished Heidish with an understanding of life on the plantation and in freedom, and the author tried to remain faithful to the idiomatic terms used by slaves in the nineteenth century.

As the novel opens Tubman is an old woman preparing for a railroad journey home to Auburn, New York. Waiting for the train, she dozes and is sharply awakened by a black veteran of the Civil War in uniform. Shadrack, a man with whom she was reared on Maryland's eastern shore, and whom she helped to escape, mocks her reputation as a daring raider of the plantations and later as scout and spy for the Union Army. Most of the people who accompanied them on their journey north when Shadrack gained his freedom are dead, he tells her, casualties of the war.

Moved to reflect on her early life, Tubman is pulled back into early memory. As a youngster in Dorchester County, Maryland, she was willful and sullen, "high-and-mighty." Before she is grown she is loaned out to "trash" who exploit and abuse her. When her father, by bowing and scraping, secures her a place in the nursery of the big house of the plantation owner, Edward Brodas, she learns to act incompetent so that she will be allowed to work outdoors, which she greatly prefers. Her many acts of defiance earn her a reputation as a troublemaker. When she aids another slave to escape, a harsh overseer throws a heavy metal implement at her, causing spells of unconsciousness and severe headaches at intervals throughout her life.

Working in the fields or cutting timber, Harriet allows herself to grow unkempt and uncommunicative, rejecting the traditional female role almost entirely. Her father, Daddy Ben, teaches her nature lore and survival skills that she will later put to use on her raids. Increasingly the ignominy of her slavery galls her. When she is forced into harness to pull a heavy barge for the amusement of white people, her humiliation is extreme. She works for wages for a time in order to buy her freedom,

Marcy Heidish

learning to her dismay that her arduous work habits have only increased her price.

In the late 1840s Harriet marries John Tubman, a free black who buys, mends, and sells used clothing for a living. Unfaithful to Harriet, he also reveals to her in a taunting way that her mother was freed by the will of her master years before, a condition that never came to pass. Harriet in anger and frustration vows to escape, and in 1848 she makes her way north to the Delaware border, aided by sympathetic Quakers. She has to overcome her natural timidity with white people as well as resist the surrounding patrollers with their "nigger dogs." A mystical fisherman-carpenter, appearing throughout the novel, encourages her on her journey north. At one point she is cared for by a deaf-mute Quaker woman who pantomimes Christ on the cross, suggesting that Christ is the one who implores her to give assistance to escaped slaves. A deep, mystical Christian current is to be found throughout the novel, faithful to Tubman's own theology and visionary experience.

Her freedom won, Tubman makes friends with Thomas Garrett and William Still at the Anti-Slavery Society in Philadelphia, seeks refuge in a black church, and gets a job as a housemaid. But her freedom fails to satisfy her when she remembers other slaves who live in bondage. On her repeated raids to Maryland's eastern shore, she leads large parties of slaves to freedom, guiding them to Canada after the Fugitive Slave Law makes their presence in northern states dangerous.

As the reward for her capture climbs steadily, Tubman persists in working her way south, hiding behind slave quarters where she sings:

> Who's that yonder dressed in red
> I heard the angels singing
> Looks like the children that Moses led.
> I heard the angels singing.

Many successive parties are led on a "journey from midnight through hope to God be praised," a code phrase exchanged by Quakers and runaway slaves. Heidish imaginatively recreates such a raid in the dead of winter, one fraught with particular difficulties as patrollers make every effort to deter the runaways, at one point burning them out of a barn.

The novel is rich in excitement and memorable in its evocation of a remarkable woman. Jeanette Lambert in *Time* praised the characterization of Harriet Tubman: "In this evocative first novel, the rescuer emerges as an invincible courageous woman, guided by a deep, mystical religious faith and a tenacious vision. Harriet Tubman used her great intelligence in the service of a passionate love for her people. She was, to the end of her days, illiterate. But she did more than read or write a book. She inspired one—and millions of followers, down to the present."

In *Witnesses*, Heidish once again has written a novel steeped in historical research, this time about Anne Hutchinson's life. Among Heidish's sources are Hutchinson and Winthrop family papers, the records of the First Church of Boston and of the region in Lincolnshire from which the Hutchinson family came. Nothing written by Anne Hutchinson or by her defenders has survived; most of the author's historical sources are unsympathetic to Hutchinson's ministry and theology. Heidish relied on four previous biographies of Hutchinson, yet she asserts: "My purpose in writing this novel was neither to examine the theological implications of Hutchinson's dispute with the Massachusetts Bay

clergy nor to develop or expound a new history of her activities; it was instead to explore the personal motivation and dilemma of Anne Hutchinson, and to create a portrait of an individual whose beliefs came into conflict with her world."

Divided into three parts and an epilogue, the novel begins from the point of view of Nell Benedict, midwife friend of Anne Hutchinson, whose narrative details the events of April 1638, during which Governor Winthrop and the colony's black-robed magistrates summoned Hutchinson to account for her refusal to end religious meetings in her home. But Nell's movement backward in time to her own emigration and Anne's furnishes the reader with an absorbing picture of early colonial life. The tension between the clergy's ideals for the new colony and the colonists' personal designs is developed, for Nell Benedict has little regard for the clergy and their theology. Her warm and homely picture of unconventional Anne, the daughter of Lincolnshire gentry but completely unpretentious herself, is a richly human and endearing one.

Anne, the mother of fourteen children, gains a reputation as a skillful and compassionate midwife. Nell remembers Anne's tender ministry to a woman who has tried to drown her child out of desperation to secure her own damnation, if salvation could not be assured. When Anne and Nell are called out late at night, ostensibly to attend a woman in childbed, they are actually called to John Cotton's house so that an assembly of clergymen can question Anne on her prayer meetings and criticism leveled at unsympathetic ministers, such as John Wilson. Anne makes her defense: "I condemn no one's words. That I do question certain teachings, that is also true. But condemnation? Nay."

Anne and the clergymen debate the balance of works and grace necessary to achieve election, and Anne persistently holds out for the measure of grace which permits the believer to find salvation. Their debate is continued when Anne is summoned before the General Court of Massachusetts Bay in Newtowne, where she is forced to argue on the scriptural basis for her teaching of theology in her home, calling attention to Deborah, Phoebe, and Priscilla as biblical precedents. Here, lies concerning her earlier testimony at John Cotton's house are recorded against her, and she is sentenced to prison.

Part two is Anne's account of her imprisonment in Roxbury from November 1637 to March 1638. Confined to a primitive cell she is often ill and suffers from an irregular pregnancy. Her conflict

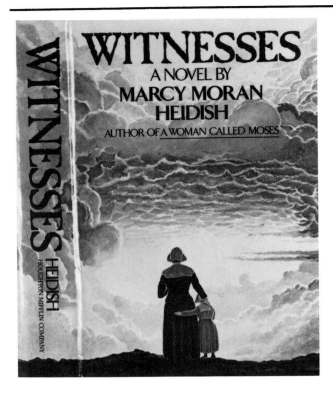

Dust jacket for Heidish's second historical novel (1980), which, she says, examines "the personal motivation and dilemma of Anne Hutchinson"

between the demands of her conscience and her responsibility to her grieving family is exacerbated by her daughter Faith's harsh condemnation of her stubbornness and pride. Many former followers denounce her, and even the occasionally sympathetic John Cotton turns his back. Her succor is Nell Benedict, the faithful midwife who visits her and tends to her physical needs.

Nell's narrative is resumed in the book's third part. Anne faces excommunication on her release from prison. Being cast out of the community of believers is a serious blow to her, but she leaves the scene of her humiliation bravely, her arm linked with that of Mary Dyer, her Quaker friend.

The striking novel concludes with pathos and dignity. Heidish's characterization of American women of outstanding accomplishments is to be admired. Her women refuse to acknowledge any but their natural limits; their transcendence of the confining roles imposed by their unrelenting societies is a mark of their human stature.

Some reviewers, though, found fault with both novels' labored didacticism. "What dilutes this inherent dramatic value is the author's inclination to pontificate and to belabor the obvious," Martin Levin wrote of *A Woman Called Moses* in the *New York Times Book Review* (20 June 1980). *Witnesses* is also didactic, but the more complicated development of Anne Hutchinson's struggle between her conscience and the needs of her family lends richness to the characterization. Barbara Bannon commented in *Publishers Weekly* (13 June 1980), "Writing with the same intensity of feeling that distinguished her novel about Harriet Tubman, *A Woman Called Moses*, Heidish gives us a heroine for all seasons, speaking as clearly to us today as she did to her own time." Webster Scott observed of *Witnesses* in the *New York Times Book Review* (14 September 1980): "The novel abounds in literary grace. It employs the voices of the times as though heard this minute. Anne Hutchinson herself often seems so alive that one feels she might walk out of the novel and ask us to define grace." Her vivid portraits of memorable women mark Heidish as an important novelist with a sharp awareness of the neglected heroines in America's past.

Evan Hunter

(15 October 1926-   )

Ralph F. Voss
University of Alabama

SELECTED BOOKS: *Find the Feathered Serpent* (Philadelphia: Winston, 1952);

Don't Crowd Me (New York: Popular Library, 1953; London: Consul, 1960); republished as *The Paradise Party* (London: New English Library, 1968);

The Blackboard Jungle (New York: Simon & Schuster, 1954; London: Constable, 1955);

Cop Hater, as Ed McBain (New York: Simon & Schuster, 1956);

The Mugger, as McBain (New York: Simon & Schuster, 1956);

The Pusher, as McBain (New York: Simon & Schuster, 1956);

Tomorrow and Tomorrow, as Hunt Collins (New York: Pyramid, 1956); republished as *Tomorrow's World* (New York: Avalon, 1956);

Second Ending (New York: Simon & Schuster, 1956; London: Constable, 1956); republished as *Quartet in "H"* (New York: Pocket Books, 1957);

Strangers When We Meet (New York: Simon & Schuster, 1958; London: Constable, 1958);

A Matter of Conviction (New York: Simon & Schuster, 1959; London: Constable, 1959); republished as *Young Savages* (New York: Pocket Books, 1966);

The Remarkable Harry (New York & London: Abelard-Schuman, 1961);

The Wonderful Button (New York & London: Abelard-Schuman, 1961; London: Abelard, 1962);

Mothers and Daughters (New York: Simon & Schuster, 1961; London: Constable, 1961);

Buddwing (New York: Simon & Schuster, 1964; London: Constable, 1964);

The Sentries, as McBain (New York: Simon & Schuster, 1965; London: Hamish Hamilton, 1965);

A Horse's Head (New York: Delacorte, 1967; London: Constable, 1968);

Last Summer (Garden City: Doubleday, 1968; London: Constable, 1969);

Fuzz, as McBain (Garden City: Doubleday, 1968; London: Hamish Hamilton, 1968);

Sons (Garden City: Doubleday, 1969; London: Constable, 1970);

Evan Hunter

Nobody Knew They Were There (Garden City: Doubleday, 1971; London: Constable, 1971);

Every Little Crook and Nanny (Garden City: Doubleday, 1972; London: Constable, 1972);

Come Winter (Garden City: Doubleday, 1973; London: Constable, 1973);

Streets of Gold (New York: Harper & Row, 1974; London: Macmillan, 1975);

Where There's Smoke, as McBain (New York: Random House, 1975; London: Hamish Hamilton, 1975);

Me and Mr. Stenner (Philadelphia & New York: Lippincott, 1976; London: Hamish Hamilton, 1977);

Walk Proud (New York: Bantam, 1979);

Ghosts, as McBain (New York: Viking, 1980; London: Hamish Hamilton, 1980);

Love, Dad (New York: Crown, 1981).

Evan Hunter is a pseudonym for one of America's most productive writers, whose successes span decades and genres with a felicity that has brought him commercial and financial success, if not artistic accolades. Since the 1954 publication of his first best-selling novel, *The Blackboard Jungle*, Hunter, whose family name was Lombino, has generated novels, short stories, screenplays, plays, and children's books—many as Evan Hunter, but more as Ed McBain. As Evan Hunter, he has authored more than twenty books. His greatest successes, in addition to *The Blackboard Jungle*, have been the novels *Strangers When We Meet* (1958), *Mothers and Daughters* (1961), *Buddwing* (1964), *Last Summer* (1968), *Sons* (1969), *Streets of Gold* (1974), and *Love, Dad* (1981). Short stories signed by Hunter have appeared in *Esquire*, *Seventeen*, *Ladies' Home Journal*, and *Playboy*. As Ed McBain, Hunter created the popular and profitable 87th Precinct police-detective series, which, at this writing, includes more than thirty-four novels and inspired an early 1960s television series. Several of the 87th Precinct novels have been filmed, including *Fuzz* (published in 1968, produced in 1972), for which Hunter wrote the screenplay. Over the years, Evan Hunter/Ed McBain has been both enormously productive and commercially successful, qualities which have won him a large, diverse readership and, simultaneously, a rather condescending critical reception, as though one who could write so much could not possibly be taken seriously.

Though many critics do not consider Hunter a truly important or serious writer, Hunter himself has long considered his writing important. Hunter says he was the "top artist" as a student at New York City's Evander Childs High School, but later, while studying art at Cooper Union, also in New York, he perceived that he was "surrounded by people who were very serious about art and who were, frankly, much better than I was." He had done a bit of writing in high school, and after leaving Cooper and joining the navy, he began to concentrate exclusively on writing. From aboard a ship in the Pacific, the eighteen-year-old Hunter sent story after story to magazines, most of them signed with pseudonyms, because he did not believe that "Lombino" would attract positive attention. None of these stories was accepted. "I sent them to all the slicks," Hunter later recalled; "I had no concept if the stories were appropriate." The lack of success did not dissuade Hunter, who returned to New York after his discharge from the navy in 1946 and enrolled in Hunter College, where he majored in English. As a college student, Hunter continued to write and later credited Prof. Francis Kolars with helping him develop his ability. While he was in college, Hunter met and married Anita Melnick, another student, in 1949. He graduated a year later with a B.A. and a Phi Beta Kappa key, determined to become a successful writer despite the additional responsibilities that were soon to come—their three children were all born in the early 1950s before the success of *The Blackboard Jungle*.

The years before *The Blackboard Jungle* saw Hunter writing a wide variety of short stories under such pseudonyms as Richard Marsten and Curt Cannon. "I think the first thing I had published was a science fiction short story in a pulp magazine for which I was paid $12," recalls Hunter. Two science-fiction novels were finished during this time, and though they were published—*Find the Feathered Serpent* (1952) and *Don't Crowd Me* (1953)—Hunter realized little profit from them and had to take odd jobs to help meet living expenses. Besides playing piano in a jazz band (an experience he was to use years later in *Streets of Gold*), Hunter sold Maine lobsters by telephone. "My deal with the boss," he later recalled, "was that I would get $5 royalty for every barrel of lobsters I sold. . . . I kept calling one restaurant for months, and finally sold them a barrel. . . . I was elated. My boss paid me the five bucks six months later, reluctantly. In many respects, selling lobsters was just like publishing." During this time Hunter also worked as an English teacher in two of New York City's vocational high schools, an experience that provided both impetus and detail for *The Blackboard Jungle*. Shortly after his teaching experience, Hunter responded to an ad in the *New York Times* for an editorship with the Scott Meredith Literary Agency and got the job. It was while he was with the Meredith Agency that he began to place his work more frequently, and it was during this time that he legally changed his name to Evan Hunter. Hunter, as Lombino, sent a draft of *The Blackboard Jungle*, signed by Evan Hunter, to Charles Heckelmann, an editor. Heckelmann told him that he wanted to meet Evan Hunter. "When I explained *I* was Evan Hunter, Heckelmann was surprised, of course, but he wanted the book, and after I asked if I should put my real name on it, he said, 'I think "Evan Hunter" will sell a lot more tickets.' I became Evan Hunter." *Evan* is short for Evander Childs High School; *Hunter* is his college. And *The Blackboard Jungle*, as Robert Dahlin has noted, "endowed the Hunter name with a full measure of legitimacy in 1954."

The Blackboard Jungle was immediately successful. All America seemed to become more aware of

Glenn Ford in Blackboard Jungle

teenage problems and delinquency in 1954. Into this atmosphere of change came Hunter's best-seller about delinquency and violence in the fictional North Manual Trades High School in New York City. The story of young teacher Richard Dadier's attempt to reach the problem students who had been more or less abandoned by the school system and shuttled to vocational school is an absorbing one in which the idealism inherent in the American democratic concept of public education comes into full clash with the cynicism and frustration of burnt-out students and teachers. Dadier, who clearly reflects the feelings and observations of Hunter's own brief experience, does not want to believe, as most of his fellow teachers do, that the students are hopeless, that the most that can be achieved is to complete the school day in an orderly fashion, without incident. "I'll tell you something, Dadier," advises Solly Klein, a veteran teacher. "This is the garbage can of the educational system. . . . Our job is to sit on the lid of the garbage can

and see that none of the filth overflows into the streets."

As the novel's plot develops, Dadier (whose students quickly begin to call him "Daddy-o") protects a provocative female teacher from being raped in the hallway, then is mugged in reprisal as he leaves the school area late one evening. Daily he struggles to find some way to make learning meaningful to his students but meets only ignorance and disdain; his brightest student chooses to use his ability to disrupt and lead the other students in revolts. Gradually, Dadier comes to realize that there is an element of truth in Solly Klein's cynical view; the education courses Dadier had taken in college had not prepared him for teaching in a vocational school, but, as Dadier muses, "Suppose the college had given elective courses titled *Teaching the Trade School Student.* . . . Would there have been a mad scramble to elect those courses? Doubtless, oh yes. Ohmyyes." In a stinging condemnation of the schools of education and people who choose teaching careers out of sheer laziness, Hunter, via the thoughts of Richard Dadier, blasts the comfortable philosophies of a system that prepares teachers only for ideal students and ideal schools, and the "meatheads . . . who drift into the teaching profession." Realizing these problems, Dadier begins to seek a separate peace with his job and his students, looking beyond education-school and idealistic orthodoxies for some means both to cope and make some important difference in his students' lives.

In the novel's denouement, Dadier, whose wife is pregnant, resists the tempting sexual favor of the teacher whom he protected from rape. There is also a confrontation with the school's principal about Dadier's use of derogatory terms for minority groups in a lesson on language and democracy. Dadier enjoys modest successes in getting his brightest student to contribute significantly to the school Christmas program and in getting his class to grasp the allegorical meaning of Heywood Broun's "The Fifty-First Dragon." Still, the novel's penultimate scene is violent, as a student who had earlier been humiliated by Dadier for bad behavior seeks revenge in a classroom attack with a knife. Dadier is wounded, but some of his students come to his aid. The willingness of the students, especially the bright leader, to help him makes Dadier believe he *has* made a difference in at least some of his students' lives, and the novel ends on a rather unconvincing upbeat note as Dadier is more confident that he is truly a teacher.

The Blackboard Jungle "breaks through the verbiage which has long clouded the facts of vocational teaching," according to *Nation* critic Stanley Cooperman. In the *New York Herald Tribune Book Review*, Barbara Klaw stated that this is "an extremely good novel," one in which Hunter displays "a superb ear for conversation, . . . competence as a storyteller, and . . . tolerant and tough-minded sympathy for his subject." The MGM film, featuring Glenn Ford as Dadier and a main-title sound track of Bill Haley's hit "Rock Around the Clock," simply added to the great success of the novel. Recalling those times, Hunter later said, "It was all pretty heady. I don't think I ever went overboard or berserk, but I *had* been waiting for a long time, and it sent me sailing over the rooftops. It guaranteed that I'd be a writer. I could freelance and write because I had some security." And write he has, work after work, year after year. *The Blackboard Jungle*, still on the reading lists in most colleges of education, may always be his best-known work, but it is doubtful that he would have it so. In the years since, in the novels signed by Evan Hunter, he has

continued to write of conflicts between generations and of family and social upheavals, but his concerns have been much broader than those he addressed in that first successful novel.

Sons is one of Hunter's most serious works and one of his favorites "because it says something very important, and I wish it could be read by everyone in America." In *Sons* Hunter traces the men of the Tyler family through three generations of personal and American history. The grandfather, Bertram Tyler, had willingly left the Wisconsin woods to fight in World War I—the war, it was claimed, to end all wars and make the world safe for democracy. The experience proved disconcerting when his own high ideals—and those that had been so enthusiastically inculcated—came into contact with the kill-or-be-killed savagery of the front. His son, Will, eagerly fought in World War II as a fighter pilot, believing he was doing the right thing even while the disillusioned grandfather began to question if America wasn't some kind of "adolescent," doomed to "make the same errors all over again." Bertram, born in the first minute of the twentieth century, represents America's need for survival with maturity and wisdom in the face of a backward and brutal world, a world which, despite technical sophistication, is doomed if America naively continues to push its piety and its system upon other cultures, because war is the inevitable result. Will represents the aggressive corporate post-World War II America that extends its business and system throughout the world, making profit beyond its frontiers, and simultaneously making any wars to protect these extensions still justifiable as defensive conflicts. Will's world is far less idealistic than his father's and much more complicated morally. It is the third generation son, Wat, who ultimately pays the symbolic cost of the family's—and America's—conflicting philosophies with his death in Vietnam.

Sons has an unmistakably urgent theme that overshadows its characters and situations, but its multigenerational view of the Tylers' painfully coming of age with America and its persistent questioning of America's myths make it Hunter's most ambitious novel after *The Blackboard Jungle*. Earlier, in *Mothers and Daughters*, he had dealt with generational intrafamilial conflict; in *Last Summer* he had portrayed bored, affluent youths who are alienated from their parents because they have been essentially ignored rather than reared; but no other work before or since *Sons* approaches the sweep of the Tyler chronicle. Technically, Hunter has frequently written better than he does in *Sons*. The first-person point of view and time perspective inventively shift chapter-by-chapter from the grandfather to the son to the grandson; but, as *New York Times* critic Richard Brickner has noted, Hunter's thesis tends to dominate each voice.

If *Sons* is Hunter's most ambitious novel after *The Blackboard Jungle*, *Streets of Gold* is probably his finest to date. The first-person account of Ignazio Silvio Di Palermo, a second-generation Italian-American who was born blind and poor in New York's Italian Harlem, *Streets of Gold* is a serious examination of America's myth of unlimited opportunity for immigrants, a myth holding that belief and hard work combine with opportunity to bring fabulous success. Ignazio tracks the myth across generations, from his immigrant grandfather to himself, and finds it more viable and inspiring as a myth than as reality, despite the fact that Ignazio is the only one who has realized great wealth.

The grandfather, Francesco Di Lorenzo, left Italy for America late in the nineteenth century when a grape blight destroyed the vineyards. Enticed by tales of rich opportunity in America, where there were "streets of gold," the grandfather at first planned to make a fortune, then return to Italy. But he never did. Rather, he labored, dreamed, saved, kept his faith, became a tailor, married the daughter of another Italian immigrant, and prospered in a

modest way that at once was better than he could have done in Italy and still was far short of the dream of great wealth that originally attracted him. His daughter, Stella, was brought up to be as "American" as possible, with English her primary language, in keeping with America's "melting pot" ideals. She married Giacomo Roberto Di Palermo, also a child of Italian immigrants, who aspired to be a professional musician—using the "more American" name of Jimmy Palmer—but who eventually settled for being a mailman during the Depression. Ignazio's parents and grandparents believed in the American Dream and lived its concomitant values of hard work, thrift, and, if not wealth, at least relative success. They took pride in their accomplishments, their faith, and their families, and they dreamed of even better lives and better opportunities for their children.

It is the blind Ignazio who realizes the great dream of success and wealth, and who finally questions it, understanding the hollowness of wealth and the poverty of values it can foster. Although his parents were not wealthy, they saw to it that he had the best possible education to overcome his handicap. This included the best instruction in piano. While Ignazio became a promising classical pianist, his older brother Tony went to war against Mussolini's Italy and died in battle. Though Ignazio's par-

Dust jacket for Hunter's 1974 novel, which examines the effect of the American Dream on an Italian family

ents felt their son had died for America, they did not tell the grandfather that an Italian had killed his grandson. After his brother's death, Ignazio began to play the jazz records that Tony left behind. These records of music that is purely American fired Ignazio's talent and ambition; he no longer wanted to play classical piano. He wanted to be a jazz pianist—"the best jazz piano player who ever lived," as Ignazio says to Biff Anderson, the black jazz pianist who becomes his new mentor. Eventually, after years of "paying his dues," Ignazio becomes an enormously successful jazz musician, and, to him, New York's Fifty-second Street, where he heard and learned from the jazz masters, was a street of "pure gold."

But his success proves costly. One cost is his name and its implicit heritage. Ignazio changes his name to Dwight Jamison—Dwight for President Eisenhower and Jamison for James's (Jimmy Palermo's) son. Another cost is the irony of how he became successful: after ten years of classical training and eleven years of playing jazz, his career-making hit record is a virtual throwaway number with a flute player, which he did not want to use. The song, hastily recorded as "filler" in a studio, becomes an instant success, with the flute contribution becoming the "distinct sound" identifying Dwight Jamison's group. Ignazio does not like the song or the sound—but they make him rich and famous, and he accepts the trade. Moreover, his once-happy, melting-pot marriage with a Jewish woman erodes, then fails altogether because, as Ignazio says, "I went along with the American fantasy . . . that anyone achieving celebrity status could call his own tune with members of the opposite sex." After one of his albums leads the nation in sales, Ignazio is visited by representatives of the Mafia, who break three fingers on his left hand when he does not allow them to become his new managers. He remains able to play, but not nearly as well. Finally, there is the inevitable: record sales decline and demand for performances wanes. Fame is transitory. The realization of Ignazio's dream of success—and that of his forebears—leaves him wealthy but alone. He feels profoundly, as he sits by his immigrant grandfather's deathbed, that much of what he has lived is a lie, but nonetheless an ideal that he betrayed. The gold of wealth, Ignazio has. The greater gold of lasting values, based upon faith, hard work, and family, he has lost. Ironically, it is the grandfather who, at the moment of his death, knows that his own life has been truly and richly blessed, for he is dying with those values still intact:

"The streets here are truly paved with gold" is his final utterance.

Streets of Gold may deal in the clichés complained of by the anonymous *Kirkus* reviewer, but the story is told with far too much verve to be glibly downgraded. More accurate is the *Publishers Weekly* critic who found it a "rich and candid novel" with "priceless vignettes of American family life." Hunter's claim to be considered a serious writer rests largely upon his stories of American families and their relationships to America's sustaining myths. In novels such as *Sons* and *Streets of Gold*, his claim is well based. But he has written so much that the truly good work's reputation is diluted. In addition to the more than twenty novels as Hunter and the more than thirty-five as McBain, Hunter has also written five screenplays: *Strangers When We Meet* (1960), based on his novel; *The Young Savages* (1961), based on his novel *A Matter of Conviction*; *The Birds* (1963), based on Daphne du Maurier's short story; *Fuzz* (1972), based on the McBain novel; and *Walk Proud* (1979), based on his novel. Hunter has also written two stage plays: *The Easter Man* (1964), retitled *A Race of Hairy Men!* in 1965; and *The Conjuror* (1969). To be sure, much of Hunter's work is uneven. But what might one expect of a seemingly tireless worker who writes from nine in the morning until six at night?

Advice Hunter gives to would-be writers in a 1978 article in the *Writer* reveals something of his method. "Set yourself a definite goal each day," he says. "*Set* the goal, make it realistic, and *meet* it." Apparently, Hunter has long practiced what he preaches, writing and rewriting until he is satisfied with results. "If it bogs down," he says, "if you're supposed to write a tender love scene and you've just had a fight with your accountant, put the anger to good use. Jump ahead and write the Battle of Waterloo chapter. *Don't stop writing!*"

Like most writers, Hunter draws upon personal experience for many of his ideas, embroidering upon them the additional elements of plot, characterization, or theme required by his story. Discussing his story ideas, Hunter says, "Some of them spring from life situations—my own life situations. Some of them are simply intellectual concepts that come to me and take a while to develop. . . . Others are based on experiences that friends or relatives may relate to me, or that I may observe." Hunter's first novel after *The Blackboard Jungle*, *Second Ending* (1956), gives a very realistic picture of heroin addiction. "My closest boyhood friend was a heroin addict," says Hunter. "He died of tetanus."

In *Streets of Gold*, Ignazio's black friend and jazz mentor, Biff Anderson, is a heroin addict who dies of tetanus. In 1973 a divorced Hunter married Mary Vann Finley and acquired a stepdaughter, Amanda Eve Finley. In 1976 one of Hunter's novels for children, *Me and Mr. Stenner*, appeared, dedicated to Amanda and relating the story, from a stepdaughter's point of view, of how she and her stepfather came to accept and love each other.

Much of Hunter's serious work carries a consistent theme of generational conflict. "I don't know why I've been attracted to writing about young people," he says. "I guess from *Blackboard Jungle* it's been a situation that's always appealed to me, the idea of adults in conflict with the young. I think part of my fascination is with America as an adolescent nation and with our so-called adult responses that are sometimes adolescent." According to *New York Times* reviewer Eliot Fremont-Smith, in *Last Summer* Hunter is able to "capture the directionless malaise of comfy youth that feels superfluous and not needed." The casual cruelty of the three friends in *Last Summer* and its sequel, *Come Winter* (1973), results in rape in the first novel and murder in the second. More recently, *Love, Dad* details the pain of a father's gradual spiritual, then physical, separation from his teenaged daughter during the turbulent 1960s. She rejects him and his values, turning to drugs and a nomadic existence. When the father divorces her mother, the daughter's alienation is exacerbated. Eventually, both father and daughter drop completely out of each other's lives. An accidental meeting years later at the novel's end only establishes that the daughter has settled down to middle-class suburban marriage and family, and that her father has been happily remarried and now lives in Greenwich Village. Their meeting is brief; each asserts that the other caused a broken heart, and in an indeterminate reconciliation, they shake hands, and the father tells his daughter that his phone number is "in the book."

Works such as *The Blackboard Jungle*, *Strangers When We Meet*, *Buddwing*, *Last Summer*, *Sons*, *Streets of Gold*, and *Love, Dad* clearly establish Hunter as a novelist who would like to be taken seriously. Other works, such as *A Horse's Head* (1967) and *Every Little Crook and Nanny* (1972), show a sense of farce and humor reminiscent of Damon Runyon. *The Remarkable Harry* (1961), *The Wonderful Button* (1961), and *Me and Mr. Stenner* show his considerable ability as a writer of children's stories. Still, he has written poor novels. His 1971 *Nobody Knew They Were There* is a completely improbable story about a presidential assassination attempt. *The Sentries* (1965), as Ed McBain, is an equally improbable tale of an attempt by a group of right-wing mercenaries to provoke World War III by seizing a U.S. Coast Guard ship and attacking Havana.

But perhaps, along with his sheer productivity, it is Hunter's wit, his ability to have fun with himself, his readers, and his critics, that has hampered his hope to be received as a serious writer. His books are sprinkled with small jabs at himself that are recognizable to his loyal readers. In *Where There's Smoke*, a 1975 McBain novel, a crow hits the narrator's car windshield and breaks it. "Birds do not appeal to me," he tells us; "I'd once written a letter to Alfred Hitchcock telling him so. Hitchcock never answered." This, of course, is more than an allusion to Hitchcock's film—it is also an allusion to Hunter's screenplay for *The Birds*. *Every Little Crook and Nanny* is a romp that twits professional book critics by telling of Luther Patterson, who becomes a kidnapper as an alternative to reviewing books. Luther proves to be a poor kidnapper, but along the way he manages to skewer some six critics, including the *New York Times*'s Martin Levin, who had been unkind about Hunter's earlier work. Levin himself reviewed this book—rather favorably—but Hunter still wrote in joking protest to the *Times* that Levin should not have been allowed to review the book because he is so prominently mentioned in it. Undoubtedly, the enjoyment Hunter has with his success and his large readership mitigates any great disappointment in the critical estimates of his work. And just as certainly, some of that work qualifies him as one of America's important contemporary writers.

If it is as Evan Hunter that he stakes his claim to be a serious novelist, it is as Ed McBain that he has won a wide following as a police-detective writer. Early in his career, Hunter chose pseudonyms because of prejudice against foreign names. "If you're an Italian-American," he says, "you're not supposed to be a literate person." Although he had used "Hunt Collins" to sign a 1956 novel, *Tomorrow and Tomorrow*, Hunter chose "Ed McBain" for the mystery novels he began writing in the mid-1950s at the urging of Herb Alexander, editor-in-chief of Pocket Books. "The mystery writer is still considered a stepchild," Hunter said. "Besides, there's an ease with a mystery. You don't have the pressure to win mainstream approval. You don't have to worry if it will be reviewed or not." Other reasons he gives for the use of the McBain pseudonym are that "I don't like to confuse critics—who are very easily

-26-

"One Heineken beer, very cold," David's waiter said at his elbow.
"Your steak'll be along in a minute, sir."

"Thank you," David said.

The tall girl with the blond hair was still sitting alone at her table ~~when David~~ when David signed for his check and went upstairs to his room.

\#

Ah, God, he thought, ah, Molly, he thought, how the hell did we get so old so young? You appeared -- long blond hair blowing in the wind, the flutter of a summer dress, a hint of petticoat below -- you appeared. And started to turn from the boardwalk railing, from the sea, green eyes flashing in the sunlight, golden sunlight splashing wanton freckles onto an Irish button nose (a ~~pretty~~ shiksa, no less), recklessly tossing freckles onto a perfect Irish phiz. You ~~suddenly~~ laughed to a girlfriend, ~~and~~ the laughter was carried by the wind far out over the sea. And you turned. You turned in slow motion, perky Dublin breasts in a flimsy summer bodice, cotton print flapping, ocean breeze lifting the skirt over long legs, your hand reached down to flatten it. All in slow motion.

You stepped out of sunlight, Molly.

And my heart raced like the swift click of your sandals on that splintered Rockaway boardwalk. I stood transfixed and watched you moving away, chattering with your girlfriend, drifting off into a crowded ~~glittering~~ distance of hot dog stands and cotton candy carts. And I thought, oh my God, I thought, <u>Move!</u> Follow her! ~~Don't~~ Don't let her get away! And I...

Page from the revised typescript of "Far from the Sea"

confused anyway. I also do not like to confuse readers." He elaborates the latter reason: "I wouldn't like a woman, for example, who had read *Mothers and Daughters* by Evan Hunter, to pick up *The Heckler* by Evan Hunter and find that it's about mayhem, bloodshed and violence. I think this would be unfair to her and unfair to me as well." It is a mark of the practiced, journeyman writer who understands his voices and his readers that Hunter has been able to sustain both Hunter and McBain for better than twenty-five years.

What distinguishes the 87th Precinct series is that, first, McBain's series protagonist is essentially an entire precinct squad; although detective Steve Carella is seen by most readers as the central character in the series, he is notably absent from some of the books and figures only peripherally in others. Other squad members play key roles in the books, many of which deal with multiple crimes/cases at once—as would actually be the situation at a precinct station in a large city such as Isola, McBain's thinly-disguised Manhattan. Second, from its earliest novels, the 87th Precinct series has been noted for its accuracy and authenticity in describing police procedures. The men of McBain's 87th Precinct investigate methodically; there are few breaks that have not been painstakingly purchased with shoe leather. McBain, whose original contract called for at least three novels in the series, knew he wanted to establish the squad as a "conglomerate hero" and that he wanted to add realism by establishing solid investigative procedure as authentically as possible. Consequently, he studied police department forms, directives, and methods so thoroughly that, according to James McClure, McBain "has become, in effect, the Norman Rockwell of the police procedural."

Detective novels are the stuff of popular culture—well known, familiar, reliable, and profitable for the producer. Hunter makes no claim to painstaking art in the generation of an 87th Precinct novel: "I write the Ed McBain mysteries in a month. I write them very swiftly with very little revision. I try to keep them entertaining, suspenseful, and exciting." Though these novels are rather hurriedly composed, they do have their stylistic moments, as in the opening lines of *Ghosts* (1980): "They might have been ghosts themselves, the detectives who stood in the falling snow around the body of the woman on the sidewalk. Shrouded by the swirling flakes, standing in snow three inches deep underfoot, they huddled like uncertain specters against the gray facade of the apartment building." The 87th Precinct series deserves its popularity for its

procedural fidelity, its general plausability, stylistic touches, and crisp dialogue. The series has sold an estimated fifty-three million copies and has been translated into nineteen languages. It is not surprising that it inspired a television series and that several of the books have been made into films, including *Cop Hater*, *The Mugger*, *The Pusher*, and *Fuzz*.

Ultimately, whether or not Evan Hunter's work will ever be critically acclaimed is probably less important than the fact that he has abundantly realized his own American dream of being a productive and successful writer.

Plays:

The Easter Man, Birmingham, U.K., Birmingham Repertory Theatre, 1964; produced again as *A Race of Hairy Men!*, New York, Henry Miller's Theatre, April 1965;

The Conjuror, Ann Arbor, Michigan, Lydia Mendelssohn Theatre, 5 November 1969.

Screenplays:

Strangers When We Meet, adapted from Hunter's novel, Columbia Pictures, 1960;

The Young Savages, adapted from Hunter's *A Matter of Conviction*, United Artists, 1961;

The Birds, adapted from Daphne du Maurier's short story, Universal, 1963;

Fuzz, adapted from Hunter's novel as McBain, United Artists, 1972;

Walk Proud, adapted from Hunter's novel, Universal, 1979.

Other:

"About that Novel," *Writer*, 91 (April 1978): 9-11;

"The 87th Precinct," as Ed McBain, in *The Great Detectives*, edited by Otto Penzler (Boston: Little, Brown, 1978), pp. 87-97.

References:

Robert Dahlin, "PW interviews: Evan Hunter," *Publishers Weekly*, 219 (3 April 1981): 6-7;

Fran Krajewski, "An Exclusive Re-Visit with Evan Hunter," *Writer's Digest*, 51 (April 1971): 24-26;

James McClure, "Carella of the 87th," in *Murder Ink*, edited by Dilys Winn (New York: Workman, 1977), pp. 301-305.

Carobeth Laird

(20 July 1895-   )

Peter A. Scholl
Luther College

BOOKS: *Encounter with an Angry God: Recollections of My Life with John Peabody Harrington* (Banning, Cal.: Malki Museum Press, 1975);
The Chemehuevis (Banning, Cal.: Malki Museum Press, 1976);
Limbo (Novato, Cal.: Chandler & Sharp, 1979).

It was not until she was nearly eighty that anyone recognized that Carobeth Tucker Harrington Laird had much to say, that she could write with passion and precision about the many things she had experienced and learned over her long life in the American Southwest. Her first published book was *Encounter with an Angry God* (1975), a memoir that records her impressions of living with and working as an unpaid assistant to the legendary ethnologist-anthropologist (and her first husband), John Peabody Harrington. *Encounter with an Angry God* is also about her love for and marriage to her second husband, George Laird, a Chemehuevi Indian she and Harrington met in the course of their work. It is a tale that renders vivid scenes and anecdotes of her arduous fieldwork among many native peoples of the Southwest in the early quarter of the twentieth century. Her descriptions of her life camping out in the deserts or living in tiny, out-of-the-way settlements are given from the perspective of someone who was always seen by the Great World as part of the background, one of the people to whom things simply happen. Yet late in life, she somehow found the strength and courage to write her story so well that Tom Wolfe was moved to say, "Never before have I heard of an exciting new literary talent bursting forth at the age of eighty. But here, I am convinced, we have one." Her second book, *The Chemehuevis* (1976), was actually made up from her first completed, book-length manuscript. Much of it was written in close collaboration with George Laird and is largely a compendium of ethnological/anthropological information about the Chemehuevi Indians and their folklore. The book is dedicated to Laird, and it includes a brief biography of him, which supplements the treatment of the Lairds' meeting, marriage, and family

Carobeth Laird

life described in *Encounter with an Angry God*. Carobeth Laird's third book, *Limbo* (1979), is a memoir of her lonely ordeal in a nursing home, which she underwent long after George Laird's death.

She was named Carobeth Tucker by her parents, James Harvey and Emma Cora Chaddock Tucker, who lived in the small town of Coleman, Texas, where she was born on 20 July 1895. Her father owned some land in the area and was a printer and publisher of the *Coleman Democrat-Voice*. She remembers growing up as an only child, "lonely, sickly, tense, introspective, and overprotected." She learned to read when she was five but did not enter school until she was nine; all her life, her education was largely informal. When she was fourteen, her family took the first of three successive summer trips to Mexico, where her father had lived as a youth. In that country, Laird exercised her talent for learning and speaking languages, an ability that later gained the attention of Harrington. In her sixteenth year, on one of the Mexico visits, she fell in love with an older man, John Dresser, whom the family had met while traveling. Their romance ended without marriage, but Laird was left with a daughter to support. The child was named Elizabeth Tucker Dresser, born 4 June 1913, and was raised primarily by her maternal grandparents in San Diego, California, where the Tuckers had moved in February of the same year.

The story of Carobeth Laird's life from that period through the 1940s is detailed in the autobiographical *Encounter with an Angry God*. The book opens with her account of her youthful excitement in the world of learning; though she had not finished high school, she talked her way into the 1915 summer session of the San Diego Normal School, and one of the courses she chose was linguistics. When her teacher walked into the room, her heart "seemed to stop. I silently and romantically exclaimed that he looked 'like an angry god.' " His deific appearance was to prove deceptive, though this man did turn out to have qualities that set him apart from other men. Carobeth Tucker would be twenty in one month; John Peabody Harrington was thirty-one and already totally involved with his work as a linguist-ethnographer. This work was also his obsession, his towering passion, his "monomania," as Tom Wolfe put it.

J. M. Walsh, Harrington's biographer, wrote that *Encounter with an Angry God* is "a must for any student of Anthropology and Harringtoniana." Frequently referred to as "the mystery man of American anthropology," Harrington was a bizarre figure whose capacity for work and, to many, perverse dedication to the task of collecting data about American Indian languages and cultures was first described in detail in Carobeth Laird's account. Though the number of readers who will come to the book out of a desire to learn more about Harrington may be limited, he is soon revealed as a character whose enormous eccentricities make him interesting even to those unconcerned with the saga of American anthropology.

Harrington was born into an old and proper New England family in Waltham, Massachusetts, on 29 April 1884. His family moved to Santa Barbara, California, when he was two. He studied philology and classic and modern languages at Stanford and

Berkeley, where he graduated at the head of his class—in a hurry, as always—after only two and a half years. He was elected to Phi Beta Kappa and won a Rhodes Scholarship, which he declined in favor of study at the Universities of Leipzig and Berlin, where he concentrated on linguistics. He never took his Ph.D., though he was awarded an honorary Doctor of Science degree from the University of Southern California in 1934. He feared that formal academic credentials would encourage offers to teach and the compulsion to publish; such demands, he felt, would impede the real work he was in such haste to further.

He "hated teaching, particularly he hated having been inveigled or coerced into teaching in this summer school," writes Laird about the circumstances under which the two first met in the linguistics class. "Even then," she continues, "he was in the grip of his grand obsession, his compulsion to record all that could be recovered of the remnants of the cultures, and most especially of the languages of the Indians of Southern California." What seemed to young Carobeth his passionate interest in her was more likely his passionate interest in how she could assist him in his task. She had attracted his attention in the first place with her talent for phonetic transcription—her remarkable ear for languages. This was a crucial skill in his work, and *Encounter with an Angry God* details how he eagerly set forth grooming her to be his helpmate—tutoring her in Russian on her lunch hour, dragging her to a sideshow to catch a few words of the Igorot Indians of the Phillipines, browbeating her into learning to drive a car for him and to type fast enough to take his dictation. All this she did, and more, moving into the field with him to study the Chumash Indians before he had mentioned the possibility of marriage.

Their wedding in June 1916 is mentioned only in passing in *Encounter with an Angry God*. Their daughter, Awona Wilona Harrington, was born 12 February 1917 (her name comes from the Zuni and means "something like God, meaning trail holder"). Children did not interest Harrington, writes Laird, nor did the ordinary comforts and trappings of success. What fascinated him and consumed most of his waking hours was his passion to "Give not, give not the yawning graves their plunder;/ Save, save the lore, for future ages' joy. . . ," as he wrote in a poem used as the epigraph to *Encounter with an Angry God*.

Their life in the field was harsh. But she was strong, as Harrington wrote in a letter quoted by Walsh: "She knows how to drive and works hard and no roughing it is too hard for her even if it comes to living like an Indian squaw." It did come to that, as she suffered from poor food, filth, and worse—the brutal parsimoniousness of her husband, a man so frugal that he wanted her to scrape out eggshells lest they waste any egg.

As Harry Lawton has summarized the contents of *Encounter with an Angry God* in its introduction, it is "an intensely personal reminiscence of the seven-year period in Harrington's life she [Carobeth] was married to him. It is a bittersweet and transcendent book, hauntingly evocative of a time now gone, a token chronicle of what it meant to be a fieldworker in the formative years of American anthropology.... The book is also a love story...." The lovers are Carobeth and George Laird.

George Laird was born 3 March 1871 in the desert near the present site of Blythe, California, to a Chemehuevi Indian woman who may have been named *Pagin nasi i* (Cloud Flower) and Thompson Porter Laird, a white man (with one quarter Cherokee blood), who had run away to the Southwest at the age of twelve from his native state of Tennessee. George grew up in a time of cultural upheaval—the Chemehuevis were being engulfed, their culture being altered by mixture with the Mohaves and by the intrusions of the Hispanics and white Americans. His mother died of smallpox when he was six, and he spent most of his early days surviving without any parental guidance. "By the time he was twelve," Carobeth Laird wrote of him in *The Chemehuevis*, he had "his own horse, his own rope and saddle and was doing a man's work and earning almost a man's wages—fifty cents a day and found." He was fluent in Chemehuevi, Mohave, Spanish, and English, though he had had no formal schooling. He knew many of the old Chemehuevi myths and songs and much of the old way of speaking; and his facility in other languages made him an ideal informant for the work that Harrington and his wife were doing.

George Laird and Carobeth Harrington met in Parker, Arizona, in 1919. Though married at the time, Carobeth had come to the Chemehuevi lands without Harrington, who was in New Mexico studying the Tanoan languages of that area. In his haste to gather material, he had previously sent his young wife on extended, solitary missions among the Indians. Her first meeting with George was "the pivot on which my life turned," she wrote in *Encounter with an Angry God*; she describes the glance they exchanged as a "moment of alchemic transformation, that 'meeting of the eyes' which committed me to another man for life—and for eter-

nity...." Her allegiance to Harrington, as *Encounter with an Angry God* reveals, had already begun to disintegrate. As they had parted shortly before her meeting with George, they had quarreled, and she had left his embrace thinking, "I called him an angry god ... and all the while he was just a dirty little boy having a tantrum."

George was very dark and a "simple laboring man," "built like the buffalo," with the broad chest characteristic of his tribe. He was in all essential points a man unlike Harrington. Their differences were soon to stand out in clear juxtaposition when Harrington summoned Carobeth—and, curiously, George as well—to Santa Fe. The love between George and Carobeth was first spoken and consummated during this period when all three lived in the same adobe house in Santa Fe. The bond between the twenty-four-year-old white woman and the forty-eight-year-old Indian grew stronger during a winter in Washington, D.C., where Harrington had to go periodically in connection with his work. By now she was no longer in awe of her husband and chose easily between the two men, rejecting the frenetic, secretive scholar for the unhurried, spiritual George. In the spring of 1920, Carobeth announced to Harrington that she was leaving him to drive back to California with George.

She finally filed for a divorce, and it was granted in May 1923; she and George were married on 23 August 1923, but her mother refused to release Carobeth's children to their custody. The couple settled down on a small ranch in Poway, California, raising grapes and tending an orchard, barely scraping by. *Encounter with an Angry God* presents this period as the happiest years of Carobeth's life: "I see sun-browned children tumbling in the dust beside a row of tall yellow and orange marigolds. I see flowers of all kinds...." Their four children are Mary Rosaleen (born 25 July 1926), Oliver Porter (born 27 April 1928), Margaret Clark (born 16 August 1931), and George Theodore (born 23 December 1932).

Following the stillbirth of a child in 1931, Carobeth Laird fell into a depression that did not lift for more than a year. Her father died, and Laird felt herself drifting "further and further into a realm of dreams...." What brought her "back to the light" was Christian Science. Her receptivity to these beliefs was probably increased by her long acquaintance, through George's agency, with "the metaphysical nature of Chemehuevi myths and shamanism...." Both of them found new strength in the church, and they were instrumental in organizing a group of believers in tiny Poway. The day

499

is a marker of some sort to remind them that their journey had a

destination and a purpose? These "helpers," ~directly related to~ those ancient shamans

who had invented the art of placing sacred symbols upon stone, came

when summoned by the song of power; but they also had wills of their

own, not always in subjection to the healer to whom they "belonged"

--or who belonged to them.

In a letter of September 20, 1981, Beverley Trupe writes: "/W/e

cannot overlook the fact that there was likely some Mohave influence

in the area and at this site /Counsel Rocks/--glyph styling alone in-

dicates two artistic methods." There is indeed every reason to assume

that, the ancestors of the Chemehuevi and the ~ancestors of the~ Mohave were neighbors a long time ago.

Then as in the more recent period, the ~there may well have been a sort of love/hate~ relationship, characterized by

~alternate~ periods of cooperation and enmity, visiting back and forth, mutual

curiosity and mutual contempt. It would appear ~is possible~ that bothxpeoplesxxx

Counsel Rocks was a locality sacred to both peoples, that both left

their sacred markings there and there participated separately in

their sacred rites. In Chemehuevi mythology Coyote was the progenitor

of the Chemehuevi (according to some sweeping statements, of all man-

kind; but always and most emphatically of the Chemehuevi) and all the

animal-people are tacitly identified with the Chemehuevi. In like

manner Chemehuevi thought identifies the Tutusiwi, the Ogres, as the

progenitors of the Mohave. This is made explicit in the commentary

which commonly followed narration of "Struggle for the Handstone" (7-2).

Cicada appears as a culture hero in Mohave mythology. But in the

Chemehuevi myth, translated into history, would seem to picture Cicada

and Horned Toad as two Chemehuevi travelers intruding upon a Mohave

fertility rite. In 12-2 ("How Chipmunk Killed the Ogres") the

Tutusiwi again appear, this time in connection with a grisly game of

wre called "cutting off raw while still a little high." Does this

A page from the corrected typescript of a work-in-progress

after the first official Christian Science lecturer came to Poway, George broke his leg when he fell from a truck. Five days later, on 13 April 1940, George Laird died of pneumonia.

In the lean years that followed George's death, Carobeth Laird saw Harrington one last time. He had "at long last" invited his daughter to visit him, and Carobeth went along to make sure it would be all right. To her middle-aged eyes he was "seedier than ever," nothing like a god; and she felt "a very faint pity mixed with superiority, because my life had been so rich and varied and his was obviously running along in the same old rut." Later, hoping that he might buy or help her find a publisher for her Chemehuevi material, she sent him a manuscript, which "consisted of a series of papers George and I had worked on together." But she heard no more of these until after he was dead. He had packed them all away with the "more than 1,000 boxes containing approximately 800,000 pages of field notes in the National Anthropological Archives of the Smithsonian alone . . ." and the other materials he had been storing here and there throughout his long career, always fearful of publication lest someone else should anticipate the great synthesis he was always postponing.

These lost manuscripts and papers, discussed in the closing pages of *Encounter with an Angry God*, eventually became the basis for Laird's second book, *The Chemehuevis* (1976). The papers had turned up among Harrington's effects after he died in 1961, and Laird retrieved copies of them around 1971.

It was the rough draft of *The Chemehuevis* that circuitously led to Laird's discovery by the world of letters. In 1971 two anthropology students were sent to conduct a survey among the Chemehuevi people in Parker, Arizona. They were told that they should interview Georgia Laird Culp; there in her home they also met her mother, Carobeth Laird. When the students made their report, their teacher, Lowell John Bean, was intrigued to see the name of Carobeth Tucker Harrington Laird. He had seen the name before when it was listed as coauthor of essays among John Peabody Harrington's papers at the Smithsonian. He arranged a meeting, and learned of her life and work and of the manuscript of *The Chemehuevis* that had by now been rejected by a university press on the grounds that it "needed to be rewritten from a contemporary theoretical perspective." But Bean, according to Harry Lawton, recognized that Laird's approach transcended the theoretical fashions of anthropology, and he began seeking a publisher.

The Chemehuevis includes chapters on the "Identity, Distribution, and Organization" of the Chemehuevi Indians, as well as on related subjects such as "Shamanism and the Supernatural," "Kinship and Personal Relationships," and much on their mythology. The introduction is a narrative account of George Laird's life, and the book is presented "as a memorial to a remarkable man, in the hope that it will serve the interests of the People with whom he never ceased to identify himself."

Her third book, *Limbo*, begins in the summer of 1974, when Laird, long widowed, was living in a mobile home owned by her daughter Georgia on the Chemehuevi reservation. She awoke one night in desperate pain from a diseased gallbladder. This book tells how she survived emergency surgery and hospitalization, first in Lake Havasu City, Arizona, and later on the Chemehuevi reservation. The first circle of Hell invoked by the title is a nursing and convalescent home in Phoenix, which she calls "Golden Mesa" in the book: "The name was painted in large letters on a sign. . . . For a moment I thought it might as well have read: 'Abandon hope all ye who enter here. . . .' " She was seventy-nine years old, in precarious health, estranged from nearly all her children, almost completely destitute, and in a strange city.

Her trials with disease and the venal bureaucracy and petty tyrants of Golden Mesa do not, as she explains, comprise "a tale of horror, of filth and overt cruelty." It is rather an articulate memoir which gives an insider's view of what it is like to live in institutionalized care. "It is," as she explains, "an account of one person's efforts to hold onto sanity and identity in an atmosphere which was, by its very nature, dehumanizing. It dwells of necessity upon those trivialities of daily routine which loom so large in the lives of the helpless and isolated."

The inflexible rules, the mind-deadening routine, and the unpalatable food were perhaps more tolerable than the maddening condescension of the staff—a matter that Tom Wolfe remarked upon: "Only after she began receiving proofs of *Encounter with an Angry God*, addressed to Dr. Carobeth Laird (she does not, in fact, have a doctorate) did the personnel stop talking to her in the language known as Cuckoo Senile Wee-wee Singsong."

In November 1974 Laird "escaped" from the Phoenix nursing home through the intervention of friends. Though fully recovered from her gallbladder surgery, she was still quite ill. Yet she had already been working on the galley proofs for *Encounter with an Angry God*, and her desire to keep writing was running high. The work was soon interrupted by more major surgery for hip implantation. Amazing her friends with her ability to recover, she resumed work on *Limbo*, even though the fifty pages she had already drafted had been lost.

In 1975, following the publication of *Encounter with an Angry God*, Laird was busy with interviews, speaking engagements, autograph parties, telephone calls, correspondence, and visitors. And still she worked on *Limbo*. But her health faltered once more. A friend, Anne Buffington-Jennings, was waiting in the intensive care unit after Laird was wheeled out of another dangerous operation: "She was chanting in a rhythmic, timed cadence—the cadence of a heartbeat: 'Live... Live... Breathe...breathe...Live...Live....'" Though she was not conscious at the time, her words communicated the "valiant life force, the power" that propels this woman to see, hear, experiment, and live so hard. Her three books, her early anthropological articles, her many articles in Christian Science periodicals, comprise a body of work that is still growing, as she continues to contribute to the *Journal of California and Great Basin Anthropology*, and expects the publication of another book, "Mirror & Pattern in George Laird's World of Chemehuevi Mythology." She continues to live where she and George Laird worked their ranch in Poway, California.

References:
Rita Rooney, "Carobeth Laird: An Old Woman Dreams—and Writes Books," *Parade* (30 July 1978): 6-7;

Jane Maclaren Walsh, *John Peabody Harrington: The Man and his California Indian Fieldnotes* (Ballena, Cal.: Ballena Press-Malki Museum, 1976);

Tom Wolfe, "Harrington's Wife," *Bookletter*, 1 (26 May 1975): 1-3.

Papers:
Many of Laird's papers are in the Carobeth Laird Collection at the University of California, Riverside.

Robert Ludlum

(25 May 1927-   )

Patricia L. Skarda
Smith College

BOOKS: *The Scarlatti Inheritance* (New York: World, 1971; London: Hart-Davis, 1971);

The Osterman Weekend (New York: World, 1972; London: Hart-Davis, 1972);

The Matlock Paper (New York: Dial, 1973; London: Hart-Davis, 1973);

Trevayne, as Jonathan Ryder (New York: Delacorte, 1973; London: Weidenfeld & Nicolson, 1974);

The Cry of the Halidon, as Ryder (New York: Delacorte, 1974; London: Weidenfeld & Nicolson, 1975);

The Rhinemann Exchange (New York: Dial, 1974; London: Hart-Davis, 1975);

The Road to Gandolfo, as Michael Shepherd (New York: Dial, 1975; London: Hart-Davis, 1976);

The Gemini Contenders (New York: Dial, 1976; London: Hart-Davis, MacGibbon, 1976);

The Chancellor Manuscript (New York: Dial, 1977; London: Hart-Davis, MacGibbon, 1977);

The Holcroft Covenant (New York: Richard Marek, 1978; London: Hart-Davis, MacGibbon, 1978);

The Matarese Circle (New York: Richard Marek, 1979; London: Hart-Davis, MacGibbon, 1979);

The Bourne Identity (New York: Richard Marek, 1980; London: Granada, 1980);

The Parsifal Mosaic (New York: Random House, 1982; London: Granada, 1982).

Knowing the truth rarely frees Robert Ludlum's characters from the bondage of conspiracy. In each of his thirteen novels truth is as elusive as freedom, and knowers of truth must repeatedly assume sole responsibility for unraveling extraordinarily complicated knots of intrigue. His superman characters tackle cabals of fanatics in

Washington and Moscow (*The Parsifal Mosaic*), international terrorist organizations (*The Matarese Circle*), narcotics rings (*The Matlock Paper*), and devious capitalists drugged by greed and power (*The Rhinemann Exchange*). Ludlum's cynicism sculptures his imagination; no tradition, institution, or organization is sacred. Power corrupts everyone from the suburbanite in New Jersey (*The Osterman Weekend*) to the pope in Rome (*The Road to Gandolfo*). No one deserves the trust implied by reputation or position, and even the heroes learn not to trust themselves. For naive readers who accept fictional truths as nonfictional facts, fictional distrust escalates into paranoia. When the Coleridgean "willing suspension of disbelief" extends beyond the printed page, Ludlum's entertaining fictions become realities.

The truth about Robert Ludlum is that he is America's best-selling suspense novelist. He is published in twenty-three countries and seventeen languages, a testament to the facts that suspenseful adventure appeals to an international audience and that Ludlum is no victim of American parochialism. His combined sales exceed twenty-five million copies, and he is one of the few writers ever to have been in the number-one position on the *New York Times* best-seller list with both a hardcover and a paperback simultaneously. His most recent adventure, *The Parsifal Mosaic* (1982), premiered in the number-one position on the *Times* best-seller list.

Ludlum did not inherit literary prowess, but his family inherited enough money from his maternal great-grandfather, Joseph Marie Jacquard—inventor of the Jacquard Loom—to buy him cultural advantages and a liberal education. Robert Ludlum was born in Manhattan and raised in Short Hills, New Jersey, until the age of nine. After his father's death, he and his mother and sister moved to Connecticut, where he attended the private schools that shaped his mind and imagination. He remembers Kent School as a "proselytizing organization run by fanatics," an early version, perhaps, of the misguided intelligence units in his later fiction. His school days were completed at Cheshire Academy, where he discovered Sir Walter Scott, Charles Dickens, Ernest Hemingway, F. Scott Fitzgerald, Robert Penn Warren, John Steinbeck, and John Dos Passos.

At seventeen Ludlum forged his mother's signature and enlisted in the U.S. Marines. His two years of service (1944-1946) fulfilled his patriotic urge, but his uneventful service must have disappointed him. Although he was stationed at the Pearl Harbor Transit Center, his assignment was as a librarian. He read history assiduously by day while

Robert Ludlum

at night he conscientiously sowed some of the wild oats of an impetuous, high-strung young man. Between Herodotus and Gibbon, Ludlum practiced judo until he could teach it and use it himself in the kind of self-defense required by barroom brawls. Both his reading and fighting inform his fiction. His early and continuing appreciation for historical facts makes possible his inspired interpretation of the facts for his fiction, and his training in martial arts and weaponry grants realism to his heroes' skills and equipment for self-defense. Lüger Sternlichts, Lupos, Graz-buryas, Remingtons, and Browning automatics repeatedly identify his protagonists and antagonists by nation and faction. Weapons also do their intended damage, but the corpses are no more significant than the heartless statistics of wartime losses. Ludlum the novelist willingly sacrifices dozens of fanatics to preserve the secret of the broken code or other fragments of truth.

In 1951 Ludlum was graduated from Wesleyan University in Connecticut with distinction in theater. Several professors served him as mentors, but none more effectively than his teacher of theater, Ralph Pendleton. Pendleton insisted that he understand the historical underpinnings of drama studied, performed, or produced, and he forced Ludlum to recognize the inadequacies of his own acting ability. Through his teacher, Ludlum was made aware of the dramatic and verbal quality of T. S. Eliot, William Saroyan, Lillian Hellman, Arthur Miller, and George Bernard Shaw, whom he now admires most for breaking all his own rules. The gratitude Ludlum owes Pendleton expresses itself in the repeated fictional portraits of generous mentors as well as in the theatrical dialogue, pace, and cues which have become the hallmarks of his fiction.

Shortly before graduation, Ludlum married Mary Ryducha (31 March 1951), now Mary Ryde, from New Britain, Connecticut. With a wife and an imminent family to support (Michael R., born in 1952), Ludlum began a career as an actor. Learning that a cast was being assembled for *Junior Miss*, he went to the stage door and read for the stage manager. Then he read for Moss Hart and, in a few weeks, was on Broadway. In a short time, so was Mary Ryde as Michelle Ryder. Both met with some success as actors on stage and television. As the family grew (Jonathan C., born in 1953; Glynis J., born in 1962), Ludlum's desire for classical theater grew greater than his opportunities for serious acting. He jokes about his acting career by saying, "I was always typecast as either a homicidal maniac or a lawyer. I've thought there must be a connection there somehow."

In 1956 Ludlum turned to producing. He brought *The Front Page* and *The Owl and the Pussycat* to Broadway and led the drive to build The Playhouse in the Mall in Paramus, New Jersey. In the late 1960s, he marketed his voice as successfully as he had his acting and producing talents. His was the voice in the commercials for Tiparillos ("Should a gentleman offer a Tiparillo to a lady?"), Braniff ("You'll like flying Braniff style"), and Plunge ("Plunge works fast"). He admits that the money from the last voice-over put one of his children through two years of college. But Ludlum had more to offer the world of show business.

At forty Ludlum established a hard regimen of writing. After eighteen months, *The Scarlatti Inheritance* was sent to ten disapproving publishers. The eleventh, World, published it in 1971, and Ludlum had his first best-seller, a Book-of-the-Month Club alternate. *The Scarlatti Inheritance*, a revision of a short story about the secret financing of the Third Reich by Western businessmen, bears some of the strains of a first novel. But despite its somewhat erratic pace and occasionally melodra-

matic characterization, *The Scarlatti Inheritance* tells a thrilling, compelling tale. It set a standard Ludlum has improved on in each of his later novels.

The Osterman Weekend (1972) unravels a complicated tale of four couples on one weekend in quiet suburban New Jersey, where the future of the United States of America and the free world hangs in balance. Ludlum modeled the insular Saddle Valley, New Jersey, on his childhood home of Short Hills. Early in the story a CIA agent poses as an FCC investigator in a meeting with John Tanner, a dedicated newsman. The agent reveals the plans of Omega, an international conspiracy of fanatics committed to economic insurgency. Tanner, whose closest friends may be members of the conspiratorial clique, is asked to pose for one weekend as "a double agent, or a Politbureau informer, or even a bona fide member of [the CIA]." If all goes according to CIA plans, Omega will reveal itself, divide, and doom itself to failure in Saddle Valley. Tanner reluctantly accepts his role, and his initial distrust inspires more. Deliberately false phone calls and messages from the CIA create havoc in the minds of his three closest male friends as well as in his own; paranoia gradually asserts its claims over all four of the once friendly couples. Beneath the weekend's lighthearted socializing, everyone tests, probes, baits, and divides one couple from another, wives from their husbands. Everyone becomes suspect, even John Tanner, the man who knows the truth. As the tension mounts, Ludlum punctuates the crises with domestic details for realism and then interrupts the realism with bizarre violence. A dead dog in a child's bedroom, a fortress in a basement, and a battleground in an abandoned depot transform the small town into an adult nightmare. John Tanner, the heroic father, is made into an American hero fighting for America's economic future. Behind this fiction, Ludlum lodges his outrage against unethical mergers, Mafia financing, and multinational corporate controls on the world's fragile economy. Tanner's hostility is Ludlum's; the CIA's admitted errors are ours to endure; the resulting violence is consistent with what we find in newspapers every day. Omega may be hard to believe, but the final truth of this fiction is not. The novel exposes the inadequacies of American intelligence operations and our deepest fears that our friends cannot be trusted. *The Osterman Weekend* was the first Ludlum novel to be made into a movie, which was directed by Sam Peckinpah and released in late 1982.

Ludlum's third novel, *The Matlock Paper* (1973), tells of other conspiracies close to home: a narcotics ring supported by college professors, a prostitution ring worked by college students. The place is Connecticut; the hero, a "flawed but mobile," highly motivated college English professor, James Barbour Matlock II, B.A., M.A., Ph.D. Ludlum's alma mater, Wesleyan University, is probably the model for Carlyle University, a bastion of truth masking deception beneath the "quiet wealth, club blazers, and alumni-sponsored regattas." The stakes are lower, but the pattern is much like that of *The Osterman Weekend*: one brave man is chosen to assist the government (this time, the Narcotics Bureau) to expose and eradicate criminal activities. The dean's reluctance to go along with the plan to expose Nimrod, a center for narcotics distribution in New England, is expected and consistent with what American readers know of the institutional loyalty of university deans. What is not expected, however, are Ludlum's imaginative reasons for why Nimrod is at Carlyle University. By the end of the novel, Ludlum has explained the real problems of drug addiction of war veterans, family and peer pressures on college students, and financial management of universities in hard economic times.

Ludlum impresses readers with his easy portrayals of character backgrounds and settings in both *The Osterman Weekend* and *The Matlock Paper*, two of his four novels with American settings. He establishes sure control of his narrative with a balance of description and dialogue. Like actors, his characters respond on cue in well-developed scenes. Whether Matlock is under surveillance or not, every gesture is carefully orchestrated and elaborated for the reader. The problem with such details lies not in their kind but their number. Suspense is controlled by delay. Stretching out the complications makes them seem more complicated. Insignificant observations cluster around the clues to obscure truths in falsehoods, appearances in realities. Ludlum writes dramatically and, as his critics are quick to point out, not always grammatically.

Always his heroes verge on exhaustion so that mistakes can be seen sympathetically. Retrospective narratives can then be daydreams or, most often, nightmares of other times of fatigue. In *The Matlock Paper*, for example, Ludlum writes:

> His body ached. His eyes were swollen and his mouth still had the terrible aftertaste of the combined dosages of Seconal, wine, and marijuana. He was exhausted; the pressures of trying to reach unreachable conclusions were overtaking him. His memory wandered back to the early days in 'Nam and he

recalled the best advice he's ever been given in those weeks of unexpected combat. That was to rest whenever he could, to sleep if it was at all possible. The advice had come from a line sergeant who, it had been rumored, had survived more assaults than any man in the Mekong Delta. Who, it was also rumored, had slept through an ambush which had taken most of his company.

Mini-narratives or flashbacks such as this extend Ludlum's fiction artificially. In his early fiction Ludlum restricted his use of them to his main characters and only occasionally buried important clues to character or plot within such minor flashbacks. In time and with practice, Ludlum uses the flashback as an important functional device for his increasingly complicated narrative structure.

Early and late descriptions of violence, however, need only be scanned. Blood rarely hides important clues. Here is "a sight no human being should ever see more than once in a lifetime, if his life must continue beyond that instant":

> On his front step was Patricia Ballantyne wrapped in a bloodsoaked sheet. Holes were cut in the areas of her naked breasts, blood flowing from gashes beneath the nipples. The front of her head was shaved; blood poured out of lacerations where once had been the soft brown hair. Blood, too, came from the half-open mouth, her lips bruised and split. The eyes were blackened into deep crevasses of sore flesh—but they moved! The eyes moved!

Half-dead bodies have significance principally when they are female and lovers of heroes. Others serve as statistics in the balance of power and the pursuit of justice. Most often Ludlum uses violence to impress upon his readers the seriousness of his outrage against his fictional conspiracy or a related social injustice. In *The Matlock Paper*, for example, Ludlum appeals for public and private funding of universities like Carlyle. He voices his outrage through Dr. Adrian Sealfont, president:

> Where were you when men like myself—in *every institution*—faced the very real prospects of closing our doors! You were safe; we *sheltered* you. . . . And our appeals went unanswered. There wasn't room for our needs . . . . What was *left*? Endowments? Dwindling! There are other, more *viable tax incentives!* . . . Foundations? Small-minded tyrants—smaller allocations! . . . The Gov-

ernment? *Blind! Obscene!* Its priorities are bought! Or returned in kind at the ballot box! We had no funds; we bought no votes! For us, the system had collapsed! It was finished!

Dr. Sealfont speaks in the italics, sentence fragments, and exclamatory voice appropriate to his outrage. His shouting staccato style characterizes many of Ludlum's fictional conversations. Rhetorical questions and one-sentence paragraphs often fill whole pages, and sometimes this kind of feature writing seems rather crude and obvious and misplaced. *The Osterman Weekend* and *The Matlock Paper* contain more than their share of such flaws. In the later novels with international settings, Ludlum gradually achieved greater control over his medium. The fanaticism and outrage remain, however, and so does the moral: "Speculations only. . . . Not the truth; nothing of the truth."

Following publication of *The Matlock Paper*, publishers realized that Ludlum sold as easily as Harold Robbins, Sidney Sheldon, Irving Wallace, James Michener, and James Clavell. He wrote rapidly (about a novel every eight months) and with a style others seem unable to copy. In 1973 he wrote two books under a pseudonym, Jonathan Ryder, as though he were testing his popularity. He even varied his three-word titles to mask his identity. Those novels, *Trevayne* (1973) and *The Cry of the Halidon* (1974), also were best-sellers. As the size of his audience grew, so did the length of his novels and the force of his outrage. *Trevayne* explodes our trust of the American power elite. Andrew Trevayne is appointed head of the congressional subcommittee to investigate defense spending. The deeper he probes into the affairs of Genessee Industries, the biggest of the defense subcontractors, the more clearly he realizes why no one dares expose Genessee. Corruption in the highest places may not surprise anyone, but the abuses of capitalism are less easily controlled than most readers might suspect. *Trevayne* considers the implications of absolute honesty and financial clout.

After *Trevayne*, Ludlum turned his imagination to international conspiracy. In *The Cry of the Halidon* and the following novels, he exposes the complications of international finance, espionage, terrorism, large-scale theft, and historical fanaticism. He returns again and again to interpretations of World War II history (*The Gemini Contenders* and *The Holcroft Covenant*), and again and again he avoids formula writing. He repeats devices with frequency (such as struck matches for signals), but he never duplicates plot patterns. The settings he

knows best—Washington, New York, Rio de Janeiro, Amsterdam, Geneva, Rome—recur, but the alleys and streets change with the needs of the characters and the requirements of the ingenious plots. His research for one novel finds its way into others, but the particular quest for truth and justice is never dependent on the search in a previous work. He claims that his method is no more formulaic or evident than that of James Michener or Leon Uris. His imagination constantly transforms old knowledge into new truths, history into fiction.

Ludlum is a disciplined writer who writes consistently each day. He rises at 4:30 A.M., walks his golden retriever, and eats breakfast. Then he settles down with his yellow legal pad and pencil to begin his minimum daily quota of 1,800 words before quitting at 11:30 A.M. In the afternoon he answers mail until his hour's nap late in the day. Then he looks at what he has written. Conscientiously, he edits out sentimental paragraphs or melodramatic phrases. He socializes easily and genially in his Connecticut home with professorial and professional friends who recognize in him a man whose love of history finds its vent in fiction. He especially enjoys his British MI-6 acquaintances who keep him from egregious errors of fact. His experience with spies is coincidental and literary, but his imaginative narratives suggest he has firsthand experience in the field. He recommends Barbara Tuchman, William Shirer, H. R. Trevor-Roper, and the German apologists. Winston Churchill's volumes provide him with a mine of topics for his fiction, and David Kahn's *Codebreakers* gives him the answers to many of his questions on espionage strategies. Research is a joy for him, but his writing is work. His plots, he says, are no more complicated than the many versions of history which inform them. In history, he believes, nothing is truly peripheral, and, in his fiction, he tries to make substance of even the smallest repeated detail.

In *The Rhinemann Exchange* (1974), for example, David Spaulding's training as an actor makes him capable of discerning truth in faces as well as in situations. Whether he is in the mountains of Spain leading the underground support for defections and escapes from wartime Germany or in Brazil directing the purchase of gyroscopes for American bombers, he is judging people by their facial expressions and relying on his instinct. Spaulding is a master dissembler. He even manages to fool the wily German expatriate industrialist, Erich Rhinemann. His trust of the embassy cryptographer and representatives of the Haganah, the Zionists who found the truth he had been forbidden to know, saves both his life and his cause: to prevent the exchange of industrial diamonds for gyroscopes to continue World War II. David Spaulding, like all of Ludlum's heroes, has a conscience shaped by justice.

The Rhinemann Exchange is the only story Ludlum did not devise himself. He heard it from a nameless stranger on a beach in St. Thomas, where he was vacationing. Perhaps the incident which began the story inhibited Ludlum's creativity, or perhaps he simply needed a change. For whatever reason, *The Rhinemann Exchange* has more excesses than his later novels. The profusion of factions strains the historical background and unnecessarily complicates the story by sheer number. Simple espionage and professional killing combine with tactics of the Gestapo, the German High Command, Zionists, big business, supercapitalists, infiltration, double-crossing, and all shades of American intelligence strategies. Even romance is complicated by embassy connections and a hostage situation. Ludlum must have recognized the inadequacies of *The Rhinemann Exchange*, for he turned next to an entirely different genre of fiction.

The Road to Gandolfo was first published in 1975 under the pseudonym Michael Shepherd. In 1982 it was reissued under Ludlum's name because his reputation was secure enough to sustain the criticism of this jeu d'esprit. The plot is bizarre, but the prose bristles with inside humor. For money and power, Pope Francesco I is kidnapped by former Gen. MacKenzie Hawkins, and the pope's cousin replaces him. While the imposter subsidizes opera companies and calls the Fifth Vatican Council, Pope Francesco enjoys retirement with his kidnapper. The kidnapping itself proceeds with reasonable ease, but Hawkins underestimates the jealousies of the curia and overestimates the value of having a competent pope as the Vicar of Christ. The result is an outrageously funny statement on how stress affects leaders and how little real significance should be ascribed to figureheads of church, state, or any powerful organization. The potential hero, former Maj. Sam Devereaux, is caught in the vortex of the hilarious scam of collecting an exorbitant ransom for the pontiff. He is forced to participate in a conspiracy he later condones. When the conspiracy fails, Sam accepts an extended vacation from the law, ambition, and even curiosity. While the papacy makes a mockery of its allocations, Sam sits comfortably high in the Alps at Chateau Machenfeld with the real pope, his kidnapper, and one of the kidnapper's five wives.

The humor in the farce-comedy *The Road to Gandolfo* comes from the parody of military postures and legal strategies. "Words of a general officer," for example, promise the impossible while legal contracts assure that no one is indictable. With strong leadership and legal controls, the possibilities for extorting the ransom seem more logical than any reader would care to admit. With Ludlum's imagination in control, no reader questions the fun of this entertainment.

Ludlum has repeatedly stressed the fact that he is an entertainer without pretensions. But the fast pace and the complexity of his latest and best books make his entertainments more than a succession of thrilling surprises. With the practice of writing at least a novel a year, Ludlum has mastered the chase of the protagonist, the function of settings, and the character of the antagonists. His thematic outrages extend the action to the world, to justice, and, as always, to truth. With an actor's eye for detail, Ludlum capitalizes on visual impressions within a tight narrative structure. After purging his desire for excesses by writing *The Road to Gandolfo*, Ludlum settled down to serious fiction writing in *The Gemini Contenders* and the five novels which followed.

As in *The Matlock Paper*, the plot of *The Gemini Contenders* (1976) turns on the disposition of a piece of paper—a final confession of Peter, Simon of Bethsaida, who was martyred in Rome 2,000 years ago. His confession describes the suicide of Jesus and the crucifixion of a nameless prisoner who resembled Jesus. Denial of the Resurrection, the central Christian belief, would invalidate Christianity and could initiate worldwide ideological warfare. The search for the document divides families, cardinals, intelligence units, and religious communities. The truth, if the parchment tells truth, remains buried. The consequences of revealing the confession are, to the modern hero, too great to bear even in the 1970s.

The novel stretches from 1939 to the present; from the Italian Alps to suburban America; from wartime to peacetime; from fathers to sons. Connecting the plethora of details are the parchment, a man with a shock of white in his hair, and descendants of Savarone Fontini-Cristi—the man who was first entrusted with the care of the parchment and twenty-six other papers related to the Filioque denials that divided the early Christian church. The home of the Fontini-Cristis—Campo di Fiori—boasts of mass murder, brutal tortures, and concealed secrets reminiscent of Gothic fiction. Fanatical priests from the Order of Xenope conduct thorough searches of the homes and minds of men connected with the documents, but their research is finally futile. For thirty years, the documents remain buried in the grave of a Jewish village boy from Champoluc in the Italian Alps.

Meanwhile in America, another ideological war begins in Washington. Andrew Fontine, grandson of Savarone Fontini-Cristi, takes up arms against the apathy, corruption, and venality pervading every branch of the armed forces. Through Eye Corps, a secret group of eight young military field officers, Andrew leads a campaign for his version of justice. His twin brother, Adrian, a Boston lawyer, opposes the campaign with one for his own version of justice. Eye Corps must be stopped before it controls the military forces and philosophy of the nation. The twin Fontines—Geminis—contend with one another in a chase leading to mortal battle at Champoluc. Individually they unravel the history of their grandfather and father, the tortures of their ancestors. Their antagonists are the same: Theodore Dakakos, a Greek descendant of Annaxas the Strong, the engineer on the train from Salonika bearing the documents to Champoluc; Enrici Gaetamo, ideological descendant of the man with the shock of white hair, a defrocked fanatic committed to the ideals of the Order of Xenope; and each other. Adrian walks in the shadow of the blood spilled by his brother to the burial mountain. There antithetical philosophies converge in violence between American brothers.

Their combat is a battle between versions of truth: Major Andrew committed to power, killing, strength; lawyer Adrian, committed to due process and weighing the consequences of truth. Mortal combat assumes epic proportions. For five pages every available weapon and force is charged with consequences—guns, fists, iron bars, and words wreak physical and psychological damage:

> Flesh and bone and blood filled his universe. The soldier was blown off the ground, his right leg a mass of red-soaked cloth. Adrian started to crawl but he could not; there was no strength left, no air in his lungs. He raised himself on one hand and looked over at Andrew.
>
> . . . .
>
> For several seconds his brother's eyes lost muscular control; they rolled in their sockets, and for an instant the pupils disappeared. Andrew's speech had the inflections of an angry child; his right hand extended into the grave. "I have it now. You can't interfere! Anymore! You can help me now. I'll let you help me. I used to let you help me, remember? You remember how I *always used to*

let you help me?" The soldier screamed the question.

. . . .

> Adrian suddenly recalled their mother's words . . . *he saw the results of strength; he never understood its complications, its compassion. . . .* The lawyer in Adrian had to know. "What should we do with the vault? Now that we've got it, what should we do with—"

This climactic scene visually matches manner and matter. The violence is warranted by the issues raised early in the novel, and the psychological dimensions of the battle are less melodramatic than the italics and ellipses suggest. Ludlum is not a stylist; he does not intend to be. He is a storyteller who knows both his art and his audience. And, most important, he knows which side of the truth he is on. The fact that his readers may be less sure is a credit to his technique of making his antagonists as real as his protaganists. With sympathy for the underdog, Ludlum makes the pain of the victim as genuine as that of the victor. The wounded man cries and writhes while the hero contemplates his deeds. If fault can be found in this element of his characterization, it is in the perseverance and stoicism of the heroes. All too often, they merely wince from traumatizing wounds as they carry on their exposure of lies and conspiracies.

Something of this imbalance remains in *The Chancellor Manuscript* (1977), where Peter Chancellor, a writer, is used as a decoy to lead a secret group of self-appointed saviors to the files of the assassinated J. Edgar Hoover. The narrative trickery of having Chancellor write the novel for Ludlum is more clever than effective, but it excuses the point of view of the victimized, just man. Chancellor is too naive to counter the hired killer, Varek, whose cover is the National Security Council, and, not surprisingly, his heroism outdistances his training.

Ludlum tackles the issue of training in *The Holcroft Covenant* (1978) by deliberately and self-consciously training his unwitting hero, Noel Holcroft, the son of Heinrich Clausen, in espionage, self-defense, and judgment. In a complicated document, Holcroft is charged by his father to make amends for the German holocaust by setting up a Swiss foundation to distribute $780 million to survivors. In a series of italicized commands, Holcroft learns his lessons: *"Carry out the lie logically, then reexamine it, and use the most credible part"*; *"even if the lie is based in an aspect of truth, make sure the person you use it on knows less than you do."* Most of Holcroft's lessons deal with distortions of truth or manipulations of half-truths, for again Ludlum has a point to make, an outrage to vent. Holcroft fends off the machinations of neo-Nazis (Sonnenkinder), international assassins (The Tinamou), vengeful disciples of Nazi opposition (Odessa), and recruiters of children of Nazis (Rache). Between the many skirmishes with death, Holcroft takes time to fall in love with Helden Von Tiebolt, daughter of one of the original members of the covenant "to make amends" for the holocaust. The protection of the survivors of the Wolfsschanze, the conspiracy that tried to assassinate Hitler, is not enough to keep Holcroft and his beloved safe from the fanatical factions vying for power. In fact, the war goes on and on, just as Holcroft's training does: *"Every action must have two alternate, split-second options."*

Love provides Ludlum with an alternative to violence and conspiracy. In his international novels, love counters the strain of extraordinary implications with the intimacy of ordinary ones. Frequently, love is as fierce as the situation which grants the respite for it, but, always, love casts out fear:

> Whatever he expected, he was not prepared for what happened. Her lips were soft and moist, parted as if swollen, moving against his, inviting him into her mouth. She reached up with both her hands and cupped his face, her fingers gently caressing his cheeks, his eyelids, his temples. Still her lips kept moving, revolving in desperate circles, pulling him into her. They stood together. He could feel her breasts pressed against his shirt, her legs against his, pushing into him, matching strength for strength, arousing him.
>
> Then a strange thing happened. She began to tremble; her fingers crept around his neck and dug into his flesh, holding him fiercely, as if she were afraid he might move away. He could hear the sobs that came from her throat, feel the convulsions that gripped her. He moved his hands to her waist and gently pulled his face from her, forcing her to look at him.
>
> She was crying. She stared at him for a moment; pain was in her eyes, a hurt so deep Noel felt he was an intruder watching a private agony.
>
> "What is it? What's the matter?"
>
> "Make the fear go away," she whispered plaintively. She reached for the buttons on her blouse and undid them, exposing the swell of her breasts. "I can't be alone. Please, make it *go away.*"

When Ludlum turns to lovemaking, he can be maudlin or silly. Then he is likely to sprinkle references to fairy tales for sexual innuendo or to make inappropriate puns on shepherd's staffs. His sex scenes are more suggestive than descriptive. Often they function as rewards, as in *The Bourne Identity* (1980) where gratitude for life leads to love:

> She was in a soft yellow nightgown, nearly white, pearl buttons at the neck; it flowed as she walked toward the bed in her bare feet. She stood beside him, looking down, then raised both her hands and began unbuttoning the top of the gown. She let it fall away, as she sat on the bed, her breasts above him. She leaned toward him, reaching for his face, cupping it, holding him gently, her eyes as so often during the past few days unwavering, fixed on his, "Thank you for my life," she whispered.
>
> "Thank you for mine," he answered, feeling the longing he knew she felt, wondering if an ache accompanied hers, as it did his. He had no memory of a woman and, perhaps because he had none she was everything he could imagine; everything and much, much more. She repelled the darkness for him. She stopped the pain.

The healing power of sex works for both men and women, but Ludlum reserves its joys for his protagonists. His villains may look seductive, but their bedrooms, if any, are closed to us. Ludlum's heroines are always more than sex symbols for his heroes. In his early novels, their function is more often revelatory than active, but, in his last and best novels, a bright woman is required for more than directions and explanations.

In *The Matarese Circle* (1979), Antonia, granddaughter of the old woman who shares her truth with Vasili Taleniekov and Bray Scofield, proves the worth of her training in the Red Brigades. The history of her rapes and tortures cannot keep her from posing as a decoy and killing those who attack Bray Scofield, the man she loves. She is drugged and tortured for information, but she refuses to reveal what she knows of the seventy-year-old conspiracy formed by Guillaume de Matarese in Corsica. Her history inures her to the massacres she hears of and witnesses; she has the strength of her murdered grandmother. While Bray Scofield pieces together the last of the information on the descendants of Matarese's conspiracy, Antonia and Teleniekov are made hostages of the son of the Shepherd Boy, the one whose voice is crueler than the wind. The Shepherd Boy killed the founder of the Matarese conspiracy, and his son became one of its leaders. Finding him is the last of the searches

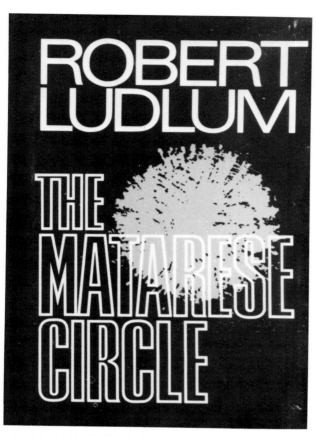

*Dust jacket for Ludlum's eleventh novel (1979), about an
international terrorist organization*

conducted by the best agents of the Soviet Union
and America; destroying him and his dominion is
the last effort of their collaboration.

The search moves to Boston, to Joshua Appleton IV, senator and front-runner for the U.S.
presidency. The family bears a marked resemblance to the Kennedy family, but its residence
looks much as the Villa Matarese must have on 4
April 1911, when the Council of the Matarese was
formed. Joshua Appleton IV, model American,
turns out to be Julian Guiderone, son of the
Shepherd Boy. He and his Council support terrorist
organizations throughout the world for the purpose of paralyzing governments, creating chaos and
a vacuum that will welcome a new generation of
Matarese philosopher-kings for the world. Their
ultimate plan is to eliminate governments altogether. Then multinational corporations will be
free to operate without restrictions, without gov-
ernmental regulations. Man, it is assumed, would
then be measured by his productivity, freed from
fear of violence by values of the marketplace. The

Matarese plan has as much truth as any utopia to its
believers, but its fanatical supporters more nearly
resemble the killer society of Hasan ibn al-Sabbah in
the eleventh century than the Oneida Community.
The combined talents of the best Soviet and American agents destroy the Matarese vision before it
overtakes the governments of every nation in the
world. The best of espionage and terrorism makes
action and reaction the pattern of every chapter.
Love of Antonia and suspicion of Teleniekov keep
Bray Scofield running toward truth. His difficulty
in finding others to believe what he and Teleniekov
know demonstrates the loneliness of power, the
perilous position of those who hold fragile truths.
Scofield deserves the woman he pines for, but
Ludlum's ending echoes Ian Fleming's humorous
passions with James Bond and his various lovers.

Without Marie St. Jacques, a Canadian
economist, Jason Bourne in *The Bourne Identity*
(1980) would never find his real identity. The story
begins with a dramatic rescue of a nameless shooting victim. His survival is just short of miraculous.
The loss of his memory seems a small price to pay
for his life. A Swiss bank account reveals his name,
but his enemies reveal themselves by gradual
shadows. The assassins of several governments, including America, haunt Jason Bourne throughout
Europe and throughout his memories of Vietnam
horrors. The repeated riddle "Cain is for Carlos
and Delta is for Cain" recalls the moment David
Webb, career foreign service officer in Vietnam,
killed one Jason Bourne to avenge the bombing of
his family and the kidnapping of his brother by the
Vietcong. Jason Bourne is an alias; Delta is the
operation founded by Webb, code name Cain; and
Carlos is the international assassin he pursues relentlessly. As Bourne-Cain recovers his memory and
skills, he abducts and then saves Marie St. Jacques
from a brutal rape. With her, then, he assumes
the responsibilities of "the chameleon," the agent
who can blend into any crowd, any scene, for any
purpose.

The presence of Marie allows Ludlum to suspend use of the rhetorical questions that mar his
earlier fiction. Instead of the hero asking himself
questions, he asks them of Marie St. Jacques, and
she comes up with better answers than those most
readers would imagine. Her contacts, her knowledge of the current events of Europe, and her
familiarity with the various cities and hotels and
countrysides they visit endow Bourne-Cain with far
more credibility than he would have alone. The
peculiarly chaste romance which punctuates the
crises humanizes the hero and strengthens the

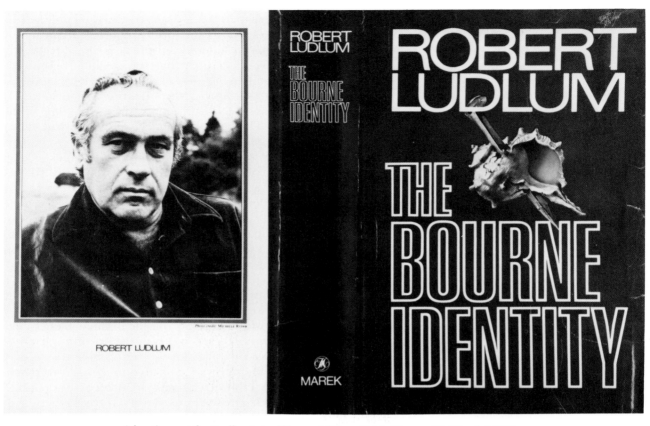

*Advertisement for Ludlum's twelfth novel (*New York Times, *23 March 1980)*

heroine. At the last moment, however, Marie fails to recognize the chameleon dressed as an old man before a New York brownstone. Cain finds Carlos and faces him alone. Armed with skills of a soldier and fragments of memories, Bourne-Cain attacks and defends himself from the knife, gun, and grip of a faceless enemy. The final confrontation extends for twelve pages with brief reminders that the combat is worth far more than two men's lives. Clandestine operations of governments around the world rest on the outcome. If Carlos lives, the world remains insecure. Global deception, called Medusa, is everywhere; "it cannot go unchallenged." Reducing it to a battle of two men simplifies entanglements, reduces complexities. The pattern is one Ludlum appreciates: if evil can be localized, it can be controlled. Bourne-Cain finds a part of his identity in the scope of *The Bourne Identity*, but Carlos—the archetype of conspiracy, the focus of deception, the embodiment of evil—lives.

Ludlum's most recent novel is unquestionably his best. In *The Parsifal Mosaic* (1982) he combines the excellences of his past fiction with new devices, such as foreign phrases and feminine partnership.

The story opens with an intelligence agent, Mikhail Havlicek (Michael Havelock), watching the supposed execution of the woman he loves, Jenna Karas, on a deserted Spanish beach. He springs the trap because he is convinced that Jenna is an agent of the Soviet Voennaya, an organization of fanatics more dangerous than the KGB. The pain of her betrayal and the necessity of her death force Havelock into retirement. Before settling down to the writing of class lectures for a New England college, he decides to travel, to "revisit all those places he had never really visited—in the sunlight." In Athens, for no reason he can imagine, "one of the most powerful men in the Soviet KGB" tells him that Jenna Karas was never a Soviet agent. In Rome Havelock glimpses Jenna in the railroad station and begins a chase for her and for the reasons he had been led to believe she deserved death. First alone and later with Jenna, Havelock travels to uncommon places in Greece, Spain, Italy, France, and the eastern United States (in all of which Ludlum seems comfortably at home). Their mutual Czechoslovakian heritage ties them to Anton Matthias, the American secretary of state. As "friend, mentor, surrogate father" to Michael, the statesman, modeled on Henry Kissinger, should know the source of deception. But Matthias does not know. He has been trapped by a malign force, code-named Parsifal, into signing nuclear first-strike treaties with both the Soviet Union and China. If either nation finds out about the other, a nuclear holocaust cannot be avoided.

Through an ingenious series of contacts and probes, murders and kidnappings, Michael Havelock unravels a conspiracy larger than any of Ludlum's earlier ones. His outrage that one man could be vested with power as great as Matthias's is revealed in his intrigue. The all-powerful Matthias is crippled by senility and the stress of his own position. Havelock, strengthened by Jenna, uncovers vast systems of infiltration and an American refugee camp with a strong resemblance to Dachau. In addition to the Voennaya, he writes of the *paminyatchiki*, Soviet children raised in America to serve as deep-cover spies. Surprises, crises, and maneuvers overlay and redefine each other with constant complications. But to Ludlum and to his devoted readers the mosaic is entertainment—not at its loveliest, perhaps, but at its most complex.

Christopher Lehmann-Haupt and John Leonard, regular reviewers of Ludlum for the *New York Times*, have answered each other's criticism of Ludlum's superman heroes, tortured plots, overwrought prose, and chaste sex scenes. Both admit that the excesses heighten the pleasure of reading the fast-paced adventures. "I like my Robert Ludlum excessive," Lehmann-Haupt admits. Ludlum, he thinks, calls up "the adolescent fantasies that hide in all of us . . . and as an exploiter of adolescent fantasies he is simply very good."

The increasing complexity of plot and structure in Ludlum's fiction has gradually added some depth to his characterization and dialogue, but his style still begs for more substance than his expletives, exclamations, and fragmented and run-on sentences contribute. Nonetheless, his readers will no doubt remain content to set aside their critical tools long enough to enjoy the imaginative search for truth in Ludlum's complicated narratives.

Interviews:

Henry Kisor, "Robert Ludlum merrily stirring a stew of spies," *Chicago Sun-Times*, 7 March 1982, pp. 24-27;

Richard Sandomir, "The Ludlum Identity," *Compass* (14 March 1982): 1-7;

Patricia Holt, "Ludlum Dashes Through," *San Francisco Chronicle*, 5 April 1982;

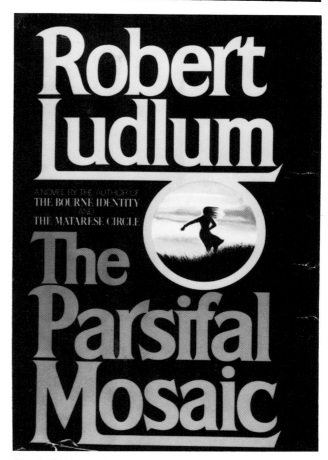

Dust jacket for Ludlum's thirteenth novel (1982), which reached the number one position on weekly New York Times *best-seller list*

George Christy, "The Great Life," *Hollywood Reporter*, 8 April 1982, p. 23;

Michael J. Bandler, "The Ludlum Mosaic: A thriller writer who escapes in history," "Book World," *Chicago Tribune*, 18 April 1982, p. 2;

Lorenzo Carcaterra, "The Ludlum Solution," *New York Sunday News Magazine*, 2 May 1982, pp. 14-15, 17, 22.

References:

Jerry Adler, "The Ludlum Enigma," *Newsweek* (19 April 1982): 32;

John Barkham, Review of *The Parsifal Mosaic*, *Middletown* (Conn.) *Press*, 30 March 1982;

Christopher Lehmann-Haupt, "Books of the Times," Review of *The Bourne Identity*, *New York Times*, 20 March 1980, III: 23;

Lehmann-Haupt, "Books of the Times," Review of *The Parsifal Mosaic*, *New York Times*, 2 March 1982, III: 10;

John Leonard, "Books of the Times," *New York Times*, 13 March 1978, III: 19;

Leonard, "Paranoia Versus Greed," *New York Times*, 5 April 1977, p. 31;

Charlie Lynah, "Robert Ludlum: Master of Intrigue," *Connecticut Today* (3 May 1982): 4-5;

Phil Thomas, "Ludlum Says His Books Popular Because of 'Age of Conspiracy,'" Associated Press, 11 April 1982.

John Nichols
(23 July 1940-)

Carl R. Shirley
University of South Carolina

BOOKS: *The Sterile Cuckoo* (New York: McKay, 1965; London: Heinemann, 1965);

The Wizard of Loneliness (New York: Putnam's, 1966; London: Heinemann, 1967);

The Milagro Beanfield War (New York: Holt, Rinehart & Winston, 1974; London: Deutsch, 1977);

The Magic Journey (New York: Holt, Rinehart & Winston, 1978);

A Ghost in the Music (New York: Holt, Rinehart & Winston, 1979);

If Mountains Die: A New Mexico Memoir, with photographs by William Davis (New York: Knopf, 1979);

The Nirvana Blues (New York: Holt, Rinehart & Winston, 1981);

The Last Beautiful Days of Autumn, with photographs by Nichols (New York: Holt, Rinehart & Winston, 1982).

John Nichols's exceptional skill with the tragicomic mode elevates his novels about ordinary people to the level of the sublimely hilarious and poignant. The everyday lives of his characters often seem extraordinary and, at times, magical.

Born in Berkeley, California, Nichols is the son of a Frenchwoman, Monique Robert, who died when he was two, and David G. Nichols, currently a psychology professor at the University of Colorado. On his mother's side he is descended from "The Bard of Brittany," Anatole Le Braz (1859-1926), the author of stories and poems depicting life in his native region. On his father's side were a number of whalers from around Salem, Massachusetts, and William Floyd, a Revolutionary War general who signed the Declaration of Independence for New York.

During his early years, Nichols moved frequently, living in California, Vermont, Connecticut, New York, Virginia, and Washington, D.C., and attending a dozen schools, but he often spent summers in his grandmother's house in Mastic on Long Island. According to Nichols's own account, that home near the sea was the center of his cultural roots. It was there, with the family treasures of several generations in the attic, that he began to understand the importance of his own history. The nearby ocean, woods, and meadows, along with the abundant natural life, stimulated the young boy's interest in the wonder and magic of nature. In *If*

Mountains Die: A New Mexico Memoir (1979), a highly personal work Nichols compiled with photographer William Davis, he says: "that estate was the most precious and dominating connection with nature I ever had. It also represented a continuity of generations—my real and tangible roots." This influence, which he contends gave him his most "palpable identity," was supplemented by his father's interest in the natural world—the collecting, stuffing, and preserving of small animals and insects. His father and his paternal grandfather were also influential in the areas of storytelling and myth. His father was something of a wanderer and would return home at intervals and tell young John "true" stories and legends, full of real or imaginary characters, all larger than life, and often set against the panorama of nature.

His grandfather's stories and exploits made a deep impression. As a noted ornithologist, biologist, and zoologist, this man for whom John Nichols was named frequently went on collecting trips, often bringing back interesting and unusual stories as well as specimens. Nichols relates one of his accounts of capturing albatrosses by "fishing" for them with hook and line: "Occasionally they would take to the air when hooked, drifting like obstinate kites. And I've often pictured that tall, gaunt, pipe-smoking man, as I remember him from childhood days, dressed in a crumpled fedora and wrinkled old suit, standing on the aft deck of a full-masted sailing vessel, reeling in those enormous birds from out of the iceberg-green air." With such images fixed in his imagination early in his life, John Nichols developed into a novelist with an ability to depict the real world and its people with an air of magic, and a tendency to treat the truly wonderful aspects of life in a matter-of-fact manner. As he states in his diary on 21 April 1969, "shouldn't *Everything* be a miracle?"

A summer spent in the Southwest when he was sixteen (1957) was doubtless extremely important to his eventual decision to move to the region and to his future direction as a writer. Nichols visited Taos, New Mexico, his present home, began to learn Spanish, and had ample opportunity to observe the local flora and fauna. He literally absorbed the environment, both the Anglo and Chicano cultures of the region, and became "westernized." Among the various odd jobs he held was that of volunteer smokechaser. In that capacity he had numerous adventures and met some undeniably wild characters, but was particularly taken by his first encounters with Chicanos. By the end of that summer he was so immersed in this culture that he thought he

would never be able to readjust to Eastern ways. Although it would be more than a decade before he returned to the Southwest to live, the spirit of the region had been firmly implanted in his spirit. He did go back, however, to a Connecticut prep school, the Loomis School, from which he was graduated in 1958. He also attended Hamilton College in Clinton, New York, where he received a bachelor's degree in 1962.

The following year he spent in Europe with relatives in Barcelona and Alicante, Spain, and in Port Blanc, a fishing village in Brittany. As a result of his visit to Spain, he became intensely interested in Hispanic culture, literature, music, and art. According to his own account, he "learned lots of songs on the guitar, got into painting, poetry, plays of García Lorca, learned Spanish, in fact, reading books such as Jimenez's *Platero y yo*." About this same time he also discovered the Nobel Prize-winning Chilean poet Pablo Neruda and became acquainted with Mexican artists such as Jose Guadalupe Posada, Diego Rivera, José Clemente Orozco, and David Alfaro Siqueiros, who "were important influences on my literature." His acknowledged list of influences is extensive—as he says, in Nichols fashion, "millions of writers"—but these are certainly among the earliest.

During this time he worked on his first novel, *The Sterile Cuckoo*. Returning to New York City in 1963, he sold his novel the following year, and it was published in January 1965. It was featured as an alternate selection of the Literary Guild and as a choice of the Doubleday Book Club and has sold well over the years in two paperback editions.

The Sterile Cuckoo is the tale of a young man, Jerry Payne, and his relationship with a girl named Pookie Adams during their college years. Jerry, the novel's narrator, is a conservative, studious boy. As time passes and he and Pookie become friends and then lovers, he experiences a brief transition into a typical, "hell-raising frat man" before emerging as a mature young man at the novel's end. Pookie, who reveals most of her kaleidoscopic life story to Jerry before she even knows his name, is bright, highly unconventional, completely uninhibited, and verbally imaginative in the style of Lewis Carroll. They are a most unlikely pair who develop a funny-sad relationship as he gropes for maturity and she, still clinging to her childhood, searches for a meaningful love. As the book progresses, the reader becomes aware of Pookie's fragile nature, her desire for stasis and obsession with death, all masked by a fun-house facade. The outcome of the novel is predictable, but the characters are so interesting and agreeable, the episodes so well written, and the youthful adventures so entertaining that this weakness does not matter. The reader finds himself fascinated by the manner in which Nichols achieves his novelistic goals. And he does so with a great deal of skill, drawing on his abilities to describe the natural world and to plumb the human spirit as he deals with the theme of death and captures life in the most poignant detail.

The young author in his first novel is capable of remarkably beautiful passages, which reveal his skillful use of imagery:

> That same afternoon in the attic, she came across an old harp her mother had once tried to learn to play. The wooden part was scrolled with leaves and several cherubs' heads, the usual stuff, but what made it very ancient and sad was it had only one string intact. All the others had snapped, and now, like electric hairs, they jumped frozenly out from either side of the frame. Every now and then, when but a little girl lying awake at night in her bed, Pookie had thought she heard a sound, a muffled twung! in the darkness over her head, and it occurred to her suddenly this winter afternoon that the sounds she had heard long ago were the harp slowly dying, and with each string, the little hope that had been her mother's youth, and most likely her own also, going with it.

Jerry serves as the first-person narrator who conveys Pookie's thoughts and feelings along with his own, and there are frequent dramatized passages. One reviewer, Thomas Curley in the *New York Times Book Review* (17 January 1965), observed that "the author's use of his narrator is fairly subtle for a first novelist."

Many people who are not acquainted with Nichols's novels firsthand have heard of *The Sterile Cuckoo* since it was made into a movie in 1968 with Liza Minelli, then emerging as a star, playing the role of Pookie. The location filming, at Nichols's recommendation, was done at his alma mater, Hamilton College. The screen version was a success at the box office, with Minelli receiving an Oscar nomination for best actress. The novel also has an international readership; it has been translated into German, Dutch, Italian, Portuguese (for a Brazilian edition), and Japanese.

In his second novel, *The Wizard of Loneliness* (1966), Nichols again portrays a sensitive young person. The protagonist is Wendall Oler, a ten-year-old boy who is forced to live with his grandparents in Vermont during the closing years of World War II. Death and war provide the thematic background as the author's talent for drawing absorbing and unusual characters, all a bit crazy and most emanating a sense of sadness and fragility, is again in evidence. Wendall's grandfather, old Doc Oler, is a troubled man, hiding behind verbal nonsense such as "detmoles in the rondo-sketiaptic dispeller." Marty Haldenstein, the town's shy, sickly librarian, becomes a friend for a brief period in a scheme to photograph hummingbirds from a tarpaper blind. Duffy Kahler, the village athletic hero presumed dead as a result of war injuries, mysteriously returns and lives secretly in the deserted railroad station as he clings to a thread of sanity. Surrounded by all the lonely townspeople, Wendall, the self-proclaimed "Wizard of Loneliness," begins to understand the world and to shed his own feelings of solitude. This novel is in the tradition of the Bildungsroman, but with a significant difference. Wendall does not quite grow up and discover his unique identity and role in life; rather, in the words of the narrator at the close of the work, "he felt supremely confident for a moment, but not because he had suddenly become a man: it was rather as if, at long last, he had succeeded in opening wide the door to his waning childhood."

Nichols's second novel received mixed reviews—mixed in the sense that almost all reviewers were enthusiastic about some aspects of the writing but were critical of others. James F. Cotter, writing in *America* (26 February 1966), praised the author: "*The Wizard of Loneliness* . . . is a flawless and controlled work of art. It balances humor and despair, symbol and event, character and theme, in a straightforward, eloquent narrative." He predicted that "another great leap forward like this, and he will be a major novelist before he is 30. If he isn't one already."

In spite of such glowing words and such a promising outlook, things were not going well for Nichols. During the period from his return to New York in 1963 through 1968, he became so involved in political organizing, anti-Vietnam war activity, and numerous social causes, that his work was affected: "My novels had disintegrated into shrill, polemical, nihilistic tracts." In an agitated frame of mind and on the pretext of gathering material for a new novel about a Western Indian major league baseball player, the author embarked, "on the day Martin Luther King was assassinated," on a whirlwind, 3,000-mile, five-day trip to the Southwest. The novel, tentatively entitled "The Man with a Coonskin Heart," was never written, but Nichols had reestablished his spiritual ties to the Southwest.

In the fall of 1968, during the filming of *The Sterile Cuckoo*, he continued to be restless, unsettled by social and political concerns. Thinking that perhaps a complete change of environment was necessary to quell his restlessness, he and his wife (whom he since divorced) considered relocating in another part of the United States but for a time could not decide where they wanted to go. As part of his involvement in radical causes, Nichols had been reading a Chicano newspaper, *El grito del norte*, published in northern New Mexico. As a result, his interest in that region and its social, economic, and racial problems was rekindled, and the relocation site was established.

During the spring and summer of the following year, Nichols settled near Taos, New Mexico, in the small community of Upper Ranchitos, where he still lives. After this move there was a lapse of some years before his next novel, *The Milagro Beanfield War*, was published in 1974. According to Nichols's account of this period, which he relates in *If Mountains Die*, he would sit "in the bathtub after dark, worrying because my life lacked energy; and my writing seemed lackluster, unemotional, dull. I found it an enormously tiring ritual, often so boring I wanted to scream. I did entire novels feeling so desperate that sometimes I was actually crying as words went down on paper. It felt as if I was working on the memory of creativity, rather than the real thing."

Nichols spent the fall and winter of 1969 reading the history of northern New Mexico, trout fishing, repairing and remodeling his house, playing hockey, and chopping wood. Gradually, his highly developed social consciousness, combined with living in Taos and his earlier influences in Spain, seem to have provided him a perspective of the Hispanic community of his region that is not often achieved by Anglos. His next group of works demonstrates this unique perspective. A lapse of eight years without having written a novel acceptable to publishers was doubtless frustrating at the time, but the resulting "New Mexico Trilogy" compensates for the frustration. Nichols's innate and particular sense of oneness with the land makes him a spiritual cousin to the Mexican Americans of New Mexico, and his intense involvement with the oppressed and their needs produced a successful novelistic series.

The Milagro Beanfield War is perhaps Nichols's best work and certainly the best of the trilogy. The conflict referred to in the title is set off by the principal character, Joe Mondragon, a handyman and jack-of-all-trades who illegally opens an irrigation canal into his small plot of land in order to water his beans. This simple act is a significant one given the situation in many Western states concerning water rights and land claims, and it provides the impetus for conflicts in the novel. The floodgates of the author's imagination are also opened, and the reader witnesses a phantasmagoria of colorful characters, ranging from Amarante Cordova, called the "human zipper" because he has had surgery so often in his long life, to one-armed Onofre Martinez, an independent man who drives around in a battered pickup truck with a three-legged German Shepherd perched on the cab roof.

Nichols's singular talent creates an original blend of myth and reality in his fictive world. Martinez is the source of a local myth, since every strange or unexplained event in town is said to be caused by "El brazo Onofre," the missing arm, which fell off one day, according to Martinez's account, releasing a huge cloud of crimson butterflies. Several other characters also achieve mythic proportions; the real merges with the fantastic, legend with history, and the ever-present social concern provides the narrative movement. The beanfield becomes a symbol of the plight of the Chicano in New Mexico—lost water rights, lost lands, and exploitation at the hands of outsiders. Wealthy Ladd Devine becomes the symbol of the white Anglo conglomerates which are taking over the people of the valley and destroying an irreplaceable way of life. This work vibrates with the wonder and the woe of human existence in the American Southwest. *The Milagro Beanfield War* is Nichols at his best.

Critical reception to this novel was mixed. The *Choice* reviewer (in January 1975) praised it, drawing comparisons with John Steinbeck, William Faulkner, and Gabriel García Márquez, the Colombian author of *One Hundred Years of Solitude*. He concluded with the statement that "Nichols has written a bawdy, slangy, modern proletarian novel that is . . . a consistently entertaining film scenario while at the same time it manages to make funny-serious sense out of a contemporary situation of endured justice and imminent violence."

Adverse reaction included comments concerning the author's heavy-handed social criticism, his tale-spinning, stereotyped characters, and folksy prose. Frederick Busch, in the *New York Times Book Review* (27 October 1974), also condemned the novel for failing in an attempt to create a myth of the common man.

The second part of the New Mexico trilogy, *The Magic Journey*, was published in 1978. Set in the town of Chamisaville, near Milagro but a much larger settlement, this novel spans the years between the Great Depression and the early 1970s. The chief Anglo villain here is Dale Rodey McQueen, "a sometime prizefighter, medicine-oil hustler, cowpuncher, flesh peddler and general all-around energetic ne'er-do-well." When McQueen's battered yellow school bus loaded with dynamite explodes, the blacksmith repairing it emerges "as tiny particles of his atomized school bus no larger than pollen flakes settled like a fine, golden gauze onto the crater floor." Cipi Garcia is "clad only in boots, and holding, in one hand, a single rose." Later, steaming hot springs burst forth from the crater. Thus begins "progress" in the sleepy, traditional Chicano community as the local entrepreneurs erect a shrine to the "Dynamite Virgin." This newly created tourist attraction provides a need for hotels, bathhouses, and restaurants, and McQueen leads a parade of politicians, developers, and speculators, all intent on amassing dollars at the expense of the Chicano. Hailed by some critics as a major revolutionary novel, *The Magic Journey* eventually focuses on McQueen's daughter, April Delaney, a marvelously well-drawn character, the embodiment of a 1960s radical leader, who finally is destroyed (ironically, in a dynamite blast) by her father and the other Anglo schemers as Chamisaville at last succumbs to what Nichols later calls the "pizza-fying of America." But the novel ends on an optimistic note as a horde of native old-timers gathers for a symbolic funeral for April. The novel's last line, "They had work to do," reaffirms the revolutionary theme and communicates a feeling that all is not yet lost.

The critical response to *The Magic Journey* was generally good but with a few qualifications. Jeffrey Burke, for example, writing in *Harper's* (August 1978), remarked that it "is a plausible history of exploitation, lush with eccentric characters, with myths, legends, ghosts, and revealing shards from the past four decades, all carried by a Dickensian narrative exuberance." He then observed that "Nichols' creative energy runs so often to comic invention, to caricature instead of character, to spates of bathos and discursive high jinks, that he entertains far more than he instructs, to use the classic formula; the imbalance makes for ambivalence."

Most critics attempt to classify this work as a "standard" revolutionary novel but fail to take into consideration the fact that *The Magic Journey*'s characters are more in the tradition of Latin America than of the United States. In Spanish-

speaking countries, personal eccentricity is the norm rather than a deviation; unusual characters or even living caricatures are much more likely to be encountered, not only in literature but also on the streets. Nichols manifests a high degree of understanding of the people about whom he is writing and whose standard he has chosen to carry. Dee Brown, author of *Bury My Heart at Wounded Knee* and a champion of social causes of American Indians, stated in a blurb for the paperback edition of *The Magic Journey* that "Mr. Nichols has a genius for creating the sort of raw comedy that has always been the sharpest weapon against injustices."

Several critics called attention to similarities between Nichols and García Márquez. This is a rather obvious comparison because of a number of resemblances in the works of the two writers—ghosts, legends, myths, inexplicable occurrences treated in a matter-of-fact manner, eccentric or unusual characters—but the influence is not necessarily that of García Márquez. Some of these same characteristics appear in *The Sterile Cuckoo* and *The Wizard of Loneliness*, both written and published before *One Hundred Years of Solitude* was printed in Argentina in 1967. Nichols's influences can probably more accurately be traced to the oral tradition passed on by his father and grandfather. Their imaginations, storytelling abilities, and love of tall tales with unusual characters are doubtless the creative source and inspiration for John Nichols.

Commenting on the matter of influence, Nichols says that he has read only one of García Márquez's books, *One Hundred Years of Solitude*, "several months after I had completed *The Milagro Beanfield War*, and I loved it, except for the ending which got a bit convoluted for me." His conclusion concerning influence is that "certainly I had assimilated a lot of the influences that influenced García Márquez. I think we are fairly different writers, but I know that his work (and also his political nonfiction, which I come across quite regularly in Spanish when friends send me stuff from Mexico) has certainly entered that huge pool of literary, artistic, poetic, graphics, musical, cultural influences from which I am constantly drawing. But I daresay no more than books like *Germinal*, *Little Big Man*, *Jean Christophe*, or *Moby-Dick*, or *War and Peace*, or *Guys and Dolls*."

Nichols's next work, *A Ghost in the Music* (1979), is a curious novel; chronologically it is sandwiched between the last two parts of the New Mexico trilogy and is set in Chamisaville, but is vastly different from those works. It is almost as if the author were returning to the same sort of

"One of the most compelling novels I've read in a long time," said Elliott Anderson in the *Chicago Tribune Book World* of John Nichols' fourth novel, *The Magic Journey*. "Long live *The Milagro Beanfield War*," wrote the Cleveland Plain Dealer of his third. Of his second, *The Wizard of Loneliness*, The New York Times Book Review said, "Author John Nichols seems to be soaring on a unique blend of humor and sadness toward a new dimension in American fiction." And *Book Week*, reviewing his first, *The Sterile Cuckoo*, hailed him as a writer "of genuine talent [with] an effervescent wit, a remarkable ear for dialogue, and a feeling for offbeat characterizations." John Nichols lives in northern New Mexico, and *A Ghost in the Music* is his fifth novel.

0 03 042576 X

Holt Rinehart Winston

Dust jacket for Nichols's fifth novel (1979), about a man who must mediate a lover's quarrel between his stuntman father and his pregnant mistress

characters and themes he dealt with in his first two novels. *A Ghost in the Music* focuses on Bart Darling, a middle-aged, third-rate movie producer, actor, director, and stuntman who calls on the novel's narrator, his illegitimate son, Marcel Thompson, to aid him in his attempt to hold on to Lorraine, the latest in a long string of wives and mistresses. She is a plain, intelligent "hillbilly" woman who refuses to remain with Bart if he proceeds with his plans to jump off the Río Grande Gorge bridge as part of a movie he is making. Her weapon is Bart's unborn child, as she threatens abortion if he does not cooperate with her. Marcel flies from his New York City graduate studies, full of reservations about his role as go-between in the confrontation. During the course of the narrative, Marcel begins to understand his father, to appreciate the man's deep love for him, and to share his exuberance for life.

Unlike *The Milagro Beanfield War* and *The Magic Journey*, this novel has a relatively simple plot and contains only a few characters. It is short—only about half the length of the New Mexico trilogy

volumes—and has nothing to do with the Chicano or his social and political problems. It is an intense character study of Bart Darling, but it is also a study of Marcel, a narrator-agent whose role and function here can be compared to those of Jerry Payne in *The Sterile Cuckoo*. It is a sound, moving novel that has not yet received much critical attention. One reviewer who has noticed it is Martin Levin, who, in the *New York Times Book Review* (28 October 1979), praised Nichols's effort, concluding that the "trick is to make this flamboyant, neon-lighted character credible and sympathetic, and Mr. Nichols carries it off. In the end, one feels that even if his hero is not capable of love, others may be capable of loving him."

In addition to using New Mexico as a setting for his novels and drawing inspiration for his characters from the Anglos, Chicanos, and Indians of the state, Nichols has done a great deal of nonfiction writing about the area. During the years between *The Wizard of Loneliness* and *The Milagro Beanfield War*, he contributed "a long investigative article almost every month" to the *New Mexico Review*, "a muckraking liberal magazine published monthly in Santa Fe." His first book-length nonfiction work is *If Mountains Die: A New Mexico Memoir*. This volume is a beautiful, poetic, poignant combination of photographs, history, and philosophy, which provides a great deal of insight into the world, both real and fictional, of John Nichols. The reader can follow, in very concrete terms, the development of the man and the writer. One so inclined may also search for clues to the inspirations for the characters in the New Mexico trilogy. The fictional worlds of Chamisaville, Milagro, and their surroundings can be seen in their real-life counterpart, since *If Mountains Die* is additionally a social, political, and cultural overview of Taos, the town where Nichols lives, and the nearby country. There are highly personal passages dealing with the author's life, his work and hobbies, his passions, and even his faults as he perceives them. The accompanying color photographs by William Davis are impressive.

There is no question that Nichols is an eloquent, knowledgeable spokesman for northern New Mexico and the Chicano people, who are rapidly losing their land, their cultural identity, and their traditional way of life. Davis's photographs depict the physical beauty of that land and stand as reminders that the Anglo world of plastic, fast foods, and asphalt may be "progress" in one sense of the word, but what may be sacrificed in securing that progress may be lost forever.

Generally, the reviews of *If Mountains Die* have been only lukewarm. John Sullivan observed in *Smithsonian* (July 1979): "His outlook reflects a naive notion of the West as a sort of psychiatric playground which must somehow be spared the irrevocability of modernization." He did, however, praise the author, stating: "The book's strengths come at those subtle moments, when Nichols melds the two most basic influences—earth and water—in recounting one man's struggles and defeats and triumphs in this strange and severe, beautiful land."

Nichols's philosophy was well-received among the liberal establishment in New York. Seymour Krim, writing in the *Village Voice* (30 July 1979), was of the opinion that the reader "will get no finer introduction to the territory than reading these words by a renegade East Villager."

It is with his latest work of fiction, *The Nirvana Blues* (1981), that Nichols draws to a close his trilogy dealing with the Mexican American. Doing so, he practically shuts the door on any hope he has for the survival of Chicano culture and traditional lifestyle. The protagonist here is an Anglo garbage

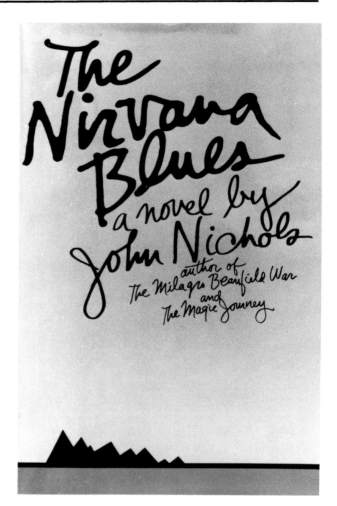

Dust jacket for the third novel in the New Mexico Trilogy

man named Joe Miniver, a modern-day incarnation of Don Quixote. Joe drives his Rocinante, a battered green Chevy pickup, around the Chamisaville area, struggling to keep his failing marriage together and juggling desperate details of his first dope deal, the proceeds of which will allow him to buy a small plot of land from Eloy Irribarren, "The Last Chicano." As in the other two volumes of the trilogy, there is a large number of characters who are eccentric or involved in weird and/or zany activities. They are a reflection in microcosm of modern Anglo America versus native New Mexico.

The reader by now has come to expect the unexpected from Nichols as characters such as a chunky, bearded angel named Lorin pop up with regularity. Nichols dazzles the reader with dozens of such characters. Some of the many comic episodes are truly hilarious, but again, as in *The Milagro Beanfield War* and *The Magic Journey*, there is

36

sitting at any one table. He much preferred to circulate
~~touching down~~ with everybody, ~~and~~ then moving on. ~~In a way~~
~~felt as if he were orchestrating all his friends and~~
~~acquaintences by moving among them so fluently.~~ He
~~felt bound to them differently, now that~~ he ~~was~~ the proud
owner of land, ~~and destined to build,~~ forge a permanent life,
~~settle down.~~ they belonged to him more, he had a bigger
stake in all their lives, ~~their triumphs, and tribulations.~~
~~He~~ touched them ~~feeling~~ ~~xxxxxxx~~ echoes of the sort of warmth
~~that he usually only felt for~~ Heidi and the kids, and ~~maybe~~
his best friend Peter Roth, ~~and of course his father--they~~
~~were family.~~

~~Joe settled~~ for a moment at a table where Ralph Kapansky, Bion Terry,
Percy Younge, jr., Larry Flagherty, ~~Larry's~~ enormous shaggy
dog, Bruno, and a woman with a green ~~colored~~ gem in her nose
~~wearing~~ a purple turban, ~~incredible~~ eye mascara, ~~and chalky~~
powder on her sallow cheeks, ~~and glistening 1950s~~ lipstick,
a bulky tie-died moomoo, and an acre of poppette beads. ~~She~~
~~was also smoking~~ a tiparello in a white plastic holder ~~provided~~
~~The woman~~ was Ralph's companion, a roady he had ~~picked up~~
in the Prince of Whales Café late that afternoon, ~~a~~
~~gypsy girl, and~~ she was on her way from Bloomington,
Indiana to Mt. Shasta, California to "Get a hit of those
powerful vibes out there, man." Ralph should have known
better, but ~~he did not. The man~~ was the most exasperating and
obnoxious guy that Joe had ever liked, ~~and a true abomination~~
~~around women.~~ A self-taught orphan who had had a remarkable
rise ~~directing in the theater, and then in Hollywood~~, at forty
~~he had started to lose~~ the thread, and ~~at forty-five~~ lived
alone in a tiny ~~house in~~ Ranchitos Abajo, that had no running
water. Frantically, dieted on molasses and lemon juice ~~in an~~
~~attempt~~ to shave off a few of his two hundred and forty
blubbery pounds, ~~took an elavil and a~~ pertophrane anti-depressant
pill every night, just to make it through the night,
wandered ~~around~~ Chamisaville, scoring one-night stands, begging
for his life to begin again, ~~terrified of~~ Bion
Terry was Ralph's travelling companion,

an underlying feeling of sadness and despair at the uncontrollable and inevitable circumstances that lead to the death of Eloy and his way of life. Nichols is laughing through his tears and causing his readers to do the same.

The conclusion of *The Nirvana Blues* must be compared to the conclusions of the other volumes of the New Mexico trilogy. The first ends on a hopeful note as Joe Mondragón and the other Chicanos of Milagro win the war over the beanfield. Death, if not defeated, is at least postponed. It appears "decked out in a sombrero, a serape, and shiny silver spurs, a spicy carnival apparition dancing over the little village, chuckled like a dove, winked in a joking, comradely fashion . . . , and jitterbugged quietly on into the resplendent and remarkably spangled horizon." In *The Magic Journey* the final melody remains a hopeful one, but the death of April Delaney indicates that there is far less reason to expect a victory over the forces bent on destruction. In the final episode of *The Nirvana Blues*, Joe Miniver and Eloy Irribarren are both killed, but in the novel's epilogue, Joe's immortal soul, en route with Lorin to select a new body, hijacks the flying machine and forces the angel to fly him over Cuba. As Joe bails out, he does so with hope for a new and better way of life: "If the soul had an eternal power, then he would land upon the courageous territory below, locate the body of anything from a butterfly to an aged cane cutter in need of animation, and try to be more worthy this time around, aided by his proximity to a more compassionate historical reality." Joe and the Chicanos are defeated and dead, but only in Nichols's rather depressing view of capitalist America.

Critical comments concerning *The Nirvana Blues* have generally been excellent. Frank Wilson, writing in the *Fort Worth Star-Telegram* (1 November 1981), stated: "Let it be known that not only does *The Nirvana Blues* have to be the best novel published in America this year, but the trilogy itself can only be regarded as the greatest literary effort by an American in decades." Other reviewers had some reservations but all concluded on a favorable note. Ed Conaway, in the *San Francisco Chronicle* (23 August 1981), for example, said: "For all these faults, this is an intriguing effort. We are reminded that the human circus has ruined a natural paradise. We are reminded that human beings routinely betray their humanity. We are reminded that we cannot be content with our neighbors or our surroundings unless we are content with ourselves. The last book of Chamisa County may fail as a traditional novel, but it succeeds as a comedy and as an inquiry into American values."

At times this seems to be the best of the New Mexico trilogy, but overall it is the weakest. Nichols points out in his introductory note that he had to write it to finish what he had begun with his two previous volumes. He felt disappointed as he realized that he had failed to incorporate the themes, mood, and message of *The Nirvana Blues* in the other works but explains that his stories "often sprint away from their original intentions like delinquent children, gallumph blindly into all sorts of unforeseen pitfalls, and finally, with luck, stagger to the finish line as total strangers to the original schemes that launched them." This statement provides an insight into Nichols's creative process but only a negative clue concerning his future directions as a writer of fiction: he is unsure and is not always in control of his characters and their actions.

As of the completion of this survey, he has returned to an early interest: the cinema. He has completed a script for the film version of *The Milagro Beanfield War* and is working on one for *The Magic Journey*. Although he does not yet have any screenplay credits, he has worked with Greek director Costa-Gavras on the film *Missing*, and he is currently working with Costa-Gavras on a film dealing with people who work with nuclear weapons.

In spite of being heavily involved in writing for movies, Nichols has continued to pursue his nonfiction work. He describes his most recent book, *The Last Beautiful Days of Autumn* (1982), as a personal account, in the vein of *If Mountains Die*, "only longer, and with 65 of my own full-page color photographs of friends and landscapes of the Taos area. This is a lovely book, and I think much more lyrical and open than *If Mountains Die*."

As far as Nichols's future fiction writing is concerned, the reader must look for clues in his six novels. Except for reviews, Nichols's work has not yet received much critical attention. It is obvious that an essential ingredient in his prose fiction has been humor. Whether he treats social and political themes as in the New Mexico trilogy or presents touching portraits of individuals in search of love, understanding, and acceptance as in his other novels, there is always a liberal sprinkling of comic characters, situations, and language. It is yet to be seen if John Nichols will fulfill humorist H. Allen Smith's prophecy that he "will likely become the best comic novel writer of his time."

References:
Richard A. Blessing, "For Pookie, with Love and Good Riddance: John Nichols' *The Sterile Cuck-*

oo," Journal of Popular Culture, 7 (Summer 1973): 124-135;

Albert Goldman, "The Comic Prison," *Nation*, 6 (8 February 1965): 142-144;

G. Kenneth Pellow, "The Transformation of *The Sterile Cuckoo*," *Literature/Film Quarterly*, 5 (Summer 1977): 252-257.

Cynthia Ozick
(17 April 1928-   )

Susan Currier
California Polytechnic State University

BOOKS: *Trust* (New York: New American Library, 1966; London: MacGibbon & Kee, 1967);
The Pagan Rabbi and Other Stories (New York: Knopf, 1971; London: Secker & Warburg, 1972);
Bloodshed and Three Novellas (New York: Knopf, 1976; London: Secker & Warburg, 1976);
Levitation: Five Fictions (New York: Knopf, 1982; London: Secker & Warburg, 1982).

Over the last two decades, Cynthia Ozick has secured her reputation in contemporary literary circles on several fronts—as New York intellectual, literary critic, political commentator, poet, and fiction writer. But it is likely that she will be best remembered for her stories. Her first collection, *The Pagan Rabbi and Other Stories* (1971), won a National Book Award nomination, and a subsequent story, "Usurpation" (1974), earned an O. Henry Prize. Ozick's stories have appeared in the 1970, 1972, and 1976 volumes of *Best American Short Stories*, and at least one critic, Leslie Epstein, considers Ozick's "to be perhaps the finest work in short fiction by a contemporary writer." She writes on a range of subjects, but her most characteristic and compelling themes are Jewish identity, Jewish history, and Jewish art.

Born 17 April 1928, Ozick grew up during the Depression in the Bronx. Her parents, William and Celia Regelson Ozick, worked long hours in their Park View Pharmacy which yielded a grudging living. They were immigrants, and their daughter grew up sensitive to their outsider status and suspect of her own behavior in the eyes of "true and virtuous Americans." In P.S. 71 she felt herself an unattractive child as well as an inept student. At home she sought fantasy for escape. Stories and novels were readily available. And so began no merely ordinary interest in fiction but an addiction to its transfiguring magic. Ozick earned a B.A. from

Cynthia O.

New York University in 1949 and an M.A. in literature from Ohio State University in 1950. There, she "committed" a master's thesis on Henry James whom she has identified as the most formative influence on her career.

After completing her M.A., Ozick went to work as an advertising copywriter. At twenty-four she sold her first article to the *Boston Globe*, but her boss forbade future newspaper stories. In the same year she married a lawyer, Bernard Hallote, with whom she later had one daughter, Rachel, and with whom she settled in New Rochelle. Apart from occasional teaching assignments, Ozick is a full-time writer who has been assisted in her vocation by grants from both the National Endowment for the Arts and the Guggenheim Foundation.

Although it was not published until 1966, Ozick began her first and only novel when she left graduate school at the age of twenty-two. *Trust*, she considers in retrospect, is "a cannibalistically ambitious Jamesian novel," an inappropriate but perhaps inevitable beginning considering that at seventeen she "became Henry James" and "for years and years . . . remained Henry James." Ozick is eloquent on her error. On James she "pins" the loss of her youth, offering herself as "an Extreme and Hideous Example of Premature Exposure to Henry James." "Listening to the 'Lesson of the Master' at the wrong time," she confused the relative merits of Life and Art, indeed misheard the Lesson itself, and opted in her own life for Art. Forsaking human entanglement, passion, and distraction, she spent those years "extravagantly," waiting for literature, "the sinewy grand undulations of some unraveling fiction, meticulously dreamed out in a language of masterly resplendence, which was to pounce on me and turn me into an enchanted and glorious Being, as enchanted and glorious as the elderly bald-headed Henry James himself," but which never did.

An appreciation of what Ozick considers the "perdition" of James's influence on her work as well as her life goes far in explaining *Trust*. Critics have suggested that while "the late novels of James offer a kind of gloss on Mrs. Ozick's intentions" in *Trust*, the result is more discontinuity between language and feeling than it is moral subtlety or psychological acuity. The book manages to be simultaneously exceptional and unfocused, for the language is brilliant but frequently unattached to a purpose. Certainly there is no simple explanation of what *Trust* is about. A young woman's quest for self-discovery shapes this long and difficult work. But Jewish-Christian themes are also at issue, and so is an intricate, elite social structure which creaks and crumbles through the length of the work.

The narrator is a hapless and graceless girl, fortunate in material opportunity but emotionally deprived by corrupt relatives who are themselves victims of the acquisitive society to which they sacrifice her. The narrator's mother, Allegra Vand, is an heiress who conceives her child during a Marxist phase and during an interval between two marriages, the first to a Wall Street lawyer, William, and the second to a Jewish intellectual and diplomat, Enoch. The interval remains more important to the mother than either marriage, but the daughter is kept ignorant of her sexually charismatic, ne'er-do-well father, Gustave Nicholas Tilbeck. A bastard with no authentic identity or experience of her own, the narrator spends the novel observing the lives of others, unraveling their intrigues, and pursuing in a desultory fashion the identity of the wretch who abandoned her mother and herself when she was still newborn. In due course the narrator is reunited with this father in a decaying mansion on a lonely island. He seduces all his female guests and attempts to seduce his own daughter. She nearly succumbs but instead contents herself with observing his lovemaking with the high-spirited young woman who is affianced to her mother's first husband's son. The long visionary description of this sexual encounter provides an extraordinary example of Ozick's best art. The narrator leaves it feeling, very convincingly, that "I had witnessed the very style of my own creation." Still, Ozick's virtuosity aside, one wonders about the narrator's new knowledge. What do all her observations teach her? Where has her quest led her? She discovers that the man who moved her mother, who diminished all life and love thereafter for her mother, is a "tawdry Muse," a cheap "holy . . . Man of No Desires" who "wants to sit in a temple full of virgins." An aging boy who skipped adulthood altogether, he dyes his hair blonde and drowns from seasickness in water soured by his own vomit. Nevertheless, even as an aging boy, he is more than the narrator, who, short of struggling into some being of her own, remains, even at the end, only a critical eye.

Jewish interests in the novel are also ambiguous and obscure. They are represented by Enoch, who refuses to play father to the narrator and so fails to attach the Jewish themes to her. Enoch, who discovers the narrator's mother during her Marxist phase, marries her at the beginning of World War II. He builds a reputation for himself as chief administrator for counting and identifying the Jewish dead at the end of the war. His stepdaughter follows him to Europe for this grisly work, and the great black ledgers with which he is usually encumbered there impress themselves indelibly in her mind. A child-witness to war-torn Europe, she is not herself Jewish; and one cannot say how the Holocaust touches her or even why it is present in her story. For Enoch, it proves more clearly significant. From it he extricates a theory that God has taken vengeance out of the hands of man and Himself and given it over to history instead, that "history is a judgment on what has happened" and that "vengeance is a high historical act." Though his wife tries to propel him into a South American ambassadorship, a government coup in his prospective host nation annuls his appointment even while the U.S. Senate confirms it. Enoch returns to his true vocation, writing history and studying the Talmud.

The remaining characters, including William; William's son; his fiancée, Stefanie; and Allegra Vand, all dramatize predictable fallacies of the privileged society to which they belong. The institutions which shape these characters, from Stefanie's school to William's law firm, ill prepare them to find satisfaction in life. Wealth cannot secure their respective loves. William loses Allegra; William's son loses Stefanie; Stefanie and Allegra both lose Tilbeck. Even wealth cannot purchase Allegra an embassy. It does, however, make her prey to Tilbeck's blackmail. These characters are in varying degrees strong, healthy, attractive, educated, cosmopolitan, and except for Stefanie, extremely witty. Their world is, by all conventions, enviable and exclusive, but they do not know how to live in it.

Ten years later, in a preface to her third book, *Bloodshed and Three Novellas* (1976), Ozick issued a modest literary credo: "Who would wish for the idea of a story in place of the story itself? But the 'what was meant' is worthwhile too . . . and a story must not merely be, but mean. Otherwise, what happens, in or out of literature, is only incident, not event. Incident is that inch of braid, the optic nerve. Event is the optic nerve's untangling report to the brain, djinn of wiliness and joy and judgment and lamentation. . . . I believe that stories ought to judge and interpret the world." It is not a surprising manifesto for a writer who fashioned herself on Henry James. But in her first and most self-consciously Jamesian book, Ozick failed on precisely those grounds. In *Trust*, language, for all its art, does not judge and interpret the world: it obscures it. On this point Ozick's critics are generally agreed. Eugene Goodheart complains in *Critique* (1967): "All is indirection, ellipsis, and 'practiced hesitation': the reader is constantly irritated, because he is denied the comfort of his stock responses. . . . In stretching

the sense of possibility, however, one must be careful not to destroy the tension with the real and the familiar, as James almost never does. In Mrs. Ozick's novel, this tension is too easily relaxed and the result is that the extravagant rhetoric doesn't so much extend the possibilities of perception as it estranges from genuine perception." Goodheart also, however, concedes that Ozick "can write like a fiend." Elinor Baumbach, writing in the *Saturday Review* (9 July 1966), would like to "dismiss, as a dismal bore, a great part of the pseudo-Jamesian concerns" of *Trust*, including its world of high finance and policymaking. She tires of the "characters and caricatures who insist upon their right to be endlessly clever with one another." But she concludes that *Trust* is an "interesting and sometimes brilliant first novel." She particularly applauds Ozick's treatment of Enoch: "His odyssey from ambition to theology is worldly but personal, and Mrs. Ozick handles it movingly." Baumbach's appreciation of the Jewish story in *Trust* proved prophetic, for in her next three books Ozick abandoned the novel and turned to Jewish stories. The Jamesian experiments were over; the language was less opaque; and all three volumes met with greater critical recognition than had *Trust*.

In her first collection, *The Pagan Rabbi and Other Stories*, Ozick concentrates on the plight of the transplanted Jew in America. It is not a new theme, but she handles it differently from most American Jewish fiction writers. In *Encounter* (September 1972) Paul Theroux observed that "she writes of people and situations who are rarely if ever seen in American novels" and that, "to her credit," "Mrs. Ozick's Jewish characters would not be at ease in the company of the people who appear in the work of Malamud, Bellow, Roth and Co." All seven stories have at least one Jewish character, and at least five must be considered so essentially Jewish that Johanna Kaplan (*New York Times Book Review*, 13 June 1971) designated their author "not as a Jewish writer, but as a Jewish visionary—something more."

The characters in these stories are victims of America as only its immigrants can be. Their most eloquent representative is Hersheleh Edelshtein in "Envy; or Yiddish in America," one of the two stories from this collection to be selected for *Best American Short Stories*. Edelshtein is a Yiddish poet with an intense mission—to save Yiddish—and an intense envy, of Yankel Ostrover, who has been translated for publication in English. Ostrover, who cannot fail to suggest Isaac Bashevis Singer, has found fame and an audience in America. Edelshtein hates him for his fame, but Edelshtein's futile quest to secure translations of his own work transcends merely personal and egocentric motives. He wants to save Yiddish poetry—in translation, if necessary—and the Yiddish language from extinction. At age sixty-seven Edelshtein tours a pitiful lecture circuit of synagogues, community centers, and labor unions. His subject is Yiddish; his thesis, that unlike any other language, "it died a sudden and definite death, in a given decade, on a given piece of soil." But his audiences fail him. They want weddings, and "to speak of Yiddish was to preside over a funeral." Edelshtein is "a rabbi who had survived his whole congregation." Edelshtein attempts to explain himself to Ostrover: "In Talmud if you save a single life it's as if you saved the world. And if you save a language? Worlds maybe. Galaxies. The whole universe." Ostrover responds: "Hersheleh, the God of the Jews made a mistake when he didn't have a son, it would be a good occupation for you." Ostrover's translator rejects Edelshtein's request to translate his poems. And finally a young Jewish girl who knows Yiddish also refuses on the grounds that the old Yiddish poets are mere "puddles" outside the literary mainstream and that they are contaminated by their own will to suffer. It is too easy to dismiss Edelshtein as if he only sought to excuse his own hard luck. On a larger, more impersonal scale, the American Jews in this story are seduced by their new country into betraying Yiddish and therefore their past. In Edelshtein's words, "whoever forgets Yiddish courts amnesia of history. Mourn—the forgetting has already happened. A thousand years of our travail forgotten." Later in her preface to *Bloodshed* Ozick reiterates the same sense of loss and dislocation in her own more tentative terms:

> Since my slave-ancestors left off building the Pyramids to wander in the wilderness of Sinai, they have spoken a handful of generally obscure languages—Hebrew, Aramaic, twelfth-century French perhaps, Yiddish for a thousand years. Since the coming forth from Egypt five millenia ago, mine is the first generation to think and speak and write wholly in English. To say that I have been thoroughly assimilated into English would of course be the grossest understatement. . . .
>
> Still, though English is my everything, now and then I feel cramped by it. I have come to it with notions it is too parochial to recognize. A language, like a people, has a history of ideas; but not *all* ideas; only those known to its experience. Not surprisingly, English is a Christian language. When I write English, I live in Christendom.

But if my postulates are not Christian postulates, what then?

A second excellent story from *The Pagan Rabbi*, "Virility," develops some of the same themes concerning the Jewish immigrant experience in America but with a feminist twist. In this case a young Jewish boy, Elia Gatoff, escapes Czarist Russia ahead of his family and travels to Liverpool to live with an aunt until his parents and sisters can join him. After news arrives that they have been brutally destroyed in a pogrom, he sails to America, where he secures work with a newspaper publisher, moving up from office boy to proofreader to police reporter. But Elia Gatoff, who changes his name to Edmund Gate, wants to be a poet—in English. Unlike Edelshtein, he masters the language, but he hasn't a crumb of poetic talent. Suddenly, however, he begins to publish beautiful poems, five volumes of them over a period of several years. He has plagiarized them from Tante Rivka, his Liverpool aunt, who writes him regularly though he never responds. The volumes of her poetry that he publishes under his own name are all entitled *Virility, I-V*. Critics rave about them on all counts, but they especially applaud their masculinity. Gatoff lectures around the world to audiences larger than Caruso's. But Tante Rivka dies—she organizes her own death by starvation when she grows too old to work. She leaves Gatoff enough poems for one extraordinary volume. But instead of pirating these also, Gatoff confesses to having plagiarized his whole career. The last poems are published as *Flowers from Liverpool* instead of *Virility VI*, Tante Rivka is pictured on the jacket, and reviewers find the collection "thin," "girlish," "fragile," "one-dimensional," "domestic," and "distaff." Elia Gatoff feels castrated, turns drunkard, and supposedly commits suicide at the age of twenty-six (though a bizarre epilogue resurrects him as a miserable centenarian). Tante Rivka, who lived out her life in a Liverpool slum without prospects, without family, without letters or financial support from Elia while he prospered from her poems, and who is denied even appropriate posthumous recognition for her art because of her sex, dies a dignified death at a ripe age. Elia Gatoff, who has youth, America, reasonable prospects with his newspaper job, as well as love and support from his aunt, disgraces and destroys himself. He suffers like Edelshtein, though in a different form, from an inability to come to terms with America. Johanna Kaplan describes these tortured protagonists as victims of an American dream: "Because America—what Edelshtein, the embittered, untranslated Yiddish poet calls 'America the bride, under her fancy gown nothing'—is so severe a disappointment to them, a lie they cannot forge a compromise with, they push out the boundaries of their imaginations and reach into territories that they know in their hearts, in their history, are forbidden."

Several of the characters from this volume's remaining stories search for their identities through the bizarre and supernatural. Rabbi Isaac Kornfield from the title story finds himself torn between Judaism and classical paganism. Passionately drawn to nature, he wanders out-of-doors at all hours of the day and night. He finally attempts to escape his body by coupling with a tree nymph. But the soul he succeeds in revealing is that of a pious and scholarly Jew. The dryad abandons him in revulsion, and he hangs himself with his prayer shawl on her tree.

In "The Dock-Witch," which is the second story from this collection to have been selected for *Best American Short Stories*, a young man is seduced by a sea nymph or ship's figurehead come to life. A lawyer, soon to become a partner in a firm that deals with shipping interests, he discovers her among the docks. First he is irritated and then intrigued by her. Soon he is addicted to her, and ultimately he is ruined and abandoned by her. Surveying his losses, he notes that his apartment is wrecked and his job gone. But another of the nymph's victims admonishes him, "That's the least of it. Believe me, buddy, the least. That's the stuff you can fix up." The worst of it will be his inability to function in the world of human beings again. He will live in a hell of unfulfilled desire for the supernatural.

Although fantasy in "The Pagan Rabbi" and "Dock-Witch" teases the reader into curious extensions of reality, "Envy; or Yiddish in America" and "Virility" are better dramatized and more substantial pieces. The entire volume earned high marks from nearly all its reviewers. Kaplan praised Ozick's new control: "In this new book . . . all that was best in the novel—that relentless, passionate, discovering and uncovering intelligence—is present and instantly recognizable, but there is now a difference in the prose. It is sharpened, clarified, controlled and above all beautifully, unceasingly welcoming." *Newsweek*'s critic (10 May 1971) ranked Ozick among the best of contemporary short-story writers: "Three of these stories are among the best written by Americans in recent years. That is a lot."

By the time her next volume, *Bloodshed and Three Novellas*, was published, Ozick was again writing longer and more opaque fictions. *Bloodshed* is the first volume Ozick chose to introduce with a preface, and her reason for doing so was the appar-

ent obscurity for gentile audiences of one of the volume's novellas, "Usurpation (Other People's Stories)." All Ozick's stories are intellectual creations built around ideas, but certain critical responses to the publication of "Usurpation" in 1974 in *Esquire* and in the 1975 O. Henry collection prompted Ozick to conclude that in this case the idea was not accessible to her readers: "I had written 'Usurpation' in the language of a civilization that cannot imagine its thesis."

"Usurpation" echoes some of Ozick's earlier stories, including "The Pagan Rabbi" and "Virility." In it would-be writers steal stories from real writers, and even the real writers demonstrate a lust for fame that belies the sacredness of their gifts. Ozick borrows two stories, one from Bernard Malamud, and reshapes them to make her point. But more important, in this story storytellers usurp God. "Usurpation" raises the question of "whether Jews ought to be storytellers" at all. The second commandment forbids idolatry or belief in magic, and "storytelling as every writer knows, is a kind of magic act. Or Eucharist, wherein the common bread of language assumes the form of a god."

The layering of stories within this story is ingenious, but the fit of thesis, audience, and story layers remains problematic in spite of Ozick's explanatory preface or, according to Ruth Wisse in *Commentary* (June 1976), partly *because* of the preface: "In her preface Miss Ozick says she has to explain the meaning of 'Usurpation' because a certain non-Jewish critic had failed to understand it. This failure she attributes not to the story's possible artistic shortcomings, but to its Jewish specificity, which puts it outside the critic's cultural range. . . . As the prophet of an indigenous Jewish culture in the English language, she might have been expected to hail the critic's failure to understand as a milestone—an authentic breakthrough in the creation of a distinctive Jewish literature. Instead, determined to have both the cake and the eating of it, she anxiously becomes her own translator."

This volume's title story, "Bloodshed," focuses many of the Jewish interests apparent in Ozick's earlier work into a key question which appears in the title story from *Levitation* also: What responsibility to the past does the Holocaust give every contemporary Jew and how does it set him or her apart from every contemporary non-Jew? Once again, the critics did not doubt Ozick's conviction or her brilliance. But some of the same judgments implicit in their reviews of "Usurpation" held for "Bloodshed" as well. It is not so obscure a story, but it is in parts more sententious than dramatic. Once

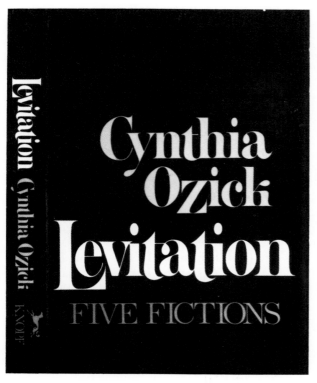

Dust jacket for Ozick's third collection of stories, five "fictions" on the themes of Judaism and art

again, however, criticism of this volume alternated with expressions of open admiration. Amanda Heller, writing for the *Atlantic* (May 1976), observed that "[these novellas] fit neatly together, demonstrating the wry humor, the quirky intelligence . . . and the eccentric beauty of language that make up the author's talent for storytelling." Julian Moynahan concluded his review for the *New York Times Book Review* (11 April 1976) confident that Ozick was leading American fiction in a profitable direction: "Wherever American writing is going now, Cynthia Ozick is a distinctive and bright part of that movement."

In *Levitation* (self-consciously subtitled *Five Fictions*, 1982), her most recent collection of stories Ozick writes, for a change, chiefly about women. One of this volume's tales, "The Sewing Harems," which had earlier publication by itself but was linked with "Freud's Room" to become "From A Refugee's Notebook" in this collection, appears on the surface to be a fable against the women's movement. In Acirema, planet of the future, colonies of women from the most sophisticated cities of the most highly developed countries sew their vaginas closed and rent themselves out to wealthy businessmen for pleasure without responsibility.

But some children are always born to each harem, the result of a few selectively snipped stitches. Over time these children develop into a dangerous sect. As a result of their upbringing, they simultaneously "fulfill themselves as irrational demons" and "idolize motherhood." Outside of their sect they are criminals, generally destroying the society that spawned them and particularly murdering sewn women. Meanwhile ecological and technological changes make it dangerous, even impossible, to remove or cut the customary thread, and "the treacherous stitch-snipping of the Sewing Harems, so long a subject of mockery and infamy among those who admired both progress and honest commitment, was all at once seen to be a lost treasure of the race."

But in the stories which precede and follow it, Ozick emerges as a feminist also. In "Shots" she sympathetically tolerates one character's affair with a married man: "I knew he had a wife, but I was already thirty-six, and who didn't have a wife by then." In "Puttermesser: Her Work History, Her Ancestry, Her Afterlife" Ozick openly supports the refusal to marry which another character addresses to her mother: "Some day all the Soviet Jews will come out of the spider's clutches of these people and be free. Please explain to Daddy that this is one of the highest priorities of my life at this time in my personal history. Do you think a Joel Zaretsky can share such a vision?" And in "Puttermesser and Xanthippe" Ozick defends the same character's preference for Plato's *Theatetus* rather than her lover in bed. Certainly Ozick's stories as a group leave no doubt as to her confidence in women artists or women lawyers even as they cast aspersions on certain professional men. "The Sewing Harems" actually expresses a very specific concern for children and a criticism of any system with a facile underestimation of their importance both to individual parents and to civilization. In Acirema pleasure without responsibility is an illusion.

The dominant theme of *Levitation*'s five fictions are, once again, Judaism and art. They get their clearest treatment in the second of two stories devoted to the woman lawyer Puttermesser. In "Puttermesser and Xanthippe" Puttermesser has left the law firm where she began her career to go to work as corporate counsel for New York City's Department of Receipts and Disbursements. She is forty-six, and while her parents no longer pressure her to marry, she is not yet "reconciled to childlessness." She fantasizes daughters and ends up creating a golem she calls Xanthippe, the first female golem in the history of Judaism. At about the same

First page of the manuscript for Ozick's forthcoming novel The Cannibal Galaxy time the mayor appoints a new commissioner to Puttermesser's department, and she loses her job in the ritual changes of the political patronage system. Xanthippe gets Puttermesser elected mayor; Puttermesser transforms New York into a model city; and Puttermesser becomes a hero. But Xanthippe grows daily as golems must; she discovers sex; and her voracious appetites begin to threaten and consume the city. She turns against her creator as golems also must; and Puttermesser is forced to destroy her, reversing the same spells and unsaying the same sacred syllables she pronounced to create Xanthippe. At the peak of their shared success, Puttermesser has a moment of recognition about her relationship with the golem: "Puttermesser made Xanthippe; Xanthippe did not exist before Puttermesser made her: that is clear enough. But Xanthippe made Puttermesser Mayor, and Mayor Puttermesser too did not exist before. And that is just as clear. Puttermesser sees that she is the golem's golem." Extended to its logical conclusion, that same statement must also read: Ozick made Puttermesser—Ozick sees that she is the golem's golem.

The magic in these fictions is equivalent to the same powers of storytelling which constitute sacrilege in "Usurpation. It comes in various forms, of which golem-creating is only one. Peopling the mind with irrational demons is another. "Freud's Room" exposes Freud's attraction to the unconscious as a desire to become a god and therefore "usurp" the only God. Not only is "the doctor of the Unconscious" vulnerable in his own right, "likely to be devoured by his own creation, like that Rabbi of Prague who constructed a golem," but he threatens civilization with his creation. The primitive stone godlets which decorate his room and which also reflect his own dream of becoming a god, goose step, "one foot thrust forward, like the men who marched afterward in Vienna." In still another of these fictions, called "Shots," the usurping magic becomes the photographer's art. Still, its contradictions remain the same.

Finally, the title story of *Levitation* rephrases relations between magic and Judaism. A New York couple, two novelists—Feingold, a Jew, and Lucy, a Jewish convert—spend their lives apparently happily, writing every evening and discussing their work. Believing themselves similar with shared "premises," "they pitied every writer who was not married to a writer," and often, as they put their work away "it seemed to them that they were literary friends and lovers like George Eliot and George Henry Lewes." One bitterness, however, rankles in this relationship. They imagine their lives and their acquaintances to be second-rate. So they decide to give a party to which they invite Norman Mailer, Susan Sontag, Alfred Kazin, Philip Roth, Elizabeth Hardwick, and a host of other literary celebrities who never show. Those who do come divide into distinct groups with all the serious Jews in the living room rehearsing history's atrocities. As one Holocaust storyteller weaves his spell, everyone in the room begins to levitate except for Lucy who is left on the floor. She grows absorbed in her own vision of classical pagan Greece, a vision in which she realizes how "she has abandoned nature, how she has lost true religion on account of the God of the Jews." Simultaneously she feels embittered by "the glory of their [the Jews'] martyrdom." She and Feingold are not the same by virtue of their writing after all. They are far more profoundly separated by religion. Assimilation and conversion are mistakes. In *Levitation* and in life Ozick champions, according to Wisse, "the idea of a Jewish literary community with meaningful ties to the past, to Israel, and to Jewish literature in Jewish languages." If Jews are to be storytellers at all, apparently they ought to take their cues from the refugee storyteller who levitates his people rather than from the famous figures who never come to the party.

Reviewers greeted *Levitation* as enthusiastically as they did *The Pagan Rabbi*. Leslie Epstein, moved by its implicit censure of Ozick's own blasphemy, idols, and golems, observed in the *New York Times Book Review* (14 February 1982): "It is awesome to watch this great and generous talent turn with such intensity upon itself." A. Alvarez, in *New York Review* (13 May 1982), described the author of *Levitation* as "a carver, a stylist in the best and most complete sense" and the writing in it as "intricate and immaculate." His single qualification doubted the curious juxtaposition of sophistication and folk magic which is precisely Ozick's strength as well as her intention: "It is in the end—despite the brilliance, despite the humor—an odd and uneasy displacement, like the Chagalls in Lincoln Center."

With the help of the Guggenheim Foundation from which she received a fellowship, Ozick will publish her second novel during early 1983. When queried about this work in progress, Ozick responded nostalgically and ambiguously: "Oh happiness without parody! Why not, why not? To drill through the 'post-modern' and come out on the other side, alive and saved and wise as George Eliot!" She is also at work on a collection of essays, "over a hundred of these, yearning to be between boards." Her gentile readers may be especially grateful for them if they help compensate for the lack of shared traditions and assumptions. Surely a question for Cynthia Ozick as well as her audience remains: what is to become of her Lucy-readers as she levitates the Jews?

Periodical Publications:
FICTION:
"The Sense of Europe," *Prairie Schooner*, 30 (1956): 126-138;
"Stone," *Botteghe Obscure*, 20 (Autumn 1957): 388-414;
"The Shawl," *New Yorker*, 56 (26 May 1980): 33-34;
"The Laughter of Akiva," *New Yorker*, 56 (10 November 1980): 50-60.
NONFICTION:
"We Ignoble Savages," *Evergreen Review*, 3 (November-December 1959): 48-52, 141-142, 144-163;
"The Jamesian Parable: *The Sacred Fount*," *Bucknell Review*, 11 (May 1963): 55-70;
"Forster as Homosexual," *Commentary*, 52 (December 1971);
"Literary Blacks and Jews," *Midstream*, 18 (June-July 1972): 10-24;
"Mrs. Virginia Woolf," *Commentary*, 56 (August 1973): 33-44;

"All the World Wants the Jews Dead," *Esquire*, 82 (November 1974): 103-107;
"Does Genius Have a Gender?," *Ms.*, 6 (December 1977): 56, 79, 80-81;
"Judaism and Harold Bloom," *Commentary*, 67 (January 1979): 43-51;
"Spells, Wishes, Goldfish, Old School Hurts," *New York Times Book Review*, 87 (31 January 1982): 9, 24;
"The Lesson of the Master," *New York Review of Books*, 29 (12 August 1982): 20-21.

References:
A. Alvarez, "Flushed with Ideas," *New York Review of Books*, 29 (13 May 1982): 22-23;
Leslie Epstein, "Stories and Something Else," *New York Times Book Review* (14 February 1982): 11, 25;
Josephine Z. Knopp, "The Jewish Stories of Cynthia Ozick," *Studies in American Jewish Literature*, 1, no. 1 (1975): 31-38;
Catherine Rainwater and William J. Scheick, eds., *Three Contemporary Women Novelists: Hazzard, Ozick, and Redmon* (Austin: University of Texas Press, 1983);
Ruth R. Wisse, "American Jewish Writing, Act II," *Commentary*, 61 (June 1976): 40-45.

Lee Pennington
(1 May 1939-)

Jean W. Ross

SELECTED BOOKS: *The Dark Hills of Jesse Stuart* (Cincinnati: Harvest Press, 1967);
Scenes From a Southern Road (Smithtown, N. Y.: JRD, 1969);
Wildflower . . . Poems for Joy (Brooklyn: Poetry Prevue, 1970);
April Poems (Brooklyn: Poetry Prevue, 1970);
Songs of Bloody Harlan (Fennimore, Wis.: Westburg, 1975);
Spring of Violets (Louisville, Ky.: Love Street Books, 1976);
Appalachia, My Sorrow (Louisville, Ky.: Love Street Books, 1976);

Coalmine (Louisville, Ky.: Love Street Books, 1976);
The Porch (Louisville, Ky.: Love Street Books, 1976);
The Spirit of Poor Fork (Louisville, Ky.: Love Street Books, 1976);
I Knew a Woman (Louisville, Ky.: Love Street Books, 1977).

As poet, playwright, folk artist, and teacher, Lee Pennington champions the culture of Appalachia, the region of his birth and a continuing inspiration for his work. "Whatever she is, wherever she touches, Appalachia symbolizes America's dream," he believes. Although Pennington has

Lee Pennington

written prolifically—in addition to his books, he has had more than 1,000 poems, short stories, and articles published in magazines and anthologies—he came closest to national prominence when his 1977 collection of poetry, *I Knew a Woman*, was nominated for a Pulitzer Prize. His books, published by small presses and in small editions, have become collector's items among his dedicated followers.

Pennington was born in the eastern Kentucky community of White Oak, ninth of eleven children of Andrew Virgil Pennington and Mary Ellen (Lawson) Pennington. Though the family lived in Baltimore briefly while Andrew Pennington worked in the shipyards there during World War II, they returned to White Oak and settled on a thirty-two-acre hillside farm. Pennington helped on the farm from an early age and planned to become a farmer—at that time no one in his family had ever gone away to college and his parents had not even attended high school. However, good teachers recognized his talent for writing and stimulated his intellectual curiosity.

The Kentucky writer Jesse Stuart was a notable influence. As principal of McKell High School in South Shore while Pennington was a student there,

he got Pennington a job covering sports and school activities for newspapers in the area. An article Pennington wrote about Stuart was published in the *Portsmouth* (Ohio) *Times* and led directly to the promise of a partial scholarship at Baldwin-Wallace College in Ohio, with work assignments on campus to cover the balance of the cost. This was the break that got Pennington into college. However, before the end of the first semester he was told that the arrangement would not cover the costs. Again Jesse Stuart came to Pennington's aid: he arranged for a mid-semester transfer to Berea College in Kentucky. At Berea, Pennington worked in all the major capacities on the school paper, served as head news-bureau writer for the college and publicity writer for the Council of the Southern Mountains, and wrote and directed *The Porch*, a one-act play. In 1962 he married a fellow student, Joy Stout, from the Tennessee mountain town of Butler.

After their graduation from Berea in 1962, Lee and Joy Pennington taught English at the Newburgh Free Academy in New York. In 1964, persuaded by Stuart that they should be teaching on the college level, they went to the University of Iowa where both earned their M.A. degrees. In 1965 they took teaching positions at Southeast Community College in Cumberland, Kentucky. This return to the mountains was a challenge to the Penningtons who refused to accept the stereotype of Appalachian students as helpless, backward products of a depressed region, unworthy of serious teaching.

As chairman of the English department at Southeast, Pennington promoted the establishment of organizations to encourage regional pride among his students and inaugurated courses in creative writing. This was a time when his own poems were beginning to gain some recognition—in 1965 he won four awards for published poems. Through his help and encouragement, his students were able to write and get their work published also. In addition to having a good representation of their poems and short stories published in national magazines, they put together four books of their own poetry. Unfortunately the fourth, *Tomorrow's People*, elicited criticism that resulted in the Penningtons' leaving Harlan County. Seen by local residents as a collection of protest poems, the students' work was in part critical of strip-mining, traditional religious teaching, and the hypocrisy of authority. Community pressure rose to the point that threats were made against the Penningtons' lives. For a time they slept on their floor in case shots were fired through the window; once they found in their furnace stoker enough dynamite to blow up the house. Finally, armed and escorted by guard cars, the Penningtons left Cumberland.

In 1967 they moved to Louisville, Kentucky, and began teaching at Jefferson Community College there. That same year Pennington's first book was published. *The Dark Hills of Jesse Stuart*, most of which had been written originally as a master's thesis, is a critical analysis of the writing of Pennington's mentor. Pennington also continued to gain recognition for his poetry, which was being published steadily; three awards in 1967 included one from the Kentucky State Poetry Society. In 1968 he won a New York Poetry Society merit award for his play *Appalachia, My Sorrow*, produced at New York City's Riverside Theatre in connection with their World Poetry Day activities and later taped and broadcast abroad by Voice of America.

Scenes From a Southern Road, Pennington's first collection of poetry, was published in 1969 with a foreword by Jesse Stuart. Though the title poem and a handful of others have Southern settings outside the Appalachians, the collection as a whole portrays the area where Pennington grew up. Louisville critic J. W. Ballman described it as "a series of mood snapshots, candid photographs of people, places and things he has seen, pictures made real through careful imagery and detail."

Local characters are the subjects of poems: Old Muley Beaton, whose blacksnake whip became part of mountain folklore after his death; Big John 9, who moved to Detroit but came back, as mountain people do; and the poet's own father and brother. Pennington derives his imagery from nature and many of his metaphors from specific local places and rivers: "Perhaps Black Mountain was the creek stop / where the sun hitched a ride on Poor Fork. . . ."

"Bloody Harlan," a seven-part poem, describes the region's physical and emotional corruption:

> Down at the edge of the world
> By the lonely waters of Poor Fork
> Time has curled
> A knot of souls.
> Someone let pride seep out.

Also in 1969 Pennington was hired by MGM to work on *The Moonshine War*, which was released in 1970. As technical script supervisor, his job was to render the script phonetically in mountain dialect.

Pennington's second book of poetry, *Wildflower . . . Poems for Joy*, was published in 1970. It is a collection of poems written to Joy Pennington

while she was in the hospital for surgery, as was *Spring of Violets* (1976), following a similar hospital confinement. Written with no intention of publication, the poems in both books express deeply personal feelings. In "You Rest," from *Spring of Violets*, the poet watches his wife sleeping after surgery:

> Tomorrow I may ask more
> But today
> To see your breath rise and fall
> is all.

Other poems note hospital details—the "forever water sound" of a fountain outside near the room, flowers brought by friends and students, a waiting room where "Someone, an old woman / Carved by age, weeps . . . ." Even more poignant than the poems that tell the anxiety of waiting for consciousness and health to return are those that chronicle the poet's lonely trips between hospital and home—rain, fog, and car problems compound his bleak mood—and describe the loneliness of the house, where even the dog Echo "worries strangely." Both books, however, end on a happy note with Joy Pennington's return home.

April Poems (1970) was written for Jesse Stuart and his wife, who were in Africa in the spring of 1969 and wrote to Pennington, "Of all the things we might miss during this spring, the one we'll miss most is April in W Hollow, Kentucky." In these thirty poems—one for each day of the month— Pennington describes the spring reawakening of winter-dormant life, as in "Maples":

> Maple is born in April on fuzzy fingers
> Which hang down like tiny hairy strings
> And the wild wind passing sends looseness
> Asunder while the rest of the tree sings.

Songs of Bloody Harlan, published first in *North American Mentor* (Summer 1971), and in book form in 1975, is Pennington's toughly realistic but ultimately loving tribute to the region that had driven him out in 1967. He wrote of the poetry's genesis, "For two years following my experience in Harlan County, I didn't say anything. But a poet doesn't have that choice either. . . . *Songs of Bloody Harlan* is my comment."

Many of the poems in this collection describe the destruction of the land's natural beauty. "Pale Silence" is one of the most striking:

> The silence I fear most is the pale silence
> Down by the river where the wind blows

Front covers for Pennington's second (1970) and fifth (1976) books of poetry, both written to his wife while she was in the hospital

The restless water into waves of cold trance
And suddenly a duck-like milk carton be-
                                        comes a rose.

It is the green silence against grey mountains.
Long sweeping scars carved into stillness.
Dry suns etched on dust where a million tons
Of coal once danced in all the dampness.

Such as men standing by the red road
Where all their goodbye hands wave
At no one in the dark night, in the cold.
Who cares anyway how empty men behave?

Some acknowledge the area's hold on its people.
The "young hunting men" go away, but the poet
knows

                    the sounds of the L & N and the
Greyhound bus bringing them back home. I
know Cleveland, Dayton, Detroit faces, all

Harlan men who went away and made good
with a $20 a week taxi job.

Others, like "Giant Man of Harlan," evoke the ancient folk rhythms and myths of the mountains:

    Giant Man of Harlan
    Tromping through the trees
    Raising young whippoorwills
    Stirring up a breeze.

Finally, in "Just Because I Want to Say It," a long
poem reminiscent of Whitman, the poet says to the
people of Harlan in all their dirt and corruption and
vulnerability:

    I love you all since I can't help it and
    Even if I could help it, I still would love you.

    I Knew a Woman is probably Pennington's

best-known collection, since it earned him the Pulitzer Prize nomination. In this book he successfully writes about woman on both a personal level and a timeless and universal level—so that on the one hand, "an ordinary woman could pick up the book and glean some pleasure of it" and on the other, "Woman in the book represented not just women but the concept of woman, the creative concept." The relation of personal to universal woman, for the poet, is expressed in these stanzas from the title poem:

> I knew a woman and she was violet shadows
> touched with honey dew, and she was woman
> everything that Lilith knew.
> . . . .
> I knew a woman carved from love dipped
>   stone
> Soft as gentle flame, and she was woman;
> Woman was her name.

Not just Lilith but other mythical figures such as Eve and Aphrodite are used to define the poet's concept of timeless woman, and the heavy natural imagery employed throughout the book helps to place woman as a part of nature in her creative aspect. These points were noted by J. R. LeMaster in his review in *Arizona Quarterly* (Autumn 1978) in which he compared the feeling of Pennington's poetry here with that of D. H. Lawrence's, calling it "detached in the sense of being primitive and elemental but committed in the sense of working with clearly delineated images." He continued, "Appeal is always to the senses: passion is there in the elements, in the woman who is the elements, and who in being so is no less a woman, is no less *Woman*."

Many poems express the poet's sense of wonder at the familiar but nevertheless unfathomable woman he loves. An example is "Moments of Ease":

> You are mysterious
> even as I know your mystery
> having lived in your gift
> of loving me beyond
> moments of ease.
> And I love you
> with all my arms
> trying to catch
> your magic
> spread on me
> like moon shadows.

Dust jacket for Pennington's sixth volume of poetry (1981), nominated for a Pulitzer Prize

Others acknowledge the darker aspects of love: pain, the possibility of separation and loss. But the overall tone of the collection is a strong affirmation of love.

Jim Wayne Miller, a poet who teaches at Western Kentucky University, has analyzed in *Mountain Review* (Summer 1978) Pennington's technical skill in adapting conventional poetic forms to achieve new effects, as he does in using the compressed haiku to achieve intense erotic imagery:

> Your tongue is the flame
> That burns in the wilderness
> Of my hungry mouth.

In "Milkweed," Miller points out, Pennington has varied the sonnet form by using slant-rhymes and run-on lines "paralleling, in the subtlety, the symbolism of the milkweed":

> Tobacco's done, she said holding brown
> Hands above her head. I turned to see
> Her standing alone by the fallen barn,
> And smiled a rose of sharon smile. She
> In turn returned with petal lips red
> Against her blushing face.

"Pennington's artistry," Miller concludes, "is in his integration of form and subject matter. Just as he can take an old form and make it new and at the same time an appropriate vehicle for his subject, he takes man's experiences of woman in every time and place and renders them with vividness, immediacy and particularity."

Pennington's seven plays, all produced, have Appalachian settings and characters. Those written earliest, *The Porch* and *The Spirit of Poor Fork*, evoke a feeling of the region but have very slight plots and momentum. Both were published in 1976, as were *Appalachia, My Sorrow* and *Coalmine*, which Pennington calls one-act plays for voices. In *Appalachia, My Sorrow* disparate voices represent the physical and spiritual wounds inflicted by a harsh and often hypocritical way of life. A young girl speaks the metaphor for all of the characters—a redbird splashing in the water of the river: "At first I thought he was takin' a bath but then I knew. He was fighting himself. Flogging the water and all against what he didn't know was himself flogging back."

Coalmine depicts the uncertainty of the miner's life. Its representative figure is a wife who anticipates her husband's death in the mine, is helpless to prevent it, and suffers a mental breakdown when it comes. The great tragedy, however, is the continuation of this way of life for miners and their families without any real hope of escape or improvement. In 1978, *Appalachia, My Sorrow* and *Coalmine* were produced at the University of Kentucky's Guignol Theatre along with Pennington's *Ragweed* and *Foxwind* as *Appalachian Quartet*. Put together with songs and poems by Pennington, the production was described by one reviewer as "a mosaic of Appalachian life—introducing a people, a land, a time, through the eyes and mind of a poet."

The Scotian Women, Pennington's only full-length play, was also produced at the University of Kentucky. Based on a 1976 Kentucky mine disaster, it shows the emotions and interaction of five women who wait for news of their husbands from the rescue workers. In mixed reviews the play was described as surreal and oppressive, though some reviewers praised the script for its lyricism. They also noted its debt to Greek drama in structure, starkness of setting, and the use of chorus and masks.

J. Robert Wills, now dean of the College of Fine Arts at the University of Texas at Austin, has directed five Pennington plays. In *Southern Quarterly* (Fall 1981), he presents an analysis of the body of Pennington's drama. "For an author so steeped in a given regional culture, Pennington's plays surprisingly reflect the mainstream of American dramatic literature during the 1960s and 1970s. He represents, for example, the return to language, the break from realism . . . the rejection of orderly logic. . . ." Wills concludes, "No other writer has explored Appalachia so consistently in dramatic form. No other writer has captured so well the complex spirit of his subject."

In 1982 Pennington and graphic designer Ben Ruiz published "The Janus Collection," a set of twelve poster-size photographs with poems superimposed on them to form what Pennington calls the "double image." Photographs and poems are by Pennington; Ruiz designed the collection. The work is named for Janus, the Roman god identified with beginnings and with gates and doors. As Janus is represented by two faces looking in opposite directions, Pennington's photograph/poems also contain faces, "thereby communicating two images," as the introductory notes on the collection's folder explain. "Likewise, each poem has a vertical, visual 'poem-within-a-poem' that also communicates twice. Basically, both the words and the pictures work together to convey the double impact that is the Janus concept." Pennington considers the creation a new genre, one that can bring poetry "out of the closet and onto people's walls."

Pennington makes frequent public appearances—as many as fifty a year—to read his poetry, sing folk songs to his own guitar or banjo accompaniment, and tell stories, another art in which his reputation is growing. Though he has enjoyed telling stories since childhood (it is a major Appalachian pastime), he did not begin doing so professionally until 1975, as master of ceremonies at the National Storytelling Festival in Jonesboro, Tennessee, which was founded in 1973. His specialty is folk yarns, in which hyperbole is encouraged. He claims to know about 500 stories, mostly from Appalachia. He has served as a board member of the National Association for the Preservation and Perpetuation of Storytelling, and in 1976 helped to found the Annual Corn Island Storytelling Festival in Louisville. It now attracts storytellers from all over the United States.

Pennington's other continuing passion, no less important to him than his writing and folk artistry, is teaching. At Jefferson Community College, where he and his wife still teach, at workshops and in special meetings with would-be writers ranging from elementary school students through retirees in their eighties, he has coaxed marketable writing from people of all backgrounds. As a teacher he is a maverick, worrying least about grammar and traditional forms, and promoting his belief that "Everyman is a poet" to the extent that he can become genuinely aware of his surroundings. A textbook he wrote, *Creative Composition: An Experimental Course in Freshman Composition*, was printed privately and has been used experimentally at Jefferson Community College.

The Penningtons' home reinforces their ties to land and tradition. Known locally as Kratz House, it was built in 1850 as a tavern. It is located in Middletown, Kentucky, an area on the outskirts of Louisville where early settlers battled severe weather and marauding Indians. Pennington's work continues to gain recognition. For his "outstanding contribution to literature," in 1979 he was awarded an honorary doctor of literature degree by World University, affiliated with University Danzig in New York. Several of his manuscripts are still unpublished, among them two novels ("Run on Seven Gravels" and "To Wake the Water") and a poetry collection that Pennington feels may be his best work, "Segovia's Fingernail." "It's very important for me to get published and get an audience," Pennington says, "but the most important thing still remains to write it down."

Plays:
The Porch, Berea, Ky., Berea College, March 1962;
The Spirit of Poor Fork, Cumberland, Ky., Southeast Community College, October 1966;

Appalachia, My Sorrow, New York, Riverside Theatre, October 1969;
Coalmine, Louisville, Ky., Jefferson Community College, April 1976;
Ragweed, Lexington, Ky., Guignol Theatre, March 1978;
Foxwind, Lexington, Ky., Guignol Theatre, March 1978;
The Scotian Women, February 1981.

References:
J. R. LeMaster, Review in *Arizona Quarterly*, 34 (Autumn 1978);
William Patteson, Jr., and Rebecca Bushman, *Collecting Lee Pennington: A Checklist* (Privately published, 1980);
J. Robert Wills, "Prevailing Shadows: The Plays of Lee Pennington," *Southern Quarterly*, 20 (Fall 1981): 25-34.

AN INTERVIEW
with LEE PENNINGTON

DLB: As a young boy in eastern Kentucky, ninth of eleven children, you didn't even think of going to college until you were in the seventh grade. When you look back on the events that led to college and a teaching career and becoming a published writer, how do you feel about it?

PENNINGTON: I think everything seems to have pleasantly and warmly and fatalistically fallen into place. Back around the fourth grade, I had my first teaching experience, and I can remember the excitement and enjoyment of it. In my little one-room school, there was one teacher for all eight grades, so she let the advanced classes teach the lower classes. When I was in fourth grade, I taught first grade for the whole year. I remember I had three students, including one very good student that I personally double-promoted to the third grade! That was my first experience of being a teacher. I had another amateur experience when I was in high school under Jesse Stuart as principal. There was a tremendous teacher shortage then, and rather than close the school down, Jesse Stuart got students with exceptionally good grades to teach some of the classes. I wound up one semester never going to a single one of my own classes—the teachers let me come by and take the exams—because I was teaching eighth grade.

I must have been in the fifth or sixth grade when one of my sisters said to me, "Someday you're going to go to college," and I thought that was the funniest thing I'd ever heard, because I had no intention of doing so. Then in the seventh grade I ran into a teacher, Robert M. Waddell, who set fire under me. I knew from then on that one way or another I would be going to college. And other people were quite influential. In addition to Jesse Stuart, there was my high school English teacher, Lena Nevison, who encouraged me in my writing. Everything seems to have fallen in place. As I look back, it's logical that it all happened the way it did and it's also a big surprise to me.

DLB: Did the urge to write come from storytelling, originally?

PENNINGTON: I don't know if I can pin it down. My first writing, I remember, was in the fourth grade. We had a history book that was not a history text but a historical novel, about an American frontier family. The novel took this family through several generations, up to the end of the 1800s, and I felt very badly that the story had not carried the family on into the twentieth century. So my first writing was taking that book and creating a new generation. As I recall, it was about seventy or eighty handwritten pages, and that's the earliest memory I have of writing. I did more writing later on in elementary school and was writing fairly seriously by the time I got to high school.

DLB: Would you comment on Berea College, both as an institution and what it meant to you personally?

PENNINGTON: The philosophical concepts of Berea were concepts that I agreed with, such as the dignity of labor—everybody at Berea College must work at least ten hours a week at some sort of job. I got a great deal of work experience, and I found that the instruction at Berea was exceptional; I didn't realize that fully until I got into graduate school and found that graduate school seemed to be pretty much a review of the work I'd done at Berea. At the time I was there, the college was almost totally for mountain students who showed good ability and could not finance their own college education without financial assistance. There was no tuition at Berea then, and room and board were relatively cheap. By saving money and working during the summers, I was able to pay my college expenses. I couldn't have done that anywhere else.

DLB: You've been very successful at teaching creative writing. How do you approach it?

PENNINGTON: I think the main job is to get students to start observing the world around them, start seeing very common things that they simply overlook. One of the things our great writers have been able to do is look at the same environment that everybody else lives in and be able to see things in it that other people have passed over. That's the first barrier that you get the students through. Then, on the college level, I feel that I have to break through the feeling about poetry that they've gotten from late elementary school throughout high school. They come to college with almost no concept of modern poetry; their concept is pretty much centered in poetry of the nineteenth-century back to Elizabethan poetry. So early in the classes they write a lot of nineteenth-century poetry.

DLB: Your belief that "Everyman is a poet" to the extent that he can see his surroundings in a fresh way is one that many writers and critics wouldn't agree with.

PENNINGTON: That's very true, but I think we've made poetry far too elite over the last few years. Poetry is the intense language which ultimately raises the level of the culture, and I don't think you can make that claim for it and exclude ninety-eight percent of the culture. Every person can have his or her level of existence raised, and in a college class it's rather absurd to think that we're all going to be Nobel Prize winners or Pulitzer Prize winners or even teachers. I think by far the largest number of students in my classes are going to be common, average American citizens. We need to have something for them.

DLB: You've tried to encourage a feeling of pride in the unique beauty of the Appalachians. Do you think Appalachian culture is becoming more widely appreciated than it used to be?

PENNINGTON: I think it's starting to come along, certainly. There's an awful lot going on in this country that seems to indicate that people are stopping and taking a look at the very valuable kind of culture Appalachia has. We in the state of Kentucky may have laughed from time to time at Phyllis George [wife of Kentucky Governor John Y. Brown, Jr.] and some of the things she's doing, but the very fact that Appalachian-made quilts are being sold in Bloomingdale's—thanks to her—indicates that people want some part of a culture that really is a high culture and a lot more permanent than some of the other things we've got around. Here in Louisville we have the Bluegrass Festival of the United States. They had to cut off attendance one year recently because too many people showed up.

But the most important thing is for the Appalachian himself to sense the value of his culture. I think that's happening, and it needs to happen more. When I started teaching in Cumberland, Kentucky, in Harlan County, I noticed right away that all of the existing programs were attempting to import "culture" to the people. They wanted to bring in the ballet and the opera, and there's nothing wrong with that, but at the same time they were saying, "The culture you have is of no value; here is the really valuable culture." Now people outside Appalachia are starting to take a look at Appalachia's culture, and this is bringing a kind of self-pride to the Appalachians, something which is absolutely necessary for them to be successful.

DLB: In *Songs of Bloody Harlan* you spoke with forgiveness, with love, for that area you and your wife had been forced out of in 1967. Has your perspective on that experience changed over the years?

PENNINGTON: I've always been happy with what I was able to accomplish there, and those were very, very exciting times. I went in there an idealistic, brassy young man. I think I may have mellowed a little bit. I probably would be, as a result of age, a bit more cautious in my approach if I were back in that situation. But I went there loving the people, loving the area, and regardless of what happened, that aspect of my feelings didn't change. Much of what took place was a result of misunderstanding more than anything else. Some people—the higher officials, in particular—thought I was trying to do one thing when, indeed, I was trying to do something else. I suspect they thought I was trying to tear down Harlan County, but my whole idea was to build up Harlan County.

DLB: One reviewer compared you to D. H. Lawrence, and the long Harlan County poems make me think of Whitman, too. What poets do you feel a kinship with?

PENNINGTON: I could go on all day about that! I feel very close to a number of poets. I think the first poet who was influential was Jesse Stuart, and, in particular, his book *Man With a Bull-Tongue Plow.* My feelings now are that *Man With a Bull-Tongue Plow* is not as good a book as Jesse's *Album of Destiny,* but *Man With a Bull-Tongue Plow* certainly had a

Manuscript for "Death Fear," written on the back
of an envelope

larger effect on me. Later on, people like Robert Frost started having a big effect on me. I know Whitman has had, but that effect did not really start until I was in graduate school. D. H. Lawrence was very influential in both prose and poetry. And the Spanish poet Federico García Lorca; he may be the largest influence on me right at the moment. I'm fascinated with Lorca because the common people in Spain can relate to him as well as people in the highest academic circles. When Joy and I were in Barcelona in 1979, I slipped out from the motel one night and went down to a Spanish bar several blocks out of the tourist area. Nobody around spoke much English and I didn't really speak Spanish. I went up to the bartender and tried to ask him about Lorca just to get his reaction. Finally someone in the bar spoke enough English to see what I was trying to do, and he told the bartender in Spanish that I wanted to know about the poet Lorca. The bartender's face lit up and he started talking about Lorca in Spanish, most of which I couldn't understand without help. He told me that Lorca was buried in Granada, and that astonished me. I thought, if we went into a typical American bar and asked about any American poet, what would the bartender's reaction be? Probably the bartender would very likely not even know someone as well-known as Frost, and he certainly wouldn't know where Frost was buried. That personal aspect of Lorca amazes me, but more than that, the literary aspect. I feel a great kinship with him.

Theodore Roethke has had an influence on me, particularly his book *Words for the Wind*. And then going back into the 1920s and 1930s, that great period, Edna St. Vincent Millay, Sara Teasdale, Carl Sandburg, Edgar Lee Masters, and many others. I suspect I would have to say that everybody I've read has had some sort of influence on me, and some people, such as Lorca and Roethke and Frost, continue to play a major role with my feeling, my existence, and ultimately, my writing.

DLB: Did you begin writing plays primarily for your students?

PENNINGTON: No. I wrote my first play quite by accident. When I was at Berea College I took every writing course I could take, and I finally ran out of writing courses. So I then designed an independent study in writing, just to get another course. I said that to complete this course I would write a short story, a poem, and a play. I don't even know why I said I'd write a play, but I hadn't written one up to that point. Well, by the end of the course I had written twelve new short stories and fifty-seven poems and a play called *The Porch*. I showed the play to the director of drama and he said, "We would like to produce it here. Would you like to direct it?" And I said, "I'd love to." So that was the first experience. It was quite exciting for me to see what happens when one writes something down, then it takes other human beings to present it to an audience.

With that first play I learned a valuable lesson about drama, and particularly about tragedy. I thought that *The Porch* was a very tragic play, and that the audience would go away absolutely wiped out. But I found out that an audience cannot stand totally serious, tragic writing for a great length of time. There was a scene in there that I thought was extremely tragic, where a man happened to look like a sheep. By that point, however, the mood had become so oppressive to the audience, they just started laughing. At first I got mad at them. I thought, "What a crazy audience. Why are they out here laughing at this?" But it was a good lesson for me that if you're going to be very serious and tragic, you also have to give the audience a chance to release their sadness—something that the Greek tragedians learned several hundred years before I did.

DLB: Reviewers and critics have certainly noticed the similarities between your plays and Greek drama.

PENNINGTON: I feel very close to the classical Greek dramatists—Sophocles, Aristophanes, and others—but I also feel very close to the Greek culture as a whole. When we were in Athens and traveling over other parts of Greece, I felt that if I weren't in heaven I certainly must be in the front yard. My last play, *The Scotian Women*, has similarities to *Trojan Women*, though I suspect it may very well have more Teutonic overtones than Greek.

I'm fascinated by the great storymakers and what they were able to do. *The Iliad* and *The Odyssey* seem to have emanated right out of the mouths of the people all around them. Those writers weren't writing outside of the culture they were living in. This is true of other cultures, too. In the English culture you have people like Chaucer, one of my favorite poets. He simply listened to what people said. One of his stories, "The Miller's Tale," which I'm sure he heard in England, I heard as a dirty joke in Greenup County. I'm sure the story I heard didn't come from Chaucer. It was just an oral tale that stayed in the culture. Chaucer heard it and made literary use of it; I heard it in 1954 in Greenup County. Shakespeare surely depended on his ear. And in this country, William Faulkner, certainly one of our giants. His story "The Bear" was an oral tradition tale before Faulkner got hold of it and made it a literary tale.

DLB: Are you traveling a lot now to sing and tell stories?

PENNINGTON: Yes, I do that all the time. Joy and I still work very hard on the Corn Island Storytelling Festival here, which was the second festival ever created in the United States just for storytelling. Last year we had about 4,000 people show up; it's getting stronger. I generally do fifty or so presentations a year—reading poetry, singing, telling stories. I enjoy doing all the things I do, and I don't really see any conflict in them, although a lot of people have advised me that I ought to settle down on one thing and quit spreading myself so thin. I don't think we have to narrow ourselves down, particularly if different things excite us.

—*Jean W. Ross*

Robert Pinsky
(20 October 1940-   )

Willard Spiegelman
Southern Methodist University

BOOKS: *Landor's Poetry* (Chicago: University of Chicago Press, 1968);
Sadness and Happiness (Princeton: Princeton University Press, 1975);
The Situation of Poetry: Contemporary Poetry and Its Traditions (Princeton: Princeton University Press, 1976);
An Explanation of America (Princeton: Princeton University Press, 1979; Manchester, U.K.: Carcanet, 1979).

In chapter eighteen of *Biographia Literaria*, Coleridge, applying William Browne's epithet for his Elizabethan contemporary Samuel Daniel, calls William Wordsworth "well-languaged" and proceeds to praise him, several chapters later, for the "weight and sanity of the thoughts and sentiments [won] from the poet's own meditative observation." Wordsworth, like Daniel, writes in "that style which, as the neutral ground of prose and verse, is common to both." Robert Pinsky belongs with these poets whose language, while obeying the idiomatic rules of their own age, is intelligible beyond the fashions of a given time. He belongs to another category as well: he is in the line of the poet-critic, an honorable class whose fountainhead in the modern age is Coleridge himself and whose members include Matthew Arnold, T. S. Eliot, and W. H. Auden.

Like these predecessors, Pinsky has been interested equally in the creation and the analysis of poetry. He has written two critical books, the first a distinguished academic investigation of the Romantic poet Walter Savage Landor, the second a speculative discussion of recent American poetry, and two volumes of verse, both published by a university press but aimed at a general literate audi-

ence. In Pinsky's poetry and criticism there lies an abiding unity, of which the principal ingredients are ethical ambition, sanity, a sense of humor, and something to say. Deeply intelligent without ever seeming pedantic or dull, Pinsky's criticism contributes to our understanding of the many modes and tones of contemporary verse; his own poetry is lucid and meditative, without ever succumbing to prosiness, and it brings together the plain and the fancy in chaste simplicity.

Pinsky was born in Long Branch, New Jersey, to Milford Simon and Silvia Pinsky. His career has followed a predictable academic curve: public education in New Jersey followed by university degrees from Rutgers (B.A., 1962) and Stanford (Ph.D., 1966), where he studied with Yvor Winters, whose sometimes eccentric or cavalier dismissal of traditional literary tastes forced several generations of students to rethink the entire notion of tradition and literary evaluation. In 1961, Pinsky married Ellen Bailey; they have two children. After Stanford and his dissertation (later his book *Landor's Poetry*, 1968) on Landor, a poet admired by Winters, Pinsky taught at Chicago, Wellesley, and Harvard and is now at Berkeley. In addition to composing his larger articulations, he has served as poetry editor for the *New Republic* and contributes to a wide variety of journals.

One never chooses what one likes for simple, objective reasons, and it is instructive to read Pinsky on Landor (or on Elizabeth Bishop or Wallace Stevens) to learn how his appreciation of other poets has affected, and been affected in turn by, his own poetry. Although he seldom writes epigrams, he often writes epigrammatically and, like Landor, he has "a special perception of what an occasion is." Part of his artistic credo, again like Landor's, "is the attractive serenity acquired by fact, even the most passionate fact, as it moves into oblivious time." Both poets force us to reexamine our notions of plainness and elegance, and both make the commonplace the convenient beginnings of their poetry.

The title poem in *Sadness and Happiness* (1975) epitomizes Pinsky's instincts for generalizations based on specific evidence, for the lure of abstraction, and for the intellectual's compulsion to move outward to larger conclusions. At the same time, the tone is informed by a secular skepticism, inherited from the tradition of Montaigne, which encourages the poet to understand that although we may speak of "sadness" and "happiness" as opposites, there are predominantly gray middle states of desire, and that the lines between categories are never crystalline. One can try to measure these two qualities, but what seems most true and surprising is how often in memory they become indistinguishable from each other: "the strangely/ happy fondling" of past failures, or the speaker's realization of "how happy I would be, or else/ decently sad, with no past."

Almost as an unconscious corollary to his focus on "the isthmus of a middle state," as Pope called the human condition, Pinsky has devised a "middle" style for this thirteen-part poem. A sinuous syntax elaborates and encompasses the poet's mental meanderings and definitions. These sentences maintain the illusion of meditative fluency or speed, while at the same time they keep the poet close (as do the short lines) to the tightness of Landor and Ben Jonson. Here, for example, are the closing lines:

> It is intolerable
> to think of my daughters, too, dust—
> *el polvo*—or you whose invented game,
> Sadness and Happiness, soothes them
>
> to sleep: can you tell me one sad
> thing that happened today, can you think
> of one happy thing to tell me that
> happened to you today, organizing
>
> life—not you too dust like the poets,
> dancers, athletes, their dear skills
> and the alleged glittering gaiety of
> Art which, in my crabwise scribbling hand,
>
> no less than Earth the change of all
> changes breedeth, art and life
> both inconstant mothers, in whose
> fixed cold bosoms we lie fixed,
>
> desperate to devise anything, any
> sadness or happiness, only
> to escape the clasped coffinworm
> truth of eternal art or marmoreal
>
> infinite nature, twin stiff
> destined measures both manifested
> by my shoes, coated with dust or dew
>   which no
> earthly measure will survive.

Although he ventures into other forms—short lyrics, reminiscences, quasi-dream poems—it is with the long meditation that Pinsky does best, for it allows him ample space to explore and savor the play of his mind. His poetic sanity encourages the "middle style," *sermoni propiora* as Horace once put it, and his professorial discursiveness forces him to think mostly in capacious and leisurely forms.

The "Essay on Psychiatrists" is clearly the triumph of *Sadness and Happiness*, for here theme and form are happily united. Surveying the field, and attempting to define and evaluate this new, modern professional, Pinsky, admittedly one who has never sought the wisdom of a psychiatrist, ranges from a contemplation of *The Bacchae* (is Pentheus or Dionysus the true psychiatrist in the play?) to Rex Morgan, M.D., to Landor's Imaginary Conversation between Fulke-Greville and Sidney, to his memory of his teacher Yvor Winters. He concludes sadly that he has "failed / To discover what essential statement could be made / About psychiatrists that would not apply / To all human beings, or what statement / About all human beings would not apply / Equally to psychiatrists." They are just like the rest of us, he proposes, in his lucid, lyric final lines:

> Even in their prosperity which is perhaps
> Like their contingency merely more vivid
>   than that
> Of lutanists, opticians, poets—all into
>
> Truth, into music, into yearning, suffering,
> Into elegant machines and luxuries, with
>   caroling
> And kisses, with soft rich cloth and polished
>
> Substances, with cash, tennis and fine elec-
>   tronics,
> Liberty of lush and reverend places—goods
> And money in their contingency and spiritual
>
> Grace evoke the way we are all psychiatrists,
> All fumbling at so many millions of miles
> Per minute and so many dollars per hour
>
> Through the exploding or collapsing spaces
> Between stars, saying what we can.

The problem of psychiatrists, "saying what we can," is everyone else's problem, but especially that of poets who, according to *The Situation of Poetry* (1976), have "a need to find language for presenting the role of a conscious soul in an unconscious world." In his critical book, Pinsky emphasizes the conscious soul, rather than the repressed or unconscious self which must be resurrected as the condition for mental or creative health. His remarks on "discursiveness," defined alternatively as wandering and explanation, go a long way toward explaining how Pinsky's own poetry came to be the way it is: rambling, like A. R. Ammons's, which he likes, as well as compressed, like J. V. Cunningham's, which he also admires. Yearning for the physical world, he says, "reminds us of our solitude . . . of the contingency and randomness of the world the senses know"; this echoes his notion, in "Essay on Psychiatrists," that although our senses can know only dis-

crete particulars, we cry out for larger, abstract categories with which to make sense of the world.

Pinsky's strongest poem is his longest, the book-length *An Explanation of America* (1979). Framed by a preparatory prologue and an epilogue in the form of a lament, the poem is an exemplary professorial performance: addressed to the poet's daughter, it attempts to instruct her about the past, in the present, for the future. Like Robert Lowell, Pinsky is interested in public life and history, but his characteristic tone is less agonized and tense, more subdued than Lowell's. And where Lowell's Rome is Juvenal's, Pinsky selects the earlier empire, Augustus's and Horace's, for his historical analogy to America. His poem affirms both the basic line of English verse, in its five-beat, largely iambic rhythms, and a native American dialectic, most clearly adduced in its debt to the tripartite structure of Wallace Stevens's "Notes Towards A Supreme Fiction." Instead of Stevens's "It Must Be Abstract," "It Must Give Pleasure," and "It Must Change," we have "Its Many Fragments," "Its Great Emptiness," and "Its Many Possibilities" to explain the "idea" of these states. Pinsky proves that explanation has its own eloquence, and pedagogy its distinctive rhythms. Walt Whitman once called America the greatest poem of all, and Pinsky possesses his precursor's speculative interest in his native land. He defines a nation as "the same people living in the same place" (an old cliché), but since we live in an America always fragmented and changing, with all things lessened and made precious with time, our nation is also "different people living in different places." Even places, paradoxically, move. Pinsky's large theme, how to make a place, a nation, or a dream useful, repeats Thomas Jefferson's early proposition that "the earth belongs in usufruct to the living." But an elegist as well (an inevitable mantle for a follower of Stevens), Pinsky reminds us that one's aspirations for oneself always differ from those for one's posterity. Like Brutus, we are committed to struggle; the Horatian dream of self-sufficiency on a Sabine farm must be reserved for our children. America, however, thwarts even our dreams of sufficiency since its boundless size encourages millennial hopes and impulses which move us imaginatively beyond "contingency" (Pinsky's own word from "Essay on Psychiatrists").

Pinsky's poem charts the development of the "idea" of America from a beginning in infinite particulars through a fall into emptiness, to the promise of "everlasting possibility." In lines generally bereft of rhetorical flourishes and full of straight speaking, Pinsky has modernized past poets Horace (one

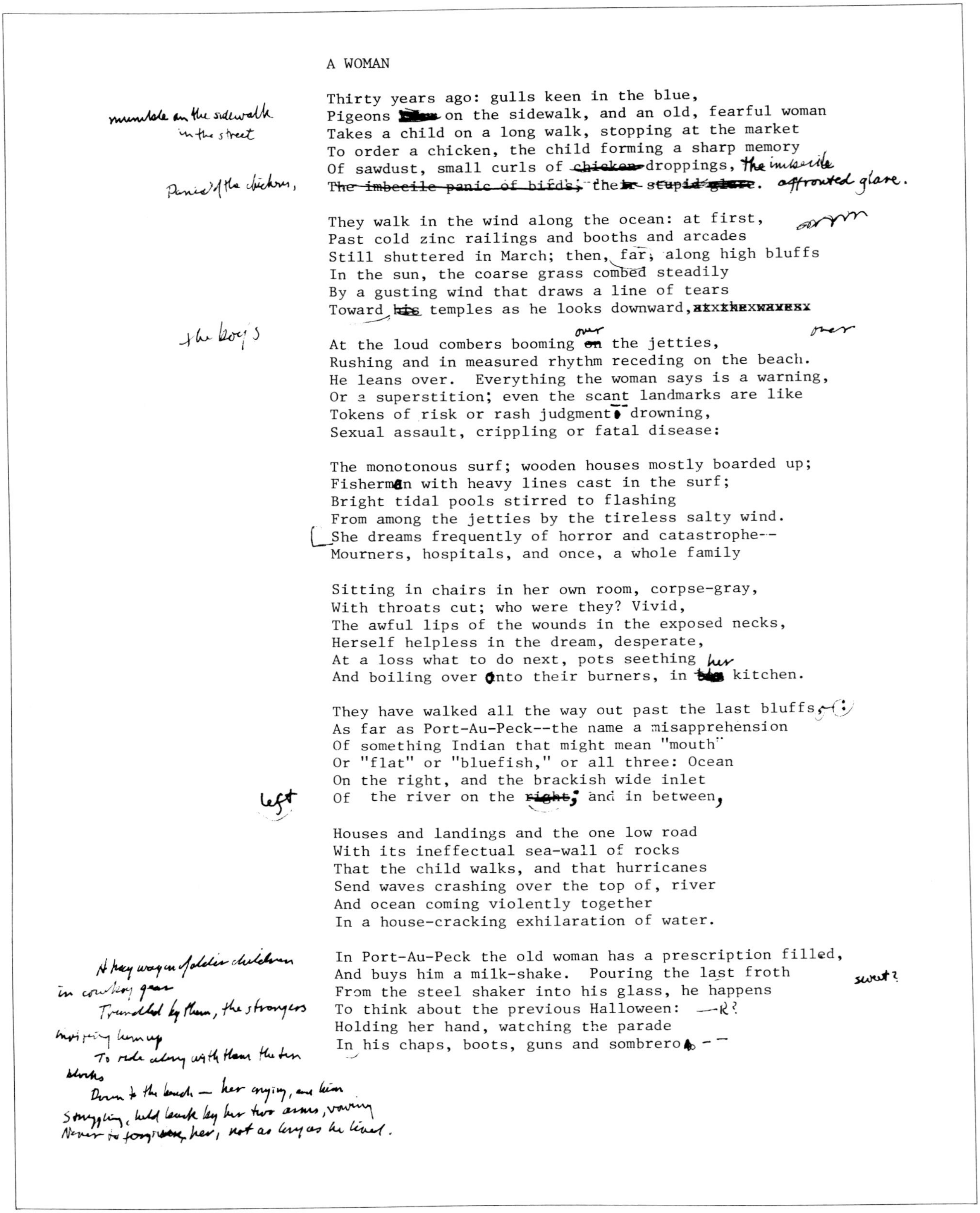

A WOMAN

Thirty years ago: gulls keen in the blue,
Pigeons ~~blue~~ on the sidewalk, and an old, fearful woman
Takes a child on a long walk, stopping at the market
To order a chicken, the child forming a sharp memory
Of sawdust, small curls of ~~chicken~~ droppings, the miserable
~~The imbecile panic of birds; their stupid glare.~~ affronted glare.

[margin: mumble on the sidewalk / in the street]
[margin: Panic of the chickens,]

They walk in the wind along the ocean: at first,
Past cold zinc railings and booths and arcades
Still shuttered in March; then, far, along high bluffs
In the sun, the coarse grass combed steadily
By a gusting wind that draws a line of tears
Toward ~~his~~ temples as he looks downward, ~~and the waves~~

[margin: the boy's]

At the loud combers booming ~~on~~ *over* the jetties,
Rushing and in measured rhythm receding on the beach.
He leans over. Everything the woman says is a warning,
Or a superstition; even the scant landmarks are like
Tokens of risk or rash judgment: drowning,
Sexual assault, crippling or fatal disease:

[margin: over]

The monotonous surf; wooden houses mostly boarded up;
Fisherman with heavy lines cast in the surf;
Bright tidal pools stirred to flashing
From among the jetties by the tireless salty wind.
She dreams frequently of horror and catastrophe--
Mourners, hospitals, and once, a whole family

Sitting in chairs in her own room, corpse-gray,
With throats cut; who were they? Vivid,
The awful lips of the wounds in the exposed necks,
Herself helpless in the dream, desperate,
At a loss what to do next, pots seething *her*
And boiling over onto their burners, in ~~the~~ kitchen.

They have walked all the way out past the last bluffs ~~,~~ :
As far as Port-Au-Peck--the name a misapprehension
Of something Indian that might mean "mouth"
Or "flat" or "bluefish," or all three: Ocean
On the right, and the brackish wide inlet
Of the river on the ~~right;~~ and in between,

[margin: left]

Houses and landings and the one low road
With its ineffectual sea-wall of rocks
That the child walks, and that hurricanes
Send waves crashing over the top of, river
And ocean coming violently together
In a house-cracking exhilaration of water.

In Port-Au-Peck the old woman has a prescription filled,
And buys him a milk-shake. Pouring the last froth
From the steel shaker into his glass, he happens
To think about the previous Halloween: ---R?
Holding her hand, watching the parade
In his chaps, boots, guns and sombrero, --

[margin right: sweet?]

[margin bottom, handwritten:]
A hay wagon of older children
in cowboy gear
Trundled by them, the strangers
inviting him up
To ride along with them the ten
blocks
Down to the beach — her crying, and him
Struggling, held back by her two arms, vowing
Never to forgive her, not as long as he lived.

of whose epistles he translates), the English Romantics, Whitman, and Stevens. His is a classic, modern, "American" performance. Indeed, the homage to the past, instead of distracting from the contemplation of the present, may remind a contemporary audience that Pinsky's own historic sense, like that of the Americans he describes, alternates between nostalgia and anticipation. Like children ("ornaments to our sentimental past, / They bind us to the future"), the joint creative enterprise of memory and expectation winds down the paths of historical and personal time. Consciousness, that great Romantic burden, is power, as Pinsky asserts when he equates the strangeness of the wide American spaces with the emptiness of a man trying to write a poem about the loneliness he shares with "the contagious blankness of a quiet plain":

> In the dark proof he finds in his poem, the man
> Might come to think of himself as the very prairie,
> The sod itself, not lonely, and immune to death.
>
> None of this happens precisely as I try
> To imagine that it does, in the empty plains,
> And yet it happens in the imagination
> Of part of the country: not in any place
> More than another, on the map, but rather
> Like a place, where you and I have never been
> And need to try to imagine—place like a prairie
>
> Where immigrants, in the obliterating strangeness,
> Thirst for the wide contagion of the shadow
> Or prairie—where you and I, with our other ways,

> More like the cities or the hills or trees,
> Less like the clear blank spaces with their potential,
> Are like strangers in a place we must imagine.

The man resembles Stevens's Snowman, becoming a part of the wintry landscape which his mind mirrors; the poet and his daughter repeat the adventure of all American immigrants confronting the vastness of the continent; the living people hear the past speak to them, as Whitman does in "A Passage to India" ("The Past—the dark unfathom'd retrospect! / The teeming gulf—the sleepers and the shadows! / The past—the infinite greatness of the past!"). This passage shows how naturally Pinsky combines grandeur of vision with intimacy of tone and execution. The ecstasy of infinite aspiration never releases the poem from its stated intention of explaining, with patience and love, an "idea" to a real audience who comes to figure as a character in its creation. Pinsky's noble achievement has been to develop an epic subject with tenderness, to define and defend his own brand of patriotism as he prepares the next generation for the historical and imaginative enterprise of understanding its country. "Well-languaged," he has maintained a colloquial tone while adhering to a grand faith "in a place we must imagine."

Pinsky's intelligent optimism, on behalf of his country, of the human heart, and of the community of poets into which he fits and for which he speaks, shines through all of his books. Critics, both other academics and other poets, have from the start admired his versatility in two areas which unfortunately seem too often hostile.

Interview:
Mark Halliday, "An Interview With Robert Pinsky," *Ploughshares*, 6 (1980): 141-169.

John Rechy
(1934-)

David G. Byrd
University of South Carolina

BOOKS: *City of Night* (New York: Grove, 1963; London: MacGibbon & Kee, 1964);

Numbers (New York: Grove, 1967);

This Day's Death, A Novel (New York: Grove, 1970; London: MacGibbon & Kee, 1970);

The Vampires (New York: Grove, 1971);

The Fourth Angel (New York: Viking, 1972; London: W. H. Allen, 1972);

The Sexual Outlaw: A Documentary. A Non-Fiction Account, with Commentaries, of Three Days and Nights in the Sexual Underground (New York: Grove, 1977; London: Futura, 1979);

Rushes: A Novel (New York: Grove, 1979).

John Rechy was born in El Paso, Texas, the son of Roberto Sixto and Guadalupe Flores Rechy. After receiving his B.A. at Texas Western College, he attended the New School for Social Research in New York. A tour of duty in Germany with the army followed his education. Before any of his novels were published, he contributed to *Evergreen Review*, where sections of *City of Night* appeared; *Nugget*; *Big Table*; *London Magazine*; and *Nation*, receiving the Longview Foundation fiction prize in 1961. When his first novel, *City of Night*, appeared in 1963, James Baldwin said Rechy was "The most arresting young writer I've read in a very long time." Terry Southern put him in the "self-revelatory school of Romantic Agony," a school which has as its basic rule "Feel everything and leave nothing unsaid." Webster Schott, in the *New York Times Book Review*, called *City of Night* "one of the landmarks in the new homosexual fiction." Rechy says that he was unable to cope with the novel's success. Cherishing his privacy, he went to the Caribbean but later returned to El Paso, staying there until his mother died in 1970. However, following his success with this first novel, he began contributing to other self-revealing collections of the 1960s: *The Moderns*, *Voices*, *Black Humor*, and *New American Story*, and then followed *City of Night* with its revealing sequel, *Numbers* (1967).

Rechy is a serious writer, influenced, as he says, by movies, Shakespeare, Proust, Milton, and Joyce, but also by Margaret Mitchell, Kathleen Winsor, and King Vidor—admiring also Dostoevski,

Hawthorne, Poe, and Faulkner. In *The Sexual Outlaw* (1977), he admits, "My life is so intertwined with my writing that I almost live it as if it were a novel." Interested in helping new writers, he has conducted writing seminars at the University of California at Los Angeles and is a member of the Authors Guild and Artists Civil Rights Assistance Fund. He admits that after discovering such places as Times Square, Hollywood Boulevard, and the French Quarter, he "turned very briefly to drugs and was almost destroyed by LSD." His novels, with homosexual themes, are full of lost angels, grotesque characters, who, in their rage against the society that has outcast them, flaunt their sexuality openly, defying the omnipresent angel of death which hovers over them.

Following the critical success of *Rushes* (1979), Rechy began writing a play based on this novel, which originated as a play but shifted to the novel form. Turning to a different medium, he has also written a screenplay based on *City of Night*. He is, as he says, "a great movie fan" and includes in his novels many famous movie scenes disguised with modern characters and incidents.

Obsessed with structure, he completed his first cycle with *Rushes*, his "benediction," his cycle of "a paradise-lost, paradise-regained sort of thing, the return to a state of a knowing purity." Now, he is in his second cycle, having completed a new novel, "Bodies and Souls." According to Rechy, there are many literary and movie references in this book of six men and six women, all disparate characters. A novel that promises to be different, it does not deal "primarily with homosexuality, though it does have homosexual characters." It is a "lush book," says Rechy, borrowing from famous movie scenes in *Gone With the Wind*, *Forever Amber*, and *For Whom the Bell Tolls*. Rechy also teaches, writes reviews, and is working on a screen adaptation of "The Mystery of Marie Roget" by Edgar Allan Poe, a writer who has influenced him "a great deal."

Rechy has one character who is present in all his books. Perhaps autobiographical, this young man evolves from a hustler who insists that he is not part of that world to a reciprocal participant who blames his inner rage on his cruel father and his

John Rechy

dominating mother who smothers him with love that he calls hate. As if to block out the dark memories of his home in El Paso, Texas, with its crushing Catholicism, he spends most of his time "scoring." Each sexual encounter not only defeats death but it also has a cleansing effect upon the bewildered young man; however, the taint of "scoring" is so engrained that he must quickly return to the streets, dark movie balconies, and alleys to expunge the rage within him. As if on a self-destructive path, he journeys through the cities of America—New York, Los Angeles, San Francisco, New Orleans, cities that have an orange-colored sky and purple landscapes. Each city in itself is a purgatory peopled with outcasts, grotesque remnants of a haunting past, and lost souls: "The world of Lonely—Outcast America."

The central character of his first novel, *City of Night*, is a lonely, remote young stud who refuses to show any emotion to his clients, terrified that his true sexual identity will be revealed to him. His "devouring narcissism" can be quenched only by sex on his own terms. To reciprocate in any way would not be masculine. It would destroy his image of the tough uncaring man who is fighting to defeat time and death—to restrain aging, a perverse insistence that stares him in the face when he sees what God and time have done to many of his clients. The professor, a bedridden man in his sixties, tells him

that "Life wrecks all illusions" and that "Like a cold card dealer, God deals out our destinies." When his first score, Ed King, "a grayhaired middle-aged man," tells him, "I was like you once. . . . the dayll come nobody wants you—then what?," the baffled young man maddeningly pursues scoring, trying to defeat death; each orgasm is a defeat of death: "the frantic running . . . for me, was Youth." To suspend youth he develops a "narcissistic obsession," and it is only the myriad ever-present mirrors that can judge him. They draw him to them like a magnet, always revealing his youthful masculine body.

In El Paso, the novel's main character lives in a world of terror dominated by a cruel father, "a strange, moody angry man" who "plunged into my life with a vengeance"; the young boy becomes the "reluctant inheritor of his hatred." Because he also hates his father, he stops going to Mass, stops believing in God: "the seeds of that rebellion . . . were beginning to germinate." When his father dies, he joins the army; when discharged, he begins his search—"looking for I don't know what—perhaps some substitute for salvation." Throughout the novel, he searches in Times Square, Pershing Square, and the parks of Chicago for this salvation, denying any emotional feelings he may have, submerging himself in an "alluring anarchic world . . . a seething world." However, wherever he goes, the memory of his father and mother lingers, and he begins to feel an indefinable guilt.

Searching for redemption, the "I" of the novel travels to New Orleans to participate in Mardi Gras, anticipating that "A religious ritual will take place in this rotting Southern city." Rechy's Catholicism, although denied by his heroes, forms a symbolic function, forcing his characters into a realization that there is hope, that there is redemption if one accepts his destiny—and in the case of his heroes, that destiny is homosexuality.

To Rechy, New Orleans is "A ghost city. . . . An almost Biblical feeling of Doom." The doom, though, is like the spectral birds ever present in this novel and others, for death looms over this section of the novel, not only in the ghostlike, rotten city but in the characters themselves. Kathy, the most beautiful drag queen the hero has ever seen, is dying. A lonely specter who has a "ghostlike quality" about her, she was disowned by her parents. Now she lives in "a little hell-hole in the Quarter," gliding throughout the bars, moving "like fog" with "doom so inexorably stamped on that beautiful face."

Another character who hovers over the ghostly city and its doomed occupants is Sylvia, owner of the Rocking Times, a bar in the Quarter, and mother to all the lost queens. When she confesses that she, too, threw her son out, she tries to drown the "insistent sounds from the ravenous past." With the plight of Kathy and Sylvia, Rechy is beginning to touch upon a theme that will be prevalent in some of his later books: an appeal to the heterosexual world to understand and accept the homosexual world.

As a male hustler in the other cities, the hero denied any possibility of homosexuality, frequently sleeping with girls to prove his manhood. Here, in this city of death, he is faced with that other "Someone" who stares at him in the mirror; he, too, becomes a "fallen angel." Redemption is brought to him in the guise of Jeremy Adams, a lonely man seeking compassion and friendship. With him, the "I" remembers his father, the hatred stored up inside himself, the rebellion, the rage, and the guilt. But he also remembers his mother and "her love like a stifling perfume." It is Jeremy who reveals the truth to this confused young man: "You want, very much, to be loved—but you don't want to love back, even if you have to force yourself not to." For the first time, feeling an intense loneliness and reaching out also for a human touch, our hero tells his last name to Jeremy Adams. No longer masked in anonymity, he responds to the warmth of another human being and says, "I leaned over him and I kissed him on the lips."

On Ash Wednesday, when all the demons and clowns are gone, he feels himself becoming a ghost, "drained of all that makes his journey to achieve some kind of salvation bearable under the universal sentence of death." For Rechy and his characters, death is the destruction of the body—youth, the only thing a hustler needs if he is to score on the streets. With the passing of youth, the hustler will become a lost angel, who, as the professor said, will one day fly away. Coming to the realization that "hope is an end within itself," he returns to El Paso. As he looks out the window, he remembers that it is spring; soon the trees will be budding with green clusters of leaves—"hinting of a potential revival."

Although *This Day's Death* was not published until 1970, it fits chronologically here in the life of the narrator of *City of Night*, for it relates the events that occurred during his three-year exile to El Paso before returning to Los Angeles in *Numbers* to purge himself. Jim Girard, as he is now called, struggles between two horrifying nightmares: in El Paso, the slow death of his mother who drowns him in a possessive love; and in Los Angeles, a long drawn-out trial in which he is accused of sexual perversion with a young married man, Steve Travis, in Griffith Park. Since the act did not occur, Jim

condemns the cop Daniels, who arrested them; the judge; the lawyers; and the courts and indicts their antiquated laws. Thus, Rechy returns to three of his themes: his mother's possessive love, his hero's feelings of guilt and his search for a true identity, and the condemnation of society's outdated mores which are supported by an uncaring, vicious group of law officials.

Jim's mother, a sixty-five-year-old devout Catholic, spends most of her time in bed, clinging to her rosary and her past. Her beloved son Salvador was killed in World War II and her first daughter, Esperanza, died of pneumonia at age twelve. Since Estela, her other daughter, lives in Los Angeles, all that she has is Jim, whom she loves with "a love which overwhelms, like sudden nausea." In trying to keep Jim with her, she succumbs to a nameless illness, which Jim realizes is her way of reducing him and his sister to children, frequently calling Jim "Salvador." To Jim, her sickness is a revenge: "She just can't forgive us for growing up." Although he realizes that she will gobble him up if he lets her, he loves her and worries about what will happen to her if he goes to prison. This war between mother and son fills him with rage and, as in *City of Night*, the rage can be stifled only through sexual release. Here, however, it is at first heterosexual sex with a pretty blonde named Caroline and later with Barbara Lewis, his girl (or rather his sexual relief) in El Paso. With Caroline, "It was as if the sexual act transformed him from the youngman capable of kindness and gentleness . . . into the violent youngman for whom sex was rage and anger." However, each sexual encounter leaves him unfulfilled, and he is "immediately ready for another such encounter. When the turbulence became excessive, he longed for his mother like an anchor to save him."

Rechy does not tell us why Jim goes to Los Angeles nor why he made the visit to Griffith Park, a gathering place for homosexuals seeking encounters. There are several brief, related episodes about his cruel father, his army service, his father's death, and his trips to New York, Los Angeles, San Francisco, Chicago, Dallas, called "sexual graveyards"—the past of "I" in *City of Night*: "His past a series of rebellious incidents that seemingly unrelated, now spliced for a summation of his life." However, it is this world of homosexual encounters that pulls Jim away from the heterosexual world in El Paso, and in an act of total defiance to the judge's sentence that he not return to Griffith Park, he goes there, where he not only hustles but, as with Jeremiah in *City of Night*, kisses a young man: "For the first time Jim felt no fury, no rage, no anger. No fear. And for the first time a hint of fulfillment." By accepting this world that he had tried to reject, he has momentarily been purged of the feelings of guilt he had stored inside—guilt about his hatred for his father and his mother and the overwhelming crush of Catholicism.

As Rechy's character matures and accepts his sexual preference, he becomes a reformer, seeing the hypocrisy of the law and society, begging for an understanding rather than a condemnation. Since the alleged act did not occur in Griffith Park, Jim rages against all the law stands for, and the trial, which drags on for months, becomes an absurdity. Daniels, the policeman who arrested Jim and Travis, has homosexual tendencies himself. There are even hints that he wants Jim: when the judge asks Daniels to identify Jim, he says, "he's the man in the blue eyes," and later when Jim raises his hand to strike Daniels, "The cop raises both hands. . . . he might as easily have been preparing to ward off Jim's blows as to strike back—or to embrace him." Yet Jim obsessively hates him with "a hatred he had never felt so keenly for anyone before."

Ironically, Jim Girard is a law student apprenticed to Lloyd Maxwell, an attorney in El Paso. Through the absurdity of the lengthy legal procedures, Jim comes to hate all that is associated with the law, even his lawyer, Alan Bryant. When he sees Bryant and Edmondson, Steve's lawyer, "speaking spiritedly, laughing, with the district attorney," he resents this camaraderie, "both sides clustered amicably like friends playing a game of pretended rivalry," and later he tells Edmondson, "don't you realize it's *our* lives—that yours and that judge's are unchanged?"

Judge Arnold Cory, to Jim, is an old man playing God. At first, he sees in this sixty-year-old, pink-faced man the image of a kindly grandfather; however, the black robe "invests him with the aura of legalistic ceremony." During the actual trial, Jim sees him for what he really is, "a petulant fat old-man" who rides in a Rolls-Royce and sits on an elevated platform with an omnipotent stare. When he presents the guilty sentence and judgment, he spews his words "like curses, smashing at his [Jim's] life."

Since the law has found Jim guilty of sexual perversion, he not only defies the law and reenters that world in Griffith Park but also when he returns to El Paso, he finally tells Maxwell the truth about his trial. When Maxwell emphatically interrupts him, telling him it didn't happen, Jim's reaction is "But even if it had, it's no crime. . . . after the trial, I

had to return to the park. . . . I wanted it to happen. . . . I wanted to face myself at last." That act of defiance in Griffith Park reveals to Jim his true nature. Leaving his job with Maxwell, he tells Barbara the truth and then leaves her, totally destroying his past, returning to his mother to wage the war between them, waiting for her death which will brand him with a brutal guilt and leave him with a terrible empty love.

Although *Publishers Weekly* said that *This Day's Death* "has dignity and depth," other critics either ignored it or scorned the immature writing style. Webster Schott, in the *New York Times Book Review* (14 January 1968), called Rechy's style "an abomination." Yet he said the book is not "wholly a failure. . . . it's possible he [Rechy] offers us more unevaluated and uncodified homosexual feeling than any writer in the United States today." Schott also believes that Rechy's *Numbers*, "as an effort toward art . . . collapses." On the other hand, Arthur Cur-

Dust jacket for Rechy's second novel (1967), about a narcissistic male hustler

351

ley, in the *Library Journal*, recommended *Numbers* to "sophisticated collections," calling it a "skillfully written novel."

In *Numbers*, Johnny Rio, Rechy's new name for his hero, returns to Los Angeles after his three-year, self-imposed exile, engulfing himself in the world of sex. However, this time it is not to hustle, for he has saved his money during his hiatus. Deciding that in ten days he must score thirty times ("30" is a newspaper printer's term for "The End"), he returns to Griffith Park, where he easily finds the willing sex partners who will accept him on his own terms, that of a passive, handsome young stud: "So Johnny doesn't even invite: never until someone expresses clear, unequivocal desire on his one-way terms."

The question in Johnny's mind is why has he come back. The answers that he discovers are the same that Rechy has already expounded in his other books. Death, the pervading theme of *This Day's Death*, is instilled in Johnny Rio's mind. On his way to Los Angeles, he encounters several bands of spectral birds on the highway "always as if courting a harsh, inevitable destiny." And their presence leads Johnny into a reflection of death which "seems determined to permeate his awareness; it does like a knife in his flesh." Ritualistically, each sexual release for Johnny is his attempt to strike back at death, which he associates symbolically with old age. As in *City of Night*, Johnny turns to the omnipresent mirror that reflects his now-strengthened, masculine, tan body made slender by his exercising diligently with weights. As long as he is admired and wanted, he will keep old age away, but if he is rejected, the old fears of death return. When his ego is deflated by a rejection, he returns to the mirror in the observatory, and seeing his handsome face, he wonders how anyone could not desire him. However, he always asks the question, "Why am I here?—To stop the flow! A stasis in time! A pause! The liberation of orgasm!"

Although Johnny Rio does not want to admit the truth, the second reason he has returned to Los Angeles and Griffith Park is to prove that his Adonis body, which must be desired by everyone, is purely masculine and that his refusal to reciprocate in the sexual encounters is proof he has no homosexual tendencies. Even though the mirror reflects for him a handsome, desirable young man, it does not lie, for there is always that other Johnny: "he looked in the mirror to dazzle himself with his smile; and he saw, instead, a depraved distortion of himself"; "He caught a glimpse of another face. . . . A face marked by enormous, bewildered sorrow."

When he visits an old friend from his hustling days, Sebastian Michaels, and sees the small group of his gay friends, he is confronted with his masked heterosexuality—that he only wants to have his body adored. When Emory Travis suggests that Johnny might be looking for *the* number, Sebastian answers, "But *the* number is death!"

When Johnny makes it with Guy Young, a member of the gay party at Sebastian's, and kisses him, as in the two previous books, he knows now that he has an "intimate knowledge of that further country." However, his masculine ego will not let him accept it. To erase that "symbolic country," he returns to Griffith Park even though he has achieved his desired number of thirty scores. Returning to the mirror and seeing something different in his eyes, he says, "*Just one more number, and I'll leave!*" But he cannot quit. Maddeningly trying to resurrect himself into the masculine hustler's world, he continues counting, knowing that he is a number, too.

Standing before the mirror, flexing his muscles, Jim, or Jerry or John as he sometimes calls himself, prepares his body for three days of sex in the homosexual underground of Los Angeles. Having now accepted his homosexuality, Rechy's character in *The Sexual Outlaw* defies society's mores and, as the title indicates, becomes a sexual outlaw, exhibitionistically participating in sex in alleys, garages, tunnels, parks, and even store entrances. Full of rage against the police who deliberately try to entrap these outlaws, Rechy believes that "Public sex is revolution, courageous, righteous, defiant revolution." It is the outlaw's way of striking back at a world that has condemned homosexuals, labeling them sex offenders. Because of the constant fear of having his "freedom . . . ripped away arbitrarily," the sexual outlaw in his rage against the law, doctors who are "perpetrators of sick myths," and preachers who "use . . . Biblical scripture to condone hatred," lives his life in rage on the brink of death.

Like *Numbers*, this work has its usual graphically written sexual encounters as Jim chalks up his scores, narcissistically flaunting his body in a tight-fitting shirt and shorts, challenging death when he has sex and fearing rejection. In the alternate chapters, which include newspaper headlines and brief stories, interviews with Rechy, and chapters in which Rechy the author speaks, there is Rechy's appeal to the hypocritical heterosexual world to abolish its legal and social constraints against the homosexual world. But the book is more than that—it is also an appeal to abolish all prohibitions against any consenting adults: "Why one wife? One husband? Why not lovers? Why marriage? . . . Why, necessarily, childen? The heterosexual world would thus be questioning, not heterosexuality itself, no, but the stagnant conformity of much of his tribal society."

The Sexual Outlaw is an appeal for action—first of all to the police and their "legally sanctioned sadism." To document this hypocrisy, Rechy presents a series of newspaper headlines and brief stories of police harassment and brutality, counteracting these with other stories of police involved in sex scandals, bribery, and theft: "Homosexuality is not a victimless crime—the homosexual is the victim, the cop the criminal." In a later chapter, Rechy visibly describes a brutal raid by the cops in Griffith Park as the police use helicopters to disband the sex hunters. The *Los Angeles Times* reports that the raid was "a sweep of fire hazard areas." Rechy laconically concludes with the statement that there was a fire in Griffith Park—"In a straight area."

Thus, the sexual outlaw continues his ancestral battle, rebelliously promiscuous, often defiantly standing against the law, flaunting his chosen way of life in a noble revolt by having sex in the streets, knowing that he is doomed to a lifetime of searching by a society which does not understand him. In an interview, Rechy says, "In my book *Numbers* there's a place where Johnny Rio thinks that if he keeps going sexually, time and death can't reach him." Relentlessly pursuing that place, the sexual outlaw challenges death through orgasm and in so doing survives the specter of aging, ritualistically sacrificing himself to survive all the "threats, repression, persecution, prosecution, attacks, denunciations, hatred that have tried powerfully to crush him from the beginning of 'civilization.'" Although many critics found the events narrated in *The Sexual Outlaw* "hellish," "raw," and "graphic," most agree with *Booklist* which thinks "it is a compelling and important one, written with authority from research and experience described in previous novels, such as *City of Night*."

In a different concept, Rechy adheres to the three unities in *Rushes*, a novel that has as its locale a macho-leather gay bar called Rushes, with the action occurring one night as the bar fills with an "astonishing array of cowboys, motorcyclists, construction workers, policemen, lumberjacks, military-uniformed men." All of these men are assuming poses, for in actuality they are lawyers, clerks, art critics, hairdressers. They have assumed this pose of the macho man to ward off the curse of effeminacy. Although the pose is "contrived, studied. Unreal," it is the new masculinity. The

former "sissies" of the 1950s and 1960s have been transformed into proud, defiant men who defy the straight marauders outside the bar, who court death and violence in the Rack, "one of the city's most popular orgy rooms" (only a few doors from Rushes), and who openly indulge in sadism and masochism.

Into this seething atmosphere come four friends who frequent Rushes. Endore, Rechy's alter ego, is "a sexually handsome dark-haired man in his upper 30s" who writes for a fashionable magazine read by many homosexuals. Chas, a proud, twenty-seven-year-old devotee of sadism and masochism, owns an antique shop. With his "sexy scar" on his left cheek, he struts in his masculinity, hating sissies and women. Don, a brilliant lawyer in his middle forties, lives in the past. He remembers the 1950s, camping, gossiping, having fun, but also the harrowing interludes of harassment and arrest. Don distrusts the openness of the 1970s. Nonviolent by nature, he detests hustlers and longs for a "beautiful lover." The only demonstration he ever participated in "was when we flew our flags half-mast for Judy." Bill, a young, slender blonde who is almost twenty-four, is a clerk. With his "mysterious Southern accent," he challenges the macho world when he lunges "into campiness." Yet, like the others, he is athletic, proud of his "lithe body."

Into this masculine world where there is a posted dress code with "a beard-stubbled man at the door nightly [who] discards the 'sissies' and other undesirables" come intruders who, during the embattled evening, cause these macho men and particularly the four friends to face themselves as they talk about macho conformity, sadism and masochism, the agony of growing old, and the fear of rejection. Like ghosts of the past, they come from the dark into Rushes, with its pool tables and erotic drawings on the wall.

Pushing their way past the protesting guard at the door, Martin, a tall, slender painter and photographer in his forties who is dressed in fashionable evening wear, and Lyndy, a fatuous designer of women's fashions who is "deceptively petite, pretty, in her thirties, slim," enter the world of this "sexual ballet" because Lyndy wants to be shocked. Her presence, for Chas, is a "violation of this macho font," and during the evening, the two confront each other with bitter hatred. Unlike the others, Chas refuses to call her "darling," referring to her instead as a "fag hag." Even Endore, who likes women, knows that Lyndy has come to Rushes for "cheap titillation: a spurt of adrenalin for boredom." The mild-tempered Bill is also hostile to her

Dust jacket for Rechy's fifth novel (1972), in which four characters engage in humiliating self-revelation

as he speaks "frostily" to her. It is only Don, the old-fashioned quiet one, who can accept her.

Like two avenging figures, two "unwelcome messengers," Elaine, a black prostitute, and Roxy, a white transvestite, stand at the door unyielding, begging to enter, for they have been threatened by a gang of thugs. When one of the men in the bar intercedes for the "two incongruous figures," they receive hostile stares; the men turn their backs spitting in disgust. When the bartender refuses to serve them, it is Endore who "enters the forbidden circle" and buys them a beer. Because they shatter this macho world, they are a greater threat than Lyndy. Roxy tells the man at the door, "The same thugs were beating on guys like you." To Chas, she vindictively says, "Don't turn your back to me. . . . I'm one of you. . . . We even wear earrings, both of us." She also stabs Lyndy with her vituperative words: "You're the manikin in your sexless drag!" And even though she speaks words of truth to Endore, spitting out her venom by reminding him how he writes about loving women but sleeps only with men, he knows that "Elaine and Roxy should have

'belonged' here—as outcasts among outcasts."

The other stranger who enters the bar is Robert, a handsome young man with dark curly hair and a "coltish body." Having to face his own homosexuality, he has defied his brother, a hustler who preys on the men outside Rushes, and entered this world he thinks is reality, for it is the world he has fantasized about. Although the theme of the heterosexual world, with its hatred and inability to understand the homosexual world, is not as prevalent in *Rushes* as it is in Rechy's other books, it is still here, like a wound that bleeds incessantly. Endore says, "He [Robert] was pushed here by his brother's hatred." And in Rechy's most devastating blow to the heterosexual world, when Robert tells Tim, his hustler brother, "I'm queer," Tim refuses to accept this jolting confession. As the confrontation between the two concludes, Robert, like an avenging angel, says, "you're as gay as I am."

The world of Rushes is a cruel world, a world of scorn for others not like them, a world of deception, a world of deliberately hurting each other with cruel words, a world of rejection. When Bill admits that they are all hollow, he adds, "But that bitchy wit saves us." Even though there is cruelty in Rushes, this bar is a haven, protecting these men from the cruelty outside—the marauders who curse them, throw bottles at them, and attack them. Chas says, "This is our island in the ocean." Labeled by Darryl Pinckney in the *Village Voice* (3 March 1980) as "Rechy's most ambitious work stylistically," *Rushes* is Rechy's plea for homosexuals to understand and accept themselves and their sexuality, to fight back against the heterosexual world, to accept their plight as one, not condemning those who have their own sexual identification.

Although *The Vampires* (1971) and *The Fourth Angel* (1972) touch upon some of Rechy's themes prevalent in his homosexual books, they are strikingly different. Like figures in *Who's Afraid of Virginia Woolf?*, *The Boys in the Band*, and the nasty episodes in *Rushes*, the characters in both of these novels play cruel games of humiliation: like pecking hens, they find out each other's dark secrets, expose them, and in so doing, reveal their repressed sexuality, which is usually homosexuality.

For *The Fourth Angel*, Rechy has chosen as his central character a young girl, Shell, a hardened, empty sixteen-year-old, who was raped by her father when she was eleven. With her are two teenaged boys: Cob, a sixteen-year-old who, like many of Rechy's characters, hides his homosexuality behind a mask—here, it is "deep-purpled sunglasses"; and a Chicano, Manny, a "well-muscled sixteen-year-old," proud of his masculinity, obviously Rechy's alter ego. However, he is combined with the fourth angel, Jerry, a young man the trio find in the park who, throughout the novel, laments the death of his mother and frequently returns to the house in which she died, but never visits her room.

Because of Shell's violation, she has become hardened, dominating; she wants to make the three boys strong so that they will have no feeling and will never cry. As her name implies, she is empty: "No one, and nothing, threatens me, nothing scares me, nothing in the world, not you, not anyone, not anything." Like an avenging earth mother, during the first part of their adventures, she controls the three boys, supplying them with psychedelic drugs which are supposed to erase all memories of the past: for her, the rape by her father; for Manny, a dominating mother who frequently sends him to a juvenile delinquency home; for Cob, a lesbian mother who hates him; for Jerry, the death of his mother. At first they play this game of exposure with a stranger, Stuart, a homosexual whom Manny deceives by pretending to hustle and whom Shell makes confess his homosexual activities. As they terrorize him with threats of turning him over to the cops for seducing teenagers, they become a "terrible jury," and Shell says she will make him become "straight." Stuart's final thrust is "You're not even kids—you're old with cruelty."

After harassing other homosexuals, they begin to play the game of pecking at each other. Because he is vulnerable, Jerry becomes the brunt of this cruel expose as they take him "in the journey to expel the pall of death." In a terrifyingly brutal section, they force him to enter the forbidden room of his mother to prove that he is not weak. Perhaps the horrifying memories of Jerry's mother with the tubes and needles in her body as she thrashes out in the last moment of death are those of Jim Girard in *This Day's Death*, for the mother image and her death permeate most of Rechy's main characters with a guilt-ridden tenacity.

When Manny and Shell make Cob reveal that Janet is not his sister, but a woman his mother has picked up, he viciously attacks Manny, telling him that his "old lady . . . hates his guts" and Shell that she's a "dike." Then the war begins. Shell must prove (by giving her body to the three boys) that she is not a lesbian. However, it is Shell who wins by revealing Cob's repressed homosexuality and by forcing Manny to rape the powerless Cob instead of her—it is her revenge not only upon Cob but upon her father and the uncaring, cruel world. Through this violent act, the vulnerability of these teenagers

is revealed. Cob is "a conquered warrior," and Manny whimpers saddeningly, "My mother *does* love me, Cob." But it is Jerry, the avenging angel, who must reveal Shell's weakness, "It's you who are sick, Shell," and at the end of the novel, this self-imposed truth-teller, "a shadow trapped in shadows," is left alone, crying for the first time since her rape.

This game of exposure continues in *The Vampires*, Rechy's most violently cruel and vindictive book. Like Shell in *The Fourth Angel*, Richard, the owner of a huge, sinister mansion on an island, instigates a game for a gathering of his grotesque friends to reveal their inner-selves. Joja, an actress and Richard's ex-mistress, says, "We've come back to be resurrected by Richard." Once they have exposed their past or their innocent feelings and have become empty, they must then try to find salvation through a play staged with props on the platform like gravestones. Before the black-draped prop on the stage is revealed to the guests as a throne, they call it "a confessional booth." Later Richard says the name of the game will be "Confessions." The removal of masks, revealing one's true identity, is, to Rechy, an act of contrition, exposing one's sins and guilts to a priest. Among Richard's guests is a priest, Father Jeremy, "A beautiful—pure—priest: as pure as the memory of love." In an attack on religion, and particularly Catholicism, which Rechy finds stifling, Richard attacks the priest by asking, "What gives *you* the right to—. . . grant absolution for living?" For even the priest has a secret hidden past; when he is forced to confess, he reveals a typical Rechy character who screams out in agony, "I loathed my mother purely."

In all of his books, Rechy says that we wear masks, "A symbol of a flaw, the origin of their blindness." As long as we are able to keep that mask intact, we are as happy as La Duquesa, a drag queen who is mourning the death of her lover, the Duke. However, when the truth is revealed that her name is Freddy and that the Duke was a punk criminal shot down in the streets by the cops, La Duquesa no longer exists. For Richard, all that is fantasy, all that is not real must be shattered by revealing the truth, which is usually ugly in Rechy's novels. The truth for Savannah, the "virgin whore" who has no flaw in her beauty, is revealed with a vicious cruelty—the showing of a porno film in which she lost her purity, "A film which captures the origin of purity," shouts Richard triumphantly. Savannah, unprepared "for a confrontation with the recorded reality of the slaughter," becomes a shell, an empty body like Tor, a bodybuilder who became "a piece of meat" by making sex movies.

As all the other characters come forward to reveal their "sacred memories," they present a lineup of Rechy's typical bizarre characters, his "fallen angels." The hustler, Blue, who cannot escape the hypnotic mirror, is a satanic angel who has committed murder. Like Bravo, the underground lesbian superstar who carries a whip; like Karen, whose translucent beauty whispers doom; and like Tarah, who tries to fill the void with young men— these people are unreal, shadows that flit in and out of the mysterious mansion. But the vampire who is the most delusive and empty is Malissa, whose "invisible shell separated her from all that was sexual." To compensate for her hatred of sex, she collects a new entourage of young men each season. With her now are La Duquesa, Tor, Rev, and Topaze, a perfectly shaped midget, and always accompanying her is Albert, a homosexual taunted by Malissa. In a revenging sequence, he reveals the truth about Malissa's using these young men's "blood" to stay young. The hatred that exudes among these detestable people is viciously revealed when they scramble for a knife, quickly placed in successive hands, each participant wanting to kill his enemy. The exorcising of evil has led them into a spewing of vile words and to an even crueler act: a desire to eradicate each other. Rechy's attempt to expunge these characters he has put into this devastatingly cruel world ends in a typical ritualistic shocker, with murder being the only purification.

Although the critics responded favorably to *The Fourth Angel*, it, like *The Vampires*, did not sell well. Both novels quickly faded into obscurity. *Kirkus Review* called *The Fourth Angel* "a concise, ugly, powerful work that may very well be Rechy's best." And Simon Karlinsky, in the *Nation* (5 January 1974), praised Rechy's style, saying that it "is written with an intensity and a driving originality that seems new in Rechy's work." Yet *The Vampires* became dismally lost in a few brief comments scattered among only a few publications. *Kirkus Review* called it "a ghastly conglomerate—say Warhol and Genet and Mary Shelley and Shelley Berman." Although the *Library Journal* recommended it since it is "Bound to be controversial as to its worth and meaning," *Publishers Weekly* found it "an adolescent fantasy novel with all the trappings of de Sade and none of the intelligence." Both novels will perhaps in time prove to be representative of John Rechy, the serious writer, and will reach a more appreciative audience for their striking originality.

References:

Alan Friedman, "Pleasure and Pain," *New York Times Book Review*, 17 February 1980, pp. 14-15;

Richard Gilman, "City of Dreadful Night," *New Republic*, 149 (14 September 1963): 21-23;

Gilman, "John Rechy," in his *The Confusion of the Realms* (New York: Random House, 1963), pp. 53-61;

Stanley Hoffman, "The Cities of Night: John Rechy's 'City of Night' and the American Literature of Homosexuality," *Chicago Review*, 17, no. 2 (1964): 195-206;

Georges-Michel Sarotte, "Three Categories of Homosexuals," in *Like a Brother, Like a Lover: Male Homosexuality in the American Novel and Theater from Herman Melville to James Baldwin*, translated by Richard Miller (Garden City: Doubleday, 1978), pp. 164-185;

Warren Tallman, "The Writing Life," *Open Letter*, third series, no. 6, (Winter 1976-1977), pp. 150-158;

David Taylor, "Loving Violence," *American Book Review*, 2 (June 1980): 9;

Keith Walker, "The Working Weekend," *Times Literary Supplement*, 11 August 1978, p. 908.

AN INTERVIEW
with JOHN RECHY

DLB: Since the publication of *City of Night*, which shocked some critics but brought approving mail from readers all over the world, you consider your novels to trace a cycle, you've said, from loss of innocence to the return to a kind of purity. How would you assess the place of that body of work in homosexual literature?

RECHY: I'd pull it out of the designation of "homosexual literature" and call it literature dealing with homosexuality. Can you imagine anyone calling *Lolita* "pedophilic literature"? Yet any book dealing with homosexuality is relegated to a subgenre today—and not as literature. The *New York Times Book Review* and the *New York Review of Books*, both notoriously homophobic in my opinion, are primary culprits. So: I've written *literature* that has often dealt with homosexuality.

DLB: You feel your work has not been fairly assessed because of this categorizing?

RECHY: Modesty is not one of my faults, and I do find self-deprecation a fault. So I'll say without hesitation that I consider myself as good a writer as any other writing today—and better than most; and, yes, I feel that it is because I have written boldly about homosexuality that I am not assessed correctly. Look—*The Sexual Outlaw* introduced a new literary form I call "the documentary"—a combination of narrative and "voice-over" essays. But critics apparently could not see beyond its heavily sexual content. My first work, *City of Night*, has a beautiful, careful structure, largely overlooked because the book deals with a male prostitute. . . . Today, young writers are being discouraged from writing about the homosexual experience because works on that subject are encountering increasing difficulty being published; those which are, aren't taken seriously. If you look back on the last ten or so years, hardly any young writer has emerged—and been praised—who identifies himself as homosexual and writes *about* homosexuality. A literary closet has been created for the homosexual writer, and a very relevant, illuminating part of the human experience is thus blocked off from literature. Paradoxically, when we had to wear a mask, we had Proust and Gide, giants. None of this means we're incapable of writing first-rate works now, not at all; it just means that the subject is shoved out of serious consideration, and therefore some tremendous writing is being ignored by the so-called "mainstream critics"—ignored or not being published at all.

DLB: Publishers might argue that, being in business to make a profit, they publish what they can expect to sell. Is the market there for writing about homosexuality?

RECHY: Quite definitely. Proof is this: Before the emergence of houses that publish only books about homosexuality, *City of Night* became a top international best-seller. *Numbers* and *The Sexual Outlaw* appeared on best-seller lists. A significant part of my mail, perhaps almost half, comes from heterosexual readers; and after *The Sexual Outlaw* appeared, I received a large number of letters from heterosexual women, praising my book.

DLB: Do you want to talk about "Bodies and Souls"?

RECHY: It's my longest book. It has a wide spectrum of characters, ranging from the top pornographic actress in films to a "Chicano" teenage boy exploring the punk-rock scene. Though it has homosexual characters, it is not primarily about homosexuality. I think of it as an epic novel of Los Angeles today—an "apocalyptic" novel. In it, through the many lives I depict, I explore what I call "the perfection of what is called accident"—the seemingly random components that come together perfectly to create what in retrospect we name "fate."

DLB: How much are you teaching now?

RECHY: Two classes, and I'm proud to tell you I'm an excellent teacher. It seems to me that I was young longer than anyone else! I feel a great concern for young people—male, female, homosexual, heterosexual, it doesn't matter. I feel a great responsibility to them—to nurture their creativity, which at that age is so fragile. Some terrific writing has emerged from my classes, writers being published consistently. It's a very good feeling.

Oh, and here's a paradox. Recently I was invited to teach a course at Columbia—the same novel-writing workshop I had been rejected for, as a student, years ago! When I got out of the army, I wanted to enroll in a course Pearl Buck was teaching at Columbia. She required prospective students to submit a sample of their work, as I do now for my classes. I submitted "Pablo!," a book I wrote as a teenager. She sent me a respectful letter saying she didn't think she could deal with my material—and it was pretty mild, very surreal and mysterious. The same novel got me into a much more "exclusive" course—Hiram Haydn's at the New School for Social Research. But it is a triumph to be asked to teach a course you've been "rejected" for. . . . I feel similarly about the negative criticism of my work. The initial shrieks about it don't matter; the works themselves will last.

—*Jean W. Ross*

Michael Ryan
(24 February 1946-   )

Willard Spiegelman
Southern Methodist University

BOOKS: *Threats Instead of Trees* (New Haven & London: Yale University Press, 1974);
In Winter (New York: Holt, Rinehart & Winston, 1981).

Michael Ryan's poems sound variations on a choral line from his second book: "No one can tell you how to be alone." In two volumes where natural description, human characterization, full meditation, ironic wit, and religious impulses often yield to naked detail or partial definitions, Ryan charts the paths of loneliness around his two obsessive themes: sexual desire and personal loss or abandonment. If one cannot be instructed in the art of loneliness, at least Ryan is bearing witness to his own mastery of the art. Found by some readers self-indulgent in

these obsessions or impoverished in his linguistic resources, Ryan has nevertheless grown considerably between the publication of his first volume, *Threats Instead of Trees* (1974), and his second, *In Winter* (1981). As a poet of the stark condition of human isolation, Ryan may not always be pleasurable to read, and large doses of his work may seem repetitive. Nevertheless, his depiction of unmotivated, unspecified fear as a chronic fact sets him apart from other poets who take as their province the sharp anguish of bitterness. For him, "intimate agonies should be wordless as birds, / small dull birds in dark scary woods." Without the searing clarity of Sylvia Plath or the bravura wit and gamy hysteria of John Berryman, Ryan sets his gaze on defining states of consciousness, which are often

removed from consistent metaphors or dramatic situations.

Born in St. Louis, Michael Ryan grew up in Allentown, Pennsylvania, a town of steel and industry. He claims that he "didn't read a book until [he] was nineteen." As a freshman at Notre Dame, where he went to study engineering and play football, Ryan experienced the two most important events of his creative life. His father, an alcoholic and failed artist, died that year; subsequently, Ryan traveled to Chicago with a friend for a weekend and stumbled into a bookstore where he discovered volumes by Plath, Berryman, Tate, and Hugo: "I had never been so moved . . . I used $27 on books [out of the $32 he had taken with him] and spent that night at the Y reading. The next day I went home."

The death of his father and the virtually simultaneous discovery of poetry were more than coincidental; they were decisive. Ryan began to study poetry and composition seriously, and in a classic twentieth-century way, the would-be Stephen Dedalus spent much of his time considering his dead parent, who turns up prominently as a theme and a character in his first book. After graduation from Notre Dame, Ryan earned advanced degrees in English at Claremont and Iowa, where he served as poetry editor for the *Iowa Review* in 1974. Subsequently, he has taught at Southern Methodist University, Goddard College, and Princeton, and held a Guggenheim Fellowship for a year in Rome.

Ryan's first volume was selected by Stanley Kunitz as the Yale Younger Poets prizewinner for 1974. In his introduction, Kunitz noticed the relentless, self-contained quality of Ryan's poetry, with its images of enclosure, suffocation, and drowning and with its exposure of "a mind that rejoices in the play of concepts, in the embodiment of 'thought as experience.' " The mobility of Ryan's mind seems to have redeemed the claustrophobia of his poetry for Kunitz, who implicitly viewed him as an heir to Eliot's speculative verse. Indeed, the two epigraphs to *Threats Instead of Trees* not only announce an inheritance from earlier poets but also define the major themes of both of Ryan's books: from Rilke, "We *are* solitary"; and from Whitman, "Even in religious fervor there is a touch of animal heat."

Most of the poems in the first volume, like the long, concluding "Negatives," in loosely related eight-line stanzas, present a bleak view of love, indeed a thinly disguised misogyny beneath a panoply of lust. The associations, sometimes random, sometimes arcane, make much of the looseness appear to

masquerade as surrealism, but the colloquial flatness of the language is often embarrassing or uninteresting:

> When fish sprout wings they aren't birds,
> and your sadness is a root.
> At first we changed touches into facts,
> nothing was private. Then tendrils
> gathering like a nest:
> evolution in the definite shape
> of your hands covering your face,
> when the only comfort is difference.

Relatively uninflected, lacking narrative or dramatic centers, presenting emblems of interior pain which seem to lack origin, the poems are at times difficult to separate from one another. The stoic coldness often covers self-pity: "This poem comes from complete sorrow / and asks almost nothing of itself" ("The Poetry of Experience").

"From embarrassments, I made statements," he confesses at one point, and for many readers of *Threats Instead of Trees*, the statements were unsatisfactory as poems. One critic (Michael Sheridan, *Southwest Review*, 1975) bridled at the heavy self-consciousness, the "thinking too much with a capital T," whereas another, in the *Antioch Review*, condemned Kunitz for demeaning the Yale prize by awarding it to "another workshop poet, full of reverence for 'darkness,' 'silences,' 'wounds,' death and other clichés of workshop poetry." While it is true that much of his poetry is well made, according to the contemporary standards of Strand, Merwin, and James Tate—austere, minimal poets—Ryan's early poetry showed glimmers of some other influences as well. Here and there a reminiscence of Stevens or an aside like something in Ashbery could suggest that Ryan might develop along other paths. Only one critic, James Atlas, writing in *Poetry*, was able to see beneath the clean language and the psychological clichés of the alienated modern ego. For Atlas, Ryan's "mannered strategies of animism, dream states, and the cultivation of a certain rhetorical urgency," his baffling metaphors (such as "Your eyes orbit the cold sun / like dead fathers circling the universe") where the theme, not the image, is what counts told only part of the story. According to Atlas's judgment, Ryan is better than the conventional style he has chosen. His unrelated images, some banal but some original, deflect rather than promote adequate consideration, and Ryan will have to winnow wheat from chaff as he continues to reap the products of his pen.

In Winter continues many of Ryan's themes but

*Dust jacket for Ryan's first volume of poetry (1974), winner of
the Yale Younger Poets Prize*

At the same time, he wittily realizes that this compulsion can lead readily to madness and asks (in "Where I'll Be Good") with a momentarily Lear-like lucidity, for protection from himself:

Wanting leads to worse than oddity.
The bones creak like bamboo in wind,
And strain toward a better life outside the
                                                body,
the life everything has that isn't human.

. . . .

If I must go mad, let it be dignified.
Lock me up where I'll feel like wood,
where wanting can't send me flopping out-
                                                side,
where my bones will shut up, where I'll be
                                                good.

Casting a backward glance at his earlier career of speculation, Ryan rehearses the dangers of questioning. Asking "Why," the inevitable temptation, always leads to disaster: "It always starts this way, / breeding inside until it swarms into things, / blackening the sky, in chorus with wind. . . ." This poem, "Why," defends Ryan's other poems and makes only half-jocular references to precursors whom he loves but dares not imitate:

Who gives a shit about carcajou
in the boscage, or pansies freaked with jet?
I'd like to write a daylight poem
that pretends the world's a good friend,
but what relation to things makes a link
that won't snap with all the shaking it gets?

Ryan's energies gather during the dark night which both inspires and frustrates his questioning:

In this thick dark the room seems blank
like a man long dead and forgotten.
I can't stop the draining of the days.
But when night edges in, and bad panics hum
like light-drunk bugs diving at the screen,
it still brings sweet expectations of return.

. . . .

Outside, the great pines face a black sky.
What can be named that is close and stays?
I know the silence of an empty house
can greet at the door with an amazing smack.
I don't want to hear what keeps me apart
when I whirl my one dance toward the edge.

This is why, he says, he writes "about loneliness, how

eliminates a good number of his irksome stylistic mannerisms. The primary focus is still upon himself ("I can't grasp exactly the feelings of anyone," he admits, perhaps including his own in this confession), although in mid-life the demands of lust are complemented by the recognition that sex is an automatic reflex action against quotidian annoyance. Psychosexual rage and despair have religious dimensions (suggested, but never carried through in the first volume, by the line from Whitman), as "Sex," the long central poem, proves. Ryan's displaced religious impulses—lacking faith, he still seeks centrality—keep him sane:

Sex, invisible priestness of a good God.
I think without you I might just spin off.
I know there's no keeping you close,
as you flick by underneath a sentence
on a train, or transform the last thought
of an old nun, or withdraw for one moment
                                                alone.
Who tells you what to do or ties you down?

it pockets me inside it, / and the longing to be freed from it / I always walk around with."

This long poem expands Ryan's earlier explorations of his fear of darkness, solitude, the outdoors, death, exposure. The person to whom the poem is addressed, sitting elsewhere, resembles one of two animals circling each other in a primeval forest. Like Robert Lowell in "For the Union Dead," Ryan longs for the dark, ancient, vegetable kingdoms, or, like Whitman, for the placidness of animal life. And yet he seems to protest too much his fears of loneliness. He is rarely bothered by impotence or by a lack of poetic creativity; he is disturbed only by the nameless horrors of the night and of an isolation which even sex can do little to abate:

> It doesn't matter that now it's summer
> and the breeze might let me forget
> if I could lie here naked and blank,
> because breeze comes easy as a sexless kiss
> and breeze won't plant me finally
> outside myself, and that is what I want.

As a poet of emptiness, of "The Pure Loneliness" as one poem's title calls it, Ryan is at his best in a group entitled "Seven Annihilations and a Slight Joke," because here a mordant wit discovers vehicles fit to bear the weight of his pessimistic concerns. Quiet, unchanging desperation, the state explored by a variety of American artists including Thoreau and Stevens, may be the one subject which distinguishes American from English verse. For writers as different as Howard Nemerov, A. R. Ammons, and Michael Ryan, geological and astronomical images (stones, black holes) offer the best equivalents of inner states. In one of his "annihilations," Ryan combines inner darkness and primeval history in the figure of a giant animal:

> Before anything else,
> before the first animal
> stumbled over a rock
>
> in the first dim light
> and growled under its breath,
> there was the Great Dark.
>
> The Great Dark never talked.
> The Great Dark only danced
> about itself, inside and out,
> and when from the energy of that
> long dance something else showed up,
> The Great Dark slipped away and sulked.

God does not play dice with the universe, as Einstein once observed, but Michael Ryan's world contains principles of creative energy which resist their own formulations. Could the poet of despair turn into a wit, an ironic sage, despite himself? As he releases some of his manic hold over certain fixations, Ryan may well relax into a slier version of himself, who moves beyond unbearable sorrow to the defenses of wit and the consolations of elegy.

Jonathan Schwartz
(28 June 1938-   )

Peter A. Scholl
Luther College

SELECTED BOOKS: *Almost Home* (Garden City: Doubleday, 1970);
Distant Stations (Garden City: Doubleday, 1979; London: M. Joseph, 1979).

Jonathan Schwartz has published a collection of short stories, *Almost Home* (1970), and a novel, *Distant Stations* (1979). His fiction and other writing have been published in periodicals including the *Atlantic Monthly*, *Redbook*, *Transatlantic Review*, *Paris Review*, and *Sports Illustrated*. In 1978 he began writing a monthly column for the *Village Voice*.

Schwartz once told an interviewer that he began his writing career when he was five years old, but that he was twenty-eight when he sold his first short story. Jonathan's interests in writing, music, and the performing arts (subjects that permeate his fiction) clearly were nurtured in his early life with his father, Arthur Schwartz. The elder Schwartz taught English, practiced law, and eventually became a well-known composer, best remembered for his collaborations with lyricist Howard Dietz on musical revues such as *The Little Show* (1929), *Flying Colors* (1932), and *Between the Devil* (1937). Schwartz

361

Jonathan Schwartz

and Dietz's best-known song is "Dancing in the Dark." Jonathan's interests in the arts were also, no doubt, encouraged and inspired by his mother, Katherine Carrington (who died in 1954), who had been an actress and singer. "I grew up around composers," Schwartz says. His mother had been in a Jerome Kern production, and as a child Jonathan knew Kern. "When I was five," he recalls, "I almost drowned in Ira Gershwin's pool. Harold Arlen pulled me out." Songs of the Gershwins, Dietz and Schwartz, and other composers of that era are often quoted in his work. (In 1977, a commercial phonodisc entitled *Alone Together: Jonathan Schwartz Sings Arthur Schwartz* was produced by Muse.)

Born to this musical and literary family in Manhattan in 1938, Schwartz attended the Riverdale Country School for Boys and, later, Columbia University. In 1959 he dropped out of Columbia and worked at radio stations WBAI and WNCN in New York. Soon afterward, he took off for Paris, where he stayed for two years, playing the piano

and singing (especially American show tunes) in cabarets. In 1980 he was still singing, playing an engagement at Michael's Pub, though he told an interviewer that he was not interested in being a professional singer. "It's a lonely life," he commented. "I'm a writer and a radio man." On 26 January 1968 he married Sara Davidson, a writer. They were divorced in 1975. Later that year he married Marie Brenner, a columnist.

His involvement in radio, like his literary career, also had an early start and continues to have great importance in his life. Like eight-year-old Michael in his story "The Immense Audience" and like the young Paul Kramer, protagonist of *Distant Stations*, Schwartz remembers "giving imaginary programs in closets when I was a child." He is often identified in print simply as a "New York disk jockey," and it is clear that his widest audiences have been listeners of radio stations in Boston and New York. In 1971 when he was thirty-two, he was described in the *Times* as "the number one disk jockey on FM radio in New York." Like his "radio idol," Jean Shepherd, Schwartz "simply loves to talk"; and he talks especially about baseball, music, and literature. "It has always been my concept," he says, "to utilize radio to say more than 'It's 38 degrees.'" Though credited in 1971 with having a "cool million listeners a week," he still "considers himself a writer first, disk jockey second."

His collection of short stories, *Almost Home*, and his novel, *Distant Stations*, both explore the lives of sensitive, intelligent city dwellers who are hurt by the inexorable sadness of living. Personal relationships seem centrally important in Schwartz's work, but stable relationships and love seem incredibly difficult to sustain, though beautiful and meaningful when discovered and held, however briefly.

In *Almost Home*, a series of male protagonists, many of them thirty years old or thereabouts, struggle to create and sustain intimacy with a lover, wife, parent, friend, or child. They often fail or find it hard to be consistently caring and reliable. These worried people and their friends frequently have trouble holding on to a sense of personal identity: they drift; they change; they often complain that they feel excessively changeable, out of focus, or even invisible. "Everything is unrelated to everything else," one of them comments. For another, "The sorrow of his thirty years lay in the burden of small decisions, daily confrontations with animate things that reflected his own feelings of uncertainty; . . . when to pacify with false affection, how to accept judgment without melancholy." Through the random drift, blur, and inconclusiveness of their lives runs the consolation of human warmth, of music and song, of performing and playing roles, and for a number of them, the ritualistic reassurance of baseball: a game with perpetual life, season upon season, with coherent rules and cloture.

Events in the lives of such characters often appear to reflect Schwartz's own experience, though it is difficult to say with how much fidelity—or even how important such resemblances are in interpreting his work. Still, it is hard to overlook such autobiographical parallels as those found in stories such as "The Raconteur," "Waiting," or "Dennicker's Love Story."

The narrator in the first story is a radio man who, like Schwartz in the middle 1960s, works in Boston. The protagonist, Roger Stern, is described in a fan letter (one of many inserted in the narrative) as a "sports fanatic," and the core of his fanaticism glows most intensely in phase with the fate of the Boston Red Sox. (Schwartz has confessed that "between 1970 and 1977 I spent nearly $15,000 listening to Red Sox broadcasts" over long-distance telephone from places like Paris, London, and Palm Springs.) Ultimately, Stern is dropped from the radio station because, as he explains in a letter to a fan in a prison, "radio is a transient business." His popularity rating has fallen off—a state of affairs that, he explains, "is endemic in such a profession." This permanent instability of the radio man works as a metaphor of wider significance. Stern writes to the prisoner: "It could be that life, like radio, is a transient business, governed by odd surveys and ratings."

The frequent use of letters in this story and the inclusion of other kinds of material that break the narrative flow in this and other works by Schwartz (such as the interpolation of quotations from the Watergate hearings heard on the radio, or pieces from the protagonist's radio interviews in *Distant Stations*) provide discrete comments, a kind of counterpoint, to the main narrative movement. They allow different points of view that help to establish the identity of the main character.

At a baseball game one day, Stern, in the midst of many changes in his personal life and career, imagines himself "being observed from high above the field by the professors, women, and friends who have passed through his life like soup through a sieve. . . ." It is also significant that this interlude is set at Fenway Park. At the ball game, Stern unexpectedly spots Richard, the estranged husband of the woman he plans to marry. Richard is not known for his interest in baseball, and he unexpectedly departs as a home run ties the scores: "He walked

out on a tie game," remarks an incredulous Stern. Here, as elsewhere in Schwartz's fiction and nonfiction, baseball functions as a metaphor: our own life "drifts by unstoppable," Stern feels. But baseball, as Schwartz wrote in a 1981 article in the *New York Times* on the players' strike, "lives in the mind, a constant amongst the twigs of broken marriages and love affairs and friendships lost and gained and glimpses of family. . . . Baseball is one season: the span of a man's life."

Fractured romances, broken families, and divorces also occur frequently in *Almost Home*—a title that points ambiguously but surely toward this theme. Dennicker, of "Dennicker's Love Story," is an American living in Paris who makes his living there playing the piano and singing. He falls in love with and arranges to marry Ghislaine, a French woman who decides at the last moment that she cannot leave Paris. He loses the woman, but as she walks out on him, he gains a long-sought glimpse of himself: "Eric Dennicker, thirty years old, saw that he was living, in these moments, through the last flickering seconds of his childhood. He felt suddenly detached from this event in which he played so large a part. It was as if he were viewing two strangers on a stage, himself alone in the audience, an invited guest."

Similar separations and recognitions, always with interesting variations and nuances, recur through the stories in this volume. As thirty-one-year-old Carol Zimmerman, protagonist of "The Shortest Vacation Ever," leaves her husband, "She envisioned herself, as she often did . . . through the eyes of a spectator who jotted down notes about her, sizing her up." Such an image recalls Stern's daydream at Fenway Park in "The Raconteur," and parallels many similar scenes in other stories. There is Jamie Orenstein, the jilted adolescent lover of Barbara in "The Deep End," for example. Rejected by the girl, he spies on her from a window opposite her apartment and sees her "pass in front of his eyes like a stage actress, remote and charming, removed from him, he as audience she as character."

In "The Voices in the Wind," twelve-year-old Tisa, a child whose mother is dying, feels that "Mom doesn't really know what I'm like sometimes. . . . It's as if another person altogether is talking and acting in a certain way, and I can see her but I can't do anything about it." Her father advises, "*Be* what you are, *all* of what you are, *all* of what you call changeable. The least interesting people I know are the least changeable."

Friedman, the thirtyish protagonist of "The Project," takes his elderly father on a drive and notes to himself how the father is now "robbed of his director's chair"; on the stage of life "They had replaced each other; as he had grown, they had drifted toward each other, merged briefly, and parted, each having assumed the other's posture." And then there is eight-year-old Michael, a child of a divorced woman, who delivers an imaginary radio broadcast of his mother's remarriage in "The Immense Audience." Such a performance, like the other related indulgences in role-playing and in the theatrical mode, seems to be a way of dealing with the problem of identity in situations where traditional bulwarks to the self—the parents, the family, the job, the lover—threaten to dissolve or disappear. The ritual of performance, like the ritual of baseball, imposes at least the illusion of order; it makes a swirling world seem "Almost Home."

In Schwartz's only published novel, *Distant Stations*, as in the stories collected in *Almost Home*, the most persistent theme appears to be that of the self as performer and the difficulty of distinguishing between what is authentic being and what is merely some sort of masquerade. All of the major characters are performers of one sort or another. Paul Kramer, the protagonist, is a radio and television interviewer and personality. His father is a retired actor and playwright. Paul's most important relationship with a woman in the novel is with Emily Keller, a writer and, as Paul discovers, a ventriloquist. A close friend of Keller's, Maggie Furth, is a voluptuous movie star. Maggie's boyfriend, Walter Decker, a millionaire candy manufacturer, wants to spend his money making films; in a television interview with Kramer he reveals that someday he would be interested in promoting the political career of Ronald Reagan, his ideal performer-as-politician.

Even when Schwartz's characters are not professional writers or entertainers, they tend to see themselves in theatrical situations or images. Especially in their sexual relationships, they function as performers. In more than one instance in *Distant Stations*, characters actually perform intercourse before an audience. On one occasion Paul prepares himself for such an encounter by watching a pornographic film.

In the opening chapter, Paul Kramer is shown as a boy living with his parents in a New York apartment. His mother is restricted to a salt-free diet, yet nevertheless is an avid reader of *Gourmet* magazine and a "brilliant and instinctive cook . . . though she could eat nothing that she made." With her elegant cookery, Paul's mother is also a performer; she says she is "like a blind man playing the piano." In his twelfth year, Paul's mother dies

(Schwartz was sixteen when his own mother died), leaving her actor-playwright husband and her son to readjust their roles in the altered drama of their family life. The morning after his mother's death, Paul ritualistically arises at his regular hour to make his imaginary radio broadcast: "My mother, Carol Kramer, died last night. . . . She was forty-one."

For Paul, even before his mother's death, "Everything's scrambled sometimes, and fuzzy. Like steam gets on all the mirrors." He daydreams, often about baseball games, and he has trouble hanging on to a sense of his own identity. "My name is Paul Kramer. Hi there, my name is Paul Kramer," he says to himself, as another boy at his school maliciously hurls a ball at him, trying to hurt him.

In the second chapter, Paul is thirty-two, and the narrative goes ahead from this point with no large chronological gaps. He is first shown leaving his media job in New York for a trip to southern California. He is still a dreamer, and his motives for his leave of absence are not clear, even to himself. Like Roger Stern, the radio man in "The Raconteur," he has found that his is a "transient business": "His programs on radio and television were removed from the air, and returned, and discontinued. Ebb and flow, Paul had observed." (Schwartz went on a mysterious and celebrated—by *People* magazine—"sabbatical" in 1980 from his radio show on WNEW after criticizing a new record by one of his favorite singers, Frank Sinatra; it was reported that Sinatra had pressured the management, though they denied the report, to take him off the air.) In California, Paul wants to see his father, now retired; but other than that, he is uncertain. "I want to drift," he admits.

His problems run deeper than he at first suspects, as he discovers through a series of relationships and adventures that recall the tenor of many American lives in the Watergate era of the late 1960s and early 1970s. Self-knowledge Paul Kramer needs most desperately, for he has no firm, internal guidelines for behavior. He feels that his father can help him, but he is ashamed to go to him; he still suffers from unresolved feelings of guilt and inadequacy and so he "lurks" outside his father's apartment, unable to "barge right in." He fills his idle hours with the resumption of a love affair with Sandi Cummings, a "vapid beauty" he had known in New York. Though he dominates, exploits, and bullies this woman, he does so more from weakness than from strength. He only impersonates manhood, going through the sexual motions. With Sandi, he is "into hitting."

He soon abandons Sandi and meets with his

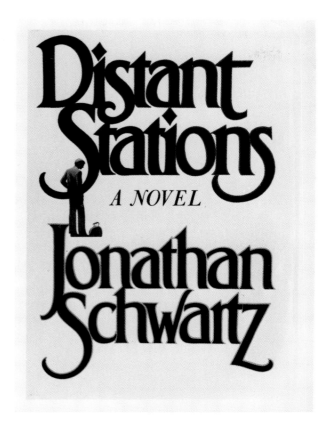

Dust jacket for Schwartz's first novel (1979), which draws on the author's experiences as a disc jockey

father, who turns out to be tolerant, wise, and understanding. Paul takes shelter under his parental wings, emerging often from his father's apartment to drift about the city. He drives the streets, loiters in anonymous motel rooms, and lingers in bars playing the same songs over and over. In a bar in Venice, he first catches a glimpse of a woman named Emily Keller, who is the other major character in the book. She is a writer and becomes Paul's consort, confidante, sparring partner, and mutually consenting adult in inventive sexual performances. (It seems more than coincidental that she lives in Venice, California, the main residence listed for Sara Davidson, Schwartz's first wife, also a writer, whose memoir, *Loose Change: Three Women of the Sixties*, 1977, includes her version of their relationship, though Schwartz is given another name in the book and many details are, evidently, intentionally altered.)

The title of the novel is elucidated by Emily Keller, who virtually lectures Paul on what she understands to be his excessive self-centeredness:

You know, Paul, I think that most of us are only tuned in to distant stations where all kinds of things are happening to other people. We listen through the static to their heartbreaks as if we were in some well-protected receiving chamber. Do you know what we overlook? That *we* are distant stations for anyone else who comes across *our* transmissions through all *our* static. It's all one network; we're all affiliates of the same conglomerate without seeing.

John Leonard found this passage "disheartening," because "a character in a novel ought not to explain the meaning of the title of that novel." Still, Leonard found that Schwartz's handling of human relationships is part of what saves the novel and caused him "to forgive Mr. Schwartz almost anything, because he is so good."

Emily, though she has a lot in common with Paul, is a station with a strong signal, but one that could be said to function on an entirely different wavelength. Paul and Emily were born on the same day; both lost their mothers when they were young; both have unusually intense relationships with their fathers.

When his father dies in an automobile crash (Paul and Emily are both passengers), Paul enters an acute phase of his protracted identity crisis. He has earlier characterized himself as "indecisive," "disconnected," "forever on the run." He has felt "tied to nothing . . . A concocter of dreams and savage pleasures." He knows that he has "meaningfully maimed" certain women. But after his father's death he also sees himself as a "killer." His self-esteem ebbs, and he is drawn deeper into amoral and self-destructive behavior, with Emily as compliant accomplice and abettor in his drift into the negative side of his personality. He takes drugs. He steals $1,000 from Walter Decker, a man too rich to notice; later (in the company of Emily), he takes $50,000 from Decker's Palm Springs home. For Emily, Paul's thievery is neither distressing nor impressive. She is, Paul learns, so far gone into a world of her own that her reactions are bound to be unusual: "I think you need psychiatric help," he tells her after he has returned to New York and his job.

The plot has no clear denouement but does provide a resolving chord that signals some hope that Paul will regain his mental balance and a vision of himself as a whole and responsible person. In the last scenes, Paul leaves Emily and returns to Palm Springs to return the money the two had so frivolously stolen from Decker. It is a gesture toward sanity and inner equilibrium in a world very much out of joint.

Schwartz's central theme of performance is certainly found in the work of other contemporary writers. Yet since this author is himself a child of performers, a professional singer-piano player, a prominent disc jockey and radio personality, an authoritative sports fan, and a writer in various genres, he can be expected to have considerable insight into this theme. His eye for detail and his well-trained ear for the emblematic phrase distinguish his writing. His evocation of a place and his handling of descriptive detail are powerful. His treatment of the novel as a form, however, is less well-developed. In *Distant Stations* there is too much material that seems digressive or merely anecdotal. Yet Schwartz grapples with a powerful theme in a convincing physical and emotional landscape, and it is clear that he is a serious and talented writer.

Recording:
Alone Together: Jonathan Schwartz Sings Arthur Schwartz (New York: Muse, 1977).

Periodical Publications:
"Day of Light and Shadows," *Sports Illustrated*, 50 (26 February 1979): 56-68;
"The Voices of the Family Tree," *Village Voice*, 24-30 November 1980, p. 32;
"Happy Talk," *Village Voice*, 17 December 1980, p. 50;
"The Strike and the Things We've Lost," *New York Times*, 26 July 1981, III: 5.

References:
Cherie Burns, "Frank Sinatra's Heat-Seeking Missive Finds Two New Targets: A Columnist and a Dee-Jay," *People*, 13 (5 May 1980): 42-43;
Sara Davidson, *Loose Change: Three Women of the Sixties* (Garden City: Doubleday, 1977);
John Leonard, "Books of *The Times*," *New York Times*, 1 March 1979, C17;
Grace Lichtenstein, "Jonathan Schwartz Still Digs Sinatra," *New York Times*, 9 May 1971, II: 7;
John S. Wilson, "A Night of Song Larceny With Jonathan Schwartz," *New York Times*, 28 November 1980, III: 5.

Betty Smith
(15 December 1896 - 17 January 1972)

Harriet L. King
Durham Academy

BOOKS: *A Tree Grows in Brooklyn* (New York: Harper, 1943); republished as *The Tree in the Yard* (London: Heinemann, 1944);
Tomorrow Will Be Better (New York: Harper, 1948; London: Heinemann, 1949);
Maggie-Now (New York: Harper, 1958; London: Heinemann, 1958);
Joy in the Morning (New York: Harper & Row, 1963; London: Heinemann, 1963).

Betty Smith is best-known for her first novel, *A Tree Grows in Brooklyn* (1943), a semiautobiographical account of tenement life at the turn of the century, which became a best-seller. In her meticulous description of urban slum conditions Smith resembled the naturalists, but she rejected their assumption that the capitalistic system had created an inescapable cycle of poverty. Her novel, which appeared during World War II, caught the imagina-

tion of a nation eager to reaffirm the values of freedom and individual courage. Because the author's background as the child of German immigrants made her sensitive to the themes of social mobility and progress, she tapped a persistent optimistic strain in American experience. Her later novels, all popular though none was as successful as her first, assert the individual dignity and valiant spirit of her protagonists, products of their environment but not doomed by it. Although Smith was by no means a feminist in the contemporary sense, she was aware of the changing roles of women and placed assertive, resilient female characters at the center of her fictional world. The wide popular appeal of her first novel rests primarily on the characterization of Francie Nolan. Almost forty years after its publication, Harper has ranked *A Tree Grows in Brooklyn*, along with *Ben Hur* and *Love Story*, among its top best-selling novels.

Betty Smith

Enjoying celebrity status, Betty Smith once commented during the course of an expensive meal at a New York restaurant that she remembered when she was growing up the only dessert they had was on Sunday: stale bread and condensed milk. Thinking back to her early years, she said, "A baby can live on bread and milk if it has love, and we had love." This remark, to writer Max Steele, characterizes Smith's novels and her life. She wrote about people who are capable—or incapable—of love, people whose survival is determined by caring relationships with those around them. Of herself she said: "I love children and dogs and cats. I love popular, sentimental songs. . . ." Those who knew her speak passionately of her loyalty, her generosity, her perseverance, and her wit. Charles Brockmann notes that "genuine introspective humility, which is a deal more than one would call modesty, is her most outstanding trait."

A shy, serious person, fearful of crowds and intensely private, she reached out to people who needed her, especially young writers. Steele remembers that she advised him after his first taste of fame: "You can't be responsible for what others say about you, but once you have published and become 'known', *you* have to be responsible for what you say, for your word carries weight." Although she was often hurt by others' unkindnesses and by reports in the press which were untrue, she enjoyed her celebrity and insisted, "The best thing fame brings you is that you can get to know anyone."

Born in Brooklyn, New York, on 15 December 1896, Elizabeth (Betty) Wehner was the oldest of three children in the family of John and Catherine Hummel Wehner, German immigrants. (There

seems to be some discrepancy in her birthdate. Her daughters claim she was born in 1896, the date recorded on her tombstone; but the Library of Congress lists her birthdate as 1904.) Her father died before she reached her teens, and her mother, whose letters to her daughter formed part of the background for *A Tree Grows in Brooklyn*, later married an Irish immigrant, Michael Keogh. At the age of eight, young Betty, or Littie as her mother called her, received an "A" on a school composition, and she later claimed that "I knew then that I would write a book someday." The greatest hardship of her early life, perhaps, lay in the fact that her formal education ended after the eighth grade, since she had to go to work to help support her widowed mother and the younger children. At fourteen she began a series of factory, office, and retail jobs in Brooklyn and New York City; she learned to cook, sew, and dance at the Jackson Street settlement house; and she acted in plays at the Williamsburg YMCA. Always in love with the theater, she wrote plays before beginning her career as a novelist, reputedly as many as seventy short dramas for stage or radio. Her early marriage to George H. E. Smith, a Brooklyn boy who was a law student at the University of Michigan, gave her the opportunity to expand her education. She received permission to take six hours of classes a week as a special student at Michigan; in 1930 she won the Avery Hopgood Award of $1,000 for playwriting. With daughters Nancy and Mary, born a year apart, the Smiths moved to New Haven, where Betty studied for three years at the Yale Drama School under George P. Baker, Walter P. Eaton, and John Mason Brown. She was active in Federal Theater projects, played in a summer stock production of *Hayfever*, and then moved back to the Midwest to write features for the *Detroit Free Press*.

In 1938, after her first marriage ended in divorce, she arrived in Chapel Hill with her daughters and a box of play scripts. Awarded a Rockefeller fellowship and subsequently a Dramatists Guild fellowship, she worked on playwriting under Prof. Frederick Koch and dramatist Paul Green. While engaged in theater and writing projects and struggling to support her family, she found time to write early every morning and put together the diarylike manuscript which she submitted to Harper by mail on 31 December 1942. Trimmed from over 1,000 pages to 400, *A Tree Grows in Brooklyn* sold 300,000 copies in six weeks, became internationally famous through translations into sixteen languages, and by the author's death had sold over six million copies in thirty-seven hardcover printings.

Writing about the composition of her first novel, Smith stated: "Some of the book is me. Every character in it is a composite of a hundred characters I've met—in Michigan, North Carolina, everywhere I've been. The dialogue, though, is Brooklyn, and I've put in things that could only happen in Brooklyn." Reiterating that the book is not the story of her life, Smith observes: "Although almost everything in the book actually happened, it did not necessarily happen to me. Some of the episodes date back to before I was born." In fact, she had been writing Francie's story in different forms for many years; one of her first plays is titled "Francie Nolan," and an early short story, "Death of a Singing Waiter," portrays Francie's father, Johnny Nolan. She credits Thomas Wolfe, however, with the direct inspiration of her novel. After reading *Of Time and the River* in 1936, she penciled in several pages of notes on the flyleaves at the back of the book and later asserted: "It all came back then, like a flood. All of Brooklyn." The following passage appears at the beginning of these notes: "Each day had its life. The anguish of today was tomorrow's reminiscences, the cruelty of today was next year's shame. But the days went on—Life was an hour by hour affair. Each minute was a stone in the mosaic, and when there was a huge pattern of it, one looked back and wept for the ugly squares, the cracked pieces, the discolored edges. One tried to tear out the pieces of gold or scarlet to hold and to finger for loveliness apart from the ugliness. But it couldn't be done. Each piece was a part of the whole. And the whole achieved a kind of glory." This statement of artistic purpose suggests the fabric of its author's life, her determination to create and succeed, her need to share a vision that was honest, universal, and triumphant.

Critical acclaim for *A Tree Grows in Brooklyn* praised its almost lyrical treatment of naturalistic setting and subject, its realistic dialogue, and its optimism in the midst of poverty. Orville Prescott in the *Yale Review* wrote: "Here is a first novel of uncommon skill . . . the work of a fresh, original and highly gifted talent. It is a story about life in the Williamsburg tenement district as lived by the Nolan family, particularly by Francie Nolan, aged one to nineteen in the course of the book—my favorite heroine for 1943." In discussing her fan mail, Smith notes that Francie had become a national figure overnight: "One-fifth of my letters start out, 'Dear Francie.'" In the novel, scene after scene builds a panorama of Francie's universe: Saturday's visit to the junk dealer and on to Cheap Charlie's for penny candy; trips to Losher's for stale bread and a five-cent pie or to the butcher's for a soup bone; afternoons in the library where the pottery-jug's flowers marked the changing seasons—nasturtiums for summer, bittersweet for fall; Tammany Hall's annual boating picnic for the district's residents; children in Thanksgiving masks begging from store to store; and the Christmas Eve when Francie and Neeley "caught" the ten-foot Christmas tree and dragged it home. Balanced opposite these bright moments, and the sense of family closeness, stand dark scenes of school humiliation—Francie's hair soaked in kerosene to ward off lice or her pants wet when the teacher refused "leaving-the-room" permission, the consequences of Johnny Nolan's alcoholism and the horror of Francie's near rape. The aftermath of this scene is starkly symbolic: Johnny rubs carbolic acid on his daughter's leg, where the rapist's genitals had touched her, and scars her for life.

Over the novel broods the image of the "tree," a type of Chinese sumac, the *Ailanthus glandulosa*: "It had pointed leaves which grew along green switches which radiated from the bough and made a tree which looked like a lot of opened green umbrellas. Some people called it the Tree of Heaven. No matter where its seed fell, it made a tree which struggled to reach the sky. It grew in boarded-up lots and out of neglected rubbish heaps and it was the only tree that grew out of cement." A tree that "liked poor people," it curls its umbrellas over the third-floor fire escape where Francie Nolan sits and daydreams. In its strong descriptions *A Tree Grows in Brooklyn* rises above sentimentalism, and its heroine encounters danger and disappointment with pride, passing her initiation rites.

It is possibly true that the novel's happy ending, its suggestion of the rags-to-riches theme, fails to maintain the authenticity of its beginning. Rosemary Dawson in the *Saturday Review* wrote: "As long as the book moves with the rhythm of life in Williamsburg and remains true to that setting it is a beautiful and moving piece of work. But toward the end of the novel the rhythm is broken." Diana Trilling in the *Nation* commented: "I am a little bewildered by so much response to so conventional a little book"; but the *New Yorker* reviewer observed: "The author sees the misery, squalor, and cruelty of slum life but sees them with understanding, pity and sometimes with hilarious humor. A welcome relief from the latter-day fashion of writing about slum folk as if they were all brutalized morons." Brockmann stated that *A Tree Grows in Brooklyn* expresses "the spiritual kinship that exists and has always existed among the poor of every nation." Such an appraisal links the specific world of Francie Nolan with a universal dream of challenge and opportunity.

In August 1943, the same month that *A Tree Grows in Brooklyn* was published, Betty Smith married Joseph Piper Jones, assistant editor of the *Chapel Hill Weekly*, when he was stationed in the army at Norfolk. Their life after the war included birdwatching, trips to the beach, and gardening. They lived in a brick and frame house on Rosemary Street in downtown Chapel Hill. Here Smith planted an ailanthus tree to remind her of the trees in the Williamsburg slums of Brooklyn, which had inspired her first novel, and she began work on the book for a musical version of *A Tree Grows in Brooklyn*. This production, written in collaboration with George Abbott, opened at the Alvin Theatre on 19 April 1951.

During the next few years Smith acquired an accountant, an attorney, and an agent in her attempt to give up a "lifelong habit" of doing everything for herself. She noted, however, "I cannot turn my writing over to a secretary. That I must do myself even to typing and word counting, wrapping the manuscript for mailing and personally buying the stamps." She discovered that change was inevitable: with her first royalties she bought the Rosemary Street house, a mink coat, and a convertible. She was paid $55,000 for the movie rights to her novel by Twentieth Century-Fox; the film was released in 1945, directed by Elia Kazan and starring Peggy Ann Garner, Dorothy McGuire, Joan Blondell, Lloyd Nolan, and James Dunn—who won an Oscar for best supporting actor in the role of Johnny Nolan. Two years later *A Tree Grows in Brooklyn* was adapted for a radio series.

An interviewer in the *Saturday Review* noted the novelist's appearance at this time: "She's petite, has a low, relaxed voice, dark hair, gray eyes, and, because 'it looks more prosperous (her words),' a year-round tan." Daily she found time to answer her fan mail personally, writing that "The thrill of someone's asking for my autograph never wears off."

Her second novel, *Tomorrow Will Be Better*, was a best-seller for 1948 although critics suggest that its tone seems dark and far less hopeful than her first book. In this story of "poverty and postponement" Margy Shannon grows to womanhood, marries a man whose homosexual tendencies are hinted at, and gives birth to a stillborn child. Always pursuing her, like the shadow of fear and failure, is the time

when she "lost" her mother. She tries, as a child, to explain to her mother why she is afraid to cross the street with the iron gates: "I don't like the way it looks at me." But she cannot communicate her terror; her mother crosses the street and walks away from her, refusing to take the five-year-old child's hand, leaving her behind. Margy, uneasy but fascinated, turns down the one-block street which ends at the gates of a charity hospital: "The gates made a long narrow cage of the street. There was a feeling that if you turned into that street, the opening would close behind you and the locked gates ahead would hold you prisoner in the city block forever." The street and its gates haunt her adult dreams, symbolizing the barrier which shuts her off from love. Though she does not share Francie Nolan's intellectual drive nor her infinite capacity for humor, Margy is resourceful and refuses to compromise her chances for fulfillment. Richard Sullivan observed in the *New York Times*: "The book makes no suggestions, answers no questions, proposes no solutions. Its intention is direct and difficult—to project, honestly and immediately, a moving image of experience. And in that purpose it memorably succeeds."

Smith's third novel, *Maggie-Now*, begun after an automobile accident in 1952, was published ten years after *Tomorrow Will Be Better* and continues its somber tone, presenting a heroine who, like Margy, lives in hope that something better will happen. The novelist had divorced her second husband in 1951, so her own mood may have influenced the sense of loneliness and expectancy that pervades Maggie-Now's existence. At the time the book appeared, Smith reported in an interview: "I am very much at ease with myself. . . . I think well of myself, which is an attitude difficult to come by." She had married Robert V. Finch, an old friend and fellow playwright, in June 1957, and was very happy, according to her close friends. In addition, her new novel won the annual Sir Walter Raleigh Award, the highest honor for North Carolina fiction.

A saga of Irish Brooklyn, complex and intensely symbolic, *Maggie-Now* creates a broad canvas with realistic details, but its heroine fails to develop into a convincing character. Maggie-Now plays a quiet waiting game with life, caring for her infant brother, her rascal father, and her husband, Claude, who appears each winter as the snow falls and vanishes with the warm chinook each spring. As the reviewer in *Newsweek* noted: "The face is familiar; the charm has faded." Maggie-Now stands only for what is present and honest in everyday life; even

Dust jacket for Smith's third novel (1958), about an Irish girl in Brooklyn

like a small sigh." The tone of *Maggie-Now* is soft and plaintive, without passion, but with pity for lost children and lost dreams. Riley Hughes in the *Catholic World* stressed Smith's perception of the sadness and courage of immigrant life, adding: "But unfortunately, she [the author] stands a bit too far off from her story, keening distantly over her characters, instead of placing herself and the reader right at their elbows. It's all remembered, not happening, and too much of Maggie-Then." Maggie-Now, the stayer and sustainer, provides life for those around her, but she herself is barren.

Smith's last novel, *Joy in the Morning* (1963), recaptures some of the intensity of youth seen in *A Tree Grows in Brooklyn*, although the scope of time and space is severely reduced, perhaps because of the criticism of *Maggie-Now*'s length. The novelist had been widowed in 1959, less than two years after her marriage, and in 1961 she was teaching creative writing at the University of North Carolina, where she had earlier been a lecturer in drama. As she told her classes about her own student experiences at the University of Michigan, she found the memories crowding back: "So I wrote a book about it and titled it *Joy in the Morning*." Later she commented: "As I wrote, I realized to my delight that the book was more than a novel of college life. It was the anatomy of a marriage; the story of victory over odds."

Much of *Joy in the Morning* is drawn from the author's own experience as the bride of a law student, a young wife with little education and a driving passion to learn. Her heroine, Annie McGairy, arrives on the train from New York to marry Carl Brown against the wishes of both families. They cope with finding shelter, food, and jobs so that Carl can finish law school at a midwestern university and Annie can audit English classes. Like Francie Nolan, Annie has a remarkable capacity for enjoying life, for interacting with and characterizing the people she meets: Goldie and her Indian husband; Henry the grocery-store owner and his squirrels; the landlady who bakes cakes for every occasion; even Jello, the fraternity dog. The reader empathizes with Annie's eagerness to learn and her delight in owning her first book, a battered twenty-five-cent copy of *War and Peace*. Details of sex and birth seem appropriate in this story of young love, and the reader is not surprised that the world beyond their cottage barely seems to exist, although Babette Hall in the *Saturday Review* criticized the narrow focus: "In the entire year in which (Carl and Annie) expressed themselves endlessly with a kind of autohypnosis there is no evidence that either of them ever saw a newspaper." Perhaps the book's more

her name insists on this presentness. Her mother says, "Hush, Maggie. Hush, Maggie, now." As the child grows up, her mother continues: "Maggie, now give me those scissors. . . . Maggie, now mind your father." In contrast, other characters represent lost dreams and the past: her father dreams of the Maggie Rose he left behind in Ireland, and Claude dreams of the parents he never knew. Smith has given the reader a kind of memory novel, like a memory play, but instead of concentrating on highly selective moments, she lets the years drag by until the last scene, where two old men scatter Claude's ashes from the top of the Statue of Liberty as the gulls wheel and scream. There are other strong scenes, alive with details, often relating to food, such as Easter dinner for Claude, where Maggie serves half a loaf of warm bread with butter for dessert: " 'Listen!,' she said. She pressed her forefinger on the eggshell-thin but crisp crust. An inch of the crust collapsed into flakes with a sound obvious flaw lies in the hint of sentimentality which pervades the young couple's consistent good luck; outsiders are invariably kind to Carl and Annie, and even the crusty Dean plays beneficent godfather. Virgilia Peterson in the *New York Times* suggested that "if we are to believe Betty Smith, it was not only the economy that was simpler in 1927, but human nature itself." Only the parents remain unforgiving, an authentic touch since Smith writes of her own experience: "When I married, my husband's father stopped sending him ten dollars a week. He said that if a man was old enough to marry, he was old enough to support himself and his wife." Close to reality, even if idealized, the novel's accurate dialogue and series of short, dramatic scenes sketch a convincing picture of marriage. Two years after the publication of *Joy in the Morning*, the film version, produced by MGM and starring Richard Chamberlain and Yvette Mimieux, premiered in Chapel Hill with some favorable reviews.

Betty Smith was awarded a Certificate of Merit by the New York Museum of Science and Industry for outstanding achievement in the arts, and she was the recipient of the Carolina Playmakers Alumni Award in 1964. There are thirty-five plays by Smith in the North Carolina Collection, with titles reflecting a wide range of subjects from historical drama, about Lincoln's life or the old West, to slapstick comedy. *The Boy, Abe* centers on a late fall morning when young Lincoln meets his new mother for the first time. Mrs. Lincoln's words will seem familiar to Smith's audience: "Yes, Abe. I'd like for you to do something for me. I'd like for you to plant this little tree out there. Where your mother is. It's a wild crabapple tree. The blossoms are mighty pretty in the spring. . . ." *Lawyer Lincoln*, a dialect folk play, revolves around a courtship-wager situation, reminiscent of Longstreet's *Georgia Scenes*. In 1961 *Durham Station*, a short historical drama, was shown on local television, sponsored by the North Carolina Confederate Centennial Commission. The theme is reconciliation in the tradition of local-color romance, with a Southern widow marrying a Union soldier. Smith also draws on biblical themes in *The Silvered Rope* and *They Released Barabbas*; but in *Wives-in-Law*, *Gandersauce*, and *Youth Takes Over* she creates situation comedy typical of her own era. Some of these plays were produced locally by amateur groups and now seem very outdated. Several of the plays were coauthored with Robert Finch, her third husband.

A widow for thirteen years, Smith died on 17 January 1972, in Shelton, Connecticut, leaving behind two copies of an unfinished autobiography,

separately titled "A Child, A Tree, A Book" and "Look Back with a Smile." In the preface to one of these manuscripts she wrote: "I came to a clear conclusion and it is a universal one: 'To live, to struggle, to be in love with life—in love with all life holds, joyful or sorrowful, is fulfillment.'"

The colorful details of ordinary life in her novels illustrate Smith's capacity for presenting "all life holds" to her readers. Her favorite modern authors were Theodore Dreiser, Sherwood Anderson, and Thomas Wolfe, all writers in the naturalist tradition. She considered her own writing part of this school, with its emphasis on objective narration, attention to detail, interest in the lower strata of society, and the environment's shaping of individual destiny. Where Smith detaches herself from naturalism, however, is in the amount of free will she allows her central characters; in the end it is not impersonal social, economic, and biological factors which rule her fictional world but the inner strength of her heroines. They are the inheritors of

Dust jacket for Smith's fourth and last novel (1963), which draws on her student experiences at the University of Michigan

nineteenth-century local-color romance and popular fiction at the turn of the century—the stories of Kate Douglas Wiggin, Gene Stratton Porter, and Frances Hodgson Burnett. Compelled to describe the ordinary happenings of ordinary people, she explained: "I loved the people I was writing about." She added: "All my life I wanted money. I thought it would cure a lot of things." Yet she pointed out in discussing the success of *A Tree Grows in Brooklyn*: "I did not write my novel to make money. I wrote it for my own pure sensuous pleasure." It is this pleasure that lies in the images which give her writing power: "We had an orange at Christmas. We were very poor. An orange meant so much to us." Like Thomas Wolfe, who subtitled *Of Time and the River* "a legend of man's hunger in his youth," Betty Smith was hungry for life and love and the drama of everyday things.

Plays:

Plays for Schools and Little Theatres, by Smith, F. H. Koch, and Robert Finch (Chapel Hill, N.C.: Bureau of Community Drama, 1937);
20 Prize-Winning Non-Royalty One-Act Plays, compiled by Smith (New York: Greenberg, 1943);
A Tree Grows in Brooklyn [musical play], by Smith and George Abbott; lyrics by Dorothy Fields (New York: Harper, 1951).

Periodical Publications:

"I'm the Girl Who Wrote about a Tree that Grew in Brooklyn," *Read*, 16 (October 1944): 27-29;

"Road to the Best Seller," *Writer*, 57 (October 1944): 291-293;
"Best-seller Aftermath: A Successful Author's Lot is a Public Life with Lovely Troubles," *Life* (6 June 1949): 5ff.;
"On Looking Back," in *Michigan*, edited by Erich A. Walter (Ann Arbor: University of Michigan, 1966), pp. 78-80.

Interview:

Robert Van Gelder, "Betty Smith on Fame and Money; an interview with the author of *A Tree Grows in Brooklyn* and *Tomorrow Will Be Better*," *Vogue*, 113 (April 1949): 186 ff.

References:

Charles B. Brockmann, "In the Shadow of the Tree," *Carolina Quarterly*, 2 (1950): 41-46;
Harold C. Gardiner, S.J., *In All Conscience* (Garden City: Hanover House, 1959), pp. 102-104;
Blanche Housman Gelfant, *The American City Novel* (Norman: University of Oklahoma Press, 1954), pp. 230, 237-241;
Orville Prescott, *In My Opinion* (Indianapolis: Bobbs-Merrill, 1952), pp. 40-49.

Papers:

The Betty Smith Papers are in the Southern Historical Collection, University of North Carolina Library, Chapel Hill. In addition, there are numerous plays by Betty Smith and articles by and about the author in the North Carolina Collection, University of North Carolina Library, Chapel Hill.

Mark Smith
(19 November 1935-   )

Gayle Swanson
Newberry College

BOOKS: *Toyland* (Boston: Little, Brown, 1965);
The Middleman (Boston: Little, Brown, 1967);
The Death of the Detective (New York: Knopf, 1974;
     London: Secker & Warburg, 1975);
The Moon Lamp (New York: Knopf, 1976; London:
     Secker & Warburg, 1976);
The Delphinium Girl (New York: Harper & Row,
     1980; London: Secker & Warburg, 1980);
Doctor Blues (New York: Morrow, 1983).

Mark Smith is a literary craftsman whose broad command of fictional technique has resulted in a canon of six novels that differ significantly from one another in structure and style. A professor of fiction writing and the form and theory of fiction at the University of New Hampshire, he gained a wide readership with the publication of his third book, *The Death of the Detective* (1974). In this work, as in each of his others, Smith upholds his conviction that the novelist's chief responsibility to his reader is to tell the truth, even if it is painful to hear. The source of Smith's most important truths, as well as the most visible point of unity among his novels, is his existential vision of the human condition. Throughout the body of his fiction, he explores the great variety of implications inherent in the theme that man is a being who defines himself through his actions in a meaningless, indifferent, and ultimately treacherous world.

The son of a boat builder, Smith was born in Charlevoix, Michigan. Spending his early childhood in this resort town on the shore of Lake Michigan in the heart of Hemingway country, Smith unconsciously absorbed a detailed knowledge of the wooded terrain and extreme winter cold of the lower peninsula which were to play an important part in his first two novels. When he was six, his parents divorced, and he moved with his mother to Battle Creek, Michigan. In 1945, when Smith was ten, his mother remarried, and the family moved to Chicago, Illinois—a city he now considers the greatest influence on his life. In high school, having little desire to study and no desire whatsoever to be a writer, he was an athlete and, by his own admission, a troublemaker. He became a "city kid," learning Chicago on the most direct level by roaming its

Mark Smith

streets and exploring its neighborhoods, from the most affluent to the most sordid. His experiences were, some thirteen years later, to form the basis of *The Death of the Detective*.

After graduating from high school in 1954, Smith earned money for college by picking up construction jobs and working both as a timekeeper and a "mucker," or tunneler, for the Chicago subway. The next year he returned to his native Michigan and spent one semester as a halfhearted business major at Western Michigan University in Kalamazoo. Coming back to Chicago, he enrolled in Wright Junior College as an anthropology major. Soon, however, he developed an intense interest in the humanities and in all forms of art and criticism. And with the inspiration and encouragement of some good teachers of literature, Smith committed himself to becoming a writer.

The summer after his second semester of college, Smith joined the merchant marine but was soon in an accident that left him with a broken pelvis. During the two years he spent recuperating, he prepared himself for his career by reading voraciously. He went through all of Hemingway and Steinbeck, much of Faulkner, and everything he could find of the Russians—Dostoevski, Turgenev, Gogol, Tolstoy. He also returned to college. Attending three institutions at once, he took only those courses in which he was interested: Greek at the downtown campus of the University of Chicago, drama and the novel at the Chicago campus of Northwestern University, and poetry at Wright Junior College. Eventually, his recovery complete, Smith realized he needed to obtain a degree; and in the fall of 1958, when he was almost twenty-three, he enrolled as a full-time English major at the Evanston campus of Northwestern.

At Northwestern, Smith came under two profound influences, the existentialists whom he studied and the respected scholars and writers who were his teachers: Richard Ellmann, whose biography *James Joyce* (1959) was published while Smith was at the university; Edward B. Hungerford, the former teacher of Saul Bellow; and John Crowe Ransom, the poet whose book *The New Criticism* (1941) is a landmark of literary critical theory. Enveloped by the aura of academe and greatly encouraged by Ransom in his poetic efforts, Smith was convinced he would pursue his career in literature as both a critic and a poet. But by the time of his graduation in 1960, he was twenty-four, married, and so weary of school that he had no wish to do graduate work.

Moreover, he was soon to see that his future did not lie in poetry, that he was writing through an academic mask he had acquired in college and would never have his own voice in that genre. Blaming not so much the university environment as his acquiescence to it, Smith abandoned poetry altogether and removed to Europe for a year. Living chiefly in Spain, he wrote his first novel—an effort wholly inspired by Joyce's *Ulysses*. Again rejecting his work as the product of a false voice, Smith returned to Chicago and began to experiment with both long and short fiction, attempting virtually every device and technique. In 1962, his marriage having ended, he moved to Boston, where he lived alone on Beacon Hill, somewhat in the style of the

bohemian artist, and continued his work. Although none of the twenty-odd short stories he produced was accepted for publication, this period of apprenticeship proved extremely valuable. Not only had he learned that fiction was indeed his genre but he had drafted the works that would become his first published novels, *Toyland* (1965) and *The Middleman* (1967), both of which he based on a single short story he had done in college; he had also written a novella that he would later expand into *The Death of the Detective*.

By 1964, Smith had remarried and was living in an eighteenth-century farmhouse in Northwood, New Hampshire. There he completed *Toyland* and, two years later, *The Middleman*. Though both of these novels are separate entities, each is most fully appreciated in terms of the other, for the action of both is centered in the same grim circumstance: Walter Wold, an eccentric recluse, has contracted by mail with a professional killer named Jensen to dispose of a young boy and girl, the newly orphaned children of Walter's brother, who are now in their uncle's charge. The one scene recounted in both novels, though in distinctly differing ways, is Walter's delivery of his niece and nephew into the hands of Jensen and his partner, a man called only by the Finnish surname Pehr. The killers come to Walter's house, meet the uncle for the first and last time, and leave shortly thereafter with the children. Each work is a first-person narrative. *Toyland*, written from Pehr's point of view, is the story of what transpires later that day in the deep Michigan woods where Jensen and Pehr take the children. *The Middleman*, written from Walter's point of view, is the story of what occurs in Walter's life and in his tortured mind during that same day.

The central conflict in *Toyland* is that which begins to arise between the killers the moment Pehr sees that their intended victims are children, a fact Jensen has purposely kept from him. Convinced that he can neither kill them nor allow Jensen to do so, Pehr resolves to kill Jensen. Yet, as Pehr eventually learns, Jensen has known all along that he would make this decision. It was, in fact, Jensen's plan. Like his choice of careers, Jensen's scheme is the product of his nihilistic belief that human life is totally devoid of worth and meaning. Voicing the novel's underlying theme, he asserts: "the system's like sodawater . . . And men? Like the bubbles of carbonation inside it. Some . . . pop at the surface. . . . Or they . . . become meaningless casualties along the way. Or they simply settle on the bottom. A high mortality rate, friend: one hundred percent." In a line of reasoning that reminds one of

Dust jacket for Smith's first novel (1965), told from the point of view of a contract killer hired to murder two children

Dostoevski's persona in *Notes from Underground* and, more particularly, of Camus's cruel and suicidal Caligula, Jensen has concluded that the only way man can protest against such a system is to imitate it, to assert his will by becoming as perverse and destructive as it is: "before you can control your fate," declares Jensen, "you've got to surrender to it."

The important focus of *Toyland*, however, is Pehr and the transformation he undergoes as a result of Jensen's plan. At first, both the reader and Pehr himself believe that Pehr is not greatly unlike Jensen. His decision to become Jensen's partner had indeed been based on an attempt to wage a revolt, but not so much against the indifference he had seen in the universe as in society: "I've said to hell with the senseless system the world's in, with its . . . dehumanized estrangements, where . . . you were only safe aping the corpselike detachment that too many people . . . possessed inately. . . . I'll go animal before I'll go machine." Forced by Jensen to see in the children the essential helplessness of all

mankind, Pehr comes to the same conclusion Camus had eventually reached: the only true revolt against the human condition is not imitative perversity but active concern for one's fellow man. Thus committing himself to humanity, Pehr strikes a blow against both the cosmic and the social cruelty which Jensen embodies.

Yet by this act, Pehr brings himself into a greater struggle with the very perversity he was attempting to transcend—a situation which leads him to the despairing recognition that despite "the unreasonable unknown" lying beyond one's actions, one is not only forced repeatedly to make and to carry out difficult choices but is also totally responsible for those acts. In Pehr's final predicament, which involves the children themselves and which Pehr handles in a way that is obscured from the reader, Smith centers the novel's major themes: the awesome contingency of man's existence, and the ultimate futility of any kind of revolt against the inherent cruelty of the world. "The whole was big enough to tolerate dissension," Pehr admits; "it didn't have to compromise."

Although *Toyland* received only a modest amount of attention when it was published, several reviewers praised it as skillful and original. It is a stylized novel, with descriptions of nature that are highly visual and poetic and with characters who habitually speak and think in metaphors and similes. While such language may be, as Glendy Culligan put it in *Book Week*, "a little too high-flown for the business at hand," the major weakness of the novel lies in the fact that it is largely a philosophical discussion. "The simple truth," wrote Culligan, "is that Smith's characters talk too much, and like certain self-absorbed acquaintances, bore and alienate us by their demands for understanding." In addition, as critics also noted, the novel is sometimes confusing as it leaps into flashbacks in which Pehr recalls the various contexts of his running dialogue with Jensen and as Pehr's interior monologues blend into episodes of fantasy and dream. As a whole, however, *Toyland* succeeds. "This is a difficult book to read at first," said Carol A. Eckberg in *Library Journal*, "but the effort is worth it."

The Middleman, which received less attention than *Toyland*, shares the same nihilistic theme of the world's inherent meaninglessness, but this novel answers a question that *Toyland* does not address: Walter's motive in having his niece and nephew killed. "I did it for no reason," he avers, "no reason at all surely, and for no feeling I'd indulged. . . . That was the reason: no reason and no feeling." Yet

Walter is not so much a man who is deliberately imitating the cruelty of the universe as one who has been engulfed by its absurdity: "Why all this?," he asks; "I mean, these somethings. Why not just *nothing*?" To Walter, the children are merely part of the useless and unnerving "clutter" of the world, which he destroys simply because there is no reason for such clutter to exist.

As an introspective study of anguish and alienation, *The Middleman* reflects the influence of the late nineteenth-century Norwegian author Knut Hamsun, whose *Hunger* Smith esteems as one of the first existential novels written in first-person and recognizes as a major influence on Sartre's *Nausea*. It is the French existentialist Sartre, however, whose presence is most heavily felt in *The Middleman*. Many of his central concepts in *Nausea* and in the closely related treatise *Being and Non-Being* are clearly echoed: that existence precedes essence, or meaning, in human beings and in objects; that objects are opaque realities which have no awareness and no essence; and that human consciousness is an invisible or transparent nonreality which gives to objects the only degree of meaning they can have but which can know itself only in its own nothingness. But whereas Sartre had gone on to maintain that the individual can transcend this nothingness within him by continually creating or defining himself through his actions, Walter has reversed the process: he has un-created not only people and objects but himself as well. "I have wasted away and become invisible," he declares, "white only upon the general and ultimate whiteness." Having retreated into the unreality of his own consciousness, where he is haunted by the viciousness and absurdity he had seen in the people of his town and in the family of which he is the last living member, Walter is "the American middleman with nothing above or below me, nothing before or behind me, nothing on either side of me." Only when he reads the words *"Poor Uncle Walter"* that the children have scrawled on a window and believes they felt true concern for him—a concern he thinks no one has had before—does he see the atrocity of what he has become and what he has done.

Despite the grim intensity of Walter's predicament, his account of it is not without humor. He mocks himself, for example, when he describes such moments as his failure to recall that nothing is growing on his head: "I had picked up the hairbrush. Just what did I think I would do with it? Massage my scalp? I dropped it on the dresser. Who put that useless object in my room?" More realistic in its dialogue and its depiction of the world than

Toyland, *The Middleman* is set in Smith's hometown of Charlevoix, a place whose people he portrays in a singularly unflattering light. Yet the novel is neither an autobiography nor an exposé but a fictional study in the psychology of estrangement that grew out of stories Smith's mother and others of his family had told him about their town when he was a child. Tenuously based in the immediate circumstance of Walter's life with his good-hearted wife and the elderly couple who run their household, the novel is a collage of interior monologues, recollections, fantasies, and hallucinations in which Walter's dead family not only participate with him in scenes from their past but also intrude into the present reality. "In its uncompromising delineation of a deranged yet highly analytical mind," wrote Peter Buitenhuis in the *New York Times Book Review*, "*The Middleman* is one of the best existential novels yet written in the United States."

In 1966, the year he completed *The Middleman*, Smith embarked on his second career as a teacher of fiction at the University of New Hampshire. He also began a new novel. But, as has been his pattern with all his books, he set it aside after a time and returned to something he had done earlier—in this case, the novella he had written in Boston. Starting in 1967, he worked for five years developing this piece into the novel which was published as *The Death of the Detective*.

The Death of the Detective reflects Smith's effort to engage a much wider canvas in his fiction, to move away from the narrow philosophical novel in the manner of Hamsun and Sartre to a broader, more naturalistic work in the tradition of Dickens and Dreiser. Setting his novel in Chicago, Smith sought, as the backdrop for his larger concerns of theme and character, to capture that city as he remembered it. All of Smith's novels give the reader a strong sense of place, and each of them is set in an area in which Smith has lived a considerable time. However, *The Death of the Detective* is exceptional in this regard. For, somewhat to Smith's surprise, Chicago is so dominant a presence in the book that Francis X. Gavin in *Best Sellers*, for example, spoke of the city as "a character itself," and Sheldon Frank in the *National Observer* called it "the major figure in the novel." Yet as other critics recognized, for all the massive and graphic detail of its portrait of Chicago, the novel goes well beyond the objective reality of its setting: "what is being presented here," wrote Barbara A. Bannon in *Publishers Weekly*, "is in all ways a microcosm of middle America."

Despite his feelings of affection for Chicago, the society Smith depicts in *The Death of the Detective* is a sick one, a world that has lost its moral balance and is sinking into the mire of its own corruption. The plot that unfolds within this "rich atmosphere of sequestered sin and naked violence" is complex and multileveled, and its characters are many. At the thematic center is Arnold Magnuson: an aging defender of good who sets out alone with a romanticized sense of destiny to conquer evil but who becomes so thoroughly integrated and confused with this force that he is ultimately swallowed up by it, his efforts rendered perverse and meaningless.

The first of the novel's four books, "Prelude to Murder," introduces Magnuson and the two men with whom his fate is intertwined. Once a detective in the true sense, Magnuson is now the wealthy, retired head of the organization into which his own detective agency had dissolved, the famous Magnuson Men—an assortment of men, from high school athletes to moonlighting policemen, hired out as guards and as ushers for crowd control at public events. Widowed, lonely, and longing for the days when he had been instrumental in curbing the lawlessness that now engulfs his city, Magnuson receives a call from Frazer Farquarson, who says only that he needs Magnuson's services. Farquarson, bedridden with a terminal illness, is an eccentric millionaire for whom Magnuson had conducted many investigations, including one some thirty years ago that had given Farquarson the evidence he needed to have his wife committed to an insane asylum. Troubled by a deep sense of guilt for a series of wrongs he had perpetrated where his wife was concerned, Farquarson fears that before his illness can kill him, he will be murdered by the man who had been caught up as a victim in the scenario of those deeds. The avenger is Joseph Helenowski, a madman who has just escaped from the asylum, where he has been confined most of his life, and who hates not only Farquarson but all mankind: "he repeats his name, 'the death-maker,' and declares this is a time of death."

Book two of the novel, "The Murders," is an account of Helenowski's one-night rampage of murder and Magnuson's pursuit of the unknown killer through Chicago and its environs, beginning at the Tudor mansion in Lake Forest where Magnuson arrives to find Farquarson dead. His sense of purpose rekindled, Magnuson vows to solve the crime without involving the police, whom he considers totally corrupt and inept. Following the trail of clues, he is led to a number of people whom he feels he must interrogate as suspects or protect as potential victims of the killer. Yet he arrives or returns in each instance to discover that the person

has been murdered a short time earlier. Soon, Magnuson begins to question his own sanity and to suspect that he is himself the murderer or that, at the very least, he is in some way causing the deaths. No longer convinced that good will prevail, Magnuson is nonetheless resolute in his mission: "he has been committed to the battle for too long a lifetime. . . . Even if he works evil instead of good, even if in the end he is not merely destroyed but damned and doomed, he cannot do otherwise."

In Book three, "Closing In," Magnuson deduces that Helenowski is the killer and comes face to face with his own guilt, both in his compulsion to solve the crimes alone and in the injustice of his investigation of Farquarson's wife. Humiliated by his failures and presumptions, he resolves to redeem himself: with the help of the Magnuson Men he will capture Helenowski, who is now known by the public to be on the loose and reputed to be headed for the park where a mammoth Polish-American picnic is being held. Throughout the novel, there are comic overtones as well as serious metaphorical intent in both Magnuson's and Helenowski's seeing themselves as personifications of cosmic powers: the former is the force of Good, the protector of life; the latter is the force of Death, the instrument of destruction. And the city of Chicago is their battleground, the intricate and menacing landscape upon which they must contend in their attempt to act out their respective roles. The final battle between these forces, which takes place at the picnic, Smith recounts with the kind of sardonic humor that he often uses when he is the most sober in his purpose: the ridiculous army of Magnuson Men completely bungles everything it attempts, and the crowd takes Magnuson himself to be the "Mad Polack" and beats him almost to unconsciousness.

The fourth part, "Discoveries," contains the resolutions to the novel's two subplots and records the last stages of Magnuson's degradation: his disappearance, his anonymous and brief reemergence on Skid Row, his death, and the public's continuing speculations about "the acute psychosis" from which he had apparently been suffering and about the degree to which he had actually been involved in the murders.

The Death of the Detective, nominated for the National Book Award in fiction, is Smith's most popular and most widely reviewed novel. It has been called everything from a " 'serious' detective novel," to "essentially a simple detective story," to a "baroque epic . . . cast in the form of the [Raymond] Chandler thriller." While the work does have af-

Dust jacket for Smith's third novel (1974), described by one reviewer as "a thoroughly depressing story of the nastiness of life"

finities with the "detective novel," or "mystery novel," both of these labels are too restrictive to apply to it, by virtue of its thematic implications alone. Described by Benjamin J. Stein in the *National Review* as "a morality tale without any hope," Smith's work is an account of madness and absurdity on the cosmic level, a dark portrait of the human condition in a world where there are no moral absolutes and no reassurances that all will be well. "As a thoroughly depressing story of the nastiness of life," continued Stein, "*The Death of the Detective* is unequaled. But that is not to take away from the book's power. To achieve this level of bleakness is not a small achievement. The writing is graphic and powerful, and if the message is grim, the medium is lively." Many other critics, however, maintained that the novel is so long and detailed, and its action so crowded and convoluted, that it loses much of its intensity. "His writing is often

wonderfully vivid," wrote Gavin in *Best Sellers*, "but after a while [it] suffers grievously from simply being too much."

After completing *The Death of the Detective* in 1972, Smith drafted a novella that he was eventually to expand into his fifth novel, *The Delphinium Girl* (1980). He put the novella aside in 1973, however, and took his family to the British Isles for a year. Traveling in England, France, and Spain, they lived in Casteltownshend, County Cork, Ireland, where Smith resumed work on the novel he had begun in 1966. Upon his return to New Hampshire, he completed the book, and in 1976 it was published as *The Moon Lamp*, a title which comes from a traditional Irish ballad.

The Moon Lamp and *The Delphinium Girl* have a great deal in common and together mark a significant change in Smith's fiction. Both works are much less violent and grotesque in character and action, less darkly intense in tone, less complex in structure, and less dense and metaphorical in style. Each is set in a small, pleasant, richly colonial community in New Hampshire, much like the one where Smith himself lived, and each reflects a more direct involvement in the concerns of everyday life. In addition, both novels have female protagonists who are essentially tragicomic figures, women whose self-delusions cause their grand purposes to dissolve into absurdly futile and meaningless gestures. Searching for fulfillment, they totally overlook their real worlds and their roles as individuals, wives, and mothers and slip into the fantasy of a nonexistent time: Winnie Linquist, in *The Moon Lamp*, into a romanticized vision of her past; Sarah Keville, in *The Delphinium Girl*, into a romanticized vision of her future. And in so doing, in refusing to be themselves and to live their lives in the present, both women simply fail to live at all.

Smith's characterization of these women is rooted in the existentialism that pervades his previous novels, most specifically Sartre's doctrine that the individual exists only insofar as he realizes himself through his actions and thus is nothing but what those actions make him. In *The Moon Lamp*, this theme appears within the context of a uniquely American ghost story, whose main characters are the Linquist family: Winnie; her husband Gene, a youthfully eccentric Dartmouth-educated drama coach; and their daughter, Penelope, a bright but uncertain girl attending Wellesley on a scholarship in archaeology.

Retiring early, Gene and Winnie had moved from Chicago to New Hampshire in order to occupy the pre-Revolutionary saltbox on an isolated tract of land Gene had inherited six years earlier. They had worked during their summers to restore the house and had thus begun their new life in an "authentic re-creation of a setting from the past." Although Gene plays his role in this setting with enthusiasm, it is Winnie who develops such a need to be a part of the social and cultural heritage of New England that she totally eschews the "traditionless" Midwest where she was born and immerses herself in the house and its history. Within that history are several of the house's former occupants, whose spirits Winnie is certain are still there.

Eventually, Winnie sees, or thinks she sees, a ghost. Yet it is not that of Gene's relative but of Sneevy, a man she had married some thirty years ago. Having completely suppressed the memory of him, Winnie now recalls that she left Sneevy when suddenly she had realized how different they were from one another: he had shown no ambition to advance in the world, and with him, she had seen herself "doing nothing, being nothing." Soon thereafter she had married Gene, a man whose educational and social status represented the terms in which she wanted to define herself. But the appearance of Sneevy, who in all likelihood is still very much alive, causes Winnie to reevaluate both her past life as Gene's wife in a well-to-do Chicago suburb and her present preoccupation with his ancestral home: "she had been a ghost. (No more substantial than a ghost, she told herself.) And no less a ghost as she stripped the paint and oiled the furniture or merely lived from day to day in this, her husband's house. She belonged to neither here nor there, to neither then nor now."

At this point, Winnie decides that she and Sneevy are alike after all: in each of them is the spirit of modern American rootlessness; they are people who have no ties to the land or to the past and who thus will sooner or later be compelled to carve out an identity for themselves by moving onward and upward in life. Sneevy's apparition, she therefore concludes, is actually a telepathic message from her former husband to tell her that he will soon come in the flesh to take her away so that together they can meet the challenge of new frontiers. In time, after Sneevy fails to appear in reality but seems to manifest himself in spirit on several occasions, Winnie retreats into her own world with her bittersweet memories of him. Eventually losing Gene to another woman, Winnie becomes a recluse in the house she has grown to hate. At the end of the novel, when two townspeople mistake her for the great-aunt who had willed the house to Gene, the reader feels a sense of complete appropriateness: Winnie is indeed a ghost, a woman who does not exist.

The Moon Lamp is a schematized novel, with ironies and reversals that are worked out in the tightly controlled manner of a Henry James short story. Perhaps Smith's most skillful uses of irony are those brought about by the novel's dual point of view. The work is framed by the narrative of a persona whose voice is the collective "we" of the New Hampshire villagers and whose statements about the Linquists reflect public speculations and judgments based on public knowledge. Skeptical but intrigued by this likable pair of "outsiders" who prefer a drafty old saltbox to a snug ranch house or mobile home, the narrator often explains the Linquist's preoccupations in the mildly mocking tone of detached amusement. The center of the novel is a third-person narrative which is limited to Winnie's point of view and which, in detailing such ironies as her attitude toward her daughter, Penelope, reveals Winnie's utter inability to see her own failings. Ambitious in a detached way for her daughter to climb the social and professional ladders on her own, Winnie is concerned when Penelope seems willing to forego her degree and subjugate herself completely to Dwight McCracken, an unconventional young man whose lack of worldly aspirations Winnie cannot accept: "How she wanted to . . . say to her, Be yourself, but whatever you do, don't be Dwight—don't be—Oh, she didn't know what, only that it was something more. . . . just don't be *him!*"

In its overall effect, however, *The Moon Lamp* is less than successful. "This is a puzzling novel," wrote Diane Parente in *Best Sellers*. "It cannot be classified as a suspense tale, an introspective novel, or a social commentary, yet it contains elements of all three, interlaced into a not altogether satisfying whole." Although it has been called "an eerie horror story," the novel contains only a few moments of eeriness and evokes no horror whatsoever. The work's real energy lies not in its Gothic trappings but, as J. L. Crain observed in the *New York Times Book Review*, in its "unfolding of Winnie's confusions and discontents." Yet it lacks the cohesion and the impact of Smith's other works. "A full-bodied story keeps wanting to materialize," commented Barbara Conaty in *Library Journal*, "but somehow the impulse is not strong enough."

In 1976, the year *The Moon Lamp* was published, Smith moved with his wife and four daughters to York Harbor, Maine, the coastal town where they live today. There he completed *The Delphinium Girl*, a work that reflects, even more clearly than its predecessor, Smith's role as an objective observer in New England. No longer writing from the powerful feelings he had attached to the landscape of his native Midwest, he makes his most conscious attempt in this novel to capture a particular time and place as he knew it and to depict a set of people whose individual and collective lives are intrinsic to that setting. In form, *The Delphinium Girl* is exposition combined with dialogue and scenes of dramatic immediacy. Deliberately restricting the narrative and concentrating on his characters themselves, Smith focuses on a small community in rural New Hampshire where the affluent professionals who are its residents enjoy "country living" at its best.

Largely the products of middle- and working-class families, they have acquired their sense of savoir faire and privilege and their European tastes on their own. Yet amid the pleasures of French cooking, gardening, and parties on the lawns of colonial houses, the modern age is making its presence felt. There are shortages and pollution, house trailers and land developers, threats of an oil refinery and a six-lane highway being built nearby. And all of these people are beginning to fear that the good life they have earned and known so brief a time will be destroyed. Many of them believe these "unhappy changes" herald the end of the human race: "Some massive annihilation by disease or human carelessness or by nothing more complicated than the massive human presence. At the very least, life . . . as man had known it for thousands of years, would be altered, and for the worse. The irreversible process, whatever it was, had already begun."

Within this growing atmosphere of "doom and danger," Smith details the interrelations and, in varying degrees, the personalities of some eighteen characters. Among them are Charles Kubilius, an anesthesiologist whose passions are his viola, his herb garden, and his family; his wife, Pokey, an accomplished but unassuming woman who has a doctorate in education yet has chosen to make her home and five children her career; Milton Cullenbine, a cynical hypochondriac and alcoholic who has a doctorate in biology and is an executive of a small chemical company; Alexander Quen, an attractive woman who had kept her maiden name when she married her rarely seen husband, Marco, and who spends most of her time reading or painting; Professor Renzi, who teaches in the humanities at the nearby university and champions the philosophy

that "active creativity" is the only route to "increased *being*"; and Robert S. Stargaard, the closest thing to a self-portrait Smith has drawn.

A writer who had abandoned poetry for the novel, Stargaard is an outsider living in the community while he tries to force himself to write his second book. Like Smith, "In college he had taken courses in existential philosophy and modern literature that featured European novelists who were studied like existential philosophers." Stargaard's first novel, begun when he was nineteen, was a Hamsunesque narrative entitled *My Underground Self*. As with Smith's own first book, it "had been favorably if randomly reviewed and if there was a consensus among its critics it was that its young author was a man of promise." Like Smith, too, Stargaard had become, in his last year of college, "discouraged with the pedantry and pettiness of the academic world," "had spent a year living cheaply in Europe," and taught writing on the college level "when he had to"; he plays tennis well, and tells himself at times, "I should have been a gardener."

An element of Smith also exists in the affable Toby Keville, who grows delphiniums and prizes them above all other flowers. Yet there the resemblance ends. For although Toby is generally well liked by his neighbors, he represents part of what they fear: he is a land developer, "enraptured at the prospect of putting up a complex of prefabricated houses overnight." Toby's wife, Sarah, whom he calls "my delphinium girl" because of her delicately blue eyes, emerges as the novel's major figure and, in her illness and death, as the focus of its only narrative thread.

In the character of thirty-six-year-old Sarah, Smith bases the two existential themes that undergird *The Delphinium Girl*: the tragic absurdity of the human condition and the insistence that the individual be constantly aware of death in order to achieve both the sense of urgency he needs to accomplish his purposes and the intensified sense of his own existence he needs to live most fully within the given moment. Having no such awareness, Sarah believes not only that she can "afford to wait" to do anything, but that her life will not actually begin until she is old. For she has only one ambition: to be a grande dame, a dignified lady of advanced years who presides over a devoted coterie of artists and intellectuals as a figure of wisdom and authority. When the talk among her friends turns to the growing number of women who are dying from cancer, Sarah asks herself, "What if I should die?" But she immediately dismisses the possibility: "She was too young and incomplete for such a fate as

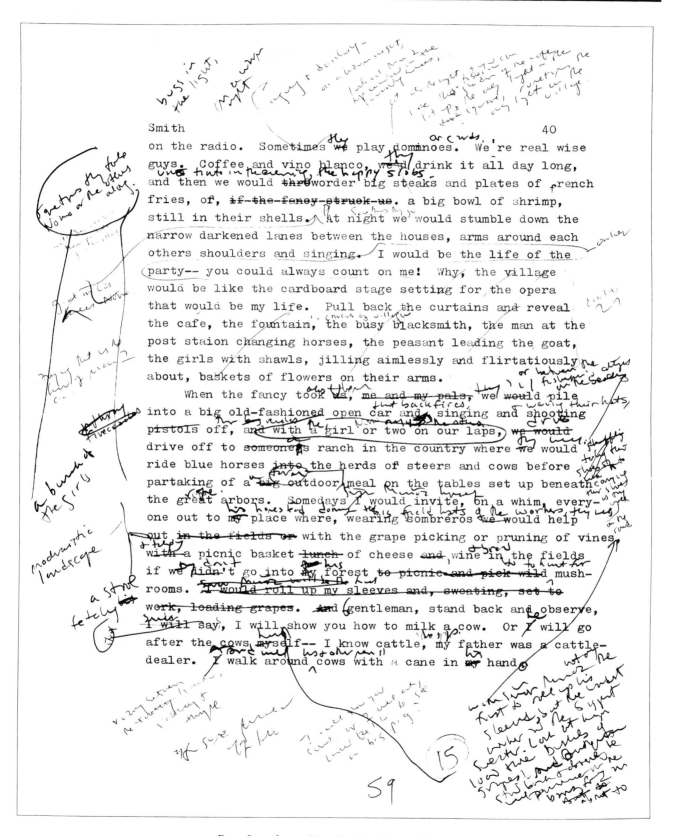

Page from the working draft for Doctor Blues

early death. She hadn't become anything, not even herself. . . . It would be stupid, cruel—it wouldn't make sense!"

After a discussion about women whose old age is lonely and miserable, Sarah begins to worry "that life could pass her by and she would miss her youth and middle years in anticipation of a later blossoming that might . . . turn out to be the worst years," and she resolves to "make the future happen" by cultivating the attributes of a grande dame now. Under the spell of Renzi, she decides her efforts must be artistic: "To be an artist was to create, and to create something was to create yourself. . . . One had to make." Yet she creates nothing. When she hears talk of the destruction of the human race, Sarah realizes she may be living for a future that does not exist and vows to "make of herself what she could, then." But still she makes nothing, and suddenly she is seized by a mysterious and ultimately fatal infection.

The hollowness and misdirection of Sarah's belief that she must create herself by creating something else is intrinsic to Smith's central thesis in *The Delphinium Girl* that the collective force of modern man, as it seeks to fulfill itself by "making" in the name of social and technological progress, is actually destroying itself and everything that it holds, or should hold, dear. Sarah Keville is the martyr of this force, the ironic victim of the very ideals of "creativity" and the grand future which she herself embraces on the individual level. Her "awfully modern death," as Dr. Kubilius puts it, was caused by an organism that was "a creation of man himself—a microscopic Frankenstein's monster": "You needed a new sort of Aeschylus and Sophocles altogether to wrestle with a retribution the like of that. A student of biology and chemistry far more than a human observer or maker of myths."

Critical opinions of *The Delphinium Girl* were manifestly at odds, and perhaps the truth lies somewhere between the extremes. Michele M. Leber asserted in *Library Journal* that the novel's "characters are deftly but fully drawn," while a reviewer for the *New Yorker* contended that they "never become more than names affixed to lists of labels." Joseph A. Keane complained in *Best Sellers* that "the author does all the talking and the characters never speak for themselves," while John Casey wished in the *New York Times Book Review* that "there

were more presence or even intrusion on the part of the author." Nicholas Delbanco in the *New Republic* called the work "a novel of manners" that is "almost perfectly composed," while Leber saw it as "A meandering tale" whose "parts are never pulled into a well-focused whole."

Susan Isaacs wrote in *Bookworld* that *The Delphinium Girl* is a novel about "death at an early age." Recognizing that "gut-churning anguish, unrelenting pain, and nearly limitless dramatic potential" are inherent in this subject, Isaacs declared that Smith's work "is impressive, but . . . not persuasive": "the novel, though complex, is well thought-out. But it is often so well thought-out that it leaves no room for spontaneity. There is little that . . . touches the reader. . . . One wants to be able to weep at the loss of Sarah. . . . Unfortunately in *The Delphinium Girl* one understands, but one rarely feels." Yet the power of Smith's novel lies in the fact that its pathos is purposely subdued and restrained. And its value lies in the fact that its subject is far more ominously universal than the death of a young woman which is its central metaphor. "In the end," as *Publishers Weekly* put it, "Smith is not gentle at all. He writes from the heart."

As Smith continues to develop as a novelist by challenging himself technically with each new work, he has become much more interested in the narrative voice than he was when he wrote *The Delphinium Girl*. In his most recent novel, *Doctor Blues* (1983), the central character is an academic who speaks both in the first person and, in certain sections of the book, in second and third persons as well.

In the course of his career, Smith has secured a following among not only the general readership but also among a group of noted authors and intellectuals, many of whom esteem him as a "writer's writer." While virtually no scholarly attention has been given to his works, he has received recognition and support from a number of sources: a grant from the Rockefeller Foundation (1965), a fellowship from the John Simon Guggenheim Memorial Foundation (1968), a grant from the Ingram Merrill Foundation (1976), and a fellowship from the National Endowment for the Arts (1978). In addition, he was appointed by the Rockefeller Foundation to serve for two years (1967-1969) as an advisor in its program of awarding grants for literature.

Herman Wouk
(27 May 1915-   )

Mark J. Charney
Clemson University

BOOKS: *Aurora Dawn* (New York: Simon & Schuster, 1947; London: Barrie, 1947);
The City Boy (New York: Simon & Schuster, 1948; London: Cape, 1956);
The Traitor (New York: French, 1949);
The Caine Mutiny (Garden City: Doubleday, 1951; London: Cape, 1951);
The Caine Mutiny Court Martial (Garden City: Doubleday, 1954; London: Cape, 1955);
Marjorie Morningstar (Garden City: Doubleday, 1955; London: Cape, 1955);
Slattery's Hurricane (New York: Permabooks, 1956; London: New English Library, 1965);
Nature's Way (Garden City: Doubleday, 1958);
This Is My God (Garden City: Doubleday, 1959; London: Cape, 1960);
Youngblood Hawke (Garden City: Doubleday, 1962; London: Collins, 1962);
Don't Stop the Carnival (Garden City: Doubleday, 1965; London: Collins, 1965);
The Lomokome Papers (New York: Pocket Books, 1968);
The Winds of War (Boston: Little, Brown, 1971; London: Collins, 1971);
War and Remembrance (Boston: Little, Brown, 1978; London: Collins, 1978).

Herman Wouk

Herman Wouk, prolific novelist and dramatist, has written nine novels and three plays. Though the critical response to his works varies as much as the subject matter, at least five of the novels Wouk wrote between 1947 and 1978 were bestsellers and two of his plays were popular and critical successes. A reading of his works makes the reasons for their popularity apparent: each displays his expertise at composing a compelling narrative.

Born in New York City on 27 May 1915, Herman Wouk is the son of Abraham Isaac and Esther Levine Wouk, both Russian-Jewish immigrants. His father began as a three-dollar-per-week laundry laborer and became the owner of a laundry chain. Herman Wouk spent most of his youth in the Bronx and attended Townsend Harris High School from 1927 to 1930. He majored in comparative literature and philosophy at Columbia University, and, in 1934, received a Bachelor of Arts degree with gen-

eral honors. It was at Columbia that Wouk began his writing career. He edited the college humor magazine, *Columbia Jester*, and wrote two popular variety shows.

In 1935, Wouk accepted a job as a radio comedy writer but was disillusioned to find that his "first literary task was copying old jokes out of tattered comic magazines on to file cards." Between 1936 and 1941, however, Wouk took on more responsibilities and began assisting Fred Allen with his weekly radio scripts. In June 1941, he began to write and produce radio shows promoting war bonds for the United States Treasury. He kept this job until 1942, when he enlisted in the navy and served as a deck officer on the destroyer/ minesweeper U.S.S. *Zane* in the Pacific for three years.

In 1943, during this tour of duty aboard the *Zane*, Wouk began his first novel, a humorous attack on radio and advertising, in order "to relieve the tedium of military service at sea in wartime." He did not complete the first part of the novel *Aurora Dawn* (1947) until he became an executive officer on the U.S.S. *Southard* at Okinawa in 1945 and did not finish it until May of 1946 while he was in Northport, Long Island.

On 9 December 1945, before the completion of *Aurora Dawn*, Wouk married Betty Sarah Brown, who converted to Judaism. The Wouks had three children—Abraham Isaac, Nathaniel, and Joseph—the first of whom died just short of the age of five in 1951.

Wouk's first novel follows the adventures and loves of Andrew Reale, who is convinced that "the road to happiness lay in becoming rich very quickly." Though the book was not received very favorably by the critics, several reviewers recognized Wouk's future potential and the Book-of-the-Month Club chose it as a featured selection in May of 1947. Spencer Klaw of the *New York Herald Tribune Weekly Book Review* called *Aurora Dawn* "a delightfully fresh and funny satire on radio advertising that never descends to mere burlesque and is all the more effective because the author—a former radio writer—refrains from grinding any personal axes," while Percy Atkinson of the *Saturday Review of Literature* appreciated Wouk's "good-natured banter and philosophic discursiveness."

Though both Klaw and Atkinson cited some of the positive qualities of *Aurora Dawn*, Wouk's exploration of the advertising world was criticized for its highly stylized manner. Russell Maloney of the *New York Times Book Review* said the novel had "no more authority than a lace valentine." Indeed, though Wouk's parody in the eighteenth-century style is fun, it fails to achieve the primary purpose of works of this kind. Whatever important social criticisms Wouk hoped to make are lost within the patterned, overly stylized, superficial story of one man's comic series of successes and failures within a farcical representation of the world of advertising and radio broadcasting. As in Fielding's *Tom Jones*, a narrator attempts to manipulate, entertain, and instruct the reader with comic diversions and witty discourse, but Wouk's diversions are either too didactic ("There is a school of philosophy which holds that there is no such thing in the world as evil, but only the absence of Being where Being should be") or too obvious ("Every novel nowadays is supposed to have a purpose . . . of correcting a specific social disorder such as capitalism, deforestation, inadequate city planning, war or religion"). Although it is predictable, *Aurora Dawn* does reveal Wouk's ability to keep his readers entertained.

Wouk's second novel was published in 1948. *The City Boy* is a maturation tale about the adventures of a plump, eleven-year-old Jewish boy from the Bronx named Herbie Bookbinder, who learns the meaning of responsibility and the joys of first love while spending a summer at camp. The theme and structure of *The City Boy* have sometimes been favorably compared to those of Twain's *Tom Sawyer*, and, indeed, Wouk does admit to a great fondness for Twain's novels. In the foreword to the 1969 edition of *The City Boy*, Wouk admits that Herbie is possibly his "favorite creation to this day," but when the book was published, "it slid off the plank, and with scarcely a ripple went bubbling down."

The reviews of *The City Boy*, however, were somewhat more positive than those for *Aurora Dawn*. Marc Brandel wrote in the *New York Times Book Review* that it made "delightful reading," and Joseph Henry Jackson of the *San Francisco Chronicle* praised the novel for being "affectionately written, enormously entertaining." Critics who disapproved of the novel, like R. B. Geham of the *Saturday Review of Literature*, concentrated upon Wouk's failure to achieve fully rounded characters due to his imitation of the styles of other authors such as Booth Tarkington, Sinclair Lewis, and, of course, Mark Twain.

In spite of the mixed reviews he received for his first two novels, Wouk was becoming well known within literary circles. Eloise Perry Hazard, in her article "First Novelists of 1947," characterized him as "tall, handsome, a good speaker, a deft writer, [who] has known from the first where he was going." Two years later, in 1949, Wouk finished his first play, *The Traitor*, a melodrama; starring Lee Tracy and Walter Hampden, it opened on Broadway 4 April 1949 to mixed reviews. Harold Clurman in the *New Republic* noted the similarity between the plot of *The Traitor* and the events of the Klaus Fuchs atom-spy case: "This is an effort to cash in on a topicality that is related to the audience's mental confusion—compounded of prejudice, indecision, and *Reader's Digest* information or ignorance." The play, which focuses upon the decisions of a scientist to release atomic bomb secrets to the enemy in the hope of gaining world peace, is often difficult to believe; nevertheless, other critics, such as Wolcott Gibbs of the *New Yorker*, found the play "continuously entertaining" in spite of its naive nature.

Wouk's greatest success, *The Caine Mutiny* (1951), is his third novel. Obviously borrowing from his experience at sea, Wouk provides a suspenseful plot and a firm thematic base. Wouk's story of young Willie Keith's fated meeting with the paranoid Captain Queeg and the events that lead to Lieutenant Maryk's eventual court-martial for assuming Queeg's command in a time of crisis create an array of themes. Though in this and both of Wouk's previous novels the protagonists have matured and learned from their mistakes, in *The Caine Mutiny* Keith's maturation process is handled with much more subtlety and honesty. Willie Keith, a Princeton graduate in comparative literature and a "mama's boy" who "is somewhat chubby, and good looking, with curly red hair and an innocent, gay face" is believably transformed into the final commander of the *Caine*—a perceptive, sensitive, responsible individual who realizes on coming home the changes the navy has made in his character: "he had felt his military personality dissolving, drifting away into the sea air like vapor, leaving a residue which was only Willie Keith. . . . He was no longer a naval officer—but he was no longer Willie Keith, either."

But in *The Caine Mutiny*, Wouk offers much more than just a maturation story. Because of Wouk's intelligent depiction of the paranoid Queeg, the book raises questions about the nature of sanity and man's responsibility to man. In the brilliantly conceived and executed court-martial scenes, Wouk skillfully shifts the reader's opinions from dislike of Queeg to pity for him, forcing the reader to examine his own judgments about the importance of appearances and the nature of cowardice.

The Caine Mutiny was warmly received by critics and the public. Edward Weeks of the *Atlantic* felt that it had "the scope and the skill to reveal how men are tested, exposed, and developed under the long routine of war," and Kelsey Guilfoil of the *Chicago Sunday Tribune* praised *The Caine Mutiny* for being "a real story, not a drab and wearisome account of the extracurricular activities of the service man." Most reviewers also pointed to Wouk's stylistic improvement in his third book. W. K. Harrison wrote in *Library Journal* that "superb writing and deft characterization make this the most exciting sea story since *Mutiny on the Bounty*," and E. L. Acken of the *New York Herald Tribune Book Review* called *The Caine Mutiny* "a provocative book, full of authentic people and atmosphere." The novel's only notable fault is the consistently sentimental shallow romance between Keith and Mae Wynn. Because Wouk spends so little time defining Willie and Mae's relationship and because Mae never shares the important experiences that Willie encounters, their relationship remains undeveloped. *The Caine*

Mutiny won the Pulitzer Prize for literature and the Columbia University Medal of Excellence. It was also on the *New York Times* best-seller list for more than two and a half years.

After seeing Bernard Shaw's *Don Juan in Hell*, Wouk decided to adapt *The Caine Mutiny* into a play, *The Caine Mutiny Court Martial* (1954). The Broadway play, with Henry Fonda, John Hodiak, and Lynn Nolan, was extremely well received.

In 1953, Wouk accepted a visiting professorship in English at Yeshiva University, where he stayed until 1957. In 1955, while he was at the university, Wouk's next major novel was published. *Marjorie Morningstar* is about the aspirations of a young, beautiful Jewish girl in New York, and the many relationships that help her to reach womanhood and to understand her heritage. More than a maturation story, *Marjorie Morningstar* also presents the conflicts inherent in attempting to live by both Jewish and American standards and the struggle young American Jews experience in coming to terms with the traditions of their elders. Like Wouk's previous novels, *Marjorie Morningstar* is immensely readable, and it became an immediate best-seller.

Despite its popularity, critics widely disagreed over the worth of this novel. F. H. Bullock of the *New York Herald Tribune Book Review* termed *Marjorie Morningstar* a "modern Jewish Vanity Fair . . . spacious, abundantly peopled, shrewd, observant, humane," and Meyer Levin of the *Saturday Review* generously called it "Herman Wouk's most solid achievement to date." While most critics felt the novel was much too long and that the tedious, repetitive conflicts dragged, few were as wholly negative as Nora Nagid of the *New Republic*, who wrote, "*Marjorie Morningstar* is a soap opera with psychological and sociological props," or the reviewer for the *New Yorker*, who called it "a damp and endless tale."

Wouk's long novel does seem melodramatic and endless because of Marjorie's patterned, moralistic conflicts, but its subtle characterization and clear prose reveal Wouk's development as a fiction writer. For example, the first sentence in the book reflects a control of style and purpose: "Customs of courtship vary greatly in different times and places, but the way the thing happens to be done here and now always seems the only natural way to do it." Although at first glance *Marjorie Morningstar* appears to be a predictable soap opera, a closer look shows that Wouk achieved his primary purpose: to write in an honest, interesting manner of customs, traditions, and the conflicts of maturity.

Wouk's third play, *Nature's Way*, was produced in 1957; it is his least successful dramatic work. *Nature's Way* is a farce about the problems of a young married songwriter who decides to leave his "too" newly pregnant wife for a while and accompany a homosexual friend to Italy in order to save his marriage and his career. Wouk's overly moralistic tone both condemns and laughs at such subjects as premarital sex, greed, and homosexuality. His inconsistent approach to these subjects prevents any humor that could be derived from the situation of the characters. Wolcott Gibbs of the *New Yorker* summed up the opinions of most reviewers when he said that "The whole enterprise, I guess, is a demonstration of the sad fact that strong moral indignation unassisted by a real detachment or urbanity, can easily be the deadly enemy of humor."

The drowning death of Wouk's oldest son, Abraham Isaac, in 1951 "deepened his father's position against 'the fashionable, unthinking agnosticism of the age.' " His religious faith is expressed in *This Is My God* (1959), an informal but detailed account of Judaism for "the many Jews who do not observe the religion, who yet would like to know a lot more about it." Obviously a "labor of love," *This Is My God* succeeds in providing the reader with an account of Jewish symbols, beliefs, customs, festivals, and holy days. It also effectively defines the conflicts that Jewish immigrants met in America and the constant struggle Jews still meet in continuing to practice the traditions that sometimes seem outdated and difficult; and it does so in a manner easily understood by the interested layman.

In 1962 one of Wouk's most important novels, *Youngblood Hawke*, was published; it became an immediate best-seller. Though he claimed that he learned both "terseness and economy" from Fred Allen, they are not apparent in this lengthy novel. A sprawling epic about a talented Southern writer's struggles to succeed in a world of publishers, theater agents, and tax collectors, *Youngblood Hawke* attacks the business policies and compromises associated with publishing works of artistic merit.

Obviously borrowing from experiences in his own life and from incidents in Thomas Wolfe's, Wouk intended for his novel to examine the pressures connected with publishing and achieving fame; but the book lapses too often into the protagonist's melodramatic struggles with his true love, his mistress, and his overbearing mother. During the final one-third of the novel, with tax collectors and moneylenders demanding payment, *Youngblood Hawke* descends into triteness and oversenti-

mentality. The critical reception was largely unfavorable. David Poroff of *Saturday Review*, for example, found that *Youngblood Hawke* possessed "an elaborate plot, a vast gallery of characters, enormous length, and a persuasive air of unreality," and W. J. Smith of *Commonweal* maintained that Wouk "plods. Sometimes he plods so doggedly that you begin to admire him more for his stamina than his story telling. . . ." Stanley Kauffman of the *New Republic* chided Wouk for characterization "constructed with the knit-browed, honest concentration of a child working with a Meccano set," while the reviewer for *Time* took offense at the obvious parallels between Youngblood Hawke and Thomas Wolfe: "Wouk has borrowed almost everything from Wolfe but his cuff links."

Youngblood Hawke, however, is not without merit. The characters, though somewhat stereotypical, are interesting and the plot, though sometimes predictable, manages to keep the reader's interest—especially in those sections of the novel which describe the devotion, doubts, and insecurities the writing profession entails.

From 1962 until 1969, Wouk served as a member on the board of trustees for the College of the Virgin Islands, a position which provided much of the experience leading to a later novel, *Don't Stop the Carnival*. Critics generally consider this Wouk's weakest novel. Published in 1965, it tells the story of a married Broadway press agent, Norman Paperman, who, tired of the pressures of New York, decides to purchase a resort hotel in a mythical Caribbean island Wouk calls Amerigo. The novel traces Paperman's minor successes and failures with the hotel until a love interest and the death of a friend force Paperman to reevaluate his life and return to New York. The thematic line, which deals with man meeting his responsibilities and his dreams, remains vague and unclear because *Don't Stop the Carnival* is replete with type characters and predictable situations. Haskel Frankel of the *Saturday Review* pointed out that Paperman moves in "a land of labels—Jew, gentile, white, Negro, homosexual." Samuel L. Simon of the *Library Journal* wrote that "*Don't Stop the Carnival* is a shoddy and absurd novel. . . . The problems are so exaggerated and comic as to border on the slapstick. . . ." When entire chapters focus upon whether the cistern in the hotel will be repaired, the reader loses interest, and *Don't Stop the Carnival* loses its audience.

Wouk's next novel, another best-seller entitled *The Winds of War* (1971), took nine years to write and much longer to research than any of his previous novels. The novel about World War II, as seen

Advertisement for the television adaptation of Wouk's historical novel about the early years of World War II

the character Pug Henry of a book called *World Empire Lost* by General Armin Von Room, "a fictitious German staff officer fictitiously imprisoned for twenty years by the very real Nuremburg Tribunal. . . ." The device of interspersing parts of the "translation" within the text of the novel provides transitions between historical events and furnishes detailed information about the German's opinions of Hitler and the war. Henry's translation of Von Roon's book also gives an account of several of the specific battles that are not contained within the rest of the narrative. This interesting device, although a bit contrived, keeps the adventures of the Henrys in historical perspective.

L. R. Andrews of the *Library Journal* congratulated Wouk for his "well-executed plot as well as believable characters acting against a fascinating background of social history," and the reviewer of the *Economist* stated that *The Winds of War* is as serious a contribution to the literature of our time as *War and Peace* was to that of the nineteenth century." Though Granville Hicks pointed out in the *New York Times Book Review* that "the failures of Wouk's style betray the failures of his imagination," he admitted that Wouk has the "gift of compelling narrative." Wouk's style may be undemanding, but his stylistic inadequacies do not detract from the power of his narrative or the effectiveness of his extensive research. *The Winds of War* provides the reader with a compelling, informative, honest picture of the brooding, threatening times, and this, in itself, is an achievement.

War and Remembrance, Wouk's sequel to *The Winds of War*, written after Wouk served as a scholar in residence at the Aspen Institute of Humanistic Studies from 1973 to 1974, is his latest novel. Published in 1978 and also an immediate best-seller, Wouk's sequel lacks the sense of balance and freshness that its predecessor has. In the foreword to *War and Remembrance*, Wouk gives the purpose for his sequel: "It is the main tale I had to tell. While I naturally hope that some readers, even in this rushed age, will find the time for both novels, *War and Remembrance* is a story in itself, and can be read without the prologue." Unfortunately, this claim does not hold true. Though Wouk awkwardly attempts to provide sufficient background material at the beginning of the sequel, the characters' motives or intentions are difficult to understand without the fully rounded characterization the earlier book supplies, and the reader who has read *The Winds of War* might be bored by the repetitive exposition. Moreover, the sequel is weighed down with interruptions for exposition of history through yet

through the eyes of the Henry family, is a sprawling, detailed epic that gives an accurate account of the moods and insecurities of both America and Europe from the early months of 1939 to the bombing of Pearl Harbor on 7 December 1941. It has been recognized as Wouk's best literary achievement since *The Caine Mutiny*.

The Winds of War has two distinct narrative lines. First, Wouk examines the lives and loves of the Henry family: Pug (a middle-aged naval attaché whose job brings him into contact with Roosevelt, Hitler, Goering, Stalin, and Churchill), his wife, his two sons, and his daughter. Through their eyes, Wouk provides diverse views and reactions to historical situations and also heightens the theme Wouk identifies in the foreword to the novel's sequel, *War and Remembrance* (1978): "Either war is finished or we are."

The second narrative line is a translation by

another fictitious book, *World Holocaust*, by General Armin Von Roon. Paul Fussell, reviewing *War and Remembrance* for the *New Republic*, said of *World Holocaust* that "the quality of the military reasoning in this document—the whole comprises about 122 pages—is impressive, and so is Wouk's scholarship in contemporary history," but Wouk's accounts of technicalities of war, though impressive, interrupt the narrative line rather than support it as they do in *The Winds of War*. Because these constant interruptions break the suspense, the narrative line and the military history together do not unify the novel.

Walter Clemons of *Newsweek* cited as the strongest point in *War and Remembrance* that it makes the reader "feel the Holocaust afresh." Wouk is at his best in *War and Remembrance* when he uses descriptive passages to serve as detailed, all-too-realistic reminders of the suffering war brings: "It may have been the worst siege in the history of the world. It was a siege of Biblical horror; a siege like the siege of Jerusalem, when, as the Book of Lamentations tells, women boiled and ate their children. When the war began, Leningrad was a city of close to three million. By the time Victor Henry visited it, there were about six hundred thousand people left. Half of those who were gone had been evacuated; the other half had died." Passages such as this one work to heighten Wouk's purpose: to move men to prevent further warfare through a careful examination of the past.

Wouk once said that "setting aside the years at war, I have had no other aim or occupation than that of writing; and it is the ambition I had when I was a boy." Like Trollope and the Victorians, he admits to being an "over-writer," usually completing 1,000 to 1,500 words a day and refusing to labor over cuts until the end of a novel. He is a man inseparably devoted to both his profession and his faith. Maxwell Geismar writes of this devotion in

American Moderns from Rebellion to Conformity, placing the novels of Herman Wouk "in a curious realm between art and entertainment." Though his less successful efforts such as *The City Boy* and *Marjorie Morningstar* may be artistically flawed because they rely too heavily on Wouk's expertise as a storyteller, his best novels, *The Caine Mutiny* and *The Winds of War*, achieve both literary and thematic merit.

Wouk lives in Washington, D.C., with his wife and two sons. He has written the screenplay for an eighteen-hour television miniseries of *The Winds of War*, which was televised on ABC-TV in February 1983.

Plays:

The Traitor, New York, Forty-Eighth Street Theatre, 4 April 1949;

The Caine Mutiny Court-Martial, New York, Plymouth Theatre, 20 January 1954;

Nature's Way, New York, Coronet Theatre, 15 October 1957.

Screenplay:

Slattery's Hurricane, Twentieth Century-Fox, 1949.

Television Script:

The Winds of War, ABC-TV, 6-13 February 1983.

References:

Maxwell Geismar, *American Moderns from Rebellion to Conformity* (New York: Hill & Wang, 1958), pp. 38-45;

Eloise Perry Hazard, "First Novelists of 1947," *Saturday Review*, 31 (14 February 1948): 12;

Jane Howard, "Herman Wouk Surfaces Again," *Life*, 71 (6 November 1971): 54;

John K. Hutchens, "Happy Success Story of Herman Wouk," *New York Herald Tribune Book Review*, 32 (4 September 1955): 2.

Charles Wright

(25 August 1935-)

George F. Butterick
University of Connecticut

BOOKS: *The Voyage* (Iowa City: Patrician Press, 1963);

6 Poems (London: David Freed, 1965);

The Dream Animal (Toronto: House of Anansi, 1968);

Private Madrigals (Madison, Wis.: Abraxas Press, 1969);

The Grave of the Right Hand (Middletown, Conn.: Wesleyan University Press, 1970);

The Venice Notebook (Boston: Barn Dream Press, 1971);

Backwater (Santa Ana, Cal.: Golem Press, 1973);

Hard Freight (Middletown, Conn.: Wesleyan University Press, 1973);

Bloodlines (Middletown, Conn.: Wesleyan University Press, 1975);

Colophons (Iowa City: Windhover Press, 1977);

China Trace (Middletown, Conn.: Wesleyan University Press, 1977);

Dead Color (Salem, Oreg.: Charles Seluzicki, 1980);

The Southern Cross (New York: Random House, 1981);

Country Music: Selected Early Poems (Middletown, Conn.: Wesleyan University Press, 1982).

Charles Wright

Charles Wright's career has been one of regular progress. He grew up in eastern Tennessee and western North Carolina, amid places that continue to nourish his work. Born in Pickwick Dam, Tennessee, where his father had been an engineer for the Tennessee Valley Authority, he was raised in Kingsport, attending local public schools. His high school years included a year at a school of only eight students, called Sky Valley (which provides the title for one of his finer poems), and two years at an Episcopal boarding school, Christ School in Arden, North Carolina, known to its students as "Jesus Tech." He studied at Davidson College in North Carolina—"which turned out to be four years of amnesia, as much my fault as theirs"—graduating with a B.A. in 1957. He then went into the army for four years, from 1957 to 1961. His last three army years were spent in Italy, serving in the Intelligence Corps, where he attained the rank of captain.

Wright did not begin the practice of poetry until relatively late, when he was twenty-five years old. While stationed in Verona, he first discovered the possibilities of poetry through the writings of Ezra Pound. "I began by using Ezra Pound's Italian Cantos first as a guide book to out-of-the-way places, then as a reference book and finally as a 'copy' book." After the army, he enrolled in the University of Iowa's Writers Workshop, receiving an M.F.A. in 1963. A Fulbright fellowship that year allowed him to return to Italy, where he lectured at the University of Rome while translating the work of Eugenio Montale and Cesare Pavese.

He has taught since 1966 at the University of California at Irvine, progressing from an assistant professor to professor of English, while living in nearby Laguna Beach with his wife, Holly, a photographer, and his son, Luke. He is clear-eyed and unpretentious about his life, acknowledging that "my biography is pretty much the biography of almost everyone here" (meaning an audience at Oberlin College in 1976). Wright seems to thrive in a structured environment; his career contains no surprises. All torment or danger or vagary has gone into the language and is to be found on the page, to our great benefit. He has varied his academic landscape by serving as Fulbright lecturer at the University of Padua (1968-1969) and as visiting lecturer at the University of Iowa (1974-1975), as well as at Princeton and Columbia universities (1978). He has been encouraged at various steps in his career by a number of awards: first, a Eunice Tietjens Award from *Poetry* magazine in 1969; then, in quick succession, a National Endowment for the Arts grant (1974); a Guggenheim Fellowship (1975); the Poetry Society of America's Melville Cane Award and the Academy of American Poets' Poe Award, both in 1976 for his book *Bloodlines*; and an American Academy of Arts and Letters grant (1977).

Wright has been very clear in acknowledging the influences on his work. Perhaps the most important, after his discovery through Pound of the basic poetic technique of compression, was the Italian poet Montale. Wright spent the formative years immediately following his formal study of poetry at Iowa translating *The Storm and Other Poems*; the result, published after Wright had established his reputation as a poet, won the 1979 P.E.N. Translation Prize. He found in Montale a certain spiritual affinity and, even more important, "a way of using hard-edged imagery with genuine sentiment." The older poet also taught him "how to move a line, how to move an image from one stage to the next. How to create imaginary bridges between images and stanzas and then to cross them, making them real, image to image, block to block." Few now do it as well as Wright.

His first major collection, *The Grave of the Right Hand* (1970), is a volume of considerable reach and promise, though with a less powerful grasp than his later work. Hands recur as a motif throughout the volume, which is more symbolic than Wright's subsequent books. In the opening poem—a successful if rather literary study entitled "The Daughters of Blum"—the unfulfilled lives of the women are called "Gloves waiting for hands." A more personal yet abstract hand is proferred in "The Offering": "An ordinary hand,/ One without pain or distinction. . . ." Yet it remains a not very successful gesture: "There is no hand for such hands, no pocket." "The Grave of the Right Hand" is properly the book's title poem, being strongly and hauntingly the

finest in the collection. It is a poem concerning America (it occurs in a section entitled "American Landscape"), though it is also about adequacy of motive. The disembodied hand of the title is the lost grip, the powerless hand that in John Keats's words was once "capable of earnest grasping." It is the trigger-hand of action, the tool-bearing hand of productivity and accomplishment, now lost. By implication, it draws attention to a society dismembered, maimed, its strength torn from the social body. The exact site of the hand's interment cannot be specified, but it is broadly located in "the American West." So all-pervasive is the loss that "No stone/ Commemorates the spot." Hopes and expectations lie buried with it, having "calcified" about the American dream with an abiding sense of futility. Even the paths of recognition, which had previously borne us through this life and land, tolerated our incursion, "suffered" our "crossing," are "faded and overgrown." Where once the land existed chiefly to serve our interests or progress, with roads existing "merely to take us there," there is now a foreseeable "end" to the West—the familiar thesis of the closed frontier. The pioneer tracks and the open, Whitmanian road are over; there is no longer purposefulness and possibility. A sense of spilled effort survives for those who persist, summarized in the tribute preserved through the poet's consciousness. The end of the poem is the epitaph of a people: "This is the grave of the right hand:/ The threshold, the woebegone." It is not a very large reward.

Yet this is a rare poem for Wright. Most of his poems are about personal, not national, woes. Despite the acknowledged influence of Pound, there are none of the epic and pedagogical ambitions of Pound in these early poems. There is interest in the past, but a personal past, and no particular sense of political community. Indeed, it might be argued that because Wright chooses not to deal with social issues directly in "The Grave of the Right Hand," there can only be an unspecified despair in the poem. Many of his poems are commemorative, titled with a place or time (time of day, season, year, even sign of the zodiac), though not necessarily "occasional" in the usual sense. That is, they are not fleeting or ephemeral; their sources lie deep in the poet and recur. His themes are consistent—mortality, the uses of memory, the irrepressible past, states of being, personal salvation, the correspondence between nature and the spiritual world, and, most broadly, the human condition. Exterior contours evoke internal landscapes. His poems seek, through language, a spiritual apotheosis from the natural world. He returns again and again to the photographic, almost petroglyphic, specificity of language, as if by vocabulary alone to purchase his way out of a failing world. His gift is creating images; his lines very often teem with them. He is pleased with their "rub and glint," though it will still be necessary for each reader to find beneath the rapids a firm rock of moral perspective by which to judge his total work. His achievement is narrative by image, though not by means of the ideogramic method of Pound's *Cantos* or a discursive persona as in John Berryman's *Dream Songs*. He comes closest to the condition of that supreme ecology of letting the images tell themselves, letting the world tell itself.

Retrospectively, no matter how accomplished the poems in *The Grave of the Right Hand* may be, a reader might find little to distinguish them from those of James Wright or Donald Justice (with whom Wright studied at Iowa) or from among dozens of other contemporaries. But rather quickly, with his next book, Wright steps into his own distinguishable authenticity. *Hard Freight* (1973) contains some of Wright's strongest work. It opens with a series of "Homages," which, as might be expected, display his influences and commitments. The first is to Pound, recalling an attempt to visit the aging poet in Venice, where the waters "assemble" and Pound the survivor walks in the "slow strobe" of the sunlight. The young poet makes his pilgrimage on "one of those days/ One swears is a prophesy:/ The air explicit and moist,/ As though filled with unanswered trees." And although the visit is not accomplished (Wright describes his following Pound around secretly for days), the devotion is expressed; the apprentice urges the old master in his waterworld of Venice to rise like the tide and "be whole again." Other tributes are to Arthur Rimbaud and Baron Corvo and, less directly, to Franz Kafka, but in them there is a cosmopolitan diffusiveness not present in the hard-grained and earthy Tennessee-rooted poems that follow in the volume.

"White" exemplifies what Wright found in Pound. It is a poem of pure image. Indeed, one stanza of it might be called Wright's "In a Station of the Metro" (Pound's Imagist classic), at the same time recalling Melville's "Whiteness of the Whale" chapter in *Moby-Dick*: "White, and the leaf clicks; dry rock;/White, and the wave spills./ Dogwood, the stripe, headlights, teeth." A previous stanza, for all its naturalism, is just as eerie (some of Wright's best poems evoke that feeling). His world is always one of correspondences: "I write your name for the last time in this mist,/ White breath on the windowpane,/ And watch it vanish. No, it stays there." As will be seen throughout his work, there are presences in his imagination that the material world alone cannot explain.

Some of the poems no less than their images are authentically visionary, as much in the visionary tradition as the work of poets who more actively cultivate and specialize in that realm. There is the intriguingly named "The Other Side," a ritual occasion in which the poet meets "the succorers" who await him on the other side of a "great noose of water" that lies before him like a bridge of sighs or blade-thin path of judgment, a soul-testing situation. We trust the speaker, we trust the experience; it is neither learned nor borrowed. He begins the ordeal triumphantly: "The first stone/ Rises like light to my hand"—literal legerdemain. The poem excels because of its timing. The encounter is not ended; the final outcome, although assured, is still in process, open to our participation. It is a poem of affirmation and mental readiness, hearkening to the reader, who is cheered ahead to his own starting line.

Occasionally the imagism is self-conscious and feeds only itself, as in "Definitions," which begins:

> The blades of the dwarf palm,
> Honing themselves in the wind;
> The ice plant, blistering red along
> Its green, immaculate skin;
> The moon, sad marigold, drooping
> On dark, attenuant waters. . . .

Here the influence is Montale rather than Pound. But poems like "Quotidiana" are more than a daring use of image; they explore the function and limits of metaphor: "The moss retracts its skin from the laced grass./ This mist is a cold address. . . ." More than traditional imagism, Wright's poems are an exploration of possibilities. The great unstated theme, as with many of the best poets, is language itself. "Nouns" is a lesson both profound and playful: "Nouns are precise, they wear/ The boots of authority . . . they know/ Whom to precede and whom to follow,/ They know what dependence means. . . ."

Wright is also open to syntactic variation. Although in these early poems he prefers the carefully controlled, evenly curtailed line (each begun with a capital) rather than an extended openness, he is capable of making excellent use of repetition. "Yellow" is such a poem, intricate and cumulative, which seeks less a definition of the color than to catalog and revel in its variety:

> Yellow is for regret, the distal, the second
> hand:
> The grasshopper's wing, that yellow, the slur
> of dust . . .
> The yellow of pencils, their black veins;
> Amaranth yellow, bright bloom;
> The yellow of sulfur, the finger, the road
> home.

There is a narrative of imagery, in which the images tell themselves, without direct egotistic mediation. That is, no narrator interjects his feelings among the subtly ordered progression of elements. At the same time, Wright is not a mere colorist or sensualist, a painter of surfaces. He is determined to engage the spirit deeper within the physical world; all the while his landscape is as palpable and crunches underfoot with the same reality as Gary Snyder's riprap of specific ravines and rivulets. "Dog Creek Mainline," the poem from which *Hard Freight* derives its title, begins:

> Dog Creek: cat track and bird splay,
> Spindrift and windfall; woodrot;
> Odor of muscadine, the blue creep
> Of kingsnake and copperhead;
> Nightweed; frog spit and floating heart,
> Backwash and snag pool: Dog Creek

—a perfectly, almost mathematically, balanced stanza. Five stanzas later, the Tennessee localities served by the railroad line emerge, their names as lushly specific as the world in which they lie embedded: "Hard freight. It's hard freight/ From Ducktown to Copper Hill, from Six/ To Piled High. . . ." The poet's specificity is his tribute to the places that have given meaning to his life. He has been the capable engine to convey these freighted facts and ladings, to bear them in celebration over whatever grades of distance and time.

The past explored through place is one of Wright's chief subjects. The next poem in the book, "Sky Valley Rider," begins: "Same place, same auto-da-fe:/ Late August, the air replete, the leaves/ Grotesque in their limp splendor. . . ." The place is wrested from inconsequence by the vigorous language. Here is the poet: "I walked these roads one, two steps/ Behind my own life. . . ." He continues the catalogue in images as unique as the setting, revealing his purpose to himself with a certain fatalism: "The past, wrecked accordian, plays on, its one tune/ My song, its one breath my breath." Wright denies oblivion its wish. His concern for the past may be a preoccupation, but it is not simple nostalgia. It is an American homesickness or loneli-

ness, though he will never state it in terms as such. There are other poems in *Hard Freight* that James Tate has said display a "Mediterranean fatalism," but these are the familiar American-abroad or Fulbright-in-Europe poems, where everything is worn decoratively rather than examined from within.

Probably the finest example of Wright's devotion to a personal past, and one of his finest poems, is "Blackwater Mountain," which mingles landscape and memory. The poet recalls hunting with a mentor, possibly his father, in the Virginia wilds. The imagery is not out of scale with its subject and represents it with immediacy: "That time of evening, weightless and disparate,/ When the loon cries, when the small bass/ Jostle the lake's reflections. . . ." He pauses in the midst of the setting, having so skillfully recreated it for us, to say outright: "This is what I remember." The allure is undeniable: "The stars over Blackwater Mountain/ Still dangle and flash like hooks." The poem is far from sentimental, even though the poet is forever in the sway of his past:

> I stand where we stood before and aim
> My flashlight down to the lake. A black duck
> Explodes to my right, hangs, and is gone.
> He shows me the way to you;
> He shows me the way to a different fire
> Where you, black moon, warm your hands.

He is drawn out like a tide, whether the moon of his departed mentor, a "black moon," is visible or not.

A poem similar in intention follows, its title again a place from Wright's youth. A note at the end of "Northhanger Ridge" identifies it as being a reliving of "Bible Camp, 1949." Its language is even more daring, pressed to its very essence, until all that is left is language's own names for itself, the terms of grammar, "sentences, sentences":

> Sunday, and Father Dog is turned loose:
> Up the long road the children's feet
> Snick in the dust like raindrops; the wind
> Excuses itself and backs off; inside, heat
> Lies like a hand on each head;
> Slither and cough. . . .
> Bow-wow and arf, the Great Light;
> O, and the Great Yes, and the Great No;
> Redemption, the cold kiss of release,
> &c.; sentences, sentences

—the meaninglessness of religious indoctrination. The poet has driven language as far as possible, with crisp new creations like "snick" and shorthand like

"&c." to get the memory set and, in this case, relieved.

"Nightdream," in its turn, marks the extreme of imagism—which is surrealism (appropriately enough for a poem of this title). Here the images are disparate, fluid, ephemeral, no matter how stark and brilliant, as one might expect from a dream. These share the weightlessness of space, the content floating off the shelves of a mind beyond gravity, making new combinations: "Your mother floats from her bed/ In slow-motion, her loose gown like a fog/ Approaching." It is what we might expect from a dream—haunting, persistent but unresolved, too fleeting to last us long through the day. Such poems, likewise, do not remain fixed in consciousness.

Rarely is Wright's use of images so vaporous and elusive. "Synopsis," though briefer, is on firmer ground, more apprehensible and consequential: nine lines in three stanzas, nine states of being embodied by nine images, which are, in fact, interchangeable. The poet could just as effectively have written, "The white crow of solitude" and "The eggshell of belief" as "The white crow of belief" and "The eggshell of solitude." Far from weak or ambiguous, however, the poem is ultimately one of methodology or ways of knowing. It exemplifies the epistemology of image—by which the poetic image, unique and irreducible, enables us to apprehend the abstract qualities of life—and also the image as ontology or study of being, where the poetic image in one sweet blow defines and delimits an abstract condition of the world. "Synopsis" yokes the concrete with the abstract as in "metaphysical" poetry, but more openly explores the way to possess, quite literally (the poem is composed entirely of possessives), the elusive abstractions, "belief," "solitude," "Lethargy," etc.—states of being, which are nevertheless being, undeniable realities of existence.

Wright's next collection, *Bloodlines* (1975), is dominated by two long, much-praised sequences. "Tattoos" is a stitching together of twenty poems (with a single page of notes at the end), each dated by the actual biographical experience which gave rise, often many years later, to the individual poems. They are not chronologically ordered according to the sequence of the experiences, but arranged in their order of writing. They are imagistic embroideries on the living skin, indelible pricks of memory, "psychic tattoos," some traumatic, some previously suppressed, all crucial. The experiences range from a premature sexual encounter to an East Tennessee snake-handling ritual, and include the death of his father (in two of the

sections) as well as recurrent dreams. The images in which they are told are so sharp and knowing that when one section concludes, "I have seen what I have seen," there is not the slightest reason to doubt the poet. He is as convincing when he speaks personally as when he writes descriptively: "I feel the gold hair of Paradise rise through my skin/ Needle and thread, needle and thread." Given the vividness of the imagery, the lines convey a psychosomatic experience, down to the bodily tingling. The notes indicate the poet fainting at the altar as a young acolyte. A different kind of poet, more hopelessly romantic, might have devoted a lifetime seeking to recapture the consequences of that experience. Wright is, in fact, more ecstatic in the poem than he allows himself to be in commenting on it in *Field*, pointing out how in church the practice had been to fast before taking communion, and that "when you're ten or eleven years old you're always hungry and you're always fainting at the altar because you're hungry. That's sort of what happened." He was given the sacramental wine to bring him around, which explains the image of the cup of wine at his lips in the poem's last line. All the "Tattoos" are personal, purgative exercises; some are confessional, in both the literary as well as psychological senses. A passionate exactness is his goal: "If you're just exact it's boring, if you're passionate it's formless, and probably boring too. If you can get the two together, you've got something memorable."

If "Tattoos" is the indelible, personal pattern made up of penetrations of real experience, "Skins," the second sequence of twenty (Wright derived the value of twenty from Montale, who included a suite of twenty "Motets" in his 1939 collection, *Le Occasioni*), is the more abstract surface upon which a life is played. Each poem is sonnet-length, though without the internal dialectic of a sonnet, in which the theme is set forth in the first eight or twelve lines and resolved in the final sestet or couplet. The sections are not resolved independently of the series as a whole. The reader must wait until the final poem for the sense of accomplishment. "Skins" seeks larger truths than "Tattoos"—hermetic wisdom, flashes from the well of profundity. Wright describes the sequence as more "conceptual," intended to balance the intensely personal quality of the previous series. It resolves the tensions created by "Tattoos" through selected rites of acceptance, rites of passage that teach one to accept the transitory nature of experience.

The sequence is more carefully structured than might at first appear. Wright reveals the surprisingly elaborate structure in his *Field* interview:

the design of "Skins" is "a ladder. Ten up, ten down. It starts at Point A, and comes back to Point A." The first section stands as the efficient cause, both driving the poet out on a quest and drawing the series home behind him. The theme is stated abstractly and encompassingly enough: "There comes that moment/ When what you are is what you will be/ Until the end." The subsequent steps are Beauty, Truth (fixed by a camera's lens "tracking inexorably toward you"), the Beginning and Destruction of the Universe, through the four elements, ascending to the Aether with number ten, "the air above the air," which Wright observes the Greeks called the fifth element. That is the top of the ladder. The poem at the apex affords "one glint of the golden stitch,/ The thread that will lead you home:" The line ends, by design, with the open gates of a colon. It is enough to encourage us to move on. The next section (eleven) begins the descent to self, its opening line guiding us with the conjunctive "then": "Upriver, then, past landfall and watertrace. . . ," until we enter "the tilt" and begin "the blind slide" home. The descent begins with five poems concerning subjects rejected by the poet—Primitive Magic, Necromancy, Black Magic, Alchemy, and Allegory. These are followed by four "acceptances," the traditional elements earth, air, fire, and water. The concluding number twenty is the existential dilemma again, the point of being and beginning. The result in the last poem is less a redeeming, synthesizing vision and apotheosis than a carefully contrived paradox. The wisdom is classical: the more things change, the more they remain the same. The "meandering man" of section nineteen becomes a "Pilgrim" in number twenty. Wright arrives where he began, at "that moment/ When what you are is what you will be. . . ." Zeno, not Plato, is his model. What he seeks is a balance between coming and going; what he gets is the illusion of rest within motion. It is a most ambitious effort, even without a dominating persona to carry the quest, a Poundian ego or at least a more directly lyrical intervention. In discussing the structure of "Skins," Wright reveals that his books themselves have an overall pattern, just as in the two series, "Tattoos" and "Skins": " 'Tattoos' was me in relation to the past. 'Skins' is me in relation to the present. *China Trace* is me in relation to the future. . . . It is even more involved: *Bloodlines* is the center of the three books *Hard Freight*, *Bloodlines*, and *China Trace*. 'Tattoos' hooks up with *Hard Freight* and the past, and 'Skins' hooks up with *China Trace* and the future." No matter how difficult the scheme is for the reader to recognize, the poet obviously benefits

from having such a sense of purpose and control.

Wright's fourth major book, and the conclusion of his trilogy begun with *Hard Freight*, is *China Trace* (1977), "a book of Chinese poems that don't sound like Chinese poems and aren't Chinese poems but are *like* Chinese poems in the sense that they give you an idea of one man's relationship to the endlessness, the ongoingness, the everlastingness of what's around him, and his relationship to it as he stands in the natural world." The opening poem ends ineffectually—"face/ After face, like beads from a broken rosary"—an image of little risk in a poem that seeks the establishment of mood by image. But the following poem, "Snow," is extraordinary. It begins with the barest dusting of religious imagery: "If we, as we are, are dust, and dust, as it will, rises." The familiar metaphor of "dust unto dust," presented in a mimetically swirling rhythm, a helical swirl, is followed by a suggestion of Christian resurrection, abetted by "recongregate" and the airy, celestial imagery of wind and cloud in the third line. It is, however, the second stanza of the poem that is so winsome, where the spiritual theme continues with a passing invocation of Original Sin and a "fallen" (as well as autumnal) world—"Things in a fall in a world of fall"—and penetrates down to rough earth, the irrefutable specificity and imperishable uniqueness of the natural world. The vision is of a transformative snow that carries its own grace. At the same time there is a larger ecology—a spiritual ecology—at work, the cycle of dust yielding to the recycling current of wind and clouds, from which, inevitably, the redeeming snow will fall. Amidst the particulars—"the spiked branches and snapped joints of the evergreens"—a larger vision is upheld: "white ants, white ants and the little ribs" on the forest floor are not images or similitudes but creatures novel and alive. It is a ghostly photograph, the familiar made strange; it may even be symbolic. It is certainly evocative.

Again, in the poem that follows, entitled "Self-Portrait in 2035," the camera works with distinct clicks. There is, for one thing, the monosyllabic snap of words into place, exact in their fit and appropriateness, bearing the authority which convinces a reader that this is a poem that *had* to be written. There is a fine and crisp metonymy, the fixating alliteration of the opening line: "The root becomes him, the road ruts . . . Recast him." The portrait is a time-elapsed shot, the camera omniscient like one mounted overhead in a space capsule, though here instead the lens is on the roof of a coffin, like some ancient Egyptian eye. The poet, any man, is almost a kenning: "Worm-waste." Indeed, all that remains is "Worm-waste and pillow tick . . . his face false/ In the wood-rot, and past pause. . . ." It is a poem of elemental processes and contrasts, of permanence within decay, not smooth urbanity or a current and replaceable fashion. The hundred-year-old body of poet-man Charles Wright, born 1935, is articulated by nature itself, relentlessly spinning on: "Darkness, erase these lines, forget these words./ Spider recite his one sin." By then, he will have merged to completeness. His "one sin" is unstated—is it that of having lived?

The stanza rather than the "projective" line is Wright's unit of measure. He comments in his *Field* interview: "Three stanzas is a good form for me and fifteen lines is a good length for me. The basketball players all have their favorite spots on the floor to shoot from, so many feet from the basket. Well, I feel comfortable at fifteen lines or thereabouts. Also, three stanzas is good because you can present something in the first, work around with it a bit in the second and then release it, refute it, untie it, set fire to it, whatever you want to, in the third." His poetry continues to be one of immaculate diction, his language strong by its display of choice (though not will and not willfulness—he is neither doctrinaire nor trivial). Instead there is an attractive decisiveness: "I'm talking about paint, about the void/ These objects sentry for. . . ." "Sentry," pressed into service as a verb, corrects the abstractions "paint" and "void." His poems, no matter how imaged, are never flatly pictorial or merely descriptive. It is a poetry more truly worthy of the designation "Deep Image"—the term originated by Jerome Rothenberg and often applied to Robert Bly's work—that is, simultaneously touching unconscious roots and the sharpest manifestations of external reality.

There is the superb balance of form and image in the poem "Dog." The dog is death, and the poem is in two stanzas. The first presents the dog of the title alone, without any trace of narrator. The second stanza almost exclusively involves the narrator (three "I"s in the first line alone). He is pitted against the menace of the dog by a careful rhetorical advance, leading with the conditional "if" followed by the assertive, existential ego: "If I were a wind, which I am, if I/ Were smoke, which I am, if I/ Were the colorless leaves, the invisible grief. . . ." The "fantailed dog of the end" is like the Old Norse Fenris-wolf, who unleashes the End of the World, or like Cerberus, guardian of hell. In any case, it is a creature to be faced. The narrator poses as something barely tangible (wind, smoke, colorless leaves, invisible grief), but is given structure by his own

assertiveness in standing up to the dog. His assurance is stressed by the double "Which I am . . . which I am." The poem owes its effect to its structure as much as to its imagery, a progression of rhetorical balances or series of doublets: "if I . . . which I am"; "if I . . . which I am"; "if I" for a third time, but followed by two images in apposition ("colorless leaves, the invisible grief"), purposely vague and abstract, before being affirmed by the double "which I am" and the counterbalance of the dog's threatening presence ("He'd whistle me down, and down"). The threat is resolved by the quickest little affirmation—"but not yet"—which ends the poem. The point is that Wright is a master of control. With such a rhythm of images, his structure is not static or syllogistic, contrived or framed. His chief skill is to achieve fluid imagery, what might be called narrative within imagism.

Wright's photographic technique reaches its representative peak in the boldly declared "Snapshot." The poet is given his image, his "ghost" or alter ego, by the flash of the full moon. Again the percussion of the language (despite the liquidity of the *l*s): "My own ghost, a lock-shot lanyard of blue flame,/ Slips from the deadeyes in nothing's rig,/ Raiment and sustenance, and hangs. . . ." The stanza hangs suspended, the craft evident. The imagery plays about, faintly nautical—a ghost ship, Wright's own *Flying Dutchman* or *Pequod* after it has been charged by lightning—and becomes specifically visual in the subsequent stanza. The narrator's ghost is "Like a noose in the night wind" or, alternatively, "Like a mouth/ O-fire" (not simply "afire" or "of fire"—the graphic pun linking that second stanza with the poem's final images of mouth followed by wine). In that form, that round, open mouth, the poet's ghost is appropriately given voice: "You are wine/ In a glass, it says, you are sack, you are silt." It is an all-denying voice, first holding out the promise of wine in a glass, then the pun of "sack" (both as wine and perhaps the dryness of cloth), then the deposit or dregs (a body without one's "ghost"?). The reader is struck with approval; the inconsistent development or shift in images, the unexpected progression from lanyard to silt, is not a distraction. The rhythm of the assertion is persuasive, all-carrying. And because there is no attempt to maintain the images simultaneously, there is never an absurd or dead-ended surrealism. How different are the endings of these poems from those in *The Grave of the Right Hand*, how much has been gained.

Among the finest poems of *China Trace*, "Indian Summer" is an album of such images. The poet is wise to have given two of his most striking lines stanzas unto themselves: "I watch the snow bees sent mad by the sun" and "The wind blows through its own hair forever." Lesser poets would end a poem on either, holding the lines aside for last lines, but Wright has gifts to spare. The poem concludes:

> If something is due me still
> —Firedogs, ashes, the soap of another life—
> I give it back. And this hive
>
> Of sheveled combs, my wax in its little box.

"Firedogs, ashes, the soap of another life" are all objects, but ones that have a purpose beyond themselves or gain an identity from an extrinsic source (the "firedogs" provide a neat and subtle parallel to the "snow bees"), as does a man whose honey is his poems. The poet has become the bee, maddened by a last sun. Wright lavishes himself on language, indulges in it, making up words in the delight of the excess of it. "Sheveled" is a back-formation of disheveled (literally, disarranged hair), thus here "hairy," with the pun on "combs" following. The subsequent "wax" is the language of the poem, itself a hive of activity and sweetness, a "little box" of meaning and delight. "Indian Summer" is a masterful blend of striking images and an incremental overall metaphor.

There may be no better way to show how Wright celebrates the physical world by means of the physicality of language than to quote his poem "At Zero":

> In the cold kitchen of heaven,
> Daylight spoons out its cream-of-wheat.
>
> Beside the sidewalk, the shrubs
> Hunch down, deep in their bibs.
>
> The wind harps its same song
> Through the steel tines of the trees.
>
> The river lies still, the jewelled drill in its
> teeth.
>
> I am glint on its fingernails.
> I am ground grains on its wheel.

There is too much logic or relatedness in the associations to be surrealism. It is assertive metaphor, rather than suggestive; devices of musicality and pattern are represented, including metonymy. The frozen trees are as bare and stiff as forks (in the economy of poetry it is only necessary to mention their tines)—although it is no romantic, Aeolian breeze that makes them sing, but a ruthless precision. The narrator is withheld from the scene until the final couplet, when he is joined with metaphor as classic as might be found in the *Song of Songs* or the folk literature of any people, all the while saving the poem from the passivity of description.

There is also the too modestly named "Sentences," an appliqué of images that recreate the physicality of landscape, at the same time allowing a "mysticality" to float clear and hover. Metaphysical matters are dealt with in Wright's work, rather than dismissed or abjectly worshipped or simply acquiesced to. Forces which are ordinarily elusive to the mind are apprehended by the imagination. Images are couplings, linking the abstract with the palpably real. They are too powerful and all-absorbing to be ignored; they fill the imagination, leaving no fissure for wasteful doubt or distraction. Wright's is a poetry of redemption, not scorn or fatigue or tentativeness. In one of his clearest possible statements (in the *Field* interview), he affirms "salvation doesn't exist except through the natural world." There is, however, a testing of alternatives. Frequently he positions himself in alternate landscapes, whether of the past or of the imagined future. "January" begins, "In some other life/ I'll stand where I'm standing now. . . ." In "Wishes," the place is "somewhere I can't remember, but saw once." There are personal crossroads as, for example in "1975," the now traditional mid-life crisis: "At 40 . . . I turn in the wind,/ Not knowing what sign to make, or where I should kneel." The quest for meaning is seen also in "Equation": "I open the phone book, and look for my adolescence." There is guilt, but the crime remains existence itself, "Something enormous, something too big to see."

Sometimes, however, states of being degenerate into mere moods ("California Twilight"). Other times the images are askew, driven into surrealism, as in "12 Lines at Midnight": "The bread bleeds in the cupboard,/ The mildew tightens. The clocks, with their tiny hands, reach out,/ Inarticulate monitors of the wind." These are foreclosures, dead ends, not convertible into familiar human associations. The weakness or limits of such poetry, the occasional failure even, occurs when the images are merely decorative, tours de force. Again in "12 Lines at Midnight," the title exposes the tentativeness of the product, which seems reluctant to step forth and claim itself as a whole and verifiable poem. Such verses are what Marco Polo, in the words of novelist Italo Calvino, quoted twice as epigraphs to both halves of *China Trace*, calls "emblems." They are no longer the things-in-

THE SOUTHERN CROSS

Things that divine us we never touch:

~~The slow growl of the moonlight;~~ *The clock sounds of the night music,*

The Southern Cross, like a kite at the end of its string,

~~invisible still from where I stand;~~

~~The black sounds of the night music,~~ _____

And now this sunrise, and empty sleeve of a day,
The rain just starting to fall, and then not fall,

No trace of a story line.

_____

~~Downtown, the past licks its thin lips,~~

~~stretched out by the boardwalk . . .~~

~~What I wanted to say is that the sea seemed its old self,~~
~~Holding its breath, beginning to turn blue.~~

~~What happened, of course, is that I took a walk on the beach~~
~~And the sea rolled its white tongue on the sand~~
~~And I wrote this down because of the empty shine~~

~~That comes and goes in my heart.~~

_____

All ~~day I've remembered~~ *day I've remembered* a lake and a sudsy shoreline,
Gauze curtains blowing in and out of open windows all over the South.

It's 1936, in Tennessee. I'm 1
And spraying the dead grass with a ~~hose~~ *hose.*

The curtains blow in and out.

And then it's not. And I'm not and they're not.

(Cont., stanza brk.)

Revised typescript of "Southern Cross"

themselves, the ineluctable, irreducible hard gain. They are less successful than the incipient naturalism of "The wind clicks through its turnstiles," which at least has the logic of a completed metaphor, no matter how eccentric. In that same poem, "Invisible Landscape," the mood is consistently ashen, depressed, the sky not just blue-grey but "Colt-colored," a gunmetal frontier in which God is "the lost/ Moment that stopped to grieve and moved on. . . ." It is one of Wright's bleaker landscapes. Other of his poems born of personal soul-wrack and a constant probing of dark water ("Born Again," "Deep Water," "Captain Dog") are efforts to affirm life. A more cynical view would be that, rather than direct outcries, they create a problematic mood by problematic language, which the poet then has the luxury to resolve. At times, a transformation is forced:

> The waters and holy ones set out . . .
> Their footprints filling with sparks
>
> In the bitter loam behind them, ahead of
>   them stobbed with sand,
> And walk hard, and regret nothing.

("Stobbed" is an invention, but it does manage to convey the resistance to be faced ahead.) The poems in the latter part of *China Trace*, all written in the mid-70s, grow gloomier, though not necessarily more desperate. Helen Vendler notes "an unrelenting elegiac fixity" to the poems. Entitled variously "Depression Before the Solstice," "April," "Noon" (many others are dated within the text, with such phrases as "August, the bones of summer" or simply "the fall"), they continue to seem time-ridden, with a vague sense of anxiety and impending darkness. Some also seem more derivative of European moods than rooted in live American experience, past or present. Indeed, one is a "Reply to Lapo Gianni" (an Italian poet from Dante's time); another is entitled "Thinking of Georg Trakl" (a German poet).

The mood changes with the ideographically titled "Spider Crystal Ascension," one of Wright's most visionary poems. The spider, with all its compressed transformative symbolism, is like an ancient god, or at least some power larger than the poet, just the thing to pull him out of himself. The spider waits for "us" to ascend, not just an autobiographical or lyrical "me," and it is "we" who "lie back in our watery hair and rock," not just the "I" (the poet). Throughout Wright's work there are poems of great spiritual yearning, like those of George Her-

bert or Gerard Manley Hopkins (whose influence Wright has acknowledged). Immediately following "Moving On" in *China Trace*, with its faint echoes of Christian symbolism ("lamb's fleece," "the fall," "The flesh made flesh and the word," "The wafer of blood"), there occurs the powerful "Clear Night." As with so many of Wright's poems, the initial stanza carefully establishes a setting, both fresh and precise: "Clear night, thumb-top of a moon, a back-lit sky." The second, somewhat unexpectedly, is a quatrain of supplication, beginning: "I want to be bruised by God./ I want to be strung up in a strong light and singled out. . . ." The prayer earns the following response in four lines of correspondingly parallel, almost Biblical, structure:

> And the wind says "What?" to me.
> And the castor beans, with their little earrings
>   of death, say
>   "What?" to me.
> And the stars start out on their cold slide
>   through the dark.
> And the gears notch and the engines wheel.

The cosmic mechanism is either eternally indifferent to the human plea, or it proves itself capable of still functioning—its only answer.

What does a poet do when faced with the vast but multitudinous unknown? He forces the unseen to materialize. What reader's attention is not going to quicken at a poem beginning: "Just north of the Yaak River, one man sits bolt up-right,/ A little bonnet of dirt and bunch of grass above his head. . . ." "Mount Caribou at Night," one of Wright's finest poems, proceeds with an entirely believable recreation of the night sky over northwestern Montana:

> Work stars, drop by inveterate drop, begin
> Cassiopeia's sails and electric paste
> Across the sky. And down
>
> Toward the cadmium waters that carry them
>   back to the dawn,
>
> They squeeze out Andromeda and the
>   Whale. . . .

It is a poem of Big Sky country, almost a billboard or tourist board scenario, but much more: it is, as so many of Wright's place poems, about man's relation to the universe. The sky is unsentimentally larger than man. The images are worthy of Pound: "cloud-gouache/ Over the tree-line." The massive mountain is

on the rise and taking it in. And taking it back
To the future we occupied, and will wake to
                              again, ourselves
And our children's children . . . ready to walk
                                          out
Into the same night and the meadow grass,
                          in step and on time. . . .

(The final ellipsis, which appears on occasion throughout these poems of process and swift transition, is Wright's.) There is the deliberate interplay of human and cosmic time—present, past, and future (seen in the tenses of the lines quoted), all in one experience. The grandeur and immensity of mountain and sky suggest an eternal presence relative to ephemeral man; yet man persists in his own right and by his own particular names—Walter Smoot and Dick Runyan and August Binder—individuals who have shared this landscape with the poet and are mentioned in the poem. These realities are the natural orders we obey or respond to, both the cosmic sweep and human specificity. Wright has visited this territory once before, in "American Landscape" in *Grave of the Right Hand*; a comparison of the two poems will reveal his growth in skill and complexity.

The earlier poem is touchingly effective, yet static; the later one is bolder in imagery and more confident in outlook. Both are set in the same northwestern Montana wilderness, where man is seen in relation to the persistence of nature. In "American Landscape," questions are raised and answered with more questions, which itself may be taken as a form of human survivability. But whereas the earlier poem ends in suspended possibility with "The clearings we might have crossed;/ The footprints we do not leave," the more recent poem ends with the poet conjoined in the fellowship of man ready to advance confidently into the future.

Personal redemption through the natural world remains one of Wright's chief themes through his most recent book, *The Southern Cross* (1981), where not only "Mount Caribou at Night" but "Holy Thursday," one of his most exemplary poems in every sense, is collected. Yet it is the abundance of nature, not the church calendar, that gives that day its sanctity. We have the bliss of life, from mourning doves and blood-sucking "hummers" to children and angels, from book-learned words to colloquial speech, all in the same breath: "Surf sounds in the palm tree,/ Susurrations, the wind,/ making a big move from the west." The natural world is so active in Wright's vision of it, bursting with glories, that his language too grows ripe, dis-

tended. His concern is to seek "salvation" not in the external orthodoxies but in the inner, natural world of language. He knows that naming is essential to creation. His impulse is religious, although he distrusts organized religion as an imposition, rejecting the orthodoxies of his youth. In this regard, too, the natural world is a comfort. In "Holy Thursday" he marks the sun of that day, "sifting its glitter across the powdery stems" of a medlar tree (he is as specific as possible always), and notes that "It doesn't believe in God/ And still is absolved./ It doesn't believe in God/ And seems to get by, going from here to there." Each time he returns to this theme, his faith in nature is unshaken and, if anything, stronger than ever, while religion continues to appear extraneous. Still, one expects Wright to have this argument with himself all his life.

Another principal theme found again in *Southern Cross*, as in all previous books, is family memory and the persistence of the past. The family is Wright's basic unit of society and must live on through his commemoration of it. He addresses none of the social issues of the day more directly. In the distinguished "Virginia Reel," he revisits "for the first time in 20 years" remnants of his family in northern Virginia. The title suggests not only a familiar folk tune and basic social activity, but, with several possible puns on "Reel," an endless loop about the same theme. The narrator, suffering slightly from a Hamlet-complex (there is an allusion to Hamlet's famous soliloquy in the lines "my flesh/ Remiss in the promises it made then, the absolute it's heir to"), burdened by purpose and seeking resolve, returns for a visit among family, where the smallest gestures of reunion have a powerful effect upon him. He tracks the past as with a photograph in hand or in memory, back to its original place:

Who cares? Well, I do. It's worth my sighs
To walk here, on the wrong road, tracking
                              down a picture back
To its bricks and its point of view.
It's worth my while to be here, crumbling this
dirt
                              through my bare hands.

His poems are an affirmation of the value of the past as a living heritage, not as nostalgia or self-pity. They survive precisely as a tribute, like the last apple blossom that "Fishtails to earth through the shot twilight,/ A little vowel for the future, a signal from us to them." He knows that this also is the poetic responsibility, and that through it something of the human race, let alone his personal history, lives on.

What distinguishes Wright from contemporaries is his risk of language. With him, language loses nothing of its sharpness and variety. His greatest accomplishment is the imagistic narrative. How he activates and propels the line of images (one thinks again of "hard freight") is his special genius, his ability to drive spirit into the matter of words. He treks the geography of the spirit, as David St. John rightly emphasizes, through its "purgatorial wastes and paradisal instants." It is a landscape shot through with spirit and the ache for ecstasy, even if there is none of the great mystics' letting go. Perhaps he is too honest-minded, in an age riddled with quacks and questers. He prefers, rather than to be transported aloft by his own light-headed imaginings, to stay among the clay and clods of earth a while, wrestling with the consequences of our days.

Other:

"Notebook from Ischia & Three Snapshots from Ponza," *North American Review*, new series, 2 (May 1965): 32-34;

"Corsica," *North American Review*, new series, 3 (May 1966): 23-26;

Autobiographical statement, in *Contemporary Poetry in America*, edited by Miller Williams (New York: Random House, 1973), p. 153.

Translations:

Eugenio Montale, *The Storm and Other Poems* (Oberlin, Ohio: Oberlin College, 1978);

Montale, *Motetti/ Motets* (Iowa City: Windhover Press, 1981);

"Improvisations on Montale," *Field*, no. 27 (Fall 1982): 46-54.

Interviews:

"Charles Wright at Oberlin," *Field*, no. 17 (Fall 1977): 46-85; reprinted in *A Field Guide to Contemporary Poetry & Poetics*, edited by Stuart Friebert and David Young (New York: Longman, 1980);

"Interview," in *Wright: A Profile* (Iowa City: Grilled Flowers Press, 1979), pp. 33-49.

References:

Kathleen Agena, "The Mad Sense of Language," *Partisan Review*, 43 (1976): 625-630;

David St. John, "The Poetry of Charles Wright," in *Wright: A Profile* (Iowa City: Grilled Flowers Press, 1979), pp. 53-65;

Pamela Stewart, "In All Places At Once," *Ironwood*, no. 19 (1982): 162-166;

Helen Vendler, *Part of Nature, Part of Us: Modern American Poets* (Cambridge: Harvard University Press, 1980), pp. 277-288.

Literary Awards and Honors Announced in 1982

AMERICAN ACADEMY AND INSTITUTE OF ARTS AND LETTERS

AWARDS IN LITERATURE
David H. Bradley, Frederick Buechner, MacDonald Harris, Daryl Hine, Josephine Jacobsen, Donald Keene, Berton Roueché, Robert Stone.

E. M. FORSTER AWARD
F. T. Prince.

GOLD MEDAL FOR BIOGRAPHY
Francis Steegmuller.

HAROLD D. VURSELL MEMORIAL AWARD
Eleanor Perenyi.

MARJORIE PEABODY WAITES AWARD
Edouard Roditi.

MORTON DAUWEN ZABEL AWARD
Harold Bloom.

RICHARD AND HINDA ROSENTHAL FOUNDATION AWARD
Marilynne Robinson, for *Housekeeping* (Farrar, Straus & Giroux).

ROME FELLOWSHIP IN CREATIVE WRITING
Mark Helprin.

SUE KAUFMAN PRIZE FOR FIRST FICTION
Ted Mooney, for *Easy Travel to Other Planets* (Farrar, Straus & Giroux).

WITTER BYNNER FOUNDATION PRIZE FOR POETRY
William Heyen.

AMERICAN BOOK AWARDS

NATIONAL MEDAL FOR LITERATURE
John Cheever.

AUTOBIOGRAPHY/BIOGRAPHY
HARDCOVER: David McCullough, for *Mornings on Horseback* (Simon & Schuster).
PAPERBACK: Ronald Steel, for *Walter Lippmann and the American Century* (Vintage).

CHILDREN'S BOOKS
FICTION HARDCOVER: Lloyd Alexander, for *Westmark* (Dutton).
FICTION PAPERBACK: Ouida Sebestyen, for *Words by Heart* (Bantam).
NONFICTION HARDCOVER: Susan Bonner, for *A Penguin Year* (Delacorte).
PICTURE BOOK HARDCOVER: Maurice Sendak, for *Outside Over There* (Zephyr/ Doubleday).
PICTURE BOOK PAPERBACK: Peter Spier, for *Noah's Ark* (Zephyr/ Doubleday).

FICTION
HARDCOVER: John Updike, for *Rabbit Is Rich* (Knopf).
PAPERBACK: William Maxwell, for *So Long, See You Tomorrow* (Ballantine).

FIRST NOVEL
Rob Forman Dew, for *Dale Loves Sophie to Death* (Farrar, Straus & Giroux).

GENERAL NONFICTION
HARDCOVER: Tracy Kidder, for *The Soul of a New Machine* (Atlantic/ Little, Brown).
PAPERBACK: Victor S. Navasky, for *Naming Names* (Penguin).

HISTORY
HARDCOVER: Peter John Powell, for *People of the Sacred Mountain* (Harper & Row).
PAPERBACK: Robert Wohl, for *The Generation of Nineteen Fourteen* (Harvard University Press).

POETRY
William Bronk, for *Life Supports* (North Point Press).

SCIENCE
HARDCOVER: Donald Johanson and Maitland Edey, for *Lucy: The Beginnings of Human Evolution* (Simon & Schuster).
PAPERBACK: Fred Alan Wolf, for *Taking the Quantum Leap: The New Physics for Nonscientists* (Harper & Row).

TRANSLATION
Robert Lyons Danly, for *In the Shade of Spring Leaves* (Yale University Press), and Ian Hideo Levy, for *The Thousand Leaves* (Princeton University Press).

BANCROFT PRIZES
Edward Countryman, for *A People in Revolution: The*

American Revolution and Political Society in New York 1760-90 (Johns Hopkins University Press), and Mary P. Ryan, for *Cradle of the Middle Class: The Family in Oneida County, New York, 1780-1865* (Cambridge University Press).

BOOKER MCCONNELL PRIZE FOR FICTION
Thomas Kenneally, for *Schindler's Ark* (Hodder & Stoughton).

CALDECOTT MEDAL
Chris Van Allsburg, for *Jumanji* (Houghton Mifflin).

CAREY-THOMAS PUBLISHING AWARD
Muriel St. Clare Byrne, for *The Lisle Letters* (University of Chicago Press).

COMMON WEALTH AWARD
Wright Morris.

DRUE HEINZ LITERATURE PRIZE
David Bosworth, for *The Death of Descartes* (University of Pittsburgh Press).

EDGAR ALLEN POE AWARDS
GRAND MASTER AWARD
Julian Symons.

NOVEL
William Bayer, for *Peregrine* (Congdon & Lattés).

FIRST NOVEL
Stuart Woods, for *Chiefs* (Norton).

FACT CRIME
Robert W. Greene, for *The Sting Man* (Dutton).

CRITICAL-BIOGRAPHICAL STUDY
Jon L. Breene, for *What About Murder* (Scarecrow Press).

PAPERBACK
L. A. Morse, for *The Old Dick* (Avon).

JUVENILE
Norma Fox Mazer, for *Taking Terri Mueller* (Avon).

SHORT STORY
Jack Richie, for "The Absence of Emily," in *Ellery Queen's Mystery Magazine*.

ERNEST HEMINGWAY FOUNDATION AWARD
Marilynne Robinson, for *Housekeeping* (Farrar, Straus & Giroux).

GOLD MEDAL OF HONOR
Barbara Tuchman.

HUGO AWARDS
NOVEL
C. J. Cherryh, for *Downbelow Station* (Daw).

NOVELLA
Poul Anderson, for *The Saturn Game*, in *Analog*.

NOVELETTE
Roger Zelazny, for *Unicorn Variation*, in *Isaac Asimov's Science Fiction Magazine*.

SHORT STORY
John Barley, for "The Pusher," in *Fantasy and Science Fiction*.

NONFICTION BOOK
Stephen King, for *Danse Macabre* (Everest House).

PROFESSIONAL EDITOR
Edward L. Ferman, editor of *Fantasy and Science Fiction*.

FANZINE
Locus, edited by Charles N. Brown.

FAN WRITER
Richard E. Geis.

IRMA SIMONTON BLACK AWARD
Ann Cameron, for *The Stories Julian Tells* (Pantheon).

JANET HEIDINGER KAFKA PRIZE FOR FICTION
Mary Gordon, for *The Company of Women* (Random House).

JOHN D. AND CATHERINE T. MACARTHUR FOUNDATION AWARD
Ved Mehta.

JOHN W. CAMPBELL AWARD
Alexis Gilliland.

JOHN W. CAMPBELL MEMORIAL AWARD
Russell Hoban, for *Riddley Walker* (Summit Books).

MAXWELL PERKINS PRIZE
Margaret Mitchell Dukore, for *A Novel Called Heritage* (Scribners).

NATIONAL BOOK CRITICS CIRCLE AWARD

FICTION
John Updike, for *Rabbit Is Rich* (Knopf).

GENERAL NONFICTION
Stephen J. Gould, for *The Mismeasure of Man* (Norton).

POETRY
A. R. Ammons, for *The Coast of Trees* (Norton).

CRITICISM
Virgil Thomson, for *A Virgil Thomson Reader* (Houghton Mifflin).

NATIONAL JEWISH BOOK AWARDS

JEWISH FICTION
Mark Helprin, for *Ellis Island and Other Stories* (Delacorte).

THE HOLOCAUST
Michael Marrus and Robert O. Paxton, for *Vichy France and the Jews* (Basic Books).

ISRAEL
Howard M. Sachar, for *Egypt and Israel* (Marek).

JEWISH HISTORY
David Ruderman, for *The World of a Renaissance Jew* (Ktav).

JEWISH THOUGHT
Robert Alter, for *The Art of Biblical Narrative* (Basic Books).

CHILDREN'S LITERATURE
Kathryn Lasky, for *The Night Journey* (Warne).

NEBULA AWARDS

BEST NOVEL
Gene Wolfe, for *The Claw of the Conciliator* (Timescape/ Simon & Schuster).

BEST NOVELLA
Poul Anderson, for *The Saturn Game*, in *Analog*.

BEST NOVELETTE
Michael Bishop, for *The Quickening*, in *Universe*, edited by Terry Carr (Doubleday).

BEST SHORT STORY
Lisa Tuttle, for "The Bone Flute," in *Fantasy and Science Fiction*.

NELSON ALGREN AWARD
Louise Erdrich, for "The World's Greatest Fisherman," in *Chicago Magazine*.

NEWBERY MEDAL
Nancy Willard, for *A Visit to William Blake's Inn* (Harcourt Brace Jovanovich).

NOBEL PRIZE FOR LITERATURE
Gabriel García Márquez.

O. HENRY AWARD
Susan Kenney, for "Facing Front."

PEN/FAULKNER AWARD
David Bradley, for *The Chaneysville Incident* (Harper & Row).

PULITZER PRIZES

FICTION
John Updike, for *Rabbit Is Rich* (Knopf).

BIOGRAPHY
William S. McFeely, for *Grant* (Norton).

GENERAL NONFICTION
Tracy Kidder, for *The Soul of a New Machine* (Atlantic/ Little, Brown).

HISTORY
C. Vann Woodward, editor, for *Mary Chesnut's Civil War* (Yale University Press).

POETRY
Sylvia Plath, for *The Collected Poems* (Harper & Row).

SCRIBNER CRIME NOVEL AWARD
Carol Clemeau, for *The Ariadne Clue* (Scribners).

SHELLEY MEMORIAL AWARD
Alan Dugan.

WRITERS ROOM AWARD
Eudora Welty.

Checklist: Contributions to Literary History and Biography, 1982

This checklist is a selection of new books on various aspects and periods of literary and cultural history; biographies, memoirs, and correspondence of literary people and their associates; and primary bibliographies. Not included are volumes in general reference series, literary criticism, and bibliographies of criticism.

Allen, Walter. *As I Walked Down New Grub Street: Memoirs of a Writing Life*. Chicago: University of Chicago Press, 1982.

Anderson, Jervis. *This Was Harlem: A Cultural Portrait, 1900-1950*. New York: Farrar, Straus & Giroux, 1982.

Arbuckle, Elisabeth Sanders, ed. *Harriet Martineau's Letters to Fanny Wedgwood*. Stanford: Stanford University Press, 1982.

Ashe, Rosalind. *Literary Houses: Ten Famous Houses in Fiction*. New York: Facts on File, 1982.

Barnstone, Willis, ed. *Borges at Eighty: Coversations*. Bloomington: Indiana University Press, 1982.

Barrett, William. *The Truants: Adventures Among the Intellectuals*. Garden City: Doubleday, 1982.

Bell, Anne Olivier, and Andrew McNeillie, eds. *The Diary of Virginia Woolf, Volume Four, 1931-1935*. New York & London: Harcourt Brace Jovanovich, 1982.

Berkowitz, Gerald M. *New Broadways: Theatre Across America, 1950-1980*. Totowa, N.J.: Rowman & Littlefield, 1982.

Berrigan, Daniel. *Portraits of Those I Love*. New York: Crossroad, 1982.

Bidwell, Bruce, and Linda Heffer. *The Joycean Way: A Topographical Guide to "Dubliners" and "A Portrait of the Artist as a Young Man."* Baltimore: Johns Hopkins University Press, 1982.

Borges, Juan Luis, and Fernando Sorrentino. *Seven Conversations with Jorge Luis Borges*. Translated by Clark M. Zlotchew. Troy, N.Y.: Whitston, 1981.

Bosco, Ronald A., and Glen M. Johnson, eds. *The Journals and Miscellaneous Notebooks of Ralph Waldo Emerson*, volume 16, 1866-1882. Cambridge: Harvard University Press, 1982.

Bowder, Diana, ed. *Who Was Who in the Greek World*. Ithaca: Cornell University Press, 1982.

Bright-Holmes, John, ed. *Like It Was: The Diaries of Malcolm Muggeridge*. New York: Morrow, 1982.

Briscoe, Mary Louise, ed. *A Bibliography of American Autobiography, 1945-1980*. Madison: University of Wisconsin Press, 1982.

Brooks, Louise. *Lulu in Hollywood*. New York: Knopf, 1982.

Brown, Edward J. *Russian Literature Since the Revolution*. Cambridge: Harvard University Press, 1982.

Bryer, Jackson R., ed. *The Theatre We Worked For: The Letters of Eugene O'Neill to Kenneth Macgowan*. New Haven: Yale University Press, 1982.

Buechner, Frederick. *Now and Then*. New York: Harper & Row, 1982.

Buechner. *The Sacred Journey*. New York: Harper & Row, 1982.

Burnett, T. A. J. *The Rise and Fall of a Regency Dandy: The Life and Times of Scrope Berdmore Davies*. Boston: Atlantic/Little, Brown, 1982.

Buttita, Tony, and Barry B. Witham. *Uncle Sam Presents: A Memoir of the Federal Theatre, 1935-1939*. Philadelphia: University of Pennsylvania Press, 1982.

Cohen, Morton N., ed. *The Selected Letters of Lewis Carroll*. New York: Pantheon, 1982.

Connelly, Thomas L. *Will Campbell and The Soul of the South*. New York: Crossroad/Continuum, 1982.

Courtney, Winifred F. *Young Charles Lamb, 1775-1802*. New York: New York University Press, 1982.

Craddock, Patricia B. *Young Edward Gibbon: Gentleman of Letters*. Baltimore: Johns Hopkins University Press, 1982.

Craft, Robert, ed. *Stravinsky: Selected Correspondence*, volume 1. New York: Knopf, 1982.

Crane, Joan. *Willa Cather: A Bibliography*. Lincoln: University of Nebraska Press, 1982.

Curtis, James. *Between Flops: A Biography of Preston Sturges*. New York & London: Harcourt Brace Jovanovich, 1982.

Darnton, Robert. *The Literary Underground of the Old Regime*. Cambridge: Harvard University Press, 1982.

Delaney, Frank, and Jorge Lewinski. *James Joyce's Odyssey: A Guide to the Dublin of Ulysses*. New York: Holt, Rinehart & Winston, 1982.

Delbanco, Nicholas. *Group Portrait: Conrad, Crane, Ford, James and Wells*. New York: Morrow, 1982.

Donaldson, Frances. *P. G. Wodehouse*. New York: Knopf, 1982.

Dreiser, Theodore. *American Diaries, 1902-1926*. Edited by Adrianne D. Dudden, Thomas P. Riggio, James L. W. West III, and Neda M. Westlake. Philadelphia: University of Pennsylvania Press, 1982.

Ehrlich, Eugene, and Gorton Carruth. *The Oxford Illustrated Literary Guide to the United States*. New York: Oxford University Press, 1982.

Eikhenbaum, Boris. *Tolstoi in the Sixties*. Translated by Duffield White; and *Tolstoi in the Seventies*. Translated by Albert Kaspin. New York: Ardis House, 1982.

Ellmann, Richard. *James Joyce*, revised edition. New York: Oxford University Press, 1982.

Fishbein, Leslie. *Rebels in Bohemia: The Radicals of* The Masses, *1911-1917*. Chapel Hill: University of North Carolina Press, 1982.

Franklin, R. W., ed. *The Manuscript Books of Emily Dickinson*, 2 volumes. Cambridge: Harvard University Press, 1982.

Fyvel, T. R. *George Orwell: A Personal Memoir*. New York: Macmillan, 1982.

Gallix, Francois, ed. *Letters to a Friend: The Correspondence Between T. H. White and L. J. Potts*. New York: Putnam's, 1982.

Gardner, Virginia. *"Friend and Lover": The Life of Louise Bryant*. New York: Horizon, 1982.

Givner, Joan. *Katherine Anne Porter, A Life*. New York: Simon & Schuster, 1982.

Green, Stanley. *Broadway Musicals of the 30s*. New York: Plenum da Capo, 1982.

Gregg, Edith E. W., ed. *The Letters of Ellen Tucker Emerson*. Kent: Kent State University Press, 1982.

Haffenden, John. *The Life of John Berryman*. Boston: Routledge & Kegan Paul, 1982.

Hamilton, Iain. *Koestler: A Biography*. New York: Macmillan, 1982.

Hamilton, Ian. *Robert Lowell: A Biography*. New York: Random House, 1982.

Hamovitch, Mitzi Berger. *The Hound & Horn Letters*. Athens: University of Georgia Press, 1982.

Harding, Walter. *The Days of Henry Thoreau*, revised edition. New York: Dover, 1982.

Hayman, Ronald. *Kafka: A Biography*. London: Oxford University Press, 1982.

Hedrick, Joan D. *Solitary Comrade: Jack London and His Work*. Chapel Hill: University of North Carolina Press, 1982.

Heineman, James H., and Donald R. Bensen, eds. *P. G. Wodehouse: A Centenary Celebration, 1881-1981*. New York: Oxford University Press, 1982.

Higgins, D. S. *Rider Haggard: A Biography*. New York: Stein & Day, 1982.

Hooper, Walter. *Through Joy and Beyond: A Pictorial Biography*. New York: Macmillan, 1982.

Hoopes, Roy. *Cain: The Biography of James M. Cain*. New York: Holt, Rinehart & Winston, 1982.

Howe, Irving. *A Margin of Hope: An Intellectual Autobiography*. San Diego: Harcourt Brace Jovanovich, 1982.

Hughes, Ted, and Frances McCullough, eds. *The Journals of Sylvia Plath*. New York: Dial, 1982.

Hyde, Mary, ed. *Bernard Shaw and Alfred Douglas: A Correspondence*. Boston: Ticknor & Fields, 1982.

Kazin, Alfred. *Contemporaries: From the 19th Century to the Present*. New York: Horizon, 1982.

Kerr, Walter. *The Shabunin Affair: An Episode in the Life of Leo Tolstoy*. Ithaca: Cornell University Press, 1982.

Kesten, Hermann, ed. *Thomas Mann: Diaries 1918-1939*. Translated by Richard and Clara Winston. New York: Abrams, 1982.

King, Larry L. *The Whorehouse Papers*. New York: Viking, 1982.

Knapp, Bettina L. *Lewis Mumford/David Liebovitz: Letters 1923-1968*. Troy, N.Y.: Whitston, 1982.

La Capora, Dominick. *"Madame Bovary" on Trial*. Ithaca: Cornell University Press, 1982.

Laurence, Frank M. *Hemingway and the Movies*. New York: Plenum da Capo, 1982.

Leach, Christopher. *Letter to a Younger Son*. New York & London: Harcourt Brace Jovanovich, 1982.

Le Vot, André. *F. Scott Fitzgerald*. Garden City: Doubleday, 1982.

Lewis, Peter. *George Orwell: The Road to 1984*. New York & London: Harcourt Brace Jovanovich, 1982.

Lindberg-Seyersted, Brita, ed. *Pound/Ford: The Story of a Literary Friendship*. New York: Norton, 1982.

Lottman, Herbert R. *The Left Bank: Writers, Artists, and Politics from the Popular Front to the Cold War*. Boston: Houghton Mifflin, 1982.

MacShane, Frank. *The Life and Work of Ford Madox Ford*. New York: Horizon, 1982.

Marchand, Leslie A., ed. *Lord Byron: Selected Letters and Journals*. Cambridge: Harvard University Press, 1982.

Martin, Brian W. *John Henry Newman: His Life and Work*. New York: Oxford University Press, 1982.

Masters, Hilary. *Last Stands: Notes from Memory*. Boston: Godine, 1982.

Matthews, James. *Voices: A Life of Frank O'Connor*. New York: Atheneum, 1982.

Maxwell, William, ed. *Letters: Sylvia Townsend Warner*. New York: Viking, 1982.

McKenna, Rollie. *Portrait of Dylan: A Photographer's Memoir*. Owings Mills, Md.: Stemmer House, 1982.

Merwin, W. S. *Unframed Originals: Recollections*. New York: Atheneum, 1982.

Meyers, Jeffrey. *The Enemy: A Biography of Wyndham Lewis*. Boston: Routledge & Kegan Paul, 1982.

Miller, Philip, ed. and trans. *An Abyss Deep Enough: The Letters of Heinrich von Kleist, with a Selection of Essays and Anecdotes*. New York: Dutton, 1982.

Miller, William D. *Dorothy Day: A Biography*. New York: Harper & Row, 1982.

Millgate, Michael. *Thomas Hardy*. New York: Random House, 1982.

Mills, Hillary. *Mailer: A Biography*. New York: Empire, 1982.

Mossman, Elliot, ed. *The Correspondence of Boris Pasternak and Olga Freidenberg: 1910-1954*. Translated by Mossman and Margaret Wettlin. New York & London: Harcourt Brace Jovanovich, 1982.

Mumford, Lewis. *Sketches from Life: The Autobiography of Lewis Mumford, the Early Years*. New York: Dial, 1982.

Myerson, Joel. *Ralph Waldo Emerson: A Descriptive Bibliography*. Pittsburgh: University of Pittsburgh Press, 1982.

Nemanic, Gerald. *A Bibliographical Guide to Midwestern Literature*. Iowa City: University of Iowa Press, 1981.

Neville, G. H. *A Memoir of D. H. Lawrence (The Betrayal)*. Cambridge: Cambridge University Press, 1982.

O'Hara, Mary. *Flicka's Friend: The Autobiography of Mary O'Hara*. New York: Putnam's 1982.

Padovano, Anthony T. *The Human Journey: Thomas Merton, Symbol of a Century*. Garden City: Doubleday, 1982.

Payn, Graham, and Sheridan Morley, eds. *The Noel Coward Diaries*. Boston: Little, Brown, 1982.

Perrett, Geoffrey. *America in the Twenties*. New York: Simon & Schuster, 1982.

Perry, John. *Jack London: An American Myth*. Chicago: Nelson-Hall, 1981.

Plante, David. *Difficult Women: A Memoir of Three*. New York: Atheneum, 1982.

Porte, Joel, ed. *Emerson in His Journals*. Cambridge: Harvard University Press, 1982.

Rivers, J. E., and Charles Nicol, eds. *Nabokov's Fifth Arc: Nabokov and Others on His Work*. Austin: University of Texas Press, 1982.

Robbins, Jhan. *Front Page Marriage: Helen Hayes and Charles MacArthur*. New York: Putnam's, 1982.

Robinson, Janice. *S. H. D.: The Life and Work of an American Poet*. Boston: Houghton Mifflin, 1982.

Rosenberg, Bernard, and Ernest Goldstein. *Creators and Disturbers: Reminiscences by Jewish Intellectuals*. New York: Columbia University Press, 1982.

Samuels, Peggy and Harold. *Frederic Remington: A Biography*. Garden City: Doubleday, 1982.

Saroyan, Aram. *Last Rites: The Death of William Saroyan as Chronicled by His Son*. New York: Morrow, 1982.

Schapiro, Leonard. *Turgenev: His Life and Times*. Cambridge: Harvard University Press, 1982.

Seebohm, Caroline. *The Man Who Was* Vogue: *The Life and Times of Condé Nast*. New York: Viking, 1982.

Shivers, Alfred S. *The Life of Maxwell Anderson*. New York: Stein & Day, 1982.

Simpson, Eileen. *Poets in Their Youth: A Memoir*. New York: Random House, 1982.

Stauffer, Helen Winter. *Mari Sandoz: Story Catcher of the Plains*. Lincoln: University of Nebraska Press, 1982.

Steegmuller, Francis, ed. and trans. *The Letters of Gustave Flaubert, 1857-1880*. Cambridge: Harvard University Press, 1982.

Thurman, Judith. *Isak Dinesen: The Life of a Storyteller*. New York: St. Martin's, 1982.

Traubel, Horace. *With Walt Whitman in Camden*, volume 6. Edited by Gertrude Traubel and William White. Carbondale & Edwardsville: Southern Illinois University Press, 1982.

Walker, Margaret. *The Daemonic Genius of Richard Wright*. Washington, D.C.: Howard University Press, 1982.

Washington, Ida H. *Dorothy Canfield Fisher: A Biography*. Shelburne, Vt.: New England Press, 1982.

Weeks, Edward. *Writers and Friends: A Memoir*. Boston: Atlantic Monthly/Little, Brown, 1982.

Weintraub, Stanley. *The Unexpected Shaw: Biographical Approaches to G. B. S. and His Work*. New York: Ungar, 1982.

Winnick, R. H., ed. *Letters of Archibald MacLeish, 1907 to 1981*. Boston: Houghton Mifflin, 1982.

Wolff, Robert Lee. *Nineteenth-Century Fiction: A Bibliographical Catalogue Based on the Collection formed by Robert Lee Wolff*, volume 1, A-C. New York: Garland, 1981.

Ziegler, Philip. *Diana Cooper*. New York: Knopf, 1982.

Ronald Sukenick:
An Author's Response

With all due respect to the author of the Ronald Sukenick entry in the *DLB Yearbook: 1981* and to the editors of that volume, I feel obliged for the record to note that this account of me misrepresents in many respects my work, critical reaction to it, and my life. In partial rectification, I append my current *Bio*, and refer the interested reader to the material in Jerome Klinkowitz's *Literary Disruptions*, revised 1980 edition, and especially to its Sukenick bibliography which, though now outdated, is yet far more up-to-date and balanced than the one included in *Yearbook: 1981*.

Ronald Sukenick: Biography

Ronald Sukenick's name is almost always included in recent serious discussion of contemporary American fiction. Sukenick's work is the subject of much critical commentary—he is listed, for example, on the cover of a new book subtitled *American Fiction Since Joyce*, among thirteen authors of the rank of William Faulkner, John Updike, Saul Bellow, and Norman Mailer (*Paradoxical Resolutions*, Craig Hansen Werner)—and he has been translated into numerous languages. He is the author of the novels *Up, Out, 98.6, Long Talking Bad Conditions Blues*, the story collection *The Death of the Novel and Other Stories*, a scholarly book on the poet Wallace Stevens, and various works of criticism, literary theory, and journalism (for the *Village Voice*, the *New York Times*, and elsewhere), and has also written for film. The movie *Out*, for which he collaborated on the script, was taken from Sukenick's novel of the same name. Sukenick is also publisher of a book review magazine, the *American Book Review*, has been active in arts administration, and is a tenured professor at the University of Colorado, Boulder. He has received a variety of awards for his fiction, including a Guggenheim and a National Endowment for the Arts Fellowship.

A critic has recently described Ronald Sukenick's writing in the following terms: "What characterizes Sukenick's fiction is its comedy, its sexual exuberance, its innovations in structure and characterization, and the accuracy of its depiction of the cultural context—namely, America of the 1960s and 1970s. His significance to literary history is double: first, his ability to refine and make current and personal his literary inheritance, Kerouac's improvisation, for example, or Miller's use of autobiography; and second, his inability to stay within a tradition, his passion for discovery of new forms, his jump outward, as he would say, to the peripheries of language where new literary language is invented" (*Contemporary Literature*, Spring 1982).

Sukenick has just finished a new novel about Los Angeles, a story about a fortune teller who gets involved in the production of a film; is finishing a book of short stories; and is writing, with its proprietor, a history of the famous New York bar, Max's Kansas City, where for years many of the most important writers, artists, and musicians gathered.

Contributors

Michael Adams ....*Louisiana State University*
Gay Wilson Allen ....*New York University*
Winifred Farrant Bevilacqua ....*University of Turin, Italy*
Ashley Brown...*University of South Carolina*
Robert E. Burkholder ....*Pennsylvania State University, Wilkes-Barre*
George F. Butterick..*University of Connecticut*
David G. Byrd ....*University of South Carolina*
Mark J. Charney...*Clemson University*
Susan Currier ....*California Polytechnic State University*
Donna Dacus ....*University of Minnesota*
Sarah English ....*Meredith College*
Lynn Felder..*Columbia, South Carolina*
Donald J. Greiner ....*University of South Carolina*
Michael Groden..*University of Western Ontario*
James Hardin ....*University of South Carolina*
Jeffrey Helterman...*University of South Carolina*
Frederick A. Hetzel ....*University of Pittsburgh*
Diane Isaacs..*University of Minnesota*
Sally Johns..*University of South Carolina*
James H. Justus..*Indiana University*
Harriet L. King..*Durham Academy*
Howard Kissel...*New York, New York*
Mark J. Lidman..*University of South Carolina at Sumter*
Dick Lochte...*Santa Monica, California*
Juan Loveluck ....*University of South Carolina*
Carol A. MacCurdy ....*University of Southwestern Louisiana*
Gary Margolis...*Middlebury College*
James O'Hara ....*Pennsylvania State University at York*
Keith Opdahl..*DePauw University*
Jacqueline Orsagh ....*Tri-State University*
Jean W. Ross ....*Columbia, South Carolina*
Hugh M. Ruppersburg..*University of Georgia*
Diane Scholl..*Luther College*
Peter A. Scholl..*Luther College*
Carl R. Shirley..*University of South Carolina*
Patricia L. Skarda ....*Smith College*
Willard Spiegelman...*Southern Methodist University*
Christopher Surr ....*New York, New York*
Brian Swann ....*Cooper Union*
Gayle Swanson..*Newberry College*
David M. Taylor..*Livingston University*
Decherd Turner ....*Humanities Research Center, University of Texas at Austin*
Margaret A. Van Antwerp ....*Columbia, South Carolina*
Ralph F. Voss..*University of Alabama*
Bernice Werner White..*Southwestern at Memphis*

411

Necrology

Harriet Stratemeyer Adams — 30 March 1982
Margaret Culkin Banning — 4 January 1982
Djuna Barnes — 18 June 1982
Nathaniel Benchley — 14 December 1981
John Cheever — 18 June 1982
Frederic Dannay — 3 September 1982
Babette Deutsch — 13 November 1982
Kurt Enoch — 15 February 1982
John Gardner — 14 September 1982
Horace Gregory — 1 March 1982
Granville Hicks — 18 June 1982
Richard Hugo — 22 October 1982
Richard Jessup — 22 October 1982
Richard Lockridge — 19 June 1982

Dwight Macdonald — 19 December 1982
Archibald MacLeish — 20 April 1982
William P. McGivern — 18 November 1982
Ayn Rand — 6 March 1982
Kenneth Rexroth — 13 June 1982
Waverley Root — 31 October 1982
Maxwell Sackheim — 2 December 1982
Howard Sackler — 13 October 1982
Cynthia Propper Seton — 23 October 1982
Red Smith — 15 January 1982
Frank Swinnerton — 6 November 1982
Thomas Thompson — 29 October 1982
Agnes Sligh Turnbull — 31 January 1982

Yearbook Index: 1980-1982

Yearbook Index

Yearbook Index